International Relations and the Euro

The New European Union Series

Series Editors: John Peterson and Helen Wallace

The European Union is both the most successful experiment in modern international cooperation and a daunting analytical challenge to students of politics, economics, history, law, and the social sciences. The EU of the twenty-first century will be fundamentally different from its earlier permutations, as monetary union, enlargement, a new defence role, and globalisation all create pressures for a more complex, differentiated, and truly new European Union.

The New European Union series brings together the expertise of leading scholars writing on major aspects of EU politics for an international readership.

The series offers lively, accessible, reader-friendly, research-based textbooks on:

Policy-Making in the European Union

The Institutions of the European Union

The Origins and Evolution of the European Union

Theorizing the European Union

The Member States of the European Union

International Relations and the European Union

The European Union: How Does it Work

International Relations and the European Union

Edited by

Christopher Hill
and
Michael Smith

OXFORD
UNIVERSITY PRESS

OXFORD

UNIVERSITY PRESS

Great Clarendon Street, Oxford OX2 6DP

Oxford University Press is a department of the University of Oxford.
It furthers the University's objective of excellence in research, scholarship,
and education by publishing worldwide in

Oxford New York

Auckland Cape Town Dar es Salaam Hong Kong Karachi
Kuala Lumpur Madrid Melbourne Mexico City Nairobi
New Delhi Shanghai Taipei Toronto

With offices in

Argentina Austria Brazil Chile Czech Republic France Greece
Guatemala Hungary Italy Japan Poland Portugal Singapore
South Korea Switzerland Thailand Turkey Ukraine Vietnam

Oxford is a registered trade mark of Oxford University Press
in the UK and in certain other countries

Published in the United States
by Oxford University Press Inc., New York

© Oxford University Press 2005

British Library Cataloguing in Publication Data

Data available

Library of Congress Cataloging in Publication Data

Data available

ISBN 978-0-19-927348-5

10 9 8 7 6 5 4

Typeset by Laserwords Private Limited, Chennai, India

Printed in Great Britain
on acid-free paper by
Ashford Colour Press Limited, Gosport, Hampshire

Outline Contents

Detailed Contents

Preface

This book is the fifth to appear in the 'New European Union' series edited by John Peterson and Helen Wallace, and inspired by Helen and William Wallace's *Policy-Making in the European Union* (now in a fifth edition, with Mark Pollack also part of the editorial team). The current editors were delighted to be invited to edit a book on the international relations of the European Union, and are grateful to John and Helen for their confidence, support, and patience.

The subject is a surprisingly neglected one, even if in recent years there has been more writing on 'European foreign policy', or on the EU as a global actor. Specialists in International Relations (IR) tend to regard the EU, even in its external mode, as a thing apart, without much to tell us about the wider system and its processes. For its part the smaller group of experts on the EU's external relations rarely reaches out to the wider field, rooting itself in the institutions of European foreign policy-making and/or the relevance of foreign policy to the historical enterprise of integration. Our aim has been to redress the balance, by explicitly bringing the discussion of the EU's world role(s) into a conversation with mainstream IR debates. We have attempted to do this by conceptualising the issues ourselves, as editors, in terms which are as much informed by our experience as teachers of International Relations as by our special knowledge of European affairs. But we have also chosen contributors who are in a position to bridge the two areas of expertise. In this respect we are particularly grateful to Andrew Linklater and to James Mayall, two distinguished IR scholars not normally on the Europeanist circuit. They were more than willing to engage with our questions and to bring their own distinctive and refreshing perspectives to bear. The book is certainly richer for their presence.

We owe just as great a debt to our other contributors, the Europeanists, who have responded enthusiastically to the bridge-building challenge we set. Filippo Andreatta did this most explicitly, by surveying IR theory and showing how it is always potentially relevant to the EU's international experience, but everyone on the team took great care to marry their specialist expertise to the broader theme of the EU as a factor, and a player, in the international system. This is a research-led text, aimed at advanced students and scholars, and we hope that readers will find that it contains creative thinking and much new empirical material, as well as a clear analysis of the central problems at stake. We are immensely grateful to all our colleagues for their insights, hard work, and amiability in what from time to time are the inevitably trying circumstances of putting together a large collective book. Reuben Wong endured the most testing time, rising superbly to the challenge of being asked to replace a colleague who had to drop out at the last minute. He deserves a special vote of thanks.

We have received much help from outside as well as from within the team. Our thanks are particularly due to the Robert Schuman Centre for Advanced Studies at the European University Institute in Fiesole, and to the East Midlands Eurocentre, the Jean Monnet Centre at Loughborough University, for hosting the workshops that respectively launched the book and then finalised its themes. The two meetings significantly assisted both editors and contributors in their work, and we very much appreciate the support and hospitality both institutions provided. We also wish to thank our editor at OUP, Ruth Anderson, for her cheerful and efficient support, especially in the last phases of this project. Finally, we are well aware of the sacrifices that our families have had to make in helping us to get to the finishing-line, and this is where our greatest debt lies.

List of Figures

List of Boxes

List of Tables

List of Abbreviations

ACs	applicant countries
ACPs	African, Caribbean and Pacific countries (of the Lomé/Continous system)
AFSJ	Area of Freedom, Security and Justice
ARENA	Advanced Research on the Europeanization of the Nation State
ASEAN	Association of South East Asian Nations
ASEM	Asia-Europe Meeting
ATTAC	Association for Taxation of Financial Transactions for the Aid of Citizens
AU	African Union
AWACS	Airborne Warning and Control System
BEAC	Barents Euro-Arctic Council
BSEC	Black Sea Economic Cooperation
CAP	common agricultural policy
CARDS	Community Assistance for Reconstruction, Development and Stabilization
CCP	common commercial policy
CDU	Christian Democratic Union
CEECs	countries of Central and Eastern Europe
CEFTA	Central European Free Trade Agreement
CELAD	Comité Européen de la Lutte Anti-Drogue
CEMAC	Central African Economic and Monetary Community
CEPS	Centre for European Policy Studies (in Brussels)
CESDP	Common Security and Defence Policy
CET	common external tariff
CFSP	Common Foreign and Security Policy
CGS	Council General Secretariat
CIS	Commonwealth of Independent States
CJTF	Combined Joint Task Force
CMEA	Council for Mutual Economic Assistance
COMESA	Common Market for Eastern and Southern Africa
COPS	Political and Security Committee
Coreper	Committe of Permanent Representatives
COREU	Correspondant Européen (EPC communications network)
CPCO	Centre de Planification et de Conduite des Opérations
CSCE	Conference on Security and Cooperation in Europe
DAC	Development Assistance Committee
DG	Directorate-General
DG DEV	DG Development
DG(E)	Directorate General of the Council Secretariat (External)
DG ELARG	DG Enlargement
DG RELEX	DG External Relations
DRC	Democratic Republic of Congo
EAC	European Affairs Committee

EADS	European Aeronautic, Space and Defence Company
EBA	Everything but Arms
EC	European Communities
ECB	European Central Bank
ECHO	European Community Humanitarian Aid Office
ECJ	European Court of Justice
Ecofin	Economic and Finance Council
ECOWAS	Economic Community of West African States
ECSC	European Coal and Steel Community
EDA	European Defence Agency
EDC	European Defence Community
EDF	European Development Fund
EEA	European Economic Area
EEAS	European External Action Service
EEC	European Economic Community
EFP	European Foreign Policy
EFPU	European Foreign Policy Unit
EFTA	European Free Trade Association
EGF	European Gendarmerie Force
EIB	European Investment Bank
EMCDAA	European Monitoring Centre for Drugs and Drug Addiction
EMS	European Monetary System
ENP	European Neighbourhood Policy
EP	European Parliament
EPAs	Economic Partnership Agreements
EPC	European Political Cooperation
ERRG	European Parliament Research Group
ERTA	European Road Transport Agreement (ECJ Judgment of 1971)
ESDI	European Security and Defence Identity
ESDP	European Security and Defence Policy
ESS	European Security Strategy
EU	European Union
EUMC	European Union Military Committee
EUMFA	European Union Minister of Foreign Affairs
EUMS	European Union Military Staff
Euratom	European Atomic Energy Community
Eurojust	European network of judicial authorities
Euromed	Euro-Mediterranean Partnership
Europol	European Police Office
FAC	Foreign Affairs Council
FAWEU	Forces Answerable to the Western European Union
FDI	Foreign Direct Investment
FPA	Foreign Policy Analysis
FSC	Foreign Sales Corporation
fYROM	Former Yugoslav Republic of Macedonia
G8	Group of 8
GAC	General Affairs Council

GAERC	General Affairs and External Relations Council
GATS	General Agreement on Trade in Services
GATT	General Agreement on Tariffs and Trade
GCC	Gulf Cooperation Council
GDP	gross domestic product
GMO	genetically modified organisms
GNI	gross net income
GNP	gross national product
GPS	global positioning system
GSP	Generalised System Preferences
HG 2010	Headline Goal 2010
HHG	Helsinki Headline Goal
HR-[/SG]	High Representative-Secretary-General (of the Council)
IAEA	International Atomic Energy Agency
IBRD	International Bank for Reconstruction and Development (World Bank)
ICC	International Criminal Court
IFOR	Implementation Force (in Bosnia-Herzegovina)
IGAD	Intergovernmental Authority on Development
IGC	Intergovernmental Conference
IMF	International Monetary Fund
IPE	international political economy
IR	International Relations
IRBD	International Bank of Reconstruction and Development (the World Bank)
IISS	International Institute of Strategic Studies
JHA	justice and home affairs
LAC	Latin America and the Caribbean countries
LDCs	least developed countries
MEDA	mesures d'accompagnement
MEP	Member of the European Parliament
Mercosur	Common Market of the Southern Cone
MFA	Multi-Fibre Agreement
MFN	most favoured nation
MINEX	Mineral Export earnings stabilisation regime
MOD	Ministry of Defence
MRA	Mutual Recognition Agreements
NATO	North Atlantic Treaty Organization
NEPAD	New Economic Partnership for Africa's Development
NGO	non-governmental organisation
NHAI	National High Authority of Intelligence
NIC	National Indicative Programme
NICs	newly industrialising countries
NIEO	New International Economic Order
NIPs	National Indicative Programmes
NPT	Non-Proliferation Treaty
NTA	New Transatlantic Agenda
NTBs	non-tariff barriers

OAU	Organization for African Unity
OBNOVA	EU renewal programme in the Balkans
OCT	overseas countries and territories
ODA	Overseas Development Assistance
OECD	Organization of Economic Cooperation and Development
OEEC	Organization for European Economic Co-operation
OSCE	Organization for Security and Cooperation in Europe
PCA	Partnership and Cooperation Agreement
PGM	Precision Guided Munition
Phare	Pologne-Hongrie aide à la reconstruction économique
PJHQ	Permanent Joint Headquarters
PoCo	(European) Political Cooperation (EPC)
PPEWU	Policy Planning and Early Warning Unit
PSC	Political and Security Committee
PU	Policy Unit
QMV	qualified majority voting
RRF	Rapid Reaction Force
SAA	Stabilization and Association Agreements
SAARC	South Asian Association for Regional Cooperation
SADC	Southern African Development Community
SAP	Stabilisation and Association Process (in the Balkans)
SAPs	Structural Adjustment Programmes
SCIFA	Strategic Committee on Immigration and Asylum
SCR	Common Service for External Relations
SEA	Single European Act
SFOR	Stabilisation Force in Bosnia-Herzegovina
SHAPE	Supreme Headquarters Allied Powers Europe
SIS	Schengen Information System
SITCEN	Joint Situation Centre (in the European Council Secretariat)
STABEX	Stabilisation of Export Earnings regime
TACIS	Technical Assistance for the CIS countries
TAD	Transatlantic Declaration
TBR	Trade Barriers Regulation
TCNs	Troop Contributing Nations
TDI	Trade Defence Instruments
TEC	Treaty of the European Community (Revised Treaty of Rome)
TECE	Treaty establishing a Constitution for Europe ('the Constitutional Treaty')
TEP	Transatlantic Economic Partnership
TEU	Treaty on European Union
ToA	Treaty of Amsterdam
TREVI	Terrorisme, Radicalisme, Extrémisme, Violence, Internationale (EPC Working Group)
TRIPs	Trade Related aspects of Intellectual Property Rights
TRNC	Turkish Republic of Northern Cyprus
UK	United Kingdom
UN	United Nations

UNCTAD	United Nations Conference on Trade and Development
UNESCO	United Nations Educational Scientific and Cultural Organization
UNSC	United Nations Security Council
US/USA	United States (of America)
USTR	United States Trade Representative
UV	unanimous voting
WAEMU	West African Economic and Monetary Union
WEU	Western European Union
WMD	weapons of mass destruction
WTO	World Trade Organization

List of Contributors

NICOLE ALECU DE FLERS — *Institute of Advanced Studies, Vienna, Department of Political Science*

FILIPPO ANDREATTA — *Università degli Studi di Parma*

GEOFFREY EDWARDS — *University of Cambridge*

CHRISTOPHER HILL — *University of Cambridge*

JOLYON HOWORTH — *Yale University*

ANDREW LINKLATER — *University of Wales, Aberystwyth*

CHRISTOPHER LORD — *University of Reading*

JAMES MAYALL — *Professor Emeritus, University of Cambridge*

SOPHIE MEUNIER — *Princeton University*

KALYPSO NICOLAIDIS — *University of Oxford*

SIMON NUTTALL — *College of Europe*

WYN REES — *University of Nottingham*

ELFRIEDE REGELSBERGER — *Institut für Europäische Politik, Berlin*

KAREN E. SMITH — *London School of Economics and Political Science*

MICHAEL E. SMITH — *University of St. Andrews*

MICHAEL SMITH — *Loughborough University*

REBECCA STEFFENSON — *DePaul University, Chicago*

LOUKAS TSOUKALIS — *University of Athens/Hellenic Foundation for European and Foreign Policy*

SOPHIE VANHOONACKER — *University of Maastricht*

REUBEN WONG — *National University of Singapore*

Editors' Note

Readers should note that most references in the text are to the consolidated list of References at the end of the book. There are, however, a few which refer to the Further Reading sections at the end of each chapter.

It may also be worth pointing out that International Relations (upper case) refers to the academic subject, and to its literature, whereas international relations (lower case) refers to the actual world of interaction between states, peoples, organizations and individuals.

Part I

Frameworks

Chapter 1

International Relations and the European Union: Themes and Issues

Christopher Hill and Michael Smith

Contents

Summary

The European Union has increasingly been studied as an international actor, but it is important to make the linkage between the Union's internal processes of integration and policy-making and the development of international relations more generally. This means that established concepts and frameworks in International Relations can be brought together with the approaches from comparative politics and public policy that have characterised study of the European Union (EU). In this way, the development of the EU as a system of international relations in itself can be related analytically to the place it occupies in the processes of international relations, and to its position as a 'power' in the international arena. Such an analysis highlights both the ways in which the EU produces international action and the ways in which the international dimension enters into EU policy-making; it can also help to expose key elements of change in the EU's international position.

Introduction

The EU has increasingly been studied as a particular kind of international actor. During the 1990s and 2000s there has been a substantial growth of attention to the ways in which the EU's international policies are made and pursued (Allen and Smith 1990, 1998; Bretherton and Vogler 1999; Ginsberg 2001; Smith, H. 2003; Smith, K. 2003, 2004; Smith, M.E. 2003; White 2001). Such a sustained and substantial interest reflects both the empirical importance of the EU in the international arena and the analytical challenge of dealing with what is a distinctive if not unique type of internationally-acting body. Empirically, the EU can be seen as one of the world's two economic 'superpowers', and an increasingly significant influence in the realms of international diplomacy, 'soft security', and broader world order. Analytically, the Union poses major challenges by virtue of its status as something more than an intergovernmental organisation but less than a fully-fledged European 'state' (Wallace 1983; Caporaso 1996). Not surprisingly, much of the attention paid to the EU in the international arena has thus consisted of charting the development of this 'partial superpower' and evaluating the ways in which it does or does not perform important 'state functions' in the changing world order (see the references cited above, plus Carlsnaes, Sjursen and White 2004).

Such a focus raises a number of important issues, most of which are touched upon later in this chapter. Yet this volume widens the perspective from 'the EU as a global actor' to 'international relations and the EU'. What does this mean? In part it refers to the fact that member states do still conduct residual foreign relations amongst themselves, as with Anglo-Spanish relations over Gibraltar, or Austrian reactions to criticisms from its EU partners of the right-wing Freedom Party's participation in government. This, however, is not our principal concern. We are mainly interested in the number of respects in which the EU constitutes part of the international/global system, and in which it can be studied through the lenses of academic International Relations (IR). This focus does not rule out consideration of the EU's credentials as an international/global actor; rather it connects this issue to the broader study of IR and of international policy-making. What we are explicitly concerned to do is to counter the tendency to assume that the EU's external behaviour can be understood through a combination of understanding the EU's *sui generis* qualities, and a reliance on the tools of comparative politics. Both are important, with the latter providing an indispensable opening to the internal dynamics of the Union and its member states, but without an understanding of the international, and its distinctive features, the analysis is bound to be superficial.

Looking at the EU's place in international relations, seen from the outside as it were, involves a new take on a number of established international relations concepts. Ideas such as balance of power, multipolarity, world system, and globalisation are relevant to understanding the contexts in which the European Union has reflected and affected major forces and changes in international relations. The EU may be interpreted in very different ways according to which dominant concept—or indeed, underlying paradigm—we employ. It may be seen as a power, a centre of gravity, a model, a magnet, a regime, and a mere arena, or various combinations of these. But whichever interpretation is favoured, this volume argues that we need to combine an understanding of the EU's internal character with an analysis of its international situation. The very conception of international 'actorness' depends on bringing 'inside' and 'outside' into a relationship with each other, just as agents and structures are mutually dependent (Wendt 1987, 1992, 1999). Thus 'International Relations and the European Union' is about both the place of Europe in the world and the way the world contributes to the shaping of Europe. At the same time, it is about the place—actual and appropriate—of the EU in the academic subject International Relations.

Such an integrated focus has not been easy for the two 'camps' that have been interested in the European integration project. On the one hand, as we have noted, the study of European integration has tended to emphasise the distinctive nature of the project, and thus inevitably to play down the ways in which it has been part of the broader development of the international arena, subject to analysis in terms of IR theory and method. On the other hand, the literature of IR has not found it easy to accommodate the EU fully in its study of the international system, its processes and its evolution, although there have been notable efforts in the area of foreign policy analysis (White 2001; Carlsnaes, Sjursen and White 2004) and in analyses of identity and order (Kelstrup and Williams 2000). Some of the most sustained study has come from those interested in regionalisation and regionalism (Telò 2001), but this has tended to neglect the ways in which the EU reaches the parts that other forms of regionalism do not—in particular the ways in which there has been a developing capacity to formulate and implement a 'European foreign policy'. Perhaps inevitably in the aftermath of the Cold War, the EU has been studied as a particular form of 'security community' or a zone of peace (Kelstrup and Williams 2000; Schimmelfennig 2003); whilst this captures some of the ways in which European integration has shifted expectations among its member states and societies, it does not fully address the ways in which the EU is more than simply an arena for the shaping of national expectations and policies. Alongside this, there has also been renewed attention to the ways in which the EU plays into the broader European order (Croft *et al.* 1999; Gärtner, Hyde-Price and Reitner 2001; Niblett and Wallace 2001), but at least so far this has not been fully extended into the study of the EU's power to shape processes and outcomes in the IR sense within the 'new Europe'. Whilst we would not claim to have remedied all of these shortcomings or areas of under-development, the attempt to address them is central to the focus of this volume.

Assumptions

In pursuing the analytical focus outlined above, we make a number of initial assumptions, three of them substantive and three methodological. For the time being they are merely asserted, so as to help render the huge universe of data and approaches more comprehensible, and we will return to them in Chapter 18 when we present our overview of the findings in this volume.

Substantive assumptions

Our first set of assumptions is substantive, in the sense that it deals with the forces affecting the development and the impact of the EU's international relations. The assumptions are as follows:

1. *The EU matters in the world and the world matters to it.* The political simplicities by which some scorn the total ineffectiveness of Europe, and a smaller number advocate a form of Euro-isolationism, are set aside. The interplay between the EU and the international system as a whole is one of the big issues of modern international relations, given that the former represents the collective weight of 25 of the richest countries on the planet, and creates an extensive demand for its foreign policy actions. Accordingly, international outcomes involving the EU are shaped by both global and domestic structures, even if the latter refers ambiguously both to trans-European and intra-state factors.

2. *EU positions, decisions and actions in the world are produced as the result of often complex interactions in a multi-level system*, involving the member states singly and collectively, as well as the common institutions. The 'three Pillars' of the Treaty on European Union (Pillar I: the European (economic) Community; Pillar II: Common Foreign and Security Policy; Pillar III: Justice and Home Affairs) represent this process to some degree, but there are also activities that cross the Pillars or occur wholly outside them, and the Constitutional Treaty of 2004 implies the eventual abolition of the 'Pillars' themselves (see Chapter 4 of this volume). Moreover, the Pillars as they currently exist are not an accurate representation of what may be termed the 'European foreign policy system', not least because they have no place for national policies. The web of activity is, however, not yet dense or homogeneous enough to be seen as a stable form of 'multi-level *governance*'.

3. *The process of EU action and reflection internationally is dynamic, if not always progressive/cumulative.* There has been a self-conscious attempt to develop a European foreign policy since the early 1970s, while the 'ratchet' mechanism—whereby each codification or treaty revision provides for further revision at a not-too-distant interval—has ensured constant movement. The progressive enlargement of the EC/EU has also brought new subjects regularly onto the foreign policy agenda and widened its geographical scope, and the widening scope of the 'internal' integration process has produced new areas of international engagement, for example in monetary or environmental policy. When combined with the dynamic but often ambiguous development of processes such as globalisation or regionalisation in the world arena, or with the shifting balance of global power, it is clear that the movement of 'European foreign policy' and the broader international relations of the EU is only part of a broader set of changes.

Methodological assumptions

Our second set of assumptions is methodological: that is to say, assumptions that we make about the components of an effective analysis of the EU's international relations, and about the aspects of IR theory that are relevant to such an analysis. They are as follows:

1. *An historical understanding of the origins of the EU's international relations is essential*, as they have highly particular characteristics and are still affected by readings of the past. What is more, given that this is a highly dynamic set of processes (see above), it is even less susceptible to synchronic generalisation than other areas of international politics. There are different and competing narratives of the ways in which the EU's international relations have been developed and understood, and it is important for analysis to reflect this plurality of 'histories'.

2. *Both ideas and material factors have shaped the development of the EU's international relations, and will continue to shape them in the future.* From the outset, there has been a dynamic relationship between processes of practical policy formation and interaction and those of identity formation and role development. Therefore both the ideational and the material need to be taken into account by attempts to explain and understand the subject, and one of the challenges is to find ways in which to apply appropriate combinations of these.

3. *A methodological pluralism is therefore required when seeking to explain and understand the EU's international relations.* No one approach, whether broad-brush as in realist, rationalist and constructivist, or more specific, as in geo-politics, intergovernmentalism or 'expectations', comes near being adequate by itself. The usual problems then arise of how to relate diverse, and possibly incommensurable middle-range, theories to each other.

As can be seen from the two sets of assumptions outlined above, we are committed to a view of the EU's international relations that is essentially problem-focused, deploying an eclectic mix of evidence and methods in an attempt to produce a rounded understanding of what is going on and how it might develop. This does not mean, however, that we do not have a point of view. Our standpoint can be summarised in terms of three perspectives on the EU's international relations, and these are outlined in the following section.

Three perspectives on International Relations and the EU

We distinguish between three key perspectives: the EU as a *sub-system* of international relations, by which we mean both the way in which it has dealt with its internal 'foreign' relations, and its capacity to generate external collective action; the EU as part of the wider *processes* of international relations, a term which refers to the legal, institutional and political mechanisms through which the problems of international conflict and/or political economy are addressed; and the EU as a major *power* impacting upon contemporary international relations, in which category we want to be able to assess the extent to which the EU shapes its external environment, is perceived by other actors as so doing and occupies a certain position in the international hierarchy of power. In the terms we have already used, these perspectives are both substantive (in that they enable us to describe key areas of the EU's international relations) and methodological (in that they enable us to think more clearly about the areas of IR that help us to analyse and evaluate the EU's international relations). The chapters in this volume focus on these three areas, albeit in varying combinations of emphasis and detail (see below). The perspectives define the EU's international existence and impact, and they help us to think about its role in a variety of global contexts. Each is explained further below.

The EU as a sub-system of International Relations

Under this heading, we are interested in three distinct issues. The first is the way in which the EU has dealt with *its own international relations*, internally. This is not a contradiction in terms. Notwithstanding the view that the European Community (EC) was initially and primarily a set of economic bargains, we hold to the position that it arose out of the need to resolve the war problem in Europe, and in particular the age-old Franco-German antagonism. It was thus, at least in one key respect, an inward-looking foreign policy device. What is more, relations between member states did not suddenly become like those between provinces overnight—and may not be so even now. French suspicion of Germany endured up to the point where Mitterrand (as well as Thatcher) attempted to prevent unification in 1989–90, while as recently as the late 1990s Italy was infuriated by the German wish to get a permanent seat on the UN Security Council, and pursued a hostile diplomatic campaign against it.

Nonetheless, there is no denying that there are much stricter limits on the tactics which member states are prepared to use against each other than on those between any random pairing of states in international relations. The Franco-German relationship has become a miracle of pacification and institutionalisation, almost at the level of the special Benelux arrangements. Britain and Ireland, likewise, have been helped to advance their difficult relationship by their common membership of the EU. These are amongst the most advanced 'democratic dyads' in the terms made familiar by the literature on the 'democratic peace', and it might be argued that this reflects the benign influence of essentially treaty-based 'civilising processes'. 'Europeanization' is not the only process at work here, though: the US has been a key player in Anglo-Irish cooperation, and relations between the Scandinavian countries have become regularised independently of EU involvement. The broader impact of the democratic peace may thus be as powerful an explanation of the stable, civil diplomacy on view as the impact of the Treaties. Yet the desire of the brittle states of the ex-Warsaw Pact to join the EU, on political as well as economic grounds, shows how the latter is seen as a 'safe harbour'—a distinctive geo-political area where the most dangerous elements of international relationships appear to have been suspended for the duration.

Second, we are interested in the way in which the EU can be considered as a set of international institutions and arrangements within which the interests and preferences of member states and other actors can be coordinated for international purposes. This is the problem of collective action and policy-formation in relation to the outside world. It is an essential part of our framework because it draws attention to the linkages between internal dynamics and external activity. External demands can stimulate internal cohesion as well as complicate it. Conversely, internal socialisation can produce increased international actorness over time, just as unpredictable upheavals inside key states can disrupt existing patterns of joint action. Key to this area are the ways in which the preferences of EU member states are articulated and the ways in which they interact, but outcomes are not only determined by procedures. The process of collective policy-formation is not an insulated one; it is penetrated or perforated by the broader activities and institutional development of the EU, and it is embedded within a variety of international/global frameworks. It is thus important not only to identify the characteristic processes of decision-making and implementation, but also to address the wider questions of legitimacy and identity. Where are the boundaries of actual and appropriate inclusion and exclusion? Turkey poses this very question at the moment in the sharpest form in relation to its potential membership of the Union.

There is a level of analysis issue to be explored here, since it might be argued that the EU—and thus its sub-system of IR—is part of an emerging system of multi-level governance in the global arena. How does EU external policy-making fit in with that of other institutions in which member states may also participate, such as the United Nations (UN), the World Trade Organization (WTO), or the Group of 8 (G8)? Lastly, there is a convergence-divergence problem to be addressed in that the differing preferences and 'weights' of the component parts of the EU's system of IR make common action often unpredictable and not straightforwardly progressive.

Third, we are interested in the ideas that bind the EU member states together. Not only is there a justifiable pride in the EU's achievement in having solved the centuries-old problem of war in western Europe, but there is also a strong emphasis in the EU's evolving approach to IR on the ideational quality of the EU's international role. This involves the development of the EU's principles and a view of its contribution to international order. The point of entry into this set of issues is the EU's association and increasing concerns with promulgating an 'ethical foreign policy'. But the more general concern of this part of the framework is to link the EU's system of IR into broader debates about these issues within the IR literature, whilst not forgetting the distinctive aspects of the EU: intense transgovernmentalism, 'civilian power', the legalisation of EU structures and processes, responsibility for the post-Cold War European security order. The European heritage, beyond the EU itself, is also relevant here: the impact of history; the ambivalent relations between Europe and the developing world; the temptation to fall back on a civilisational view of European identity in the face of external (and internal) challenges; the continuing role of national foreign and development policies. What is more there is a 'second image reversed' factor to take into account: the extent to which participation in international relations feeds back to effect changes in the EU's own political system—fostering or hindering integration, constituting common identity and determining the distribution of resources. Less portentously, various kinds of interference, intervention, complication, or mere noise may occur in the internal affairs of the EU and member states as a consequence of international relations. For the most part this will affect the capacity to generate collective action, but it may also act directly on the complex political, social, and intellectual processes by which 'Europe' comes to decide on what in the world it stands for.

The EU and the processes of International Relations

From the outset, the European project has been intimately related to the processes of international relations, by which it will be remembered, we mean the common mechanisms, formal and informal, through which international problems are confronted. During the Cold War, European integration can be seen as performing a vital role in the stabilisation of the West, and in forming the basis for a 'Europe between the Superpowers', a conception of the continent that emphasises its dual role both as a stake and as a participant in the Superpower confrontation. This duality of status was not simply a matter of high politics and security, although that was not absent: the European Economic Community (EEC) played a vital role in the evolution of the political economy of the Western Alliance. The process of détente during the 1960s and 1970s created a new context for the European project, but one in which it continued to play a central shaping role; in the 'Helsinki' process after 1975, the position of the EEC, and the evolution of European Political Cooperation, were of increasing significance, and the ways in which the development of the European political economy took place during the 1970s and 1980s had a strong shaping influence both on the Atlantic Alliance and on emerging East-West relations in Europe (a matter of some concern to successive Washington administrations).

From the mid-1980s onwards, it became part of conventional wisdom that the EC and then the EU were an emerging 'economic Superpower' and that this had implications for the roles played by the Europeans (both nationally and collectively) within the changing international order. During the current period, it is clear that the EU is intimately related to the co-existing and intersecting processes of globalisation and regionalisation, that it plays a key role in a variety of inter-regional contexts and that it is increasingly (and literally) a force to be reckoned with in the matter of international security relations, despite its continuing limitations.

This rough sketch naturally raises as many questions as it answers. If the EU is increasingly prominent, central and influential, exactly *how* has that come about and why are there still evident gaps in its capacity to shape its external environment? We shall address some of the issues arising from these questions in the third part of this chapter, but here the key focus is on the nature of the EU's activities and their links to the major global issues of the contemporary era. We are interested in four issues arising from a focus on the EU and the process of international relations.

First, we ask how the EU comes into contact with these issues, how does it contribute (differentially) to their pursuit, treatment, and resolution and how it projects 'European' interests as defined by the EU's system of international relations in interaction with the international environment. In light of what has already been said about the complexity of the EU's internal processes, we would expect that an answer to this question would depend crucially on the specific issue area in which the EU was engaged, and on the fluctuating constellation of preferences among the Union's member states and other institutions.

Second, we explore the nature of the EU's capabilities when participating in and shaping contemporary international processes. Here, the questions to be asked overlap with those we shall address when considering the EU as a 'power' (see below), but they relate sharply to its capacity to enter into the process of IR as well as to its attainment of a particular international position or impact. In particular, how does the EU muster 'hard' and 'soft' power, the 'capacity to act' in specific and diverse issue areas and the ability to regulate or to set common standards? There has been considerable discussion in both the European integration and the IR literature about exactly what the EU brings to the international table, and studies of its resources have identified a number of problems relating to the EU's 'carrying capacity' and its 'mobilisation capacity' relative to the resources available to and used by its member states. There is, though, significant evidence that the EU's institutional resources and its ability to act within key international organisations, especially in the global political economy, have strengthened and broadened over time.

Third, we enquire into problems of status and legitimacy confronted by the EU when participating in processes of international relations. What is the EU's status within international organisations and institutions, how are the roles of the EU affected by its engagement with processes of global governance, and how can EU collective action be sustained in the fact of external resistance or temptation? Because of the multilayered nature of EU policy-making, and its engagement in processes of multi-level governance within the global arena, it is clear that the potential for member state defections or deviations, or for the emergence of shifting coalitions within the Union itself, can be a key issue, affecting its capacity to maintain common positions or convey a consistent message. This inevitably links with issues of credibility and the ability to match expectations.

Finally, we explore what is (and what should be) the extent of EU involvement relative to other actors. This is a matter of intense interest and debate within the EU, but also more broadly in the international arena and international institutions. How much can the EU hope to aggregate the interests of its members, to express the 'European interest' and also to displace the activities of other international bodies such as the Organization for Security and Cooperation in Europe (OSCE), the North Atlantic Treaty Organization (NATO) and the like? Is it possible to identify the EU's distinctive (inter) 'national interests'? The Union exists in a 'multi-institutional' context, where there are always alternative channels for the pursuit of national or 'European' policies. Not only this, but the EU has powerful competitors for international influence and status, most obviously the United States at the global level but others in specific regions or sectors of activity. Most analysts would describe the EU-US contest as balanced in some areas (political economy in particular) but massively unbalanced in others (especially matters of 'hard security'). Equally, however, analysts would draw attention to the changing terms and conditions of competition between the EU and its key competitors.

The focus here is thus very directly on the EU as an 'international actor' and as an 'international interactor' within the current international arena, and on the attempt to evaluate its effectiveness not only in taking action but also in participating in or competing with other available international structures. We should be able to arrive at some broad estimate of the extent to which the EU achieves effectiveness or participation, but we must also be aware of the ways in which this feeds through into perceptions of the EU as a 'power' in international relations (see below) and into problems of world order more broadly defined. We should also be sensitive to the ways in which effectiveness is inevitably uneven, patchy and unpredictable, given the conditional legitimacy and the under-developed policy instruments in a number of key areas of the EU's makeup.

The EU as a power in International Relations

The notion of the EU as a 'power' is particularly related to the impact of the EU on the international arena. We have already discussed the notion of the EU's power resources and the issues that arise from their mobilisation or targeting. Now we need to explore the way in which the EU impacts on the 'shape' of the global arena, on specific targets in terms of external groupings or actors, and on the substance of key issues. We take the basic position that in international relations the impact of particular structures or groupings is conditioned by a number of critical variables, many of which have been touched upon already but which can be dealt with here in a more focused way.

First, the EU's international activity reflects a consistent search for settled frameworks within which to define and pursue international relationships. The EU (as noted in respect of other issues) has been a relentless generator of strategies and proposals for framework agreements, both in terms of political economy and in terms (more recently) of political/security issues. Some might link at least part of this to the EU's character as a 'trading state', seeking a stable and predictable environment in which to pursue its civilian activities (and thus not developing to a high degree the capacity, to deal with the unexpected and the fluid). The EU can be seen as expressing a fundamentally conservative bias in its approach to international relations, and as having a profound desire to systematise or pigeon-hole its growing set of relationships.

There is a persistent tension between this desire to systematise, the growing expectations of EU intervention and the persistent or growing fluidity of international order—a tension putting increased pressure on the EU and underlining the problems of attention and resource allocation pointed to earlier. It is of course possible to resolve this tension in the direction of increased EU collective capacity, but it is also quite possible that it will be resolved in favour of withdrawal from challenging areas of international relations in the wake of traumatic failures.

The issues noted above also relate strongly to issues of 'European identity' and the understandings that the EU and its member states have of its international role. Is it an inward-looking and self-referential security community, constructed not only by its institutions but also by the interactions and discourses within them? Or is it the prototype of a new form of international order founded on the management of large-scale complex systems both in the political/economic and the political/security domains?

These factors say something about the orientation of EU collective action (as well as raising questions about the extent to which the EU can or should capture the international preferences and actions of its member states and other groupings or actors). They also raise issues about impact—that is to say about the ways in which the EU impresses itself on regional and world order, the extent to which it wishes to do so, and thus the extent to which it is a force for change or consolidation.

When it comes to impact, we are interested in the following issues. First, how does the EU's impact relate to the resources deployed, to its stated preferences and to the required levels of collective action and solidarity? In principle, given the EU's propensity for explicit statements of strategy noted above, these elements can be measured and a comparison made between expected and actual performance in specific theatres of operation (for example, the Asia-Pacific, or global environmental issues). Second, how is the impact of the EU viewed by the 'recipients' of EU actions? One of the paradoxes of the EU's international role is that often it appears very much more impressive to the outsider than to the insider (or perhaps to the relatively distant rather than the intimately involved, whether they are formally outside or inside—thus it is not always apparent that the US is impressed). The actual or potential gap between understandings about the EU's international performance and impact is likely to be implicated in more general estimates of the EU's success or failure in international relations.

This links with a further question: How can we deal with variable impact across a number of different dimensions of activity? We have already seen that the EU's participation and effectiveness are uneven and patchy, and this clearly implies that impact will also be uneven and patchy. We do need to remember though that the impact of 'absence' can be as important as the impact of 'presence' (US foreign policy in the 20th century, with its fluctuating balance between isolationism and internationalism, shows ample evidence of this).

Finally, how do we frame the EU's conception of world order, and in particular the relationship between order in the near neighbourhood and order more broadly defined? Several different versions are available: a 'stabilisation of the near neighbourhood' model, an 'inter-regional' model involving competition as well as collaboration, a 'global values' model involving the elevation of global institutions and norms, and the 'conservative trading state' model noted above. The impact of the EU's changing membership is felt here, for example in the influence of the 1995 entrants. One factor that also enters into the equation is a 'costs and risks' element, in which the benefits and potential dangers of particular developments need to be weighed within the EU's institutions and among its members; another factor is a 'self-actualisation' element, in which the search for greater recognition of the EU's international status is central, and a third is an 'export model' element, in which the institutional and policy frameworks of the EU are seen as the basis for an extension of the preferred European or world order.

It is thus not clear that the EU has a unified view of the model of world order it would wish to bring about (although as will be seen later in the volume, it now has an explicit statement of security as well as economic interests), and this is one of the most serious problems of the EU's international relations. Moreover, the complexities of the post-Cold War period have made the quest for an open, rule-based, and interdependent international system based on the EU example less easy to pursue. But there are examples to be found of the ways in which the long-term nature of the world order is being modified by tendencies not far removed from those expressed in the EU (in world trade, the environment, even in the Middle East).

Structure of the volume

As noted above, in constructing this volume we have asked contributors to take into account the questions raised in this initial chapter. Thus the reader will find that in each of the following chapters there is attention to the substantive and methodological issues raised by a study of the EU's international relations. It will also be apparent that in a variety of ways, each chapter focuses on the three perspectives we have outlined above (the EU as a sub-system of international relations, the EU and processes of international relations, and the EU as a 'power' in international relations). What we have not done is to impose a strait-jacket on individual contributors: thus, the balance between substantive and methodological issues, and between the three perspectives, is different for each chapter, reflecting the focus and orientation of the topic it covers.

The chapters are grouped into four Parts. Part I, including this chapter, deals with the broad framework for understanding the EU's international relations. In this chapter, we have set out a broad framework for analysis, inevitably generating more questions than answers. In Chapter 2, Filippo Andreatta focuses explicitly on theory and methodology, asking how International Relations theory can inform our study of the EU's international relations, and indicating some of the key ways in which theory has to be adapted for the study of this area. Chapter 3, by Geoffrey Edwards, focuses on the substance of the EU's international relations, drawing attention to the key patterns of international activity and engagement, geographical and functional, and forming a foundation for more detailed study in later chapters.

Part II of the volume addresses the institutions and processes that surround the EU's international relations and that give rise to the EU's international policies. Here, the focus is inevitably more on the 'internal' characteristics and policy-making processes than on the international context, although in all cases the chapters draw attention to the ways in which the 'internal' and the 'external' are intimately linked. In Chapter 4, Sophie Vanhoonacker deals with the institutional framework for EU international policies, and explores the significance of institutional change for the character and substance of policy. Chapter 5, by Simon Nuttall, addresses a key problem in EU international policy-making, that of consistency and coherence within a complex policy-making process, especially one organised around three distinct 'pillars', in a changing global arena. In Chapter 6, Christopher Lord explores an emerging issue for all international policies, that of accountability and legitimacy, and shows how it takes specific forms within the EU's international relations. Chapter 7, by Reuben Wong, investigates the extent to which the international activities and policies of EU member states have become 'Europeanized' through a process of convergence around distinct European positions and procedures, while in Chapter 8, Michael E. Smith deals with the problem of policy implementation and shows how the EU presents a particular manifestation of some key general problems in this area.

Part III of the volume is focused on key areas of policy substance, and has the general aim of exploring the ways in which EU policies are pursued and have effects within the international arena. Chapter 9, by Jolyon Howorth, describes and analyses the dramatic ways in which the EU has moved from a generalised foreign and security policy towards a common defence policy during the late 1990s and 2000s, at least at the aspirational level. In Chapter 10, Wyn Rees takes up and investigates a different aspect of security policy, by focusing on the linkages between internal and external security in the EU—a matter of great significance in the era of the 'war on terror' and other novel security challenges. The next two chapters address the ways in which the EU relates to the global political economy: in Chapter 11, Loukas Tsoukalis deals with the relationship between the regional integration process and key areas of international interdependence in a globalising world, whilst in Chapter 12, Sophie Meunier and Kalypso Nicolaïdis take this further by exploring the conception of the EU as a 'trade power' in the global arena. There follow two chapters dealing broadly with matters of international order: Karen Smith, in Chapter 13, deals with the ways in which the enlargement of the EU has contributed to the development of a new 'European order', whilst James Mayall, in Chapter 14, addresses the relations between the EU and the developing world in light of the processes of decolonisation which have marked many member states and which have run alongside much of the European integration project. Finally, two chapters focus on specific types of relationships within the EU's international relations: in Chapter 15, Elfriede Regelsberger and Nicole de Flers investigate the ways in which the EU has developed inter-regional relations as part of a broader global strategy, and in Chapter 16, Michael Smith and Rebecca Steffenson explore the single most important bilateral relationship in the EU's international relations, that with the United States.

Part IV completes the book with two 'overview' chapters, each with a different focus. In Chapter 17, Andrew Linklater looks closely at the ways in which the EU's international relations reflect a dominant set of normative assumptions, in particular those connected with 'civilising' processes, while in Chapter 18, Christopher Hill and Michael Smith return to the initial framework set out here, reassessing it in the light of the evidence provided by the intervening contributions, and advancing a number of themes that can be extracted from them.

Conclusion

The European Union is undoubtedly a crucial dimension, as well as an important geographical area of modern international relations. It has internalised and domesticated a significant amount of previously 'foreign', and dangerous, inter-state relations. It has been drawn ineluctably into wider processes through its successes as a customs union and a commercial actor, to the point where it now aspires to a common defence and foreign policy, and the prime minister of a key member state has called for the EU to become a superpower. Whether this new phase of international activity reflects the perceived need of Europeans to do more to ensure their own security, or whether it implies the willingness to risk more through taking on responsibilities for international order, remains to be seen. One of the important tasks for academic observers and for students both of IR and of the EU now is to conduct an audit of how much has been achieved, in what areas and what it amounts to. How far are the achievements cumulative and how far variable according to issue-area? This should enable us to make judgements both on particular enterprises like the European Security and Defence Policy (ESDP) and the dynamics of the overall project. Where is the EU going in international relations? What kind of entity is it, might it be and in our judgement will it be? In this context the normative agenda must not be neglected; that is, those principles or discourses which have been historically or are currently dominant in Europe's relations with the outside world, and those that represent possible futures. We hope that by using this book, students and those with a broader interest will be enabled to answer—or at least define more sharply the questions: who and what is the EU for, in its international relations? What should it be trying to achieve and how might this be done?

Perceptions of European foreign policy—in the broadest sense—are important entry-points both for charting actual progress and for understanding the reasons for disagreement over the EU's role. Domestic opinion, national and transnational, as well as the views held by outsiders, generate capability-expectation gaps, which may or may not then narrow according to homeostatic processes. How the EU looks from beyond its borders is a particularly important area to investigate. As noted above, this involves the images held by non-EU citizens both of the EU in general, and of its differentiated roles by region and issue area. By focusing on these areas, this book should provide the basis for more detailed appreciation of the ways in which the EU has had and will have an impact on the international arena.

We hope that the questions and general framework, as well as the more focused contributions, provided in this book will take further a detailed deconstruction of the issues involved in understanding the EU's international relations, and encourage others to pursue the questions raised in greater depth. Academic International Relations has perhaps tended to leave this subject for too long to a coven of specialists, when it has a great deal to offer to the wider study of international relations, as well as much to take from it.

Further reading

The following list provides an initial set of perspectives on international relations and the European Union. Thus, it contains the key 'standard' introductions to the international relations of the European Union (Bretherton and Vogler 1999; Ginsberg 2001; Smith, H. 2002; Smith, K. 2003, 2004; White 2001), together with selected works taking further some of the key issues: foreign policy analysis (Carlsnaes, Sjursen and White 2004), security and order (Kelstrup and Williams 2000; Schimmelfennig 2003) and regionalism (Telò 2001). Many of the issues touched on in this chapter are taken up in more detail and fully referenced in later chapters.

Bretherton, C., and Vogler, J. (1999), *The European Union as a Global Actor* (London: Routledge).

Carlsnaes, W., Sjursen, H. and White, B. (eds) (2004), *Contemporary European Foreign Policy* (London: Sage).

Ginsberg, R. (2001), *The European Union in International Politics: Baptism by Fire* (Lanham, MD: Rowman and Littlefield).

Kelstrup, M., and Williams, M. (eds) (2000), *International Relations Theory and the Politics of European Integration: Power, Security and Community* (London: Routledge).

Schimmelfennig, F. (2003), *The EU, NATO and the Integration of Europe: Rules and Rhetoric* (Cambridge: Cambridge University Press).

Smith, H. (2002), *European Union Foreign Policy: what it is and what it does* (London: Pluto Press).

Smith, K. (2003), *European Union Foreign Policy in a Changing World* (Cambridge: Polity).

Smith, K. (2004), *The Making of European Union Foreign Policy: the case of Eastern Europe*, 2nd edn (Basingstoke: Palgrave/Macmillan).

Smith, M.E. (2003), *Europe's Foreign and Security Policy: The Institutionalization of Cooperation* (Cambridge: Cambridge University Press).

Telò, M. (ed.) (2001), *European Union and New Regionalism: Regional Actors and Global Governance in a Post-Hegemonic Era* (Aldershot: Ashgate).

White, B. (2001), *Understanding European Foreign Policy* (Basingstoke: Palgrave Macmillan).

Web links

Basic information on the international activities of the EU can be found on the Commission web site: http://www.europa.eu.int, where there are pages for all of the many international involvements of the Union, especially those dealing with external relations generally, with foreign and security policy and with external trade and development. For more detailed and specific information on various aspects of 'European foreign policy', see especially the Fornet web site, http://www.fornet/info and the web site of the European Foreign Policy Unit at the London School of Economics and Political Science, http://lse.ac.uk/Depts/intrel/EuroFPUnit.html.

Chapter 2

Theory and the European Union's International Relations[1]

Filippo Andreatta

Contents

Summary

This chapter places the study of the EU's international relations into two related theoretical contexts. First, it explores the ways in which the classical explanations of European integration—federalism and functionalism—incorporate the international dimension, and highlights their limits. Second, the chapter moves on to explore the ways in which a range of International Relations theories can account for the processes by which the EU frames its external policies and for the EU's impact on the international arena. The chapter concludes by focusing on the role played by the EU in international relations, and on the possible future development of a European foreign policy.

Introduction

Theoretical work on international relations is characterised by a high degree of heterogeneity. It is divided along paradigmatic lines between realism, which is pessimistic about progress in political relationships, liberalism, which is more optimistic about the possibility of avoiding conflict, and various alternative approaches, which reject realist and liberal traditional views about the centrality of states in international affairs. It is also divided along cultural lines between American scholars, who tend to emphasise the role of power, European scholars, who highlight the role of values and rules, and non-Western scholars, who tend to concentrate on issues of political, economic, and cultural development. Finally, theories of international politics are very much the product of the times in which they are developed, and one could easily distinguish at least four different periods: the inter-war years, the aftermath of the Second World War, the final phase of the Cold War after the late 1970s, and the contemporary, post-Cold War, period.

Despite this diversity, there is a paradox in the relationship between the theoretical study of international politics and the development of a common European foreign policy, defined broadly as the attempt of the European Union and its member states to ensure that their many and various external relations present as coherent a face as possible to the outside world. On the one hand, the study of international relations has always been considerably eurocentric, as it developed strongly in Europe after the First World War, and even when, after the Second World War, it mainly shifted to the United States, the Cold War kept the focus on the problem of European order. On the other hand, the development of a common European foreign policy has been largely ignored by international relations theorists, or treated as a purely empirical event (Rosamond 2000a). Somewhat surprisingly, even when Europe is dealt with, it is treated mainly from a general integration point of view rather than in terms of foreign policy. For this reason, the study of European institutions is more easily found in international political economy (IPE) syllabi, because of the more advanced integration which has taken place in the trade and monetary fields, than in traditional international politics courses.

The reasons for this paradox are threefold. Firstly, whereas most mainstream theories of international politics deal with states and their relations amongst each other, the European Union is neither a state nor a traditional alliance, and it therefore represents a heterodox unit of analysis. Secondly, since IR theory has a bias towards the explanation of broad phenomena it tends towards generalisations, while the European Union is, at least so far, a unique example of international cooperation and integration (Wallace 1994). As will later be argued, the precise nature of European foreign policy and the attempt to view its explanations in a general, rather than specific, framework, are the questions at the heart of the theoretical debate on the subject. Thirdly, the achievements of treaty-based integration (Pillar I of the Treaty of European Union), whether in trade, agriculture, or money, seem more substantial than those in the area of the Common Foreign and Security Policy (i.e. CFSP, in Pillar II), which is intergovernmental and will remain so, even if the Pillars are formally abolished.

This chapter will firstly review the main schools of thought which have advanced an explanation for the emergence of European institutions in general and a common European foreign policy in particular. It will begin with an account of the two classic accounts of European integration—federalism and neofunctionalism—and then move on to discuss the views of the main traditions in IR theory: realism, liberalism, and alternative approaches. The analysis of the causes of the emergence of a European foreign policy will be followed by a discussion of its consequences, with a review of the most important suggestions about the role and impact of European foreign policy with respect to the global international system. A final section will deal with the likely future developments, and the light cast on them by theory. It should be borne in mind that different theories highlight different aspects of the EU's international role and capabilities. Federalism and realism, for instance, tend to focus on high politics, while neofunctionalism and liberalism inherently cast the net wider, to include the cultural and political economy aspects of external activity.

Classical explanations: Federalism and neofunctionalism

The classic account of European integration derives from federalism. For this school of thought, the main problem in international relations is international anarchy, because the independence of multiple nation states brings mistrust, reciprocal threats, rivalry, and conflict. Federalists were concerned about events in the first half of the twentieth century, which had brought about two world wars, and thought that the decentralisation of sovereignty had been the root cause of conflict. They were therefore sceptical about traditional remedies for interstate anarchy, such as diplomacy or the balance of power, and suggested a truly revolutionary solution which tackled the very essence of the international system: the abolition of national independence and the fusion of different political entities into one. According to Altiero Spinelli (1972, 68; see also Lodge 1984, Pinder 1991) 'the national states have lost their property rights since they cannot guarantee the political and economic safety of their citizens'. Federalists therefore built on the tradition dating back to the Enlightment's schemes for perpetual peace (Hinsley 1963), as well as on the American example, in which the Union allowed the thirteen colonies to defend each other, but also to avoid mutual attacks (Deudney 1995).

Federalists believed that a union would bring Europe to solve conflict among different groups by an institutional *deus ex machina*, since no group would any longer enjoy the liberty to resort unilaterally to arms. The autonomous use of force, or even the liberty to raise independent armies, would be legally forbidden. A supranational form of government, according to a domestic analogy, would regulate relations among states as governments do internally among citizens (Suganami 1989). The reasons for unification, according to federalists, are ultimately political, and have to do with the objective of tackling international anarchy and the conflicts it tends to produce. According to the classical distinction between 'high politics', which concerns life and death issues of political order and violence and 'low politics', which revolves around economic and social questions, federalism is situated firmly on the first side.

Federalism typically sets up two tiers of government, the parts and the whole, and distributes specific functions to each (Friedrich 1968). However, a federation must enjoy ultimate control of the instruments of violence, otherwise there is the risk that the parties fight with each other or with the central, supranational power. The achievement of a common defence and foreign policy is therefore the main aim of the federalist project. However, the federalist approach to the question is more normative than analytic in nature, as it could be expected from a tradition firmly rooted in political philosophy. It is more a discussion of why states should form a union rather than an explanation of why they would eventually surrender their sovereignty, despite the fact that such a voluntary transfer has been extremely rare in history, and even in the European case is still far from certain. It nonetheless remains true that one of the strongest arguments for federalism, theoretical and practical, is the perceived need to have an effective European foreign policy.

The other classical approach to European integration derives from the functionalist school. Functionalists believed that modern society was increasingly dominated by matters of 'low politics' such as the welfare of citizens and economic growth and criticised federalists because of their neglect of such issues. The fundamental motive for integration would not therefore concern the legal relationships between political communities, but would stem from the inability of nation states to provide essential services to their citizens. While the first school deals with groups, the latter stresses the importance of individuals. According to functionalism, political functions must be performed at the most efficient level, and its logic ultimately leads to the whole world being unified. Mitrany therefore criticised European federalists for their narrow geographical focus. 'Between the conception of continental unions and that of a universal league there is a difference not merely of degree but of essence. The one would proceed in the old way by a definition of territory, the other by definition of functions; and while the unions would define their territory as a means of differentiating between members and outsiders, a league would select and define functions for the contrary purpose of integrating with regard to the interests of all' (Mitrany 1933, 116; see also Mitrany 1943, 1975).

The neofunctionalists, who became a significant factor in political science in the 1960s, utilised Mitrany's framework of analysis, and its emphasis on 'low politics', but agreed with federalists, in contrast with Mitrany, on the desirability and feasibility of a continental union and of a superstate, eventually with its own foreign and defence policy. For the most prominent neofunctionalist, Ernest Haas (1958, 16; see also 1964, Nye 1971) integration brings 'loyalties, expectations and political activities toward a new centre, whose institutions possess or demand jurisdiction over the pre-existing national states. The end result of a process of political integration is a new political community, superimposed over the pre-existing ones'. Neofunctionalists believed that the process of integration is endogenous, meaning that the current level of integration determines—by facilitating and amplifying them—future levels. The expectation is therefore of an 'ever closer Union' based on original intentions as well as on the integration already reached. The mechanism behind unification is radically different from that identified by federalists. There is in fact no conscious and explicit attempt to introduce a new federal constitution, as, according to Haas, '[a] new central authority may emerge as an unintended consequence of incremental earlier steps'. Neofunctionalist integration proceeds incrementally and spontaneously by a process of spillover. Integration—even in a secondary and technical area—creates pressures to integrate contiguous areas for which the original area is crucial and which, therefore, can no longer be controlled at the national level. Functional spillover, from one area to the next, generates a technical spillover, which enlarges at the supranational level the dimension fit to deal with the issue. Technical spillovers—in turn—can create a political spillover, meaning that formal control is necessarily transferred from the national level, and political loyalties and attentions are shifted to the supranational level.

The increasing difficulty in dealing with technical issues at the national level, and the tendency of integration to generate spillovers, can be exploited by supranational agencies, which could therefore promote a strategy for further integration 'from above'. Integration in coal and steel would therefore have generated conditions for the wider customs union, which eventually has brought about the single market. From the single market would have emerged the demand for monetary coordination, firstly, and, secondly, for a monetary union, which would now generate pressure for closer coordination of economic policies. Just as a rock can provoke an avalanche, integration in a specific and technical area, such as coal and steel, can eventually lead, by a series of small and gradual steps, to integration in a very wide area crucial for national sovereignty. The process follows an incremental path, in the sense that there is no single moment, unlike the introduction of a federalist constitution, which can be identified as the point of no return. The functionalist framework even allows for non linear paths of integration. According to Schmitter (1974) integration could happen in wider areas but without institutional deepening (spill around), or with institutional deepening but without involving other areas (buildup). In certain extreme circumstances, integration could even recede by reducing the institutional deepening in a certain area due to national resistance (retrenchment) or by returning authority in an area to the national level (spill back).

In the neofunctionalist framework, because of its emphasis on 'low politics' and its traditional distaste for power politics, foreign policy is relegated to an ancillary position, and it is generally expected that political spillovers, will follow economic and social integration. The failures of the EDC and the Fouchet Plans, of 1952–54 and 1961–62 respectively, could be ascribed to a failure to wait for natural spillovers. However, there remains one possibility for integrating foreign policy even before the completion of the process in other fields, as is demonstrated by the arrival of European Political Cooperation in the 1970s, well before the main thrust of integration in the 1980s and 1990s. That is, other states outside the integration process can provide a stimulus for integration in the foreign policy field, a process known as 'externalization', due to non members' pressures to negotiate with a single partner rather than with all member states individually (Schmitter 1969). In this case also then, a functional demand could lead to a decision on the part of European states to pool their resources for maximising efficacy, facilitated by the fact that foreign policy does not involve legislation and usually implies low sunk costs.

European integration and IR theory

The two classic approaches have been criticised mainly on two counts. On the one hand, their emphasis was too eurocentric. Both schools were in fact formulated in general terms, but they highlighted characteristics of the process of European integration which were not to be found in other regions of the world. Federalism and neofunctionalism appeared more specific 'local' theories apt to explain events in Western Europe than general models of behaviour in international politics. On the other hand, they employed a teleological approach, taking eventual full integration for granted, and underestimating both the potential resistance of the nation state as well as the possibility of forms of integration which could stop short of the creation of a superstate. For these reasons, the theoretical debate in the 1970s shifted towards accounts more in tune with the broader paradigms in international relations theory (Hoffmann 1964), which gave more importance than the classical theories to the role of states in the international system and which utilised variables having a broader empirical base of application. In particular, most of these accounts specify exogenous causes for integration, pointing out that each further step in integration must rest on actors' interests rather than on an inertial and teleological process leading to a predefined—and superstate—result. It follows that these approaches could also take into account the possibility that integration could lead to various possible outcomes.

The beginning of European Political Cooperation (EPC) in the 1970s—as well as the resilience of the wider process of European integration—constituted a turning point in the conceptualisation of the foreign policy of European institutions. These first timid attempts contradicted expectations, as for example those of the Tindemans Report, that a common European foreign policy could happen only when basic integration had been achieved. EPC demonstrated that there was indeed a foreign policy dimension to the EEC, and it therefore forced those theorists who had hitherto ignored the issue to consider the subject. On the other hand, the limits of EPC also forced the enthusiasts for integration to reconsider their position as it became clear that European institutions would not soon acquire the cohesiveness of a superstate. These reasons induced the two main schools of thought in international relations theory, realism and liberalism, belatedly to come to terms with European integration in general and with the role of European institutions in the world in particular.

Realism, which will be dealt with more in depth below, was the dominant 'paradigm' in the study of international politics and was based on three main assumptions:

1. The state is the dominant actor on the international scene, and is capable of acting as a coherent, unitary and rational unit.

2. Since states recognise no authority above them, international relations are in a state of anarchy, or lack of hierarchy, which forces states to self help.

3. In anarchy, politics is dominated by military considerations and by the fragility of trust and cooperation. War is therefore always a possibility.

Realism is therefore concentrated—like federalism—on 'high politics' and shares much of its analysis on the conflictual consequences of anarchy, although it is not optimistic on the ability of states to develop sufficient trust to enter into a federation.

Liberals, who had already abandoned their utopian roots, responded with different assumptions which allowed for a more flexible, and positive, view of the world:

1. States are not the only actors in world politics. Other types of actors are important at the supranational (international organisation, such as the EEC), transnational (for example, multinational corporations or religious organisations), or subnational level (for instance, interest groups or political parties).

2. Interstate anarchy can therefore be tamed by a network of relations between states, between states and other types of actors, and between other types of actors themselves.

3. International politics is not fully determined by the distribution of military power. Other issues, namely of an economic nature, can be crucial. There is more room for choice than in realist accounts, allowing for cooperation and the development of international institutions.

Liberals envisaged a more complex model of international politics, which could more easily account for the role of European institutions in world politics. In particular, liberals tended to share neofunctionalist assumptions about the importance of 'low politics' and the necessity of interstate cooperation, although they also shared realist scepticism about the ultimate abandonment of national sovereignty.

It is therefore possible to sketch a typology of the main theories of European integration according to two variables (see Table 2.1). On the one hand, while realists and federalists concentrate on high politics, liberals and neofunctionalists give more emphasis to the importance of low politics. On the other, while federalists and neofunctionalists believe that the end result of the process of integration will be a fully fledged Union, realists and liberals argue that integration could well stop short of the creation of a superstate. According to Karl Deutsch (Deutsch *et al.* 1957, cf. also Deutsch 1968, Adler and Barnett 1998) integration brings states into a 'security community', which is a group of states among which war is so improbable as to

Table 2.1 Main approaches to integration

		Motive for integration	
		'high politics'	'low politics'
End result of integration	'pluralistic security community'	Realism	Liberalism
	'amalgamated security community'	Federalism	Neofunctionalism

become unthinkable. If integration brings about a unified state, it leads to an 'amal-gamated' security community, while it is termed a 'pluralistic' security community if it maintains the independence of members.

Realist views of European foreign policy

Realists are in general sceptical about the possibility of international cooperation, given the constraints of anarchy. In particular, realist theories assume that 'the most basic motive driving states is survival. States want to maintain their sovereignty' (Mearsheimer 1994/5, 10). For these reasons, 'realism [. . .is not. . .] well designed to ex-plain the political integration of Western Europe' (Wayman and Diehl 1994, 17). Yet the success of European integration and the beginning of a 'European' foreign policy have somehow forced realists to give an explanation to these phenomena, even at the cost of adapting their main theories. According to Grieco: 'the interest displayed by the European countries in the EU creates a problem for realist theory' (Grieco 1997b, 184; see also 1995, 1996).

The founder of neorealism, the most influential contemporary version of realism, Kenneth Waltz, has advanced a 'local' solution to the question of European integra-tion. For Waltz, integration is an exceptional event:

> Although the integration of nations is often talked about, it seldom takes place. Nations could mutually enrich themselves by further dividing not just the labor that goes into the production of goods, but also some of the other tasks they perform, such as polit-ical management and military defence. Why does their integration not take place? (Waltz, 1979, 105)

There are exceptions to this rule, as there is 'the fact that some states may persist-ently seek goals that they value more highly than survival; they may, for example, prefer amalgamation with other states' (Waltz 1979, 92). However, even if it even-tually took place, integration could only alter the distribution of power among different units (for example, the United States of Europe would become a world superpower), but it could not alter the basic characteristics of the international sys-tem, as the fusion of several states into one does not alter the anarchic relationship between the new unit and all the other ones which have not participated in the union (Waltz 1987, 226). When asked to comment on the future of international polit-ics after the end of the Cold War, Waltz states that 'the emerging world will neverthe-less be one of four or five great powers, whether the European one is called Germany or the United States of Europe' (Waltz 1993, 70). In a 2000 article, Waltz suggests that Europe will not become a great power 'in the absence of radical change' (essentially Europe becoming a state). He is dubious about the prospects of this and, therefore, predicts a European great power is unlikely (Waltz 2000, 31–32).

Although Waltz's attempt to conceptualise the EU may help to save the general propositions of the neorealist model, it does not account for the causes which may have brought integration about. Other realist theories have thus provided hypotheses in this respect, which are consistent with the realist framework in general and in particular with its emphasis on rational state strategies and the constraints imposed by the international system. In other words, integration may be seen as a rational response to the peculiar systemic position, and the consequent war exhaustion, in which European countries have found themselves after 1945. While one group of theories concentrates on the position of Europe within the wider international system, another group analyses the systemic conditions within Europe itself. Of these, the first is the role of American hegemony within the Western camp. According to Robert Gilpin (1981), international cooperation is possible only when a state is capable of imposing order in the international system by virtue of its superior power. When there is a clear hierarchy of power, there are few or no clashes of interests, as the stronger state can impose its will and the weaker ones have to conform to its wishes. The United States during the Cold War wanted to increase the power of the Western coalition against the Soviet Union and wished Western Europe to contribute to its own defence, and therefore favoured measures—such as integration—which reduced inter-allied conflicts and increased collective economic and military efficiency.

Other theories emphasise the role of the post-war bipolar structure of the international system. According to Joanne Gowa (1989), in bipolar systems agreements between states are stable and durable because alignments are structurally determined, allowing for a higher degree of cooperation and trust. By contrast, alignments in multipolar systems are the result of choice among multiple options and can therefore change over time. Cooperation is therefore inhibited by the risk that today's friends will become tomorrow's adversaries. The main point of the theories linking European integration to the Cold War international system is that, with the end of bipolarity, the structural conditions for the emergence of European cooperation will be altered.

This could have ambivalent effects on European cohesion. In John Mearsheimer's pessimistic view, even the established achievements of integration may be subject to revision: 'Without the Soviet threat or an American night watchman, Western European states will do what they did for centuries before the onset of the Cold War, look upon one another with suspicion. [...] Cooperation in this new order will be more difficult than it was during the Cold War. Conflict will be more likely' (Mearsheimer 1990, 46). However, the end of bipolarity might also be seen as a stimulus for deeper European cooperation in the foreign policy sphere. With the end of the Soviet threat, the Western alliance which was created to counter it would also lose its rationale. Kenneth Waltz (1993) has suggested that NATO, like all other alliances, will not eventually survive the loss of the threat which gave rise to it in the first place. The end—or the weakening—of transatlantic ties could spur Europe to a more active role in the world, or even to an attempt to 'balance' American power, which after the demise of the Soviet Union has become preponderant and may have inaugurated a 'unipolar' world awaiting challengers. In the view of realists, a stronger Europe would anyway contribute to the weakening of the relationship with the United States. For example, according to Henry Kissinger (1966, 232) 'European unity is not a major cure-all for Atlantic disagreements. In many respects it may magnify rather than reduce differences. As Europe gains structure, it will be in a better position to insist on differences whose ultimate cause is structural rather than personal.' More recently, Lawrence Kaplan (1996, 29) has argued that: 'If the European movement ultimately embraces a military component, it could be the final act in NATO's history.'

The other group of realist theories concentrates on international relations within Western Europe itself, and is therefore less dependent on broader systemic conditions. In particular, Joseph Grieco, elaborating on an earlier insight by Hans Morgenthau (1973, 509), suggests that European integration may be the result of the attempts of other member states to constrain Germany, especially after it has emerged potentially stronger after unification. According to Grieco, 'if states share a common interest and undertake negotiations on rules constituting a collaborative arrangement, then the weaker but still influential partners will seek to ensure that the rules so constructed will provide sufficient opportunities for them to voice their concerns and interests and thereby prevent or at least ameliorate their domination by stronger partners' (Grieco 1995, 34; see also 1996, 1997a). Robert Art agrees on the fact that 'the desire for security vis-à-vis one another has played a role in the Western European states' second great push for closer union in the 1990s, just as it did during their first great push in the late 1940s and early 1950s' (Art 1996, 2). Agreement was therefore possible because 'if other nations did not completely trust Germany, neither did Germans completely trust themselves [and this is why they chose] a strategy of voluntary self-entanglement' (Art 1996, 24).

More generally, the efforts to create a common European foreign policy could be conceptualised as a strong and permanent form of alliance. Paul Schroeder (1976; see also Gelpi 1999) has suggested that alliances are formed for two main purposes: 'capability aggregation and the control of allies'. In order to gain on these two fronts, states are willing to limit their own autonomy and follow the prescriptions of alliances and other international agreements (Snyder 1997). Integration could represent a more dramatic loss of autonomy justified by an equally dramatic increase in common capabilities and in the capacity for mutual control. After all, as Stephen Krasner (1999; see also Caporaso 1996) argues, absolute 'Westphalian' sovereignty is an abstract concept which has in history tolerated many exceptions. Given the drastic changes in Europe's international position after the Second World War, and in particular the realisation that continental anarchy could have near suicidal consequences and that European states had no longer the critical mass to compete with the superpowers decision to begin integration become logical. Where this realisation was clearer, such as in the defeated Axis countries—Italy and Germany—the propensity to integrate was higher than in the victorious continental powers—such as France and the Benelux countries, which had been subject to German occupation—and higher still than in the United Kingdom, which had not even been invaded.

The importance given by realists to security considerations as a key motive for integration seems substantiated by historical experience. On the one hand, Goertz and Diehl (1992, 54) have shown that integration is indeed a rare phenomenon. Of all territorial changes, only 5% have happened by political unification, while 72.4% have happened by the more traditional means of conquest, annexation, and secession. On the other hand, in his study of federalism, William Riker (1964, 1975, 1996) has analysed all the 35 successful cases of political unification until 1975, finding that in all cases there was an internal or external military threat. In those attempts in which a threat was absent, political unification was unsuccessful.

Liberal views

The liberal paradigm is more easily adapted to explain European integration and the emergence of a European common foreign policy for two reasons. On the one hand, liberals adopt a more flexible approach than realists on the question of the actors in international politics, allowing also for a role of supranational organisations. On the other hand, liberals are generally more optimistic on the prospects of interstate cooperation, and are therefore more willing to acknowledge the successes of the European Community and the European Union. There are three main liberal groups of theories which can be applied to the subject in question: republican, commercial, and institutional.

The first group of theories is based on the importance of domestic regimes in the formulation of foreign policy. Democracies (or Republics, in Kantian language) behave differently from non-democracies in the international scene, because they are forced to take the electorate's view into account, because they are governed by a complex institutional mechanism, and because they are based on norms prescribing peaceful conflict resolution (Doyle 1983, Russett et al. 1993, Lynn-Jones and Miller 1996, Russett and Oneal 2001, Lipson 2003). In particular, democracies tend, for these reasons, not to go to war with each other, forming a democratic security community, in which a separate peace rules. European integration would therefore be a result of the democratisation which has taken place after the Second World War in the Western half of the continent.

One interesting work which employs a similar line of thought is Mancur Olson's *The Rise and Decline of Nations* (1982), which emphasises that, in democratic politics, younger regimes are more capable of engaging in policies which favour general interests, while older regimes are more prone to be influenced by particular interests, which have had more time to organise their collective action. In the case of European integration, it would follow that the timing of the process would be influenced by its proximity with the end of the Second World War, given that most European countries had to rebuild their political systems after the conflict. This would also help to explain the different propensities of the various countries (Koenig-Archibugi 2004), with the most recent democracies—Italy and Germany—more enthusiastic than the older ones, and with the oldest, the United Kingdom, least eager of all. History thus plays an important role in explaining integration. Those countries which suffered defeat in 1945 were able to establish new democratic institutions as well as European cooperation, while in other areas of the world democratisation has been either not as fast or not contemporaneous.

Olson's more general theory of public goods is also useful to highlight the limits of Europe's common policies. When a collaborative arrangement produces a public good, each party to the agreement has an interest in free riding; that is, in enjoying the benefits without paying the costs. Given that all parties are subject to this incentive, however, there is a tendency to underproduce public goods as most or all will defect, producing a suboptimal result. With respect to Europe's common foreign policy, this means that even if all members agreed on a basic policy and found it desirable to implement it, it could still fail since each would prefer that others shoulder the cost of its implementation. Christopher Hill (1996, 7) suggests that European states 'find it genuinely difficult to reach agreement on group strategies and then to hold to these strategies once agreements are reached'.

The theory of public goods could also help to explain why European integration has advanced much further in the economic sphere than in the field of foreign policy. On the one hand, the latter area is less divisible and it is therefore more prone to collective action failures than economic development, which provides incentives for everyone to participate. On the other hand, American military preponderance in the Western alliance, which was necessary (and sufficient) to deter the Soviet Union, gave no real incentives to Europeans to spend intensively on defence, because their security was already guaranteed, and led to the frequent debates about burden sharing within NATO, as the United States were contributing a disproportionate amount of resources to the collective defence effort (Oneal 1990, Lepgold 1998). Liberals, unlike realists, believe that NATO is based on common values and ideologies, and that it can therefore survive both the end of the Cold War and a stronger European profile. According to Olson and Zeckhauser (1966, 279) 'a union of smaller members of NATO, for example, could be helpful, and be in the interest of the United States. Such a union would give the people involved an incentive to contribute more toward the goals they shared with their then more nearly equal partners. Whatever the disadvantages on other grounds of these policy possibilities, they at least have the merit that they help to make the national interest of individual nations more nearly compatible with the efficient attainment of the goals which groups of nations hold in common'.

The emphasis on domestic structures has also produced the so-called intergovernmentalist school. Building on the model of two-level games first developed by Robert Putnam (1988; see also Evans, Jacobson and Putnam 1993, Milner 1997), this tradition envisages a world in which governments act on two arenas simultaneously: the domestic and the international. Andrew Moravcsik, who more than any other scholar can be associated with intergovernmentalism, argues that—on the one hand—governments negotiate at the supranational level only on those issues which are favoured by their domestic constituencies, since their primary interest is in being re-elected. Indeed, in these models the government is designated as 'agent' of a 'principal' which is the social coalition supporting them. On the other hand, Moravcsik suggests that: 'international negotiations and institutions change the domestic context in which policy is made by redistributing [...] political resources [...]. The reallocation of control over domestic political resources [...] generally favours those who directly oversee national involvement in international negotiations and institutions, generally executives. [...] This shift in domestic power resources feeds back into international agreements, often facilitating international cooperation' (Moravcsik 1998, 3). In other words, by delegating certain policies to a supranational level, governments can increase, rather than decrease, their power because they gain extra resources against their domestic adversaries. Integration is therefore a process under strict governmental planning, and proceeds only when governments judge it in their interest to resort to supranational strategies and to reinforce their control over a certain issue. In this view, foreign policy would remain outside the 'community' integrated framework which characterises monetary or commercial policy, and could remain rigidly separated from integration in general. Conversely, once major commitments are made, they are difficult to back out of, which makes a genuinely collective foreign policy an important Rubicon to cross.

This line of thought is substantiated by the historical enquiry of Alan Milward, who has argued that European integration—far from eroding national sovereignty—has helped to reinforce European states in the reconstruction era. Regarding the origins of the EC, Milward (1992, 12; see also 1984) writes that 'nation-states have played the dominant role in its formation and retained firm control over their new creation'. In this view, foreign policy has undergone less integration than other areas, such as monetary or agricultural affairs, because governments already enjoy a high degree of autonomy in that particular field. This position also explains the emergence of a so-called 'democratic deficit', according to which decisions at the European level are not subject to the same controls as decisions at the national level (Kaiser 1971, Sharpf 1999, Koenig-Archibugi 2002).

The second group of liberal theories is based on the commercial tradition and stresses the importance of economic processes (Rosecrance 1986). According to this school of thought, the recent growth in transnational flows has created interdependent modern societies which have altered the traditional conception of 'national interest' (Keohane and Nye 1977). In particular, security matters have lost their preeminence vis-à-vis economic considerations and the latter force governments to unprecedented levels of collaboration. The difficulty in controlling transnational interdependence with the scale of the nation-state has even created an incentive to pool political resources together by building institutions with a sufficient critical mass to deal with the new issues. European integration would then be a byproduct of this more general process, given Europe's tighter web of transnational relations and the relatively small dimensions of its states, for example compared to the United States. The interdependence school borrows from functionalist logic, although it does not share its teleological conclusions, and its insights regarding foreign policy depend on the extent that contemporary interdependence creates a demand for a common and unified European role in world affairs. For example, this approach could help to account for the different levels of success in developing a common position in the various fields, with a higher propensity to integrate foreign economic policy than military capabilities, for which, given Europe's relative sense of security, there is a less intense feeling of urgency. Relations on security matters with the United States have also mainly remained close (with the exception of 'out of area' problems), whereas more frequent conflict has arisen in trade issues, given Europe's wider and deeper capabilities in economic affairs.

The last group of liberal theories concerns the development of international institutions. According to neoliberal institutionalists, conflict in the international system is an effect of the lack of trust between states in a condition of anarchy. Although this places them close to realists, cooperation is still presumed to be possible. Using simple game-theoretic reasoning, this school of thought shows that negotiations can lead to suboptimal outcomes, even when there exists a common interest in cooperation. However, it is possible to reinforce the prospect of cooperation by enhancing the commonality of interests among players, by reducing the number of uncertain variables, and by reiterating the interaction in a more structured setting (Keohane 1984, Axelrod and Keohane 1985, Hasenclever et al. 1997; for an application to the European Community, see Martin 1992). These conditions can be created by establishing international institutions, aimed at reducing uncertainty and mistrust in interstate relations. When transaction costs are prohibitive, and ad hoc institutions are not economical, states may even resort to integration (Lake 1996, Weber 1997, Koenig-Archibugi 2000). The institutionalist model has been applied to European common security policy by Carsten Tams (1999), who argues that European institutions serve the purpose of ameliorating collective action problems emerging from cooperation in the military field. In particular, while France and Germany wish for stronger European institutions because the more ambitious the project the more acute are the collective action problems, the United Kingdom prefers weaker institutions because it wants a more limited role for European foreign policy.

Alternative approaches

A number of critiques have been developed over the years against the mainstream debate between realists and liberals, which has been considered by some too rigid to capture the essence of international politics. In particular, in the last two decades a number of alternative approaches has emerged emphasising the importance of cognitive factors in the elaboration of foreign policy, which had been ignored by the more 'scientific' and 'positivist' methodology of both realists and liberals. On the one hand, while the traditional theories assume the rationality of actors, some middle range theories based on the foreign policy analysis tradition employ notions of 'bounded rationality', which take into account the cognitive constraints facing decision-makers. The limited amount of time to gather information, its possible bias and the limited capacity to process it, lead to decisions based on less than full rationality. On the other hand, other theories, influenced by postmodernism, question the ability to observe social events objectively, opting for a more 'reflective' approach based on the fact that even theories are an inextricable part of social reality. More than the explanation 'from the outside' of international events, scholars should therefore concentrate on the understanding 'from the inside' of the point of view of decision makers, reconstructing the objective as well as the subjective milieu in which they operated (Hollis and Smith 1991). Both groups of theories—in short—agree that the emphasis placed by realists and liberals alike on 'exogenous' objective interests is misplaced and that it is better to consider actors' motives as an 'endogenous' variable dependent on certain cognitive conditions. This would allow us to overcome a rigid agent-structure divide and to conceptualise agents and structures as 'mutually constitutive' (Wendt 1987).

   These approaches tend to consider European institutions as more than a simple set of rules, and can be organised into three groups, all of which might be seen as loosely associated with the burgeoning school of thought known as 'constructivism', in that they ascribe importance to the social origins of behaviour, and to the power of ideas (Bretherton and Vogler 1999, 28–36). Firstly, although states do not transfer sovereignty to institutions and retain, in theory, ultimate control over their policies, in practice states tend to conform to the institutional rules and 'scripts' to which they have subscribed (Hall and Taylor 1996). In other words, states adopt the logic of appropriateness according to which they follow institutional rules, unless this explicitly infringes one of their vital interests, because they fear being considered untrustworthy or 'inappropriate' (March and Olsen 1998). Institutions can therefore penetrate into a foreign policy standard operating procedure and influence decisions by, for example, fostering common platforms which are then followed by national policies in the absence of better alternatives. A process of 'Europeanization' could follow which, like a coordinated reflex, could progressively draw national positions closer. Furthermore, policy networks and epistemic communities can influence decision-making in an institutional context (Haas, 1992). Belief systems can also be viewed from a post-positivist viewpoint as a means of identifying 'general lines in a country's foreign policy', as for example in the form of national attitudes and discourses on European integration (Larsen 1997, 10).

Secondly, other approaches emphasise that states do not seek only material objectives, but are also inspired by ideological motivations. European institutions are therefore to be considered in this light as a normative entity. At a minimum, the fact that the EU exists creates pressures to preserve its unity, and develops a consistent bias toward common, rather than national, positions. At a maximum, the existence of the EU as an institution which embodies certain principles—democracy, the rule of law, human rights, free markets—creates an incentive for states to sustain those same objectives and constitute a 'European' identity. States which are part of the process become socialised with institutional aims and with those of other members. According to Wayne Sandholtz (1996, 406), institutions 'allow [. . .] governments to become intimately acquainted with the goals, aversions, tastes and domestic constraints of each other'. Having provided a normative and ethical framework for relations within Western Europe, the EU could then project these same instincts externally, constituting an 'ethical power' on the world stage.

Thirdly, institutions and norms can be seen as part of the international environment facing states. In particular, the presence of a tight network of rules in Western Europe can approximate the traditional conception—introduced by the English school of international relations—of an international society. Unlike in an international system, in which interactions between states occur in a normative vacuum, in international society there are conventions which guide foreign policy and limit eventual conflict. Western Europe, also due to its institutions, could be considered as the most developed example of an international society. A more radical view sees the international system itself, and its characteristic anarchical condition, as a 'social construction' which can be altered or transformed by finding an alternative lens through which to conceptualise international relations (Wendt 1992). Seen in this light, European integration could represent an experiment in the construction of a different type of international order, in which conflict is replaced by cooperation and suspicion by mutual trust. For example, Robert Cooper sees the Treaty of Rome as the pillar of 'postmodern Europe'. According to Cooper (2003, 27), 'the postmodern system does not rely on balance; nor does it emphasize sovereignty or the separation of domestic and foreign affairs. The European Union is a highly developed system for interference in each others' domestic affairs, right down to beer and sausages.'

The last approach which may be considered 'alternative' is that of neo-Marxism, which is different from the paradigms of mainstream international relations because it believes that political institutions are governed by economic interests. In particular, states and international organisations are part of a superstructure governed by and in the interest of capitalist elites. The European Union is therefore seen—in a centre-periphery model—as yet another instrument by which the former is capable of exploiting the latter, and of maintaining its subordinate status (Holland 1980; see also Galtung 1972, Wallerstein 1979). Particularly interesting from this point of view would be the attempts to develop a common development aid policy via the Lomé Conventions, as well as the suggestions for a higher European profile in global financial organisations such as the International Monetary Fund (IMF) and the World Bank.

The role of Europe in the world

Having reviewed the most important causes suggested by theoretical accounts for the emergence of European integration and a common foreign policy, attention should now shift to the effects of these phenomena on the international system. For this purpose, it is useful to introduce two key distinctions. On the one hand, one should distinguish between the role of the European Union inside its own borders and its impact on the outside world as a power or as a participant in the general processes of international relations. On the other, one should distinguish between those theories which analyse Europe's role as an actor in its own right and those which conceptualise the Union as an institution whose influence is mainly felt through the foreign policies of member states (Wolfers 1962, 21; see also White 2001). The current status quo is in fact quite unsatisfactory. According to Christopher Hill (1993, 316) 'the cartoon which once showed 12 Prime Ministers voting on whether or not to press the nuclear button pithily summarized the impossibility of having a genuinely intergovernmental defense community'. It is therefore clear that Europe has to choose one of two paths: either it strengthens the institutional backbone behind a common policy, or it decides to value flexibility, informality, and subsidiarity instead.

The theories which envisage Europe as an independent actor are quite sceptical on the possibility of projecting power abroad without the characteristics of statehood. In particular, they tend to emphasise the two special factors which set international politics apart from other policies and require a 'communitarian' and integrated approach. Firstly, the rhythm of decision making cannot be set by cumbersome intergovernmental processes because the pace of action is determined by outside events demanding urgent responses. Secondly, since foreign policy can—ultimately—lead to the use of force, no real foreign policy can be worthy of the name unless it has a military component, which in Europe's case cannot be guaranteed until there is a transfer of democratic legitimacy and of sovereignty to the European level. For example, according to David Allen (1998, 42), there must be a level—national or common—which is ultimately responsible: 'the determination to preserve national foreign policies is ultimately at odds with the ambition to create a European foreign policy'.

On the contrary, the proponents of the 'Europe as an institution' approach believe that significant levels of cooperation can be attained even without transforming the EU into a state. Sovereignty in the field of foreign policy can therefore be shared between the national and the community level as other policies, including for example commercial or agricultural policies, have been in the past. According to this position, while speaking of a European superstate is either unrealistic or undesirable, it is possible instead to imagine a 'foreign policy system' in which a European common policy and national foreign policies converge and combine in their impact on international events and which represents, in Hill's view, 'the sum of what the EU and its member states do in international relations' (Hill 1998a, 18). As a corollary, while the first position would prefer the full institutionalisation of European foreign policy, this position values the flexibility of an intergovernmental arrangement, and the possibility of resting on ad hoc coalitions, directories and variable geometries in the conduct of international affairs.

From these distinctions it is possible to construct the typology in Table 2.2, which identifies four possible ways to reason about Europe's international role.

The first way is to emphasise the internal effects of integration in the foreign policy field as a necessary step toward the creation of a supranational—or statal—actor. This would be the way preferred by federalist and neofunctionalist theories, or by those realist theories which imagine the European Union becoming a fully fledged superstate. Particular attention is devoted to the transfer of sovereignty from member states to the Union level, with the analogy in mind of what has happened to another traditional area of state control, monetary affairs. Particularly relevant for this view is integration in the field of defence, with the creation of a common European industry, headquarters and even an army.

The second way to conceptualise Europe's impact on the international stage is to concentrate on its internal effects but without necessarily imagining the creation of a superstate. While the previous conception concentrates on the relationship between member states and the Union, this focuses on the states' relationships with each other. Such a view—which builds on the 'democratic peace' tradition emerging from republican liberalism—stresses the importance of European integration

Table 2.2 Europe's international role

	Significance for members	Significance for wider world
Europe as independent actor	EU taking on the characteristics of a state	'Superpower in the making'
Europe as institution of national actors	Security community	International Alliance or 'Civilian power'

on the pacification of the continent, with the creation of a 'pluralistic security community' among Western European countries (Hassner 1968, 21, Keohane *et al.* 1993, Hoffmann 1995).

A third position highlights Europe's role in the outside world and considers its impact as if it was a power endowed with its own autonomous resources — in Johan Galtung's phrase, a 'superpower in the making' (Galtung 1973, Buchan 1993). This view generally concentrates on Europe's potential aggregate capabilities, which are indeed considerable both in economic and even in military terms. For example, the EU comprises the largest single market in the global economy, it has the largest gross national product and is the biggest commercial power and aid donor in the world. Even the combined military resources of European states are, on paper, impressive, with about a quarter of global military expenditures being spent by EU members, a higher proportion than the Soviet Union during the Cold War.

Finally, a fourth position imagines Europe's impact on the wider international system not as an autonomous actor, but as an institution capable of influencing the various foreign policies of member states. Although the most classical instance would be that of an international alliance, less traditional solutions are also possible. The idea is that of a European 'presence' or, more abstractly, a European 'identity' (Allen and Smith 1990, Whitman 1998). The most influential definition is that of Europe as a 'civilian power' which utilises non military means to uphold civilian ends such as the defence of human rights and the support for the consolidation of democracy or of an open global economy (Duchène 1972, Bull 1982, Hill 1990, for a critical view; see Aron 1966, ch. 10, s. 3). A prototypical example is that of Europe's sanctions against South African apartheid, which employed economic means to further a human rights goal (Holland 1995). Clearly, such an approach depends on a non-realist view of the world, in which non-military means and goals have a significant impact on international outcomes.

Given the Union's quite formidable limits in terms of military power, which have so far not allowed the development of common capabilities, at least for high intensity conflicts, most of the attention has been devoted to the last approach. In particular, a useful distinction has been introduced (Nye 1990) between the 'hard' military power of coercion and 'soft' power, which rests more on the political and economic instruments of persuasion. Since the European comparative advantage is less military and more economic, being in this field almost as strong as the United States, the possibility of influencing events by 'soft' power is crucial for Europe's role in the world.

The future of European foreign policy

There is one area in which the application of soft power has an impact second only to that of military conquest, and that is the enlargement of the EU. The entry of new members into the EU changes the geopolitical context of the continent and has a profound impact on political equilibria and outcomes, as it relegates the iron curtain to the past, and ensures the consolidation of transition, so important in order to avoid other collapses into violence like the one experienced in former Yugoslavia.

Even if it has rarely been conceptualised as such, enlargement is therefore first and foremost a foreign policy action, as it permanently changes the international environment. However, it is atypical because it is reached mainly by the extension of domestic policies rather than with traditional foreign policy instruments. Enlargement also modifies the traditional concept of foreign policy because it creates porous borders; today's neighbours could become tomorrow's members and any rigid distinction between outside and inside collapses. A debate has therefore begun on the eventual 'final' borders of the EU.

But there are two reasons why Europe is pushed to assume a more traditional role if it wants to exert influence beyond the continent. Firstly, Europe's atypical policy of enlargement and civilian power could emerge only because American protection during the Cold War guaranteed continental order even without a European contribution. Where this order is wanting, as for example in the Middle East or in the Caucasus, more traditional means—such as the ability to use force—are necessary. Secondly, while Europe's importance as a strategic theatre has diminished in recent decades,[2] Europe must now concentrate on global issues because some of the risks it faces, such as terrorism or the proliferation of weapons of mass destruction, originate in extra-European regions and therefore require a power projection capability (Piening 1997). This has been noted through the elaboration of a European Security Strategy (European Council web site, December 2003).

Much will depend, as during the Cold War, on the transatlantic relationship. Robert Kagan (2003) predicts that the differences between the United States and Europe will grow, due to the weakness of a 'European' foreign policy. The United States will therefore be forced to use its power globally to preserve international order, while Europe will retrench itself behind its prosperity and relative security after enlargement. Charles Kupchan (2003) takes the opposite view and believes that Europe will acquire the instruments of hard power which it still lacks, not least because the world is becoming multipolar, and the foreign policy of the United States will become more parochial and unilateralist. It will therefore no longer seem attractive in terms of protecting European interests. John Ikenberry (2002), finally, takes a middle position by arguing that—unless the traditional American multilateralism is abandoned—the transatlantic relationship and NATO could prosper for some time to come. Accordingly Europe will continue its incremental steps toward integration without being affected by—or provoking—sea changes in global alignments.

If Europe wants to develop a foreign policy based on both hard and soft power, this will ultimately and intimately be linked to the more general process of integration. European democratic institutions cannot in practice withstand the possibility of war being declared by common institutions without full democratic legitimacy, while it is impossible to conduct a war unless control is transferred to the collective European level. It is difficult to imagine a high intensity military operation being conducted through the cumbersome decision making procedures of intergovernmentalism, with 25 veto powers and/or with rotating presidencies. Ultimately, only the establishment of a federation can approximate the foreign policy of a state (Hill 1993, 316).

Notes

1 I am indebted to Mathias Koenig-Archibugi for many of the ideas here presented. I am also grateful to Christopher Hill for his patience in waiting for, and improving, the various drafts of this chapter.

2 According to Hinsley (1963, 8) European integration was possible only because of Europe's decline. 'The [eventual] success of [European integration] will have taken place in a changed situation which renders it irrelevant to a solution of the international problem, and will have taken place because of that changed situation.'

Further reading

The most orthodox theoretical treatment, from a realist standpoint, of European integration and EU foreign policy is Grieco (1996, 1997). Hill (1993) explains the conditions for an effective single European foreign policy. White (2001) and Whitman (1998) are broad analytical discussions of the way in which it operates. Kagan (2003) and Cooper (2003) discuss contemporary international politics with a special emphasis on Europe: while the first is critical of European attitudes, the second believes they are a model for other parts of the world.

Cooper, R. (2003), *The Breaking of Nations: Order and Chaos in the Twenty-First Century* (New York: Atlantic Monthly Press, London: Atlantic Books).

Grieco, J. (1996), 'State Interests and International Rule Trajectories: A Neo-Realist Interpretation of the Maastricht Treaty and European Economic and Monetary Union', *Security Studies*, 5/3.

Grieco, J. (1997), 'Systemic Sources of Variation in Regional Institutionalization in Western Europe, East Asia and the Americas', in Mansfield; E.D.; and Milner; H.V.(eds) *The Political Economy of Regionalism* (New York: Columbia University Press).

Hill, C. (1993), 'Shaping a Federal Foreign Policy for Europe', in B. Hocking (ed.) *Foreign Relations and Federal States* (Leicester: Leicester University Press), 268–83.

Kagan, R. (2003), *Paradise and Power: America and Europe in the New World Order* (London: Atlantic Books).

White, B. (2001), *Understanding European Foreign Policy* (Basingstoke: Palgrave).

Whitman, R. (1998), *From Civilian Power to Superpower? The International Identity of the European Union* (London: Macmillan).

Web links

The most useful web sites for initial exploration of thinking about the international relations of the European Union are those of the Fornet network (http://www.fornet.info/) and the European Foreign Policy Unit at the London School of Economics and Political Science (http://www.lse.ac.uk/Depts/intrel/EurFPUnit. html). Each of these presents current debates about the nature of the EU's international relations, and has links to additional academic resources. More generally on international relations theory and foreign policy analysis, see the following: http:// www.isanet.org/sections.html (the International Studies Association), http://www. bisa.ac.uk/groups/groups.htm (the British International Studies Association) and http://www.essex.ac.uk/ECPR/standinggroups/ir/index.htm (the Standing Group on International Relations of the European Consortium for Political Research).

Chapter 3

The Pattern of the EU's Global Activity[1]

Geoffrey Edwards

Contents

Summary

This chapter provides a broad survey of the activities of the European Communities, now the Union, since their beginning in 1958. It approaches the problem as foreign ministries do, through both geographical and functional categories. The EU has recently been most active in its own region, but its first historical priority was the far-flung ex-colonies of France and Belgium, to which those of Britain were later to be added. From the mid-1970s the Mediterranean had a high profile until over-shadowed by the newly independent countries of eastern Europe while, for a multitude of reasons, the Atlantic has also proved of persistent importance. Functionally, the chapter identifies the main elements which have pushed forward the EU's international role, and those which have held it back. These often turn out to have been the same things. Some are institutions, such as the European Commission and European Council; others are processes such as the Community method or Political Cooperation. The most important of all, both pushing and pulling, have been the member states. Their ambivalence, combined with external complications such as the actions of a distinctly ambivalent United States, present the contemporary EU with a difficult set of tensions, and accompanying choices.

Introduction

So far in this volume we have analysed the inherent problems of thinking about the place of the European Union in international relations (Chapter 1), and what may be usefully taken from the academic subject of International Relations in approaching this task (Chapter 2). It is now time to survey the empirical reality of EU actions in the world. The current chapter covers the pattern and scope of the EU's global activity, in the sense of providing an overview of what the European Communities/Union have done, where and when. This is to serve as a backcloth to the more specialised accounts of institutions and processes on the one hand, and particular issue-areas on the other, which make up Parts II and III of the book.

The chapter begins with a narrative of the historical evolution of the impact of European integration on the rest of the world, and vice versa, from the beginnings in the mid-1950s, through the emergence of a common policy on development aid, and then in the 1970s, of Political Cooperation, to a new plateau of Maastricht and the Common Foreign and Security Policy (CFSP) in 1993. The attempts since to achieve further institutional refinements, culminating in the acceptance of a military dimension to the EU, are also followed.

The central part of the chapter is divided in two. Firstly it focuses on the main geographical areas in which Europe has been active, namely Africa and other ex-colonial theatres, Europe's own regional environment, the north Atlantic region and to a lesser extent Asia. Secondly it surveys the main 'drivers' of Europe's external relations, whether common institutions, procedures, or particular member states, while taking into account at the same time the fact that these very same drivers can also at times exert a braking force on the common venture. This is the complex and dialectical nature of European cooperation, not only in the external area, whereby change is not only never linear but also evokes contradictory political instincts within the various actors involved—sometimes even within individual personalities.

The chapter proceeds by identifying the major tensions which arise from these dialectics. They are fivefold, between rhetoric and achievement, Europeanization and national foreign policy, small and big member states, old and new Europe, and finally the concept of civilian Europe and the growing militarisation of the EU. It concludes with a reminder of the considerable variety and scope of Europe's international relations, especially in an era of continuing enlargement, and with the cautionary observation that such a fast-changing and patchy system cannot be expected to resolve the tensions arising from internal complexity and external suspicions in the near future.

Historical evolution

A Belgian Minister's remark that the EU in the global system added up to little more than 'an economic giant, political dwarf and military worm' has long haunted the EU. The scope and pattern of the EU's international role was determined by the initial decision that the Economic Community should be a customs union with a Common External Tariff rather than an industrial free trade area. A common commercial policy thereby became inevitable. The fact, too, that several of the member states still had colonies meant that trade concessions had to be made to enable them to have continued access, while Community aid was also regarded, especially by France, as a condition of membership. If these two elements provided the bases for the EC/EU external relations, their development and expansion has been rapid.

The economic weight of the EU brought with it greater opportunities for the exercise of political influence or 'structural power' (Keukeleire 2003), with, frequently, the aim of regime development if not regime change over the longer term. The EU, after all, has particular values to promote such as economic liberalism, international law (particularly the sanctity of contracts and freedom from arbitrary change) as well as its own legal order in the protection of the *acquis communautaire*. Effective multilateralism (to use the language of the EU's 2003 Security Strategy), whether in the UN, WTO, or inter-regional relationships, has long been a cornerstone of the EC/EU's foreign external relations—whether to protect or promote its interests. That is not to say that the EC has not often used its weight bilaterally in reaction to increased competition—whether from the Newly Industrialising Countries (NICs) in the 1960s or from the United States and Japan in the 1970s and 1980s. But whether in reacting to or itself shaping the issues and pressures bound up with globalisation, adapting to change in an increasingly interdependent system has been critical: forcing the pace of completing the internal market, bringing Treaty reform or establishing new patterns of relationships. Foreign economic policies are in a very significant sense at the 'core of EU "foreign policy"'; to ignore them excludes possibly less dramatic but certainly no less consequential developments (Smith, M. 1998b).

And yet the idea that the 'flag follows trade' does not capture the conception that many within the governments of the original six member states had of the nature and objectives of the EC. From the outset there were plans for Europe to become a political entity, beginning with the proposal in 1950 for the establishment of a European Defence Community. That initiative, and the Political Community proposal that accompanied it, may have been killed off by the French National Assembly in 1954, but the idea lived on, not simply among small groups of Euro-federalists but in a number of European parties in and out of government—not least the Christian Democrats in Germany and in Italy. It took on a new lease with the creation of European Political Cooperation (EPC) in 1970. EPC was very clearly limited to a procedure for coordinating foreign policy based on intergovernmental cooperation rather than supranational decision-making, but the rhetoric accompanying it saw it as the first step towards Political Union.

If the EC's foreign economic policy gradually widened in scope with the transfer of competences to the European level through successive Treaty revision, EPC also developed although at a rather different pace. While the former often led to a pro-active change in the EC's relationships with third countries, EPC was frequently criticised for its limitations and its reactive and declaratory characteristics (Edwards 1997). The need to react to international events, especially crises, frequently caused immobilism and failure even if it then led to new efforts to deepen commitments and refine procedures and policy instruments. Conceptualising it as a single system was difficult even when attempted (by, for example, Ginsberg 1989). This remained the case with EPC's transformation into the Common Foreign and Security Policy within the second pillar of the Treaty on European Union (TEU) signed at Maastricht, even though the Treaty also called for a 'single institutional framework'. Clarity in terms of the EC/EU's 'foreign policy' was further complicated by the increasing pressures to complement, externally, moves to promote the EU's internal security within Maastricht's third pillar on Justice and Home Affairs. Even under EPC in the 1970s, issues such as terrorism had been increasingly dealt with—on an intergovernmental basis—within the so-called TREVI group (Terrorisme, Radicalisme, Extremisme, Violence, Information) agreement on internal security cooperation. While the incorporation of that group and others dealing with the management of borders, asylum, and immigration within pillar III may have reinforced the role of the European Council as the only body capable of overseeing all aspects of the EU, it did little to bring any greater coherence to the conception of an EU foreign policy.

Subsequent Treaty reforms at Amsterdam and Nice saw a greater emphasis on the single decision-making framework and new instruments of policy such as common strategies—and this has been extended further in the Constitutional Treaty. Member states have clearly recognised not only the need for greater efficiency in decision-making and more effective policy implementation but also the need for greater popular acceptance of collective action. On the other hand, in retaining an intergovernmental base for the CFSP, and the European Security and Defence Policy agreed at Nice in December 2000, member governments have ensured that they can still take autonomous action in the event of a lack of common agreement. As a result there remain a number of conceptual problems to bedevil Europe's foreign policy, not least consistency, coherence and continuity. While the use of such terms varies, Nuttall has suggested a three-fold set of distinctions: 'horizontal' as between the different policies of the EU, whether across the Maastricht pillars, or even within pillar I between foreign economic policy, aid and development or between different regions; 'institutional' consistency as between the intergovernmental and Community bureaucratic structures; and 'vertical' consistency between EU and national policies (Nuttall, Chapter 4 below).

To expect such coherence at the European level is doubtless unrealistic when at the national level there are frequently interdepartmental rivalries between Ministries of Foreign Affairs, Trade, Development and Defence, and Treasuries. Not all member states have effective governmental coordination mechanisms, thereby compounding problems at the European level when there are already pressures within different Councils to reach agreement on the merits of each case according to their own acquis. Nonetheless, frequent ringing declarations by Heads of State and Government—on the need for greater European unity and coherence—do tend to raise expectations. This has a particular resonance in periods of crisis when 'joined up' decision-making may be at a premium. In the aftermath of 11 September 2001, for example, European efforts in the fight against terrorism extended across all three pillars and beyond in that, within the EU's competence, there was agreement on policies such as better coordination through Europol and Eurojust, the introduction of anti-terrorist clauses in agreements with third countries, and better targeted assistance with the declared emphasis on preventative measures and diplomacy. The aim of strengthening the relationship with the US, however, proved more problematic, with participation in the US-led anti-terrorist coalitions in Afghanistan and then Iraq only on an individual member state basis.

As for problems of continuity, it had long been a complaint about EPC as well as the CFSP that leaving the organisation and representation of the EU on foreign policy matters to a Presidency of the Council that rotates every six months undermined the EU's weight and credibility in the world. While in 1981 a ministerial troika of the current, immediately past and immediately future Presidencies (together with the Commission) was a step taken forward, it was not until the Amsterdam IGC of 1996 that it was finally agreed that there should be a senior figure able to speak for the EU on foreign policy issues. However, as respected as Javier Solana has become as the Council's High Representative in bringing much needed continuity, the EU remains susceptible to counter pressures especially from the member states. The proposal within the Constitutional Treaty to establish an EU Minister of Foreign Affairs (EUMFA), who would take on the roles of both the High Representative and the Commissioner responsible for external relations, supported by an integrated external service, would go further in meeting criticisms—though, critically, the EUMFA would remain the servant of the Council and the member states.

Geographical scope

Africa, the Caribbean, and the Pacific

From the beginning, the colonies and overseas territories of the member states were incorporated into a close network of relationships, strongly institutionalised and covering not only trade but also aid and technical assistance. The French, indeed, had been insistent on such a relationship in the negotiations establishing the Economic Community. The result was the beginnings of what has been described as a 'pyramid of privilege' in terms of preferential relationships with third countries (Mishilani *et al.* 1981).

If, initially, the colonies and former colonies were largely French and Belgian possessions in Africa, with the accession of the UK, former British colonies in the Caribbean and Pacific as well as Africa were included, grouped after 1975 within an institutionalised framework governed by successive Lomé Conventions. Despite their disparate nature and discrepancies in size, the African, Caribbean and Pacific countries (ACPs) have proved to be an enduring group in international affairs. Lomé, signed at the height of the New International Economic Order, placed considerable emphasis on ideas of partnership despite the inequality of dependence, non-reciprocity of trade concessions and need for aid and assistance (Twitchett 1981; Ravenhill 1985; Grilli 1993). The asymmetries were only too obvious insofar as the EC development policies determined access to the largest market in the world and the largest source of assistance. The scope of successive Lomé Conventions was gradually widened to take into account the growing concerns about abuses of human rights, especially in Africa—expressed clearly and continuously by, *inter alia*, the European Parliament. The influence of the 'Washington institutions' (the IMF and World Bank) in the shift towards structural adjustment, as well as member government concerns about the effectiveness of aid and the need for greater respect not only for human rights but for democratic principles and the rule of law, found expression in Lomé IV (1995–2000) (Holland 2002). Although there have been criticisms of a lack of even-handedness in dealing with developing states and with others—raising questions about the EU's unequivocal commitment to upholding human rights norms (Ward 1998)—Lomé provided for the possibility of dialogue on non-compliance. This increased focus on political conditionality was extended in the Cotonou Agreement, which replaced Lomé in 2000 (Smith, K. 2003). The Agreement signed by 77 states continued the trend of the politicisation of the aid relationship with its emphasis on good governance, and the role of civil society and the private sector, and on conflict prevention (Hilpold 2002; Hill 2001b).

The pyramid of privilege in the EC's relations with the rest of the world gradually emerged, determined by a combination of member state interests—individual or collectivised—historical ties, strategic and geopolitical considerations and, frequently, crises—coups, civil wars, state failures, natural disasters, and in the Mediterranean, the Arab-Israeli conflict. But relations were affected, too, by both the EC's own enlargement to include Greece, Spain, and Portugal and changing political-economic theories or fashions, including the increased emphasis on good governance and political conditionality. The result inevitably was a very much stronger political dimension to foreign economic policy, encapsulated in the concept of political dialogue and which has become applicable to the EU's relationships with a wide range of other regional groupings, from the Association of South East Asian Nations (ASEAN), via the Gulf Cooperation Council (GCC) to the Common Market of the Southern Cone (Mercosur) (Edwards and Regelsberger 1990; Monar 1997b; de Flers and Regelsberger, Chapter 15 below).

The Mediterranean

A similar pattern of politicisation is discernible in the EC/EU's relationship with the countries of the Mediterranean. The area's strategic importance was obvious. While in 1957 Algeria was still a part of metropolitan France, with independence, the French sought to maintain a close relationship. Other member states, only too well aware of the tension generated by the Arab-Israeli conflict, the need to ensure oil and gas supplies and supply routes, and the size of the Mediterranean market, were keen to ensure stability in North Africa. If the ACP countries had initially been at the top of the pyramid of privilege, the countries of the Mediterranean had rejected the idea of similar provisions in order better to exploit their geographical proximity. In practice this failed to materialise, despite or because of the mosaic of different types of agreement negotiated after 1961 which gradually encompassed all the countries of the Mediterranean, firstly through a complex series of individual agreements that ranged from Association with the prospect of a customs union and presumed future membership with Greece and then Turkey (1961 and 1963) to preferential trade agreements (as with Israel in 1964) to association agreements with the countries of the Maghreb. From 1972 onwards, the mosaic was always subject to European attempts to impose more global principles of free trade between the EC/EU and individual Mediterranean states—beginning, i.e., with free access for industrial goods (with exceptions for more sensitive goods such as refined petroleum products, as well as agricultural produce).

While the end of the Cold War meant that EC/EU attention shifted increasingly towards the countries of Central and Eastern Europe, there was also an acute sense of insecurity engendered by continued instability in the Mediterranean region and an ever growing rate of migration, legal and illegal, from and through North Africa. The first Gulf War of 1990–91 increased the intensity of that concern. Thus, while other member states were preoccupied with similar migration flows via the Balkans and through Eastern Europe, as well as increasing aid and investment flows, France, Italy, and Spain determined on the need for a more holistic approach to the Mediterranean region. Their efforts culminated in 1995 in the so-called Barcelona Process, with its three 'baskets' that mirrored the Conference on Security and Cooperation in Europe (CSCE)'s Helsinki Final Act of 20 years earlier, covering security, economic relations and humanitarian and cultural relations. It clearly reflected a multidimensional view of security in which migration, terrorism, and drug-trafficking took precedence (Barbé and Izquierdo 1997, 122) and which required cross-pillar coordination. It was, for one EC/EU veteran:

> reduced to its elementary political substance, . . . nothing but a political deal with Europe offering its advice, its moral presence, its vast political and economic experience and, of course, sizeable financial cooperation to those determined to tackle their problems effectively. (Rhein 1996, 83)

The Barcelona Process has not, however, been regarded as particularly successful. While the economic dimension has been foremost, it has not provided the expected leverage in other fields. The security dimension has made little headway with the Arab-Israeli conflict rarely separable and frequently to the fore, preventing meetings in Arab countries or emptying them of much significance (de Vasconcelos and Joffe 2000).

Central and Eastern Europe

If Italy and Spain had been pushing for some time for an improved relationship with the countries of the southern Mediterranean, French reluctance to see a more encompassing European relationship in an area in which it held itself privileged was overcome in part by increased security concerns, and in part by a perception of the growing imbalance in the EU's relationship with its European neighbours. The end of the Cold War resulted in the countries of Central and Eastern Europe (the CEECs) looking both 'to return to Europe' by acceding to the EC/EU and to join NATO for fear of the uncertainties further East, in Russia, Belarus, and the Ukraine.

The EC's reaction reflected a distinct lack of coherence and vision. On the one hand, it—or rather the European Commission—seized on the invitation proffered by the US to coordinate the West's aid effort. The EC's *Phare* programme (*Pologne-Hongrie: Assistance à la Restructuration des Economies*) became particularly significant even if it lacked a clearly-defined strategic purpose. Policies tended to emerge by default rather than by design (Zielonka 1998c). In part this was because the EU and its member states had no conception of 'Europe', and, as Zielonka argues, in the absence of any vision, EU policies towards the CEECs were dominated by the internal agenda. This was to be seen not only in the conditions laid down in the Europe Agreements, where despite high-flown rhetoric on the part of many EU leaders on the importance of helping in the transition process, protectionist interests held sway, but also in the determination of the European Council in Copenhagen that the CEECs themselves had to converge on EU norms (i.e., democratic systems, market economies capable of coping with EU competition, and the administrative capability to take on obligations of membership) before accession could be possible. It can also be seen in the inability of the member states to fulfil the fourth of the Copenhagen criteria, i.e., their own institutional reorganisation, to meet the likely demands of enlargement. Having failed in 1997, they resolved the so-called 'Amsterdam left-overs' of Council and Commission reform at Nice in 2000, but in such a minimal manner that, although the reforms were considered to be enough for the accession of the 10 applicants to take place, further reform was still considered necessary—hence the Convention on Europe's Future of 2002–03 and the Constitutional Treaty of 2004.

Although accession by the 10 was finally achieved in 2004, the process was seen as fraught with difficulties. It took considerable time for the member Governments, despite agreement at Copenhagen in 1993 on the criteria to be met by any new members, to settle on a coherent policy that looked effectively to the future. Given the other events of the 1990s, whether the move towards Economic and Monetary Union and the single currency, the collapse into conflict of Yugoslavia, the implosion of the Soviet Union and the uncertainties surrounding the prospects of democracy in Russia, it was not surprising that domestic interests successfully asserted themselves in the policy making processes (Tewes 2002). It was also the case that member governments were often divided about the wisdom of moving towards further enlargement to include so many CEECs, despite the rhetoric. The UK was exceptional among the EU states furthest from central Europe in pressing for speedy enlargement, although given its belief that a wider Europe meant a looser Europe, it was a position that inevitably reinforced concerns elsewhere, as in France and Germany. But differences only slowly resolved, about who could join and when, did little to enhance the EU's reputation for coherence and vision.

The new neighbours

It was a sentiment that inevitably gave rise to a certain concern among those to the East, notably Russia. The enlargement process to include the countries of central and eastern Europe, may ultimately have been regarded as a successful EU foreign policy action, yet it created its own problems for EU relationships with those beyond the EU's prospective new borders. That meant not just Russia but the Ukraine, the

Balkans, towards Turkey and onwards to the Caucasus (Jenkins & Smith 2003). The need to bring Russia into a more inclusive relationship with the EU had long been a goal of member states, not least of Germany. The Soviet Union had proved particularly ambivalent towards Western European integration, seeking to ignore and bypass it as much as possible. Neither Presidents Yeltsin or Putin have appeared much more enthusiastic, but continued integration within the EU suggested few alternatives to establishing a more comprehensive relationship, even if only slowly. This was reinforced by the EU's enlargement (and, indeed, by that of NATO), which intensified Moscow's ambivalence while creating new problems over Kaliningrad. For the EU's part, there were not only sensitive trade issues to negotiate in the Partnership and Cooperation Agreement (PCA), but, after 1995, also increasing concerns over Russia's policies in Chechnya. The EU imposed some delays in implementing the PCA, but for the most part it has tended to seek to maintain channels of communication rather than to foreclose them, not least since 9/11 when Russian governments have sought to identify dissident Chechnians with terrorism in general. Although Russia has sometimes appeared to play with the idea of possible membership (as during the visit of the Russian Prime Minister Chernomyrdin to Brussels in 1998), it has more often been a case of keeping its distance, not least when criticisms of its Chechnyan policies have been particularly vociferous. Successive governments have also been anxious to prevent Ukraine and Belarus from following others too closely on the track towards EU membership, particularly Ukraine, which has a Partnership and Cooperation Agreement on similar lines to that of Russia but which has also a strong political movement in favour of entering the EU.

On the other hand, the prospect of membership has been an integral part in the reconstruction objectives in the Balkans. The collapse of Yugoslavia presented the EC/EU with an existential challenge as much as a strategic one, for the destruction and bloodshed seemed 'the antithesis of everything the EU stood for' (Pentland 2003, 145). Strategically, it was a serious defeat made worse by initial certainty that 'This was the hour of Europe, not of America' as the then Luxembourg Foreign Minister was reported as saying (Edwards 1997, 176). The lack of coherence among the member states and the inability of the EC/EU to resolve the conflict meant that it was left to the United States to bring about the temporary peace with Slobodan Milosevic at Dayton in 1995. Dependence on the United States was only too clear during the Kosovo crisis of 1998–99, when it was left to the United States and NATO to take the lead. And yet the outcome was not only the move towards a European Security and Defence Policy, but also, gradually, the consolidation of various plans and programmes into a coherent policy towards the Balkans as a whole. The initially reactive Regional Approach gave way in 1999 to the very much more proactive Stabilisation and Association Process (SAP) that has included recognition of the Balkan states' vocation as possible EU members. If the emphasis was initially on economic reconstruction, it became more highly politicised and interventionist in order to ensure that political norms compatible with those of the EU were introduced and maintained (Pippan 2004). Such has been the relative success of the SAP, that both Croatia and Macedonia have applied for membership of the EU. Both remain a part of the Stabilisation process, while EU forces are also still present in Macedonia as part of Operation Concordia, thus helping to ensure the implementation of the 2001 Ohrid Framework Agreement between the Macedonian Slavs and the Albanians.

The collapse of Yugoslavia and the loss of control over border traffic, and even the disruption of visa and other arrangements that accompanied enlargement negotiations meant that, as a CEPS Report on Reshaping Europe's Borders put it:

> Political conflicts and discontents, migration and criminal problems, and a sense of exclusion and frustration associated with the difficult transformation of former communist countries could be exacerbated without careful development of relations with all the countries of the region. (CEPS 2001, 1)

Yet here the issue of possible EU membership has been particularly difficult for the Union. For countries beyond Turkey, which, after considerable pressure and much division within the EU, became a candidate for membership during 2004, the prospects of being drawn more closely to the EU have sometimes been seized with greater alacrity than perhaps the EU had anticipated or had been prepared for. Within the Mediterranean region, for example, while Morocco's bid for membership was rejected by all member governments, there has been less unanimity on the question of Israel (the Italian government in particular making some ambiguous declarations). Further afield, the European aspirations of governments in the Caucasus has also proved a sensitive question—in part also because of the continued involvement of Russia. For the EU, the need to be rather more successful than its attempts at a more holistic approach in the Mediterranean, to create an alternative to membership, has become increasingly clear. While PCAs have been negotiated with an increasing number of former Soviet states, and aid and technical assistance provided through an extended Phare programme, TACIS (Technical Assistance for the CIS Countries), the EU clearly hopes that its alternative to full membership will find acceptance through its proposed new Neighbourhood Policy of 2004.

The Atlantic

Although the United States has been the EC/EU's most important trading partner and ally, no formal relationship was established between the EC and the US until the Declaration of 1990. US support for European integration had frequently been tempered by spats over trade, less often resolved within the General Agreement on Tariffs and Trade (GATT) than in the WTO, and concerns over burden sharing in terms of security. In the past, the EC/EU's relationship with the US had been successfully compartmentalised—though with occasional efforts such as that of Dr Kissinger in 1973 in his 'Year of Europe' to bring them together within one 'ball of wax' (Smith, M. 1984). Successive US Administrations have run with both an integrating Europe and with its member governments (particularly those of the UK and Germany), against a background of particularly dense non-governmental links and relations, and, of course, NATO. From the EU perspective, the 1990 Declaration was succeeded by the New Transatlantic Agenda signed in Madrid in 1995, which included what was termed a confidence-building process on the resolution of bilateral trade issues, together with a wide ranging agreement on promoting global peace and stability, working towards common responses to global challenges and expanding world trade. A Transatlantic Economic Partnership agreement followed in 1998. On the other hand, moves towards deepening and widening European integration and establishing a distinctive European identity have frequently led to US demands for compensation (altruism has its limits even for a hegemon), while US involvement in resolving conflicts in the Balkans have invariably shown up European weaknesses and the continued dominance of the US. Concern over US reluctance to continue its involvement in European security issues as in the past, as well as a more unilateralist approach in general led the incoming government of Tony Blair to move towards a radical shift in British policy, with the build-up of the Kosovo crisis proving decisive (Hoffmann 2000; Shearer 2000; Howorth 2001). The outcome, the Franco-British declaration at St. Malo in December 1998, which presaged the European Security and Defence Policy, wrong-footed the Clinton Administration, whose Secretary of State, Madeleine Albright disapprovingly spoke of 'no duplication, no decoupling and no discrimination' on the EU's part against NATO and its non-EU allies (Edwards 2000, 9). That ambiguity and a mixture of concern, scorn and scepticism towards the venture continued in the aftermath of the events of 9/11 and in the consequent invasions of Afghanistan and Iraq, the latter in particular threatening to divide the enlarging EU.

Asia

The density of the EU's relationship with the United States has been in marked contrast with the relative weakness of EU-Asia links—and, indeed, Asian-US ties. The last, since 1989 in the form of the Asia-Pacific Economic Cooperation of some 21 states, had agreed in 1994 to move to free trade by 2020 creating a strong incentive on the part of the EU to take a more proactive role, which met an equally interested Asian (and especially Singaporean) interest (Forster 1999). Biannual Asia-Europe meetings were launched in 1996 under the telling slogan of 'Towards a New Asia-Europe Partnership for Greater Growth' (Wiessala 2002, 76). Trade issues have invariably been the catalyst for EC/EU involvement, whether in meeting the competitive challenge of the NICs and Japan in the 1960s–70s, or inspiring hopes of new markets in Japan (disappointed, especially since the financial difficulties of the late 1990s) and more recently in China with its phenomenal growth figures—the last leading to consistent EU support for Chinese accession to the GATT/WTO (achieved in 2001). Even in the EC-ASEAN relationship, which dates back to 1978, economic interests have usually complemented any political interests (Nuttall 1992). On the other hand, regional insecurity combined with strong historical ties have frequently tempered EU enthusiasm, reinforcing what Dent has called 'value system friction' (Dent 1999, 51). The relationship with ASEAN became subject to increased difficulty after 1991 over the issue of East Timor because of Portuguese concerns, and over Burma/Myanmar's membership of ASEAN given its human rights record. Human rights—and their active pursuit by the European Parliament as well as by individual member states—have also provoked antagonism, not least after Tian'anmen Square in 1989, and over Tibet. Tensions over Chinese-Taiwanese relations have further complicated relations with China, in part because of the added complication of US involvement, while similar circumstances have determined the difficulties of coping with North Korea under its unpredictable leader, Kim Jong-Il.

Drivers and brakes

The development of so many varied relationships across widely diverging geograph-ical areas has inevitably been subject to a range of forces and players. Many have sought to drive forward integration in Europe's external relations, both for its own sake and as a means of exerting international influence. Others have been con-cerned, sometimes in conjunction with interested non-EU parties, about the implic-ations for already-existing national foreign policies, or for other international insti-tutions. This section analyses the main elements which have pushed for cooperation in the external field, while showing how almost every positive initiative has had an equal and opposite reaction. The focus here is on the intra-European forces at work, while in full awareness of their perpetual interaction with outsiders, notably the United States.

The general EC framework

The dubious legal and political standing of much European 'foreign policy' indicates the core importance of the general EC framework, i.e., pillar I, which represents the principal driver of the process. The agreement of the original six member states to es-tablish not simply a customs union, but also a common market with four freedoms relating to factors of production, and certain common policies, particularly agricul-ture and competition, inevitably determined the basic structure of the EC's interna-tional relations. It necessitated not only the negotiation of bilateral trade agreements within the pyramid of privilege, but also almost continuous negotiation within the framework of the GATT and later the WTO. Moreover, as the EC became an increas-ingly genuine single market, so, as the size and scope of the acquis communitaire makes abundantly clear, it led to the creation of a regulatory regime with few par-allels elsewhere (Majone 1996). The consequence of this has been the promotion of the acquis beyond the EU's borders in trade agreements and in a host of multilat-eral fora, which has led to innumerable disputes bilaterally and multilaterally (Mayes 1993; Weiler 2000; Hocking and Smith 1997; Young 2002).

As the EC has agreed a number of common policies so it has also sought to pro-tect its own producers against others. Pre-eminent among the common policies since the 1960s has been the Common Agricultural Policy (CAP). While mutual interests, notably among the US, Europe and Japan, kept agriculture off the GATT (General Agreement on Tariffs and Trade) agenda until the 1990s, the CAP has frequently been a complicating factor in relations with the United States and other temperate producers, and developing producers—with the example of bananas suggesting the complexities of the negotiations in that the EU had to modify its banana regime at the behest of the WTO in favour of Latin American producers supported by the US against its traditional (ACP) suppliers. And if the CAP and the Common Commercial Policy (CCP) have been foundational elements of the EC/EU, there are a range of other policies, such as competition policy, industrial, R&D, and environmental policies that have either developed or been gradually added to the EC/EU agenda. Moreover, even in areas where there has been little Community competence such as culture and education, there has been increasing coordination among member states, whether through 'television without frontiers' directives or the so-called 'Bologna process' relating to education. In part this has been in order to protect European cultures, in part to enhance Europe's global competitiveness—but all further extend the international policies of the EU, on the basis of the belief that when Europe speaks with one voice it carries considerably greater weight than any individual member state.

On the other hand, as the unsteady and sometimes difficult expansion of the Community's competences has shown, member states have on a number of occasions been loath to allow the Community a single voice simply because they do not believe that their interests are being adequately protected. This has been particularly the case in the area of services, especially culture and intellectual property where differences among the member states (notably on the part of France) have left the EC's position unclear. While the Community's competence in trade matters was established early, thus allowing the Commission to negotiate on behalf of the EC/EU as a whole, the challenge to further transfers led by the French resulted in the involvement of the Court of Justice in Case 1/94. The Court, even while seeming to back away from the preemptive nature of European law laid down in the *ERTA* case, concluded that competence in some sectors such as intellectual property remained with the member states. Nonetheless, the Court emphasised the 'duty to cooperate' on the part of the member states where such issues of mixed competence were involved, which it regarded as imperative in the WTO context given the close interlinkage of different issues. The matter was not wholly resolved at Amsterdam or even at Nice—largely because of French opposition (Meunier 2001). Given such particular differences, there remains the concern that if such issues could not generate common positions despite being within the EC's competence, an individual member state would, in effect, then be left without a voice. It has reinforced a reluctance to allow for further transfers of responsibilities to the EC/EU in subsequent Treaty revisions (Young 2000, 101).

This kind of blockage occurred from the outset of the EC, even within those areas ostensibly always within the competence of the EC, such as trade policy (Hayes 1993, 123). As Hayes points out, even on trade member states have taken full advantage of Article 113 (now 133) of the EC Treaty, which lays down that the Commission will undertake trade negotiations within the framework of directives agreed by the Council. However, while the role of the so-called 133 Committee of (senior national) officials has frequently been critical in terms of oversight or management (Johnson 1997), it has often proved inadequate. The Commission has appeared to be beyond control during actual negotiations and government suspicions of the EC/EU central institutions have remained or been reinforced. French ministers have been far from reticent about complaining at subsequent meetings of the Council—although as an example, Hayes quotes the Italian Trade Minister in 1990 on a GATT Trade Negotiation Committee:

> The Commission was practically conducting the negotiations alone. Indeed, 24 frustrated Community Ministers, 12 for trade and 12 for agriculture, were milling around hoping to capture rumours and bits of information on what was occurring... (Hayes 1993, 124)

This has otherwise been described as 'the mushroom treatment': ministers 'are kept in the dark, and every so often the door is opened and a bucket of manure is thrown over them' (ibid. 125). French hostility to successive—especially British or other too

liberal—Trade Commissioners and, more seriously, to the extension and development of Community competences, as in the case of culture and intellectual property,
has frequently been the result of this kind of behaviour.

European Political Cooperation

This suspicion of the Community framework and the role of the Commission was
particularly apparent in the establishment of European Political Cooperation (EPC) in
1970, which soon became the focal point for aspirations for a common foreign policy.
The Gaullist legacy inherited by Georges Pompidou as President of France necessitated a separate intergovernmental procedure, albeit linked via its membership to the
EC, but which excluded the Community institutions. As a result, EPC had perforce
to rely on the commitment of the member states: EPC procedures were designed for
them, maintained by them and developed by them. The role of the Presidency was
critical. It was, indeed, only in 1986 that a small secretariat was established in support, despite the sometimes onerous burdens placed on member states, especially
the smaller ones, when they held the Presidency. The secretariat, enlarged under
Maastricht to service the CFSP, and brought within the general Council Secretariat,
remained the alternative but still limited institutional infrastructure to that of the
Commission. The changes brought about by the Amsterdam Treaty of 1997 in creating the High Representative and his Policy Unit enormously strengthened the Council Secretariat's role, a process likely to be developed further under the Constitutional
Treaty when the roles of the High Representative and the Commissioner responsible
for foreign policy in the form of an EU Minister of Foreign Affairs will be merged.

   The drive to keep EPC and CFSP intergovernmental in terms of its structure and
procedures may have meant a continued separateness from the EC and the Commission but outcomes often remained limited so far as policy was concerned. Decisions
may not always have been based on the lowest common denominator but neither
were they adequate or effective enough to match the growing expectations that the
member states would and should act in common. The result especially for the bigger
member states was either to remain protective of their own bilateral relationships
and *domaines réservés*, or a tendency on the part of the big three to act as a *directoire*.
In consequence, Italy and the smaller member states often found EPC a useful means
by which to try to constrain the big three. And they were also to be found encouraging the communitarisation of foreign policy, both on grounds of principle and on
the more pragmatic basis that keeping EPC separate from the EC was self-limiting if
not self-defeating.

The Commission

The artificiality of the division between EPC and EC policy-making gradually therefore broke down and, in an important sense, the Commission became an active if
not always successful partisan on the side of a more coherent foreign policy. As a
driver of foreign policy integration it had the advantage, at least from the mid-1980s
on, of being able to bring the economic and political aspects of policy together. It
alone could initiate Community action over the widening range of policy instruments within the EC framework, not least sanctions and aid programmes—and this

even though ministries of foreign affairs might have wished to retain the distinction between high and low politics. Moreover, under the Single European Act (SEA) as re-affirmed by Maastricht, the Commission shared with the Presidency of the Council the responsibility for ensuring consistency between EC external policies and those agreed under EPC. To quote Nuttall: 'It would be misleading. . .to give the impression that EPC has been purely intergovernmental, as the emphasis on coordination of policies might have led one to expect (1994, 85). Ultimately, indeed, the Commission came to enjoy a formal shared right of initiative in the CFSP, although this was not a power it found possible to exploit.

The Commission's role has not simply been a question of its presence under the Treaties, but has also reflected the expanding scope and scale of the EU's activity and the concomitant growth in the EU's overseas representation (in marked contrast to the experience of the Member States where cutbacks have been rather more com-mon (Hocking and Spence 2002). The representation of the Commission has been steadily expanding—the Commission in 2001, for example, was accredited to 158 countries and organisations and represented by 107 heads of delegation (Allen and Smith 2002). Its delegations have diplomatic functions and their political reports have been of increasing significance. The Commission, in other words, has its own sources of information in the formulation of policy at the European level, some-times rather more extensive than the sources available to many of the smaller mem-ber states. At the same time, the Commission has the capability to implement ex-ternal policy (in contrast to internal policies which are largely implemented by Mem-ber governments) as well as negotiating on behalf of member governments in the GATT/WTO etc. As Pollack has pointed out following Putnam, this places the Com-mission at both the internal and international negotiating tables, providing it 'with the possibility of using external pressure to strengthen its negotiating position in-ternally, and vice versa' (Pollack 2003, 270). While Pollack restricts his analysis to eco-nomic and commercial issues, the spillover effect in terms of foreign policy making is equally significant—as can be seen in the Commission's participation together with the original and the reformed troika of EU representation. Even if, within EPC/CFSP, it has not been in the interests of the Commission often to appear above the inter-governmental parapet, its role as a policy entrepreneur and policy driver should not be underestimated.

Member states

The representation of the EC/EU by the troika, and the essentially economic and com-mercial instruments of policy at the disposal of the EC/EU, led to much discussion of whether Europe could be or should be anything but a 'civilian power', a concept widely discussed in the literature (see, for example, Hill 1990; Whitman 1998; Tewes 2002). As Hill and Wallace have suggested, European diplomacy steadily became asso-ciated in the public mind with a distinctive set of principles—including a preference for diplomacy over coercion, mediation to resolve conflicts, the patience to look to long term economic solutions (i.e., an open, liberal economy) for political problems, and the promotion of human rights (Hill & Wallace 1996). The problem came when crises and conflicts continued and member states could not, or would not, move be-yond declarations, towards common action, including more coercive policies such as sanctions. All too often in the face of crises and despite their Treaty commitment, member governments would resort to unilateral action, whether before discussions were completed at the European level, or even in some cases afterwards.

And yet, just as often, member governments committed themselves to developing foreign policy cooperation further. In this sense they have been both a driver and a brake, with no given country falling neatly into one category or the other. Balancing the EC/EU's economic strength with political clout has remained a constant in the EU's development—whether in the interests of more effective external/foreign policy or deepening European integration. With every setback, from the 1973 Yom Kippur War, to the first Gulf War, and the collapse of Yugoslavia from 1991 on, member governments have sought to bring about reform, whether through successive reports within EPC or Treaty reform as in Maastricht (which introduced the CFSP itself), Amsterdam or Nice. At the Nice Council in December 2000 the Heads of Government also agreed to the establishment of a European Security and Defence Policy (ESDP), although this was not part of the Treaty. As a minimum this envisaged the use of a military option in support of humanitarian actions, even if not immediately a common defence (a possibility allowed by the 1993 Maastricht Treaty).

The key states in this long process towards a security and defence policy have been France and Germany. Indeed, Peterson saw the Franco-German alliance as key to the development of European foreign policy; when the two were in harmony, advances were possible (Peterson 1998). Certainly a strong Franco-German relationship was one frequently emphasised in Germany's European discourse—Wolfgang Schäuble (long a leading figure in Germany's CDU) declaring in 1997, for example, that if France and Germany cannot agree, 'things will go wrong in Europe' (Aggestam in Manners and Whitman 2000, 77). Franco-German initiatives had frequently provided the motor both in terms of integration in general and foreign policy in particular, not least in their joint initiative for an IGC on Political Union in April 1990, even if the CFSP was the result of both domestic political pressures and the need to mend the rift that reunification had caused in their relationship: 'To Paris and Bonn, the CFSP was more important as symbol than as substance' (Nuttall 2000, 271).

During the 1990s, the differences between the two seemed to sharpen as France came to terms with a 'new' Europe that included a reunified Germany (and, indeed, three new smaller and neutral member states). Accordingly the French believed 'their position and status had been devalued while those of Germany had been enhanced' (Szukala and Wessels 1997, 78). The search for alternative allies may have temporarily led France to look to other Mediterranean states and to the initiation of the Barcelona Process, albeit without tremendous enthusiasm and reverting soon enough to bilateral relations with individual Mediterranean states. There was even a minuet with NATO, with France coming closer to but ultimately shying away from full reintegration. Nonetheless, this led to the agreement on Combined Joint Task Forces and to debates over a European Security and Defence Identity within the NATO framework (Cornish 1997).

Even on CFSP, there appeared to be differences, with Germany much keener on reducing the distinctions between the Maastricht pillars, while the French reemphasised the role of the Council through the appointment of a Mr/s CFSP. Even so, efforts continued, not least through bilaterals under the rubric of the Elysée Treaty of 1963, to attempt to steer European Council meetings—even when little of substance seemed to emerge. There was common ground throughout the 1990s, for example, on the need to merge the Western European Union (WEU) into the EU, a proposal blocked consistently by the UK, including the new Labour Government in its first forays at Amsterdam in 1997. But reports of the demise of the Franco-German tandem proved either premature or exaggerated. In the autumn of 2002, for example, the British and others appeared surprised by the reassertion of Franco-German pressure within the Convention on the Future of Europe, even though mutual support in opposition to the US-led invasion of Iraq had been increasingly evident. France and Germany (together with Belgium) also pressed for a new security and defence headquarters to be set up in the Brussels suburb of Tervuren in their mini-summit in April 2003, creating pressure for a planning, command, and control structure for European actions which could be autonomous, if not wholly separate from that of NATO.

The British cannot be excluded from those driving towards a more effective and coherent EU foreign policy, despite the frequency with which they have sought to apply a brake, especially where NATO seemed to be under threat. As Hill (1996) and Forster (2000) have noted, the UK has been a strong supporter of both EPC and CFSP, even if for the most part as a supplement to its national foreign policy positions. In terms of EPC, for example, UK support can be seen in the London Report of 1981 and later in the Howe proposals for reform that transmuted into the Franco-German proposals leading up to the SEA (Nuttall 1992). The value of coordination on an intergovernmental basis—even while calling for greater coherence and effectiveness—has been frequently noted, culminating in Blair's call in October 2000 for Europe to become 'a superpower but not a superstate', with not only a 'more' coherent foreign policy, but 'the military capability we require without which common defence policy is a chimera' (in Leonard 2000, 26–27). That was in the optimistic aftermath of St. Malo (December 1998) and the rapid movement thereafter towards the creation of the ESDP, which was declared operational at Laeken in 2001. It was also before the disarray of the EU member states over the invasion of Iraq in 2003.

The UK and other member states have also sought to drive the process from two other standpoints, by frequent references to bridge-building and a persistence in attempting to set the agenda. Bridge-building has often been a significant element in the way the new member states, in particular, have conceived their value to the EC/EU, but it has also been used to try to set a particular path for coordinated action by the EU. Perhaps the most obvious example has been that of the UK in its 'special relationship' with the United States—even if others, too, such as the Irish, Italians and Germans, have their own special relationships. The idea that particular member states could be *interlocuteurs valables* has a long history, even if one fraught with difficulties, as the British discovered in the aftermath of the second Gulf war. Other member states have also sought to use historically close relationships such as Spain's with Cuba and the countries of South America, or Italy's with Libya. The persistence with which Portugal put the issue of East Timor on the EU agenda, or other member states have pursued human rights concerns, has tended to force the pace of what otherwise has been a slow-moving or non-existent diplomacy. This tendency has been especially pronounced during a member state's Presidency. The outcomes, however, have not always been those intended. While smaller member states have frequently held the Presidency with enthusiasm, relishing the opportunity to represent the EU in the world, and frequently seeking to move the agenda on, the effect has sometimes been only the reinforcement of the tendency towards closer relations among the big three.

The moves from 1998 onwards towards the creation of an ESDP inevitably raised serious questions about Civilian Power Europe. Some member states, such as Denmark with the opt out granted at Maastricht, and Ireland with efforts to ensure recognition of its (military) neutrality, have tended towards the position that such moves weaken the EU's distinct profile both domestically, inside the EU and in relation to other states (Sangiovanni 2003). The debate, especially with the US, has thus mostly related to the higher end of the Petersberg tasks, of peace-making rather than simply humanitarian assistance. When reinforced by 'French references to the importance of replacing unipolarity with a multipolar world and creating a counterweight to America's hyperpuissance' (Kupchan 2000, 19), this has increased uncertainty and generalised anxiety. As Heisbourg pointed out, 'a certain studied imprecision about the eventual destination has also been essential to the progress of ESDP' (Heisbourg 2000, 5). It has also been clear from the outset that the member states have been keen to see ESDP as part of a balanced parallel development of military and civilian capabilities so as to bolster their own role in crisis management. Indeed, the first operations of ESDP were almost exclusively for civilian means, policing as part of a reconstruction process rather than simply military intervention (Rummel 2002). To the same ends, the Commission drew up plans for improving the EU's capacity for conflict prevention, including a Rapid Reaction Mechanism to ensure a more effective civilian response in crises. The EU's programme was launched under the Swedish Presidency in 2001. For the cynics, such an emphasis on preventive diplomacy was more a question of making a virtue out of necessity given the ambiguities and differences over quite what the ESDP should be for. On the other hand, the emphasis on coordinating all the instruments available to the EU, both military and civilian, was strongly supported by all member states.

Nor was it a matter of coordinating only across pillars I and II. Efforts to give Europe a political presence commensurate with its economic weight have been matched by an increasingly strong pressure to complement, externally, moves to promote the EU's internal security. The fight against terrorism, for example, began in the aftermath of the 1972 terrorist attacks at the Munich Olympic Games. Meetings of Interior Ministers and officials may have begun in an ad hoc way within the framework of EPC but were soon institutionalised within its own process, TREVI. This was joined by other groups, on immigrations, asylum, organised crime—drug smuggling, people smuggling etc—all of which were given legal recognition in the third pillar of Maastricht (Mitsilegas *et al.* 2003). One of the main driving forces behind the discussions that led to the Amsterdam Treaty, along with enlargement towards Central and Eastern Europe, was how to make the EU more relevant to its citizens, particularly through enhancing a sense of security, with proposals that led ultimately to the 1999 Tampere proposals for an 'area of freedom, justice and security'.

Such internal preoccupations inevitably had external consequences, recognition of which increased further concerns over horizontal coherence across the Maastricht pillars. Such coherence was less a luxury than a growing necessity as, for example, the United States pressed steadily for a closer relationship with the EU on such issues as the fight against terrorism, even before the events of 11 September 2001. Similarly, even while some member governments or elements within member governments (particularly some Interior ministries) were reluctant to see Europol established and developed (den Boer 1997), the US was keen to see increased cooperation between it and its agencies. But the internal/external dimensions of the fight against terrorism and other international crimes, including people and drug trafficking, have increasingly blurred distinctions between the pillars.

The European Council

Inevitably, problems inherent in trans-pillar coordination have enhanced the role of the European Council. For many leaders, since the EU's legitimacy derives from the member states, it is proper for heads of government to take the major, strategic decisions. Thus the Council became increasingly important in shaping and voicing the EU's international position from the 1980s on. The development of CFSP and moves towards ESDP necessarily involved heads of governments—whether the proposals came via Foreign, Trade, or Interior Ministers prepared by the Commission within an EC framework, or were drawn up by the High Representative in pillar II as with the appointment of an EU Counter-terrorism Co-ordinator in March 2004 within the Council Secretariat. With the development of the European Council's role, so the inadequacies of the system of rotating Presidents became more apparent and the move towards a more permanent elected chair irresistible (despite some anxiety on the part of smaller member states and/or the more federalist governments). The Constitutional Treaty's provisions for a more permanent Presidency, together with an EU Minister for Foreign Affairs (with an integrated external service eventually at his or her disposal) reflect a further step in the evolution of a more coherent European foreign policy. It can be argued that the European Council epitomises the paradox of European foreign policy cooperation: that it takes place at ever higher levels, and with a higher profile, while remaining through that very fact resistant to the Community method.

The European Parliament

A second source of legitimacy within the EU is the European Parliament. Much in the tradition of the executive role in foreign affairs at national levels, it has only been slowly that the EP has found more than a voice in foreign affairs. Within the EC framework, its role initially was merely a consultative one, extended by the SEA of 1986 to allow the EP to assent to accession and Association agreements. Where these have budgetary implications the role of the EP is significantly enhanced and it has used its position to halt or delay financial protocols etc. The SEA also provided for the EP to be regularly informed by the Presidency on specifically foreign policy issues—or at least 'on the main aspects and basic choices' of policy. Parliamentary efforts to exploit such vague language have not always garnered success—much has depended on the attitudes of individual Presidencies—but the right to have its views taken into consideration has been important. While its formal powers might still be regarded as largely inadequate (Viola 2000), the EP has sometimes managed to exercise significant influence through providing a 'grand forum' for debate and inviting leaders to address it. Its emphasis on human rights has made it a particular focal point for non-governmental organisations (NGOs) and others, and a voice that has often had to be taken seriously even when it challenges the coherence of the EU's position. It is generally a force for enhanced cooperation, but can also represent a rival international voice within the system.

Enduring tensions

The growing number of civilian and military operations being carried out by the EU suggests a certain coming of age. There remain, however, a number of not wholly resolved tensions.

First, is the tension between rhetoric and achievement. Despite the continuous re-iteration of the aims of speaking with one voice in a common foreign policy, commensurate with the possession of economic 'superpower', the EU continues to lack credibility, both domestically and on the international scene. On the one hand, there has been the agreement on a Security Strategy, and the examples of successful policing operations in the Balkans and central Africa. On the other hand, awareness of these successes—a vital precursor to acceptance and legitimacy—remains limited. Differences among member states tend still to grab the headlines. The possibility of EU inaction as a result of lack of government confidence in carrying popular opinion remains high. The temptation to fall back on caution and/or the more familiar tradition of bilateral action is reinforced. As in the past, the repetition of lofty aims has done little to promote common actions—the split over Iraq being the most glaring example. A capability-expectation gap remains, and remains to be exploited by others, thereby ensuring that the EU's credibility as a strategic international actor is continuously in question.

Secondly, there remains a tension between the processes of Europeanization and national foreign policies. There are a number of different levels and dimensions involved. One of the fundamental drivers of integration, for example, was 'the German question', which became again a vital issue on Germany's reunification in 1989. Fears arose over the degree that Germany had become Europeanized, or even Europe becoming Germanised, with the Intergovernmental Conference (IGC) on Political Union and the CFSP among the results. Since Maastricht, Germany's competing discourses on responsibility have maintained a sense of ambiguity: one tends to see Germany as a 'normal' state, emphasising its national interests, while still committed to multilateral solutions and playing to a large domestic audience, which Chancellor Schroeder exploited in 2002; a second tends to emphasise responsibility to partners and allies, even if it now leads to military intervention, as in Kosovo and Afghanistan, which still creates anxiety within Germany. The balance struck by Fischer over support for intervention in Afghanistan, followed as quickly as possible by peace proposals, was indicative of the latter.

Closely related, but more generally applicable, is the process of socialisation within EPC and the CFSP, especially among officials (Nuttall 2000). In the first instance, this was because foreign ministry officials were enjoying the flexibility of the EPC process and the new opportunities for diplomats. The blurring of the distinctions between EC, Justice and Home Affairs (JHA), and CFSP after Maastricht, and the 'turf-fights' that followed, which left 'victory' with the Committee of Permanent Representatives (Coreper) as the final negotiating forum at official level, changed the process but still left an 'interesting' form of Brusselsisation in which to operate. Meanwhile at the political level, Foreign Ministers were being Europeanized in a rather different way, if only through being overloaded with responsibilities. Not only did Foreign Ministers have to cope with collective foreign policy-making, they were also responsible for the coordination of the expanding work of the EC/EU as a whole in the General Affairs Council—with the result that they were regarded as inefficient and ineffectual (Gomez and Peterson 2001). Various reforms have been suggested over time to divide up their labour more efficiently, as at Seville in 2002. But the trend over time has been to accentuate the role of heads of state and government in the European Council, both in resolving conflicts within and across the pillars and determining the parameters of foreign and security policy.

Policy-making at heads of state and government level reveals even more clearly the tensions between the logic of common policy making and that of national separateness. Heads of state and government have not always proved as predictable as might have been expected from their ever-growing familiarity through European Councils, informal Council meetings, other summit meetings and the growing number of bilaterals. On the one hand, they have frequently confirmed if not set Europe's agenda, becoming more formally institutionalised in the interests of collective leadership. And yet, they necessarily have to look back to their national constituencies if they wish to retain their position, especially when elections are imminent. They also have limited time, depending on Foreign and Finance Ministers to prepare the Councils together with the Presidency and Council Secretariat, and have many other distractions, whether political, financial, media, or personal.

A third area of tension that became particularly explicit during the Convention on Europe's Future—although it has frequently lurked in the background—is that of small versus big states. It is not simply a question of the big having more global interests or, rather, the conceit of being a global power against the more limited and parochial interests of the small. Small states have frequently shown that they have particular interests in and knowledge of regions outside Europe (whether through past colonial links, trade or aid). Moreover, despite the burdens of the Presidency, they have frequently enjoyed the 'political tourism' of representing the EC/EU, whether on the steps of the White House or in the UN (Rummel 1990). This has often been to the irritation of the big states, not least since the smalls have often regarded EPC/CFSP as a way of exercising at least some restraint on the big. The latter have become more restless now that the number of smalls has increased through successive rounds of enlargement. It has posed a challenge especially perhaps to France and the UK, both of which have tended to regard EPC/CFSP as an instrument of their own national foreign policies. While London and Paris have often been made aware that their global credibility rests heavily on their membership of the EU, that only rarely influences their foreign policy discourse, at least as articulated through their national media.

Given the circumstances, it is not surprising that, not only have the big three often found the pressure to work together irresistible, but they have positively sought such a *directoire* (often with the Germans acting as informal intermediary with the smaller member states). This self-characterisation as a triumvirate of the willing and able, has not been easily accepted either by the Italians—who have frequently sought very determinedly to be a participant, as in the so-called Quint (i.e., with the United States as the fifth member) on the Balkans (Gegout 2002)—or the smaller member states. The meeting of the big three at Ghent before the October 2001 European Council alienated most other leaders; Mr Blair compounded the problem when he invited French and German leaders to Downing Street in November 2001 to discuss further the intervention in Afghanistan—eventually finding himself entertaining the Belgian President of the Council, the Italian and Dutch Prime Ministers, and the High Representative, all of whom gate-crashed the party.

A fourth set of tensions derive from characterisations of 'old' and 'new' Europe. This is not to accept the characterisation of US Defense Secretary, Donald Rumsfeld, on the divisions between those who supported US action in Iraq and those who opposed it, since a number of 'older' European states including Denmark and the UK became a part of the US-led coalition. There is, nonetheless, a tension that derives from the enlargement to Central and Eastern Europe, which may have an important impact on the development of the EU's foreign, security, and defence policies. Many of the new member states, retaining vivid memories of Soviet domination, looked for and found strong American support in their search for security. Although their preoccupation with territorial defence may have been challenged by the way in which, since 2001, the US has come to regard NATO as having a global mission, they still do not see the EU as a realistic alternative in terms of defence. That is not to say that the new member states have not been involved in, or supportive of present EU missions and the ESDP in general, but there remains a continuing sense of gratitude towards the US and NATO, that is different from the attitudes of the older members of the EU.

A fifth set of tensions revolves around the question of the continued relevance of the concept of Civilian Power Europe and the scope and nature of the EU's ESDP. So far, the EU's growing participation in policing/peacekeeping missions in the Balkans and the Democratic Republic of the Congo have been viewed with satisfaction. The search for balance in the Security Strategy of 2003 between civilian and military means of responding to threats, risks, and crises won significant support. But there remain elements of constructive ambiguity and tension, for example over concepts of pre-emption rather than prevention. Even as the divisions over Iraq emerged, Robert Kagan's widely-debated article seemed designed to exacerbate them by exaggerating the differences between Europe and the US (Kagan 2002). While the concept of 'soft power' was generally regarded in Europe as a European strength, Kagan's critique of Europe's weakness, and his characterisation of Europe as from Venus (and the US from Mars), was widely resented, not least because it was believed to be commonplace in Washington. Such a division of labour nonetheless has its adherents, albeit for possibly different reasons, as Menon and Nicolaïdis have suggested (2004). Moreover, there remains debate over the direction of the ESDP. While the Constitutional Treaty contains a solidarity clause similar to that of the WEU and of NATO, the latter is also referred to, indicative of the continuing reluctance of many states either to forego NATO's collective defence or to risk alienating the US by seeming to challenge NATO.

The relationship with the United States can thus be seen to be of particular salience in the continuing development of the CFSP and ESDP. The issue of how to live with a hyper-power in an economically multi-polar world continues to tax the member states. France, even with its frequent steps back, continuously dwells on the need for Europe to accept multipolarity even at the risk of appearing a rival to the US. American responses to Chancellor Schroeder's opposition to the war in Iraq engendered further German questioning of the value of NATO as it existed. In marked contrast, the UK government seemed determined to prove its loyalty as an ally, seemingly regarding it as inconceivable that the UK would fight a war without the US—creating some confusion as to the UK's commitment to the development of the ESDP given the reasons put forward for the initiative at St. Malo. Insofar as the United States has been wary of a European caucus on security and defence matters in the past, and looks to NATO either to accept a more global role in the future or at least to provide a coalition of the willing, the EU will continue to be subject to strain as a foreign policy actor.

Finally, and in part as a response to such differences, provisions for greater flexibility or enhanced cooperation are developed further in the Constitutional Treaty. Those member states 'whose military capabilities fulfil higher criteria and which have made more binding commitments to one another with a view in this area with a view to the most demanding missions shall establish permanent structured cooperation within the Union framework' (Article I-41, 6). Insofar as the EU has had varying elements of such flexibility in the defence field since it was created (with the WEU, NATO, Eurocorps etc, on the one hand, and the Danish opt out, or Irish military neutrality on the other), this creates little that is new. It can be seen, however, as both opportunity and danger: it provides an opportunity for the EU to act even if not all the member states are wholly in agreement—increasingly important in an EU of 25. Yet it also creates dangers, at least in relation to the orthodox view that the declared aim of the EU is to develop 'mutual political solidarity... and the achievement of an ever-increasing degree of convergence' (Article I-40).

Conclusions

While it has become commonplace to agree with the characterisation of the EU as economic giant, political dwarf, and military worm, this underestimates, as this survey suggests, the scope and variety of the EU's international relations. The scope of the EU's relationships was in a very real sense laid out by the very nature of the Economic Community and the colonial legacy of the member states. It remains inevitably patchy in its depth and intensity insofar as its concerns have been determined not simply by its own volition, difficult though that has often been, but by its need to react to change, whether over the longer term or in short term crises. The end of the Cold War and the need to respond to the new demands of the countries of Central and Eastern Europe led, if initially clumsily and without much sense of purpose, to the successful accession of ten states to the EU in 2004, with Bulgaria and Romania on track for membership in 2007. Croatia, Macedonia, and Turkey have also applied, with the Stabilisation and Association Process geared to further Balkan accessions.

Such an enlargement process contains its own foreign policy problems, not least in what to do with the EU's new neighbours, some of which wish to join but whose eligibility under existing criteria is in doubt. Whether the EU's new 'New Neighbourhood Policy' meets the demands of such varied demands of Morocco and other Mediterranean states, Georgia and the other states of the Caucasus, Ukraine, Belarus, and Russia and eastwards to the other former parts of the Soviet Union, remains critical. Stability and security on the EU's borders is an obvious goal but one the EU failed to engender in the past. It remains to be seen whether the new emphasis on preventive diplomacy, and the extension of the EU 'tool box' to include the military elements of a security and defence policy, proves adequate.

Certainly the tensions that have accompanied the evolution and development of the toolbox are likely to remain, both external and internal. The US, for example, is likely to remain ambivalent about working with the EU rather than through individual member states. Russia similarly has made much of its particular relationships with Germany, and to a lesser extent, France. China is perhaps the most interested in European integration as a phenomenon. Internally, despite the signature of the Constitutional Treaty, the ratification process may not be a smooth one. Even if member governments have shown themselves willing to provide a new framework for integration, they manifest different levels of enthusiasm, while their publics are even less predictable. In terms of implementing a more coherent external policy, governments are likely to retain an element of schizophrenia—well aware of the advantages of a politics of scale, but nonetheless reluctant to give up all pretence of individual weight and importance, especially in areas where they have traditionally been strong or with a particular contribution to make. Despite the attempts to provide solidarity clauses and more clarity over who is speaking for the Union abroad, there remains a lack of certainty about the sources of EU action—and consequently a lack of legitimacy, particularly if the use of force is envisaged. The growing number of EU foreign policy interventions may create a familiarity and gradually, if they continue to be successful, a wider acceptance. But the fundamental tension remains, between the conceptions of Europe as a civilian power, and as a potentially more forceful actor. This is endemic in the extraordinary adventure which is European integration and enlargement. The historical process has been in continual movement, and the scope has ever-widened. But the strains have grown in parallel, with the result that incrementalism and inconsistency are likely to be the order of the day in Europe's external activity for some time to come.

Note

1 I am grateful to Joyobroto Sanyal, Marie Curie visiting fellow in the Centre of International Studies at Cambridge, for his suggestions and help with references.

Further reading

The substantive geographical and functional patterns of the EU's international relations are generally well covered in the standard texts. See, for example, Bretherton and Vogler (1999), Ginsberg (2001), Piening (1997), and K. Smith (2003). The problem of 'drivers and brakes' and of the roles played both by member states and EU institutions can be approached from a number of different angles. See, for example, Peterson and Sjursen (1998) and Nuttall (2000) on the contending forces in the evolution of the CFSP, and Hill (1996) and Manners and Whitman (2000) on the influence of member states. More specific studies of policy issues demonstrating the different patterns of EU activity include Holland (2002), Keukeleire (2003), K. Smith (2004), and M. Smith (2004).

Bretherton, C., and Vogler, J. (1999), *The European Union as a Global Actor* (London: Routledge).

Ginsberg, R. (2001), *The European Union in International Politics: A Baptism by Fire* (Lanham, MD: Rowman and Littlefield).

Hill, C. (ed.) (1996), *The Actors in Europe's Foreign Policy* (London: Routledge).

Keukeleire, S. (2003), 'The European Union as a Diplomatic Actor: Internal, Traditional and Structural Diplomacy', *Diplomacy and Statecraft* 14/3, 31–56.

Manners, I., and Whitman, R. (eds) (2000), *The Foreign Policies of European Union Member States* (Manchester: Manchester University Press).

Nuttall, S. (2000), *European Foreign Policy* (Oxford: Oxford University Press).

Peterson, J., and Sjursen, H. (1998), *A Common Foreign Policy for Europe? Competing Visions of the CFSP* (London: Routledge).

Piening, C. (1997), *Global Europe: The European Union in World Affairs* (Boulder, CO: Lynne Rienner).

Smith, H. (2002), *European Union Foreign Policy: What It Is and What It Does* (London: Pluto Press).

Smith, K. (2003), *European Union Foreign Policy in a Changing World* (Cambridge: Polity).

Smith, K. (2004), *The Making of EU Foreign Policy: The Case of Eastern Europe*, 2nd edition (Basingstoke: Palgrave).

Smith, M. (2004), 'The European Union, the United States and Asia: A New Trilateralism?' in Cowles, M.G., and Dinan, D. (eds) *Developments in the European Union 2* (Basingstoke: Palgrave).

Web links

For general information on the patterns of the EU's international activities, the best sources are the web sites of EU institutions and delegations, especially the Europa web site, http://www.europa.eu.int/ and the web site of the EU delegation in Washington DC: http://www.eurunion.org/. On the foreign policies and priorities of the member states, the best sources are the national government web sites and especially those of foreign offices, for example: http://www.fco.gov.uk/(Britain) and http://www.foreign.ministry.se/(Sweden). For more academic analysis, see the web sites of FORNET, http://www.fornet.info/ and the European Foreign Policy Unit at the London School of Economics and Political Science, http://www.lse.ac.uk/Depts/intrel/EuroFPUnit/.

Part II

Institutions and Processes

Chapter 4

The Institutional Framework

Sophie Vanhoonacker

Contents

Summary

Although both the Treaty on European Union (TEU) and the Treaty establishing a Constitution for Europe (TECE) talk about a single institutional framework, there is in fact a complex institutional context for the evolution of the EU's international relations, within which the roles of the Council, Commission, European Parliament, and European Court of Justice in various areas and on different policy issues differ considerably. Such marked variations reflect differing paths of evolution, and the different roles of institutions in the integration process. This chapter focuses on the institutional basis of the international policy role of the EU, asking initially how we should think about the roles of institutions and reviewing some of the key ideas about the ways in which the EU's institutions work. The chapter then reviews three key areas of EU international policy, and finally returns to ideas about institutions and their effects on policy, with particular reference to the potential effects of the Constitutional Treaty.

Introduction: institutions and why they matter

The European Union manifests itself on the international scene in many different ways: through its trade policy, development cooperation and humanitarian aid, as well as through the Common Foreign and Security Policy (CFSP) and the emerging European Security and Defence Policy (ESDP, now more frequently known as the CSDP or Common Security and Defence Policy). Being the logical consequence of the establishment of the customs union and the Common External Tariff (CET), the Common Commercial Policy is one of the Union's oldest and most integrated policies. Decision making in the area of trade is organised according to the supranational Monnet method, whereby the Commission has the exclusive right of initiative and the Council decides by qualified majority voting (QMV). The same applies for development cooperation although in contrast to the Common Commercial Policy (CCP), development is not a truly common policy but an area where individual member states have maintained a high level of sovereignty. The TEU as well as the Constitutional Treaty stipulate that EU action in this field is complementary to that of the national capitals. Cooperation in the area of foreign policy started from the 1970s onwards, but only took off after the end of the Cold War when the Union started to tackle the sensitive question of security. Although it has been catching up since the 1990s, the level of institutionalisation in the foreign policy area has historically been lower than in trade and its mode of governance continues to be primarily intergovernmental.

This chapter focuses on an institutional analysis of the international relations of the Union. It looks not only at formal constitutional entities and decision rules as defined in the TEU, but also examines political practices and forms of informal interaction—in other words, institutions in the broadest sense. As the institutional frameworks of the above-mentioned policies (commercial, development, foreign and security, defence) came about at different periods and developed along various tracks with their own integration logic, each policy will initially be treated separately. Contrary to what the Treaty on European Union (TEU) claims, there is in effect no single institutional framework for EU external relations—in fact, this is reflected in the labels given both to the CFSP and CSDP. They are *common* policies, not single policies. Even if the institutions are to some extent the same, the rules of the game between the various policy areas of external relations vary considerably, and the Constitutional Treaty agreed in 2004 does not change this. But it must be remembered that although there are apparently separate institutional tracks for the handling of the EU's international relations, some of the key issues in external policy making are concerned with the interactions and the tensions between the different tracks. The questions of 'consistency' to which this co-existence of institutional frameworks gives rise are dealt with specifically in Chapter 5 of this volume.

Why and how do institutions matter, both within the process of European integration more generally and more specifically in relation to the EU's international relations? The role(s) of institutions both broadly and narrowly defined has been a continuing preoccupation of scholars dealing with the integration process in its 'internal' aspects (Pollack 2003, 2004; Peterson and Shackleton 2002; Stone Sweet,

Sandholtz and Fligstein 2001), and this has been extended by others into the field of international policy-making (Smith, M.E. 2003). From this work, and from what has been said already in this chapter, it can be seen that institutions can matter in a number of significant ways to the international relations of the EU:

- First, institutions in their most formal sense reflect the prevailing conceptions and levels of agreement among member states and other significant bodies about the scope and nature of the EU's international relations. Most formally of all, they are encapsulated in the successive treaties that have been concluded among the member states and which thus incorporate successive institutional bargains at the intergovernmental level. In this form, institutions can be said to reflect the power and preferences of the member states and to be the product of inter-state bargaining within a broadly rationalist framework (Moravcsik 1993, 1998, etc).

- Second, institutions, as indicated above, say something important about the history of the European integration process and about where the international relations of the EU have been as well as where they might be going. Analysts who emphasise 'historical institutionalist' approaches have drawn attention not only to the impact of successive institutional bargains but also to the ways in which prior bargains and institutional arrangements shape what is seen to be possible or appropriate at a given time. This analysis has given rise to ideas of 'path dependency' in which the evolution of EU policies can be read off from the institutional bargains concluded often years beforehand (Pierson 1996).

- Third, institutions and institutional changes can reflect the changing political complexion of the EU and of its engagement with the outside world through a process of 'multi-level governance' (Marks and Hooghe 1996). In other words, the institutions through which—in this case—the EU frames and conducts its international relations are partly a response to the changing internal makeup of the Union and partly a response to external demands and opportunities. Thus, some of the changes that have taken place in the EU's institutional framework as it relates to international relations have reflected the growth of the Union itself and the needs or assets of new member states. Equally, some of the external demands and opportunities themselves emerge from the institutional frameworks that surround the EU, in the shape of organisations and rules associated with (for example) international trade, the global environment and global security issues.

- Fourth, institutions are not inert, 'neutral' mechanisms that simply obey orders. Rather, they can profoundly shape the ways in which EU policy-makers develop their preferences, their priorities and their understanding of what is possible for the Union in the international arena. The proponents of 'sociological institutionalism' have thus assessed the institutions of the EU's international relations in terms of the ways in which they shape and respond to expectations, the ways in which they reflect 'social learning' on the part of those engaged in them and the ways in which they shape the framing ideas of EU external policies. Here, the definition of an 'institution' is clearly a long way from the idea noted above that institutions are what is formally laid down in the treaties or other treaty-like arrangements: the nature of institutions broadly defined can include informal norms and conventions as well as formal institutional frameworks or rules that can be written down and are subject to judicial interpretation (Risse 1996, 2004).

Not surprisingly, therefore, there has been a continuing tendency, which has become especially marked in the past decade, to analyse and evaluate the development of the EU's international relations in terms of institutionalist approaches (Smith, M.E. 2003; Joergensen 2002). Seen in this light, and with admittedly considerable variation among adherents of different schools of thought, the growth of the Common Commercial Policy, of development and humanitarian assistance policies and of the Common Foreign and Security Policy/Common Security and Defence Policy are reflections of the ways in which institutions emerge, expand, and shape or re-shape the activities of those operating with them or within them. The rest of this chapter will deal successively with the broad institutional frameworks for the three central strands of the EU's international relations, and will then return to the issues raised here in terms of the impact and implications of institutions.

Institutions and their impact

In this part of the chapter, the key concern is to analyse and evaluate institutional trends in three main areas of the EU's international relations. Key to this analysis is the fact that within the three areas at issue—the Common Commercial Policy, development and humanitarian aid policy, and CFSP/ESDP—institutional change has occurred to different degrees, in different directions and with different impacts. To put it simply, the origins, the trajectory, and the implications of the institutional developments that have taken place in the three areas are markedly different, suggesting that the insights from different areas of institutionalist analysis will be a fertile source of comparative analysis. Thus, the story of institutional development in the Common Commercial Policy has a long historical basis, coinciding with the initiation of the European integration project itself and reflecting an extended engagement with the development of the global political economy. In development policy and humanitarian assistance, the story is only slightly shorter, but also draws upon a host of other influences ranging from decolonisation in the 1960s to the ending of the Cold War in the 1990s. The institutional developments in the field of CFSP and ESDP were initially more incremental and less formalised, but since the end of the Cold War they have seen a major acceleration and deepening. In light of the general thrust of this chapter it is important to describe how the institutional foundations of these polices have taken shape and developed or been transformed, in line with the views of historic institutionalism that initial policy choices have an impact on further institutional evolution. Equally important is the focus encouraged by institutionalist approaches on the ways in which both at the formal and the informal level institutional changes have shaped the expectations and actions of the actors involved, whether they be states, non-state organisations, or the European institutions themselves. As can be seen from other chapters in this volume, the institutional environment is not the only variable explaining the variety of policy outcomes in the field of EU external relations, but it deserves close attention and analysis because it creates certain possibilities and constraints, as well as facilitating comparative analysis and evaluation. The final part of this chapter will return explicitly to evaluation of the impact of institutions on the Union's external policies.

The Common Commercial Policy

The Common Commercial Policy is one of the oldest EC policies as well as a policy with a high level of integration; it has often been argued that the inevitable institutional consequence of the establishment of a customs union was the need for a common commercial policy with the delegation of authority over trade negotiations to the Community and the Commission. Its central objective is to contribute to 'the progressive abolition of restrictions on international trade' (preamble, TEC, and Article III-292 and 314, TECE). In the early years of European integration, it was primarily tariff issues, subsidies, and anti-dumping duties that dominated the agenda, reflecting the predominance of trade in goods in the international economy. The creation of a customs union implied the establishment of a common external tariff (CET) and required that the member states spoke with one voice in international trade rounds. From the 1970s onwards the focus of the debate and of international trade negotiations shifted from tariff issues to non-tariff barriers (such as quotas or technical barriers to trade), and in the 1980s it was broadened to trade in services, intellectual property rights and investment (Woolcock 2000, 374). In contrast to trade in goods, which is an exclusive EU competence, these areas were of mixed EU and national competence and only certain aspects fell under the CCP (Nicoll and Salmon 2001, 213). The changing nature of international trade thus had a key impact on the ways in which the European institutions were configured and operated (see below).

The main institutional actors in the CCP decision-making process are the Council and the Commission (see Figure 4.1). The European Commission initiates proposals (usually but not always for trade negotiations) and the Council acts by QMV (Article 133, TEC). The role of the European Parliament (EP) is consultative. Having the exclusive right of initiative, the role of the European Commission is pivotal. With regard to anti-dumping measures, it even has decision-making powers: it determines whether to start an investigation following a complaint and decides whether or not anti-dumping duties will be imposed. It also plays a crucial role in the conclusion of international trade agreements. The portfolio of the Commissioner for trade is therefore an important one. The Trade Commissioner necessarily works in close coordination with the Directorate General for Trade (DG Trade). This DG distils the overall Commission position and works in close co-ordination with other DGs such as DG External Relations, DG Agriculture, Consumer Protection, Environment, etc. As these DGs have their own priorities and concerns, this coordination process is often difficult and time consuming.

Within the Council it is primarily the General Affairs and External Relations Council composed of the Ministers of Foreign Affairs (GAERC) that coordinates the trade-related dossiers. There is no formal Council of Trade Ministers, but they can attend the GAERC if trade matters are on the agenda (Woolcock 2000, 383). In addition, the external dimension of different policies is also discussed in sectoral Councils such as the Agricultural Council. Before reaching the GAERC, trade issues are discussed by the so-called 133 Committee and by Coreper. The 133 committee is composed of high-level officials specialised in trade matters, and has responsibility for monitoring the progress of trade negotiations and other activities in the trade area. Coreper or the Committee of Permanent Representatives is composed of the Ambassadors of the member states to the EU and goes through all issues on the GAERC agenda. All levels in the Council are chaired by the rotating Presidency, assisted by the Council General Secretariat (DG (E)).

In the EP, trade issues are followed by the committee on international trade. The purely consultative role of the EP has led to criticism that the CCP lacks transparency and is undemocratic (see the chapter by Christopher Lord in this volume). Nonetheless, the Parliament has not been afraid to voice its opinions on issues such as those of human rights, which often have a close link to the CCP. It also has a power of assent in the case of trade agreements that create new institutional or financial obligations, such as the agreements resulting from the Uruguay Round, which led to the creation of the World Trade Organization. The role of the European Court of Justice (ECJ) goes often unnoticed but is crucial. Through a series of judgements it has extended the scope of the CCP and it is also at the basis of the 'doctrine of implied powers', meaning that where Community institutions have the power to regulate a matter internally, they may also act externally (Young 2000, 102). This has been a major factor for example in negotiations on air transport or trade policy aspects of the environment.

As one of the central aspects of the EU's trade policy is the conclusion of agreements with third countries or international organisations such as the World

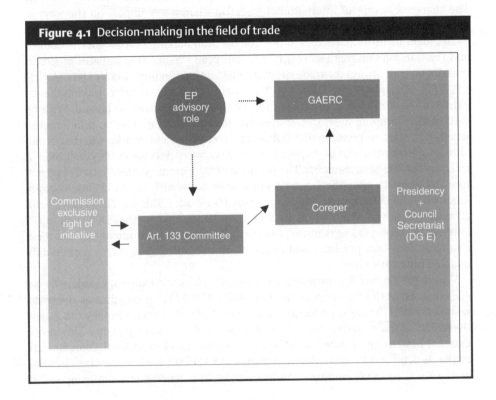

Figure 4.1 Decision-making in the field of trade

Trade Organization (WTO), it is important to describe in more detail how the different EU institutions interact in this process. The legal bases for such negotiations are to be found in the treaties establishing the European Community: Article 133 (trade), Article 300 (agreements with a broader scope than trade) or Article 310 (association agreements).[1] In all cases it is the Commission that represents the member states. It does not act autonomously but on the basis of a mandate adopted by the Council. The Commission also negotiates on behalf of the Council when the issue is of shared national and EU competence (for example, trade in cultural and audiovisual services). During the negotiations there is a continuous dialogue between Council and Commission through the Article 133 or another specialised committee (when the scope is broader than trade). When the negotiations take place in Geneva (WTO), the delegations of the member states to the WTO are consulted. This allows member states to monitor the process and if necessary to adjust the mandate. Third parties sometimes accuse the Commission of inflexibility, because of the need for continual consultation with the member states. At the same time one should recognise that one single point of contact is preferable to dealing with 25 players.

The Treaty does not foresee any formal role for the EP in the development of the Commission mandate. Following pressure, both the Council and Commission have agreed to inform the EP *post facto* about the mandate and the negotiation process (Nicoll and Salmon 2001, 195). The Constitutional Treaty foresees that the Commission should regularly report to the EP during the negotiations, but does little to expand the powers of the EP. The consultation of national parliaments is left to the individual member states and is limited (Woolcock 2000, 380). In recent years the Commission has also made efforts to include the views of non-governmental organisations (NGOs) and interest groups.

Most agreements are adopted by the Council deciding by QMV (Articles 133 and 300). There are however exceptions such as agreements relating to trade in cultural matters and audiovisual services, and services related to education, social and human health. They still require unanimity and ratification by the member states (Decision 1/1994 ECJ;[2] Article 133, paras 5 and 6, TEC). In the case of association agreements (Article 310), the member states need unanimity and the assent of the EP by simple majority. Under Article 300, as noted earlier, the EP has to give its assent for agreements with important institutional or budgetary implications or touching upon EC legislation adopted by co-decision. The results of the Uruguay Round were a case in point (Woolcock 2000, 388). Political control by national parliaments is rather limited and ad hoc and does not compensate for the limited role of the EP.

Representing a market of 475 million customers, the EU is an important player on the international trade scene. From the beginning, the European Commission has occupied a central position. Being the body that drafts international negotiation mandates, it undoubtedly is an institution that matters in the field of trade. Not all member states are happy with this situation and they have tried to regain some of their powers in new policy areas such as trade in services and intellectual property rights. The Nice Treaty stipulates that agreements relating to trade in cultural matters and audiovisual services, educational and social and human health services fall within the shared competence of the Community and its member states. Hence they are subject to unanimity. The Constitutional Treaty confirms this rule (Article III, 315, TECE), but it should be noted that as a result of agreements finalised in the Nice Treaty (2000) for all practical purposes the Commission now acts as the agent of the Union in those areas covered by the remit of the World Trade Organization (WTO).

The concentration of power in a small community of experts (DG Relex and Article 113 committee) has added to the efficiency of the CCP, giving it a decidedly technocratic air at times (Smith and Woolcock 1999). The penalty that is paid, though, is a lack of transparency and accountability, which has often been a source of criticism. In a period of increasing globalisation where NGOs have become active players on the international scene as well as in the domestic economies of member states, such an approach is hard to maintain. The Constitutional Treaty makes a small step in the direction of enhanced accountability and transparency, first by requiring the Commission to report regularly to the EP on the progress of international trade negotiations. Secondly, the principle of participatory democracy is introduced, urging the Commission to give citizens and representative associations the chance to express their views. Practice will show to which extent these changes will make a difference.

Development cooperation policy and humanitarian assistance

Although the provisions on development cooperation (Articles 177–181, TEC) were only introduced into the core treaties of the EU with the adoption of the TEU in Maastricht, formal relations between the EC and the developing world are almost as old as the Communities itself. Due to their colonial past, several member states had historic links with the developing world and they therefore had significant interests in using the EC as a vehicle for their continuing relationships with their previous colonies as well as more generally supporting these countries in their battle against poverty. Today the EU and its member states provide 55% of international development aid and two thirds of global humanitarian aid. As regards development aid, the member states provide the bulk of the funds (45% by the member states and 10% by the EU), whereas for humanitarian aid, the EU is the main provider (30% by the EU and 25% by the member states) (Holland 2002, 109 and Commission 2000, 3).

One of the most important instruments of EU development policy are the cooperation and association agreements that have been concluded with countries and regional groupings all over the world. While the EEC initially focused on the (sub-Saharan) African, Caribbean, and Pacific (ACP) countries, today EU development policy is global in scope. Nonetheless, the Cotonou Partnership Agreement with the ACP countries continues to be the most elaborate and institutionalised form of cooperation.[3] Building on the *acquis* of the Lomé Conventions (1975–2000), this 20-year agreement entered into force in April 2003 and provides the basis for political dialogue, development cooperation, and closer economic and trade cooperation. In contrast to Lomé, Cotonou also imposes political conditionality, emphasising respect for human rights, democratic principles, the rule of law, and good governance. As with the case of the Common Commercial Policy, it can be seen from this brief sketch that the significant institutions for the EU's international relations are not all to be found within the EU itself; it is the interaction of the EU's institutions with those of the broader global arena that makes for important complexities and tensions.

> **Box 4.1** Institutional framework for the Cotonou Partnership Agreement
>
> - **ACP–EU Council of Ministers:** composed of one minister of each of the participating countries as well as a representative of the Commission. It meets once a year and is chaired alternately by an EU and an ACP country. It is responsible for the implementation of the agreement and its decisions are binding. The Council is assisted by committees and ad hoc working parties.
> - **Committee of Ambassadors:** composed of a representative of each EU and ACP state and a representative of the Commission. It meets at least every six months and assists the Council with its implementing tasks.
> - **ACP–EU Joint Parliamentary Assembly:** composed of an equal number of members of the EP and ACP parliamentarians and meets twice a year alternately in the EU and in an ACP country. Its role is purely consultative.

The cooperation between the EU and the ACP countries is supported by a number of joint institutions, which have been seen by many as unique in the global political economy (see Box 4.1). Some have argued that this high level of institutionalisation contributes to the stability and the effectiveness of the relationship (Holland 2002, 49).[4] Others have argued that what matters in the stability of these arrangements is the power of the EU, and its capacity to sustain commitment to the kinds of partnership that has developed; if this view is accepted, then the institutions become the symptom of this power, rather than the generators of stability in an independent sense.

Unlike the CCP, development cooperation is not a common policy. It has its centre of gravity in the member states and their bilateral aid programmes. In Maastricht, the EU countries agreed to coordinate their policies and to consult each other (Article 180, TEC), but in practice, it proved difficult to implement the principle of complementarity. Lack of political will and diversity in traditions and working methods are important obstacles. But in addition, and with particular relevance to the focus of this chapter, the weaknesses of the internal EU institutional structure are a significant explanatory factor.

As in the area of trade, the two principal institutional players in development policy are the Council and the European Commission. The role of the Commission is much weaker than in the CCP, and for the Council development cooperation is not often high on the agenda. It is certainly not a priority for the European Council, which waited until November 2000 to adopt its first general statement on development policy. At the level of the Council, it was for many years the Development Council that dealt with development cooperation. With the reduction of the number of Councils (European Council of Seville, June 2002), development policy has been integrated into the GAERC and is now discussed twice a year.[5] Decisions by the GAERC are prepared by Coreper II (the Permanent Representatives of the member states to the EU) and by the working groups. Under the provisions of the Constitutional Treaty, development policy will fall under the Foreign Affairs Council, chaired by the Union Minister for Foreign Affairs. The fact that this person will be nominated for a five-year period, and will deal with all aspects of the Union's external relations, may have a beneficial impact on the coherence and consistency of the EU's development policy. On the other hand, poverty reduction may be less central and become subservient to the realisation of foreign policy objectives such as security.

The European Commission has a wide range of responsibilities in the area of development policy. On behalf of the member states, it negotiates cooperation and association agreements with third world countries, it manages the EU aid budget and the European Development Fund (EDF) (see Chapter 8 by M.E. Smith), and it can undertake initiatives to coordinate the policies of the EU and the member states. Nonetheless, its role is much weaker than in the area of trade. Partly this has to do with the reluctance of the member states to cede sovereignty, and partly it can be explained by the Commission's hybrid organisational structure. Within the Commission the responsibilities for development cooperation are shared out by geographical region. DG Development (DG DEV) deals with the ACP and Overseas Countries and Territories (OCT); DG Enlargement (DG ELARG) is responsible for pre-accession aid to the candidate countries; and DG External Relations (DG RELEX) provides assistance to the remaining non-ACP countries (North Africa, Latin America, most of Asia, the Middle East, countries of the former Soviet Union). In the Commission's most recent study of development policy, this diffusion of institutional responsibilities was the subject of a decidedly negative judgement.[6] The dispersion of responsibilities over different DGs led to 'lack of transparency, a waste of human resources and a compartmentalisation of methods' (European Commission, 2000, 6).

The reforms undertaken by the Santer and the Prodi Commissions tried to address this situation. One of the most important impulses for reform came from the decision to try to reunify the project cycle (from programming to evaluation), which is a central part of the largely project-based funding mechanisms for EU development policy.[7] With the establishment of the Common Service for External Relations (SCR) in 1998, all services responsible for implementation and evaluation of aid projects (the two last phases of the project cycle) were brought together. The first part of the project cycle (programming, identification, appraisal and the financing decision) remained however with DG RELEX and DG DEV. The Prodi Commission replaced the SCR in 2001 by the EuropeAid Cooperation Office and made it responsible for all the phases of the project cycle (from identification to evaluation) except for the programming phase that stayed with DG DEV and DG RELEX (see Box 4.2). For some observers, these reforms do not go far enough: they argue for a single DG, under a development Commissioner responsible for both policy and programming functions (House of Lords 2003, point 43). Whether the Commission will ultimately embark upon that road remains to be seen. As historical institutionalism argues, entrenchment of institutional arrangements makes a radical overhaul a daunting task. This might be seen as even more daunting in light of the ways in which the internal arrangements intersect and interact with the external institutional arrangements for dealing with such groupings as the ACP countries; quite simply, there is a great deal of investment or vested interest in the existing arrangements, and thus a natural reluctance to accommodate radical change.

Another important element of the reform in development assistance activities was the decision to devolve more responsibilities to the more than 120 delegations of the Commission's External Service. Being based on the spot, their staff is generally better placed to manage aid projects and to take into account the needs of the partner

> **Box 4.2** The EuropeAid Cooperation Office
>
> ■ Established in January 2001.
>
> ■ Successor of the Common Service for External Relations (SCR) (1998–2000).
>
> ■ Responsible for all the phases of the project cycle that follow the programming phase.
>
> ■ Consists of eight Directorates (of which five are responsible for geographical programmes).
>
> ■ Does not deal with pre-accession aid,[8] humanitarian aid, macro-financial assistance, actions under CFSP, and the Rapid-Reaction Mechanism.
>
> ■ The Management Board is composed of the five Commissioners that are members of the Relex Group[9] and chaired by the Commissioner for External Relations. The Commissioner for Development and Humanitarian Aid is Chief Executive.

countries, as well as acting in some ways as 'EU embassies' in the coordination of aid with other areas of policy.

The role of the EP and its Committee on Development and Cooperation is weak. The EP budgetary powers are limited to the aid that is funded from the EU budget. The European Development Fund (EDF) providing aid to the ACP countries consists of national contributions and escapes control by the EP. Development cooperation falls under Article 251, TEC, but as there is little legislation in this area, there is not much to co-decide. When the Council concludes a trade agreement with a developing country, the EP has no formal role (see above). The Committee on Development and Cooperation can address oral and written questions to the Council or Commission and can adopt resolutions trying to influence the course of the negotiations, but it has no competence to approve the results. This is different in the case of the association agreements and some cooperation agreements where the EP has the power of assent.

Finally a few words should also be said about EU humanitarian aid, managed entirely through the European Commission and more particularly by the European Community Humanitarian Office (ECHO—see Box 4.3). ECHO is a separate agency because it has to respond rapidly and effectively to humanitarian crises. It is primarily a financing body and has to limit itself to providing emergency aid. Contrary to DG DEV and DG RELEX, it is responsible for the management of the full project cycle (from programming to evaluation). A lot of the management functions are devolved to staff in the field.

Relations between the EU and the developing world have changed considerably since the signature of the first Yaoundé agreement in the 1960s. While the EEC primarily concentrated on the ACP countries, EU external assistance today has a global reach. Furthermore there is also a trend to increasingly link aid to political and economic conditions. On the institutional side, developments have been less spectacular, and some would argue that this can be explained predominantly by intergovernmental processes and the kinds of institutional arrangements they produce. Many member states still see the relations with the developing world as

---

Box 4.3 ECHO

- Established in 1992.
- Provides humanitarian assistance to populations of third countries affected by disasters or conflicts.[10]
- Funds are mainly drawn from the Commission budget and from the EDF in the case of the ACP countries.
- Implementation is done through third parties: humanitarian organisations (NGOs and international organisations such as UN agencies).

---

their *domaine réservé* and are reluctant to see a strong role for the Commission and even the Council. In the GAERC, development is in competition with the many other aspects of external relations and is not a priority. The position of the Commission is much weaker than in the field of trade. This is partly because development cooperation is only a complementary policy, but it is also due to the Commission's poor internal organisation. Through reforms in the management of external assistance, both the Santer and Prodi Commission have tried to turn the tide. Much progress has been made but the process is far from being completed. For the EP the balance is mixed. It has to give its assent in the case of cooperation and association agreements but its power of the purse is seriously curtailed because the EDF falls outside the Community budget. As in the area of trade, the accountability question remains a burning one.

The rather weak institutional foundations of European development cooperation are thus in large part a reflection of the member states' reluctance to cede sovereignty in this area. The bulk of decisions related to development aid continue to be taken in the national capitals. As regards the questions dealt with by the EU, we see an increasing attempt by the Commission to exploit the possibilities of its powers by becoming better organised. If successful, this could give the Commission some of the influence as a 'policy entrepreneur' that has been discerned in other areas of policy-making, and would reflect a significant shift in institutional balance within this policy area.

European foreign policy and defence cooperation

The third leg of EU external relations is that of cooperation in the field of foreign policy and defence. Foreign, security, and defence policy are issues that reach to the core of the sovereignty of the nation state, and as a result the member states were for many years extremely reluctant to integrate (as opposed to cooperating) in this area. In line with the argument in this chapter, it is to be expected that this would have important impacts on the pattern of institutional development in European foreign, security, and defence policies. Moreover, most Western European countries in the Cold War period had chosen an Atlantic rather than a European framework for the organisation of their security and defence cooperation; the key institution for many was thus not the European Community, but the North Atlantic Treaty Organization (NATO). The end of the Cold War, uncertainty about the future of transatlantic relations and the outbreak of the Yugoslav conflict re-launched the debate on a European foreign policy in the early 1990s and opened up the institutional as well as the political field of play. At Maastricht (1991) the member states agreed on the creation of a Common Foreign and Security Policy (CFSP) and from the late 1990s onwards security and defence were also put high on the agenda. The chapter briefly examines the institutional underpinnings of European Political Cooperation (EPC), the predecessor of CFSP, and then moves on to examine CFSP and ESDP in more detail. Finally, a few words will be said about the institutional provisions for foreign and defence policy in the Constitutional Treaty.

European Political Cooperation was a loose form of foreign policy cooperation between the member states of the EC and it was not until the adoption of the Single European Act (SEA), that it received a Treaty basis.[11] The mode of governance in EPC was that of intergovernmentalism; the key players were the member states and their Ministers of Foreign Affairs deciding by consensus.

EPC was kept as much as possible outside the realm of the supranational Community institutions. The European Commission, despite its key role in external economic relations, was initially excluded from foreign policy meetings and was only consulted if EPC affected the EEC's work. In practice it proved hard to sustain this artificial separation between economic and political aspects of foreign policy and in the London Report (1981) it was agreed to fully associate the Commission with EPC 'at all levels'. The attitude towards the European Parliament (EP) was even more reticent. MEPS were only consulted and informed about foreign policy discussions through the Presidency. The realm of EPC was also excluded from the jurisdiction of the European Court of Justice.

The limited role of the Commission put a heavy burden on the Presidency. To support the chair, the troika system was introduced, bringing together representatives from the Presidency, its predecessor and successor and the Commission. With the SEA, a small secretariat was established in the buildings of the Council General Secretariat (Nuttall 2000, 20). The EPC machinery grew in a gradual and pragmatic way. As new practices such as a Group of European Correspondents and their telex network, better known as Coreu developed, they were codified in successive reports. Gradually the cooperation also extended to the member states' embassies abroad and to their representations to international organisations such as the UN.

EPC existed for 23 years. Although it had many weaknesses, it created a habit of consultation and cooperation and allowed the member states to get acquainted with each others' working methods and foreign policy traditions. As several diplomats and scholars have argued, one of its principal benefits has been that it created a kind of 'co-ordination reflex' (Nuttall 1997, 38; Regelsberger, de Schoutheete and Wessels 1997, 3), through a form of what sociological institutionalists and social constructivists would characterise as 'social learning'.

The pragmatic world of EPC was abruptly shaken by the end of the Cold War. Uncertainties about the future developments in Central Europe and the US role on the European continent meant that the EC member states no longer had the luxury of ignoring security questions. The European difficulties in speaking with one voice during the first Gulf war (1990–91) and the outbreak of the Yugoslav conflict in June 1991 catapulted security to the top of the European agenda, inevitably raising the question of new institutional arrangements.

In the framework of the 1991 Intergovernmental Conference (IGC), culminating in the Treaty on European Union, the Twelve adopted a series of provisions laying the basis for the development of a Common Foreign and Security Policy (Title V, TEU).[12] On the institutional side, two major issues were discussed. Firstly, the Twelve examined how to reduce the gap between the EC institutions and the foreign policy machinery. Secondly they tried to reach an agreement on the institutional framework underpinning the adoption and implementation of security and defence decisions.

As concerns the first question, the outcome was mixed. The Maastricht Treaty referred to a single institutional framework but at the same time it placed the CFSP provisions in a separate, so-called second pillar. The institutions playing a role in the EC and CFSP became to a large extent the same but their competencies and the way they interacted continued to be different. For the supranational institutions the changes were minimal. The European Commission received a so-called 'non-exclusive' right of initiative in CFSP (Article J.8), and its membership of the troika was confirmed (Article J.5).[13] Its role, nonetheless, remained much weaker than in the first pillar. The powers of the EP remained purely consultative and foreign and security policy continued to be excluded from supervision by the Court (Article L, TEU).

It was at the level of the Council that the artificial separation between external economic and political relations was addressed most directly. The General Affairs Council, meeting in Brussels, was entrusted both with EC and CFSP matters. The former EPC secretariat was merged with that of the Council General Secretariat (CGS) and within its DG E, a CFSP unit was established. At lower level, the Political Committee was maintained as a central player but Coreper, formally in charge of preparing the Council agenda, also became involved. After some initial tensions, it was agreed that Poco would continue to be responsible for content matters, while Coreper would primarily look at the institutional, legal, financial and Community aspects of the documents prepared by Poco (Nuttall 2000, 183 and 245–8; Regelsberger 1997, 76).[14] Coreper would be assisted by a group of so-called CFSP counsellors (today known as Relex counsellors) based in the Permanent Representations. By attending both the meetings of Coreper and Poco, they would in principle serve as a bridge and fulfil an important role in examining the consistency between the pillars (Nuttall 2000, 245–8, and Chapter 4 of this volume). The distinction between EC and EPC working groups was also brought to an end and EPC working groups with counterparts in the Council structure were merged (Nuttall 2000, 249–50; Regelsberger 1997, 76–9). These detailed changes, however, made relatively little difference to the distribution of institutional responsibilities, as shown in Box 4.4 below.

CFSP decisions including the new instruments of common positions (declaratory statements) and joint actions (operational actions) continued to be taken by unanimity. When implementing a joint action, there was scope for QMV, but first the member states had to agree by unanimity which aspects it concerned (Article J3)!

The extension of CFSP to 'all questions related to the security of the Union' was one of the most sensitive issues of the IGC (Article J4, para. 1). While Atlanticists such as the British pleaded for a strengthened European security role within NATO, Europeanists saw the end of the Cold War as an opportunity to develop an independent European security identity. Neutral countries such as Ireland, though, were not eager at all to embark on the security path. The compromise consisted of bringing in the Western European Union (WEU). Becoming an integral part of the development

Box 4.4 Comparison of main players in EPC and CFSP

EPC	CFSP
European Council	European Council
Meeting of Ministers of Foreign Affairs	Council
Chairmanship by rotating Presidency	Chairmanship by rotating Presidency
Support by EPC Secretariat	Support by CFSP unit of the CGS
Political Committee	Political Committee and Coreper
EPC working parties	Merged working parties
Commission: fully associated	Commission: co-right of initiative
EP: fully associated	EP: fully associated
Court: excluded	Court: excluded

of the Union, this Western European security organisation, first established in 1955, was given the task of elaborating and implementing the decisions with a defence dimension (Article J4, para. 2). At the same time it had to serve the objective of strengthening the European pillar of the Atlantic Alliance—a provision insisted on by the British and others (Declaration No. 30, TEU). All EU members were invited to join the WEU or to take observer status, while those who wished could (and did) remain outside. European NATO members not belonging to the EU were given the status of associate member.[15] In terms of the discussion in this chapter, this can be seen as a significant institutional innovation, but one that in principle remained closely linked to the preferences of key EU member states.

In June 1992 the WEU member states adopted the Petersberg declaration defining the possible security tasks for the WEU. It concerned humanitarian and rescue tasks, peacekeeping tasks and tasks involving combat forces in crisis management including peacekeeping (*Europe Documents*, No. 1787, 23 June 1992). To facilitate closer cooperation between the EU, the WEU, and NATO, it was decided to move the WEU Secretariat and the Permanent Representatives to the WEU to Brussels—a first step on the road to what some have called 'Brusselsisation' (Allen 1998). The one-year Presidency of the WEU was reduced to six months and synchronised with that of the Council of the EU. The main challenge remained how to increase the WEU's operational capacities. The WEU member states agreed to organise twice-yearly meetings of the WEU Chiefs of Defence Staff, to create a planning cell, to set up a satellite centre in Torrejon (Spain) and to define a list of forces answerable to the WEU (FAWEU) (Jopp 1997, 160–2). One of the first operations included the sending of naval forces to the Adriatic to monitor observance of the UN embargo against Serbia and Montenegro.

The introduction of CFSP in Maastricht had led to high expectations, but the poor performance of the EU in the Yugoslav crisis made it clear that the Union still had a long way to go before becoming a mature player on the international scene. As a result, and also because the Maastricht Treaty had explicitly provided for a review of the institutional arrangements after five years, CFSP was again high on the agenda during the 1996–97 IGC leading to the Treaty of Amsterdam. Four issues dominated the debate: the use of QMV; the introduction of the principle of flexibility; institutional reform; and amendments with regard to security and defence.

QMV in the area of CFSP again proved a bridge too far but a reinforced QMV (at least ten member states in favour) was introduced for implementing measures that had first been agreed by unanimity such as joint actions, common positions and the new instrument of common strategies (Article 23.2, TEU). However, in case of 'important and stated reasons of national interest' a question can always be referred to the European Council for a decision by unanimity. In addition there was introduced a possibility for member states to abstain and not obliged to apply a decision while allowing the others to go ahead (constructive abstention).

Some of the most visible IGC results were the institutional novelties. In an attempt to give more visibility and continuity to CFSP, the post of High Representative (HR) for CFSP was created, to be supported by a new Policy Planning and Early Warning Unit (see Figure 4.2). The tasks of this so-called Mr/s CFSP were not intended to be performed by a member of the Commission as some had proposed but by the Secretary General of the Council (Article 26, TEU). The main tasks consist of assisting the Council with the formulation, preparation and implementation of foreign policy decisions. Upon request of the Presidency, the HR can also perform representational tasks and is part of the reformed troika (Article 18.3, TEU—this consists usually of the Commissioner for External Relations, the President of the Council at a given time and the High Representative). By appointing Javier Solana, the former Spanish minister for Foreign Affairs and former Secretary General of NATO, the member states chose a strong and experienced personality. Solana was able to give shape to the function and acquire an important place in the formulation and implementation of CFSP. Even the relationship with the Commissioner for external relations was much smoother than expected, perhaps because of the good personal relations between Solana and Commissioner Chris Patten (Müller-Brandeck-Bocket 2002, 271).

In the area of security and defence the most important achievement was the introduction of the so-called Petersberg tasks into the Treaty (Article 17.2, TEU). The proposal of France, Germany, and the Benelux countries and Spain to gradually integrate the WEU into the EU was not taken forward at this time, but by a process of institutional convergence given formal expression at the Nice IGC in 2000, the WEU became effectively the defence policy arm of the Union by the early years of the new millennium (see Howorth, Chapter 11 of this volume).

At the Nice summit of December 2000, the issue of CFSP was formally not on the agenda. Under pressure from the upcoming enlargement, the member states decided to concentrate on three issues left over from Amsterdam (extension of QMV; future composition of the European Commission; re-weighting of votes) and to revisit the issue of 'enhanced cooperation'. Besides reviewing and relaxing the existing enabling clauses on enhanced cooperation in the first and the third pillar, the Fifteen also introduced it in an extremely limited form in the area of CFSP.[16] The scope was confined to the implementation of joint actions and common positions (Galloway 2001, 135).

The most important CFSP amendments in Nice were however related to the issues of security and defence (Galloway 2001, 155–6). The new bodies, first created *ad*

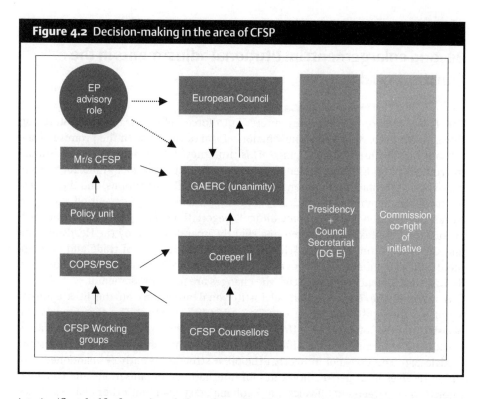

Figure 4.2 Decision-making in the area of CFSP

interim (first half of 2000) and then formally (European Council of Nice, December 2000) include the Political and Security Committee (PSC), the European Union Military Committee (EUMC) and the European Union Military Staff Organisation (EUMS). The Political and Security Committee, better known under its French acronym COPS, is the successor of the Political Committee. Contrary to Political Cooperation it is a permanent and Brussels-based organ.[17] Besides ambassadors of all the member states, it is composed of representatives of the European Commission (DG RELEX), and the Council General Secretariat (DG E and the Policy unit).[18] Under the chairmanship of the rotating Presidency,[19] it meets at least twice a week to monitor and analyse the international situation (Kiessler 2003, 40–41).[20] It organises evaluation and planning and gives political advice to the Council. It is also the body that is in charge of the political control and strategic direction of crisis management operations (Article 25, TEU). Its meetings are being prepared by the so-called Nicolaides group, composed of officials based at the various Permanent Representations (Kiessler 2003, 43–4). Being a relatively new body it is still in the process of finding its working habits (Kiessler 2003, 45).

The other bodies created in Nice are dealt with in Chapter 11 by Jolyon Howorth and it is not necessary to rehearse them in detail here. But it is important to note that these decisions, and others taken later to implement the operational side of the ESDP, have led to a further elaboration of an essentially intergovernmental approach to defence coordination. A host of new institutions has thus either been created or 're-invented' by being given new tasks or put into new relationships with other bodies.

Beyond enlargement: institutional adjustments in the Constitutional Treaty

The Treaty of Nice had not even entered into force before the Heads of State and Government embarked upon a new major reform of the EU with the promise of significant further institutional change. This time they did not rely on the traditional instrument of an IGC but convened a Convention (February 2002–June 2003), composed of representatives of national parliaments, the EU institutions, and the governments of the member states and the candidate countries. The Convention agreed on a draft constitution and after some difficult negotiations during the Italian and Irish Presidencies the text was adopted in a slightly amended form by the Heads of State and Government in June 2004. The amendments in the area of trade and development policy are minimal (see above) but for CFSP and ESDP, renamed as the Common Security and Defence Policy (CSDP), the changes are more fundamental.

A merit of the Treaty is that all institutional provisions on the EU's external action are brought together in one Title (Part III, Title V).[21] The text repeats the Maastricht provisions that 'The Union shall be served by a single institutional framework' (Article 18) and that the different areas of external action should be consistent (Article 193). This does not imply that the pillar structure is entirely abandoned. The Union receives legal personality, can join international organisations and conclude international agreements (Everts and Keohane 2003, 169), but other characteristics of the pillar structure persist. Decision-making procedures and instruments still vary depending on the policy area. In other words, the intergovernmental mode of governance continues to apply both for CFSP and CSDP, reflecting the persistent influence of member state preferences and their reluctance to relinquish control of areas seen as central to the national interest.

The Constitutional Treaty proposes a number of significant institutional adjustments. One of the most debated ones is the introduction of a longer term Presidency for the European Council and the Foreign Affairs Council.[22] By appointing the chair of the European Council for two and a half years (once renewable) and Minister of Foreign Affairs for five years, it is hoped to address the problem of lack of continuity in the foreign policy field. The risk of conflict and overlapping competencies between the Relex Commissioner and the High Representative will disappear as both functions are merged into the new position of Minister for Foreign Affairs. New challenges may however crop up. Competition may arise with the President of the European Council, responsible for defining the strategic interests and objectives of the Union. Another question is whether the new post will further strengthen the intergovernmental character of CFSP. Some fear that the loyalty of the Minister who is nominated by the European Council will in the first place be with the member states. Others consider that the Minister's membership of the Commission and its right of initiative will contribute to the supranational character of CFSP.

A further institutional novelty proposed by the constitution is the creation of an European External Action Service (EEAS), an EU diplomatic service composed of officials of the Commission, the Council General Secretariat and national diplomatic services. It will operate under the authority of the Minister for Foreign Affairs (Article III-296, TECE). The role of the EP and its committee on foreign affairs continues to be consultative, although the nomination of the Minister for Foreign Affairs is subject to its approval. As before, the 'decisions' in the area of CFSP[23] are not enforceable by the European Court of Justice.

The most important changes in the former second pillar relate to the area of security and defence. Flexibility, which used to be a taboo in this area, is now omnipresent. Firstly, the implementation of the Petersberg tasks (Article III-310) is left to the willing and the able. Secondly, the constitution foresees the possibility of structured cooperation amongst a more ambitious group of countries with the necessary military capabilities (Article III-312). Finally, member states can also establish closer cooperation as regards mutual defence (Article I-41).

It is true that the Constitutional Treaty largely consolidates existing institutional practice. However, there is more. Newcomers such as the Minister for Foreign Affairs and the earlier mentioned European External Action Service may further contribute to the Brusselsisation of foreign policy (see above and Chapter 7 by Reuben Wong). In the field of security and defence, the most interesting novelty is the explicit recognition that countries have different ambitions and capabilities, and that this requires flexible arrangements.

Conclusion: how and how much do institutions matter?

Having given an overview of the institutional foundations of EU external policy and of the key developments in three core areas, the argument now returns to the more theoretical question posed at the beginning of this chapter: how and to what extent do institutions matter? It was proposed earlier that institutions mattered in four key ways:

- First, they expressed the limits of intergovernmental agreement and successive 'bargains' encapsulated in the various treaties (the intergovernmentalist position).

- Second, they embedded historical bargains and in that way could constrain or shape subsequent institutional developments in the EU's international relations (the 'historical institutionalist' position).

- Third, they reflected the changing nature of demands and opportunities within the EU itself, especially for example through the process of enlargement, and at the same time the interaction between the institutional developments taking place within the EU and the influence of broader institutional frameworks in the global arena (the 'governance' position).

- Fourth, they provided a context for 'social learning' and the development of expectations and understandings through the interaction of the various groups engaged in the international relations of the EU, from NGOs through to national governments and the European institutions (the 'sociological institutionalist' or the social constructivist position).

What can we say about these four propositions, in light of the evidence gathered together in this chapter? First, in general it is clear that be it in the fields of trade, development, foreign policy or defence, EU external relations go beyond interaction amongst member states and their foreign counterparts. Supranational players such as the European Commission, the EP and the ECJ play an important role and the way they are structured undeniably has an impact on the political debate, on the expectations of significant actors and on policy outcomes. It is for example impossible to understand the sometimes rigid EU position in the WTO without any knowledge about the central role of the Commission and its interaction with the Council and the 133 committee (see Meunier and Nicolaïdis, Chapter 12 in this volume). Likewise, one cannot comprehend the large number of often vague and aspirational EU foreign policy declarations if one is not familiar with the intergovernmental mode of decision-making in the field of CFSP.

As would be expected by historical institutionalist analysis, the high degree of institutional complexity and diversity in EU external relations can to a large extent be explained by the ways in which the different policies developed. As one of the oldest and most integrated policies, the CCP is highly institutionalised and even if some member states would like to recapture some of their powers, the traditionally strong position of the Commission makes it difficult to realise this goal. The institutional framework is not only embedded in a series of treaties; it has been strengthened by practice and by the evidence that especially in global trade negotiations, the member states are stronger acting collectively than they ever could be acting apart. The bargains made in the 1950s have been cemented not only by the evidence of policy effectiveness but also, sometimes with some reluctance, in the face of change at the level of the global political economy expressed in the WTO and other multilateral institutional frameworks. Historical institutionalists would also point to the evidence provided by the development and humanitarian aid policy area, to indicate that the relative weakness of the historical bargains among member states has made it difficult to overcome the essentially mixed nature of the policies adopted. To a degree, the same goes for foreign policy cooperation. Having embarked upon the intergovernmental path, successive IGCs have not been able to communitarise this policy. This said, however, it has been pointed out by a number of analysts that the development of powerful informal norms and working practices has also enabled cooperation in the foreign and security policy area to be consolidated, and by others that the foreign policies of member states have been increasingly 'Europeanized' and 'Brusselsised' (Nuttall 2000; Allen 1998).

The chapter also provides evidence that change in the composition of the EU itself and in the institutional arrangements surrounding the EU within the global arena has important implications for the development of the EU's 'internal' institutions. EU activities in all three of the areas discussed here have been affected by the enlargement of the EU, through which new constellations of member states with new preferences and priorities have been introduced into the development of external policies. The introduction of Britain in the 1970s created new directions in the framing of trade policy, aid policy, and foreign policy because of the powerful influence wielded by the historical experiences and international connections of the 'awkward partner'. In perhaps a more subtle way, the introduction of Sweden, Finland, and

Austria during the mid-1990s gave greater salience to institutional arrangements in the area of human rights, development policies and the broadening nature of security policies. But neither of these sets of developments can be taken in isolation from other areas of institutional development within the EU or from the changing international scene itself. In particular, the post-Cold War era and the changing nature of 'global governance' has given new salience to attempts to institutionalise EU policies in areas such as asylum and immigration (see Wyn Rees, Chapter 10 of this volume), defence policy (see Jolyon Howorth, Chapter 9) and the management of the global political economy (see Loukas Tsoukalis, Chapter 11). For some observers this means that in a host of new and old policy areas, the EU should be seen increasingly as part of a global system of 'multi-level governance'.

The strong degree of path dependency noted above does not imply that institutions in the field of external relations are static—or that formal institutions tell the whole story. Adjustments take place but they have to be negotiated both formally and informally, and rarely reflect an entirely novel institutional design. The reforms in the management of external assistance under the Santer and Prodi Commission are a case in point, and the increasing trend to Brusselsisation in the area of CFSP shows that adjustments are possible, even if they are slow. Very often, these adjustments in formal institutional processes actually lag behind the development of new degrees of mutual understanding and 'social learning' that would be emphasised by the adherents of sociological institutionalism and its near relative, social constructivism. This means that there has to be an emphasis not only on the formal rules and institutions in examining the international relations of the EU, but also on the informal games and interactions that take place.

Looking at the way formal institutions interact and informal institutions have evolved in the EU's international relations, we see that the game is primarily played by the Council and the Commission. In the CCP, the initiative is often said to lie very much with the Commission, especially in areas where the prevailing need is for technocratic types of policy formulation—although in a number of instances the increasing politicisation of trade-related issues such as human rights and environmental concerns have modified the picture. In development policy and humanitarian assistance, the picture is essentially one of mixed institutional roles, with key significance attaching to the interaction between preferences, institutions and resources both of the member states and of the relevant EU institutions. In the case of CFSP and ESDP, it is still very much the Council that sets the tone, despite significant institutional innovation in recent years, and it is the cooperation between member states that shapes both the institutional framework and the more specific policies undertaken. Despite its right of assent in certain cases and the co-decision procedure in development cooperation, the role of the EP continues to be weak. This raises important questions regarding the legitimacy and the accountability of EU action in the field of external relations, with major implications (as some institutionalist analyses would put it) for the effectiveness and transparency of delegation and control among the EU's key institutional frameworks (for detailed discussion see Lord, Chapter 6 in this volume). A further challenge is that of consistency (see Nuttall, Chapter 5), reflecting the uncertain boundaries between the EU institutions, the interests and actions of member states, and the wide range of international contexts in which EU actions can now be taken. The institutional framework for the EU's international relations is complex, reflecting a variety of histories, trajectories, and innovations, but questions such as these remain central to a full understanding of its implications.

Notes

1 The corresponding articles in the TECE are: Art. III-315 (trade); Art. III-323 to 325.

2 Opinion 1/1994, European Court Reports I 5267 (15 November 1994).

3 The text of the Cotonou Partnership agreement is available at: http://europa.eu.int/comm/development/body/cotonou/overview_en.htm

4 On the instruments of the EU development policy, see Chapter 8 by Michael E. Smith.

5 When development policy is on the agenda of the GAERC, the meeting is also attended by the Development Ministers.

6 During the period 2000–2004, the seats were divided as follows: DG External Relations: Chris Patten; DG Development: Poul Nielson; DG Enlargement: Gunther Verheugen. In the 2005–2009 Commission, the players are: Benita Ferrero-Waldner (External Relations and European Neighbourhood policy); Louis Michel (Development and Humanitarian Aid); Olli Rehn (Enlargement).

7 The different steps of the project cycle are: programming, identification, appraisal, the financing decision, implementation, evaluation.

8 The pre-accession instruments are managed by a single administrative structure, namely DG ENLARG.

9 These are the Commissioners for CFSP, Trade, Enlargement, Development and Humanitarian Aid, and Economic and Financial Affairs.

10 See Council Regulation (EC) No. 1257/96 of 20 June 1996, *Official Journal L 163*, 2 July 1996.

11 On EPC, see: S.J. Nuttall (1992) *European Political Cooperation* (Oxford: Oxford University Press); E. Regelsberger, Ph. De Schoutheete de Tervarent (1997) *Foreign Policy of the European Union. From EPC to CFSP and Beyond* (Boulder: Lynne Rienner Publishers); M. Holland (ed.) (1991) *The Future of European Political Cooperation. Essays on Theory and Practice* (London: Macmillan).

12 For an overview of the Maastricht negotiations on foreign policy, see S.J. Nuttall (2000).

13 In 1993, a new DG responsible for external political affairs (DG IA) is set up and the CFSP portfolio was entrusted to Commissioner van den Broek. With the Santer Commission (1995–99), DG I (trade) and DG IA are merged, bringing together the management of the political and economic aspects of external relations (Cameron 1997, 99–102).

14 On 29 October 1993 the European Council adopted a text outlining the working relations between the two bodies. For the text, see Martin Westlake (1999), 178.

15 Greece joined the WEU, while Ireland and Denmark became observers. Turkey, Norway, and Iceland became associate members.

16 De facto there was already flexibility in the second pillar: in Maastricht, Denmark had received

an opt-out on defence and the Amsterdam Treaty had introduced constructive abstention.

17 The PSC can still meet in the formation of the Political Directors. There are four to five such meetings per Presidency.

18 The policy unit is the successor of the PPEWU.

19 In certain cases the meetings can also be chaired by the HR/SG.

20 For a full list of the tasks of the COPS see 'Annex III to Annex VI. European Council, Nice, 7, 8, 9 December 2000', in Rutten (2001: 191–3).

21 This title brings together provisions on CFSP, CSDP, as well as on the CCP, and cooperation with third countries (development, economic, financial, and technical cooperation) and humanitarian aid.

22 The functions of the General Affairs and External Relations Council (GAERC) will respectively be taken over by the Foreign Affairs Council (foreign affairs) and the Legislative and General Affairs Council acting in its General Affairs function.

23 The constitution no longer speaks of joint actions, common positions, common strategies, but replaces them by 'European decisions'.

Further reading

For general approaches to and analysis of the EU's institutions, see especially Peterson and Shackleton (2002); for analysis of EU policy-making in areas including trade, development, CFSP, and ESDP, see the relevant chapters in Wallace, Wallace and Pollack (2005). On the Common Commercial Policy, see Saunders and Triggs (2002). On development cooperation, see Holland (2002); Cosgrove-Sacks (2001). The development of EPC and CFSP is comprehensively covered by Nuttall (1992, 2000) and by M. E. Smith (2003); the latter focuses especially on institutional approaches and developments. For a collection of relevant documents on CFSP, see Hill and K. Smith (2000). On ESDP, see Duke (2000). For a legal approach towards EU international relations, including all of the main policy strands, see Eeckhout (2004).

Cosgrove-Sacks, C. (2001) (ed.), *Europe, Diplomacy and Development: New Issues in EU Relations with Developing Countries* (New York: Palgrave).

Duke, S. (2000), *The Elusive Quest for European Security: From EDC to CFSP* (Basingstoke: Macmillan Press).

Eeckhout, P. (2004), *External Relations of the European Union. Legal and Constitutional Foundations* (Oxford: Oxford University Press).

Hill, C., and Smith, K.E. (2000) (eds), *European Foreign Policy: Key Documents* (London: Routledge).

Holland, M. (2002), *The European Union and the Third World* (Basingstoke: Palgrave).

Nuttall, S. (1992), *European Political Cooperation* (Oxford: Oxford University Press).

Nuttall, S. (2000), *European Foreign Policy* (Oxford: Oxford University Press).

Peterson, J., and Shackleton, M. (eds) (2002), *The Institutions of the European Union* (Oxford: Oxford University Press).

Saunders, C., and Trigg, G. (2002) (eds), *Trade Cooperation with the European Union in the New Millennium* (The Hague: Kluwer)

Smith, M.E. (2003) *Europe's Foreign and Security Policy: The Institutionalisation of Cooperation* (Cambridge: Cambridge University Press).

Wallace, H., Wallace, W., and Pollack, M. (eds) (2005) *Policy-Making in the European Union*, 5th edition (Oxford: Oxford University Press).

Web links

On the Common Commercial Policy, see http://www.europa.eu.int/comm/trade/. A useful broad-based web site on 'European foreign policy' is: http://www.fornet. Fornet is an academic network focused on research and teaching, and the web site includes a bulletin, documentation, and news items. For data and documents on development assistance, see especially http://www.europa/eu/int/comm/development/. See also (especially for defence issues) http://www.iss-eu.org, the web site of the European Union Institute for Security Studies, which includes text of policy papers and documentation.

Chapter 5

Coherence and Consistency

Simon Nuttall

Contents

Summary

This chapter deals with what some have seen as a pervasive problem in EU international policy-making: that of 'coherence' and 'consistency'. The focus is particularly on the issues as it relates to the development of the Common Foreign and Security Policy (CFSP), although the problem can be discerned in almost all areas of the EU's international activity, reflecting the institutional complexities outlined in Chapter 4. The chapter identifies three types of coherence/consistency: 'horizontal', 'institutional', and 'vertical'; it illustrates the ways in which these can be discerned in the policy-making and implementation processes; and it evaluates the ways in which successive EU treaties have attempted to deal with the problems. It concludes by discussing the implicit assumption that coherence/consistency is either attainable or a 'good thing', identifies its implications for different types of EU foreign policy activity, and relates this to the broader development of the EU as a foreign policy actor.

Introduction

'Coherence', otherwise known as 'consistency', has acquired a specialised meaning in the context of EU foreign-policy making. In the early legal texts it referred to the advantages accruing to member states which agreed to pool their foreign policies and thereby increase their international clout. Later, however, it came to refer most frequently to the perceived need to bind together the institutions and procedures of the intergovernmental European Political Cooperation (EPC) and the integrationist European Community. Subjacent to this was a bureaucratic power struggle: which set of civil servants was to gain the upper hand? On a more elevated plane, which of the two approaches—intergovernmentalist and integrationist—was to prevail?

This, however, is not the only manifestation of consistency. In this chapter, a tripartite categorisation is proposed: 'horizontal' consistency means that the policies pursued by different parts of the EU machine, in pursuit of different objectives, should be coherent with each other; 'institutional' consistency, the sort described above, denotes the problems which arise because the EU has chosen to handle a single policy sector, that of external relations, by two sets of actors applying two sets of procedures; 'vertical' consistency comes into play when one or more member states pursues national policies which are out of kilter with policies agreed in the EU. Each of these categories of consistency is examined in turn, in the light of three approaches: legal instruments and practices (provision in the treaties for interaction, combined recourse to separate instruments); structures (organisational arrangements encouraging consistency); and obligations (exhortations to practise consistency). The analysis covers developments since the Maastricht Treaty, including the complications created, especially for 'institutional' consistency, by the appointment of a High Representative for the CFSP, following the Amsterdam Treaty. It ends with a first evaluation of the likely impact on consistency of the Constitutional Treaty adopted in 2004 (considerable for 'institutional' consistency, negligible if not negative for 'horizontal' consistency, and no change for 'vertical' consistency).

The conclusions suggest that the debate about 'consistency' has been vitiated by three mistaken assumptions. The first is that 'consistency' is a single phenomenon, whereas it is in reality a nexus of different problems the solutions to which are various and not always compatible. The second mistaken assumption is that the concept of 'consistency' must by definition be awarded a positive value, whereas a case can still be made for preserving a distinction between two different kinds of foreign policy, one being closer to traditional diplomacy, the other, what is now called 'structural foreign policy', being distinctive to the EU and based on longer term, essentially economic relationships. The third mistaken assumption is that, when problems of consistency arise, foreign policy considerations must prevail. It may well be that domestic considerations gain the upper hand, and that this represents the more democratic outcome. The EU is, in that case, engaged in a classic defence of its domestic interests in a hostile international environment, and thus does indeed have the capacity to articulate its distinctive concerns in the international system.

'Consistency' and its importance

The more the institutional structure of European foreign policy-making has developed, and become complex, the more complaints there have been about a lack of coherence in the process, sometimes to the point where serious failures of foreign policy have been ascribed to it, even if the criticism has amounted to little more than the truism that the member states could not agree to follow a common political line. What is more, references to a supposedly technical problem of 'consistency' have been included in some of the most important official texts governing the Union's external relations since 1974, which shows that national governments have increasingly sought to improve their collective performance through institutional and procedural changes.

This chapter examines the meaning of the terms 'consistency' and 'coherence', in the context of the institutions and processes employed by those responsible for conducting the external relations of the European Union, and assesses the importance of the issues for outcomes. The question of how far the EU manages to make multi-level governance work coherently is at the heart of an understanding of both its current international behaviour and its potential for greater effectiveness in the future.

It does not, however, attempt a distinction between the terms 'consistency' and 'coherence', since they are frequently interchangeable in the texts, and attempts to distinguish between them risk ending up in linguistic pedantry. What can be said is that while 'consistency' is the officially preferred term in English, 'coherence' is used in French, and many other European languages, and may well have a broader signification.

The scientific examination of the problem of consistency is from the start beset by difficulties because of the emotional baggage it carries with it. We should all like our policies and actions to be characterised by consistency, if only because the logical alternative is inconsistency, a concept which carries almost exclusively negative baggage. Indeed, exhortations to pursue consistency, which abound in the EU texts, are as often as not indications that someone with an axe to grind wishes to make a point about inconsistency.

This is not a phenomenon unique to the European Union. All forms of government, with the possible exception of pure dictatorship and pure anarchy, have to deal with problems of consistency created by the coexistence of different forms of policy-making. Different issues call forth different policy responses, which need (according to the devotees of consistency) to be rendered compatible with each other; different policy-making circles and levels produce different answers to the same or similar problems, which need to be coordinated. The difference between the European Union and a conventional state is that the latter is by and large a recognisable unit for decision-making, with well-tried procedures for arbitration. Its resolution of cases of inconsistency is an internal process, often obscured from the public view. In the European Union, however, the corresponding process is external, conducted in the full glare of publicity, and through mechanisms which are not only imperfectly developed, but reflect diverging views about the proper form of European governance.

Does this matter? Yes and no. It can be argued that consistency in EU foreign-policy making is desirable, if not for its own sake, then for the credibility of the Union as a foreign-policy actor and thus its capability of defending its interests and values on the international stage. In other words, it may not matter very much whether a given policy is consistent with another policy, but it matters a great deal if the perception of inconsistency brings the Union into contempt and thereby impairs its effectiveness to act. An example of this is the war in Iraq. Differences among the member states may well come to be seen as historically insignificant, but their existence deprived the Union of the credibility it needed to play an effective role.

On the other hand, the common foreign and security policy of the EU—too often mistakenly taken to be the sole expression of the Union's external persona—is *sub specie aeternitatis* of relatively minor significance. Not only do other aspects of the Union's external relations (now present in all three pillars) often have much more substance than CFSP actions and positions, but it certainly cannot be assumed that the CFSP provides the element of commonality, or coherence, which the EU by definition aspires to. It cannot even be assumed that the external aspects of policy must always prevail over the domestic ones. To the extent that 'consistency' is a codename for the supremacy of the CFSP, it may well not matter, therefore, except to closet-bound specialists, whether it is achieved or not.

What does matter is that 'consistency' as a topic for discussion in the foreign policy context is the product of the institutional development of the European Community and later Union. It coexists with EU structures and changes as those structures change. It will only disappear if the structures become unified, or themselves disappear.

This chapter begins with a sketch of the historical background to the phenomenon of consistency, suggests a categorisation of the concept, and ends with a discussion of implementation—the means of dealing with the problems to which consistency gives rise.

Historical background

'Consistency' as a concept in European foreign-policy making has a long history. The word makes its first appearance in an official document in the Communiqué of the Paris Summit in December 1974:

> Recognising the need for an overall approach to the internal problems involved in achieving European unity and the external problems facing Europe, the Heads of Government consider it essential to ensure progress and overall consistency in the activities of the Communities and in the work of political co-operation...
>
> ...In order to ensure consistency in Community activities and continuity of work, the Ministers of Foreign Affairs, meeting in the Council of the Community, will act as initiators and co-ordinators...

However, the concept behind the word flows from the earlier recognition by the member states that the Community's considerable achievements in internal construction required it to play a more ambitious international role. The Heads of Government meeting at The Hague in December 1969 declared that:

Entry upon the final stage of the Common Market ... also means paving the way for a united Europe capable of assuming its responsibilities in the world of tomorrow and of making a contribution commensurate with its traditions and mission.

Faithful to the instructions given by the Summit, the Foreign Ministers in the Luxembourg Report of October 1970 set out as one of the guiding principles of political union:

...Europe must prepare itself to exercise the responsibilities which to assume in the world is both its duty and a necessity on account of its greater cohesion and its increasingly important role.

This was recalled in the Preamble to the Single European Act (SEA) of 1987:

Aware of the responsibility incumbent upon Europe to aim at speaking ever increasingly with one voice and to act with consistency and solidarity in order more effectively to protect its common interests and independence...

The concept of cohesion and responsibility was clear. Member states needed to stick together to bring their weight to bear on international events and to exercise international responsibilities. Consistency in this sense was thus more a matter of political solidarity than institutional technique. A certain congruence of approach was necessary for credibility. The need for consistency, however, in the more technical sense of the Paris Summit Communiqué arose from difficulties in the institutional implementation of the underlying principle. European Political Cooperation (EPC), set up in 1970 as the first step towards political union, modelled its ethos and procedures on the experience of diplomatic coordination gained during the Fouchet negotiations. At the insistence of France, EPC and the Community were kept as far as possible in hermetically sealed compartments. As time went by, the distinction proved increasingly difficult to apply in practice. The objective links between diplomatic and economic foreign policy asserted themselves, and EPC cast longing eyes on the possibilities of action afforded by the Community. The two phenomena combined led to interaction; 'consistency' became the art of managing the interface.

The responsibility for managing 'consistency' was defined in varying terms in successive documents. The SEA provided that:

The external policies of the European Community and the policies agreed in European Political Co-operation must be consistent.

The Presidency and the Commission, each within its own sphere of competence, shall have special responsibility for ensuring that such consistency is sought and maintained.

For the first time, the Treaties had created an obligation of consistency, and had conferred responsibility for ensuring its observance on the Presidency and the

Commission. It is interesting to note that the original draft spoke of the member states' obligation to ensure observance; the obligation was transferred to the Presidency in order to be more operational. The provision was taken up, amplified, and slightly altered in the Maastricht Treaty (TEU):

> The Union shall in particular ensure the consistency of its external activities as a whole in the context of its external relations, security, economic and development policies. The Council and the Commission shall be responsible for ensuring such consistency. They shall ensure the implementation of these policies, each in accordance with its respective powers.

The new formulation was not an improvement. The operational sharpness of the SEA ('Presidency and Commission') was blunted by the change to 'Council and Commission', and the proviso that these institutions should act in accordance with their respective powers was transferred from the observance of consistency to the implementation of policies, thus replacing the challenging (a new function of coordination) with the banal (the status quo). The amendment of this text by the Amsterdam Treaty, which added the words 'and shall cooperate to this end' after '...ensuring such consistency' reflected the member states' annoyance at the perceived lack of cooperation on the part of the Commission, but did little to improve the management of consistency. And as long as the Union organises its affairs in separate Pillars, consistency will need to be managed.

Categorisation

Discussions of consistency usually take it in the sense of the organisation of the interface between the largely intergovernmental EPC/CFSP and the largely integrationist external relations of the Community. This reflects the reality of the historical debate, as can be seen from the outline given above. But even in that limited sense, different layers of meaning are present, and the debate is often broadened to cover wider aspects of consistency. These subtle differences must be understood if the debate is not to be characterised by misunderstandings. To that end, a dual characterisation is attempted here.

There are three levels of understanding of 'consistency' in its limited sense: the banal, the benign, and the malign (Nuttall, S. (2000), 25–6) (see Box 5.1). The *'banal'* sense is the literal one of policies agreed in one pillar not cutting across or contradicting those in another pillar. This rarely if ever occurs. An exception was when the Foreign Ministers in New York decided to break off cooperation with Haiti, unaware that such an action was ineligible under the terms of the Lomé Convention. The *'benign'* sense is otherwise known as 'interaction': the instruments of the Community are made available for the accomplishment of policy objectives defined in the second pillar. Classic early examples are EC sanctions on the Soviet Union following the imposition of martial law in Poland, and the provision of additional EC aid to improve security in Central America. The *'malign'* signification is about the struggle for institutional power—the question as to whether the representatives of

Box 5.1 Restricted categorisations of consistency

1.1 banal: absence of literal inconsistency

1.2 benign: interaction EC/CFSP

1.3 malign: turf wars

the member states in the second pillar should be able to give directives as regards EC external policies, and at its most base, the question as to which set of bureaucrats gets to decide. Two examples shrouded in the decent mists of time are the attempts by some member states to prevent the Commission from giving aid to schemes of agricultural restructuring in Marxist Ethiopia, and the petulant reaction of the Ambassadors in Pretoria to their exclusion from an operational role in the distribution of aid to the victims of apartheid.

There is, however, a second, more extended, categorisation of consistency, which can be superimposed on the first categorisation and which more completely represents the debate as it has developed over the years. This second categorisation is also divided into three: 'horizontal', 'institutional', and 'vertical' consistency (see Box 5.2).

This new set of categories requires some explanation, since they are often confused in discussion, and remedies adapted to one category are not always, and not necessarily, adapted to another.

Horizontal consistency means that the policies pursued by different parts of the EU machine, in pursuit of different objectives, should be coherent with each other, or at least not involuntarily incoherent. This implies the existence of an effective arbitration mechanism. The most frequently quoted example of inconsistency in this sense is the coexistence of the common agricultural policy, which subsidises exports and on occasion protects the European market, and the EU's development policy, which encourages its partners to develop their agricultural sectors with a view to exports.

Institutional consistency could have been presented as a sub-category of the above, but has so many special characteristics of its own that it makes sense to treat it separately. It denotes the problems which arise because the EU has chosen to handle a single policy sector, that of external relations, by two sets of actors each applying a different set of procedures. Inconsistencies which arise in this category are the result, not of different policy objectives, as is most frequently the case with horizontal consistency, but of different approaches to the same problem. It closely resembles, but is not coterminous with, the 'malign' sense of consistency in the first categorisation.

Box 5.2 Extended categorisations of consistency

2.1 horizontal: between different EU policies

2.2 institutional: between the two different bureaucratic apparatuses, intergovernmental and Community, operating in the field of external relations

2.3 vertical: between EU and national policies

It is the category of consistency on which the historical debate has centred, and to which most reforms have been directed.

Vertical consistency comes into play when one or more member states pursues national policies which are out of kilter with policies agreed in the EU. Reforms have also been made to improve discipline in this respect, albeit not under the heading of 'consistency' in the texts.

The EU has tackled in various ways the problems to which the requirement of consistency gives rise. The three main approaches are legal instruments and practices, structures, and obligations (see Box 5.3).

Box 5.3 Fostering consistency

3.1 Legal instruments and practices: provision in the treaties for interaction; combined recourse to separate instruments

3.2 Structures: organisational arrangements encouraging consistency

3.3 Obligations: exhortations to practise consistency

These three approaches will now be discussed with regard to each of the categories (horizontal, institutional, and vertical) in turn. Institutional consistency will be taken first, because it is the one which historically has given rise to most concern, and which comes up most frequently in the texts.

Institutional consistency—legal instruments and practices

The EU is a treaty-based organisation, founded on the rule of law. The great change which EPC underwent in the Single European Act was to become a subject of international law, whereas previously it owed its existence to informal agreement among governments. The trend continued in the Maastricht Treaty, which endowed the new CFSP with its own legal instruments (Common Positions and Joint Actions), as well as subsuming it into the European Union. It might therefore be expected that the new treaty would also provide legal instruments to give expression to consistency, if only in the 'benign' sense. Surprisingly, the only such provision which has been made to this day is that concerning economic sanctions. If the EU wishes to impose sanctions, it must adopt both a Common Position or Joint Action, through CFSP procedures involving unanimity, and a Council regulation, through Community procedures which may involve qualified majority voting (Articles 228A and 73G of the TEU).

The procedure is important because it recognises and organises competences shared between the first and second pillars. So why is it unique? (The Common Strategy, which might be thought to present similar characteristics, will be discussed later.) One explanation is that the tension between those favouring an intergovernmental and those favouring an integrationist approach was in general too great to allow compromise. The procedure for imposing sanctions slipped through because it represented established practice. This practice began in 1982, if not by accident then by a concatenation of unrepeatable circumstances, with the imposition of sanctions on the Soviet Union following the declaration of martial law in Poland, and was strengthened and continued in response to the Argentinian invasion of the Falkland Islands and the persistence of apartheid in South Africa. It was in connexion with the latter case that Willy De Clercq, then Commissioner for External Relations, declared that, in cases with strong political implications, the Commission would refrain from making a proposal for a Community act until it was assured of prior consensus in EPC, thus signifying the Commission's acquiescence in a dual procedure which apparently violated its prerogatives.

A similar construction, although one not specifically provided for in the treaties, was used in 1994 to place restrictions on the export of dual use goods (goods which potentially had a military as well as a civil use). A Joint Action decided in the Common Foreign and Security Policy (CFSP) was accompanied by a Regulation adopted in the Community framework. As in the case of sanctions, the dual track was established through the use of two separate legal instruments, one for each pillar. Both derived from precedent: sanctions from the practice culminating in the De Clercq doctrine, described above, and the dual use measure from practice in the late 1980s regarding the treatment of the precursors of chemical weapons. It may be surmised that the 'malign' category of consistency is at work here, since when the dual use regime was renewed in 2000, a Council Regulation alone was used, on grounds of improved efficiency, and the CFSP element was dropped.

It may be thought that the legal instruments specific to the CFSP introduced by the Maastricht Treaty—Common Positions and Joint Actions—can contribute to the maintenance of consistency. Indeed, some people believed at first that Joint Actions in particular should not only set out the political approach to a given problem but indicate the action to be taken to implement it, regardless of who was the 'owner' of the instrument. This interpretation was hotly contested by the Commission, determined to protect its treaty independence; on paper, it had right on its side, since the new instruments came in Title V of the Treaty dealing with the CFSP, and the Treaty specifically provided that nothing in the new pillars could have an adverse impact on the Community. Several member states took a different view. The early experience of framing Joint Actions, in the months following the entry into force of the Maastricht Treaty in November 1993, was marked by ferocious battles over this point. As the months and years went by, however, a *modus vivendi* appears to have been established whereby the Commission is not required but invited to do this or that, an invitation it is the readier to follow for having itself been closely involved in the framing of the joint action.

Similar concerns were raised by the introduction of the new instrument of the 'Common Strategy' in the Amsterdam Treaty. This too was placed only in Title V, and so was technically just another CFSP legal instrument. The reality was rather different, in that not only did the Treaty provide that 'Common Strategies shall set out...the means to be made available by the Union...', thus implying that means from all pillars could be requisitioned, but also the decision was reserved to the European Council, whose political preeminence in the EU system could not be challenged. Difficulties like those encountered in the early days of the CFSP were, however, avoided. The Commission saw to it that it remained largely in control of the process, thus demonstrating that 'ownership' can most easily be secured by whoever presents the first draft. This proved to be the case with the Common Strategies towards Russia and the Mediterranean; it proved more difficult to maintain (institutional) consistency with the Common Strategy towards the Ukraine. Vertical consistency proved impossible (see below); the member states could not be persuaded to make their national means available to the common enterprise. The question is not current, given the disrepute into which the Common Strategies have fallen as a result of the damning analysis of their imperfections presented by High Representative Solana at the end of 2000.

Institutional consistency — structures

In compensation to the integrationists, who had failed to prevent the perpetuation in the Maastricht Treaty of the pillar system, the TEU introduced a 'single institutional framework' designed to safeguard consistency in the Union's external action taken as a whole:

> The Union shall be served by a single institutional framework which shall ensure the consistency and the continuity of the activities carried out in order to attain its objectives while respecting and building upon the *acquis communautaire*. (Art. 3, Consolidated)

While applying in theory to the full range of EU activities, this provision was in fact aimed principally at the external relations of the Union in the strict sense — the dossiers handled so far by the EPC machinery on the one hand, and the Commission's Directorate General for External Relations on the other. The introduction of a 'single institutional framework' meant in fact that the old EPC Ministerial Meetings, which had so far maintained a separate existence, finally ceased to exist and were absorbed into the meetings of the General Affairs Council, in which the Foreign Ministers met in the Community framework. This brought in its wake the disappearance of the EPC Secretariat, composed exclusively of seconded diplomats from the member states, which had been set up by the Single European Act. It was replaced by the Council Secretariat performing its normal function of servicing the Council and the Council machinery, under the authority of the Presidency. Here then was a step towards greater institutional consistency, in that the number of competing bureaucratic populations was reduced. All was not plain sailing, however. Although it took on a number of member state diplomats with experience of EPC, the Council Secretariat found it difficult to adjust to its new tasks and to make applicable to EPC-type foreign policy the expertise it had acquired in very different surroundings. The fact that the responsible Directorate General of the Council Secretariat was divided into two sections, political and economic, did not help matters. The situation improved over the years, however, especially after the appointment of Javier Solana as High Representative (see below), and the Secretariat now provides a high-performance foreign policy machine.

Structural change designed to encourage institutional consistency remained, however, limited to the measures described above. The Maastricht Treaty explicitly postponed a decision on the relationship between the Political Committee and Coreper, and on what was to happen to the EPC Working Groups and the Working Parties of the Council, whose agendas sometimes overlapped. The sensitivity of the question is shown by the fact that it took several years to work out a *modus vivendi* between the Political Committee (now replaced by the Political and Security Committee, commonly known as COPS) and Coreper. The convention now is that Coreper forwards to the Council without comment political analyses prepared by the COPS, but can and does intervene if EC business, especially finance, is involved. It is helped in this task by a new Group of Advisers (formerly CFSP Advisers), who are experts in financial and institutional questions. All this elaborate construction is necessary because of the continued existence of different and competing bodies, and the requirement for institutional consistency, even within a single institution, to which they give rise.

Similarly, the attempt by the Belgian Presidency in the early days of the CFSP to merge the old EPC and the Council Working Groups, while successful on paper, continued to present problems in practice. The difficulty lay in agreeing who was to represent the member states in the merged groups, and above all who was to chair the meeting. Was it to be someone from the Permanent Representation, as was the usual Council practice, or someone from the national capital, as in EPC? A temporary solution was found, which has endured to the present day: the 'Council' practice was followed for 'Council' agenda items, and the 'EPC' practice, sometimes in separate meetings, for 'EPC' items.

Experience over the years nevertheless highlights a trend towards 'Brusselsisation'. This is a loose concept, used in different ways by different scholars. One thing it does not mean is the application of Community procedures to pillar II foreign policy decision-making. Rather, it is the evolution of a new atmosphere in which the focus of European foreign policy shifts from the national capitals to Brussels. It is an amorphous and elusive process which can best be grasped through structural changes like those described above, apparently unimportant in themselves but which collectively effect a transformation in *mores*. It is important in encouraging consistency, because it is conducive to a shared mindset.

The shift towards Brusselsisation was accelerated by the creation in the Amsterdam Treaty of the position of High Representative/Secretary General and his attendant apparatus—essentially the Policy Planning and Early Warning Unit, now renamed the Policy Unit, which for the first time set up an indigenous foreign-policy making capacity within the Council.

These developments had their effect on the Commission. In order to be better equipped to play its role in the new CFSP, the Commission decided at the end of 1992 to set up a new Directorate General (DG IA), separate from DG I which had hitherto been responsible for all aspects of external relations, to cover the political aspects only and be responsible for contacts with the new CFSP machinery. The new DG thus lost control over the deployment of EC instruments, creating new problems of consistency within the Commission. At the same time, a Political Director was appointed who no longer regularly attended Coreper, breaking the personal link which had previously been so valuable. Although the split between the political and economic aspects of the Commission's work was rectified two years later, the creation of a political counter-culture within the Commission made institutional consistency harder to handle. The decision at the beginning of the Prodi Commission to regroup the larger part of the external relations DGs in a single DG under one Commissioner went some way towards reversing this trend, although this was countered, for reasons of internal efficiency, by the setting up of EuropeAid as a separate body responsible for the management of the EU's aid programmes. DG Relex has as a consequence felt the loss of immediate control of the financial levers of power.

Institutional consistency — obligations

As was noted in the section on the historical background, the Treaty contains an obligation to ensure consistency, particularly as regards external relations:

> The Union shall in particular ensure the consistency of its external activities as a whole in the context of its external relations, security, economic and development policies. The Council and the Commission shall be responsible for ensuring such consistency, and shall cooperate to this end. They shall ensure the implementation of these policies, each in accordance with its respective powers. (Art. 3, Consolidated)

Similarly,

> The Council shall ensure the unity, consistency and effectiveness of action by the Union. (Art. 13.3, Consolidated)

These obligations apparently refer to institutional consistency only, i.e. consistency within the range of the external action of the EU in a limited sense. This results from the list of areas covered in the first reference, and from the positioning of the second reference in the chapter dealing with the CFSP. Performance of the obligations depends entirely on the goodwill of the Institution concerned, since there is no judicial oversight of Title V. It is assisted by some technical arrangements. For example, the Troika, which brings together the Presidency (and usually the incoming Presidency), the High Representative, and the Commission, carries out some representational activities on behalf of the EU, but it does not act as a collective organ; its members have separate briefings prepared by their own administrations, not a collective briefing prepared by the CFSP Secretariat. Again, the Commission forwards to the Council Secretariat all reports from its external delegations; traffic is, however, less dense in the reverse direction.

Ironically, institutional consistency, especially in the benign sense of 'interaction', was easier to manage before the reforms introduced by the Maastricht and Amsterdam Treaties. In those days, the links between member states in the first and second pillars were scanty to the point of non-existence. The Commission almost alone provided a link between the two pillars, and was able by the exercise of its Treaty functions to translate a political consensus in EPC into action on the Community side, while at the same time warning EPC of potential difficulties in the Community. This was embodied in the fact that the same official represented the Commission in the Political Committee and in Coreper. Constitutional responsibilities were clear, and the allocation by the SEA of responsibility for the management of consistency to the Presidency and the Commission made operational sense. If there was to be a battle for turf, it helped that the turf boundaries were clearly defined.

Of course, life was simpler in that prelapsarian age. The amount of business was less, and so, consequently, was the interface between EPC and the Community. The profile of European foreign policy was lower, which meant that less attention need be paid to consistency. Nevertheless, there is no doubt that the organisational changes, described above, in both the Commission and the Council Secretariat were a negative factor in the search for consistency. In particular the creation of the office of High Representative, and the new machinery dependent on him, has made the problem of institutional consistency more difficult to handle. What had previously been a fairly obscure institutional difficulty has now been mediatised as a personal duel, Solana versus Patten, which has carried the question to a higher plane of public attention. In spite of the good working relationship between the two men, and frequent protestations of cooperation on their part, the number of learned articles and press commentaries on the subject has been on the increase, as has the number of occasions on which foreign countries profess to be 'confused' by the EU's institutional arrangements. A more substantive element of confusion comes from the High Representative's need for his own policy back-up staff, which is provided by the new Policy Unit. This difficulty was introduced by the Amsterdam Treaty; the Maastricht Treaty had indeed brought about the absorption of the EPC Secretariat into the Secretariat General of the Council, but the Council Secretariat did not thereafter provide, any more than its predecessor, independent policy advice. Instead it performed its traditional role of advising the Presidency on the best way of handling a problem, given the existence on the table of a policy proposal submitted by another body (Commission, Presidency, or member state). The Policy Unit, on the other hand, for the first time became a provider of autonomous policy papers in potential competition with the Commission, and indeed with member states. The problems which inevitably arise have not so far come to the light of day, although it may be noted that in February 2004 the press reported that a paper on Russia which had been jointly prepared by the Policy Unit and the Commission services was presented under the sole imprint of the Council Secretariat, President Prodi's cabinet having vetoed, on ideological grounds, the public association of the Commission.

Whatever progress may have been made in practical cooperation on the ground, the fact is that, as long as two bodies with overlapping responsibilities coexist, there will be a problem of institutional consistency. The problem will be compounded when it is a question of individuals, given the increasing personalisation of modern diplomacy. The Constitutional Convention was right to identify the relationship between High Representative and Commission as critical to the future development of the CFSP.

Horizontal consistency

The topic of institutional consistency has been dealt with at some length because it occurs most frequently in the texts and is most frequently the subject of discussion. Horizontal and vertical consistency, although arguably of greater importance, can be dealt with more briefly.

It is worth recalling here the distinction between institutional and horizontal consistency: institutional consistency refers to external relations policies worked out in different parts of the EU machine, while horizontal consistency refers to EU policies in general, adopted in pursuit of different objectives but with external implications which are not always taken into account. This applies to many important areas of EU activity. Agriculture, the environment, transport, competition policy, consumer protection, public health, are but the most striking examples. All these policies, domestic in origin, can have significant impact for the world outside the EU, which needs to be managed if negative consequences are to be avoided.

The Treaty contains a general obligation of consistency (Article 3, 1st para., Consolidated, quoted above), although it is not expressed with the same clarity and detail as for the specific field of external activities. In particular, consistency does not figure so much as an obligation as both the objective and result of the single institutional framework introduced by the Maastricht Treaty ('...a single institutional framework which shall ensure the consistency...'). Of the three means of fostering consistency (Box 5.3), therefore, horizontal consistency has to rely to a limited extent on legal instruments and practices, but mainly on structures, and on obligations hardly at all.

It might be expected, given its position at the apex of the pyramid, that the European Council would be best placed to arbitrate over competing policy objectives and would have at its disposal the legal means to enable it to do so. This seems, however, not to be the case. The only instrument reserved to the Heads of government is the Common Strategy, which as we have seen is in theory a solely CFSP instrument. Even if it is accepted that this is a legal nicety, and that in reality the European Council has the power to call on all aspects of the life of the Union, as was shown for example by the inclusion of justice and home affairs cooperation in the Common Strategy towards Russia, the fact remains that this instrument is limited in scope, and soon became discredited to the point where it disappears in name, though not in substance, in the Draft Treaty of 2004.

A more promising approach is the European Council's power to set political guidelines for the CFSP, including for matters with defence implications (Articles 4 and 13.1, Consolidated). There have been some good examples of this. The programme of measures adopted by the European Council following the terrorist attacks of 11 September 2001, which included contributions from most branches of EU activity, surprised everyone by its comprehensiveness. The Heads of government even found the courage at a later stage to reprimand the Ministers of Justice for their tardiness in implementing some parts of the programme which lay within their jurisdiction. And the new Security Strategy, adopted by the European Council in December 2003, sets parameters which are designed to be observed by all who carry on the EU's business, not just those active in the field of foreign affairs.

Both these examples, however, show the European Council drawing on all the resources available to the EU in order to achieve an essentially foreign policy objective. To arbitrate between conflicting policies is, however, a different matter, and one in which the European Council has shown little inclination to become involved. That is rather the task of the General Affairs Council, and there is general dissatisfaction at the way in which it is being carried out.

In the early days it was natural that the General Affairs Council should play the leading role in managing the affairs of the Community. Composed of the Foreign

Ministers of the member states, it reflected the political reality of the time, that EC business was a matter for foreign relations. However, as the work of the Community grew and became ever more diversified, other departments of government became involved and the sectoral Councils took on a life of their own. The extent to which the General Affairs Council was able to control them depended on the influence Foreign Ministers wielded in their national governments. If some control over the activities of the less prestigious Councils remained possible, this rapidly proved illusory when it came to the big beasts like the Economic and Financial Affairs (Ecofin) or the Agriculture Councils. The situation was further complicated by the fact that each formation of the Council was legally entitled to take its own decisions, no reference to the General Affairs Council for endorsement being necessary. To the extent that coordination took place, it was carried out by Coreper at the preparatory stage.

Nor were the Foreign Ministers interested in the politically unrewarding grind of day-to-day coordination. A Foreign Minister would attend an EPC Ministerial Meeting for the 'high policy' agenda items it had to offer, but he would leave a junior Minister in his place for the session of the Council, even when the two were organised back-to-back. This situation did not change with the Maastricht reform whereby the EPC Ministerial format was merged with the General Affairs Council. Foreign Ministers still attended for the politically interesting items, and left the rest to their deputies. The fact that a forum controlled by Foreign Ministers was less than ideal as an arbitrator between the domestic and external aspects of an issue only added to the difficulties.

Various proposals have been advanced in recent years to remedy the situation. One would be to give the European Council the means to strengthen its function of issuing policy guidelines, either by making the High Representative directly responsible to the European Council, on the lines of the original French proposal, or by appointing a President of the European Council to hold office for a period of years. The recommendations of the Constitutional Convention on this question will be discussed below.

Another proposal was to set up a standing body in Brussels composed of senior national politicians, for example Deputy Prime Ministers, to supersede the General Affairs Council in its coordinating role. Given the position held by Deputy Prime Ministers in their national governments, this would certainly solve the problem of horizontal consistency. The political objections to it proved too great, however; for example, it was not clear how to persuade Foreign Ministers to agree to be sidelined, nor Deputy Prime Ministers to divert their attention from national affairs.

The problem created by the existence of multiple Council formations, which of course went further than the exclusively foreign policy angle, was tackled by the European Council at Seville in June 2002. The number of Council formations was, at least nominally, reduced, and the General Affairs Council was rebaptised the General Affairs and External Relations Council, it having proved impossible to separate the two. The net effect on problems of consistency has been minimal, the practice of Foreign Ministers regarding attendance having remained unchanged.

It is appropriate at this stage to pause a moment for thought. In the discussion in this chapter so far, as well as in the historical debate, it has been taken as axiomatic that consistency is a good thing, and its absence a problem to be solved. Furthermore, since the debate has been in the hands of foreign policy specialists, it has been assumed that, in the case of a clash between policies, foreign policy considerations should be given preference. But an effective arbitration mechanism could well, depending on the case, come to the opposite conclusion and decide that domestic policy considerations should prevail. This would solve the problem of consistency, but the solution would not be to the taste of those who seek a coherent and effective EU foreign policy.

Here I introduce a further consideration, which casts doubt on the generally accepted idea of the nature and objectives of European foreign policy. It is based on a new version of the concept of 'structural power'.[1] As used here, 'structural power' means the capacity to take, for domestic reasons, policy decisions which have a significant impact on foreign countries, without having to pay undue attention to any ensuing negative reaction. Examples are the EU's decisions on hormones in beef and on genetically modified organisms, both of them being decisions which would have been taken regardless of whether or not the external implications were realised at the time. The United States and the European Union have such power; China may have it in the future, but it is doubtful whether any other country or organisation does. What it lacks in international morality, structural power gains in domestic legitimacy. It has the significant effect of transforming the concept of EU foreign policy from being an autonomous activity with on the whole worthy objectives to being a diplomatic effort directed at attenuating the effects abroad of EU domestic-policy making—in other words the classic defence of sovereignty, but at the EU level.

Vertical consistency

Vertical consistency, or consistency between EU and national policies, gives rise to the greatest political difficulties and, perhaps for that reason, is least frequently the object of attention. The question is, to what extent are member states prepared to bind their national foreign policies to the outcome of the CFSP and the EU's other external relations policies, thereby strengthening the EU's position as a force in international diplomacy? Of the three means of fostering consistency (Box 5.3), structures only apply to vertical consistency in the broad sense in which the structure of the EU as a whole provides the framework for implicating the member states in the EU's action.

Legal instruments and practices, although some exist, are scarcely more promising. As already mentioned, Common Strategies 'shall set out...the means to be made available by...the Member States', but this has proved difficult to implement and is unlikely to provide a way forward. The reluctance of member states to contribute national means to the Common Strategy towards Russia is a good example. Likewise, the EC Treaty makes specific provision for synergy between EU and member states' development cooperation policies:

> The Community and the Member States shall coordinate their policies on development cooperation and shall consult each other on their aid programmes, including in international organisations and during international conferences. They may undertake joint

action. Member States shall contribute if necessary to the implementation of Community aid programmes. (Art. 180, EC)

This has, however, been more honoured in the breach than the observance: there are, however, a number of general obligations to which the member states are subject in the context of the CFSP:

> The Member States shall support the Union's external and security policy actively and unreservedly in a spirit of loyalty and mutual solidarity.
>
> The Member States shall work together to enhance and develop their mutual political solidarity. They shall refrain from any action which is contrary to the interests of the Union or likely to impair its effectiveness as a cohesive force in international relations.
>
> The Council shall ensure that these principles are complied with. (Art. 11.2, Consolidated)
>
> Member States shall ensure that their national policies conform to the Common Positions. (Art. 15)
>
> Joint Actions shall commit the Member States in the positions they adopt and in the conduct of their activity. (Art. 14.3)

Respect of these obligations is sporadic because there is no credible provision for policing it. The European Court of Justice has no jurisdiction; although examples of the breach of the obligations set out in Article 11.2 are not hard to find, there has been no example of the Council 'ensur[ing] that these principles are complied with'. Indeed, the authors of the Treaty seem to have been more concerned with providing the member states with ways of avoiding their obligations; the texts are full of escape clauses which have increased in number over the years. The Maastricht Treaty contained a provision which indicated that commitment to a joint action was not absolute:

> Should there be any major difficulties in implementing a joint action, a Member State shall refer them to the Council which shall discuss them and seek appropriate solutions. Such solutions shall not run counter to the objectives of the joint action or impair its effectiveness. (Art. 14.7, Consolidated)

The Amsterdam Treaty went further and introduced an opt-out in the form of 'qualified abstention' (Article 23.1, Consolidated), whereby by formally abstaining a member state could absolve itself from the obligation to apply an EU decision.[2] And the Nice Treaty, by extending to the CFSP the treaty provisions on flexibility or 'enhanced cooperation', made it possible for fewer than all the member states to engage in an intensified form of cooperation—or, seen from another angle, for some member states to acquiesce in being dissociated from such cooperation.

None of these devices has been used so far. They were designed to afford the member states some protection against such potential violations of national sovereignty as qualified majority voting or the constitution of core groups, but since the danger has never arisen, the defence has never had to be deployed. The fact is that the procedures followed in the second pillar will de facto lead to decisions which can usually be accommodated in national policies without too much difficulty. This is an advantage for some parts of the CFSP, but not necessarily for all.

National commitment to policy positions worked out in common in the CFSP is clearly an advantage; the credibility of such positions depends on the degree to which they are shared by all the member states, and their effectiveness on the assiduity with which they are propagated by national diplomats. The case is altered, however, when it comes to actions rather than positions. Here, the involvement of all the member states in implementation is not always indispensable. The EU may appoint an agent to act on its behalf, and a member state which has contributed to the decision-making procedure does not necessarily have to engage itself nationally in the further process. In this case vertical consistency can, at a pinch, be dispensed with, especially given the great diversity of member states in terms of the number of missions, and other foreign policy resources.

This casts a fresh light on the need to 'solve' the problem of vertical consistency. There is only one solution the success of which can be guaranteed, and that is to make the CFSP a common policy like the Common Commercial Policy or the Common Agricultural Policy, i.e. an exclusive competence of the EU with oversight by the Court of Justice. This would eliminate the problem at a stroke, since there would be no more national foreign policies, but apart from being politically unattainable in the foreseeable future leaves unanswered the question of how to secure the input of the national diplomatic establishments.

A second option would be to stay with the status quo. This has considerable attractions. The big political difficulty under this heading is not so much consistency as how to keep the Big Three broadly corralled inside the European political order. The dangers are real, as the activities of extra-EU formations like the Contact Group and the Quint demonstrate. Forms of *directoire*, either inside or outside the EU, are ultimately destructive of European foreign policy-making and should be guarded against. Excessive insistence on consistency could imperil this objective.

A further option could be to exploit the distinction between positions and actions in the sense explained above, seeking ways to enhance vertical consistency for the former while neglecting it for the latter, so that that part of the EU's external relations became the autonomous foreign policy of the Union, with its own priorities and interests, detached from the national policies of the member states. I shall return to this question in the conclusions.

The Constitutional Treaty

At the time of writing (November 2004) it was uncertain whether the Constitutional Treaty agreed by member states in June of that year would eventually be ratified. In the treaty as signed, however. those recommendations which affected the EU's external action were approved with few if any changes. The provisions include the appointment of a Chair of the European Council for a number of years, the introduction of Presidencies for the sectoral Councils lasting at least a year, the merger of the posts of High Representative and External Relations Commissioner, and the creation of a single External Action Service. The overall effect on consistency is likely to be considerable for institutional consistency, negligible if not negative for horizontal consistency, and no change for vertical consistency.

Box 5.4 Impact of the TEU and the Constitutional Treaty on Consistency

A. CRITERIA	B. TEU	C. CONSTITUTIONAL TREATY
Unity of decision taker	YES European/General Affairs Council	YES European/Foreign Affairs Council
Unity of decision-making procedure	NO Pillar I and II methods	NO Pillar I and II methods retained
Unity of bureaucratic community	NO CFSP and Commission	YES if common service, but ?ESDP
Unity of external representation	NO Presidency, HR and Commission (President and Commissioner)	NO EC Chair, Commission President and EU Foreign Minister

A. Criteria for institutional consistency
B. Situation under TEU
C. Situation under Constitutional Treaty

The situation regarding institutional consistency is shown in Box 5.4. There is no change in the identity of the decision-taker, which has been the General Affairs Council since the Maastricht Treaty. The decision-making procedure remains the same before and after. The major change is brought about by the merging of the posts of High Representative and External Relations Commissioner, which by eliminating two of the EU's representatives on the international scene (Presidency and Commissioner) reduces correspondingly problems of consistency. However, what the Constitutional Treaty giveth, the Constitutional Treaty taketh away: two new representatives are introduced. One is the new Chair of the European Council, who will find that his/her appearances on the international stage constitute the only rewarding political activity, and that there is competition with the Foreign Minister for the leading role. The other is the President of the Commission, who could be presumed to make up a single actor with the External Relations Commissioner, but with the latter gone will assert his independence vis-à-vis the Foreign Minister, given the latter's ambiguous position half in and half out of the Commission. The most important change may well turn out to be the creation of a joint External Action Service, merging the relevant services of the Council Secretariat, the Commission, and the Commission's Delegations, thereby creating over time a unified bureaucratic ambience. And even here it may well prove that the section dealing with the ESDP retains its particular and separate bureaucratic status.

Horizontal as opposed to institutional consistency benefits for the first time from specific recognition in the texts:

> The Union shall ensure consistency between the different areas of its external action and between these and its other policies. (Art. III-193.3)

The commitment to consistency in general remains the same, but no new machinery is set up to ensure that it is respected. The responsibility is awarded to the new

Legislative and General Affairs Council (a Convention recommendation unlikely to be adopted in that form), but that body's task is made immeasurably more difficult by the decision to attribute the Presidency of the sectoral Councils to the various member states on a longer term and rotating basis. The disappearance of the single six-month Presidency with its unifying influence, imperfect though that may have been, can only encourage the sectoral Councils to develop their separate agendas and resist coordination with other policy areas. If the task of coordination is to be done at all, it will have to be done by a combination of Coreper and the new Chair of the European Council, who will find the tools for such an action sadly lacking.

The existing exhortations to vertical consistency are repeated. There are no significant innovations in this area.

Conclusions

The study carried out in this chapter enables us to perceive more clearly that the debate about 'consistency' has been vitiated by three mistaken assumptions. The first is that 'consistency' is a single phenomenon. On the contrary, it is a complex one, being in reality a nexus of different problems the solutions to which are various and not always compatible. The distinction between different kinds of consistency must be made, even if it is not always present in the texts.

We are led into the second mistaken assumption by the nature of language. 'Consistency' is a 'yes-word'; it carries within it a presumption in its favour, to deny which is to assign a positive value to its opposite, inconsistency. But in the more closely defined sense of institutional consistency, for example, a case can be made for inconsistency. It can be argued that for many years the division between the first and second pillar regimes represented a genuine difference between two different kinds of foreign policy, pillar two being closer to classic diplomacy while pillar one conducted a new type of foreign policy, distinctive to the EU and based on longer term, essentially economic relationships—what some scholars now call 'structural foreign policy' (Keukeleire 2003, 2004). This is what led some observers to describe the EU as a 'civilian power'. Recent developments, especially the EU's acquisition of a defence personality and the changed climate of international relations after the end of the Cold War, make this position less tenable. It is recognised that conflict prevention, going as far as peace-keeping, has become a prime responsibility of the Union. This strengthens the objective case for institutional consistency, and correspondingly erodes the civilian power model. The point is not whether institutional consistency is desirable *per se* or not, but the extent to which it serves external objectives fixed by the public authority, and ranked by them in order of priority.

The third mistaken assumption derives from the fact that the academic and political debate on consistency has been conducted exclusively by the foreign policy community. This has not surprisingly encouraged the view that foreign policy, including ethical foreign policy, considerations should prevail over all others. As we have seen above with regard to horizontal consistency, this cannot always be assumed to be the case. It may well be that, in an arbitration, domestic considerations gain the upper hand, and that this represents the more democratic outcome. The implications of this for the nature of EU foreign policy have been discussed above in the section on structural power—that the EU is, at least in part, engaged in a classic defence of its domestic interests in a hostile international environment. In other words, the European Union does indeed have the capacity to articulate its distinctive concerns in the international system.

Notes

1 This concept has had various uses in the International Relations literature. Susan Strange used the term in contrast to 'relational power' (i.e. of X over Y) to denote the capacity to shape the direction of the overall system, and in particular the international economy. In this she harked back (if indirectly) to Marx; see Strange (1986). Equally influential has been the work of Kenneth Waltz, which stressed the key role of the balance of power in structuring the international system. The dominant powers in the system accordingly shape the structure in which the less powerful have to operate (Waltz 1979). See also Buzan, Jones and Little (1993), and Chapter 18 of this volume.

2 This is often known as 'constructive abstention', as it was designed to allow a majority to proceed while respecting the wish of a particular state not to be associated with a given decision.

Further reading

The following references deal with the evolution and characteristics of the 'consistency' problem since the early 1990s. The best historical treatment is in Nuttall (2000), whilst Keukeleire (2003) places the issue into a broader framework for the analysis of European Union diplomacy. The more legal and institutional aspects, as expressed in the Maastricht and Amsterdam Treaties are well treated in Neuwahl (1993) and Schmalz (1998), whilst more policy-centred treatments are in Krenzler and Schneider (1997), Missiroli (2002), and Nuttall (2001, 2004).

Keukeleire, S. (2003), 'The European Union as a Diplomatic Actor: Internal, Traditional and Structural Diplomacy', *Diplomacy and Statecraft*, 14/3, 31–56.

Krenzler, H.-G., and Schneider, H. (1997), 'The Question of Consistency', in

Regelsberger, E., de Schoutheete de Tervarent, P., and Wessels, W. (eds), *Foreign Policy of the European Union: From EPC to CFSP and Beyond* (Boulder, CO, London: Lynne Rienner).

Missiroli, A. (2002), "Coherence, Effectiveness, and Flexibility for CFSP/ESDP", in Reifer, E., Rummel, R., and Schmidt, P. (eds), *Europas ferne Streitmacht* (Hamburg: Mittler).

Neuwahl, N. (1993), 'Foreign and Security Policy and the Implementation of the Requirement of "Consistency" under the Treaty on European Union', in Twomey, P., and O'Keeffe, D. (eds), *Legal Issues of the Maastricht Treaty* (Oxford: Hart).

Nuttall, S. (2000), *European Foreign Policy* (Oxford: Oxford University Press).

Nuttall, S. (2001), ' "Consistency" and the CFSP: A Categorisation and its Consequences', LSE European Foreign Policy Unit Working Paper No. 2001/3 (London: London School of Economics and Political Science).

Nuttall, S. (2004), 'On Fuzzy Pillars: Criteria for the Continued Existence of Pillars in the Draft Constitution', *CFSP Forum* 2/3, http://www.fornet.info.

Schmalz, U. (1998), 'The Amsterdam Provisions on External Coherence: Bridging the Union's Foreign Policy Dualism?', *European Foreign Affairs Review*, 3(3), 421–42.

Web links

The best web sources for discussion of the 'consistency' issue are the Fornet web site, http://www.fornet.info/ and the web site of the European Foreign Policy Unit at the London School of Economics and Political Science, http://www.lse.ac.uk/Depts/intrel/EuroFPUnit.html.

Chapter 6

Accountable and Legitimate? The EU's International Role

Christopher Lord

Contents

Summary

This chapter focuses on the role of accountability in legitimating the international policies of the Union. Yet it also notes how heterogeneous are present arrangements and proposals for further development. On the one hand, they vary across the different types of international policy to be found at Union level: trade, aid, policies towards accession countries, and the Common Foreign and Security Policy (CFSP). On the other, they vary across modes of accountability and levels of governance, with the European Parliament, national parliaments, and administrative and judicial standards, all shaping the relationship between the legitimacy and accountability of the Union's international policy.

Introduction

Institutions are legitimate where their right to make collectively binding decisions is acknowledged by their policy addressees. Accountability, on the other hand, is an obligation to justify decisions and their management on pain of being sanctioned through loss of office, powers, resources, or reputation. Legitimacy and accountability are intimately related in systems governed by liberal democratic values. Since such systems require that decisions can only be legitimate if they are made on behalf of the public, high levels of accountability are also needed to ensure that decision-makers act as authorised delegates or trustees of the public, or with public needs and values in mind. All of this is well rehearsed in the analysis of single state political systems and now even in relation to the internal politics of the European Union. But what issues are raised by the relationship between accountability and legitimacy in the external dimension of the EU? This chapter begins with a brief discussion of how far the Union faces distinctive issues of legitimacy when it makes policy towards the outside world. It then assesses how far the European Parliament, national parliaments, wider politicisation and agreed governance standards contribute to the accountability of the Union's international actor. In the final section of the chapter concluding lessons are drawn for the link between legitimacy and accountability.

The external dimension: a source of distinctive legitimation issues?

Legitimacy is a complex phenomenon. In societies with liberal democratic values it has at least three dimensions: the performance of the political system, popular identification with the system, and the acquisition and exercise of power according to democratic values (Beetham 1991). These dimensions are cumulative and interactive: where each is present, it reinforces the others in producing legitimacy: where any is lacking, it cannot entirely be compensated by a super-abundance of either of the other two.

The complexity of legitimacy interacts with the complexity of the EU itself (Beetham and Lord, 1998). At least two levels of governance—the Union as a whole and its member states—are mutually implicated in one another's legitimacy. Thus Fritz Scharpf (1996) has written eloquently of how well-functioning Union institutions have become a part of the output legitimacy (performance) of the state itself. On the other hand, many of the input conditions for legitimacy—identity and, in his view, democracy—continue only to exist at national and not Union level. Either level may, therefore, find itself needing to 'borrow' missing aspects of legitimacy from the other. Up to a point, legitimacy follows policy. To the extent each policy touches ordinary lives in different ways, it raises different issues about what is right and wrong in the exercise of power, and requires the compliance of different actor types who may vary in how they conceive legitimacy.

It should not, however, be too quickly assumed that one way in which legitimacy is likely to vary across types of policy is that any policy whose impact is external to a political system is going to be easier to legitimate than one that reallocates values within it. First, international policy faces the added complication of needing to be justified to outsiders and not just to domestic audiences. This is of special interest in the case of the EU, since for some players in the international system the legitimacy of Union policies towards the rest of the world may be increased by the fact that it is a novel form of non-state international actor, while for others it may be reduced. Second, external issues of war and peace, and of democracy and human rights in the international system, are also internal values. They are often divisive, they often require the expenditure of scarce resources on foreigners, and they often affect judgements publics make of their own political systems. Third, the legitimacy of a polity may only be fully tested when it faces crisis or policy failure. Here the history of states contains a cautionary tale for all would be international actors, the EU included: domestic legitimation crises derive as often as not from the international system (Bobbitt 2002), its peculiar configuration of risk, and mistakes (of omission and commission) in designing policies and institutions to deal with those risks. The last two points mean there is a double blurring—of value and of performance—between the legitimacy of power deployed internationally and the legitimacy of power exercised domestically.

It is not, however, just on account of variations in their 'outputs' that policies vary in their legitimacy, but also on account of 'input' differences in how decisions are made. This is of special relevance to the Union because it employs so many different methods to make its decisions. Yet once again, differences are not between internal policies on the one hand and international ones on the other. Table 6.1 shows how decision-making procedures—who has the initiative, voting arrangements in the Council of Ministers, and the extent of parliamentary and judicial control—differ across nine Treaty articles that govern how the EU makes policy towards the outside world on matters as diverse as development aid, trade, international monetary, and environmental agreements, and the Common Foreign and Security Policy. Three patterns emerge:

• Procedures used to make or control different international policies of the Union involve no uniform distribution of power within or between Union institutions. Only some policies allow member states to bind one another by qualified majority votes (QMV) (Column 5). Only some allow the European Parliament (EP) agenda-setting or veto powers (Co-decision and Assent) (Column 6). Only some allow the Commission to 'gate keep' choice by giving it an exclusive right of initiative (Column 4). Only some allow the ECJ jurisdiction (Column 7). It follows that different international policies of the Union tap into different conceptions of input legitimacy. They vary in how far they draw on indirect legitimation through the unanimous agreement of member states; on parliamentary legitimation through the scrutinising and controlling powers of a representative body; on technocratic legitimation through a role for 'independent experts' (the Commission); or on judicial legitimation by a court able to ensure legality and the protection of rights in the pursuit of the Union's international policy (Lord and Magnette 2003);

• The Treaties vary in how far they empower the Union to make single, common, or coordinated policies in international matters (Column 3). Single policies exclude all action by member states. Common policies allow for parallel national policies on condition that Union policies take priority in the event of conflict. Coordinated policies involve no more than the mutual—and voluntary—adjustment of national policies. Not only do the international policies of the Union span the range, but CFSP on its own occupies an ambiguous status. It is a common policy to the extent that

Table 6.1 Inter-institutional distributions of power over six different international policies of the EU

	1	2	3	4	5	6	7
	Area of international policy	Treaty Articles EC = European Community Treaties EU = European Union Treaty	EU competence: Single, common or co-ordinated policy?	Power of initiative	Council voting rule QMV = Qualified Majority Voting UV = Unanimous voting	European Parliament participation	European Court of Justice Jurisdiction
	Development Cooperation	EC177-181	Common/ Coordinated	Commission	QMV	Co-decision/ Assent	Y
	Environment. International agreements	EC174	Common	Commission	QMV	Assent	Y
Pillar I External Polices	Monetary policy. Exchange rate agreements with issuers of non-EU currencies	EC111	Single for Eurozone members	Commission or European Central Bank (ECB)	UV	Consultation	Y
	Trade/Commercial Policy	EC131-4	Single	Commission	QMV	Consultation	Y
	EC International Agreements	300(2.3)	Common	Commission	UV	Consultation/ Assent (See Box 6.1 on p. 20)	Y
	Association agreements	300(3)	Single	Commission	UV	Assent	Y

continues

Table 6.1 continued

	1	2	3	4	5	6	7
	Area of international policy	Treaty Articles EC = European Community Treaties EU = European Union Treaty	EU competence: Single, common or co-ordinated policy?	Power of initiative	Council voting rule QMV = Qualified Majority Voting UV = Unanimous voting	European Parliament participation	European Court of Justice Jurisdiction
Pillar II Foreign and Security Policy	Common Foreign and Security Policy	EU11–28	Common/Coordinated	Shared initiative. Commission or Member States	Mainly UV (QMV only possible if prior agreement by UV)	Consultation	N
	European Security and Defence Policy	EU17	Coordinated	Member States only	UV	No assured role	N
	CFSP International Agreements	EU24	Coordinated	Presidency of Council	UV	No assured role	N

member states have committed themselves by Treaty to ensure 'national policies conform to the common positions' of the CFSP (Article 15, EU Treaty). In practice, however, it often appears to be a coordination of national policies at best, since the 'obligation of loyalty' is hard to enforce in the absence of any ECJ jurisdiction over CFSP.

- The combined effect of the two foregoing differences is that the international policies of the Union vary in how far they transfer power to EU institutions, rather than retain control in the hands of individual member states. This is, once again, a reason for expecting issues of input legitimation to vary across the different international policies of the Union, since it is, of course, only where there is an exercise of power of one actor over another, as opposed to voluntary action, that legitimacy becomes an issue.

On the other hand, it would be a mistake to exaggerate likely differences in the politics of legitimacy across the international policies of the Union. Where the public does not make fine-grained distinctions between types of Union policy, it may be enough for a decision to be made in 'Europe's name' for it to be implicated in the Union's legitimacy, even where member states retain high levels of control. Even significant transfers of powers over international policy to Union institutions may, conversely, be conditional only. Union institutions can only act internationally where authorised to do so by the Treaties. Even then, they have to anticipate that member states can—singly or collectively—seek to rein in unwanted international policies through future Treaty changes, decisions about Union resources and appointments, or a grudging approach to the delivery of the policy in question (Pollack 1997; Kassim and Menon 2003).

What, then, are the possibilities of legitimating the international policies of the Union along the three dimensions of performance, identity, and democracy? Beginning with performance, or output legitimacy, there are at least three reasons for believing Union policies might be able to achieve things internationally that uncoordinated national policies cannot. First, a decision to make international policy through the Union may offer benefits of scale, notably where high fixed costs mean that individual member states struggle even to cross minimum resource thresholds for effective foreign or security policy provision (Ginsberg 1989). Second, there may be gains from removing inconsistencies between national policies. This may be a simple housekeeping act of avoiding duplication. But it can also be a matter of safety and stability. Successful coordination can reduce risks of member states constructing inconsistent notions of what it is to be secure such that one can only feel more at its ease at the price of another feeling less so ['Security dilemmas' (Jervis 1976, 66)]. It can also anticipate relationships with outsiders that risk entangling member states in third-party disputes in a manner that only aggravates the latter while provoking spill-back frictions in the Union itself.

Third, 'positive externalities' may be involved in pouring different kinds of international policy (security, economic, humanitarian and so on) through the Union, even if different institutional means are used in each case. Each aspect of policy might, in other words, have 'spin-off benefits' for the others. Thus part of the thinking behind the development of the CFSP was that access to the single market—and even EC membership itself—could be used as foreign policy leverage in the resolution of security problems with third states. Security thus conceived is not just a matter of accumulating military capabilities. Rather it requires 'joined up' government across all policy instruments (commercial, environment, judicial, and so on) if the complex causes of security problems are to be tackled (Smith M. 1996b, 249). In so far as those 'other policy instruments' have been vested in EU institutions 'joined up security governance', in turn, presupposes discussion of security issues at Union level. In addition, third party incentives to cooperate with the EU's distinctive non-state political system may be sufficiently different from those associated with dealings with any of its component states to open up new sources of foreign policy leverage. For example, a Treaty agreed with the EU can only be changed or set aside with the unanimous approval of EU member states and the assent of the European Parliament, as opposed, for example, to a simple majority of a single national parliament. This allows member states to 'increase the credibility of their promises' by structuring relationships with third countries through EU Treaties. It also allows third countries to benefit from more entrenched agreements.

Whether the Union can turn the foregoing into 'output legitimation' through superior performance depends in practice on institutional effectiveness. It is often argued that transaction costs associated with the complex character of Union institutions cancel out at least some of the gains from using them to solve collective action problems in international policy. The CFSP has been charged with losing credibility by raising expectations beyond its capabilities to deliver (Hill 1993). The coherence of the EU's contribution to the World Trade Organization (WTO) has been criticised on account of the multiple veto points and complex interest politics of the Union's internal political system (Van Oudenaren 2001, quoted in Keohane 2002, 749). The EU's potential as the world's single donor of development aid has, in the view of many, been stymied by poor institutional capacity on the ground, with the result that only a small proportion of the aid has reached those it is supposed to benefit.

Turning to the question of identity, any policy is more likely to be seen as legitimate where it is underpinned by a 'we' feeling: by a feeling amongst a group that it is 'we' who are agreeing to act together, rather than 'they' who are imposing some unwanted policy on us. Much has been written about the EU's ability to ground its international policy in an agreed view of its own identity. A common theme in that literature is that the international identity of the Union is, or ought to be, associated with a new approach to international relations. That is to say, with an external projection of the Union's own internal identity politics and institutional structures aimed at changing the very nature of statehood, territory, and boundaries (Manners and Whitman 2003; Keohane 2002). Another theme—this time an external counterpart to the notion that the Union should build its internal identity around a 'constitutional patriotism' of shared political values (Habermas 2003)—is that the Union is, or should be, a force for democracy, human rights, the rule of law, and, therefore, multilateralism in the international system. As Ian Manners and Richard Whitman put it (2000, p. 390), the latter theme goes beyond familiar categories of 'civilian' and 'military' power to represent the Union as a 'normative power'.

Yet it is between the categories of 'civilian' and 'military' power that the international identity of the Union often seems most uneasily poised, whilst that of 'normative' power poses difficulties of its own. In particular, attempts to use the Union

---

Box 6.1 The assent procedure

The assent of the European Parliament is needed for:

■ Treaties that admit new states to the EU (Article 49), by a majority of all MEPs.

■ Association agreements with other states or organisations that create 'reciprocal rights and obligations' (Article 310), by a majority of votes cast.

■ Other international agreements that 'establish a specific institutional framework', have 'budgetary implications for the Community' or 'entail amendment to an act' adopted under Co-decision.

---

to promote democracy elsewhere in the world may lack legitimacy with external audiences in so far as the Union is not democratically controlled. Public opinion within the Union likewise appears anxious that all EU decisions should be publicly controlled in some way (Lord and Beetham 2001). Accountability—in the manner we defined it on pages 113-14—is an obvious mechanism of public control. Apart from delivering one half of the definition of democracy ('public control with political equality' [Beetham 1994; Weale 1999]), accountable decisions are less likely to be arbitrary (Pettit 1997), and thus, once again, more likely to be legitimate. Given this double link to legitimacy, the remainder of the chapter concentrates on arrangements for bringing the international policies of the Union to account. Such arrangements may involve obligations to give accounts of decisions before (*ex ante*) or after (*ex post*) they are made. They may involve the extraction of justifications for international policies at the moment that Treaties are concluded, ordinary legislation is passed, budgets are agreed, the execution of policy is scrutinised, or even, *in extremis*, where political leaderships are threatened with dismissal. They may operate at both Union and member state levels. They can, finally, be mediated through structures of representative government (parliaments and elections at both European and national levels) or, conversely, through administrative standards of good governance that are either judicially enforced or self-enforced by decision-makers on themselves.

The European Parliament

EU institutions and Member Governments often claim that Union decisions are doubly accountable, through the European Parliament on the one hand and national parliaments on the other. The following paragraphs show briefly how accountability to the EP varies across four areas of international policy: trade, relationships with candidate countries prior to accession, development aid, and the Common Foreign and Security policy.

Trade

At the time of writing the EP does not enjoy Co-decision over Commercial policy. It can, however, use the Assent procedure to extract accounts from both the Commission and the Council of how they conduct the Union's international trading policies. The reason for this is that trade policy is heavily governed by bilateral treaties with non-member states and by multilateral treaties with international organisations such as the World Trade Organization (WTO). As shown in Box 6.1, all such treaties require the approval of the Parliament. Although the procedure is a 'take it or leave it' vote that does not allow the EP to propose amendments of its own, the risk of the Parliament rejecting international treaties means that the Parliament is in practice consulted throughout the course of their negotiation (European Council 1983) (Corbett *et al.* 1995, 214–15).

Enlargement

The EP also has to give its Assent to treaties enlarging the Union to include new member states. A crucial difference, however, is that a majority of the EP's membership (and not just of those voting) is needed to approve the accession of new states to the Union. In practice this means that parliamentary Assent to an accession will require an over-sized majority of about 70 to 75 per cent on normal turn-outs for EP votes. This high hurdle adds to the incentive to take the views of the EP into account in developing Union policies towards countries that might one day become members. A possible justification for the high hurdle is that an accession amounts to an agreement to terminate a foreign policy relationship and admit a state to the EU's own internal system of shared rules. It is thus a kind of 'end-game', and virtually irrevocable. In contrast, international agreements and protocols short of accession frequently need revision and renewal. This gives the EP repeat opportunities to use its powers of Assent (Corbett *et al.* 1995), so softening the impact of the rule that it has no powers of amendment in relation to any one use of the Procedure.

Whether used to exert parliamentary control over enlargement or other international policies such as trade and aid, assent is most likely to be an effective instrument of parliamentary accountability and control where international dealings fall 'within the shadow of any veto' that the EP might one day exercise on attempts to formalise external relationships into a treaty. Up to a point, the Council has scope to call the Parliament's bluff knowing that it would not lightly veto a treaty that it itself values. On the other hand, there are some questions on which a threat of a parliamentary veto carries special credibility, notably human rights and democracy in third countries, either of which can emerge as conditions for EP ratification of commercial or accession treaties. It is also worth mentioning that the EP has developed signalling techniques, designed to encourage the Commission and Council to justify third country relationships and adjust them to future threats of failed assent procedures on an almost continuous basis. Apart from procedures for consulting the EP during the negotiation of treaties that require assent, the Parliament drafts annual reports on accession states. The appraisals reached, the amendments tabled, and the size and composition of majorities for and against those amendments in both committee and plenary, are all clues to how the Parliament could decide an assent vote.

Aid

Treaties such as the Cotonou agreement that regulates relations between the EU and 77 developing countries in Africa and the Caribbean are covered by what has just been said about the Assent procedure. In addition, the EP has Co-decision with the Council on ordinary legislation covering development aid. Most obvious, it is the need for parliamentary approval of annual budgets that allows the EP a measure of control of the various kinds of financial aid offered by the Union to third countries. International policies belong to the 'non-compulsory' parts of annual budgets, where the EP has most scope to shape and control priorities. It is important, however, to understand what is and is not possible here. The EP's powers over any one annual budget are tightly constrained by five-year agreements between the member states, which set a limit to how far the Parliament can vary expenditure overall or between individual categories. Still, the EP can make a difference by targeting just one or two international priorities in successive annual budgets (Corbett *et al.* 1995). Thus the 1999–2004 Parliament repeatedly increased funding for stabilisation programmes in the Balkans. Moreover by adding so-called 'remarks' to international budget lines, the EP can shape the procedural and substantive conditions under which allocations can be spent on international policies. This can be a powerful weapon of accountability. First, because the Parliament can vote to keep funds in reserve, until the Commission satisfies it further on how it is proposed money should be spent. Second, because the approval of the EP is needed to discharge the Commission's accounts, or, in other words, to certify that all money has been spent as intended and authorised. The EP has made it clear that criticism of how programmes have been managed in the past is grounds for scaling them back in the future (European Parliament 2001c).

CFSP is where successive European Parliaments have been least satisfied with arrangements for parliamentary control of foreign policy. The Treaty requires the Council Presidency to 'ensure' the fomulation of the CFSP takes 'the views of the European Parliament . . . into consideration'. It also allows the EP to recommend foreign policy objectives. However, the obligation to consult the Parliament amounts to less under the second and third pillars than the first (Fortescue 1995, 23). Only the first pillar is covered by the ECJ ruling that the Council must allow reasonable time for the EP to submit a written opinion for member states to consider in their own deliberations (Isoglucose, 138/79, 1980). Indeed in CFSP matters, the Council decides for itself what form its obligation to consult should take and when it has been satisfied. The Parliament has thus complained about only being consulted at an excessively high level of generality. Whilst the Council has always consulted it on the broad priorities set out in its annual report on CFSP, consultation on the specific instruments of CFSP (common strategies and positions, and joint actions) has, in the EP's view, been more patchy. The following summarises its discontent:

> From Parliament's view [the Council's reporting on CFSP] is useful but insufficient. It is useful because it summarises CFSP action over the past year and sets guidelines for the following year, but it is insufficient because formal consultation once a year is not appropriate. Parliament and its Foreign Affairs Committee certainly welcome the regular

contact with the Presidency of the Council, the High Representative and the Commissioners responsible for external relations and enlargement, but do not see this as a substitute for the consultation provided for in the Treaty. One field that lends itself particularly well to consultation of Parliament is the Common Strategies. Parliament should be consulted on a preparatory document so the Council takes due account of the opinion of the democratically elected institution when it takes its decision. (European Parliament 2000a, 29)

In addition to questioning the adequacy of parliamentary control over its formulation, the EP complains that unaccountable patterns of delegation are used to carry out the CFSP. Although CFSP has not yet spawned ad hoc executive agencies to the same degree as Justice and Home Affairs (JHA), proposals for a rapid reaction force and an arms procurement agency imply that three forms of delegation will soon be relevant to CFSP: delegations to CFSP agencies formed through the secondment of personnel from equivalent national bodies; delegations to specific individuals, notably the Secretary General of the Council in his or her role as the High Representative for CFSP, but also peace envoys; and, finally, delegations in which member states effectively entrust tasks to one another. It should, however, be noted that the new Constitutional Treaty dispenses with Common Strategies, partly on the very grounds of their public aspect.

In the view of several EP reports, much of the foregoing amounts to a form of 'off-balance sheet governance' in the sense that is not covered by normal practices of accountability. Second and third pillar delegations to agencies or individuals do not link to parliamentary powers of censure of designated office-holders as would, for example, be the case if the High Representative for CFSP were a Vice President of the Commission rather than an appointee of the Council. Nor are such delegations covered by general legislation on administrative standards in Union institutions such as the regulations on the processing of personal data and access to documents (European Parliament 2001b). Even the delegation of tasks to specific member states amounts to a form of mutual recognition of the standards of accountability national actors follow domestically, without any attempt to deliberate on the minimum standards for a policy agreed by all and affecting all.

Yet, cross-pillar differences in EP control of international policy are not always as stark as they appear. Even where the external policies of pillar one are co-decided by the Parliament, power passes to implementing committees (Comitology)—which bring together representatives of the Commission and member states to the exclusion of the EP—once decisions have been made. Conversely, the EP has some scope to control CFSP indirectly, through the budget, or, conceivably, through a threat to veto an accession or trade treaty with a third country if a CFSP priority is not changed. The Parliament has used the Union's financial 'rule of unity'—that income and expenditure are best monitored where included in a single budget—to resist the funding of the CFSP from outside the Commission's budget, and thus its own purview. When, for example, the Council proposed to fund CFSP peacekeeping envoys from its own budget, the EP threatened to terminate the 'gentlemen's agreement' by which the Council and Parliament have abstained from intervening in the other's budget since 1970 (European Parliament 2000b, 26).

A little noticed complication is that 'inter-pillar spill-overs' contain the converse risk of developments within CFSP threatening parliamentary control of pillar one business. This is one reason why the Parliament has been anxious that there should be an adequate parliamentary base for any European Security and Defence Policy (ESDP). Plans to use ESDP for crisis management and to give it access to the 'entire spectrum of civilian and military instruments' available to the Union (European Parliament 2000b) mean that *ex ante* scrutiny may be the last practical opportunity for elected representatives to scrutinise an initiative whose implications for other Union policies could unfold quickly in an emergency. It is perhaps in the absence of any provision for deployment of force in the Union's name to require a vote of the European Parliament that the latter most obviously has fewer powers than the US Congress over international policy.

National parliaments

International policies related to both pillars one and two are covered by a Treaty protocol requiring documents to be made available to national parliaments six weeks before they are decided by the Council of Ministers. In principle, this allows national parliaments significant potential to control all international policies of the Union, since, even where QMV is available to the Council, it prefers to decide by a consensus of its members. For example, a roll-call analysis of votes in the Council compiled by Mikko Mattila and Jan-Erik Lane (2001) indicates that 99% of votes on the Common Commercial policy between 1995 and 1998 were decided by unanimity. Yet, as Box 6.2 shows, national parliaments differ in how far they avail themselves of opportunities to control Union level decisions through the scrutiny, or even instruction, of their own governments.

Box 6.2 National parliamentary scrutiny and control

National parliaments differ widely in the time and resources they pour into the scrutiny of EU matters. Some have European Affairs Committees (EACs) that meet weekly with ministers to discuss and decide national positions on Council agenda items for the coming week. Other EACs only have a handful of meetings a year. However, only national parliaments representing a small proportion of the EU population are able to turn their scrutiny into any power of control over what their governments agree in the Council. Only the Danish and Austrian Parliaments can issue legally binding mandates, and only the Finnish and Swedish politically binding ones. An interesting divergence between the pillars is to be found in the Netherlands, where Parliament has the right to issue mandates for JHA decisions but not those made in CFSP.

Indeed, the case of CFSP shows that if QMV between member states does not preclude national parliamentary control of the Union's international policy, unanimous voting does not guarantee it. It is arguable that CFSP is an area of policy where the influence of national parliaments is weaker, not stronger, than average. The following is the assessment of the UK's House of Lords:

Our involvement in the formation of the CFSP is negligible. As a Parliament we are informed after the event and there has been no occasion whatsoever since our arrangements for scrutiny of both pillars were set up on which we have been consulted about any CFSP document or decision before it was finalised. (House of Lords, 1996)

Even those national parliaments that participate in the inputs their own governments make to CFSP face structural constraints. First, practices of national parliamentary control have built up around legislative activity where the main parameters of a decision can usually be summarised in a text that can be considered at length if not at leisure. In contrast, foreign policy decisions and declarations require quick responses. Second, any parliamentary supervision is constrained by asymmetry of information. Executives simply know more about their own policies and intentions than do representative bodies (Krehbiel 1991). The complexity and opacity of CFSP compounds the problem by raising the cost of monitoring. National parliaments have struggled to respond, some by linking their specialist Foreign Affairs Committees to their more generalist EACs, others by counterbalancing intergovernmental cooperation in the formulation of CFSP with inter-parliamentary cooperation in its monitoring. The EP has, in turn, seen the latter as an opportunity to promote meetings between the chairs of the foreign affairs committees of all parliaments in the Union, the Presidency of the Council, the High Representative of CFSP and the Commissioner with foreign policy responsibility. There is, however, a possible trade-off between the development of inter-parliamentary solutions and the extension to more member states of the (largely) Scandinavian model of national parliamentary participation in the formulation of national government positions on CFSP: the 'Scandinavian model' presupposes a measure of confidentiality to avoid disclosure of national negotiating positions in the Council of Ministers, to the point at which the national parliaments involved do not even open their discussions to their own publics, let alone to MEPs or parliamentarians from other member states.

Even where they have information and control, national parliaments may feel constrained in how far they can object to CFSP decisions. As suggested by the above quotation from the House of Lords, opportunities to object may come late in the day with the result that there is a transaction cost in unravelling decisions that other member states consider agreed. National Parliaments from some small states may also feel the pressure of maintaining the credibility of CFSP in so far as alternative sources of foreign policy influence are restricted. On the other hand, it is precisely national parliaments from states that arguably need CFSP most that are least likely to be able to shift its decisions closer to their own preferences. Where there are multiple veto holders, it is those who need to cooperate least who are best placed to dictate the terms of collective action (Moravcsik 1998).

Before concluding that the combined powers of the EP and national parliaments are inadequate, we need to anticipate counter-arguments to the effect that international policy can be legitimated without high levels of parliamentary control. One is that the public has an interest in accepting less accountability and more secrecy in international policy-making. A second recalls the earlier argument (see pp. 114–15) that internal standards of legitimacy may not apply to policies that are external in their impact. A difficulty with the first objection is that the secrecy/accountability trade-off is itself made problematic by the moving of international policy responsibilities into the EU arena. Political systems that have combined secrecy with political responsibility in the management of international problems have done so through intangibles of political culture, namely trust and a powerful internalisation of agreed norms that actors enforce on themselves. It may take time to reproduce these standards at European level. As for the second objection, it is arguable that some international objectives of the Union, such as the external promotion of democracy and human rights, belong as much in the legislative branch of government as others requiring speed and secrecy belong in the executive. What it is to promote democracy and human rights is, after all, a matter of value, interpretation, and deliberation.

Politicisation?

The previous two sections examined the powers of the European and national parliaments over the international policies of the Union. To appraise 'public control' it is, however, necessary to go beyond an analysis of the powers of representative bodies. Those powers need, in turn, to be linked to public opinion. This section accordingly discusses what little we know about the attitudes of the public and of parliamentarians towards the international policies of the Union. It then concludes with an assessment of the link between the two.

When asked whether they prefer 'joint action' by member states and the EU to 'national action only', respondents to successive Eurobarometer opinion polls have shown that public support for Union participation varies across types of international policy. Table 6.2 sets out the data for the three areas included in recent Eurobarometers: humanitarian aid, foreign and defence policy. One way of reading the figures is that across the Union as a whole public opinion would seem to be comfortable with a civilian rather than a military model of European power. Yet the slightly lower level of support for Union involvement in humanitarian aid than foreign policy in general indicates that even unambiguously civilian instruments may enjoy less appeal where they have financial costs, or where there has been some history of under-performance: Union development aid programmes have been criticised for non-delivery on the ground.

The case of defence policy illustrates the further possibility that public opinion from different member states might be split on whether the Union should be involved in particular forms of international policy even where it is agreed that it

Table 6.2 Balance of those favouring joint decisions by the EU and member states over those favouring national decision-making only. Eurobarometer 57 (2002)

	EU	Aus	Bel	Den	Fr	Fin	Ger	Gr	Lux	It	Ire	NL	Por	Sp	Swe	UK
Humanitarian aid	+39	−1	+56	+16	+48	−4	+39	+43	+41	+67	+48	+36	+37	+60	−22	+21
Foreign	+51	+38	+66	+23	+56	+39	+58	+35	+58	+70	+54	+56	+37	+67	+11	+19
Defence	+6	−12	+28	−19	−3	−80	+13	−32	+41	+35	−25	+18	+8	+35	−62	−23

should be active in foreign policy in general. Across the Union as a whole the balance of support falls by 45 points (out of a possible 200) once respondents are asked about Union involvement in defence rather than foreign policy. Amongst those with some degree of neutral status it falls by 50 points (Austria), 73 points (Sweden), 79 points (Ireland), and 119 points (Finland). Provision in the Treaties for constructive abstention from CFSP actions would thus seem to be a wise reflection of variations in what kind of external involvements public opinions from different states are prepared to accept through the medium of their EU membership.

Yet, it is difficult to know what to make of public opinion data without also knowing how well formed is public opinion on Union involvement in different areas of international policy. Ill-formed preferences are untested and unreliable guides to what public opinion is likely to support when confronted by specific policy choices. Subjective measures show the public does indeed feel ill-informed on EU issues in general (various Eurobarometers), whilst studies of the flow of information to the public via the media show that Union policies towards the rest of the world are poorly covered relative to internal aspects of EU membership (see Box 6.3). Evidence of low public awareness of the Union's international policies is also provided by focus groups recently arranged by the European Commission. Groups in just four out of the then 15 member states associated external security with the Union. Those in seven identified trade as a policy where the Union is active. In contrast, groups in 13 countries recognised more domestic concerns—agriculture, fisheries and monetary policy (the Euro)—as Union responsibilities (European Commission 2001c [The 'Optem' Report]).

Box 6.3 Media coverage of EU international policy

On the basis of a study of five member states, Guillaume Garcia and Virginie Le Torrec (2003) estimate that foreign and defence policies feature in 13 per cent of television news items with some EU content. This compares, for example, to 19 per cent for agriculture, fisheries and hunting. All EU items, in turn, make up 7.5 per cent of average TV news coverage, implying that the EU's international dimension is mentioned in just one per cent of news stories.

How do these public attitudes towards the Union as an international actor link to those of parliamentarians? The only direct data relates to MEPs, not their national counterparts. Table 6.3 analyses the results of a survey by Simon Hix. The third column of the table shows the level of support amongst MEPs for different international policy choices and institutional means of realising them. The fourth column shows how 'contested' or 'politicised' is each choice, since it measures how varied are MEPs' views. The fifth column measures the strength of the relationship between MEPs' views on international questions and their description of themselves as 'left' or 'right'. Column 3 suggests that the international policies most likely to be supported by representatives are development aid and international cooperation on environmental questions. However, development aid is also amongst those policies where MEPs are most likely to compete (probably because it involves money), whilst international environmental cooperation is amongst those where they are most likely to agree.

Table 6.3   MEP attitudes towards international questions. Source: the European Parliament Research Group (EPRG) questionnaire of MEP attitudes

1. TOPIC	2. MEPs asked to indicate how far they agree to the following:	3. Average level of agreement expressed as index from 0 to 1	4. Variance of responses in column 3: the lower the figure the higher the level of agreement between respondents	5. Correlation of answers in column 3 with left-right self placement of MEPs
Development aid:	Spending on Development aid should be increased	0.67	2.31	0.5
Refugee aid:	Financial support should be given to member states receiving most refugees	0.63	2.47	0.36
Free Trade:	The EU should support global free trade at all costs	0.21	1.58	−0.43
World Trade Or-ganization:	The EU should abide by all WTO rules and rulings	0.30	1.44	−0.32
Global Labour Standards:	The EU should support uniform global labour standards	0.35	1.29	0.43
Global Environ-mental Standards:	The EU should support global environmental standards	0.49	0.78	0.24
EU-US Trade Relations:	All trade barriers between the EU and the US should be abolished	0.28	1.2	−0.28
Mr/s CFSP powers:	Mr/s CFSP should have the power to set the EU Foreign Policy Agenda	0.08	1.29	0.13

continues

Table 6.3 continued

1. TOPIC	2. MEPs asked to indicate how far they agree to the following:	3. Average level of agreement expressed as index from 0 to 1	4. Variance of responses in column 3: the lower the figure the higher the level of agreement between respondents	5. Correlation of answers in column 3 with left-right self placement of MEPs
Commission powers on CFSP:	The Commission should have the power to set the EU Foreign Policy Agenda	0.21	1.49	0.12
Majority voting on CFSP:	The Council should vote by majority when adopting 'joint actions'	0.30	1.50	0.17
EU Military role:	The EU should have its own military units available for rapid reaction	0.65	1.56	−0.04
EU or NATO:	The EU rather than NATO should be responsible for Europe's defence	0.29	1.85	0.25

A general criticism of the link between public and European parliamentary opinion that goes well beyond international policy is that European elections are 'second order' in nature with low voter participation and little attention to European, as opposed to domestic, issues (Reif and Schmitt 1980). This criticism is not, however, decisive. Even where European elections fail to discuss EU issues, the EP may have some representative qualities if the same dimension of political choice—such as left-right—dominates both domestic and Union politics (see Lord 2004 for further discussion of both the importance and shortcomings of this insight). Indeed, it is a feature of representative government that we do not expect the views of representative and represented to coincide on each and every issue but to match one another at a higher level of abstraction. This allows voting to be simplified into one or two key dimensions of choice. Jacques Thomassen and Hermann Schmitt (2000) show that the left-right preferences of MEPs and their voters do, indeed, correlate. In turn, column 5 of Table 6.3 above shows significant correlations between MEPs' 'left-right' positions and their views on some aspects of international policy such as development and trade questions. However, the relationship is more mixed on security issues, with support for an EU military role scarcely correlating with the left-right preferences of MEPs at all, while attitudes towards independence from NATO are only modestly correlated to left-right views. MEPs' preferences on institutional questions raised by the future development of the Union's international policies are likewise only weakly correlated with their left-right positions, but, then, these are matters that continue to be decided by Treaty change, and not by the European Parliament.

Standards

So far we have only examined the accountability of the EU's international policies through institutions of government, as opposed to processes of governance (Harlow 2002). As seen, the former involve political leaderships accounting for themselves to parliaments and voters. The latter involve all decision-makers accounting to all policy addressees in terms of agreed procedural standards (transparency, consultation, due process and so on) that may be enforced by courts or independent arbiters such as Ombudsmen. Once again, there are variations in how far this particular approach to accountability is applicable to the Union's different international policies. As seen, the ECJ is excluded from consideration of CFSP decisions, and the Ombudsman is technically only empowered to investigate *Community* institutions. It has likewise proved difficult to apply the EU's administrative standards to CFSP. The most striking example concerns transparency. Carol Harlow (2002, 39–40) tells the following story about the recent regulation laying down uniform rights of public access to documents of the Parliament, Commission, and Council: 'A security classification was introduced furtively by the Council, apparently at the request of the Council and without adequate consultation with the European Parliament'.

A difficulty in applying governance modes of accountability to all of the Union's international policies—and not just CFSP—is that they rely, as Adrienne Héritier puts it (1997, 110), on the involvement in policy of diverse actor types who are both mutually 'suspicious' and equally 'knowledgeable'. In other words, they presuppose a well-developed system of competitive interest politics as much as 'government' approaches presuppose well-politicised elections and competition between representatives. In practice it is engaged organisations of civil society—monitoring groups and advocacy coalitions—that are most likely to set off alarm bells about the transgression of administrative standards or bring complaints to the courts or Ombudsmen. Once again, the international dimension of Union-policy making would seem to be the poor relation. Table 6.4 shows that out of 700 organisations of civil society to have registered with the Commission 'Connect' data-base, 30 express an interest in the EU's External Relations (the only broad foreign policy category), 42 in its International Development policies and 45 in its Human Rights policies. This compares with 91 interested in Agricultural policy and 214 in Enterprise policies. Moreover, different actor types seem to colonise different international policies of the Union rather than adopt a critical attitude across the range or engage in mutual monitoring across the range. NGOs, for example, comprise 60 and 90 per cent of those interested in Development Aid and Human Rights respectively, while

Table 6.4 Organisations of civil society expressing their interest in different aspects of the EU's international policy. Source: the 'Connect Data Base' of the European Commission

	TOTAL	NGOs as proportion of total	Professional associations+ producer interests as proportion of total
Development Aid	42	70%	22%
External Relations	30	47%	53%
Trade	61	14%	73%
Human Rights	45	90%	5%

producer/professional associations comprise 74 per cent of those with an interest in international trade.

A particular form of 'governance accountability' is the notion of 'stakeholder accountability', viz. that all those affected by a policy should have rights to compel institutions to account for their compliance with agreed standards. In the case of international policy, however, this raises the special difficulty that those most immediately affected are often those without rights or legal standing within the political system itself. This difficulty can only be overcome by outsiders acquiring internal champions. Paul Magnette provides an example of how this might work in the case of the EU. Following French nuclear tests in the Pacific in 1995, environmental lobbies within the EU complained to the Ombudsman on the grounds that the Commission had failed in its duty under the Euratom Treaty to ensure member states observe standards of public health in their handling of radio-active materials (Magnette 2003, 143). Although the Commission was, of course, powerless to do more, it was a useful surrogate target for an NGO that really wanted to complain about the behaviour of a particular member state.

Conclusions

The design of the policies and institutions that define the European Union as an international actor stand in a circular relationship with understandings of its legitimacy. At any one time, those policies and institutions are constrained by beliefs about the necessary and sufficient conditions for the legitimate exercise of political power by the Union. Yet beliefs about EU legitimacy are, in turn, influenced by Union policies towards the outside world. Those policies impact on appraisals of the Union's performance, on understandings of its international identity, and on assessments of its accountability. The success of the Union in managing this 'feedback loop' will be a factor in its further development as an international actor. Legitimacy is a 'capability', and, like others, it has to be developed in line with 'expectations' raised by the policy it is supposed to support.

A particular aspect of this challenge is ensuring that the international policies of the Union are accountable. Yet present arrangements for accountability are differentially institutionalised. In some areas of international policy, they rely to varying degrees on the European Parliament, on national parliaments, and on administratively-enforced standards. In other areas none of the foregoing assume a significant role and it can be argued that the Union's international policies remain only weakly accountable. Whether this heterogeneity is sustainable will be affected by two questions: first, are the differences in accountability arrangements justifiable in terms of the standards the Union's policy addressees require if its international activities are to be legitimate? Second, are the different approaches competitive, such that there is a real possibility of one eventually prevailing over the others, or are they better conceived as complementary? National and European parliaments may, for example, have more scope than at present to divide their labours in scrutinising the Union's international policies while sharing information in ways that would reduce the costs of monitoring at both levels. Governance approaches may be best placed to provide the fine-grained rights of accountability that individuals, and, arguably even non-EU actors, have in the delivery of the Union's international policies, while parliamentary approaches are needed for forms of public control that cannot be reduced to individual interests and preferences.

Further reading

Little has been directly written on the legitimacy and accountability of the Union's international policies, though much has been written on the legitimacy and accountability of the Union in general. Beetham and Lord (1998) extend the idea that legitimacy will be a product of performance, democratic control, and identity to the case of the Union. Scharpf (1997) applies the distinction between input and output legitimacy to the EU. Harlow (2002) discusses the relevance of different notions of accountability to the Union. Lord (2004) assesses the accountability of different Union institutions and policies.

Beetham, D., and Lord, C. (1998), *Legitimacy in the European Union* (London: Addison-Wesley Longman).

Harlow, C. (2002), *Accountability in the European Union* (Oxford: Oxford University Press).

Lord, C. (2004), *A Democratic Audit of the European Union* (Basingstoke: Palgrave Macmillan).

Scharpf, F. (1996), 'Democratic Policy in Europe', *European Law Journal*, 2/2, 136–55.

Web links

The European Parliament web site, http://www.europarl.eu.int/ provides much good material including the reports of relevant committees and other bodies; many individual MEPs also have their own web sites, which can be accessed through the sites of their political groups. Much of the general material on attitudes towards the EU can be found through the Europa web site, http://www.europa.eu.int/ and through sites offering access to Eurobarometer reports; Eurobarometer carries out regular surveys dealing with international issues, and its reports are available (for example) on the web site of Economic and Social Data Services in the UK, at http://www.esds.ac.uk/ or via the Euractiv web site at http://www.euractiv.com/. More general material on issues of accountability at the EU level can also be accessed via the web sites of member state governments or through those of political parties or pressure groups. See also the web sites dealing with CFSP/ESDP and related issues cited by Chapters 3 and 4 in this volume.

Chapter 7

The Europeanization of Foreign Policy

Reuben Wong

Contents

Summary

After an initial review of the possible meanings of 'Europeanization', the chapter seeks to establish an operational definition of the phenomenon, linking and contrasting it with the paradigmatic European integration theories—neo-functionalism and intergovernmentalism. It goes on to ask if 'Europeanization'—so often understood as a process of transformation in domestic politics and institutions—can be identified in EU member states' foreign policies, and proposes three relevant dimensions of the process: top-down policy convergence, bottom-up national projection, and socialisation. An operational definition of Europeanization is proposed, using a number of parameters to understand and measure the extent, and variability, with which the process shapes the making and content of member states' foreign policies.

Introduction

'Europeanization' is a relatively new, fashionable, and ill-defined concept in the scholarly literature of European Studies/International Relations. Like globalisation theory, there is much debate over the nature, causes and effects of Europeaniza-tion, and precious little agreement on what exactly Europeanization is (Olsen 2002; Harmsen and Wilson 2000). The term often refers to the political and policy changes caused by the impact of membership in the European Union on the member states. Europeanization theorists draw on ideas found in institutionalism as well as in globalisation theories and what might be termed 'rationalisation'—or a way of op-timising outcomes in an increasingly challenging external environment. Some see Europeanization as an 'institutionally thick form of rationalisation within the global economy' (Rosamond 2000b, 179–80). Borrowing from institutionalist theory's hy-pothesis that international institutions have 'persistent and connected sets of rules that prescribe behavioural roles, constrain activity, and shape expectations' (Keo-hane 1989, 161), various Europeanization scholars argue that sustained membership and participation in the EU leads to the convergence of national policy-making, both in style and content (Cole and Drake 2000; Hanf and Soetendorp 1998; Ladrech 1994).

As Hill and Smith argued in Chapter 1 of this volume, established concepts in In-ternational Relations are increasingly being brought together with approaches from Comparative Politics and Public Policy. This cross-disciplinary trend is evident in the 'Europeanization' approaches in European Studies, even in studies of the European Union's international relations. This chapter proposes Europeanization as an altern-ative approach to understanding EU member states' foreign policy. It seeks to de-velop an operational theory of Europeanization in order to better understand the extent of the influence, opportunities and constraints on member states' choices afforded by the European Union.

The meanings of Europeanization

Alistair Cole and Helen Drake identify four different usages of the concept ('Euro-peanization' as: an independent variable, emulative policy transfer, smokescreen, and imaginary constraint). The two strongest definitions are (i) as a constraining, independent variable—where the EU imposes policy orientations on national gov-ernments—e.g. in public services and industrial policy, and (ii) as a source of policy transfer and learning—where states look to other EU member states for policy ideas. The other two uses of Europeanization—as 'smokescreen' and imaginary constraint—paradoxically empower EU governments by giving them manoeuvring room to make politically difficult domestic reforms under the cover of the EU. For example, French governments used the European Monetary Union convergence cri-teria to justify domestically sensitive reforms to pension and welfare schemes. These uses focus on the manipulation of Europeanization in political discourse. Harmsen and Wilson identify as many as eight distinct, if partially overlapping, senses of the term 'Europeanization' in current usage. Most of these senses are dependent variables, or effects, of other phenomena, such as European integration, democratisation, or modernisation (Cole and Drake 2000, 39–41; Harmsen and Wilson 2000, 13–18). The concept of Europeanization is thus beset by different uses of the term and ambiguities about independent and dependent variables. I would group these different usages and varied meanings of the concept 'Europeanization' into a taxonomy of five categories.

National adaptation

One of the oldest and most widely received conceptions of Europeanization is by Robert Ladrech, who defines Europeanization in terms of national adaptation to EU membership (Ladrech 1994, 69):

> An incremental process *reorienting* the direction and shape of politics to the degree that EC political and economic dynamics become part of the organizational logic of national politics and policy-making.

This 'reorientation' or national adaptation school of Europeanization championed by Ladrech suggests that Europeanization is a top-down process translating change from the supranational/European level to the national level in decision-making politics. This school understands Europeanization as a process in which 'Europe, and especially the EU, becomes an increasingly more relevant and important point of political reference for the actors at the level of the member-states' (Hanf and Soetendorp 1998, 1). It is, however, *not* a Haasian process (to use neo-functionalist language on integration and convergence) that follows a self-perpetuating integrationist logic, where political actors in Europe 'shift their loyalties, expectations and political activities toward a new centre, whose institutions possess or demand jurisdiction over the pre-existing national states' (Haas 1961; Tranholm-Mikkelsen 1991), and where the end result is a supranational state. In other words, Europeanization as understood by Ladrech is a process in which the state is reactive, and where the state adapts and makes adjustments in its domestic politics and policy in compliance with the constraints and requirements of European institutions. Similarly, other scholars have all understood Europeanization as an incremental process of adjustment and adaptation reorienting member states' politics and policies towards the EU (Mazey and Richardson 1996, 44–45; Hanf and Soetendorp 1998, 1–9).

Christian Lequesne's detailed study of the iterative process of French EU policy-making and the interaction between Paris and Brussels also makes an argument for the national (in this case, French government's) reorientation of domestic politics and structures. Focusing on the institutions of the EU and joint policy-making in the EU framework between Brussels and the national capitals, Lequesne and others have used the lenses of Comparative Politics in suggesting an incremental 'iterative process' of Europeanization in the national administrations as governments adapt their mechanisms and practices of policy-making in politics, administration and law. Incrementalism and 'muddling through' are the main processes in this model of Europeanization. Adaptations are ad hoc and there is no thought-out, coherent plan. Moreover, the extent and nature of the EU influence depends on endogenous factors in the member states which affect their capacity to adapt. National institutions may clash with, or conform to, European integration; in particular, their capacity to accommodate, refract, or resist pressures for change are key to understanding distinct national and sectoral trajectories of Europeanization (Lequesne 1993; Goetz and Hix 2001; Kassim 2000, 2003; Guyomarch 2001; Hanf and Soetendorp 1998, 188).

National projection

In contrast to the national adaptation school of Europeanization, a bottom-up understanding of Europeanization is also common currency. In this conception, which I will call the 'national projection' school, nation states are the primary actors and agents of change rather than passive subjects. Alan Milward argues that the early construction of the EU was achieved by, and contributed towards, the post-war construction of European nation-states. European integration was viewed as a means and vehicle for the achievement of nationally defined goals. For Simon Bulmer and Martin Burch, Europeanization is a process of 'seeking to export domestic policy models, ideas and details to the EU'. In the place of a reactive state being constrained to change its policy-making processes, this notion of Europeanization sees the state as being pro-active in projecting its preferences, policy ideas, and models to the European Union. This conception of Europeanization shares many similarities with rational-choice, interest-based accounts of national preferences and national élites using the EU as an instrument to further national interests (Milward 1992, 2000; Bulmer and Burch 1999; Guyomarch et al. 1998; Laffan and Stubb 2003).

The 'national projection' school of Europeanization at first glance provides a countervailing antithesis to the national adaptation/policy convergence school. The latter fails to appreciate the roles played by member states themselves—especially the larger and more powerful ones, in fashioning EU structures and policies. These states, in 'projecting' their national policies and policy styles onto the larger European structure, 'Europeanize' their previously national priorities and strategies and create a dialectical relationship. By exporting their preferences and models onto EU institutions, they in effect generalise previously national policies onto a larger European stage. This has several benefits. First, the state increases its international influence. Second, the state potentially reduces the risks and costs of pursuing a controversial or negative policy (e.g. sanctions) against an extra-European power. As some scholars have noted, even small states within the European Union may pursue integration as a way of 'formalizing, regulating and perhaps limiting the consequences of interdependence' (Milward 2000, 19). At any rate, a strong European presence in the world is potentially beneficial to all in increasing individual member states' international influence. In the same vein, scholars have argued that Germany 'Europeanized' its low-deficit, fiscally disciplined macro-economic policies into the EMU convergence criteria, that the UK Europeanized its sanctions on Argentina during the Falklands conflict in 1982, and that France projected its institutions into the early EC and its predecessor, the High Authority of the European Coal and Steel Community (Regelsberger et al. 1997). These examples also suggest that foreign policy-making is as susceptible to Europeanization as domestic policy, politics, and processes, i.e. foreign policy is *not* a special case immune to Europeanization pressures on member states.

Identity reconstruction

A third meaning of Europeanization refers to the reconstruction of identities in contemporary Europe. This usage is predominantly employed by anthropologists and social constructivists. Europeanization is typically defined 'as a strategy of self-representation and a device of power' which is 'fundamentally reorganizing territoriality and peoplehood, the two principles of group identification that have shaped the modern European order' (Harmsen and Wilson 2000, 17; Bellier and Wilson 2000). Studies of this type of Europeanization have focused on the redefinition and negotiation of identities within EU institutions such as the European Commission and the European Parliament. They envisage a teleological movement: the fading away of member states' monopoly on the loyalties of their citizens over the long term, to the benefit of *European* attitudes and objectives. This meaning of Europeanization is akin to neo-functionalist theory in stressing a gradual transfer of identity and affective affiliation towards a new supranational Europe. The identity reconstruction thesis finds echos in the old Deutschian idea of political communities. Europeanization here is a way of blending the national and federal impulses to create a transnational and culturally integrated Europe.

Élite socialisation is a phenomenon frequently associated with national officials attached to the Commission and other EU institutions in Brussels. Research undertaken in recent years by Jakob Øhrgaard, M.E. Smith, and Kenneth Glarbo suggests that officials are increasingly thinking in 'European' rather than 'national' terms. Anthropological studies of European Commission officials suggests that these officials were exhibiting traits of cultural 'hybridisation' whereby their 'national being' was becoming a 'European being' (Harmsen and Wilson 2000, 149–50). Most scholars agree that intense and repeated contacts have socialised not only EU officials, but also national officials working in EU institutions. Even national diplomacies are becoming more 'European' and displaying a 'coordination reflex' in foreign policy-making (Øhrgaard 1997; Glarbo 1999). Hill and Wallace point out the potential transformational effects of élite socialisation within this complex network (Hill 1996, 6):

> From the perspective of a diplomat in the foreign ministry of a member state, styles of operating and communication have been transformed. The COREU telex network, EPC working groups, joint declarations, joint reporting, even the beginning of staff exchanges among foreign ministries and shared embassies: all these have moved the conduct of foreign policy away from the old nation-state sovereignty model towards a collective endeavor, a form of high-level networking with transformationalist effects and even more potential.

Whether or not national officials have indeed been 'localised' or 'captured' by EU interests to think 'European' rather than 'national', most studies indicate that officials in Brussels work with both the national and the European interest in mind. In their study of the impact of the EU on Irish officials, Laffan and Tannam note that 'public officials are no longer just agents of the Irish state; they are participants in an evolving polity which provides opportunities for political action but also imposes constraints on their freedom of action' (Hanf and Soetendorp 1998, 69; Tonra 2001). Research in this school suggests convergence as "prolonged participation in the CFSP feeds back into EU Member States and reorients their foreign policy cultures along similar lines'. The main agents for convergence include élite socialisation, bureaucratic reorganisation, and an institutionalised 'imperative of concertation' (Smith, M.E. 2000; Glarbo 1999, 650).

Modernisation

A fourth meaning of Europeanization is the political, economic, and social modernisation set in motion by prospective membership in the European Union. This sense of Europeanization is often applied to economically less developed states on the geographical 'periphery' of Western Europe as they are being brought into the 'core' through EU membership. This modernisation meaning of Europeanization is common in works on Ireland, Greece, Spain, and Portugal and the 2004 accession countries (Featherstone 1998; Corkill 1999; Morata 1998). Similarly, the term is also taken to mean 'joining Europe' and applied to the Central and Eastern European accession countries in the context of EU enlargement (Ágh 1999). This applies to the adoption of a West European state model and involves the firm anchoring of democratic institutions and market economies. Ágh has suggested a variation of the concept of Europeanization as describing a successfully completed process of transition in which some or all of the candidate countries become fully integrated into the entire range of West European and Trans-Atlantic cooperative institutions.

Studies of the EU's effects on national foreign policy in the enlargements of 1986 and 1995 have also demonstrated new member states 'modernising' their foreign policies upon accession by jettisoning outmoded national policies to align themselves with established European norms. Thus Spain changed its position on the Western Sahara and recognised Israel, and Austria revised its neutrality policy (Barbé 1996; Luif 1998).

Policy isophormism

Policy isophormism is a fifth and final meaning of Europeanization. Arising as a logical by-product of advanced policy adaptation and convergence (School A, see Table 7.1) and socialisation (School C), this variant is concerned with the degree of convergence in substantive policy areas. Claudio Radaelli has suggested that the Europeanization of policy has two dimensions. On one hand there is the 'direct' Europeanization of various areas of public policy to the extent that regulatory competence has passed from the member states to the European Union.

On the other hand, there has been an 'indirect' Europeanization of policy learning where member states begin to emulate one another regarding particular policy choices or policy frameworks. Advocates of this school of Europeanization as isomorphism draw on the work of DiMaggio and Powell from the 1980s, arguing that over time, particular organisational forms or policy choices come to be perceived as 'legitimate' by the actors concerned, to the exclusion of other choices. They argue that in the present context, the type of intensive transnational cooperation fostered by European integration may lead to the emergence of such shared senses of legitimate (and illegitimate) choices (Radaelli 1997, 2000; Lodge 2000).

Table 7.1   Five schools of thought on Europeanization

Schools of thought on Europeanization	Direction of change/ related processes	Major proponents
National Adaptation (A)	Top-down/Globalisation, policy convergence	Ladrech (1994), Kassim (2000, 2003), Cole and Drake (2000), Lequesne (1994), Goetz and Hix (2001)
National Projection (B)	Bottom-up and sideways/Policy projection, Policy learning, Policy transfer	Bulmer and Burch (1999), Moravcsik (1993, 1998), Guyomarch *et al.* (1998), Laffan and Stubb (2003)
Identity Reconstruction (C)	Top-down/Elite socialisation	M.E. Smith (2000), Hill & Wallace (1996), Nuttall (1992, 2000), Øhrgaard (1997), Zielonka (1998a), de Schoutheete (1986)
Modernisation (D)	Top-down/Democratisation, Economic Development, 'Westernisation'	Ágh (1998, 1999), Corkill (1999), Featherstone (1998)
Policy Isophormism (E)	Top-down and sideways/Policy learning, emulation and transfer	Radaelli (1997, 2000), Lodge (2000)

Three dimensions of foreign policy Europeanization

What do we mean by 'foreign policy' in the context of an EU member state which takes part in a complex European foreign policy-making mechanism? The notion of a 'foreign policy' is problematic as it often carries with it the conceptual assumptions of the state-centred view of world politics. Although the international system is populated by important non-state actors, the dominant paradigm in international relations still conceives of foreign policy as essentially the *domaine réservé* of sovereign governments and therefore exclusive to states. One of the most comprehensive definitions of 'foreign policy' in the International Relations literature, by K.J. Holsti, characterises foreign policy as 'ideas or actions designed by policy makers to solve a problem or promote some change in the policies, attitudes, or actions of another state or states, in nonstate actors, in the international economy, or in the physical environment of the world'. The essence of foreign policy is often understood as the definition of national ends, objectives, or interests, and the pursuit of these interests. Foreign policy is therefore seen as 'an attempt to design, manage and control the external activities of a state so as to protect and advance agreed and reconciled objectives' (Holsti 1992, 82; Allen 1998, 43–4).

The main problem with using either notion of 'foreign policy' is that the EU is not a unified state actor with identifiable 'European interests'. Despite habits of policy consultation and coordination through EPC since 1970, the EU is still a 'flexible and disaggregated series of patterns, arrangements and institutions which express a collective yet pluralistic identity, and of which others are increasingly aware' (Allen and Smith 1990, 23). If we use a working definition of foreign policy as 'actions and ideas designed by policy makers of an *international actor* (rather than state actor) to promote a change in the attitudes of other actors or in the environment', we will be justified in characterising the EU as a significant international actor which not only makes foreign policy, but also exerts a significant influence on world politics, whether in interactions with other states, regional or international organisations from ASEAN to the UN, or international regimes like the WTO (Allen *et al.* 1982; Devuyst 1995).

'EU foreign policy' (EFP) is thus a much more encompassing concept than the narrow focus of intergovernmental politico-diplomatic activities under the Common Foreign and Security Policy (CFSP), which was established by the Maastricht Treaty and succeeded European Political Cooperation (EPC) in 1993. As the EU is not a single unified actor, 'EU foreign policy' will be understood in this essay as the sum and interaction of the 'three strands' of Europe's 'external relations system', comprising: (a) the national foreign policies of the member states, (b) EC external trade relations, and (c) the CFSP (Hill 1993; Ginsberg 1999). National foreign policies have of course always existed side by side with, sometimes in competition to, collective EC/EU policies, e.g. on issues as diverse (and often divisive) as dealing with the US, China, Russia, the Middle East, nuclear disarmament, UN reform, and WTO negotiations. On the economic front, the record of Community policies (mainly economic and trade policies) has generally been a success while the record of politico-security policies under EPC/CFSP has been mixed. Whatever the record in each area, it is clearly perceived that 'Europe' does act in various issue areas and that Europeans also act as individuals, groups and nations, actions sometimes interpreted by outsiders as representative of Europe as a whole (Hill 1998b).

To answer the question of how much a member state's foreign policy has been affected by the EU, this writer proposes three concepts of Europeanization applicable to national foreign policy: (i) a top-down process of **policy convergence**; (ii) a bottom-up and sideways process involving the export of national preferences and models, **national projection**; and (iii) the socialisation of interests and identities, **identity reconstruction**. The first concept of Europeanization is used predominantly in the literature to explain the top-down adaptation of national structures and processes in response to the demands of the EU. This concept predicts cross-national policy convergence between EU states after a sustained period of structural and procedural adaptation. A second Europeanization concept refers to the bottom-up projection of national ideas, preferences, and models from the national to the supranational level. Third, Europeanization in its broadest sense means a process of identity and interest convergence so that 'European' interests and a European identity begin to take root alongside national identities and interests, indeed to inform and shape them.

The three aspects of Europeanization and their expected indicators are summarised in Table 7.2.

Table 7.2   Three dimensions of Europeanization in national foreign policy

Aspects of Europeanization	National foreign policy indicators
I Adaptation and Policy Convergence	a) Increasing salience of European political agenda b) Adherence to common objectives c) Common Policy outputs taking priority over national *domaines réservés*
II National Projection	a) State attempts to increase national influence in the world b) State attempts to influence foreign policies of other member states c) State uses the EU as a cover/umbrella
III Identity reconstruction	a) Emergence of norms among policy-making élites b) Shared definitions of European and national interests

Common Foreign and Security Policy vs. national foreign policies

The lack of a coherent 'European' foreign policy has often been attributed to the absence of a centralised decision-making state-like executive. EFP decisions are often arrived at as compromises between national foreign policies of member states. As such, European foreign policy as a subject of enquiry up till the end of the 1990s tended to be either dismissed out of hand by realists as non-existent, or idealised teleologically as an inevitable end-product of European integration, quite divorced from the realities of persistent (and often divergent) national foreign policies. Within European foreign policy studies, one school sees member states as the principal actors while another emphasises the role of supranational institutions (e.g. the Commission) and the emergence of a 'European interest'—a kind of pan-European national interest. Neither school has developed good causal theories of EU foreign policy because they tend to be highly normative and to advocate positions on what the EU should be rather than what the EU is actually doing in world politics.

The study of the foreign policy of EU member states is thus split into two rival camps. In one camp is the traditional approach, focusing on the foreign policy of individual member states as utility-maximising, selfish, and purposive actors—let us call this the 'state-centric' school. The 'hard' position in this tradition claims that states are the only essential and salient actors. Any study of EU foreign policy is thus unproductive as the 'real' Europe is the one of state governments. As Hedley Bull claimed, '"Europe" is not an actor in international affairs, and does not seem likely to become one' (Bull 1983). Bull felt that only an independent European nuclear deterrent and military power (represented by a West European military alliance led by France and Britain) would give Europe a real capability in foreign affairs. Of course, Bull's assessment was coloured by the escalating Cold War tensions of the 1980s between the USSR and Reagan's USA, but his prognosis for a European military capability independent of the US and NATO is still shared by many states (chiefly in some quarters of France and Britain) and analysts today in the aftermath of Bosnia, Kosovo, and Iraq.

Not all scholars in the state-centric tradition dismiss the EU as a serious international actor because of its lack of state-like qualities, nor do they agree with Bull's military-security conclusion. Neorealist intergovernmentalists privilege the centrality of the state while acknowledging the EU's influence, albeit only as a forum in which governments meet periodically to negotiate new contracts that enhance their interests and power. They view the EU as merely representing an advanced forum for negotiations at intergovernmental conferences (IGCs). The 'Harvard approach' of liberal intergovernmentalism, represented by Andrew Moravcsik, believes that the member states can raise the common interest in EU policy-making. It has a materialist and rationalist bias in its stress on "interstate bargain", deals and side-payments between member states' governments who at certain times come to common agreements when their preferences converge. In this conception, decisions at the European level are viewed as 'conventional statecraft' between sovereign states—the key actors in all EU activities (Moravcsik 1991).

In the other camp—which I will call 'European-idealist'[1]—is the perspective which treats European Foreign Policy as given, i.e. as a foreign policy that already exists, has a consistent personality that makes an impact on world politics, and is taken seriously by other actors (Smith, H. 2002; White 2001; Nuttall 2000; Zielonka 1998b; Carlsnaes and Smith 1994). While this approach does not deny the continued importance of individual member states' foreign policies and accepts that EFP will not supplant national foreign policies any time soon—especially in defence and security matters—it often presumes that EFP's scope will expand eventually to subsume national policies in almost all other functional areas (Smith, M.E. 2000). Walter Carlsnaes and Steve Smith in 1994 made the bold prediction that the essentially 'multilayered character' of the new Europe would mean that 'differentiated as to function, and maybe implicitly acknowledging suzerainty-like hierarchies, they will develop kinds of diplomatic relations and foreign policies that we best anticipate by reading about "proto diplomacy" in Der Derian's *On Diplomacy* (1987) and by searching even further away in time and space—among the empires of antiquity, the Chinese and Indian diplomatic traditions...' (Carlsnaes and Smith 1994, 271).

The European-idealist perspective downplays the realist emphasis on state power and national interests, and privileges instead the role of supranational European institutions in building a common 'European' identity, and a distinctive moral presence in world politics. François Duchêne, the first major spokesman in this school, envisaged the EU as a 'civilian power', a kind of 'soft power' which wields civilian instruments on behalf of a collectivity which has renounced the use of force among its members and encourages others to do likewise (Duchêne 1973). Taking as their starting point Duchêne's premise that the EU should and can become a 'civilian power' and a model of reconciliation and peace for other regions in the world, European-idealists posit that EU foreign policy should focus on the promotion of democracy, human rights, and security cooperation. Many have advocated the German model of using economic leverage focusing on issues such as environmental concerns and open trading rather than military power as the way forward for the EU after the Cold War. Karen Smith lists propaganda, diplomacy and economic instruments as three of the four instruments (excluding military) that the EU could and should exploit as a civilian power (Smith, K. 1998). Acknowledging that the European Union may never possess a common defence policy, others have suggested that the EU has unparalleled foreign policy strengths as an 'attractive power' at the pivotal point between overlapping international clubs (Richard Rosecrance 1998).

Attempts since the early 1980s to bridge this divide have focused almost entirely on comparing individual member states' foreign policies, albeit *within* the framework of the EPC/CFSP (Hill 1983, 1996; Manners and Whitman 2000; Tonra 2001). Scholarship along this vein argues that there is something 'distinctive' about the foreign policies of EU member states. These states' foreign policies are made under opportunities and constraints qualitatively different from that of the US, hence a distinctive foreign policy analysis method to study EU member states' foreign policies is necessary (Manners and Whitman 2000; Carlsnaes and Smith 1994). It clearly matters if a state is a member of the EU or not; relations between that state and the EU (and its member states and its policies, e.g. the Common Agricultural Policy) can pass overnight from being 'foreign' to domestic policy.

Foreign policy analysis and Europeanization

Instead of getting bogged down in the debate of whether foreign policy can really exist for the EU as a non-state actor, and how to identify and evaluate a debatable 'policy', it may be more fruitful to conceptualise EFP in terms of a process, and of the EU's actorness, presence, and impact in international affairs (going back to Holsti's definition of ideas or actions aimed at making changes in the environment). In this regard, the two concepts indispensable to the study of European foreign policy are actorness and presence. Although the precise qualities (and indeed composition!) of 'Western Europe' have remained obstinately resistant to definition or analysis and EFP is certainly produced in a messy manner, the reality is that there is a cohesive European impact on international relations. Thus the EU is an actor in issues ranging from the UN Human Rights Charter and the NPT, to China's WTO membership, NATO expansion, and the plight of refugees fleeing wars in Africa, Asia, the Middle East, or indeed the Balkans. The EU is present and active both as an actor in itself and through its member states at both bilateral and multilateral discussions and negotiations on these issues.

'Europeanization' in foreign policy is equated by many scholars to mean 'adaptation' (School A in this chapter). Europeanization theorists argue that over time, there is a dilution of the national in favour of the European. Ben Tonra defines Europeanization in foreign policy as '. . .a transformation in the way in which national foreign policies are constructed, in the ways in which professional roles are defined and pursued and in the consequent internalisation of norms and expectations arising from a complex system of collective European policy making' (Tonra 2000, 229). This 'transformation' usually translates as adaptation to EU norms and standards, an 'incremental process orienting Member States' politics and policies towards the EU'. Manners and Whitman conclude that 'Member States conduct all but the most limited foreign policy objectives inside an EU context' (Manners and Whitman 2000, 245). If this generalisation is true, then the foreign policies of EU states must, with the cumulative weight of the *acquis* of EPC/CFSP/ESDP—to name but one of the three arenas of each member state's participation in EFP—increasingly show some discernible impact on the foreign policies of these states. I would argue that the logical extension of the Manners and Whitman thesis is foreign policy convergence (both in substance and in process) over the long term, although the process may suffer periodic setbacks and reversals.

Applying Europeanization theory to national foreign policy

Is foreign policy immune to Europeanization (if we understand the process as policy convergence)? Stanley Hoffmann, observing the reassertion of nationalist sentiment in the EC/EU by France under de Gaulle in the 1960s and Chirac from 1995, made the realist claim that states remained the basic units in world politics (Hoffmann 1966, 2000), and that France today remains fiercely jealous and protective of its foreign policy independence. Intergovernmentalists like Hoffmann privilege the role of national governments in defining their national interests independently of the EU, and then bringing these interests to the table for negotiation. Andrew Moravcsik, the chief scholar arguing for liberal intergovernmentalists, argues that 'the primary source of (European) integration lies in the interests of the states themselves and the relative power each brings to Brussels' (Moravcsik 1991, 75). The key actors are governmental élites and the motivation for integration is the preservation of executive capacity at the national level, *not* its erosion (Moravcsik 1993, 515):

> The EC provides information to governments that is not generally available… National
> leaders undermine potential opposition by reaching bargains in Brussels first and present-
> ing domestic groups with an 'up or down' choice… Greater domestic agenda-setting
> power in the hands of national political leaders increases the ability of governments to
> reach agreements by strengthening the ability of governments to gain domestic ratifica-
> tion for compromises or tactical issue linkages.

Control by the Council and/or the Commission represent 'two cultures' competing in the European foreign policy-making process. The EPC had been devised essentially along the lines of the Gaullist Fouchet Plan, to prevent Brussels from becoming a foreign policy centre and to keep foreign policy as a national competence within the Council. Even so, the 'Brusselsisation' (steady enhancement of Brussels-based decision-making bodies) of foreign policy shows no sign of abating, and even member states jealous of their foreign policy sovereignty have not been immune to this process (Allen 1998; Peterson and Sjursen 1998; White, 2001).

Europeanization theory (especially School C) privileges the role played by European institutions in changing the interests, politics and policy-making of its member states over time into a more convergent whole. In this sense, it shares insights and assumptions with sociological institutionalism, which suggests that the EU's common policies, or *acquis politiques*, have encouraged new conceptions of interest and identity among its member states. Sociological institutionalists believe that institutions play more than a cost-minimising, information, and utility-maximising coordinating role in ensuring reciprocal cooperation for the collective good. The 'sociological institutions' in EFP are found in the form of unwritten rules, norms and practices, found in both pillar I and CFSP, and include the 'Gymnich formula' (foreign ministers' informal retreat held every six months or so by each Presidency), and the premium placed on consultation and consensus. Sociological studies from the late 1990s indicate that EPC/CFSP institutions have a strong 'socialisation' effect; élites involved even in the intergovernmental bargaining process of EPC/CFSP show surprising signs of internalising supranational norms and interests, feeding these back to their national capitals (Øhrgaard 1997; Smith, M.E. 2000; Bellier in Harmsen and Wilson 2000, 147–50). CFSP is today an essential component of member states' foreign policy formulation. Between 1974 and 1999, over 74 'Gymnich' meetings were held at foreign minister level, i.e. an average rate of three times yearly. At the official level, the intense activity of some 30 CFSP Working Groups in Brussels had become an integral part of each member state's foreign policy. The process of formulating CFSP—if not always the results—is clearly becoming Europeanized.

How far does the Europeanization perspective explain member states' recent foreign policy? We are thus faced with a dichotomy. The Europeanization perspective portrays the member state subject to the strains, constraints, opportunities, and influences of EU membership as a 'member of the club' and obliged to behave and play a certain role in the EFP regime. In contrast, the intergovernmental perspective (with its realist and liberal variants) views the member state as an independent power driven by its national interests, a state that shapes, influences, and sets the pace of European foreign policy, and determines its level of cooperation according to its interests in the issue at hand. The two paradigms and their major characteristics are summarised in Table 7.3.

Of course, the table above exaggerates the differences between the two perspectives. The supranational-intergovernmental divide has narrowed considerably today as member states adjust to the increasing Brusselsisation of foreign policy-making. Britain and France, the two most 'independent' member states in the EU, increasingly accept that they can no longer assure their own national defence nor pursue an independent global role today. Even Britain, the member state traditionally most opposed to European supranational integration and in favour of intergovernmental decision-making in the EU, shows characteristics of moving towards foreign policy decision-making at the European level (White, B. 2001).

Convergence vs. the logic of diversity

A key question for Europeanization theorists is whether the process would lead to a convergence of the EU member states' foreign policy trajectories and an emergence of shared norms and notions of European interests. This writer expects convergence to be the dominant tendency over the long term. Several factors contribute towards this Europeanization of national foreign policies.

First, European states in general have become less powerful in the 21st century with the rise of competing centres of power such as the United States, Japan,

Table 7.3 Europeanization versus intergovernmentalism in the study of national foreign policy

	Europeanization theory	Intergovernmentalism	
		Realist variant	Liberal variant
Central variables	Knowledge/learning/ roles	Power	Domestic interests
Role of institutions	Strong (Sch.A) Medium to weak (Sch.B)	Weak	Weak
Meta-theoretical orientation	Sociological (Sch.C, A) Rationalistic (Sch.B, D)	Rationalistic	Rationalistic
Behavioural model	Role-player	Concerned with relative gains	Concerned with absolute gains
Main actors	European élites, member states (Sch.B), institutions, IOs, interest groups	State	Government élites, domestic interests
Actors' preferences	Socialised and negotiated (A,C,D,E)	Exogenously given and fixed	Dynamic, rising from processes in national polities

and China. Smaller member states such as the Netherlands, Ireland, Portugal, and Denmark have been forced to adapt to the changing world environment by aligning themselves with EU positions so as to amplify their voices in international trade and politics. The 'post-neutral' member states Austria, Sweden, Denmark, and Finland have had to redefine their defence policies in response to the CFSP in 1991 and the ESDP in 1999. This does not mean that the EU always smothers the smaller states' foreign policies—it sometimes gives small states the necessary institutional resources to profile themselves in 'new' regions, or to project their own interests as *European* interests. Thus Portugal found that the Mediterranean, especially North Africa, became part of its foreign policy agenda, and that it was able to draw effective attention to East Timor through the EU (Tonra 2000, 2001; Phinnemore 2000; Miles 2000; de Vasconcelos 1996).

Second, the EU provides even the larger states (especially those with colonial histories), a means to re-engage in areas of former colonial influence in Africa and Asia. Britain could re-engage with its former Southeast Asian colonies through the ASEAN-EU dialogue in 1980. France was able to re-engage with all the countries in the East Asia region through the vehicle of the Asia-Europe Meeting, launched in 1996 and effectively a summit meeting of EU and East Asian leaders. The EU offers a means or cover in affording a 'politics of scale' to support member states' interests (Ginsberg 1989). By acting as an agent of European foreign policy, Britain, France, Belgium, Portugal, and the Netherlands could claim more credit for their dual national/European roles in troubled areas in the African Great Lakes regions, Southeast Asia and even discussions on North Korea. Many large operations in the Balkans, Asia, and Africa are not confined to CFSP, but require pillar I resources and member states' contributions, e.g. peace-keeping forces. In seeking to Europeanize their national approaches, these key states needed support from allies in the EU, as seen in French and German efforts to upgrade political dialogue with China and to end the arms embargo imposed since 1989, or British efforts to enlist EC help in the Falklands war in 1982.

Of course, such convergence processes are not irreversible or pre-determined. Member states continue to resist being locked into a fixed path of identity and policy convergence. French and British policies are often contrasted to that of Germany, supposedly the model of a 'Europeanized' state with a European identity. Yet even Germany showed a clear preference for national interest over agreed EU policy in its recognition of Slovenia and Croatia in December 1991 (Marcussen *et al.* 1999; Rummel 1996). National interests, as defined by incumbent national élites, still play a decisive role in national foreign policy-making. But while national élites may resist the institutionalisation of EU practices and a reflex of working for the collective interest, changes in the international context, venues of decision-making (increasingly oriented towards Brussels) have incrementally altered even the definition of what constitutes the 'European' or the 'national' interest.

Commercial policy is a prime example of this shift. The Commission's 1991 'Car deal' with Japan undertook to dismantle, over 10 years, quotas for Japanese car imports in the protected markets of France, Italy, and Spain. Member states share the same interests of improving access to world markets and habitually entrust the Commission to take the lead in multilateral negotiations with strong economic powers such as the United States, Japan, and China, especially at the WTO (Devuyst 1995; Smith, M. 1998b). Economic convergence is not limited to top-down processes proceeding from the Commission. The successful national policies of other member states are often copied. British and Dutch successes in attracting Japanese FDI in the 1980s, and Germany's export success in China in the 1990s, are two examples of policies emulated by other (more protectionist) EU governments (Lehmann 1992; Nuttall 1996).

The Union's Human Rights policy throws up an even more complex picture of convergence and diversity. The EU has suffered from conflicting interests and coordination problems between the General Affairs Council (GAC), the member states, the Commission and the European Parliament (EP) on dealing with human rights situations from Chad to China. While the formal locus of effective decision-making on human rights issues is the Council—empowered by the Maastricht Treaty to ensure the 'unity, consistency and effectiveness of action by the Union'[2]—deliberations on human rights action in practice impinge on other policies across the three-pillar structure (affecting *inter alia* development assistance, Trade and Cooperation Agreements, enlargement, justice, and immigration), and thus involve a multiplicity of intra-EU actors, not to mention interactions with the US, UN, Council of Europe, human rights lobbies, etc (Clapham 1999; Smith, K. 1999, 2001).

Theories of rational-choice institutionalism admit that 'institutions make a significant difference in conjunction with power realities' (Keohane and Martin 1995, 42). States may however withdraw from multilateral cooperation if the benefits accruing from cooperation do not compensate the costs incurred. Such a conception will lead us to think that CFSP actions have continually to contend with intergovernmental bargaining, coordination and the constant threat of collapse as the costs to each member state are variable. But the nature of even CFSP, one of the most intergovernmental of EU institutions, has over the last 30 years moved a long way from its original anti-*communautaire* approach towards a *réflexe communautaire*. It is not just another rational-choice institution, but has become a critical sociological force and venue that shapes perceptions, structures policy choices, and privileges certain courses of national and collective action while constraining others.

Conclusions

The five major meanings of Europeanization are: a top-down process of national adaptation (School A), a bottom-up and sideways process of national projection (B), the multidirectional processes of socialisation (C) and modernisation (D), and policy isophormism (E). The five schools are not mutually exclusive but share many overlapping assumptions about causes, effects and processes. For example, the top-down school of national adaptation (School A) would accept that member states play critical roles in forging 'European' policies (School B) in the first place. The notion of Europeanization thus lacks paradigmatic consistency. Unlike major schools of integration theory such as neo-functionalism or intergovernmentalism, Europeanization does not put forward a series of inter-related premises concerning the dynamic or the end-state of the European integration process. Europeanization is a concept which can be criticised as lacking 'core tenets, common to all or most usages of the term, which might serve as the basis for constructing a common paradigmatically defined research agenda' (Harmsen and Wilson 2000; Olsen, J. 2002, 2003). The growing currency of Europeanization in recent years could be attributed to the concept's utility in two areas. First, it evokes parallel and interconnected processes of change at both the national and European levels. The concept recognises and captures more accurately than the paradigmatic theories the significant changes that are taking place at the national level, fostering at the same time convergence and diversification at various levels of European polities and societies. Second, the concept has a strong focus on the interrelationship of institutions and identities. It shows how institutional change and development may affect identities and interests, as well as how changing identities may create pressures for new institutional forms and modes of behaviour.

The wide range of usages of the term Europeanization in the literature touches on most aspects of political, societal, and economic change in Europe today and can be applied to foreign policy analysis. This chapter proposed that three of the five schools of the Europeanization concept, outlined in the literature survey, could be useful in explaining the changes taking place in foreign policy-making in an EU member state. Under the CFSP, 'Europeanization' can be understood as a process of foreign policy convergence. It is a dependent variable contingent on the ideas and directives emanating from actors (EU institutions, statesmen, etc) in Brussels, as well as policy ideas and actions from member state capitals (national statesmen). Europeanization is thus identifiable as a process of change manifested as policy convergence (both top-down and sideways) as well as national policies amplified as EU policy (bottom-up projection). Identity reconstruction (towards a 'European' identity) is a closely related effect observable over time.

For scholars such as Ladrech and Kassim, Europeanization is national adaptation to pressures arising from European integration. For Harmsen and Wilson, it is an effect on national institutions, identities, and citizenship. The primary usage of the Europeanization concept—that of capturing the top-down adaptation of national structures and processes in response to the demands of the EU—is of course critical in testing if national policy-making has indeed been affected by EU membership, and in what ways. Europeanization scholars may debate the institutional forms and distinctive national responses to EU pressures. Some may note that Europeanization as adaptation has actually increased divergence within the EU (Mazey and Richardson 1996). Over the longer term, however, a sustained period of structural and procedural adaptation would necessarily result in cross-national policy convergence between EU states. Convergence in policy style and content is expected as EU institutions prescribe roles and constrain activities. Coupled with the second and third processes of national projection and identity reconstruction, the overall picture expected is one of converging rather than diverging policy outputs, whatever the differences between national structures, preferences and policy inputs.

The second process, that of the projection of national ideas, preferences and models from the national to the supranational level, can be expected of states which command larger resources, strong domestic pressures or dogged commitment to change or forge a certain EU policy. National preferences are expected to be projected onto the European structure by the more powerful member states which seek to structure EU institutions and policies according to their interests. This was the case of CAP for France and industrial competition for Germany.

Third, Europeanization in its broadest sense of identity and interest convergence—so that 'European' interests and a European identity begin to take root—does not mean that the European will simply supplant the national over time. National identities and interests in Europe have evolved and grown over centuries and will not go away after just a few decades of European integration. However, European identity shapes and is increasingly incorporated into national identities.

We could measure the degree to which a state's foreign policy has been Europeanized over time according to three criteria:

a) *National adaptation/Policy convergence*

- Has convergence and/or adaptation of national policy with EU norms and directives taken place?

- Is convergence in substantive policy areas visible in the 'direct' Europeanization of public policy where regulatory competence has passed from national capitals to Brussels; or the 'indirect' Europeanization where member states learn from one another through transnational cooperation and policy transfer?

- Have national institutional structures and policy-making processes been adapted in response to European integration?

b) *Projection of national policy onto EU structures ('National projection')*

- Has the state pushed for its national foreign policy goals to be adopted as EU goals/policy?
- Has the state benefited from the 'cover' of the EU?
- How indispensable is the EU to the achievement of national foreign policy goals?

c) *Internalisation of 'Europe' in national identities ('Identity reconstruction')*

- Has there been a reshaping or hybridisation of identities which relativises national identities and privileges a European identity?
- What kinds of European norms have arisen among national officials and how do they apply to foreign policy?

As a top-down process, Europeanization is the process of policy convergence caused by participation over time in foreign policy-making at the European level. This produces shared norms and rules that are gradually accumulated (Sjursen 2001, 199–200; Øhrgaard 1997). As a bottom-up process, it is the projection of national preferences, ideas and policy models into Europe. A third aspect is the redefinition of national interests and identity in the context of 'Europe'. Europeanization is thus a bi-directional process that leads to a negotiated convergence in terms of policy goals, preferences and even identity between the national and the supranational levels (Smith, M.E. 2000).

When there is convergence between member states and EU institutions, this could result in a raising of the common interest, e.g. encouraging the development and consolidation of democracy and human rights abroad by trading and having full political/diplomatic relations with governments that respect minimum human rights standards. At other times, it is the lowest common denominator decision/preference that prevails and becomes EU policy. This could be the case in legitimising one member state's interests by raising EU protectionist barriers against other trading countries/groups of states.

If Europeanization is a dependent variable or effect, what is/are the independent variables driving the process? I would argue that we would have to cast the net for explanatory variables farther than the current Europeanization literature in Comparative Politics/Public Policy, and deeper into time for an answer. Europeanization is ultimately driven by European integration, which itself can be traced to the underlying political and economic imperatives for highly coordinated cooperation between member states that early integration theorists identified (Haas 1958).

Unlike intergovernmentalism, Europeanization theory acknowledges the important roles played by non-state actors and Europeanized élites in formulating national foreign policy. But contrary to integration theory, Europeanization theory does not foresee a supranational centre eclipsing the national capitals. The Europeanization process is just one—albeit a significant one—among many effects in the domestic politics, processes and foreign policies of EU member states. Furthermore, variables at the global, European, national, and sub-national levels interact in intricate ways, so that to claim pressures from European integration as the deterministic or dominant causal variable would be overstating the case.

The key proposition of Europeanization is that membership in the European Union has an important impact on each member state's foreign policy and that this impact is increasing in salience. States that join the European Union have to and do adapt to pressures for changes in their foreign policies—frequently even before formal membership. The overlapping and inter-related forces of Europeanization (policy convergence, national projection, and identity reconstruction) interact with often surprising results. The ensuing foreign policy of each member state is the end product of a complex series of negotiations between governments, EU institutions (Commission, Council and Parliament), officials, and member state representatives, as well as a process of policy learning and emulation between individual member states.

Notes

1 Here, I am using 'European-idealist' in the sense of believing in, arguing for and advocating a coherent and powerful European actor in international politics in place of a Europe of nation states.

2 The Maastricht Treaty states that one of the goals of CFSP is to 'develop and consolidate democracy and the rule of law and respect for human rights and fundamental freedoms' (Art. 11(1) of the consolidated Amsterdam Treaty, cited in Clapham 1999, 636).

Further reading

Some of the best literature surveys of the uses of the concept 'Europeanization' are found in Harmsen and Wilson (2000), Olsen (2002) and Olsen (2003). To better understand how Europeanization relates to earlier debates between neofunctional integrationists and intergovernmentalists, refer to extracts of two classic texts on European Integration and Intergovernmentalism: Haas (1958) and Hoffmann (1966) in Nelsen and Stubb (2004), Chapters 16 and 18 respectively. For assessments of the impact of EU integration on the domestic politics and policies of member states, see Goetz and Hix (2001), which contains a very good introduction and a number of papers on Europeanization (also published as a special issue in *West European Politics*, 24/3, 2000). Similar

is Mény, Muller and Quermonne (1996). Also see Hanf and Soetendorp (1998), which discusses the impact on smaller member states. The best books dealing with the European Union's impact on member states' foreign policies (and vice versa) include Hill (1996), Manners and Whitman (2000), Tonra (2001) and White (2001).

Goetz, K., and Hix, S. (eds) (2001), *Europeanised Politics? European Integration and National Political Systems* (London: Frank Cass).

Hanf, K., and Soetendorp, B. (eds) (1998), *Adapting to European Integration* (London: Longman).

Harmsen, R., and Wilson, T. (eds) (2000), *Europeanization: Institutions, Identities and Citizenship* (Amsterdam: Rodopi).

Hill, C. (ed.) (1996), *The Actors in Europe's Foreign Policy* (London: Routledge).

Manners, I., and Whitman, R. (eds) (2000), *The Foreign Policies of European Union Member States* (Manchester: Manchester University Press).

Mény, Y., Muller, P., and Quermonne, J.-L. (eds) (1996), *Adjusting to Europe: The Impact of the European Union on National Institutions and Policies* (London: Routledge).

Nelsen, B., and Stubb, A. (eds) (2004), *The European Union: Readings on the Theory and Practice of European Integration*, 3rd edition (Boulder: Lynne Rienner).

Olsen, J.P. (2002), 'The Many Faces of Europeanization', *Journal of Common Market Studies* 40/5, 921–52.

Olsen, J.P. (2003), 'Europeanization', in Cini, M. (ed.), *European Union Politics* (Oxford: Oxford University Press).

Tonra, B. (2001), *The Europeanization of National Foreign Policy: Dutch, Danish and Irish Foreign Policy in the European Union* (Aldershot: Ashgate).

White, B. (2001), *Understanding European Foreign Policy* (Basingstoke: Palgrave).

Web links

Conferences on the 'Europeanization of national foreign policies' (2002) and 'European Foreign Policy' (2004) yielded many useful research papers, available on the European Foreign Policy Unit (EFPU) web site of the London School of Economics and Political Science. http://www.lse.ac.uk/Depts/intrel/EuroFPUnit.html. The web site of Advanced Research on the Europeanization of the Nation State (ARENA) at the University of Oslo includes relevant papers on Europeanization: www.arena.uio.no. See also the materials and links at http://www.fornet.info/, the Fornet web site.

Chapter 8

Implementation: Making the EU's International Relations Work

Michael E. Smith

Contents

Summary

The EU has developed a wide variety of policy instruments to translate its common interests into collective action in the international system. It also possesses its own financial resources to help fund those policy instruments, an important attribute not found in any other regional organisation. While there is wide variation across different types of policy instruments in terms of their sophistication and external influence, the EU now enjoys a capability for global action—including military operations—that was nearly unthinkable just a few years ago. However, this unique capacity for policy implementation is still quite dynamic, and with every policy decision the EU must constantly balance the competing incentives for cooperation among its member states with their inherent desire to act unilaterally in world affairs.

Introduction: the problem of implementation in foreign policy

Foreign policy, which includes security and defence policy for the purposes of this chapter, involves a unique array of problems that set it apart from most domestic-oriented policy domains, such as social welfare policy. This is true whether speaking of national foreign policy-making or foreign policy cooperation among nation states. Most importantly, the stakes are perceived to be much higher in the realm of foreign policy, up to and including the very survival of the state itself. Compared to domestic policy, foreign policy is not easily regulated through the use of forward-looking legislative instruments owing to the limited availability of information about global affairs and the need to preserve flexibility in the face of changing circumstances. This often results in the delegation of wide-ranging authority to executive bodies and may make it difficult for opposition parties or other actors to criticise certain decisions (Pollack 1997). Foreign policy also involves a large mix of policy tools and institutional procedures that can undermine the coherent behaviour of any global actor, whether a state or a regional institution like the EU. Similarly, it is often very difficult to assess and distribute the gains, if any, from foreign policy actions. All of these problems in turn also present challenges to the democratic oversight of foreign policy, where the watchdog role of legislators and the media is often undermined by the strict controls on information maintained by foreign policy-makers.

The EU's persistent attempts to manage these kinds of problems in the hopes of transforming itself into a global actor represent a unique experiment in world politics. However, if we conceive of the EU as a regional sub-system of international relations, there are strong reasons to expect such cooperation. The Western European states which founded the EU in the 1950s share powerful historical memories, cultural values and norms, and even a vision, however shadowy, of a common destiny (Haas 1958). The EU's position, geographic and ideological, between a (relatively) 'benevolent hegemon' to the West and potential threats to the East and South help contribute to a base of common interests to promote joint action. A rejection of balance-of-power politics in Western Europe since 1945, and the promotion of reconciliation among former enemies, also represent a fundamental break with previous patterns of interaction in this region (Deutsch et al. 1958). Finally, high levels of social, economic, and political interdependence also contribute to the idea that common European problems can be solved effectively only through common European policies.

Yet this pool of common values and interests is embedded within a larger system of international relations subject to its own dynamics of action. Fundamentally, the EU is still a system of sovereign states bound in a treaty-based regional institution. Although EU member states may have delegated certain aspects of their foreign policies to the EU, they still reserve the right to act unilaterally in foreign policy and they often do so. A demand for action based on common interests alone does not automatically lead to the supply of collective action in world politics (Keohane 1983). In many cases, EU states still must be convinced of the need to act together, even when common interests seem self-evident. This propensity to cooperate can also vary between economic issues (such as trade or aid), 'soft' political issues (such as human rights and civilian security), and 'hard' political issues (such as military defence). Cooperation in economic affairs represents a clear goal—such as the elimination of trade barriers—that can be explicitly measured according to agreed timetables. Many economic issues also involve a fairly high degree of consensual knowledge about the effects of economic conditions on national welfare, such as the relationship between inflation and economic activity. A common foreign policy, however, does not share these characteristics; it can mean only a constant process of policy coordination on a case-by-case basis. This often involves the creation of entirely new mutual standards, sometimes at the expense of existing national foreign policy positions.

Even when states may agree on general common goals, such as the promotion of human rights or democracy, they may fundamentally disagree on the specific tactics or means to achieve those goals. This is especially true among the larger EU member states, particularly the UK and France, and in areas where EU states claim a 'special relationship' or unique national interest (such as relations with former colonies). Although the EU has gradually managed to diminish the influence of many of these '*domaines réservés*' in its conduct of external relations, EU member states are not likely to delegate most aspects of their foreign policies to the EU. Moreover, coordination among all foreign policy missions, once chosen, must be decided and managed. Cooperation must be organised and, often, paid for. If it is to be sustained and monitored in any coherent fashion, it must also be institutionalised. This results in a constant process of negotiation for every policy decision taken by the EU, even in fields like trade policy where EU organisations (chiefly the Commission) possess a fairly high degree of negotiation authority. And in cases where the details of policy implementation are left to EU member states, compliance may become an issue since those states vary widely in their ability to uphold common policy decisions in a timely and efficient manner. As outright opposition to commonly agreed foreign policies is actually quite rare in the EU, compliance is more frequently undermined by commonplace domestic political issues such as election campaigns, parliamentary rules, budgetary limits, party competition, and bureaucratic disputes (Smith, M.E. 2004).

Even so, the EU still manages to act coherently in world politics through the use of various policy instruments. Although most EU policies involve some external component, directly or indirectly, the objective in this chapter is to explore how the EU executes its key foreign policy decisions, or cooperates in various areas of foreign policy, through the use of common resources and policy tools. Before turning to this question in detail, we should note several other general features of the EU's ability to implement common policies. First and most obviously, this ability varies widely across policy tools, ranging from diplomatic to economic to military instruments. Each of these instruments, with representative examples, will be explored below. Second, the EU's capacity for action has not developed according to a grand institutional blueprint, although all policy sectors have become more institutionalised since the Treaty of Rome in 1957 (Stone Sweet and Sandholtz 1998). Instead, processes of trial-by-error learning and crisis-induced decision-making have strongly influenced EU action in world politics. The EU's institutional arrangements

Table 8.1 The EU's Pillars and external policy instruments[1]

	Diplomatic tools	Economic tools	Military tools
I. European Community	Yes	Yes, including a very large budget	No
II. Common Foreign and Security Policy	Yes	Yes, including a limited budget	Yes (through the ESDP/RRF)
III. Justice and Home Affairs	Yes	Yes, including a limited budget	Limited to police/customs cooperation

for external action clearly reflect this fact, as all three Pillars of decision-making (EC, CFSP/ESDP, and JHA) involve overlapping competencies in many areas of foreign policy (see Table 8.1).

This leads to our third general point: the EU's repertoire of policy tools cannot be understood fully by examining treaty articles and formal institutional arrangements alone; the EU has managed in many cases to do more than we might otherwise expect by a reading of EU treaty documents. This often involves creative 'cross-pillar' policy coordination, moving funds across different budgetary lines, arranging national contributions to common policies on a case-by-case basis, and even the creation of new informal rules to handle situations where a breakdown occurs between deciding a policy and actually implementing it (i.e., the 'slippage problem'). While instances of deliberate national defection are fairly rare in the EU, other cases of involuntary defection do occur (most often due to domestic political procedures) and can interfere with effective implementation. Fourth and finally, all of these dynamics must be understood in light of the changing domestic politics of EU member states, whose foreign policy machinery and national political processes both contribute to and complicate the EU's own efforts in world politics. These processes include not only governmental decision-making inputs at the EU level, but even domestic ratification processes in certain areas of EU policy not subject to supranational procedures. While these complex dynamics make it difficult to measure the EU's true capacities as a global actor, they also make the EU a fascinating laboratory for exploring the dynamics between comparative domestic politics, European integration, and international relations, the primary theme of this volume.

The EU's own resources in external relations/third countries

Why is the EU such a unique actor in world politics? One of its most important attributes involves a capacity to finance its own policy decisions. In fact, the EU possesses a larger pool of independent legal/institutional, technical, and financial resources than any other regional organisation on the planet. This capacity, known as the EU's 'own resources', has gradually expanded over a period of four decades. Under the 1957 Treaty of Rome, national contributions at first provided the bulk of financial re-sources to the emerging European Community (EC), but with a view to giving the EC its own budgetary resources. Article 201 was a key provision of this Treaty; it stated that: 'Without prejudice to other revenue, the budget shall be financed wholly from own resources.' Such resources are understood to be a source of operational funds separate and independent of EU member states, such as tax revenue assigned to the EC to fund its budget without the need for any subsequent decision by the national authorities. EU member states would be required to make these payments available to the EC for its operational budget.

This process took longer than expected to achieve as some EU states (particularly France) adamantly resisted the requirements of the Treaty. It was not until the Hague summit in 1969 that EU member states, in the face of the first-ever EU enlargement, finally took the decision to fully implement Article 201. This inaugurated a system of independent financing based on 'traditional' own resources (customs duties and agri-cultural levies) and an additional resource based on the value-added tax (VAT) applied across EU member states. These two traditional own resources are considered the 'natural' own resources of the EU, since they are revenue collected by virtue of Com-munity policies rather than revenue obtained from the member states as national contributions. However, these traditional resources were not enough to balance the EU's budget, so a new source of revenue, VAT own resources, came into use in 1980. In 1988 the Council decided to add a fourth own resource, based on a GNP scale, which was meant to replace the VAT as the resource for balancing the EU's budget. All of these instruments were consolidated into a new own resources system follow-ing a report by the Commission in 1998. Inaugurated in 2002, this new system set a cap of own resources at 1.27% of the EU's GNP and reduced dependence on the VAT as a source of revenue. It also provided that no new own resource would be introduced, although this question will be revisited in light of the EU's recent enlargement. And although the EU endured some difficulties in managing the budgetary procedures of its CFSP and JHA pillars in the 1990s (Monar 1997a), today there is more effective co-ordination between the EU organisations and member state financing procedures in most areas of external relations.

To summarise, the EU at present controls a total budget of about €100 billion a year, making it one of the most powerful (in financial terms) international or-ganisations in the world. In comparison, the budget of the United Nations is about $2.5 billion a year, plus another $2 billion a year for peacekeeping operations. Moreover, the main source of UN funds is the contributions of its member states; it does not possess its own resources. However, although only a portion of the EU's large budget is explicitly devoted to external policies (see below), the EU's ability to finance its projects, and the ability of the Commission and Parliament to help im-plement the budget, give the EU a source of influence far beyond any other regional economic organisation. Now that financing for the EU is relatively secure, the more recent challenge for the EU has been to find a way to marshal its financial and other resources in service of common foreign policy goals.

National resources and EU external relations

Beyond its own budgetary authority based on the revenue sources noted above, the EU is also able to draw upon the experience and resources of its individual member states. Bilateral and multilateral special relationships based on colonial or cultural connections are still important for EU states, especially the large ones (the British Commonwealth; France's International Organisation of the Francophonie). Britain and France also enjoy unique responsibilities as permanent members of the UN Security Council, while other EU member states rely on close interest-based ties by virtue of their geographic locations (the Nordic countries, the Mediterranean countries, etc). These relationships will not disappear with the pursuit of the EU's global ambitions and they have the capacity to both frustrate and inspire action at the EU level (Hill 1996; Manners and Whitman 2000). For example, Britain's special relationship with the US certainly complicated the EU's search for a common policy on Iraq, while Sweden and Finland successfully pressed for a new 'Northern dimension' to EU foreign policy after their accession to the EU in 1995.

However, EU member states still must pursue these relationships in the context of EU norms and structures, which make them an indirect source of power for the EU in three ways. First, EU norms require its member states to consult on all major questions of foreign policy before forming their own policies. All EU member states recognise, though to varying degrees, that they will have more impact on world affairs if they act in common, and the EU foreign policy system attempts to reinforce this understanding by ensuring regular communications on all major subjects of foreign policy. This 'consultation reflex', which is highly institutionalised in the EU, often promotes the creation of common foreign policy positions and even joint actions. Such collective diplomacy, or the EU's *communauté de vue* on important foreign policy questions (de Schoutheete de Tervarent 1980), draws upon a large reservoir of policy goals and actions that must be taken into consideration by all EU member states. In fact, wholly unilateral foreign policy actions taken without consultation are disdained by other EU states and usually do not gain much internal support. As former British foreign minister Douglas Hurd once noted (1981, 389): 'Perhaps one reason why these unilateral efforts now usually come to nothing is precisely that they are unilateral.'

Second, the EU has produced additional rules for areas where national and EU competencies overlap. These are especially prominent in cases of economic policy, where the notion of 'mixed agreements' was developed to find a way to combine the competencies of the Commission and those of EU member states in areas not governed by the EU treaties. For example, all of the 'Europe agreements' negotiated with the Central and Eastern European countries in the 1980s were mixed agreements, as they involved both economic aspects (governed by the Commission) and political aspects (governed by EU member states and the Commission). Thanks to this type of arrangement, the EU can always draw upon the formidable diplomatic and intelligence resources of all of its member states and the Commission, even where formal treaty authority for implementing collective action is lacking or incomplete. Such agreements may also include a financial component contributed by EU member states, depending on the question at hand. The EU's administration of the Balkan city of Mostar, for example, relied on special contributions by EU member states calculated according to a GNP scale. Yet the complicated logistics of organising such contributions (a key example of slippage between policy-making and policy implementation) ultimately resulted in greater use of the EU budget, as a normal rule, for such mixed agreement policies. As EU member states themselves delegate more economic policies to the EC, such as trade in services and trade-related aspects of intellectual property rights, then European foreign policy actions will have to rely on EU budgetary resources even more.

Third, the EU's most recent ambitions to field an independent military force are promoting new experiments in permitting states to contribute to operations on a case-by-case basis. The commitments from 30 European states inside and outside the EU amounted to about 100,000 ground troops, 400 aircraft, and 100 ships in line with the so-called 'headline goals' agreed at a Commitment Conference on 20 November 2000 (see Table 8.2). All six European NATO members outside the EU at the time (Czech Republic, Hungary, Iceland, Norway, Poland, and Turkey) also showed a willingness to contribute to the force (Salmon and Shepherd 2003).

Note that these force commitments do not involve the raising of new troops; they are existing forces already committed to national and/or NATO operation plans. They are now 'separable' from NATO for the ESDP on a temporary basis but are not quite 'separate' from the alliance. In addition, although the recent Nice Treaty failed to provide details about greater European arms cooperation and more defence spending to support the ESDP, EU member states have worked to consolidate their arms industries and engage in numerous joint procurement projects. Several EU states even managed to create the European Aeronautic, Space, and Defence Company (EADS) in mid-2000; this was followed in July 2000 by a 'framework agreement' between Britain, France, Germany, Italy, Spain, and Sweden intended to ease export controls and other restrictions to promote cross-border mergers and joint ventures among European defence firms. And the new European constitution has more details regarding the creation of a European Armaments, Research and Military Capabilities Agency. Although these efforts are more modest in comparison to NATO's resources (much of which are supplied by the US), they do represent a considerable expansion of the EU's policy toolkit compared to the situation just a few years ago, when the idea of an independent EU military force was unthinkable for some of its member states.

The instruments of EU foreign policy

With the addition of the ESDP, the European Union today possesses many of the major foreign policy instruments of a state. In fact, the EU's main problem in foreign policy implementation is not so much the lack of effective instruments, but in the

Table 8.2 Projected national commitments to ESDP forces by selected EU members

	Ground forces	Naval forces	Air forces
Austria	2,000 troops		1 transport helicopter squadron
Belgium	1,000 troops	9 vessels	1 squadron F-16s (24) 8 C-1302 Airbus
Denmark	Opted out of EU defence cooperation		
Finland	2,000	1 mine-sweeper	
France	12,000 troops	12 vessels (inc. 1 submarine and 2 aircraft carriers)	1 air naval group 75 combat aircraft 1 AWACS 8 tankers, 27 transports
Germany	18,000 troops	14 vessels	6 combat squadrons 8 air defence squadrons
Greece	4,000 troops		1 combat helicopter unit 1 transport helicopter unit 42 combat aircraft 4 transports, 2 air defence units
Ireland	850 troops		
Italy	12,000 troops	19 vessels (inc. 1 submarine and 1 aircraft carrier)	26 Tornado and AMX combat aircraft 6 combat search and rescue helicopters 4 C-130J aircraft 2 tankers, 3 multipurpose, 2 air defence
Luxembourg	100 troops		1 A-400M (future)
Netherlands	5,000 troops	3 vessels	1-2 F-16 squadrons 1 Patriot missile battery
Portugal	4,000 troops	5 vessels (inc. 1 submarine)	12 F-16 aircraft 4 C-130 Hercules 4 Puma helicopters 12 transports, 3 multipurpose
Spain	6,000 troops		Air-navy unit 2 F-1/F-18 squadrons 1 transport squadron
Sweden	1,500 troops 1 MP company	3 vessels	12 aircraft
United Kingdom	12,500 troops	8 vessels (inc. 2 submarines and 1 aircraft carrier)	72 combat aircraft 58 transports and helicopters

Source: The Center for Defense Information, *Military Reform Project* (Washington: 23 May 2002); and Gustav Lindstrom, *The Headline Goal* (Paris: European Union Institute for Security Studies, July 2004).

Note: these figures are subject to change.

difficulties involved in finding the will to use those instruments in a strategic, coherent fashion. Part of this problem is political: finding a consensus among 25 EU member states can be difficult, especially in areas involving security or defence. Another part of the problem is institutional: the effective implementation of EU foreign policy often requires decision-making across two or more EU pillars, which invites turf battles or other disputes among EU member states and between EU states and EU organisations, such as the Commission and Parliament. Economic sanctions are especially problematic, as they require decision-making in both the first (EC) and second (CFSP) pillars. Yet the EU's ability to find a consensus on any question of foreign policy is a testament to the effectiveness of its institutionalised policy mechanisms in facilitating international cooperation. These instruments of policy coordination can be grouped under three general headings: diplomacy, economic tools, and military tools.

Diplomatic capability

The question of diplomatic capability can be examined in terms of who speaks for the EU, on what subjects, and with what authority and resources. Finding specific answers to these questions has taken much time and energy in the EU, and this capability is still in development. Yet there is little doubt that the EU is perfectly able, though not always willing, to speak with a single voice on an expanding array of subjects relevant to international politics.

General diplomacy

The 1957 Treaty of Rome did not provide for common diplomacy on foreign policy problems, although it did include a minor provision for consultation on foreign policy issues, such as war, that might impact the functioning of the EC. At the time, EU member states were preoccupied with a debate over whether to include a defence component to European integration. This idea was eventually abandoned in favour of a weak intergovernmental system, European Political Cooperation (EPC). EPC was created in 1970 to facilitate discussion and, if possible, joint action, in matters of foreign policy (Nuttall 1992). Its functioning, which included agenda-setting and diplomacy, was dominated by the EU member state holding the six-month rotating EU presidency. Later provisions under EPC allowed for a system of joint representation (the 'Troika') involving the immediate past, current, and immediate following holders of the EU presidency. By the 1980s, the Commission was a full participant in EPC and could help implement EPC's two main policy tools, declarations and *démarches*. Declarations merely express the EU's opinion on an issue, while *démarches* are formal presentations of the EU's position on an issue made to representatives of third states and international organisations. This is done in hopes of encouraging a corresponding change in the behaviour of those third states or organisations. EU ambassadors to non-EU states make dozens if not hundreds of such *démarches* every year, on an increasingly wide range of subjects. The number of EPC declarations made each year has expanded as well since the creation of EPC, ranging from only a few in 1975 to well over 100 by the late 1990s. A final general point is that the EU has the capacity to impose diplomatic sanctions, such as recalling its diplomats or preventing officials from third countries from travelling to the EU. Such sanctions often require the coordination of all three EU pillars, although a new title in the 1997 Amsterdam Treaty mandated that policy on border controls, immigration, asylum, visas, and judicial cooperation in general (all originally handled through the JHA pillar) would gradually become subject to EC rules and procedures. Although the impact of such diplomatic sanctions on outsiders is likely very minimal, they do provide a low-cost way for the EU to signal displeasure in cases where more robust measures cannot be agreed.

While the original EPC framework did not specify any topics for discussion, EPC participants in member states (and eventually in the Commission) gradually defined a number of areas suitable for diplomatic cooperation. Major examples include the Arab-Israeli conflict (through the Euro-Arab Dialogue) and relations with the Soviet bloc through what became the Organisation for Security and Cooperation in Europe (OSCE). EPC also helped the Community enhance its reputation as a defender of human rights by facilitating its collective condemnation of South Africa's system of *apartheid*. By the time of the Maastricht Treaty on European Union, EPC was replaced by the CFSP and two new policy instruments were institutionalised in addition to the declarations and *démarches*: CFSP common positions and joint actions. In principle, common positions were to be implemented through the use of coordinated national action and joint actions were to be implemented through the use of EC instruments, such as aid and sanctions (see below). In practice, however, this distinction was lost as it became more effective to rely on EC procedures and resources rather than coordinate the diplomatic activities of 15 EU states. The record of common positions and joint actions in fact shows a great deal of similar activity in key areas, such as ex-Yugoslavia; various African states; Central/Eastern Europe (including Russia and Ukraine); and the Middle East. One important example of a successful joint action involved the large network of agreements under the single heading of a 'Stability Pact' to stabilise borders in Central and Eastern Europe. Several positions and actions involved general security issues as well (see below).

Since the Amsterdam Treaty of 1997, the EU has bolstered its general diplomatic capability in three ways. First, the distinction between CFSP common positions and joint actions has been overshadowed by much greater use of first pillar (EC) resources and policy tools. Second, Amsterdam provided for the creation of common strategies to help provide greater coherence to the EU's major external policies, especially where the instruments cross EU pillars. The first such strategy, for Russia, was agreed in 1999 and others have followed for Ukraine and the Mediterranean region. Third, the Treaty created the position of 'High Representative for the CFSP' to help give the EU/CFSP a single voice. Former NATO Secretary General Javier Solana of Spain was appointed to this position in 1999 and he clearly has raised the public profile of the EU's diplomatic activity. His most prominent action perhaps was the joint diplomacy with George Robertson, Secretary-General of NATO, in working to prevent civil war in Macedonia in 2001. This action ultimately led to the EU's first-ever military mission (see below). However, the EU still relies on a re-constituted Troika mechanism in many areas of diplomacy; the Troika now usually comprises Solana, the foreign minister of the state holding the EU presidency, and the European Commissioner for External Affairs. The EU also appoints special representatives for areas of important interest, such as the Great Lakes region of Africa, the Middle East, Central/Eastern Europe, the Former Yugoslav Republic of Macedonia, Ethiopia/Eritrea, and Afghanistan.

A final point on the general diplomatic activity of the EU, which largely involves the CFSP, is that the CFSP budget is fairly small relative to spending in other areas of external relations: about ε 63 million for 2004 for the CFSP by itself. However, many of the decisions taken in the context of the CFSP, particularly during its early years, have instead been funded through other EU budgetary resources, such as those for development cooperation, human rights, and even agriculture. This trend has continued and it is therefore quite incorrect to rely on the CFSP budget alone to judge the EU's overall diplomatic resources and activities.

Cultural diplomacy

Among other foreign policy innovations, the 1991 Maastricht Treaty created a new EC competency for culture in order to both respect the cultural diversity among EU states and promote cross-cultural projects among them. Although most of this activity is inward-directed, the cultural competency does include an external relations component. Indirectly, culture-related actors are encouraged to participate in every EU contract competition that involves external relations. Participants have included Southeast Europe; countries of the former Soviet Union; countries of the Mediterranean, South America, and Asia; the African/Caribbean/Pacific (ACP) countries, Canada, Mongolia, and the United States. The EU also participates fully in the cultural activities of the UN Educational, Scientific, and Cultural Organization (UN-ESCO) and the Council of Europe.

The most prominent policy tool directly involving European cultures is the Culture 2000 programme, which was established for five years (2000–2004) with a total budget of ε 167 million. Unlike previous EU cultural projects, Culture 2000 provides grants to cultural cooperation projects in all artistic and cultural fields. Among other things, a key objective of Culture 2000 is to promote the dissemination of art and culture, intercultural dialogue, and knowledge of the history of the European peoples. It also accords culture a social integration and socio-economic development role. The Commission implements the programme with the advice of the opinions of a panel of independent experts. So far, participants from 30 European countries have taken part in the Culture 2000 programme. Activities supported by this programme, such as festivals, exhibitions, and tours, are intended for artists and cultural operators as well as for a broader audience, in particular young people and those who are socially or economically disadvantaged. Of course, just as with foreign policy in general, many EU states retain their own influential mechanisms for promoting their own cultures abroad. Yet here again the EU is a very unique regional actor in light of its legally-based authority to promote cultural cooperation as part of its broader efforts in global diplomacy.

Economic capability

Although the EU's diplomatic capability has expanded considerably since the creation of EPC, its real strength lies in the economic tools found primarily in the first pillar: the EC. Through the development of this policy domain, and its formal links to other EU pillars, the EU has managed to evolve from a relatively inward-focused regional economic organisation to a more outward-focused global political actor. Although the EU is still sometimes accused of being an 'economic giant' but a 'political dwarf', its foreign policy capabilities range far beyond what might be expected of an organisation primarily devoted to regional economic integration. In the economic realm, this capability involves both 'carrots' and 'sticks', or positive and negative policy tools.

Before examining these tools individually, an overview of all EU spending in external relations might be useful. According to official EU sources, the EU's external relations budget seeks to support the objectives of the EU external policy by means of development aid, conflict prevention, human rights programmes, and the CFSP. As Table 8.3 reveals, total EU spending on its major external relations programmes (not including pre-accession aid, trade, or relations with the ACP countries) amounts to just over Ɛ 5 billion a year.

Development aid

The EU's first and perhaps most prominent economic carrot for foreign policy involves its devotion to development aid, particularly among former colonies of EU member states. Africa was the recipient of its first such aid programme, beginning in 1963 in the form of the Yaoundé Convention between the EC and 18 African states. This programme was replaced in 1975 by the Lomé Convention, which also expanded the programme to a total of 46 ACP states. Today Lomé (now known as the Cotonou Agreement since June 2000) covers 71 ACP states, making it the largest coherent aid programme for non-members of the EU. It is funded directly by EU states by national contributions to a 'European Development Fund' (EDF) and a 'European Investment Bank' (EIB) and is not part of the EU budget, so the figures in Table 8.3 do not fully reflect the EU's resources in this area. The most recent financial commitments amount to about Ɛ 15 billion in EDF grants and EIB loans for developing countries. The overall goal for development aid is to reduce and eventually eradicate poverty by supporting sustainable economic, social, and environmental development in all developing countries and regions in a consistent manner. This programme includes their gradual integration into the world economy.

As Figure 8.1 shows, spending by the EU (including the Community budget and the 15 EU member states prior to the 2004 enlargement) represents over half of all official development assistance (ODA) by 22 of the world's most developed countries, as measured by the Organization for Economic Cooperation and Development (OECD).

As we can see, US ODA spending pales in comparison to what the EU provides, and America's aid as a percentage of gross national income (GNI) is the lowest of all DAC countries. Individually, four of the 15 EU member states even manage to meet or exceed the UN target of providing 0.70% of their GNI in development assistance: Denmark, Luxembourg, the Netherlands, and Sweden. In addition, much US foreign aid requires the purchase of American goods or services (such as surplus grain), which may be more costly than local supplies.

In terms of aid recipients, Community ODA is spread across a number of regions, as shown in Figure 8.2.

Although these commitments are admirable as a potential source of 'normative power' for the EU (Manners 2002), it must be noted that implementation problems

Table 8.3 The EU's external relations budget (rounded up to the nearest million euros)[2]

ACTIVITY	2003 budget	2004 budget	Change from 2003–2004
Food aid and support operations	426	419	−1.6%
Humanitarian aid	442	490	10.9%
Cooperation with Asian developing countries	563	616	9.4%
Cooperation with Latin American developing countries	337	312	−7.4%
Cooperation with the countries of Southern Africa	127	134	5.5%
Cooperation with Mediterranean countries and the Middle East	754	842	11.7%
Assistance to partner countries in Eastern Europe and Central Asia	507	535	5.5%
Cooperation with countries of the Western Balkans	685	675	−1.5%
Other cooperation measures	505	519	2.8%
European initiative for democracy and human rights	106	126	18.9%
International fisheries agreements	193	194	0.5%
External aspects of certain EC policies	86	91	5.8%
Common Foreign and Security Policy	48	63	31.3%
TOTAL	€ 4.772 billion	€ 5.016 billion	5.1%

Source: European Commission, *General Budget of the European Union* (Luxembourg: Office for Official Publications of the European Communities, 2004).

Figure 8.1 Official Development Assistance: OECD Development Assistance Committee (DAC) members (current USD equivalent)

	$ millions	as % of GNI
Australia	989	0.26
Canada	2,006	0.28
Japan	9,283	0.23
New Zealand	122	0.22
Norway	1,696	0.89
Switzerland	939	0.32
United States	13,290	0.13
(15) EU member states	29,949	0.35
EC budget	6,561	
TOTAL	**64,835**	

Source: OECD figures for DAC countries, 2002.

Figure 8.2 Regional distribution of Community aid, $ millions

1. Sub-Saharan Africa	2,028
2. Europe	1,413
3. Middle East/North Africa	635
4. Latin America/Caribbean	552
5. South/Central Asia	419
6. Other Asia/Oceania	323

Source: OECD 'Aid at a Glance' charts for DAC countries, 2002.

frequently delay or even prevent the delivery of aid. Domestic political situations within EU member states and within target countries often complicate the disbursement of funds, especially when national EU budgets are strained. To be fair, however, this problem is not unique to the EU; the entire system of aid delivery from the North to the South, through the OECD, the G-7/8, and the UN system itself, can be criticised for lacking sensitivity to the problems of developing countries. Yet the EU does consciously attempt to improve its aid delivery through the use of institutionalised frameworks such as Cotonou (Holland 2002).

Humanitarian aid

The EU also spends about ε 400 million a year on general humanitarian aid, primarily through the European Community Humanitarian Office (ECHO) within the Commission. This amount of financing makes the EU the world's largest donor of such aid. ECHO is especially concerned with handling 'forgotten crises' neglected by other donors, as well as unstable post-crisis situations where other donors may be reluctant to get involved. Key examples include aid for crisis-management in the Great Lakes region of Africa and in Afghanistan following the US-led war on that country in 2001. In fact, the EU was the largest reconstruction and humanitarian aid donor to Afghanistan, spending about Ɛ 800 million in the year after the war and committing a further Ɛ 1.9 billion for 2002–2006 at the January 2002 donor conference in Tokyo. This represents nearly half (44 per cent) of all aid pledges to that country. And, like most other EU foreign policy tools, ECHO spending is also intended to mesh with the EU's broader normative or political goals, such as democracy and human rights.

Trade policy

Finally, a note about trade policy, which is covered in more detail elsewhere in this volume. Although most efforts here involve breaking down internal barriers to trade and coordinating a common external tariff toward non-member states, the EU also manages to incorporate free trade pacts into many of its most important external relationships. Today the EU, largely through the Commission, increasingly tends to structure its most important foreign policies into broad dialogues or framework agreements, which involve economic, political, and even security dimensions. These cooperation agreements are made with regions (such as the 'Europe Agreements' with Central/Eastern Europe and the 'Euro-Arab Dialogue' in the Middle East) or individual countries (such as South Africa, Russia, Mexico, and the 'New Transatlantic Agenda' with the US) (see, for example, Allen 1978; Holland 1995; Smith, H. 1995; Smith, K. 1999). Trade agreements often form the centrepiece of these dialogues, and this incentive encourages non-EU states to accept other political goals important to Europe, particularly democracy, respect for the rule of law, and human rights (Szymanski and Smith 2005). These arrangements also enable the EU to promote regional integration in other key areas of the world, such as the Middle East, Latin America, and Asia. This capacity to 'package' all EU external policies toward an important outside actor into single comprehensive deals may be far more important for the EU's global power than the implementation of any single policy area alone, although the EU has yet to fully exploit this capability.

In addition, each of these positive measures (financial aid or favourable trade agreements) involves a negative component as well: the EU's ability to stop aid or suspend trade negotiations (at a minimum), or impose diplomatic or economic sanctions, including weapons embargoes, on third parties (at a maximum). The EU's willingness to use this negative power developed gradually; during the first two decades after the Treaty of Rome, economic sanctions were imposed in only two cases: against Rhodesia (1965) and Greece (1967). Following the creation of EPC in 1970, the EU began to impose various sanctions and/or suspend trade negotiations against a number of other countries: Iran, the Soviet Union, Argentina, Poland, Libya, South Africa, Yugoslavia, Iraq, and even one of its own members (Austria). In May 1995 the EU decided to institutionalise the principle of political conditionality with a standard clause incorporated as Article 1 of every framework agreement signed by the EU; it is thus compulsory. Such agreements can be suspended if either side violates this clause, which reads in part: 'Respect for democratic principles and fundamental human rights, as proclaimed by the Universal Declaration of Human Rights, underpins the domestic and external policies of both Parties and constitutes an essential element of this Agreement.' In its relationships with other countries, the imposition of sanctions by the EU involves close coordination between all three EU pillars, usually following an initial decision by the CFSP pillar. The greatly expanded use of sanctions since the 1970s clearly demonstrates the EU's ability to use its formidable economic power for political ends.

Military capability

The question of whether the EU requires its own military force is one of the longest-running, and most divisive, debates in the history of European integration. An initial attempt for a defence capability, the European Defence Community (EDC), failed in 1954, as did subsequent efforts to revive such a plan in the 1960s. Until the Maastricht Treaty, most of Europe's defence capability was coordinated in NATO and, to a much lesser extent, the Western European Union (WEU) and various loose arrangements among smaller groups of EU states (such as the 'Eurocorps'). Following the revolutions in Eastern Europe, the Persian Gulf War, and the disintegration of Yugoslavia, the negotiators of the Maastricht Treaty made the first successful attempt to mention the possibility of a defence capability (through a weak link to the WEU) in the EU. This decision did not lead to any concrete EU-WEU policies through the 1990s, although the WEU did participate in the EU's administration of Mostar. In addition, a number of CFSP decisions did touch upon security matters, including both common positions (on blinding laser weapons; biological and toxic weapons; the creation of an emergency travel document for EU nationals; and plans for the rescue of EU diplomatic missions) and joint actions (renewal of the Nuclear Non-Proliferation Treaty; action against anti-personnel landmines; the Korean Peninsula Energy Development Organization; and controls on dual-use technology).

Following the 1997 Amsterdam Treaty, which mentioned the possibility of a European Security and Defence Policy (ESDP), the successful NATO attack on Kosovo, which was largely dominated by American forces, prompted another intra-European debate about the necessity for a military capability independent of NATO. Even before the military action in Kosovo, in 1998 the 'St. Malo agreement' between the UK and France paved the way for concrete plans for the ESDP and a merger between the EU and the WEU, long a point of contention for the EU's neutral states (Austria, Ireland, and Sweden). A major focus of the ESDP would be the so-called 'Petersberg tasks': humanitarian and rescue missions, peacekeeping, and crisis management, including peacemaking. In terms of policy tools, the ESDP would comprise three general elements: military, civilian, and conflict prevention.

• Military element: a *Political and Security Committee* of senior national officials, a *Military Committee* of EU chiefs of staff, a *Military Staff* of 136 officials, and an *EU Rapid Reaction Force* (RRF) of at least 60,000 troops based on the national commitments discussed above.

• Civilian element: *police cooperation* with up to 5,000 policemen; *strengthening the rule of law* with up to 200 judges, prosecutors, and other experts; *civilian administration* to establish or guarantee elections, taxation, education, water supplies, etc; and *civil protection* by assisting humanitarian actors through emergency operations.

• Conflict prevention element: overseen by the Commission by concentrating on improving the consistency and effectiveness of all of the EU's actions. With the goal of promoting peace and stability, the four main objectives here are: to make more systematic and coordinated use of the EU's instruments; to identify and combat causes of conflict; to improve the capacity to react to nascent conflicts; and to promote international cooperation in this area.

However, implementation of the ESDP proved difficult during its initial phase despite several opportunities at the time between 1999 and 2002: Macedonia, Afghanistan, and Iraq. In each case, several EU states suggested sending the EU's RRF to the conflict, yet other EU states opposed joint EU action in favour of national contributions. Since the 2001 Nice Treaty, which further codified the ESDP plan, the EU has managed to implement several concrete ESDP policy decisions. The first official ESDP action involved a contribution to civilian police forces in Bosnia starting in January 2003, taking over from the UN's International Police Task Force. The total annual budget of Є 38 million for this three-year operation includes Є 20 million from the EU budget. This was soon followed by an ESDP decision to take over a military operation from NATO in Macedonia, implemented between 31 March and 15 December 2003. Operation 'Concordia' was requested by the government of Macedonia to help implement an internal peace agreement; it made use of NATO assets and 350 military personnel. A third recent ESDP deployment is Operation 'Artemis' in the Democratic Republic of Congo (DRC), which ran between June and September 2003. France served as the 'framework nation' in organising the mission, which involved about 1,800 troops. All three of these deployments were authorised under UN auspices and involved both EU and non-EU forces. However, the question remains whether the ESDP will lead to greater defence cooperation and thus take over some of NATO's functions, a major topic of discussion during the EU's constitutional convention (see below and also in Chapter 9 of this volume by Jolyon Howorth).

Credibility and capability gaps

Does EU foreign policy really matter? Before answering this question, we should first reiterate the highly unique nature of the EU's role in world politics. What began as a weak system to manage common coal and iron resources has grown into a stable, highly complex, supranational policy-making system with its own governing institutions, financial resources, diplomatic network, monetary system, and military force. No other regional economic organisation has achieved such success in expanding its functions, and in linking its foreign economic policies with greater cooperation in related fields of external relations, such as development policy, human rights, humanitarian aid, environmental policy, security affairs, and defence cooperation. In addition, the EU's growing ability to target these disparate policies toward a single goal (such as dealing with the break-up of Yugoslavia; see Box 8.1) in a coherent, even strategic, fashion is a unique accomplishment in world politics. This achievement alone should lead one to view the EU as an unqualified success in the history of international cooperation, and every assessment of the EU's 'performance' in world politics should acknowledge that fact.

However, we might also ask whether the lofty ideals represented by Europe's global ambitions are in fact matched by solid policy successes in the real world of dip-lomacy. In other words, does the EU's substantial policy cooperation actually produce effective results? Here we must be more critical, and the truth is that numerous gaps between capability and expectations do exist in the EU's conduct of foreign policy, although these vary across different policy domains and specific initiatives. In terms of policy implementation, the key divide is between the 'low politics' of economic affairs, where the EU is able to wield considerable influence, and the 'high politics' of security/defence affairs, where the EU is still finding its way. In economic affairs, policies over trade in goods and development cooperation are handled almost exclus-ively at the EU level and national inputs to this process are often decided by various forms of majority voting, not consensus. Trade policy in particular is the founda-tion of regional economic integration, and here the EU's supranational approach has succeeded far beyond other experiments with regional common markets. If the EU manages to reform its Common Agricultural Policy to make it more compatible with free trade in general and the promotion of economic growth in the developing world in particular, the EU could reap a huge amount of goodwill in the poorer countries of the world, and perhaps even gain a major edge, in both rhetorical and material terms, over the US.

The area of high politics is more problematic. As security/defence affairs still largely involve consensual decision-making among EU states, and a limited role for the Commission (compared to economic policy), common policy initiatives can be limited or even blocked by the actions of just one EU member state. This often happens because of lingering divisions between EU member states over the

---

Box 8.1 Yugoslavia: implementation in action

The EU's response to the Balkans conflict after 1990 is often cited as a failure of European foreign policy. However, it is questionable whether any international organisation could have prevented either the self-destruction of that country or the widespread violence that resulted from its break-up. Despite a rough early start that coincided with the negoti-ation and difficult ratification of the Maastricht Treaty, the EU did manage to forge a fairly coherent (though not equally *effective*) set of policies toward the region. These involved diplomatic, economic, and even military tools, each decided according to appropriate EU procedures yet all in the service of a common position. Since 1991, these EU-led policies have involved trade and cooperation agreements, humanitarian aid, financial sanctions, arms/trade embargoes, customs patrols, conflict resolution/diplomacy, public administra-tion (Mostar), civilian policing in Bosnia, and military peacekeeping in the former Yugoslav Republic of Macedonia. As always, these efforts were coordinated through a range of EU ini-tiatives, such as ECHO, the PHARE, OBNOVA, and CARDS programmes,[3] and Stabilization and Association Agreements with certain countries of the region (in process). Although the practical implementation of these programmes has been difficult and time-consuming ow-ing to the multiplicity of goals, the EU has done far more than any other international organ-isation to help stabilise, rebuild, and repatriate the region. And while the future of the west-ern Balkans is still uncertain, the EU's proactive attention toward this region today (which amounts to hundreds of millions of euros in funding) is a far cry from its limited, reactive ap-proach to similar crises elsewhere during the 1970s and 1980s.

basic rationale for an EU military force (i.e., whether for defence or peacekeeping tasks), and because of more specific opposition to giving EU institutions an operational role in any security/defence policies. Both of these disputes are further complicated by a need to specify the division of labour between the ESDP, NATO, the UN, and other arrangements with non-EU member states (such as 'Contact Groups'). Yet the EU is perfectly aware of its shortcomings in this area, and it continues to take steps to close this gap through institutional measures, such as the High Representative for the CFSP, a CFSP Policy Planning and Early Warning Unit, a Rapid Reaction Force, a more efficient system for imposing economic sanctions, plans for crisis management/response, more reliance on 'coalitions of the willing', and other measures. The EU clearly attempts to learn from its mistakes and has never rolled back its foreign policy ambitions in the face of a perceived policy failure.

These efforts do not go unnoticed by the international community. In fact, cooperation in the EU is now so entrenched that the EU often seems to receive more attention when it fails to cooperate than when it acts collectively. We might also recall that even during EPC's early years, when foreign policy cooperation was expressed only in the form of declarations and *démarches*, non-EU states (particularly in the developing world) took note of Europe's attitude toward various global issues. And as EPC/CFSP developed its policy tools in the form of economic aid and sanctions, its influence has broadened (for a detailed examination, see Ginsberg 2001). This has been demonstrated in crisis situations (such as the Falklands War), long-range security issues (such as the OSCE process), and in areas where the EU has attempted to institutionalise a long-range policy into a dialogue (such as the Middle East, Eastern/Central Europe, South Africa, and Central America). Moreover, these efforts are important for internal cohesion, in terms of helping to prevent foreign policy disputes from interfering with economic integration over the past three decades. In this sense EU foreign policy has an important confidence-building function within Europe, while outside the EU it symbolises Europe's identity in the international system, and (possibly) represents a major alternative to the hegemony of American foreign policy.

The capability-expectations gap is widest in the area of military/defence affairs. The Kosovo operation in particular, where a NATO air force dominated by the US coerced Yugoslavian President Slobodan Milosevic to halt his attacks on ethnic Albanians in that province, helped instigate more detailed plans for the ESDP and the RRF. Similarly, the EU's highly public split over the Iraq war in 2003 encouraged its member states to push for a formal security strategy statement under the direction of the High Representative for the CFSP, Javier Solana. Even with its disunity over Iraq, the EU's internal deliberations challenged the US to articulate its case for war in the UN and at home. The EU's first-ever military operations in Macedonia and the Congo demonstrate that virtually no policy tool is completely off-limits in achieving its ambitions. Still, it is questionable whether the ESDP will ever include the key elements of a true defence pact, such as a formal security guarantee for EU member states, a unified command and control structure, and a policy on nuclear weapons (see below). Lacking these elements, the EU might find it difficult to deter, compel, and defend (i.e., war-fighting) outsiders in any coherent fashion, although it is clearly starting to cope with some of these issues on a small-scale basis. In the meantime, the EU will continue developing its strengths in the area of long-term conflict prevention with mostly economic tools rather than short-term crisis management with military means.

Conclusion: what kind of power does the EU possess?

The EU's foreign policy capabilities are as complex and varied as those of its 15 member states. Despite its trappings of a supranational superpower, the EU is still a treaty-based regional organisation designed to promote international cooperation primarily through the use of 'soft' power. When its member states manage to cooperate, the EU's power can be quite formidable. It certainly has the power to defend its economic interests through the use of economic power. This power can be seen most clearly in forums such as the World Trade Organization or policy areas such as competition (or anti-trust), where the Commission has challenged major American economic interests such as General Electric and Microsoft. By presenting itself as an alternative to American hegemony, the EU builds upon and reinforces its social democratic normative goals. Here there are considerable risks for the EU, but also potential benefits as well. In fact, the EU has shown increasing willingness, even before the war with Iraq, to confront the US on a number of contentious foreign policy issues: national missile defence, the Kyoto Protocol on global warming, the international campaign to ban landmines, the International Criminal Court, the sale of genetically modified foods, and many others. This US-EU opposition even extends to domestic policy issues, such as the use of the death penalty and the war on drugs in the US (Manners 2002).

All of these issues present opportunities for the EU to articulate its own set of global political goals. The EU's capacity to defend these political interests, such as democracy and human rights, has also grown in recent years, especially through the use of specialised framework agreements with key regions. These experiments could go a long way toward the creation of zones of democracy, or at least stability, in many troubled areas of the world. Here again the EU is at odds with the US approach to free trade pacts, which tend to avoid the inclusion of important political elements such as the development of civil society (although that may change). The next challenge for the EU is to bolster its economic and political goals with an effective military capability, and even here the EU has made considerable progress in just the past few years. The operations in Bosnia, Macedonia, and the Congo, although small in scale, have proceeded without major complications, and they should help build confidence in the EU's ability to implement the ESDP.

Yet the EU's efforts to speak with a single voice in world politics will face major stresses in the very near future. The international role of the euro, the war on terrorism, and most importantly, the largest expansion of the EU in its history will provide Europeans with numerous opportunities for either cooperation or discord. These factors motivated the EU's first-ever constitutional convention, where foreign policy was just one of many difficult items on a complex agenda. Among the key questions that required attention were: how to balance between the EU's development of soft and hard power, how to balance between national and EU-level decision-making in foreign policy, and how to balance various national interests in a community of 25 or more member states. To its credit, the convention paid increasing attention to security and defence policy issues in light of general concerns about terrorism and the specific wars in Afghanistan and Iraq. And the eventual Constitutional Treaty of 2004 managed to finalise several potentially significant reforms in this domain: a new EU foreign minister post, a European armaments agency, investing the EU with 'legal personality' (to facilitate its ability to sign international agreements), an EU diplomatic service, and perhaps most important, a new mutual defence clause. However, if past experience is any guide, the true impact of these reforms, assuming the constitution is ratified, will remain a mystery until the EU attempts to utilise them on a case-by-case basis. As always, the EU will thus 'learn by doing' and then institutionalise these lessons into its existing system for foreign policy. In doing so, the EU will continue its erratic though progressive development as a unique global actor, helping to shape not only the regional future of Europe but also the international environment on which that future depends.

Notes

1 The 'Pillar system' has been substantially altered by the draft European constitution. If ratified as written, it will eliminate the third Pillar (JHA) and transfer most competences in this area to the EC.

2 These figures do not include preaccession aid for the Mediterranean countries (€ 25 million in 2003) and aid budgeted for the reconstruction of Iraq (€ 160 million in 2004).

3 PHARE is the Poland-Hungary Assistance for Recovering Economies programme. CARDS is the Community Assistance for Reconstruction, Development and Stabilization programme. The OBNOVA programme takes its name from the Serbo-Croatian term for 'renewal' or 'regeneration'.

Further reading

Many of the arguments in this chapter are drawn from M.E. Smith (2003). For general overviews of EU foreign policy-making processes, see Cameron (1999), White (2001), and H. Smith (2002). In addition to the titles listed in the references above, specific EU foreign policy actions are covered in Ginsberg (1989), Monar (1998), Youngs (2002), and Wiessala (2002). For a more critical analysis of the EU's foreign policy capabilities, see Zielonka (1998).

Cameron, F. (1999), *The Foreign and Security Policy of the European Union: Past, Present and Future* (Sheffield: Sheffield Academic Press).

Ginsberg, R. (1989), *Foreign Policy Actions of the European Community: The Politics of Scale* (Boulder: Lynne Rienner).

Monar, J. (ed.) (1998), *The New Transatlantic Agenda and the Future of EU-US Relations* (The Hague: Kluwer).

Smith, H. (2002), *European Union Foreign Policy: What it is and What it Does* (London: Pluto Press).

Smith, M.E. (2003), *Europe's Foreign and Security Policy: The Institutionalization of Cooperation* (Cambridge: Cambridge University Press).

White, B. (2001), *Understanding European Foreign Policy* (Basingstoke: Palgrave MacMillan).

Wiessala, G. (2002), *The European Union and Asian Countries* (London: Sheffield Ac. Press/Continuum).

Youngs, R. (2001), *The European Union and the Promotion of Democracy: Europe's Mediterranean and Asian Policies* (Oxford: Oxford University Press).

Zielonka, J. (1998), *Explaining Euro-Paralysis: Why Europe is Unable to Act in International Politics* (London: Macmillan).

Web links

Details of all EU programmes can be found at http://www.europa.eu.int/ which has links to the international activities of all of the main EU institutions and agencies. Analysis and links to academic materials can be found at http://www.fornet.info/ and at http://www.lse.ac.uk/Depts/intrel/EuroFPUnit/html. Links listed for other chapters in this volume will in many cases carry information about the implementation of EU activities in specific areas.

Part III

Activities and Impact

Activities
and impact

Activities

Chapter 9

From Security to Defence: the Evolution of the CFSP

Jolyon Howorth

Contents

Summary

This chapter is concerned with the ways in which, between the late 1990s and the early 2000s, the EU moved from a predominantly 'civilian' foreign and security policy to a much more muscular and 'harder' common defence policy. It begins by reviewing the ways in which International Relations theory would explain the limitations of the CFSP up to the late 1990s, and then moves on to show how the development of the EU's defence policies challenges established explanations. The chapter then examines the institutional and operational changes that have occurred since the late 1990s, and identifies a number of continuing tensions and problems. The final parts of the chapter address some of the long term and continuing problems in development of a European strategic vision and culture, and return to some of the conceptual issues raised in the early stages.

Introduction

When the notion of an EU Common Foreign and Security Policy (CFSP) was first floated in February 1990,[1] sceptics asked where the 'S' component of the acronym lay hidden. The EU, since the early 1970s, had been attempting to coordinate a common foreign policy—mainly in the guise of European Political Cooperation (EPC). However, there was not, in the early 1990s, any serious attempt among the then EU-12 to coordinate *security* policy. The Western European Union (WEU), a little-known and even less-understood body which, since its creation in 1955, had informally acted as a security and defence liaison mechanism both between France and NATO and between the UK and the EU, had been 'reactivated' in the 1980s (Deighton 1997). Its Ministerial Council asserted in October 1987 that 'the construction of an integrated Europe will be incomplete as long as it does not include security and defence', but it then proceeded to define WEU's mission as 'to strengthen the European pillar of the Alliance' (WEU 1988, 41). The main institutions of WEU (the Council and the Secretariat) were relocated in 1992 from London to Brussels to enhance coordination with NATO. Although WEU carried out some joint European minesweeping actions in the Gulf in 1988–90 and monitoring or police activities in former Yugoslavia in the early 1990s, it did not presume to deliver EU 'collective defence'. That remained, throughout the greater part of the 1990s, the exclusive role of NATO. What was true of WEU was even truer of the EU itself. Although some European states—again mainly through the WEU—sought to create a European Security and Defence Identity (ESDI) from inside NATO, any notion of an autonomous EU role in the field of security (let alone defence) was virtually unthinkable for most of the 1990s. Yet between 1998 and 2004, the evolution from an essentially 'civilian' notion of the CFSP towards a European Security and Defence Policy seemed almost to portend a revolution in the concept and operation of a 'European foreign policy'. By 2004, the EU was involved in several military or quasi-military operations, not only in the 'new Europe' but also in Africa, and had developed its own formal Security Strategy as a guide to the further development and implementation of what the Constitutional Treaty described as the Common Security and Defence Policy.

The aim of this chapter is to place this set of developments not only in the context of changes within the EU and the international arena, but also in the context of thinking about security and defence policies in International Relations more generally. It begins with a review of the ways in which International Relations theory might approach the problem of a European Security and Defence Policy (ESDP), and then proceeds to analyse the ways in which the developments of the late 1990s and 2000s challenge established notions of essentially national defence policies. Next, it explores the continuing tensions in EU security and defence policies in terms of resources and institutions, and identifies the evidence from and prospects for operational implementation of an EU defence policy. Finally, the chapter turns its attention to the longer term, and to the elaboration of a strategic vision and a strategic posture for the EU.

European security and defence in theoretical perspective

Mainstream international relations theory would regard the situation of European defence up to the late 1990s situation as entirely normal. For neo-realists, state actors alone can engage in security and defence—that is, military—activities, either individually, or as part of a military alliance. A body such as the European Union, in this conception, is not only inappropriate for but also quite incapable of engaging in security and defence (Bull 1983). Liberal institutionalists have similar difficulties in conceptualising such a role for the EU. The characteristic of intergovernmental institutions, in this theoretical approach, is that they bargain in the currency of national interest and, while they may strike deals (primarily in the field of trade and economics) which can produce a positive sum game, they are not in the business of pooling—let alone abandoning—'sovereignty' (Moravcsik 1998). The notion of the European Union as a security and defence actor is hardly catered for in mainstream IR theory. And yet, as the present chapter will chronicle, from 1999 onwards the EU made enormous strides towards grasping the nettle of security and defence cooperation (and even integration) confounding the theorists from both mainstream schools.

To the extent to which the recent wave of constructivism has addressed these issues, it has been to suggest that international relations can be 'socially constructed' in more value-based or normative terms (rather than as a clash of interests), and that in this sense EU security integration is theoretically unproblematic. Yet constructivists are, for the most part, somewhat ill-at-ease with the EU as their focal point.[2] However, this school has, since the mid-1980s, succeeded in broadening national concepts of security (Buzan et al. 1998) with the result that there has been some measure of convergence between mainstream approaches on the one hand, and the newer, sociologically-derived theories of international relations on the other, not least because constructivism has made some significant concessions to rationalism. There has also been a convergence between the IR security literature and the EU's civilian power mentality (Whitman 1998). The EU is increasingly being conceptualised as taking part in the processes of IR and is even being perceived as a 'power'. It is perhaps too soon to see it as a coherent system of IR in its own right.

As far as EU integration theory is concerned, both liberal intergovernmentalists and supranational institutionalists have striven to stake out a territory fenced by a dominant or monocausal explanatory factor for European cooperation (the former) or integration (the latter): on the one hand the sovereign state as a unitary actor involved in political bargaining; on the other hand supranational institutions with diverse actors at multiple levels involved in functional integration. The key element here is that each of these two camps believes that *its* dominant explanation trumps that of the other. However, it is not clear why scholars would wish to detect mono-causal or even dominant drivers behind complex political and historical processes. When, in 1958, the UK prime minister was asked by a young journalist what can most easily steer a government off its chosen course, Harold Macmillan replied: 'Events, dear boy! Events!' Since 1989, and especially since 11 September 2001, 'events' have run way ahead of the capacity of politicians—even strong ones—to determine their course. In the area of security and defence, events have also ridden roughshod over most of the established theories of European integration.

In an early study of ESDP, I coined the concept of 'supranational intergovernment-alism' (Howorth 2000, 36, 84). By that I meant the phenomenon whereby a profu-sion of agencies of intergovernmentalism take root in Brussels and, through dialogue and socialisation processes, reaction to 'events', and a host of other dynamics, gradu-ally create a tendency for policy to be influenced, formulated, and even driven, from within that city. This is close to the idea of Brusselsisation used by other comment-ators, including in this volume. Governments, often against their wishes, are being forced in directions they had not anticipated. Vivien Schmidt (2002, 63–7) has out-lined a variety of 'mediating factors' which help explain such changes in govern-ment policy on major issues. Although her factors were devised for the European political economy, they are easily adaptable to other policy areas. *Vulnerability*—in strategic terms—is a factor which, in the last 15 years, has risen dramatically to the top of security policy-makers' agendas. It is largely exogenous and a prime example of 'events'. *Political-institutional capacity*—an endogenous ability to impose or negoti-ate change—has also evolved markedly in the field of ESDP. European statesmen, even the most powerful, have demonstrated time and again that national institu-tions are inadequate to the task of driving forward a coherent European response to the external environment. New European institutions and agencies have recently popped up like mushrooms to fill the gap. *Policy legacy and preference*—the extent to which long-standing approaches remain valid—is likewise a factor where even the most powerful statesmen have been forced to adapt.[3] Above all, *discourse*—the ability to change preferences by altering actors' perceptions of the available op-tions—has proven to be an immensely powerful factor in driving forward the ESDP process (Howorth 2004). Policy preferences which, only a few years previously, would have seemed unimaginable to many a leading actor, have in recent years and in this crucial policy area, rapidly been embraced, constructed, and integrated into the mainstream. It is here that constructivism comes into its own as a theoretical lens (Katzenstein 1996). In Article I-41 of the EU's 2004 draft Constitutional Treaty, it is even stated that: 'The common security and defence policy *shall* include the pro-gressive framing of a common Union defence policy.' However, while policy can be constructed, impact cannot.

The moves towards pooling that last bastion of 'sovereignty'—security and de-fence policy—with all their limitations and *caveats*, constitute a sea-change in the way the EU and its member states will henceforth relate to the outside world. The reality is deeply empirical and lends itself awkwardly to theoretical speculation. It be-lies the prescriptions of both main EU integration schools of theory. Liberal intergov-ernmentalists have long assured us that, especially in this area of 'high politics', such developments cannot and should not happen (Moravcsik 1998). Supranational insti-tutionalists, on the other hand, can scarcely begin to explain such major progress in a policy area which is overwhelmingly associated with the European Council and its agencies (Sandholtz and Stone Sweet 1998). And yet, by any measure, it seems to be working. The process is worth keeping under review.

From foreign policy coordination to a European Security and Defence Policy (ESDP)

By the turn of the century, the EU had begun to ride roughshod not only over IR theory, but—rather more importantly—over its own previous diffidence in the field of security and defence. No longer content with the quest for a security and defence *identity* from inside NATO, and no longer prepared to use the WEU as a proxy, the European Union itself now sought to generate a European Security and Defence *Policy* (ESDP), which, as it arose from the Saint-Malo Declaration of December 1998, explicitly called for the 'capacity for autonomous action, backed up by credible military forces'. The story of how the EU got to this point has been told (Howorth 2000; Hunter 2002; Quinlan 2002). But some milestones in the shift from ESDI to ESDP—and above all their explanations—seem appropriate. Two important explanatory sets of variables underlie the EU's move towards assuming a security and defence remit. The first set, of exogenous factors, derives from the shifting tectonic plates of the international system in the aftermath of the Cold War. The second set, of endogenous factors, derives from the internal dynamics of the European project. When combined, these explanatory variables amount to a forceful drive towards ESDP.

When the Berlin Wall fell on 9 November 1989, it brought down with it a Eurocentric reading of international relations which had been unquestioned since the Treaty of Westphalia in 1648. Europe had been the fulcrum of world history since the sixteenth century as its internal wars and external expansion dictated the fates of countries and peoples around the globe. The very discipline of IR was built around analysis of European conflicts. All of that came to an end in 1989, even if it was not immediately apparent. For the United States and for much of the rest of the world, the 'dawn of peace in Europe' (Mandelbaum 1996) shifted the continent to the margins of the international radar screen where it featured as little more than a blip. In particular, the focus of policy-makers and military planners in Washington DC switched to Asia, to the Gulf, to the Middle East. Europe (with the irritating but hardly strategically significant exception of the Balkans) was simply no longer a problem.

The corollary to this realisation was that US troops were not best employed sitting about in tens of thousands in bases in Germany training for a war which now could never happen. The security of the European continent should logically be delivered through Europe's own resources. In the first instance, that involved efforts to define a European security identity (ESDI) from inside NATO. Why was this problematic? The biggest difference between US forces and European forces as they emerged from the Cold War derived from geography. The Europeans, perched on the front line of the Iron Curtain, were configured for static line defences, based on mass mobilisation of conscripts, artillery and tanks. The Americans, coming from across the ocean, were configured for distant force projection involving strategic transport facilities, rapid mobility, and sophisticated 'stand-off' weaponry.

The crisis management missions of the 21st century required specific kinds of assets. The US possessed them; the Europeans did not. Europe suffered from a 'capabilities gap'. While the Europeans discussed ways to convert their lumbering militaries into useful—and usable—instruments (in 'out of area' places like the Balkans), it seemed sensible that they should seek access, through NATO, to available US assets which would allow them—temporarily—to plug the capabilities gaps between their past and their future. This would take the pressure off US forces more urgently needed elsewhere, and would allow EU forces, pending their professionalisation and modernisation, to take over peace-keeping missions in areas such as the Balkans where the US had no identifiable interests. The drive to force European militaries to take responsibility for their own back yard began unequivocally in Washington DC. Unless the Europeans 'got serious' about rendering their armed forces usable, the message from DC read, the Atlantic Alliance was finished. Two powerful exogenous forces then combined to galvanise that seriousness of EU purpose: the prospect of US disengagement and the re-emergence of insecurity and instability on the EU's periphery.[4]

The second set of explanatory variables behind ESDP stems from the dynamic processes unleashed within the EU itself by the developments of the late 1980s and early 1990s. However long delayed may have been the community's embrace of 'actorness', there was never any doubt that the European project was a political project. Its fundamental objective was the resolution of a double conundrum: how to bind together the fates of Europe's core nations in a way which would both render intra-European war unthinkable and maximise European influence in the outside world. Indeed, the European project began with this same defence conundrum. The Treaties of Dunkirk (1947) and Brussels (1948), the Anglo-French plan for a Western Union in which Europe 'should be independent both of the United States and of the Soviet Union' (Gaddis 1985, 78), the debates over the European Defence Community (1950–54), all aimed to provide solutions. Failure in those endeavours produced NATO—which took the issue of European security autonomy off the agenda for almost 40 years. Yet the notion that the European states might look to their own interests—in contradistinction to those of the USA—predated the fall of the Berlin Wall, as nervous European leaders pondered the security dilemmas posed by a US president who, in 1981, appeared to be contemplating nuclear war and then, in 1986, appeared to have converted to unilateral nuclear disarmament.[5] As European integration gathered speed in the late 1980s, impelled by the Single Market project, by plans for a single currency and by the Schengen process, the internal forces behind foreign policy convergence (the majority of 'foreign' policy being commerce-related) meshed with those suggesting the need for greater security policy autonomy. These dynamics were intensified after the fall of the Berlin Wall by the growing awareness of the strategic challenges posed by enlargement to the countries of Central and Eastern Europe (CEE). Moreover for some, enlargement presupposed deepening—itself charged with political dynamics.

The immediate European security challenge in the 1990s was essentially twofold. Institutionally, it involved thinking through the complex relationship between the

European Union itself (which several member states, led by the UK, wished to deny any active involvement in security or defence discussions), the WEU (which was too small and increasingly too diverse in membership to be effective), and NATO (which most analysts were declaring obsolete if not moribund). Militarily, it involved developing a serious EU military capacity which would allow the Union to assume responsibility for crisis management tasks. At a meeting at Petersberg, close to Bonn, in June 1992, the WEU had defined three such tasks: 'humanitarian and rescue tasks; peacekeeping tasks; tasks of combat forces in crisis management, including peace-making'. The latter might even include war-fighting such as the Kosovo operation of 1999—that is, 'high-end Petersberg tasks'.

The EU's initial attempt to meet these challenges involved using the 'good offices' of the WEU to work with NATO in generating European Combined Joint Task Forces (CJTFs— Terriff 2003, 39–59) drawing on ear-marked NATO troops (Howorth and Keeler 2003, 3–21). This involved the so-called 'Berlin Plus' arrangements (see Box 9.1) whereby the EU could enjoy 'assured access to NATO planning', 'presumed access to NATO assets and capabilities' and a pre-designated Europeans-only chain of command. This awkward process proved unsatisfactory in several ways. First, the WEU was too insignificant a body to be entrusted with the major *political* responsibility for oversight of European military operations. Second, the unresolved nature of the political relationship between the EU and WEU failed to demonstrate who owned the process. Third, the mechanics of Berlin Plus proved extremely difficult to nail down.

Box 9.1 Berlin Plus

Deriving from a NATO summit in Berlin in June 1996, the 'Berlin Plus' procedures referred to the mechanisms whereby the EU would be able to borrow assets from the US in order to carry out regional crisis management missions. They include 'assured access' to NATO operational planning capabilities (essentially the services of SHAPE at Mons); 'presumption of availability' to the EU of NATO capabilities and common assets; and NATO European command options for EU-led operations. It took over four years to reach formal agreement on the details of these arrangements, which remain tightly classified. The resolution of this issue allowed the EU and NATO to make a landmark Declaration on ESDP (16 December 2002), providing a formal basis for a strategic partnership between the two organisations in the area of crisis management and conflict prevention.

By the spring of 1998 (as Kosovo was poised to erupt) Tony Blair, whose first year in office had been dominated by domestic politics, began to look seriously into defence issues. A group of senior officials in Whitehall, liaising with their opposite numbers in Paris, had come up with a solution (Howorth 2004). Since the inadequacies of WEU were clearly a large part of the problem, they suggested that the organisation, whose 50-year treaty base was up for renewal in 1998, should be scrapped. The EU should take on direct political responsibility for deciding on and overseeing military operations. And, in the hypothesis (which the experience of Kosovo rendered increasingly likely) of an EU-only operation in which the US wanted no part, it should develop autonomous forces in order to escape dependence on complex borrowing arrangements such as Berlin Plus. That was the Rubicon crossed by Tony Blair at the historic meeting with Jacques Chirac in St. Malo in December 1998.[6]

St. Malo raised a number of challenges which the EU collectively and the member states individually have been grappling with ever since. The institutional implications were rapidly resolved and the EU has successfully implanted in Brussels a raft of new bodies—the High Representative for the CFSP (HR-CFSP—Javier Solana) and his advisory Policy Unit (PU); the Political and Security Committee (COPS from the French acronym) comprising ambassadors from each member state's permanent representation in Brussels; the European Union Military Committee (EUMC) formally made up of the Chiefs of the Defence Staff of all member states; and the EU Military Staff (EUMS) comprising some 150 senior officers from across the Union. This institutional nexus, modelled largely on NATO, has already demonstrated its ability to work and to work well. It is set to be fine-tuned by the institutional innovations of the EU Constitutional Treaty (Duke 2003).

More problematic was the resolution of the EU's working relationship with NATO. This involved two interlocking issues. The first was the implementation of the 'Berlin Plus' arrangements for transfer to and from the EU of NATO (meaning US) military assets (see Box 9.1). The second was the involvement in ESDP of non-EU NATO members such as Turkey and Norway. The latter problem dominated the headlines, while the former was tackled behind closed doors. Turkey was particularly disturbed by the ESDP project for three reasons. First, while Turkey had been fully involved in intra-European security discussions as an associate member of the WEU from 1992, ESDP offered no such facility. Indeed, the six non-EU European member states of NATO[7] not only found themselves excluded from the EU's institutions, but forced to watch as four former neutral countries (Austria, Finland, Ireland, and Sweden) assumed full membership. Second, Turkey feared that it was witnessing a process whereby the US (in which Ankara had enormous faith) transferred responsibility for European security to the EU (in which Ankara had very little faith). Thirdly, this was all the more unpalatable for the Turks in that most scenarios for armed conflict and crisis management in the European theatre were situated in the South-Eastern parts of the continent, which Turkey regarded as its own 'back yard'. In particular, Ankara feared the use of ESDP military assets to intervene in Cyprus in support of Greece. Turkey therefore decided, in spring 2000, to block the entire Berlin Plus process by threatening to veto the transfer to the EU of those indispensable NATO assets without which the EU could hardly embark on any military operation.

It took almost three years of high level negotiations to reach an agreement acceptable both to Ankara and to Athens (Tofte 2003). This involved mutual guarantees of non-aggression between NATO and ESDP, agreement on intensive consultation procedures between the non-EU NATO states and the COPS, acceptable arrangements for the involvement of such countries in EU-led military operations and the exclusion from such operations of both Cyprus and Malta (Haine 2003, 136–40). On 16 December 2002, the EU and NATO issued a 'Declaration on ESDP', announcing their strategic partnership, and asserting that, while the EU would ensure 'the fullest possible involvement of non-EU European members of NATO within ESDP', NATO, for its part, would guarantee the EU 'assured access to NATO's planning capabilities'. On paper, at any rate, the EU had finally solved the conundrum of its complex relationship with NATO. This opened the way to the launch of EU military operations in 2003. However, the fine print of the EU-NATO relationship remains highly classified and the specific details of the Berlin Plus arrangements have never been made public. Many analysts

Table 9.1 EU member states defence expenditure (2003)

Country	US$m	US$ per capita	% of GDP	Forces (000)*
USA	404,920	1,391	3.7	1,427
1. France	45,695	765 (1)	2.6 (2)	259.0
2. UK	42,782	722 (2)	2.4 (3)	212.6
3. Germany	35,145	426 (10)	1.5 (18)	284.5
4. Italy	27,751	481 (8)	1.9 (10 =)	200.0
5. Spain	9,944	242 (15)	1.2 (22)	150.7
6. Netherlands	8,256	509 (7)	1.6 (16 =)	53.1
7. Greece	7,169	671 (3)	4.1 (1)	177.6
8. Sweden	5,532	618 (5)	1.8 (14 =)	27.6
9. Poland	4,095	107 (22)	2.0 (8 =)	163.0
10. Belgium	3,923	379 (11)	1.3 (21)	40.8
11. Denmark	3,334	619 (4)	1.6 (16 =)	22.8
12. Portugal	3,173	311 (13)	2.1 (6)	44.9
13. Austria	2,488	309 (14)	1.0 (23)	34.6
14. Finland	2,300	441 (9)	1.4 (19 =)	27.0
15. Czech Rep.	1,871	183 (19)	2.2 (5)	57.0
16. Hungary	1,589	157 (20)	1.9 (10 =)	33.4
17. Ireland	803	204 (17)	0.5 (25)	10.4
18. Slovakia	627	117 (22)	1.9 (10 =)	22.0
19. Slovenia	378	192 (18)	1.4 (19 =)	6.5
20. Lithuania	342	99 (24)	1.8 (14 =)	12.7
21. Cyprus	294	382 (12)	2.3 (4)	10.0
22. Latvia	194	84 (25)	1.9 (10 =)	4.9
23. Luxemb'g	233	520 (6)	0.9 (24)	0.9
24. Estonia	172	127 (21)	2.0 (8 =)	5.5
25. Malta	95	237 (16)	2.1 (6 =)	2.1
EU-15 Totals	198,528 m			1,605,900
EU-25 Totals	208.185 m			1,863,600
EU-15 Av	13,235	485	1.91	
EU-25 Av	8,327	361	2.2	

Note: * Forces figures are 2002.
Source: The Military Balance 2004–2005, International Institute of Strategic Studies (Oxford: Oxford University Press, 2004).

believe that, in the event of two crises arising in the world simultaneously, one vital to the US and one vital to the EU, the likelihood of the latter being able to count on the availability of key military assets belonging to the former is slim indeed. Such a situation stimulates the European drive for genuine autonomy in the area of military capacity.

European military capacity: the rhetoric and the reality

Spending patterns and defence budgets

The first factor to consider when analysing Europe's military potential is the *volume* of current and future expenditure. The EU-15, in 2003, spent almost US $200 billion on defence, almost half the US defence budget for that year—$404 billion (Tables 9.1 and 9.3). That is more than three times the defence budget of the second biggest military spender on earth (Russia at $65,200 bn) and more than that of the *five* next biggest spenders put together (Russia, China, Japan, Saudi Arabia, India—$198,238 bn). And yet, the EU collectively gets very little bang for its euros. Out of that sum, the EU-15 attempted to fund 15 separate armies, 14 air-forces, and 13 navies. If one includes in the equation the ten accession countries, the total EU spend rises to $208 billion, equivalent to the *six* next biggest military spenders. But that sum funds 25 armies, 21 air forces and 18 navies. The only one of the new accession states with any significant military clout is Poland, which ranks (at $4,095 m) in ninth place out of the EU-25, ahead of Belgium, Denmark, Portugal, Austria, Finland, Ireland, and Luxembourg among the existing member states. Of the armed forces of the EU-25, only seven are fully professionalised, the others relying to varying extents on conscripts, even if the trend is clearly towards the abolition of the draft (Table 9.2). Furthermore, just three countries in the EU (France, the UK, and Germany) together spend 62% of the combined EU-15 defence budgets and 60% of the EU 25. If Italy is added to the trio, the four nations alone contribute almost 75% of the EU-25 budget. The average defence expenditure of the lowest-spending 21 states comes to just $2,705 m. That is less than the defence budget of Vietnam! One might ask exactly what those nation states believe they are buying with their money.

For as long as this situation exists, return on investment will be sub-optimal. A major rationalisation of the EU's defence spending is overdue. It is not necessarily greater spending that is required, as is so often asserted. Wiser spending would certainly help. But only once has the EU clearly established what it hopes to achieve, with what force levels and with what state of equipment, can it have any clear idea about how much money is needed. Other problems require urgent resolution if the EU is to maximise the impact of its defence spending.

The Helsinki Headline Goal (HHG) and European military capacity

The HHG, established at the European Council in Helsinki in December 1999, was conceived as a broad 'force catalogue' from which would be drawn appropriate

Table 9.2 European armed forces 2002–2003					
Country	Prof/Consc	Army	Navy	Air Force	Total
Austria	Conscript	34,600	—	6,850*	34,600
Belgium	Professional	24,800	2,450	10,250	39,200
Cyprus	Conscript	10,000	—	—	10,000
Czechy	Conscript	39,850	—	13,100	49,400
Denmark	Conscript	14,700	4,000	3,500	22,700
Estonia	Conscript	2,550	440	220	5,000
Finland	Conscript	19,200	5,000	2,800	31,800
France	Professional	137,000	44,250	64,000	260,000
Germany	Conscript	191,350	25,650	67,500	296,000
Greece	Conscript	114,000	19,000	33,000	177,000
Hungary	Conscript	23,600	—	7,700	33,000
Ireland	Professional	8,500	1,100	860	10,500
Italy	Conscript	116,000	36,000	48,000	216,000
Latvia	Conscript	4,000	620	250	5,500
Lithuania	Conscript	7,950	650	1,150	13,500
Luxembourg	Professional	900	—	—	900
Malta	Professional	2,140	2,140**	2,140**	2,140
Netherlands	Professional	23,150	12,130	11,050	49,600
Poland	Conscript	104,050	14,300	36,450	163,000
Portugal	Conscript	26,700	10,950	7,250	43,600
Slovakia	Conscript	13,700	—	7,000	26,000
Slovenia	Conscript	6,500	—	530	9,000
Spain	Professional	95,600	22,900	22,750	177,900
Sweden	Conscript	13,800	7,900	5,900	33,000
United King	Professional	116,670	42,370	53,620	210,400
Norway	*Conscript*	*14,700*	*6,100*	*5,000*	*26,600*
Turkey	Conscript	402,000	52,750	60,100	514,850

Note: * Austrian air service is part of the army.
** Maltese armed forces cover all three services.
Of **EU-15,** Austria and Luxembourg have no navy and Luxembourg has no air force.
Of **EU-15,** eight still field conscript armies (although Italy is phasing it out).
All EU Accession states (except Malta) have conscript armed forces.
Source: The Military Balance 2004–2005, International Institute of Strategic Studies (Oxford: Oxford University Press, 2004).

resources for a range of hypothetical European missions, including the three levels of 'Petersberg Tasks'. The force catalogue envisaged 60,000 troops, 100 ships and 400 air-craft, deployable within 60 days and sustainable for one year. Via a series of 'Pledging Conferences'—Capabilities Commitments Conference (November 2000) and Capabilities Improvements Conference (November 2001)—this pool of resources was refined and deficiencies identified. A third conference took place in May 2003 at which the package was fine-tuned and the precise contributions of participant states agreed. The European Council meeting in Laeken (December 2001) boldly declared that the EU 'should be able to carry out the whole range of Petersberg tasks by 2003'. It went on to note, rather less assertively, that it 'will be in a position to take on progressively more demanding operations as the assets and capabilities at its disposal continue to develop' (Rutten 2002, 120–2). This declaration of 'operationality' was severely criticised by most serious strategic analysts.

There were several basic problems with the HHG. The first was the methodology itself. Voluntary, bottom-up contributions might (just) secure the raw numbers. They do not guarantee the delivery, still less the mobilisation, of a coherent fighting force. By way of comparison, we might note that, for the 2003 Iraq conflict, the most efficient and best equipped *unitary* member state—the UK—took 70 days (as opposed to Helsinki's prescribed 60) to deploy a force of only 45,000 combat troops. The list of forces notionally committed to the Helsinki Force Catalogue by each member state is known (Venusberg 2004, 67). But we have no real idea to date precisely what such forces could collectively accomplish. The key concept is usability. There are almost 1.7 million European troops 'in uniform'. Of that number, about 10% (170,000) are adequately trained for serious peace-keeping operations, and of those probably a maximum of 50,000 could be used for the type of peace-making operation needed in a conflict such as that in Iraq. Factoring in the requirements of rotation, the number falls to a maximum of 20,000 who are genuinely usable in serious military missions (Venusberg 2004, 27). Bottom-up methodology can produce raw numbers. But that does not equate to genuine military capacity. The solution to the methodological problem is to move towards a top-down mode. This could come both via the constitution of a formal Council of Defence Ministers and via the future European Defence Agency, as well as via mechanisms such as structured cooperation.

The second problem with the HHG has to do with the division of labour for procurement of strategic systems. Beyond raw numbers, the three Capabilities Conferences allowed the EU to identify the main areas of strategic deficiency—currently ten[8] (Missiroli 2003, 94). But in order to generate an effective EU capacity in the area of unmanned aerial vehicles, or strategic transport, or air-to-air refuelling, it is not enough to rely on voluntary efforts, or even to appoint a lead nation to chair a working group. These strategic enabling capabilities are unaffordable at national level, even for the best endowed nations. The problem is not one of science or technology. Despite collectively spending only one third of the US spend on Research and Development (R&D), the EU faces no purely technological or scientific impediment to the pursuit of such high technology programmes (Grant 2000). But there must be collective political agreement to drive the process forward towards agreed targets. That means top-down, pooling, and specialisation. The EU is moving towards the recognition of 'coordination responsibility' for key procurement projects (Germany:

strategic air lift; Spain: air-to-air refuelling; UK: Headquarters; Netherlands: PGMs for delivery by EU F-16s). This approach needs systematisation. Five years after Helsinki, in December 2004, progress had been slow.

The third—and potentially biggest—problem with the HHG process is the absence of clear debate about the nature of the military operations the EU intends to mount. The original thinking behind the HHG derived from Kosovo. What the EU had in mind—especially in the context of the use, in the Saint Malo Declaration, of the notion of autonomous forces—was the ability to carry out a Kosovo-type operation with minimal reliance on US inputs. But this has two different implications. The first would be that the EU could, with existing capacity, mount a Kosovo-type campaign. It would be a different type of military operation from 'Operation Allied Force'. It might involve the use of pilot skills instead of precision-guided weaponry for the suppression of enemy air defences. It would almost certainly involve the early use of ground forces and the acceptance of significant numbers of casualties. Many military analysts have insisted that such an operation was—and remains—within the capabilities of the EU. A second implication of the 'Kosovo objective' would be that the EU would need to develop a US-style capacity to fight high-level network-centric warfare (Arquilla & Ronfeldt 2001).[9] As we saw not just in Kosovo, but even more clearly in Afghanistan and Iraq, only the US currently has the capacity to engage properly in such war-fighting. Even the UK cannot fully interoperate with the most advanced US systems. The question is whether it is possible to acquire such a capacity 'with half a loaf'. European experts are increasingly promoting the cause of 'network-enabled' facilities.[10] However, there is considerable debate as to whether such a compromise would actually work effectively on the battlefield.

This poses the crucial question of the type of warfare the EU intends to fight. According to one analysis (Venusberg 2004, 68), the average US soldier, trained for high intensity warfare, operates at levels 8 to 10 on an intensity scale of 1 to 10. If forced to, he can 'operate down' to level 6 but is uncomfortable with that, owing to lack of training in the art of peace-keeping and nation-building. Many UK and French troops as well as some crack German, Italian, Spanish, and Dutch special-forces can operate up to level 8, but the vast majority are more comfortable lower down the intensity scale dealing with irregular forces in a peace-keeping environment. Most other EU troops cannot operate much above level 5 on the US intensity scale and are therefore incapable of assuming peace-keeping duties such as those required in 2004 in Iraq. The discussion of this 'what for?' series of questions is all the more urgent in that the EU has decided that it wishes to engage in the global war on terrorism. Article III-309 of the draft Constitutional Treaty extended the Petersberg tasks to include 'joint disarmament operations, humanitarian and rescue tasks, military advice and assistance tasks, conflict prevention and peace-keeping tasks, tasks of combat forces undertaken for crisis management, including peace-making and post-conflict stabilisation'. It added that 'these tasks may contribute to the fight against terrorism, including by supporting third countries in combating terrorism in their territories'. Yet the war on terrorism requires different instruments from those involved in driving the Serbian army out of Kosovo. Can Europe afford both when currently it seems unable to afford either? These internal contradictions at the heart of the HHG process required urgent attention. Some initial progress was made in 2004 with the announcement of a new 'Headline Goal'.

'Headline Goal 2010'

At the European Council meeting on 17 June 2004, the new Headline Goal 2010 (HG 2010) was adopted. Building on the HHG, the HG 2010 commits the Union 'to be able by 2010 to respond to a crisis with rapid and decisive action applying a fully coherent approach to the whole spectrum of crisis management operations covered by the Treaty on the European Union'. Inter-operability, deployability, and sustainability are at the heart of the project and the member states have identified an indicative list of specific milestones within the 2010 horizon, including the establishment of the European Defence Agency (EDA) by the end of 2004; the implementation of an EU strategic lift joint coordination by 2005; the ability by 2007 to deploy force packages at high readiness broadly based on the EU 'battle-groups' concept;[11] the availability of an EU aircraft carrier by 2008; and 'appropriate compatibility and network linkage of all communications equipment and assets' by 2010. The project was accompanied by a Capability Improvement Chart which detailed progress on meeting the main capabilities requirements in every area. HG 2010, by focusing on small, rapidly deployable units capable of high intensity warfare, shifted the objective from quantity to quality. It also resolved (at least partially) the contradiction between a Kosovo-style capability and the requirements of the 'war on terrorism'. The newly created battle-groups, of which up to thirteen are projected for 2007, can be used for both types of operation. The battle-groups model was inspired by the first ever experiences of the EU in armed combat, which took place in 2003.

2003: The EU becomes a military actor

On 31 March 2003, the EU launched its first military operation—a peace-keeping mission in the Former Yugoslav Republic of Macedonia (FYROM), taking over from a NATO force. Operation Concordia deployed 357 troops (from all EU states except Ireland and Denmark, and from 14 additional nations—an average of 13 troops per participating member state) into a small mountainous country and successfully kept the peace between bands of lightly-armed irregulars and the Macedonian 'army' which boasts a defence budget less than half that of Luxembourg. This was an operation high in political symbolism and modest in terms of military footprint. The mission was challenged in early September 2003 by growing unrest in northern villages but the EU successfully re-established order. By the end of the mission, it was clear that the biggest problem in Macedonia was no longer armed conflict but criminality—hence Concordia was succeeded on 15 December 2003 by an EU police operation: Proxima. Concordia's primary value was that it allowed the EU to test its recently agreed procedures covering every aspect of the mounting of a military operation—albeit on a very modest scale—from command and control, through use of

Table 9.3   World military expenditure 2003

Military spend '03	Expend. $millions	$ per capita	% of GDP	
1. United States	404,920	1,391	3.7	↑
2. Russia	65,200	455	4.9	↑
3. China	55,948	37	4.1	↑
4. France	45,695	765	2.6	↑
5. Japan	42,835	337	1.0	—
6. United K'dom	42,782	722	2.4	—
7. Germany	35,145	426	1.5	↓
8. Italy	27,751	481	1.9	—
9. Saudi Arabia	18,747	832	8.9	↓
10. India	15,508	15	2.6	↓
11. South Korea	14,632	305	2.8	—
12. Turkey	11,649	165	4.9	—
13. Australia	11,758	591	2.3	↑
14. Israel	10,325	1,544	9.5	—
15. Spain	9,944	242	1.2	—
16. Brazil	9,274	53	1.8	↓
17. Netherlands	8,256	509	1.6	—
18. Taiwan	7,479	336	2.7	↓
NATO	626,033	773	2.8	↑
[NATO Europe]	[221,113]	[426]	[1.9]	↑
[EU 25]	[208,185]	[365]	[1.9]	↑
ME & N.Africa	54,148	165	6.0	↓
C.& S. Asia	24,388	16	2.6	—
E. Asia + Australia	164,379	79	2.1	—
Carib + C/S Am	25,145	47	1.4	↓
Sub-Sah. Africa	7,716	11	1.9	↑

US expenditure = $405 bn.
The next 14 combined (Russia to Spain = $408 billion).
'Axis of Evil' states + Russia + China + Japan + NATO Europe (= $395 bn).
The rest of the entire world (minus NATO Europe) (= $371 bn).
NB: US expenditure in 2007 = $470 bn.
Source: The Military Balance 2004–2005, International Institute of Strategic Studies (Oxford: Oxford University Press, 2004), pp. 353–8.
↑ or ↓= budget rise or fall as % GDP (2002–2003).

force policy, to issues such as logistics, financing and legal arrangements and memoranda of understanding with host nations.

From June to September 2003, the EU launched its first ever autonomous operation. Operation Artemis, in the Democratic Republic of Congo, offers even richer lessons about EU capabilities than Concordia (Cornish 2004). The initial assessment suggests that the mission, which involved rapid force projection to a distance of 6,500 kilometres into unknown and non-permissive terrain, was a success. France was the 'framework nation', supplying 1,785 of the 2,200 troops deployed. Sixteen other 'troop contributing nations' (TCNs) were involved, above all providing strategic air lift (Germany, Greece, United Kingdom, Brazil, and Canada) engineers (UK), helicopters (South Africa) and special forces (Sweden). Operational planning was conducted from the French *Centre de Planification et de Conduite des Opérations* (CPCO) at Creil, to which were seconded officers from 13 other countries, thus demonstrating the potential for multinationalisation of a national HQ. The operation was exemplified by rapid deployment (seven days after UNSC Resolution 1484 on 30 May), a single command structure, well and appropriately trained forces, clear rules of engagement allowing for tactical evolution in the theatre, good incorporation of multinational elements, excellent inter-service cooperation, and adequate communications. NATO procedures were copied throughout. The twin challenges of command chain and logistics were successfully met, even though deficiencies were noted in certain aspects of secure communications as well as transmissions and manning at the force HQ. Artemis demonstrated conclusively that the EU can undertake a peacekeeping operation, and on a significant scale, even at some distance from Europe.

The transfer (from NATO to the EU) of responsibility for the Stabilisation Force (SFOR) in Bosnia-Herzegovina (BiH), in December 2004, represented an even greater test of the EU's military muscle. The initial NATO force deployed in BiH (IFOR, December 1995) involved some 60,000 troops. This was scaled down constantly to a January 2003 total of 12,000. Projections for 2004 foresaw a further reduction to about 7,000 troops centred on ten battle-groups of around 750 soldiers each. It was in part this reduction in scale which made it possible for the EU to consider taking over the peacekeeping role from NATO in late 2004. Over 80% of the troops in NATO's SFOR were already from EU member states. Operation Althea is the EU's most ambitious military mission to date.

Through these missions, the EU has demonstrated its ability to break out of its self-imposed conceptual paralysis concerning military operations. Despite the weaknesses and deficiencies discussed earlier, the EU is clearly not without considerable potential in relation to the use of force. In addition to the ground forces which have been—and will increasingly be—deployed in overseas missions, the EU could with no difficulty take on naval or air-combat missions against any conceivable adversary. Officially, the EU's agreed strategy involves the ability to intervene—essentially on humanitarian grounds and at the invitation of the UN—anywhere in the world. But before that can happen, the EU needs to resolve a range of political dilemmas.

Political developments and dilemmas

The 'European Security Strategy'

The European Security Strategy (ESS), approved by the European Council on 12 December 2003 (Solana Strategy Paper 2003), was an initial attempt to think through the real political objectives behind ESDP. It aimed to harmonise the different views of the current and future member states without falling into lowest common denominator rhetoric. The Strategy, entitled 'A Secure Europe in a Better World', inevitably constitutes something of a compromise between different cultures and approaches among the EU's member states. However, it also reflects the humanitarian intervention theses which have long been associated with UK diplomat Robert Cooper, a key influence in shaping the document (Cooper 2003). Overall responsibility for developing the ESS lay with Javier Solana.

The Strategy begins with the recognition that Europe has never been 'so prosperous, so secure nor so free'. This derives both from the benefits of European integration and from the US security guarantee delivered via NATO. It identifies five key threats: terrorism, weapons of mass destruction (WMD), failed states, organised crime, and regional conflicts. The document has been criticised in some quarters for its alleged alignment, via this focus on threats, with US security policy. But it is nevertheless more nuanced than its US equivalent (US National Security Strategy, 2002), paying greater attention to the root causes of poverty and global suffering, and stressing the 'complex' causes behind contemporary international terrorism. It recalls the destabilising effects of regional conflicts such as Kashmir, the Great Lakes, and the Korean peninsula, all of which feed into the cycle of terrorism, WMD, state failure, and even international criminality. Nonetheless, it is unequivocal in stating that the EU faces the same challenges as the United States. The main differences are that the ESS explicitly states not only that the United States cannot solve these problems on its own, but also that the only solution is what it calls, echoing President Bush, 'effective multilateralism'.

The second section outlines the EU's 'strategic objectives', asserting at the outset the EU's existing record in tackling the new threats. Two features of the strategy are also stressed: that 'the first line of defence will often be abroad'—via conflict prevention; and that none of the new threats is 'purely military' or manageable through purely military means. The strategic objectives rest on two main pillars: building security in the European region, and creating a viable new international order. The former is absent from US policy, the latter only fleetingly entertained. The EU document is strong in its assertion of a commitment to upholding and developing international law and in recognising the UN as the main source of international legitimacy. However, the most innovative aspect of this section is the new emphasis on using its powerful trade and development policies in a conditional and targeted way. The final section addresses the policy implications for the EU, which needs to be 'more active, more capable and more coherent'. One of the boldest statements of the document (which guaranteed applause in the US) was the need to develop a strategic culture that fosters 'early, rapid and, where necessary, robust intervention'.

Intervention implies the entire panoply of instruments at the EU's disposal, including political, diplomatic, military, civilian, commercial, and developmental tools. The document also insists that the Union be able to sustain several operations simultaneously. In order to do this, greater capability implies more defence resources, more pooling of assets, greater intelligence sharing, and joint procurement—a central challenge as the EU attempts to develop its security and defence policy. The document concludes by insisting on partnership—with the United States and NATO first and foremost, with Russia as a second priority, and with all other regional partners throughout the world. The strategy, it is claimed, will contribute 'to an effective multilateral system leading to a fairer, safer and more united world'.[12] This document is already an important milestone in the EU's move towards a coherent security and defence policy. It must be understood in the context of the parallel political dilemmas addressed by the Convention on the Future of Europe, that is, the issues of political coordination, effectiveness and solidarity.

The 'European Union Minister for Foreign Affairs' (EUMFA)

The EU's constant quest for greater political coordination led to the creation of the post of Union Minister for Foreign Affairs. The EUMFA emerged in 2004 from the Convention and the subsequent IGC as—at least potentially—an immensely powerful figure.[13] The post-holder will combine the current responsibilities both of the HR-CFSP and of the Commissioner for External Relations, thus having one foot in the Council and one (as Vice-President) in the Commission. This will allow him or her[14] to coordinate the two main thrusts of the EU's external policy: security and overseas aid. The UMFA will also contribute both to the preparation of and to the implementation of CFSP/ESDP and will chair the new Foreign Affairs Council (FAC). S/he will represent the Union in international organisations and at international conferences, will 'conduct political dialogue' on the Union's behalf, and can convene an emergency meeting of the FAC within 48 hours (or, in a real crisis, even sooner). The post-holder, elected for a five-year term, will replace the previous semestrial rotating Presidency, thus accumulating even more authority. Moreover, the EUMFA will preside over an EU Diplomatic Corps—the 'European External Action Service'—which is intended to be introduced within one year after entry into force of the Treaty (Duke 2002). If delegation can be properly organised, the advantages of having this central pillar of cohesion will out-weigh the disadvantages of inter-agency complexity. But the bottom line is clear. The requirements of coordination in the broad field of CFSP and in the more critical field of ESDP are now so urgent that the creation of this post practically imposed itself. The crucial issue raised by the very existence of this post is whether the urgency of coordination necessarily implies the inevitability of integration. The EUMFA seems like the first genuine incarnation of 'supranational intergovernmentalism'.

'Structured Cooperation' and the 'Solidarity Clause'

Two further issues were tackled by the Convention/IGC: how to maximise the political coordination of military capacity, and whether to move towards some statement of European collective defence. A new instrument which emerged from the

Convention/IGC was 'structured cooperation'. This involved an attempt, promoted by France and Germany, to go beyond 'enhanced cooperation' as provided for in the TEU and to allow a small number of militarily well-endowed states to drive forward ESDP in the name of the entire Union. The Draft Constitutional Treaty specifies that 'those member states whose military capabilities fulfil higher criteria and which have made more binding commitments to one another in this area with a view to the most demanding missions shall establish structured cooperation within the Union framework'.[15] While this would allow the more 'muscular' member states to forge ahead with coordinated EU military capacity and even to form coalitions with a view to mounting EU missions, the procedure was seen by many member states, including the UK, to carry two main dangers. The first was that membership of 'structured cooperation' would be restricted to a small band of self-selected countries and would be overtly 'exclusivist'. The second was that it would be seen as an alternative to NATO.

As a consequence of Britain's desire to mend fences with its European allies after Iraq, a trade-off was reached in September 2003 between France, Germany, and the UK whereby the latter dropped its objections to structured cooperation in exchange for explicit commitments by the former two countries that the scheme would be as inclusive as possible and that it would work in harmony with NATO. The smaller EU and NATO countries, especially the new accession states, were reassured by the lead taken by the UK and objections to structured cooperation effectively vanished. Some EU neutrals may well have continuing reservations about their own eventual membership, but most EU member states will probably aspire to join. This is all the more likely in that the capabilities required for membership have been identified as either a specialist 'niche' contribution or participation in one of the battle-groups currently being planned under the new Headline Goal 2010. Most EU member states, given the political will, should be able to find a way of joining.

What this means in practice is that the EU has given itself the political wherewithal to organise, from among its member states, a number of high intensity combat units for intervention overseas in crisis areas calling for rapid response, normally at the behest of the United Nations. The emphasis is on inter-operability, deployability, sustainability, and concurrence. These military operations will attempt to spread the load among the EU's member states, through the instrument of structured cooperation, which aims to maximise the number of member states which are militarily 'up to speed', and as rapidly as possible. It is all about capacity. What use the EU makes of that capacity is entirely up to the Council, acting unanimously. No member state will be forced to do anything. But the potential to act—in the name and under the flag of the EU—is considerable. This is a minor revolution in EU affairs.

It was complemented to some extent by another innovation: the introduction into the Constitutional Treaty Draft of a 'mutual assistance' clause stating:

> If a Member State is the victim of armed aggression on its territory, the other Member States shall have towards it an obligation of aid and assistance by all the means in their power, in accordance with Article 51 of the United Nations Charter Article I-41.

This was a highly sensitive issue. An early version of this arrangement had been vetoed by Tony Blair as his first act of security policy at the Amsterdam Council in June 1997. The Atlanticist states feared it would lead to a downgrading of the Alliance. The 'neutral' states feared they would be sucked into something they did not agree with.

On the other hand, the Europeanist states had hoped for a much more robust statement. The final text was a largely common sense recognition that, in the event of attack against a member state, the others will do what they feel they can (or wish to) do to help out. It is a small step towards the recognition of common interests, rights, and responsibilities. In the context of a Constitutional Treaty which has already enshrined structured cooperation, the very fact that a specific clause on mutual assistance is included in the text at all acquires real political significance. At the same time, a new 'solidarity clause' in the event of a terrorist attack or a natural or man-made disaster, was also introduced into the Treaty. The EU is explicitly attempting to pull ever more closely together, even in these areas which were once the last (and indeed the first) bastion of sovereignty.

Operational and planning issues

Procurement and defence planning

Armaments cooperation has hitherto taken place rigorously outside the EU framework. Two main reasons lie behind a 2004 decision to change tack. The first is the relative failure of previous attempts to coordinate procurement and armaments cooperation. The second is the accelerating reality of the European Security and Defence Policy (ESDP) agenda and the concurrent perceived need to link capabilities to armaments production. It is increasingly recognised that national defence markets in Europe are too small to sustain a viable defence industry, and that there is a need for more transparency and intra-European competition. The urgency of these drivers is reflected in the fact that, at the Thessaloniki European Council in June 2003, it was agreed to establish a European Armaments, Research and Military Capabilities Agency, commonly known as the European Defence Agency (EDA). The agency was to be created immediately. In early 2004, an Agency Establishment Team set about clarifying its objectives and role and narrowed down four basic purposes:

- To work for a more comprehensive and systematic approach to defining and meeting ESDP's *capability* needs.
- To promote *equipment collaboration*, both to contribute to defence capabilities and to foster further restructuring of European defence industries.
- To encourage the widening and deepening of regulatory approaches and the achievement of a European defence *equipment market*.
- To promote defence-relevant *research and technology* (R&T), 'pursuing collaborative use of national defence R&T funds' and 'leveraging other funding sources, including those for dual use or security-related research'.

The EDA is subject to the authority of the Council and guided by a Steering Board meeting at the level of the 25 Defence Ministers, nominally headed by the High Representative-CFSP (Javier Solana). It is managed by a Chief Executive, Nick Witney, the former head of the UK MOD's International Security Policy Division. The EDA offers the first real opportunity for the EU to bring its defence planning, military capability objectives and armaments coordination in line with the urgent tasks it is facing on the ground. Nobody expects the Agency (at least in its early years) to engage in radical restructuring of key sectors such as fighter aircraft. Rather, it will have to be highly pragmatic, concentrating on creating synergies through which it can make a real difference. The EU governments are poised to take a major step forward towards more rational armaments and defence planning. The dynamics of ESDP suggest that they will progressively situate their national plans within a European framework. The seven nation project for the construction of a European heavy transport plane—the A400M—is a case in point.

Operational planning

Another 2004 breakthrough came in the field of operational planning. The UK, throughout the debate on EU planning arrangements, had always prioritised national headquarters as the most appropriate facility for EU-only operations almost certain to be led by a 'framework' nation, as was the case with the French-led mission in Congo. The model here is the UK's permanent joint headquarters (PJHQ) at Northwood in Middlesex. This is a highly pragmatic joint headquarters, geared to operationality and readily multi-nationalisable, working directly with NATO planners at SHAPE. In addition, the UK argued in favour of an EU facility to be integrated into SHAPE (Strategic Headquarters for Allied Command Operations). French operational planning assumed rather more ambitious objectives, explicitly presented as only being achievable at EU level. In September 2002, the *Centre de Planification et de Conduite des Opérations pour la France et l'Europ*, known as the 'pre-CPCO', was launched. This is intended both as a strategic and as an operational planning facility enjoying unprecedented access to the necessary intelligence, information, and command structures (C3R) required of a major EU military operation involving up to 50,000 troops. Multinationalisation is taken as a given and great emphasis is placed on improvements in intelligence gathering. In addition, France, together with Germany, Belgium, and one or two other countries, pushed for a dedicated EU planning facility to be sited in Brussels.

The arrangements which were agreed at the European Council in Brussels in December 2003 involve a compromise between these approaches which has its own distinctive flavour. Two parallel developments are envisaged. An EU cell will be established inside SHAPE ensuring total transparency between the EU and NATO in preparation for operations taking place under the Berlin Plus procedures. NATO will also establish liaison arrangements alongside the EU Military Staff. In addition, an autonomous EU planning cell, which will be overseen by Javier Solana and will grow from 30 to about 100 staff, will be established within the EU Military Staff facility in Brussels. It will feature planning for both civil and military EU operations and will work in close cooperation with the existing national joint headquarters, which are explicitly recognised as constituting the facility of choice for EU-only missions. Under 'certain circumstances', the EU Council of Ministers will be able to call upon the EU cell for missions with both a civilian and military component and where no national headquarters appears either available or appropriate. The cell will work in close cooperation with the NATO liaison officers. It will not have a standing permanent headquarters as such, but will have the ability rapidly to establish an operations centre for a particular mission (IISS 2003). In short, in 2004 the EU acquired planning facilities for every conceivable type of mission—in principle.

Intelligence

Another potential breakthrough in 2004 came in the field of intelligence gathering. The agreement between the EU and the US for the coordination of the Galileo satellite navigation system with the US's GPS system potentially constitutes a major step forward on the road to EU autonomy in intelligence gathering (Lindstrom 2003a). I say 'potentially' for two reasons. First, because Galileo is explicitly configured as a civilian programme. Although it has considerable military potential, the political decision to develop that potential has yet to be taken. Secondly, for the EU collectively to forge an integrated intelligence capacity (not to mention an intelligence agency) several major hurdles would have to be cleared—not the least of which is the intimate relationship between the UK and the US intelligence services. However, even well short of any EU-dedicated intelligence capabilities, a recent report suggests that much can be done vastly to improve the current level of intelligence coordination, including expansion of the existing SITCEN, extending the competencies of Europol and establishing a European network connecting the National High Authorities of Intelligence (NHAIs) and improving cross-agency cooperation at national level (Muller-Wille 2004).

Towards a long-term vision?

A longer term vision was proposed in May 2004 by the 'Venusberg Group' of strategic researchers (Venusberg 2004). The new proposals call for the EU to develop 'a holistic, strategic civil-military vision that combines achievable means and ends'. The EU, it argues, must be able to carry out 'a far broader range of missions than currently envisaged, over far greater distance, at potentially higher levels of conflict intensity and for longer periods'. New institutions such as an EU Security Council, an EU Security Minister, and an EU Homeland Security Agency are envisaged. This would require intensive cooperation with NATO and the US but also robustly autonomous EU facilities such as operational planning, including an EU Permanent Combined Joint Headquarters, as well as satellite-based intelligence 'eyes and ears', jointly trained special forces, and the development of a 10,000 strong European Gendarmerie[16] to bridge the gap between combat soldiering and policing. It calls for an EU Joint Intelligence Committee as well as a European Security and Defence College, a common research and technology budget coordinated through a robust European Defence Agency and even a 'Buy European First' strategy for the procurement and rationalisation of existing spending through a Defence Business Affairs Programme. These radical and sweeping proposals, published as this chapter was going to press, are likely to constitute a major sounding board for the debate on European security and defence developments over the next ten to 15 years.[17]

They were complemented by the proposals of a private group reporting to High Representative Solana, in a document entitled 'A Human Security Doctrine for Europe'. The proposals built on ESDP's traditional care to combine civilian and military instruments. Noting that 'Europeans can no longer feel secure when large parts of the world are insecure', the report defines human security as 'freedom for individuals from basic insecurities caused by gross human rights violations'. The doctrine comprises three elements:[18]

- Seven principles for operations in situations of severe insecurity: the primacy of human rights, clear political authority, multilateralism, a bottom-up approach, regional focus, the use of legal instruments, and the appropriate use of force. The report puts particular emphasis on communication, consultation, dialogue and partnership with the local population in order to improve early warning, intelligence gathering, mobilisation of local support, implementation and sustainability.

- A 'Human Security Response Force', composed of 15,000 men and women, of whom at least one third would be civilian (police, human rights monitors, development and humanitarian specialists). The Force would be drawn from dedicated troops and civilian capabilities already made available by member states as well as a proposed 'Human Security Volunteer Service'.

- A new legal framework to govern both the decision to intervene and operations on the ground. This would build on the domestic law of host states, the domestic law of sending states, international criminal law, international human rights law and international humanitarian law.

The Human Security Response Force would be under the direction of the new Union Foreign Minister. If implemented these significant proposals would help clearly to distinguish the EU's security strategy from that of the United States.

Conclusions: from the short to the medium term and beyond

Any overall evaluation of European military capacity has to be set within a very clear timeframe. Anyone who had predicted in 1999 that the EU would be mounting autonomous military missions by 2003 would probably have been laughed out of court. Much has been accomplished very rapidly. However, over the next five years (the short term), the EU will need to absorb the lessons of its military missions, concentrate on plugging the gaps in strategic assets, develop genuinely integrated operational capacity, and perfect command, logistics and communications procedures. This will limit actual operations to the type and style of those we have already witnessed and are about to witness. During this period, however, the EU will also need to plan procurement projects for the medium term (the following 15 years). This will necessitate tough political decisions about the ultimate size, scale, and style of EU military ambitions. How far down the road towards US-style network centric warfare will the Union wish to go? How many new generation platforms and other strategic systems will it require, and for what purposes? How far afield does it anticipate intervening? In parallel, the Union will have to develop a holistic Strategic Concept along the lines of the proposals discussed above. Without clear guidelines as to its ultimate objectives and purpose, progress will be stalled. In the longer term, only two factors prevent the EU from developing genuinely autonomous and seriously credible military muscle: one, its ability to cooperate and to integrate, and two the political will to implement its decisions, by acting robustly in support of the values and interests outlined in its evolving Security Strategy. That is the challenge facing the next generation of Europeans.

Notes

1 The concept was first used by President François Mitterrand and Chancellor Helmut Kohl in February 1990 in a joint letter to the Irish Presidency of the EU. It was incorporated into the Maastricht negotiations (and, later, Treaty) as a new chapter in EU policy-making.

2 It is not insignificant that two of the major tomes of constructivist theory (Wendt 1999; Katzenstein 1996) fail to address the European Union as such.

3 Consider the irony of it being a *Gaullist* president, Jacques Chirac, who reversed his socialist predecessor's inhibitions about bringing France back into the NATO fold in 1995; or of it being a British prime minister, Tony Blair, who, at Saint-Malo in 1998, acted as midwife to European defence integration.

4 In fact, it should be noted that the territory of former Yugoslavia is situated within the spatial boundaries of the EU, between Greece to the south, Austria to the north and Italy to the West. The issue of the Eastern boundary remains open.

5 In October 1981, Ronald Reagan, in response to a journalist's question about NATO's plan to deploy a new range of nuclear missiles in Europe, stated that he could imagine fighting a nuclear war in Europe without it spreading to the territories of the superpowers. In 1986, at Reykjavík, he informally agreed with Mikhail

Gorbachev to scrap all nuclear weapons from the face of the earth.

6 The text of the 'Saint-Malo Declaration' of 4 December 1998 is published, along with other 'Core Documents' of ESDP, in Rutten 2001, 8–9. (Further Core Documents of ESDP in Rutten 2002; Haine 2003; Missiroli 2003).

7 Turkey, Norway, and Iceland—joined in April 1999 by the Czech Republic, Hungary, and Poland.

8 Air-to-Air Refuelling; Combat Search and Rescue; Headquarters; Nuclear, Biological and Chemical Defences; Special Operations Forces; Theatre Ballistic Missile Defence; Strategic Air Mobility; Space; Unmanned Aerial Vehicle/Surveillance and Target Acquisition Units; Interoperability.

9 'Network Centric Warfare enables the military to leverage extensive information to their advantage in an effort to dramatically increase combat effectiveness and efficiency through self-synchronization across the host of entities operating on the network. [. . .] The real-time theatre-wide battlefield management system coupled with intelligent collaborative scenario planning systems will create the ability to retask units or division in seconds. (Coleman 2004). See http://www.iwar.org.uk/index.htm for full details on information warfare.

10 This would simply allow EU forces to 'plug in' to certain segments of the US network (Venusberg 2004, 43).

11 Battle-groups are units of 1,500 troops for combat in jungle, desert or mountain conditions and will be deployable within 15 days and sustainable in the field for up to 30 days.

12 Two good analytical critiques of the Solana document are Biscop & Coolsaet 2003 and Haine 2003a.

13 The post-holder's basic functions are laid out in Article I-28 of the Constitutional Treaty.

14 In fact the first post-holder—Javier Solana—was appointed in June 2004 before the post itself had been created.

15 Constitutional Treaty, I-41(6). & III-312.

16 In September 2004, this proposal became a reality with the establishment of the European Gendarmerie Force (EGF) involving cooperation between France, Spain, Italy, Portugal, and the Netherlands.

17 Another forward-looking report was published in June 2004 (White Paper 2004), analysing scenarios for EU troop deployment and methods of combating capabilities deficiencies.

18 The following extracts are taken from *A Human Security Doctrine for Europe: the Barcelona Report of the Study Group on Europe's Security Capabilities*, presented to EU High Representative Javier Solana in Barcelona, 15 September 2004. The document can be found on-line at http://www.lse.ac.uk/Depts/global/ Human%20Security%20Report %20Full.pdf.

Further reading

Treatments that look at the long-term evolution of European security and defence policies include Deighton (1997) and Van Eekelen (1998). Howorth (2000), and Howorth and Keeler (2003) are important sources for analysis of the debates that characterised the late 1990s and the new millennium, whilst Quinlan (2002) provides a transatlantic perspective. The best sources for documentation and policy debates from the mid-1990s onwards in general are the various publications of the European Union Institute for Security Studies (formerly the WEU Institute for Security Studies—see also Web links below): the collections directed by Rutten (2001, 2002), Haine (2003), and Missiroli (2003) pull together the key documents relating to the evolving negotiations and institutional developments, providing an invaluable record and collections of 'raw material' for analysis.

Deighton, A. (ed.) (1997), *Western European Union, 1954–97: Defence, Security, Integration* (Oxford: St Antony's College).

Haine, J.-Y. (dir.) (2003), *From Laeken to Copenhagen: European Defence—Core Documents III*. Chaillot Paper 57 (Paris: EU Institute for Security Studies).

Howorth, J. (2000), *European Integration and Defence: The Ultimate Challenge?* Chaillot Paper 43 (Paris: EU Institute for Security Studies).

Howorth, J., and Keeler, J. (eds) (2003), *Defending Europe: The EU, NATO, and the Quest for European Autonomy* (New York: Palgrave).

Missiroli, A. (dir.) (2003), *From Copenhagen to Brussels: European Defence—Core Documents IV*. Chaillot Paper 67 (Paris: EU Institute for Security Studies).

Quinlan, M. (2002), *European Defense Cooperation: Asset or Threat to NATO?* (Washington, DC: Woodrow Wilson Center Press).

Rutten, M. (dir.) (2001), *From Saint-Malo to Nice: European Defence — Core Documents.* Chaillot Paper 47 (Paris: EU Institute for Security Studies).

Rutten, M. (dir.) (2002), *From Nice to Laeken: European Defence — Core Documents II.*

Chaillot Paper 51 (Paris: EU Institute for Security Studies).

Van Eekelen, W. (1998), *Debating European Security, 1948–1998* (Brussels: CEPS).

Web links

The most useful source of documentation and discussion about the ESDP and its development is the web site of the European Union Institute for Security Studies in Paris: http://www.iss-eu.org; here you will find full text of all newsletters, discussion papers and the extensive series of Chaillot Papers (several of which are cited in Further Reading). Other sources include the European Commission web site; http://www.europa.eu.int, which has links to defence policy sources as well as official documentation, and the Fornet site, http://www.fornet.info.

Chapter 10

The External Face of Internal Security

Wyn Rees

Contents

Summary

This chapter seeks to examine how the development by the EU of an internal security regime has had implications for external policy. The EU has identified growing security challenges from outside the territory of the member states, in the form of international crime and drug trafficking, terrorism and illegal immigration. The responses that the EU has made to these challenges, in the form of judicial and police cooperation, as well as the creation of common frontiers, have generated important foreign policy consequences. Furthermore, the EU has sought cooperation from third countries in countering some of these problems. The evolving EU security regime has demonstrated the interconnectedness between internal and external security.

Introduction

Over the last decade the EU has developed a role as an internal security actor. The Justice and Home Affairs (JHA) portfolio, or 'third pillar' of the Treaty on European Union (TEU), has been one of the fastest growth areas of EU activity in that period. EU member states perceive that they face growing security challenges that can only be addressed through common, or at least coordinated, policies.

The remit of internal security extends across a wide variety of fields. At one end of the spectrum are measures to counteract transnational organised crime, drug trafficking, and cross-border terrorism. At the other end of the spectrum are measures to counter illegal immigration and unfounded asylum applications and preserve the integrity of external borders. EU member states have been developing a range of policies to meet these challenges to their internal security. Amongst these policies are police and judicial cooperation across the territories of the Union, the coordinated management of borders and common policies towards immigration. In addition, the member states have established dedicated agencies to facilitate police and judicial cooperation, in the form of the European Police Office (Europol) and 'Eurojust', as well as monitoring agencies for drug control such as the European Monitoring Centre for Drugs and Drug Addiction (EMCDAA) in Lisbon.

Although the development of JHA has been intimately concerned with debates about national sovereignty and the powers of member states, a neglected dimension has been the way in which internal security issues raise important external policy considerations. There has always been recognition of the fact, to a limited extent, that internal security has possessed an external dimension and vice versa. For example, the extradition of criminal suspects between states, agreements to allow 'hot pursuit' by police across national borders, customs cooperation and the sharing of criminal intelligence between countries, have all blurred the boundary between internal security affairs and foreign policy cooperation. In the 1990s, the dramatic expansion in the scale of JHA activities focused attention to an unprecedented extent on the nexus between internal and external security.

This chapter attempts to illuminate the international relations dimensions of the EU's JHA activities. In the first section it begins by looking at the limited cooperation that occurred in this field prior to the signing of the Treaty on European Union. It then proceeds in the second section to chart the growth of the JHA Third Pillar in response to the perceived external post-Cold War threats. In the final section the chapter investigates the pattern of JHA-related activities that the EU has pursued with third countries, including allies such as the United States, as well as prospective new members of the Union.

The history of internal security cooperation

Cooperation in the field of internal security, prior to the construction of the JHA pillar, was fragmented and shallow. The member states of the European Community (EC) recognised that they shared mutual interests in protecting their territories, but they lacked an overarching framework in which to systematise their cooperation. This was principally because the overwhelming security preoccupation during the Cold War was the threat of military aggression from the Soviet Union and its Warsaw Pact allies. Within such a paradigm, little attention was accorded to cooperation over internal security when the external military threat was so pressing.

Nevertheless, there were three main stimuli for the EC's development of an internal security framework. One of these was the increase in international terrorism from the early 1970s, conducted principally by Palestinian groups. European governments, amongst others in the west, came to recognise their shared vulnerability in the face of a rising international menace. The EC created TREVI (*Terrorisme, Radicalisme et Violence Internationale*), in 1976, as a bi-annual forum for interior ministers to share intelligence on the threat from international terrorism. Trevi remained an intergovernmental form of activity that was carried out under the aegis of the nascent 'European Political Cooperation' (EPC). The linking of Trevi to EPC served as acknowledgement of the blurred boundary between internal security matters and foreign policy. Trevi's competences were expanded in 1985 when a working group was established to focus on drug trafficking and subsequently on organised criminal activity.

The second stimulus to the development of EC internal security cooperation was the decision to create a Single Market by 1992. The Single Market project conceived of the territory of the member states as a unified space and the accompanying Schengen agreement of 1985 (signed in 1990) was designed to facilitate the free movement of goods and people within this area. Both the Single Market and Schengen initiatives recognised that free movement raised questions about the vulnerability of the European space to criminal activity and outside penetration. The founding members of Schengen—Germany, France, Belgium, the Netherlands, and Luxembourg—agreed to remove their internal borders in favour of a common external frontier. Measures to control immigration were agreed in the Dublin Convention of 1990 which laid down common standards for processing asylum applications across the territory of the member states. Each member state had the obligation to test the eligibility of an asylum seeker if they were the first territory on which the applicant arrived.

The Schengen and Dublin Conventions had major implications for the internal security of the EC member states. On the one hand, the internal security of the participants was made interdependent as all had to rely on the enforcement of the common external frontiers. In the words of Geddes, 'the "low politics" of economic interdependence seemed to have spilled over into the "high politics" of border control and state security' (2000, 3). Schengen proved to be a powerful motivator for new governance structures and security mechanisms amongst its signatories. The seriousness with which this has been taken was exemplified by the fact that after acceding to Schengen, Italy was made to wait for several years until its border controls were judged to be compliant. On the other hand, the ramifications of Schengen have been felt by the EC's neighbours. Countries bordering Schengen frontiers have been forced to interact with a group of EC member states who act in concert on security matters. Neighbours have been made to feel that they represent a dangerous 'outside', from which the citizens of the Community must be protected; thereby contributing to a perception of a 'Fortress Europe' being constructed.

A third powerful stimulus to the EC's internal security framework was the end of the Cold War. The fear of military conflict in Europe diminished as the Warsaw Pact collapsed and then the Soviet Union imploded. Conflicts have still afflicted the continent: but they have remained localised, and have not raised for Western Europe the dilemmas of survival that characterised the Cold War. This has enabled the emergence of a broader security agenda which the EC has been well placed to address. The fact that the EC represented a multi-level polity with competences in fields such as law enforcement has made it an appropriate actor to combat new transnational security challenges. Narrowly configured military organisations such as NATO have been less well suited to coping with non-military risks.

Post-Cold War internal security challenges

The justification for the development of internal security structures and policies by the EC/EU has resulted from perceived threats to the territories of the member states. These problems did not suddenly materialise in 1990: many European states, for example, experienced indigenous terrorist groups. Similarly, countries such as Italy have long suffered with domestic organised crime problems. What has occurred in the 1990s has been a re-prioritisation of the security agenda as military threats have diminished in importance. The environment of post-Cold War Europe also served to amplify the risks arising from these new threats. The collapse of former socialist states; the economic turbulence and corresponding social dislocation surrounding the transition to market economies in the east; the opening up of borders and the emergence of inter-ethnic conflicts all served to increase the sense of vulnerability in western Europe.

Challenges from international terrorism, transnational crime, and illegal immigration have been elevated to a level whereby they are discussed as security threats to the European space. The actors responsible for activating and obtaining legitimacy for this security discourse (Buzan, Waever and de Wilde 1998) have been a mix of both representatives of national governments—interior ministry officials and law enforcement officers—and officials from the EC/EU. A complex process of interaction has occurred between national agencies and representatives at the European level. This interaction has grown commensurately with the expansion of the Union's competences in the internal security field. The need to counter perceived threats, real or exaggerated, has justified EU cooperation and the establishment of agencies, such as Europol and the EMCDAA, have created a bureaucratic constituency in support of this cooperation. This has developed into a dynamic of the European integration process with countries that are advocates of closer union proposing greater powers for EU agencies.

Several analysts have expressed concerns about the process of 'securitisation' that has taken place in relation to new challenges. Bigo has observed that the manner in which the crime threats have been constructed, namely as external to the EU, have served to justify a Europe-wide response (1999, 67). Similarly, den Boer notes that the 'construction of a common threat may have become an instrument in the formation of a common identity' (1999, 18).

These suspicions about the underlying motivations for the approach to internal security challenges are borne out by the EU response to the problems of illegal immigration and unjustified asylum applications. These issues have also become part of the securitisation process. This is in spite of the fact that immigration and asylum usually involve people from poor and economically stagnating regions of the world searching for better economic prospects. The concept of 'harm' inflicted on recipient states is difficult to measure, other than in the pressure that may be placed on employment and social security provisions, or the risk of unskilled migrants failing to obtain work and resorting to crime. 'Harm' by such immigration is different in nature to that which might be inflicted by acts of terrorism. Yet the two have become conflated due to the fear that illegal residents in a European country could perpetrate terrorist acts. In numerous EU documents, problems as diverse as terrorism and bogus asylum applications are grouped together as part of the new security challenges. The result has been the actuation of an all-embracing security discourse that fails to differentiate between problems and tends to justify blanket responses.

Transnational crime and drug trafficking

One of the foremost post-Cold War European security concerns has been the increase in crime carried out by organised gangs across international borders. The types of interstate crimes that are conducted are diverse in nature. They include commodity crimes, such as cars or cigarettes, which are frequently stolen in the west and then smuggled to neighbouring regions to be sold on the black market, or smuggled weapons or sensitive materials. Organised crime groups are involved in much of the trafficking of human beings as well as other crimes such as the evasion of import taxes on goods, prostitution, and fraud. Certain crimes are associated with organised groups due to the scale of the activity and the infrastructure and sophistication required to execute them. The creation of a common external frontier within the EU has provided an added incentive because it has meant that once this outer barrier is breached, then there are no other obstacles to prevent criminal groups from moving throughout the European space.

Money laundering is another form of illegal activity that requires high levels of organisation. Laundering is a process by which criminally derived funds are passed through the international financial system in order to render them as legitimate. The scale of this problem has been increasing dramatically: partly because of the speed with which it is possible to transmit money electronically and partly because of the proliferation of new banks in the eastern half of Europe that have been established with only rudimentary regulatory oversight. The laundering of money represents a major problem for law enforcement authorities because if it flows across several financial jurisdictions then it becomes extremely difficult to trace. Neverthe-less, money laundering also represents an opportunity for the law enforcement com-munity because it exposes the criminal to possible detection and arrest.

Those countries at the eastern edge of the European Union have felt the most vul-nerable to the rise of organised crime groups penetrating from central and eastern Europe. It has been difficult to determine how much of the perceived rise in or-ganised crime activity has resulted from groups extending their activities from east to west as compared to domestically grown groups in the west operating beyond their borders (Europol: 2001). However, those EU states in proximity to the Balkans and Europe's eastern borders have expressed concern at evidence of organised crime gangs exporting their operations from these areas. The war in the Balkans and the disintegration of the states of the former-Yugoslavia had the effect of engendering a very permissive environment for illegal activities. Organised crime, for example, de-veloped entrenched positions in Albania, Serbia, Montenegro, and Bosnia. Russian, Chechen and Ukrainian crime groups have also achieved particular notoriety in the west, not only for the range of activities in which they are engaged but also for their ruthlessness.

The flow of illegal drugs into western Europe rose during the 1980s and the range of sources diversified (Ruggiero and South 1995). Heroin has long been smuggled from states in the 'Golden Triangle' and 'Golden Crescent', such as Afghanistan, My-anmar, Thailand, and Laos. It follows several routes into western cities, often traf-ficked by ethnically homogeneous gangs: one through the Balkans, another through Turkey and a third through Russia and the Central and East European Countries (CEECs) (Stares 1996) (see Figure 10.1 on heroin seizures in Europe, 1990–2002). Co-caine consumption rose substantially in the 1980s as a result of inflows into southern Europe from the Andean states of Colombia, Bolivia, and Peru. Europe's importation of cocaine is only about one third of the level in the United States but it still amounts to a sizeable hundred tons per year. Other types of drugs, such as cannabis, are impor-ted from North Africa whilst some synthetic drugs are now entering Western Europe from countries like Poland.

Evidence has suggested that there is more cooperation between drug trafficking groups in an expanding market, especially in cocaine and synthetic drugs. Greater co-operation is consistent with the trend within organised crime where activity by large, ethnically homogeneous groups seems to be giving way to more opportunistic and mixed nationality groups. Albanian and Turkish groups are still heavily involved in the trade in drugs and are able to channel supplies along their established smuggling routes. In addition, they can draw upon help from diasporas of their fellow country-men in most European cities.

The EU has responded energetically to the problem posed by drug trafficking. As an issue it has grown to account for nearly 60% of the requests for information re-ceived by Europol (Europol 2000). Not only has the EU created cooperative structures, such as the Mutual Assistance Group and the *Comité Européen de la Lutte Anti-Drogue* (CELAD), it has also undertaken regular four year Action Plans, starting in 1990, in or-der to establish EU-wide priorities in combating the problem (European Monitoring Centre for Drugs and Drug Addiction 2000).

States are poorly prepared to counter the threats posed by organised criminals and drug trafficking organisations. Securing prosecutions, when criminal activity

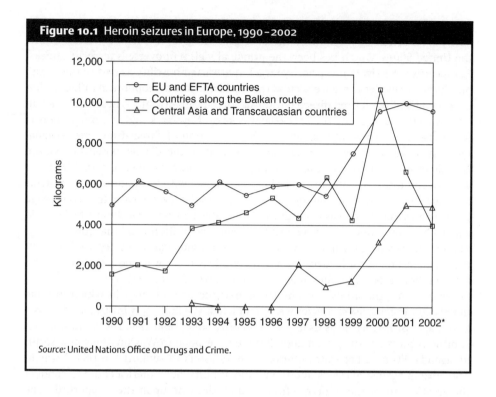

Figure 10.1 Heroin seizures in Europe, 1990–2002

Legend:
- EU and EFTA countries
- Countries along the Balkan route
- Central Asia and Transcaucasian countries

Source: United Nations Office on Drugs and Crime.

may have been carried out across several legal jurisdictions, demands the admissibility of evidence between national judicial systems as well as the willingness of courts to respect judicial decisions from neighbouring countries. In contrast to the inherent fluidity of transnational criminals, states are relatively inflexible agents that must engineer cooperation and remain constrained by legal processes. States are limited by the means that police forces can employ to obtain evidence and have to draft special legislation to counter organised forms of criminal activity. It has been widely acknowledged that law enforcement activities must break free of their national frameworks if they are to deal with the challenge effectively. This thinking has underpinned efforts to develop the necessary structures at the EU level to counter international crime.

The challenge from terrorism

European states have been vulnerable to sporadic terrorism that results from their political and colonial histories, such as France's experience of Algerian-inspired violence and the UK's troubles in Northern Ireland since 1969. The issue of terrorism has proved traditionally to be more capable of dividing than uniting European states. Apart from the modest example of TREVI, the divisive nature of the terrorist phenomenon was evident in the poor record of European bilateral cooperation, such as over extradition, and their failure even to agree upon a common definition of terrorism. It was not until 1999, for example, that Europol was given the right to become involved in the EU fight against terrorism.

The poor European record on cooperating against international terrorism was partly a reflection of the limited threat it presented to EU member states. Unlike the United States, which has been the principal victim of overseas terrorist attacks, Europe was a relatively low priority target. It attracted hostility as part of the 'west', but Europe's smaller presence around the world and lower geopolitical influence has inspired less of the hatred directed towards its transatlantic ally. These European attitudes were shattered by the al-Qaeda attacks on New York and Washington on 11 September 2001. These attacks altered the perception of threat from international terrorist movements by exposing the full extent of the danger posed by extremist religious movements seeking to inflict the maximum number of casualties upon western countries. Had these attacks been conducted with weapons of mass destruction, such as chemical or radiological devices, then the level of casualties could have been even worse. There was a recognition in western Europe that these attacks could equally have been undertaken against Paris, London, or Berlin and that concerted action on the part of the whole international community was necessary. In the event, the terrorist attack on Madrid in March 2004 in which over 200 people died confirmed that Europe was vulnerable to the new wave of atrocities.

Furthermore, the attacks on the US altered the environment in which international counter-terrorist strategies were conducted. The Bush Administration declared a 'War against Terrorism' as its foremost security policy objective. The result was that enormous pressure was placed upon Europe to respond to Washington's new security agenda. EU member states offered military assets to support the US-led war in Afghanistan against al-Qaeda and their Taliban hosts, but America chose to conduct the greater part of the military effort without drawing upon this support. Europe accepted a major role in the post-conflict policing of Afghanistan as part of the International Security Assistance Force. The EU has been spurred into more proactive policies towards states designated by the US as state-sponsors of terrorist groups. EU member states have led efforts to change the policies of countries such as North Korea, Iran, and Libya who have been regarded as 'states of concern' by the US in relation to terrorism and the development of weapons of mass destruction.

EU members have taken a range of measures to improve their own internal security. Border controls and the security of their airports have been increased through more stringent checks on documents and additional measures and an information exchange on visas as a direct response to the *modus operandi* of the 9/11 bombers. This has been complemented by greater intelligence sharing on terrorist matters both with other EU states and with third countries. The EU was able to secure agreement upon a common definition of terrorism (Council of the European Union 2002), which had hitherto eluded their efforts. A Common European Arrest Warrant was put into effect, allowing a warrant for the arrest of a suspect to be issued in one EU state and acted upon in another. The warrant included terrorism but also stretched to include 31 other offences that involve jail sentences exceeding three years, including the illicit trafficking of people and participation in a criminal organisation. Finally, systematic efforts have been undertaken to target terrorist sources of finance, by the freezing of assets of organisations linked to terrorism and by action to combat the laundering of money. In cooperation with the US, the EU members have undertaken to ratify all the existing conventions on terrorist financing and states joining the Union in the future will also be expected to comply (European Council 2001b).

Immigration and refugees

Concern over immigration into Europe is not a new phenomenon. Spain and Italy, for example, have long experienced migration pressures from the poor states of North Africa where people have been attracted by high western standards of living. The problem was compounded by the policy of European governments since the 1970s of refusing to accept migrants for reasons other than family unity. With the end of the Cold War, there were fears that mass migration pressures would shift from the south to the east and that waves of economic migrants would emerge from eastern Europe. It was envisaged that not only would people from the states of Central Europe seek to emigrate to the west but that the region as a whole could become a holding area for millions of migrants from central, southern, and eastern Asia (Lavenex 1998, 288). As Schengen dismantled the borders between EU countries it was likely to be more attractive for migrants to attempt to breach the Union's single common frontier.

Large-scale immigration flows from east to west did not materialise in the 1990s. Yet concerns regarding immigration were exacerbated by the rise in refugee flows from conflicts on the periphery of the continent. The conflict in Bosnia, for example, generated 2.75 million refugees between 1991 and 1995 (United Nations High Commissioner for Refugees 1999). EU members such as Germany bore the main brunt of the refugee flows and this influenced the decision of European governments to intervene in the conflict in 1995, through NATO, and attempt to restore stability. The conflict in Kosovo in 1999, although it led to much lower levels of refugee movements into western Europe because the problem was contained in the region, raised similar concerns. In addition, asylum applications to West European countries have grown rapidly in numbers and have contributed to a perception of an immigration crisis. Legitimate asylum applications have increased as people have sought to flee countries in domestic turmoil, such as Afghanistan, Iraq, and Sri Lanka. But there has been a corresponding increase in illegitimate asylum applications as people have claimed they are fleeing from persecution when in fact their motivation has been to improve their economic circumstances (see the Table: 'Asylum claims submitted to the European Union, 1990–2003).

There has also been a rise in the orchestrated trafficking of people for profit into the territories of the EU member states. Human beings are trafficked onto European shores as a result of people seeking to escape from lives of extreme poverty and deprivation elsewhere in the world. Sometimes women and children are trafficked against their will and sold into prostitution in the west—a form of modern day slavery. Three principal trafficking routes are known to exist into Europe. One is through the Balkans bringing people from that region, as well as from further afield such as South East Asia and China. The traffickers are mainly Chinese and Albanian organised crime groups. A second route, involving traffickers from Russia and the Caucasus, moves people through parts of Russia, Ukraine, Belarus, and the Baltic states. A third route comprises people from North Africa who seek to cross the Straits of Gibraltar and land in Spain (Mitsilegas, Monar and Rees 2003, 81). These smuggling paths often mirror established drug trafficking routes and confirm that organised crime groups treat human trafficking as another form of income alongside

Table 10.1 Asylum claims submitted in the European Union, 1990–2003			
Country	Total	Share	Per 1,000 population
Sweden	349,700	6.6%	39.4
Austria	249,800	4.7%	30.8
Belgium	283,400	5.3%	27.5
Netherlands	433,500	8.1%	27.0
Germany	2,168,000	40.7%	26.3
Denmark	117,900	2.2%	22.0
Luxembourg	9,700	0.2%	21.7
Ireland	59,300	1.1%	15.2
UK	851,930	16.0%	14.4
France	485,700	9.1%	8.1
Finland	29,600	0.6%	5.7
Greece	47,000	0.9%	4.3
Spain	113,100	2.1%	2.8
Italy	118,800	2.2%	2.1
Portugal	6,400	0.1%	0.6
Total	5,323,830	100.0%	14.0

Source: 'Asylum Levels and Trends 2003,' United Nations High Commissioner for Refugees.

illegal drugs or stolen goods. The scale of the activity and the growing sophistication of counter-measures by states has led to larger groups becoming involved. Parts of Europe that have been particularly vulnerable to inflows of people include the coast of southern Italy and eastern Austria. Although immigration and criminality are separate issues, the two have become linked in the minds of the public, due in large part to the activities of the popular press and to hard right political parties desirous of fomenting protest votes.

Creating and developing the EU's Justice and Home Affairs Pillar

The creation of the 'third Pillar' in Justice and Home Affairs as a part of the Treaty on the European Union was a response to the internal security challenges outlined above. The Treaty marked the beginning of the EU's formal involvement in a range of issues including asylum and police cooperation, mutual assistance in civil and criminal law and the establishment of a judicial network. The TEU built upon the modest foundations in internal security cooperation that had evolved bilaterally between European governments as well as the nascent multilateral efforts that were embodied within TREVI.

Originally, the third pillar was purely intergovernmental in nature: a reflection of the fact that there was little stomach amongst states such as the UK for a Community approach towards internal security. Member governments retained tight control over the remit of JHA, namely organised crime, illegal immigration, drug trafficking, asylum and immigration. A working group dealing with international organised crime and drug trafficking was established within the powerful K-4 coordinating committee framework (Chalk 2000, 178). The Treaty represented no more than a potential framework for the future. The Commission possessed only a limited right of initiative in JHA and only weak, non-legally binding instruments were made available — 'Common Positions', 'Conventions', and 'Joint Actions'. The European Commission's report to the Reflection Group in May 1995 reflected this sense of disappointment with the ineffectual powers that had been created at Maastricht.

It was inevitable from the structure created by the TEU that there would be issues that would overlap between the third pillar and other parts of the Union. For example, even though drug policy resided in the JHA portfolio, many of the instruments by which the EU could conduct counter-drug activities with other countries resided within the first and second pillars. This was exemplified when the EU agreed to control the sale of precursor chemicals for illegal drugs that drew upon trade powers within the first pillar. Similarly, terrorism remained outside of JHA because some member states were concerned about the implications for their sovereignty and counter terrorist policies were conducted under the Common Foreign and Security Policy (CFSP). The problem of so-called 'cross pillar' issues illustrates both the artificial nature of the EU structure and the difficulties of dealing with internal and external security issues in a coherent way.

Two other sources of tension have compounded difficulties inherent within the third pillar. First, the decision-making processes in all three pillars are different. This has rendered it difficult to obtain agreement on complementary steps in the first and second pillars when an initiative is undertaken in the third pillar. Second, the record of member state cooperation in the sensitive sphere of CFSP has not been a happy one and it has frequently proved problematic for the external aspects of internal security policy to be addressed adequately. Indeed, in the Treaty on European Union, provision had not been made for the EU to make treaty agreements with other countries on JHA matters. This was remedied in the Treaty of Amsterdam (ToA) so that new provisions in relation to CFSP made it possible for the EU to conclude agreements with third countries on policing and judicial issues. Such a development enabled the EU to play a full part in the drawing up of the UN Convention on Transnational Organised Crime, which was signed in Naples in December 2000.

Ironically, the lack of progress in CFSP matters proved to be an indirect source of benefit to the third pillar when the time came to assess the progress of the TEU. When an Intergovernmental Conference was convened in 1996 for the purpose of revising the TEU, the inability of the member states to achieve significant progress in the area of the CFSP led to a greater political will to advance integration in other sectors. This factor, coupled with a perception of a growing risk to internal security from organised crime and illegal immigration, provided a stimulus to achieving substantial steps forward in JHA. The Treaty of Amsterdam created an 'Area of Freedom, Security and Justice' (AFSJ) and asserted the aim of 'provid(ing) citizens with a high level of safety' (Title VI, Article 29, Treaty on European Union). The ToA, and the subsequent Vienna Action Plan of December 1998 which clarified the Treaty's aims, established free movement and the maintenance of a secure internal environment, as core Union objectives. To provide free movement as well as a secure and just internal space meant that EU citizens had to be protected from external threats such as international crime and terrorism. This reinforced the linkage that had been made at Maastricht between crime and immigration. More than ever before, the EU was drawing a sharp distinction between a safe and secure internal space and a threatening and dangerous external area.

The ToA 'communitarised' key aspects of the JHA portfolio. Matters relating to asylum, immigration and external border controls were removed from former Title VI, TEU and placed in the first pillar, under a new Title IV. This meant that Community instruments could be used in relation to these issues after a transitional period of five years. Certain intergovernmental features were retained in Title IV, such as a shared right of initiative between the European Commission and the member states as well as limited powers for the European Parliament. Pastore notes that interior ministries retained their primacy over asylum, immigration and external border controls through the creation of a Strategic Committee on Immigration, Frontiers and Asylum (SCIFA), rather than let the subjects fall under the control of Coreper (2001, 8).

The desire to make progress in the field of immigration reflected two factors. First, that the envisaged policies on migration and asylum had not borne fruit in the early 1990s. Second, that immigration pressures over the last decade had rendered several member states much more receptive to the idea of European cooperation on this subject. The UK, for example, has recently been in the vanguard of those states arguing for an equitable distribution of asylum seekers amongst EU members due to the rapid increase in its number of applications. The need for a common EU asylum policy is now widely agreed upon.

Another important step within the Treaty was the incorporation of the Schengen Convention on internal and external frontiers. At a stroke this simplified the framework for EU internal security by ending the artificial split between matters relating to immigration, asylum and visas from the vital issue of the control of borders. Three states, the UK, Ireland, and Denmark, chose to remain outside of the Schengen provisions and continue their own national arrangements. Nevertheless, Schengen brought a vital ingredient in the Union's relationship with its neighbours inside the EU *acquis*. A practical result of this decision has been that the Schengen Information System (SIS), with its approximately fourteen million records and fingerprints of individuals, has been made available to Europol (Bort 2000, 3). The inclusion of Schengen into the *acquis* also had important implications for EU external relations. Norway and Iceland had previously negotiated special border arrangements with the Schengen members in order to ensure that their citizens did not need to apply for visas to visit the EU. With the signing of the ToA both of these countries had to draw up an agreement with the EU to preserve their special status.

Box 10.1 Key aspects of the Tampere Conclusions, October 1999

- The creation of an 'Area of Freedom, Security and Justice'
- The establishment of a common European asylum system
- Cooperation on the management of migration
- Mutual recognition of judicial decisions
- Agreement on common definitions of crimes
- The creation of 'Eurojust' and a 'European Police College'
- EU action against money laundering

Policing and judicial cooperation issues were not communitarised in the Amsterdam Treaty as they were considered too sensitive to be included in the first pillar and were kept within Title VI, TEU. The intergovernmental nature of the former Third Pillar was circumscribed, however, by new powers of consultation that were afforded to the European Parliament as well as a role granted to the European Court of Justice. Police and judicial matters were placed under the auspices of the new Article 36 Committee, which replaced the former K.4 Committee. Thus, the Amsterdam Treaty left the EU with a mixed intergovernmental and communitarised internal security regime, but one in which there was momentum towards closer integration.

At the special EU Summit at Tampere in October 1999 (see Box 10.1), a road map for future EU priorities in JHA was agreed. The operational role of Europol was strengthened in relation to the fight against organised crime: the mutual recognition of member states' judicial decisions was endorsed as an alternative to seeking the harmonisation of laws: an EU judicial body, 'Eurojust', would be created to coordinate multi-jurisdictional prosecutions and joint investigative teams could be established in relation to terrorism, drugs and the trafficking in people. There was thus substantial progress in enhancing the law enforcement powers of the EU, but critics contended that insufficient attention was paid to issues of democratic accountability through the European Parliament, questions of legitimacy and safeguards for judicial rights through the European Court of Justice (Monar 2000, 160). As it has moved forward in cooperation on JHA matters, the counter-balancing of the Union's repressive powers with guarantees of protecting freedoms has frequently been overlooked.

Tampere also acknowledged that there was a strong external dimension to the issue of internal security and that the AFSJ could only be built effectively if this dimension received adequate attention. Section D of the Tampere Conclusions focused directly on the need to build 'Stronger External Relations in the Field of JHA'. This was recognition of the need to enhance the powers of the Union in the international aspects of its internal security agenda. Priority areas were deemed to be EU accession states, the Balkans, relations with source countries of migrants to the EU, and developing cooperation with third countries in tackling international terrorism, transnational organised crime, and drug trafficking.

Cooperation with third countries

Antonio Vitorino, EU Commissioner for JHA, stated in 2001 that:

> The Union cannot limit itself in improving law enforcement and judicial cooperation between its Member States. It will have to develop external priorities in the field of justice and home affairs, which must be incorporated in the Union's overall external strategy (2001, 6)

EU cooperation with third countries has increasingly reflected the needs of its own internal security agenda. Whether in the fight against crime, the combating of international drug trafficking or migration, the EU has embedded internal security objectives into foreign policy agreements. The 1997 Action Plan against Organised Crime, for instance, contained measures to improve cooperation with third countries and offered them EU assistance with their efforts. The EU has also encouraged states to enter into cooperative relationships with Europol.

These priorities have been evident in the EU's relationships with various neighbouring regions. In the case of the EU's 'Common Strategy on the Mediterranean Region' and the 'Stability Pact' for the Balkans, measures against organised crime, drug trafficking, and terrorism were embedded in these initiatives. The Union was particularly concerned at the flow of migrants and soft drugs from north Africa: five EU members and acceding states met with five countries of the Mahgreb Union in Tunis in December 2003 to discuss these issues (European Council 2003, 12). In the case of the Balkans, the principal sources of concern have been over people trafficking, drugs such as heroin, and small arms. The EU has responded by contributing towards the training of judicial and police agencies and has established mechanisms for information sharing.

EU policies towards Russia and Ukraine have contained important elements focused on improving internal security cooperation. Due to the proliferation of organised criminal gangs since the collapse of the Soviet Union, measures such as the EU 'Action Plan on the Fight Against Organised Crime' in Russia in March 2000 have concentrated on the main risks that are thought to emanate from the country. Attention has focused on combating money laundering and the criminalisation of many of the new banks in Russia, efforts to target commodity crime, and countering the trafficking in women and children. Exchanges of information have been agreed between Europol and both the Russian and Ukrainian law enforcement authorities (Smith 2003, 189).

In the case of policies towards South America and the Caribbean, the EU has needed to be more circumspect because these are areas of vital interest to the United States. Whilst the US has actively tried to engage the EU in collaborative policies towards these areas, the Union has not shared the robust policy prescriptions advocated by Washington. The EU and the US have collaborated in drug interdiction programmes in the Caribbean and efforts to improve judicial structures and police techniques. But in South America, the EU and the US have largely pursued separate programmes. The US government has supported crop eradication in the principal coca growing states of Bolivia and Peru and initiated a major programme, 'Plan

Colombia', to provide military assistance to the Colombian government to counter guerrilla groups that were protecting some of the coca-growing areas. The EU has preferred to offer funding to farmers for crop substitution to avoid the growing of coca and has expressed disquiet at US funding that may be channelled to governments with poor human rights records.

One factor that has excited comment has been the growing willingness of the EU to exert pressure on third countries over internal security issues. An example has been the linking of EU aid to matters of asylum. Since the June 2002 Seville European Council, which focused on issues of illegal immigration, every agreement that the EU concludes with third countries must contain a clause on managing migration and on the readmission of illegal immigrants. This was a diluted form of what some countries had been pressing for before the negotiations began. The 2003 Brussels European Council reaffirmed its commitment to 'the use of all appropriate instruments of the EU's external relations . . . including strengthened partnerships with the third countries concerned, in pursuit of the EU's strategy to combat illegal migration' (European Council 2003, 9). The EU designated certain countries as safe from persecution, with the result that asylum-seekers from these states are immediately determined to have an unfounded claim for sanctuary. The Union has shown itself to be capable of linking the provision of development aid to agreements in which states sign readmission arrangements.

The USA

While the EU has usually been in a powerful position over internal security matters towards third countries, the reverse has been the case in its relationship with the United States. Here, for much of the post-Cold War period, the pattern has been one of the US pressing for increased cooperation and the Union reacting negatively to these advances. The US looked upon the EU as the most viable organisation for sharing its policy priorities in countering international crime and terrorism. But for much of the 1990s the EU was preoccupied with building its own internal security structures through the Treaties of European Union and Amsterdam. The EU experienced the difficult situation of being pressed to cooperate with the most powerful state in the international system at a time when its own internal structures were not ready. Its response was largely to deny American requests.

This is not to ignore the fact that some progress was achieved in the post-Cold War period between the US and Europe. Bilateral Mutual Legal Assistance Treaties were negotiated between Washington and all the European capitals, promoting the extradition of suspects across the Atlantic to face trials in the countries in which their crimes were committed. In a complementary fashion, Europe hosted the highest density of US law enforcement and judicial officials, whose job has been to liaise with their European counterparts on criminal matters and to facilitate judicial cooperation.

Yet the more ambitious frameworks for cooperation that the US sought to instigate received little support from the EU. The New Transatlantic Agenda (NTA) of 1995 attempted to refocus transatlantic energies onto a range of American global concerns that included transnational crime, drug trafficking, and international terrorism. The US believed that linkages were developing between the threats. It had traced relationships between drug traffickers and the supply of weapons to revolutionary groups and identified terrorist linkages with rogue states. But this concerted attempt by Washington to get the EU to adopt the same agenda was unsuccessful. Instead, cooperation has tended to be tied to initiatives by successive EU Presidencies. These initiatives have been worthy in their own right but they have reflected short-term considerations and have often lacked long-term commitment.

A transformation in the US-EU relationship occurred after the 11 September 2001 attacks on the United States. In their aftermath the political imperative for the EU to cooperate with the US was overwhelming. As a consequence a new framework has been emerging and cooperation has stretched beyond the field of anti-terrorism to a host of other issues including fighting international crime and illegal immigration. One aspect of this cooperation has been a growth in the volume of intelligence information that has been shared across the Atlantic. Second, authority was granted to the EU Presidency to negotiate a multilateral judicial agreement between the US and the EU that would supplement the existing bilateral arrangements. This 'Agreement on Extradition and Mutual Legal Assistance' was eventually signed at the EU-US Summit in Washington in June 2003 and makes it possible for the allies to create enhanced joint investigative teams as well as mechanisms to identify terrorist bank accounts. Third, there has been significant new transatlantic cooperation to combat various forms of money laundering. Fourth, has been the opening up to cooperation and participation of US representatives in working groups of the Council, in Eurojust, and Europol. A long-standing deadlock in sharing information with US authorities was overcome with the signing of an agreement in December 2001 by the Director of Europol, Jürgen Storbeck. Differences between Europol and the US government over data protection had prevented any previous cooperation, but these were overcome after significant concessions from the side of the Union.

States seeking accession

Perhaps the most important external dimension of EU internal security has developed in relation to the enlargement process. The objective of the candidate countries to accede to the EU has granted the member states the capacity to insist that new adherents adopt the Union's entire internal security model. Internal security considerations have been used to structure aspects of the EU's relationship with Central and East European Countries and have been at the heart of the accession negotiations (Lavenex 1998, 285). The EU's approach has been to emphasise the importance of providing a free and secure internal space for its citizens and has consequently treated the accession of new members as potentially putting these objectives at risk.

The CEECs are of particular importance to the future of the JHA regime. As states situated on the eastern border of the EU, they occupy zones through which organised criminals, illegal drugs and economic migrants may pass *en route* to the territory of the existing member states. The EU has feared that it will import the crime and immigration problems not only from the CEECs when they become members, but also their eastern neighbours, such as Belarus, Ukraine, the Russian enclave of Kaliningrad, and the Balkans. Although the applicant states currently possess less sophisticated means for policing their borders, they will nevertheless serve as the EU's 'frontline'. In addition, they bring with them new approaches to internal security that the pre-existing members will have only limited ability to modify. Thus the EU member states regarded it as imperative to enhance the internal security provisions of the aspirant states prior to them acceding to the Union in May 2004.

The challenge for the CEECs of adopting the EU *acquis* in JHA, including the Schengen provisions, is considerable. The law enforcement and judicial officers in these countries have experienced low salaries and relatively low social status, due to the hangover of their association in the public mind with unpopular former regimes. There have been shortages of experienced judges and senior officials because of the dismissal of previous figures linked to the old regimes. Since the end of the Cold War, the countries have been subjected to a process of rapid transformation whilst simultaneously suffering grave financial pressures. Raising their internal security standards to those of the rich western democracies has meant the imposition of considerable burdens. The CEECs have been expected to amend their domestic legislation; create new administrative organs, judicial structures, and liaison bodies to interface with EU agencies; re-train their police and border guards; and adapt new practices in relation to judicial and customs services. They have also been called upon to purchase sophisticated equipment, such as heat-sensitive appliances and data base management systems for border areas, that has squeezed limited budgets (Storbeck 2003, 287).

In order to assist the applicant states in adopting the JHA *acquis*, the EU brought to bear all its pre-accession instruments: the Structured Dialogue, the Europe Agreements, and the funding of technical assistance through the Phare, Grotius, Oisin and Falcone programmes—the last three of which, all training and coordination programmes in the fight against organised crime, were merged under the name AGIS in 2003 (Mitsilegas, Monar and Rees 2003, 150). Both the European Commission and the EU member states expressed concerns over the ability of the CEECs to attain the necessary standards. Two evaluation processes were initiated; the 'collective evaluation' in 1998 by the Council and the other by the Commission. Both processes assessed the implementation by the accession states of the *acquis* with a particular reference to JHA.

A 'Pre-Accession Pact on Organised Crime' was agreed in May 1998 between the EU and the applicants. This aimed to provide the accession states with specialised knowledge that had been amassed within the EU; to assist with training and equipment, and to draw the newcomers into a cooperative relationship with Europol. Furthermore, the Pact agreed to draw up an annual strategy document, agreed between the existing and future members, that would be focused on combating the threat from transnational crime. This linked the accession states with the EU's own Action Plan on Organised Crime that had been endorsed by the June 1997 Amsterdam European Council. As part of the Pact the applicant states had to join the judicial network and participate in the information exchange process.

Yet despite the EU's efforts to ensure that the CEECs were ready to assume the full obligations of the JHA acquis, there remained fears amongst the member states as to what would happen after 2004. Although by the time of accession the countries were legislatively compliant with the *acquis*, the EU member states were concerned that their ability to implement the provisions would be limited. To some extent the EU must share the blame for this because not only did it take an inordinate amount of time to make the CEECs aware of the existing JHA framework, but it has subsequently been expanding the *acquis* at a significant rate. The CEECs have therefore been chasing a moving target. The risk is that the accession states will represent a weak point in the EU's internal security system. As a result, the EU has notified the accession states that it will implement transition arrangements so that new members will not experience the benefits of incorporation into the JHA *acquis* for some time. As in the earlier cases of Greece and Italy, the new members may have to wait for some time before they are regarded as 'Schengen mature'. This has led to resentment as the CEECs rightly perceive that they have been accorded second class membership.

Policing roles in external interventions

The role of policing in post-conflict situations is the final area in which the EU has recognised the nexus between internal security and external affairs. This area of policy has exemplified the cross-pillar nature of contemporary conflicts by drawing together the JHA portfolio with the CFSP and the emerging European Security and Defence Policy (ESDP). Although the 'hard' military prowess of the EU remains modest, its law enforcement capabilities provide it with considerable potential influence. This has enabled the Union to develop its 'soft' power instruments, something that resonates with the historical image of the European Community as a civilian power. In the contemporary context, these soft power instruments are regarded as a necessary complement to coercive instruments, rather than an alternative. It was envisaged that some sort of non-military capacity might accompany the deployment of an EU Rapid Reaction Force.

In the Treaty of Amsterdam, the so-called 'Petersberg tasks', relating to humanitarian operations and crisis management, were amalgamated into the EU. This encouraged the member states to look for ways to contribute to such tasks from their array of capabilities. At the EU Council in Santa Maria de Feira, in June 2000, the intention was announced to be able to deploy a force of up to 5,000 police officers in support of a crisis management operation. JHA working groups, from the third pillar, have assisted in shaping the sorts of roles and missions that such a policing force could perform. Consistent with the EU's stated priority that the rule of law must be an integral element in a region's progress towards democracy, the contribution of a force of police officers could be especially important. It was later agreed that a smaller force of 1,000 officers should be available at short notice.

Policing roles in post-conflict situations have thus been regarded as a source of opportunity. The EU demonstrated its willingness to address such specialised tasks before the signing of the Dayton Accords in Bosnia. At that time the EU tasked its defence arm, the Western European Union, to undertake the training of a multinational police force in the Muslim-Croat city of Mostar. Since then, the need has arisen to help train a police capability for the whole of Bosnia Herzegovina as an integral element in its post-conflict reconstruction. The EU accepted this challenge and deployed a Police Mission in Bosnia, beginning in January 2003.

Conclusion

The post-Cold War period has witnessed a growing recognition of the need to build JHA objectives into the external action of the EU. This has arisen from two sorts of pressures. First, the need to react to perceptions of increasing challenges from organised crime, drug trafficking, and illegal immigration. The threat from international terrorism was perceived to be particularly acute following the September 11th attacks. These growing perceptions of external threat have resulted in responses at the EU level. The trend has been accelerating as European interior ministers have appreciated that only through concerted action can they have an impact on these problems. Thus the EU has been pressing forward with police and judicial cooperation against a range of challenges that are considered to be linked.

Second, the EU member states have come to accept that they must enhance the Union's capacity to act externally in order to protect their internal security. The separation of EU instruments into foreign policy and internal security categories is no longer appropriate in the face of a variety of transnational challenges that defy such distinctions. Instruments to combat these challenges must be available from the first and the second pillars as well as in JHA. The EU's weakness has been the slow pace at which the capacity for cross-pillar action has developed. The European Council has put pressure on the General Affairs Council to play more of a coordinating role in the use of EU instruments to fight terrorism and international crime, but its success has been modest. It has remained difficult to marry up the machinery for external affairs with that of internal security.

The EU has sought to improve its cooperation with other states by making internal security objectives an explicit element in its foreign relations. This point was formally acknowledged in the Conclusions to the Tampere summit and has been pursued in various trade and other agreements with states in eastern Europe as well as outside Europe. Countries that are regarded as sources of danger to the EU, such as through migration, transnational crime or terrorism, are particular targets of the EU's approach. Developments in the international environment have also played an important role in shaping this agenda. The aftermath of September 11th, for example, has dramatically increased the attention accorded to international terrorism and provided a major stimulus to developing cooperation with the United States.

At the behest of its member states, the EU has been developing an internal security regime that is becoming the model for the rest of the continent. This model consists of a 'safe' EU internal space that must be protected from an 'unsafe' external environment. With the JHA *acquis* expanding, areas of cooperation are becoming mutually reinforcing and as a result, greater organisational coherence is evident. Due to its economic power and influence and because of the attraction of membership, the EU is emerging as a 'power' in the domain of internal security. The EU's internal security regime is effectively being exported to its neighbourhood because of its insistence that those countries that wish to become members of the Union must sign up to its strictures on JHA. Not only is this regime being transferred to Eastern Europe but it is also serving as an example to the wider international community because of the unique nature of the EU as a polity. There exists no international organisation capable of constructing an alternative, comprehensive model to that of the EU. In this way the internal security of the EU has taken on a powerful external dimension.

Further reading

For the background debate about internal security within the European Union see Anderson *et al.* (1995) and Anderson and Bort (1998). For analysis of the Justice and Home Affairs portfolio see Peers (2000), and Mitsilegas, Monar and Rees (2003). For an overview of the drugs problem in Europe see Dorn (1999); for immigration issues see Geddes (2003); and for the theory of 'securitisation' see Buzan, Waever and de Wilde (1998).

Anderson, M., den Boer, M., Cullen, P., Gilmore, W., Raab, C., and Walker, N. (1995), *Policing the European Union* (Oxford: Clarendon Press).

Anderson, M. and Bort, E. (eds) (1998), *The Frontiers of Europe* (London: Pinter).

Buzan, B., Waever, O. and de Wilde, J. (1998), *Security: A New Framework for Analysis* (Boulder, CO: Lynne Rienner).

Dorn, N. (ed.) (1999), *Regulating European Drug Problems. Administrative Measures and Civil Law in the Control of Drug Trafficking, Nuisance and Use* (The Hague: Kluwer Law International).

Geddes, A. (2003), *The Politics of Migration and Immigration in Europe* (London: Sage).

Mitsilegas, V., Monar, J. and Rees, W. (2003), *The European Union and Internal Security: Guardian of the People?* (Basingstoke: Palgrave Macmillan).

Peers, S. (2000), *EU Justice and Home Affairs Law* (Harlow: Longman, 2000).

Web links

Interesting material relevant to the issues covered in this chapter can be found on the websites of the EU, specifically that of the Commission DG responsible for Justice and Home Affairs (http://europa.eu.int/comm/dgs/justice_home/index_en.htm) and its agencies such as Europol (http://www.europol.eu.int/) and the European Monitoring Centre for Drugs and Drug Addiction (http://www.emcdda.org).

Chapter 11

Managing Interdependence: The EU in the World Economy

Loukas Tsoukalis

Contents

Summary

This chapter explores the EU's broad roles and impact within the world economy, and evaluates the impact of recent developments. The history of European integration is characterised by continuous expansion in terms of functions and membership. It started essentially as an economic affair, although with broader political objectives, graduating from an incomplete common market to a regulatory state, which has also acquired in the process a redistributive dimension and, last but not least, a single currency. This has had important implications for the role of the EU in the world economy: a powerful and expanding trade bloc which has not always been successful in translating internal integration into external common policies. Relations with the United States and the link between regional integration and globalisation remain key factors in this respect.

Introduction

Implicit in many other chapters of this volume is a set of key questions about the re-lationship between the European Union and the world political economy. In reality, there are three sets of questions, relating to the three themes identified in Chapter 1:

- How has the EU as a sub-system of the world economy developed within the broader global economic context, and how has the 'internal' process of European integration reflected more widespread processes of economic change?
- How has the EU and the European integration process contributed to the changing processes of international economic development, and in particular to the ways in which the world economy has been subject to processes of management or governance?
- How can the EU be seen as a 'power' in the world political economy, and how has that power been deployed and applied in an increasingly globalised world?

This chapter addresses these and related questions by exploring the EU's role in the management of interdependence, and by doing so it confronts some of the central issues of international political economy. The continuous deepening of integration has produced higher levels of economic interdependence in Europe. In the context of complex, mixed economies, this has in turn raised questions about joint manage-ment and about rules governing the interaction between different national models of capitalism. In turn these rules reflect a constantly changing balance of forces inside member countries and the EU more generally, economic ideas and the international environment. Internal policies influence the role of the EU as an international actor and vice versa. The Union is big enough not to take the rest of the world as given. This is, of course, more true when it is united in its dealings with the rest of the world, and when as a result it can undertake significant collective actions with substantial inter-national impacts. The transition from a common trade policy to a common foreign economic policy, fulfilling key economic functions in the global arena, has proved to be both difficult and painful.

The chapter proceeds in several stages. First, it reviews key elements in the de-velopment of the contemporary world economy and relates these to the process of European integration up to the 1980s. Second, it explores the emergence of the Single Market Programme in the 1980s and the move towards Economic and Mon-etary Union in the 1990s, with particular reference to their implications for Europe and for the world economy. Third, it analyses the relationship between the changing (and expanding) processes of international exchange and regulation and the ways in which the EU enters into key activities of management and competition. Finally, it addresses the ways in which current changes in the EU and in the world economy mesh (or do not mesh) together—in particular, the expansion of the EU and the continuing processes of regionalisation and globalisation that characterise the world economy in the twenty-first century.

Integration and mixed economies

The process started more than fifty years ago, with coal and steel. Of course, nobody would choose those two sectors now; they have both been declining rapidly in importance for quite some time. In the late 1940s, though, they were a core part of managed capitalism and the mixed economies that were emerging in post-war Western Europe, and the choice of these two sectors also reflected their long history of government intervention and cartelisation. The next, more ambitious step had to be more liberal in its economic approach. The Treaty of Rome, signed in 1957, led to the establishment of two more Communities, the European Economic Community (EEC) and the European Atomic Energy Community (Euratom). The latter proved to be stillborn, while the former was essentially about the establishment of a common market, albeit highly incomplete, with the emphasis on the elimination of cross-border controls on the movement of goods.[1]

During the 1950s and early 1960s, the foundations of European governance were laid through the operation of common institutions and joint rule-setting. The incomplete common market in goods was complemented by the first attempts at a common competition policy, mostly of an anti-trust character inspired by American experience, and a common commercial policy which bound the Six together in the General Agreement on Tariffs and Trade (GATT), thus turning them into a major international actor in trade negotiations (see also Chapter 12 in this volume). This incomplete common market also included a highly interventionist agricultural policy as a key element of the overall package deal supporting the EEC, and as the only possible way of incorporating a sector which represented a very significant part of national output and of the labour force of continental economies. Indeed, the overall package deal of European integration at the time appeared to make little sense in terms of neo-classical economics; but did national economic reality make any more sense seen through the eyes of neoclassical economists?

The post-war Golden Age for the Western European economies lasted until the early 1970s, and produced rapidly rising levels of prosperity.[2] The growth rates and unemployment levels achieved during that period have never been matched since (Figure 11.1). It was truly exceptional, with average annual growth rates of real GDP reaching 5%, while unemployment was close to 2%. Things have changed dramatically since then. The only macroeconomic variable that has improved in recent years, as compared with the Golden Age, is inflation; and this improvement has been far from dramatic, since annual rates of inflation remained around 3–4% in most Western European countries until the late 1960s.

International trade grew faster than output during that period, and intra-EEC trade grew faster than international trade. Economists were very quick to try to establish links between these variables. To the extent there can ever be unanimity among economists, they achieved it on the relationship between trade liberalisation as a result of regional integration efforts, and the growth of regional trade. Moreover, economists agreed that most of this trade was the result of trade creation (a good thing) as opposed to trade diversion (a bad thing), the latter being associated mainly with the CAP. There was, however, less agreement about the link between the growth of

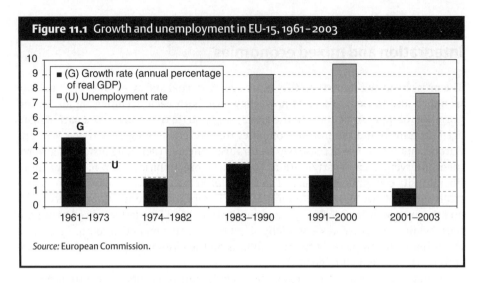

Figure 11.1 Growth and unemployment in EU-15, 1961–2003

- ■ (G) Growth rate (annual percentage of real GDP)
- ▫ (U) Unemployment rate

1961–1973   1974–1982   1983–1990   1991–2000   2001–2003

Source: European Commission.

trade and GDP. Early studies on integration suggested that the welfare effects of trade growth were very small. If true, this would imply that, after all, integration had little to do with economics, since trade cannot be an economic good in itself. Later, economists began to study the so-called dynamic effects of trade and, in so doing, they were able to establish a much closer link between intra-European trade on the one hand and growth and welfare on the other. They probably still underestimate those effects.

The causal link between trade and growth is not only one-way, as is usually assumed. The rapid elimination of intra-EEC trade barriers between 1958 and 1968 was made possible largely by the favourable macroeconomic environment, characterised by high rates of growth and low unemployment. Increased exposure to international trade brings with it adjustment costs for both labour and capital. These costs are much more easily absorbed in times of rapid growth, thus minimising resistance from potential losers. This suggests a virtuous circle: the favourable macroeconomic environment of the 1950s and 1960s, attributable to various factors such as catching up with the more advanced US technology and high investment ratios coupled with wage moderation, created the conditions that permitted the signing of the Treaty of Rome and the successful implementation of its trade provisions. Liberalisation then led to more trade and this, in turn, contributed to the remarkable growth rates of the period.

So far so good. But another piece of the puzzle challenged conventional thinking. Trade liberalisation, much faster at the regional level but also quite significant at the international level, with GATT as its main vehicle, coincided with the emergence of mixed economies and welfare states, especially in Western Europe. They were national mixed economies and welfare states. During that time, the role of the state became increasingly pronounced at both micro and macro levels. 'Keynes at home and Smith abroad', as someone very ingeniously put it. While Western European countries were eliminating their border controls, mostly affecting trade in goods, they

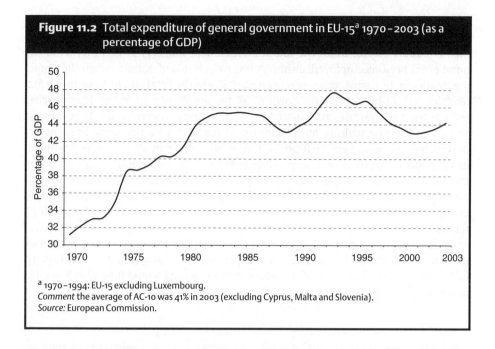

Figure 11.2 Total expenditure of general government in EU-15[a] 1970–2003 (as a percentage of GDP)

[a] 1970–1994: EU-15 excluding Luxembourg.
Comment the average of AC-10 was 41% in 2003 (excluding Cyprus, Malta and Slovenia).
Source: European Commission.

were busily developing domestic instruments for macroeconomic stabilisation, redistribution, insurance against risk, and the provision of public goods. In some countries, notably France and Italy, the state also directly controlled whole sectors of the economy, ranging from public utilities to the banks.

General government expenditure as a percentage of GDP is a simple yet quite reliable indicator of the size of government. With small ups and downs, there was a clear, long-term upward trend in all Western European countries during the Golden Age; and it continued all the way until the mid-1990s. Figure 11.2 shows the rise of general government expenditure as a percentage of GDP for the average EU-15 country between 1970 and 2003, the period for which there are comparable data. For the average EU country, that measure rose by more than a fifteen points between 1970 and the early 1990s, reaching almost 50% of GDP; since then, it has fallen a little, although remaining around 45%—still not bad for capitalist economies! The political contract of the post-war period was the apotheosis of social democratic values, usually coupled with the growing power of trade unions and heavy regulation of labour markets.

At the time, the Keynesian state facilitated trade liberalisation and European integration, not the opposite, as economic purists might have thought. The mixed economy and the welfare state helped to smooth domestic adjustment resulting from the opening of borders and greater international competition; it also helped to buy social acceptance by alleviating the effects of adjustment on potential losers inside each country. It was therefore part and parcel of the virtuous circle: the domestic political contract was inextricably linked with the international economic environment and regional integration.

It was only in the agricultural sector that the main responsibility for intervention and adjustment was, from early on, transferred to the European level. In the 1950s, the agricultural sector in all the founding members was very large in terms of the numbers of persons employed, although less so in terms of output. When the founding treaties were signed, farmers represented 23% of the total labour force in the Six, reaching 35% in Italy. It is now down to 4% for the Fifteen, although much higher (13%) in the ten countries that joined in 2004. It would therefore not have been at all easy to leave agriculture out of the overall package deal. Given the long history of intervention in and external protection of agriculture in all European countries, intra-regional liberalisation was possible only through the establishment of a common policy, which was bound to reproduce at least some of the elements of the national policies it replaced. It thus had little to do with laissez-faire. The price was to be paid by consumers and taxpayers alike, as well as by foreign producers. High intervention prices for European farmers were coupled with a very effective system of variable levies on imports. But the overall cost of the CAP skyrocketed as productivity growth accelerated and European self-sufficiency in food products also rose rapidly. In a sense, this was the price of success; but for how long would it be worth paying, as overall CAP expenditure kept rising?

A new economic orthodoxy

The Golden Age of high growth and monetary stability lasted for almost thirty years after the end of the war—the *trente glorieuses* frequently referred to by the French. A subsequent period of stagflation brought with it new protectionist pressures and tensions. This period of stagflation coincided with the first round of enlargement, with the accession of three new members in 1973. It also prepared the ground for a change in prevailing economic ideas and the inauguration of a new phase of European integration. This centred on the programme for an internal (or single) market, which was introduced in 1985 (Tsoukalis 1997).

The internal market programme was first of all an acknowledgement of the highly incomplete nature of the common market, by far the most important economic achievement so far of European integration. It recognised the uneasy symbiosis between free trade and mixed economies, in which state interventions in the domestic economy unavoidably create distortions in cross-border transactions, whether in the form of state aids or different kinds of regulation: all those things that used to be bundled together in economics textbooks as 'non-tariff barriers' to be eliminated sometime before the second coming.

The decision to deal with the large variety of non-tariff barriers (in other words, with the multiple manifestations of the European mixed economy) ushered the EC into a new phase of deregulation and re-regulation at the European level (Majone 1996). Since then, much joint European decision-making and legislation has been about new regulatory frameworks concerning technical standards for industrial products, telecommunications, transport, or financial services. This has expanded economic integration beyond trade in goods to include services and capital, which had been, to all intents and purposes, previously left out. Services had a long history of public regulation; and the uncoordinated (and often explicitly protectionist) character of national regulation had meant that most services had been virtually excluded from cross-border transactions. As for free capital movements, they were supposed to be one of the so-called four fundamental freedoms that lawyers are so fond of (the other three being freedom of trade in goods and services, and freedom of establishment, meaning the freedom to take up and pursue activities as self-employed without any discrimination on grounds of nationality). Yet any capital liberalisation that had taken place inside the EC before the internal market programme was adopted had been introduced unilaterally by individual member countries. A key element of the internal market programme was precisely the complete liberalisation of intra-EC and extra-EC capital movements.

The new economic reality had brought about a shift in economic ideas in Western Europe. The new emphasis on macroeconomic stabilisation, including fiscal consolidation after several years of large budgetary deficits, coupled with supply-side measures and deregulation of markets, lay behind the internal market programme. The accumulation of budget deficits pointed to the limits of expansionary fiscal policies as a remedy for the recession, while the first years of the European Monetary System (EMS), created in 1979, confirmed German monetary policy as the anchor of monetary stability for all members. Meanwhile, big business in Europe came to perceive the fragmentation of the European market, caused by persisting government intervention and various forms of non-tariff barriers, as the main reason for the lack of competitiveness in international markets. Thus, economies of scale and cross-border restructuring became the key objectives, and the elimination of intra-European barriers the main instrument to achieve them. Supply-side measures and deregulation were ideas mostly imported from the United States of President Reagan, with Margaret Thatcher acting as the main and highly energetic European agent. Academic economists had laid the groundwork earlier.

Thus, the national mixed economy was no longer untouchable: a new formula would have to be found for John Maynard Keynes to be able to coexist with Adam Smith. Intruding into the mixed economies of individual member states implied that national economic sovereignty would become a more relative concept. This was true, but up to a point. In the process of translating economic ideas into policy, this new economic orthodoxy had to be adjusted to the political realities and diversity of European mixed economies, much to the regret of neo-liberals.

The internal market programme helped to create a new virtuous circle, involving both governments and the marketplace. The internal market and the Single European Act (SEA) signed in 1986 coincided with a steady improvement in the economic environment. But, like all good things, the economic boom was soon to end. Virtuous circles are not for ever; and this particular one was short-lived. The programme was meant to rely as much as possible on the principle of mutual recognition, in turn consistent with subsidiarity, while common legislation was to be limited to essential objectives and requirements. In practice, there has been much more EU legislation than generally expected. People had clearly underestimated the complexity and diversity of Europe's mixed economies, which require some degree of European re-regulation as a pre-condition for the establishment of a true internal market (Pelkmans 2001). European legislation has taken much longer than anticipated; it has often provided for differentiation and different timetables in the application of common rules; and, most important of all, it has highlighted the implementation problems inherent in a highly decentralised system. EU institutions often legislate, but they never implement. Implementation is still exclusively the responsibility of national institutions, and the result is both imperfect and variable.

Although the internal market programme has not produced the quick and spectacular results predicted in some economic studies, it has certainly given a fresh boost to the growth of all kinds of economic transactions across national borders, including now services and capital, thus bringing a quantitative and qualitative change in intra-European economic interdependence. Today, exports of goods and services represent approximately 35% of GDP for the average EU member, and between 25 and 36% for the big countries. The opening of European economies was, indeed, spectacular during the second half of the twentieth century. Exports of goods and services, expressed as a percentage of GDP for the Fifteen, registered a very large increase—more than doubling in most cases—between 1960 and 2003 (the UK being an exception to this rule, having registered a relatively small increase in trade openness during this period). Ireland and the Benelux countries are by far the most open economies, while Greece is the least open. Even before officially joining the club, the ten new members already had very open economies. Nowadays, close to 70% of total trade in goods (it is difficult to find corresponding statistics for services) is done with other members of EU-25. Thus, we are dealing with highly open economies whose prosperity crucially depends on developments outside their borders and predominantly on what happens in the rest of the Union.

This high degree of economic interdependence (or integration) is manifested not only in trade but also increasingly in terms of capital flows and production. The large number of cross-border mergers, acquisitions, and various other forms of economic cooperation, ranging from the much publicised mega-mergers like that between Vodafone and Mannesmann to the thousands of small- or medium-sized trans-European firm marriages or joint ventures, are daily changing the corporate map of Europe, while also marking the death (and subsequent reincarnation?) of long-established and much-venerated national champions. Cross-border mergers and acquisitions reached a peak before the bursting of the financial bubble of the 1990s. The period of sobriety that followed may not last long. People do not always learn from experience. There is, however, little doubt that cross-border mergers and acquisitions will continue to be a key feature of further restructuring in Europe.

The new approach to regulation, introduced with the internal market programme, was later taken one step further with the so-called Lisbon process. The objective was to make the EU 'the most competitive and dynamic knowledge-based economy in the world by 2010', and this was to be achieved through a set of economic reforms aiming at further liberalisation and the creation of a more business-friendly environment in the new e-economy. The emphasis would henceforth be on the 'open method of coordination', relying mostly on benchmarking and peer pressure, instead of the traditional 'Community method', which was deemed too constraining for those new areas of policy. Some European leaders at least appeared determined to employ the Union—and peer pressure—as an external catalyst and facilitator for domestic reforms. It has not worked well so far. Soft coordination of the intergovernmental kind has produced meagre results; this may have something to do with the method adopted, but it could also reflect strong resistance within European societies to the kind of changes promoted by the Lisbon process.

One of the very few markets that remain predominantly national is the labour market, not so much because legislators at the European level have not tried to eliminate remaining barriers to cross-border mobility, but rather because of linguistic and cultural barriers that are difficult to legislate away. The operation of national welfare states constitutes another significant impediment to labour mobility across frontiers. Professionals with exportable qualifications and students have benefited most from the elimination of legal and other such barriers. An integrated labour market is, indeed, beginning to emerge in places like London, Brussels, or Frankfurt, but only for a small and successful transnational elite. The paradox is that the large majority of foreigners in European labour markets come from countries that do not benefit from the freedom of movement that EU membership brings with it, including those that have recently joined. People who have the established right to move rarely do so, while many others on the immediate or more distant peripheries of the Union are only too keen to jump the barriers, legally or otherwise. The labour market, at least at its lower end, is very much supply-driven.

Thus, with the major exception of labour, the EC/EU has become a more truly common market. It has also developed into a regulatory state. Albeit of a modest character, redistribution was added to the European package deal after the adoption of the Single European Act of 1986. In Community jargon, this is called 'economic and social cohesion'. Thus, liberalisation has become directly linked to redistribution, and in practical terms it has meant significant transfers of funds to less developed countries and regions of the Union through the Structural Funds and, later, the Cohesion Fund.

A single currency

At the time of writing, twelve European countries have already replaced their national currencies with a new single currency, the euro. And in so doing they have also transferred a big chunk of their sovereignty, and the symbols that go with it, to the EU. Money is at the heart of national sovereignty: the currency has always been a key symbol of nationhood, while monetary policy and the exchange rate constitute major instruments of economic policy. Economic and monetary union is therefore the most important thing that has happened in Europe since the fall of the Berlin Wall; and there is surely nothing in its fifty-year history of integration comparable to EMU in terms of political and economic significance.

Few people would have dared to predict such a development as late as 1993, when bilateral exchange rates in the EMS came under massive attack in international markets, while European societies greeted the Maastricht Treaty with remarkably little enthusiasm. EMU has, in fact, a long and turbulent history of ups and downs. It was born at the same time as European Political Cooperation, the predecessor of the Common Foreign and Security Policy (CFSP); and both were meant as bold attempts to venture beyond low politics. Their trajectories have been very different so far: while EMU has already reached the final (irreversible?) stage, the CFSP still has a long road to travel.

So important a project deserves an explanation. How is it, after all, that a slow and conservative system—an apt description of the European political system—operating under extremely complicated rules and requiring very large majorities, has produced such a revolutionary decision followed by remarkable political commitment? Three main driving forces can be identified in the long process of European monetary integration.

The first has been the search for stability: of intra-European exchange rate stability seen as a precondition for the proper functioning of the European market, to which the objective of price stability was later added. Thus, European monetary integration came to be seen as a way of imposing external discipline on those unruly members with a poor record of monetary stability, with their governments willingly tying themselves to the European mast in order to be protected from the Sirens (and macroeconomic mismanagement). Once again, a major project of economic integration became directly linked to a particular set of ideas, with the EU acting as a facilitator of the new orthodoxy.

The second driving force has been the search for symmetry: inside the Union, thus going beyond the DM standard which had characterised the early phases of regional monetary integration, and vis-à-vis the rest of the world—a diplomatic way of referring to the US dollar. The instability of the international monetary system and the perceived need to insulate Europe from the vagaries of the US dollar played an important role in the 1960s and 1970s. The third driving force has been the search for further integration: money has been repeatedly used as an instrument for achieving deeper economic integration in Europe, and most importantly, political integration; hence a means to an end rather than just an end in itself.

As EMU entered the European political agenda in the end of the 1980s, it was perceived by advocates as the final and irrevocable confirmation of the reality of the single European market and of a unified European economy. A common currency was seen as the means of welding national economies together, but also, very importantly, the means of accelerating the movement towards political union. This was familiar stuff to the integrationist lobby; but, arguably, nothing much would have come of it had it not been for the fall of the Berlin Wall and German unification, which provided the unexpected catalyst.

The economics of EMU has been much debated by economists.[3] There is certainly no consensus that the economic advantages of a single European currency outweigh the disadvantages resulting from the loss of important policy instruments at the national level. Of course, the balance sheet for Belgium would be substantially different from that for the UK. It has to do with the openness of the national economy, among other things. The EU is not an optimum currency area, far from it, though such an optimum currency area could be created *ex post*. The European economy is not yet sufficiently homogeneous, which means that different countries and regions can be subject to asymmetric shocks. And there are no adequate adjustment mechanisms, such as flexible labour markets, high labour mobility, or large budgetary transfers, to act as effective substitutes for the exchange rate. But how effective is the exchange rate as a policy instrument in a world characterised by highly mobile international capital and highly unstable financial markets? Financial globalisation clashes with the persisting diversity of national economic systems, institutions, and cultures. Can there be a true European market with constantly fluctuating exchange rates linking its national components?

The economics profession gave no decisive answer, although an increasing number have now come to the view that optimum currency areas are not determined by exogenous factors; they are created. With EMU, the broad answer was given at the highest political level and mostly on the basis of political arguments; then it was left to the experts to negotiate the technical arrangements. It had been different with the internal market programme, which enjoyed wide support among the economics profession (Dyson 2000; Tsoukalis 2005). The construction which came out of the Maastricht Treaty was compatible with the strong tradition of elitism and depoliticisation in European integration. The key decisions were taken at the very top behind closed doors; the texts were drafted by central bankers and diplomats making of the European Central Bank (ECB) a fortress for the *cognoscenti*; big business was allowed a say in later stages, while the wider public was simply expected to acquiesce. After all, the management of money had traditionally been a matter reserved for experts; and it was all compatible with monetarist ideas prevailing at the time. As for the wider implications of EMU, they were meant to be subsumed under the general goal of European integration, which of course could work well in the case of Italy or Greece, but not necessarily so in Denmark or the UK.

The euro arrived at a time of low growth and further rapid restructuring, which naturally brings with it adjustment costs and political resistance from potential losers. In earlier years, liberalisation measures at the European level had helped to create a favourable economic environment, which not only contributed to growth and welfare but also helped to shape positive popular perceptions of integration. Thus, virtuous economic circles kept the European project spinning. It has been very different since the early 1990s.

The management of the euro raises fundamental questions about governance and legitimacy, which have been left unanswered by the architects of EMU. The link between monetary and fiscal policy at the European level, the degree and kind of coordination of national fiscal policies, the powers of common institutions and their democratic accountability feature among the key questions. On the other hand, there is no universal membership of EU countries in the eurozone. Does this point in the direction of a European system with different classes of members?

Trade policy—and more

European integration does not take place in an international vacuum. Size and history combine to ensure that what happens within the region does not go unnoticed outside. The EC started as a trade bloc; its nature as a customs union, incomplete though it had remained for many years, long determined its external dimension.

This was enshrined in the treaties, and the Commission was given the power to represent the Community in international trade negotiations. As regional integration deepened, covering an ever-increasing number of policy areas, relations with the rest of the world were bound to be affected, raising some fundamental questions about external representation and the definition of the common interest in relation to others.

Between trade and high politics, relations with the United States have been the single most important determining factor of a common European policy. This has been true of GATT negotiations, in which the Americans were very critical of what they described as European protectionism and the repeated violations of multilateralism and the most-favoured-nation clause of GATT; and it is even more true of attempts by EU members to develop a common foreign and security policy (see Chapters 9, 12, and 16 in this volume).

The EU is big and influential in trade matters—and there is a large difference between trade and most other aspects of relations with the rest of the world. The reason is simple, namely that in trade the EU has a common policy that operates along federal principles, with a single representation ensuring that its negotiating power is commensurate with its collective weight. This does not apply as yet to other areas of policy.

For many years, the EC/EU had been one of the worst, if not the worst, offenders against the principle of multilateralism in international trade, because of the large number of preferential agreements signed with other, mostly developing, countries. It had done so because of old habits and sometimes in an absent-minded fashion; but preferences also often served as a substitute for a more encompassing policy, unattainable because of the internal limitations of the EU. The share of trade of the Union's privileged partners among developing countries has been declining in contrast with the share of, say, South-East Asian countries, which have traditionally been the object of negative privileges from Europe. This may therefore suggest that some countries trade and others sign trade agreements. But surely preferential access to markets is not the only determining factor for export success, not to mention economic development more generally.

European attitudes and policies have evolved; in the process, they have become more compatible with the multilateral system, as many EU protective barriers came down and preferences began to fade. European policies have also retained a distinct European flavour relating to the protection of the environment, labour standards and human rights, although with limited practical effect. European integration has also served as a model for many developing countries, and the Europeans have consciously promoted its export; but again, with poor results so far, essentially because European conditions are not easily reproducible in other parts of the world.

There is broad consensus among economists, drawing from numerous econometric studies, that trade creation resulting from European integration has been much greater than trade diversion, thus having a positive welfare effect for those inside the regional bloc as well as for those outside it. This is true of earlier studies in the 1960s and it is also true of subsequent studies on the trade effects of the internal market. Agricultural goods are the main exception: the CAP operates partly at the expense of outsiders, with trade diversion far outweighing trade creation, although in this respect the EU is not very different from many other developed countries.

The extension of the European integration agenda has often gone hand in hand with the GATT agenda, although the results remain substantially different. The latest example was provided by the Uruguay Round, which started officially in 1986 leading to a final agreement signed in Marrakesh in 1994. There was close similarity between the European internal market programme and much of the agenda of the Uruguay Round, dealing with the multitude of the so-called non-tariff barriers (NTBs), usually coming under the label of economic regulation, and the extension of jurisdiction to new areas and most notably services.

Although the Uruguay Round has produced important concrete results, leading also to the creation of the World Trade Organization (WTO), it is hardly surprising that these results are far short of what has been achieved in the context of the Union. There is a big difference between what is feasible at the regional (more precisely, the European) level and the global level; and this difference has to do with the similarity of economic and social values, the long history of cooperation, the existence of an elaborate institutional machinery and a well-established legal order, among other things. There is much greater reality and scope for joint governance of the economic interdependence achieved within the EU than is the case at the global level; and this should have long-term consequences for market integration within Europe and globally.

Trade in services has been growing faster than trade in goods in recent years, and this has bitten harder into Europe's mixed economies because of a long record of extensive state intervention and/or state ownership. Financial markets in particular have acted as a driving force of economic globalisation. Internal EU measures have followed suit through the internal market programme and subsequent legislation. In this area, the Union seems to have adjusted to external events rather than trying to shape them. Regional integration has therefore become part and parcel of—and in some cases, virtually indistinguishable from—global developments. Is there really so little scope for regional differentiation in the context of increasingly global financial markets, or is this more due to the inability so far of Europeans to adopt a common policy?

There is, in fact, a more general problem arising from the continuous extension of the international trade agenda, which has not been matched by a corresponding transfer of powers to EU institutions as regards external policy. The Commission still has legal powers to negotiate on behalf of the Union only with respect to trade in goods. New areas of policy, such as services, intellectual property and investment as well as labour standards, cultural issues, and the environment, are either the subject of so-called mixed competences, where the Commission does not have exclusive responsibility for representing the Union and decisions in the Council have to be taken by unanimity, or they remain in the hands of member states. One example among several are the bilateral 'open skies agreements' concluded by individual member countries and the US, later to be found contrary to EU law by the European Court. The result has almost invariably been a much weaker power of negotiation for the Europeans. Illusions of national sovereignty die hard.

An expanding agenda

Although regional integration may indeed have influenced the relationship between the state and the market in Europe, it has not fundamentally changed, as yet, the mixed character of European capitalism(s). It should not be surprising therefore that for many Europeans globalisation, essentially a market and technology-driven process, raises fundamental questions of governance. It is certainly not the heavenly glow that we can all lie back and enjoy. Together with its undeniable wealth-creating effects, globalisation often brings along greater inequalities, social disruption, and environmental damage, the kinds of negative externalities that those benefiting from globalisation prefer to ignore.

Their collective experience in regional integration, relying heavily on common rules and institutions, and their long political traditions, in which the mixed economy, public goods, and solidarity occupy a prominent position, has made Europeans naturally much more inclined than the other big power in the international economic system, the United States, to contemplate multilateral rules and institutions for the management of global interdependence. Several examples prove the point, such as the creation of the WTO and its dispute-settlement procedure, a successful European initiative, and the Kyoto Protocol on global warming which the Bush Administration has refused to endorse.

True, consistency has rarely been the main characteristic of political and social behaviour. This also applies to Europeans, who started with a propensity for regional preferences until they gradually discovered their limitations, while also sometimes collectively succumbing to the temptation of unilateral action when they felt strong enough to do so. One prominent example of unilateral action in the absence of internationally recognised rules is the use of anti-dumping, an important instrument of so-called commercial defence, the other being the extra-territorial dimension of the common competition policy, both in the hands of the Commission. Yet, despite such qualifications, there is a considerable, and apparently widening, gap between the two sides of the Atlantic with respect to multilateralism and global rules, a gap which is even wider in what international relations theorists refer to with awe as 'high politics'.

The Europeans have values as well as goods and services they would like to export. These values include a developed sensitivity for the environment, the rights of workers, and distributional justice. They form part of the European model, if there is to be one. They therefore need to be reflected in common European policies and linked more closely to the objective of further trade liberalisation in the context of the WTO and the new multilateral trade round launched in Doha in November 2001, as well as in other international forums. In Doha, as before, the United States talked mostly about free trade and the EU about governance. Admittedly, the difference has been much greater in the rhetoric employed by the two sides than in terms of concrete policies.

More recently, European integration has generally developed in parallel with globalisation: witness the liberalisation of capital and financial services. In some cases, the Europeans were simply swept along with the current, while in others they succeeded in developing a collective regional response to globalisation (Kierzkowski 2002). EMU could be seen as an example of the latter, although how consciously so remains to be seen. Although symmetry with the US dollar has been all along one of the implicit aims of European monetary integration, the Maastricht Treaty contained precious little in terms of provisions for the external representation of the eurozone. The twelve members have now elected Mr Euro, initially in the person of the Prime Minister and also Finance Minister of Luxembourg, Mr Juncker. He will preside over the Euro Group and represent the eurozone in international forums. He is also likely to act as the political counterpart to the President of the ECB. How the relationship develops between the two still remains to be seen. Mr Euro will have a task on his hands in trying to create harmony out of the cacophony of uncoordinated voices which has often characterised the eurozone, with obvious negative consequences for negotiating power and credibility of the new single currency in financial markets.

Do Europeans have common views and interests to defend with respect to the role of international financial institutions and the rules governing the financial system? Experience again suggests that, as long as European views and interests on such issues are represented separately, they will continue to have only a small impact on global economic governance, not commensurate with the relative weight of the Union. Such considerations have historically provided one of the main driving forces behind EMU in an international system still characterised by US hegemony. It remains to be seen whether the Europeans will be able collectively to rise to the challenge of the euro growing into a major international currency, and thus assume the responsibilities that go with it.

The Europeans have been learning from experience—some faster than others—that regional cooperation/integration usually enables them to deal more effectively with global interdependence. They have the size and the degree of self-sufficiency that enables them to establish collective forms of management and regulation in place of ineffective national ones. And they also have the collective power to influence international decisions; individually, (most) European countries count for little in international economic affairs. The continuous deepening of regional integration has not always been accompanied by a corresponding transfer of powers to the external policies of the Union, and this has been clearly reflected in European weakness in international negotiations.

Relations with developing countries are very important: Europe's colonial past, having left behind accumulated knowledge, some vested interests, and feelings of collective guilt strengthened by traditions of solidarity and social justice in European societies, will probably continue to compensate for the declining economic importance of much of what is still euphemistically called the developing world. The European regional bloc has made repeated, albeit often half-hearted, attempts to establish a new model of North-South economic relations, thus trying to satisfy at least some of the demands made by less developed countries. Admittedly, those attempts are not universally deemed as successful, to put it mildly (see Chapter 14 of this volume).

There are several difficult issues which need to be tackled in this context. One is surely the further reform of the CAP. As long as the European agricultural fortress keeps many of the exports of the less developed countries out of European markets, the credibility of the image of Europe as the generous partner of poor countries will continue to be severely tested. Albeit partial, successive reforms of the CAP have been in the right direction; and this is even more true of decisions taken in 2003 which should lead to a substantial reduction in trade-distorting domestic support. On the other hand, some kind of privileged relationship with groups of developing countries is most likely to continue. History and geography will continue to militate in this direction. But the privilege is likely to continue to shift from trade to aid. This should also help to further reduce the negative trade discrimination against non-privileged partners in the Third World.

The EU is already a big aid donor; in fact, by far the biggest in the world if we include aid provided by member states. With time, EU financial assistance has arguably become the single most important element of preferential agreements with developing countries. However, the efficiency of EU development assistance leaves much to be desired, suffering for long from lack of coherent strategy as well as from heavy bureaucratic procedures and a serious shortage of Commission staff entrusted with the management of multilateral assistance. It has not been very efficient in terms of the use of economic resources and the outputs delivered. Furthermore, the considerable amounts of money spent have generally bought the Europeans little political influence in the recipient countries, for better or worse. Have the Europeans been willing to part with their money just in order to keep their collective conscience clear? Or is this poor result yet another by-product of their highly imperfect political system? Having finally realised the shortcomings of their external aid policies, the Europeans have recently begun to take some measures to make the system more efficient.

Aid recipients almost invariably prefer multilateral to bilateral aid because the latter usually has political and other strings attached. EU aid is multilateral, yet conditionality need not be confused with political strings. In order to avoid wasting European taxpayers' money, external aid needs to be given with strict conditions linked to development. And the Europeans now also seem to have fewer qualms about imposing political conditions related to democracy and human rights, although in practice they experience great difficulties in applying them consistently in many parts of the Third World suffering from very low standards of governance. They need to find the political courage to do so. Otherwise, redistribution will mostly take place from the European middle classes and workers to the benefit of corrupt rulers in very poor countries—and also a small number of European consultants. It is a question of political courage; it is also a question of coherent policy and efficient management and monitoring of EU external aid.

An ever increasing membership

The Union exerts its strongest influence on other countries through the prospect of membership. This is the most effective way of extending *Pax Europea*, which carries with it peace, democracy, welfare, and a highly advanced form of joint management of interdependence. Membership of the Union comes with several preconditions; these have become increasingly difficult over time and, once a country has joined, socialisation (and Europeanization) becomes an ongoing process. Sharing sovereignty can only be learned the hard way, not through the texts prescribed for candidates. With repeated rounds of enlargement, the Community and now the Union has been spreading *Pax Europea* to an increasing number of European countries; and it has been gradually transformed as a result of new accessions. This time, the challenge is greater than ever before.

Until the 'big bang' of 2004, there had been three rounds of enlargement, with three new members joining in each round: the first group of Eftans, led by the UK, in the 1970s; the southerners in the 1980s; and the second group of neutral Eftans in the 1990s. Three, therefore, appeared to be the magic number, although, as with everything else magic, it had emerged from some sleight of hand. To be more precise, the southern enlargement took place in two installments, since Greece joined on its own—an event highly unlikely to be repeated; and there is also the very important enlargement of 1990, when the eastern *Länder* joined Germany and the Community, although this does not officially count as enlargement but only as an internal German affair. The numbers are now very different: ten new members joined in May 2004, while several others have been exercising their patience in the waiting room. The reasons that so many countries want to join the EU are obvious: they want to secure access to European markets, access to private and public funds, access to a reliable insurance policy for security and democracy, and also their share of influence and prestige associated with membership of the most important club in town. It is to be hoped that they also want to play an active role in the construction of the still unfinished common European home.

Surely enlargement means, first and foremost, an investment in democracy, security, and prosperity, in other words an extension of *Pax Europea* to the whole of the European continent (see also Chapter 13 in this volume). This is what is really at stake and little less than that. But for the immediate future, enlargement will cost money in times of financial stringency; it will threaten vested interests, be they farmers or net beneficiaries from EU Funds; it will make decisions and the running of the EU much more difficult; and it will require painful internal reforms. In other words, while the benefits of enlargement for the Union are mostly long-term and intangible, the costs are perceived to be more immediate and concrete. This is hardly the combination to mobilise politicians in a democracy, let alone in the highly complex system of the EU. It largely explains the wide gap between official rhetoric and action as well as the slow pace of enlargement.

There is widespread fear (mostly exaggerated) among Union citizens that enlargement will lead to large new flows of immigrants. Immigration has already become a major political issue, and is often linked in the public mind to the increase in criminality. It is therefore not surprising that justice and home affairs ministers have been meeting all too frequently, and it is also not surprising that existing members have insisted on—and obtained—long transitional periods before allowing free movement of people for the new members.

Europe is crowded, rich, and ageing. It is mostly surrounded by countries with much poorer and younger populations, countries with high birth rates, weak political institutions, and uncertain economic prospects: an explosive combination indeed. The poor are at the gates. Some are already climbing over them. Immigration policy has become an integral part of foreign policy—and also enlargement policy. European governments, separately and (more so with time) jointly, continue to experience great difficulties in reconciling economic interests with social and political constraints; and immigration has unequal effects on their societies—there is no point in pretending otherwise. Some will be tempted to look for a scapegoat in Brussels, while there is no certainty at all that a common policy would also be effective in dealing with the problem. As the EU expands further to the east, an increasing number of those young and worse-off will be turned into privileged citizens of the Union, although after long transitional periods intended to placate the fears of those already in. Immigration will remain a hot political issue, and much will depend on how the economic situation develops.

It will be a big challenge to integrate successfully a large number of much poorer countries, with weak administrative and regulatory structures, not to mention a relatively short experience of markets and democracy (Mair and Zielonka 2002). The enlarged EU risks turning into an unmanageable affair. And there is also the politically awkward question: how much diversity (and how many more new members) can the EU take before it becomes totally unrecognisable and unable to deliver the goods? This is the kind of question that most European politicians have until recently avoided asking (at least in public), for obvious reasons. Asking the question unavoidably leads to a discussion about the final objective and the ultimate boundaries of this ever-enlarging Union—and we all know that there is no agreement on either of them, and that a discussion on boundaries is guaranteed to insult some of our more or less distant neighbours.

Europeanization and globalisation

European integration can be seen as a highly developed system for the joint management of interdependence. This interdependence started with trade and steadily extended into many other manifestations of cross-border interaction and exchange in a crowded continent with a long and turbulent history, relatively scarce natural resources, and a wide diversity of cultures, political traditions, and economic systems. Nowadays, the welfare of European citizens is intimately linked with this system of regional interdependence, and so more generally is their quality of life to the extent that it too depends on the freedom to travel, study, or work anywhere inside the Union, and to the extent that it depends on access to a wide variety of goods and services and greater security, among other things. One may be tempted to add the ability to preserve a certain way of life, although this remains a controversial argument for the minority who still prefer to emphasise diversity rather than commonality of values and models of society.

Many aspects of the everyday life of European citizens now depend on decisions taken beyond their national borders, albeit with the participation of their representatives. A key characteristic of European integration has been the attempt to combine liberalisation of markets and the elimination of national barriers in general with the establishment of common rules and institutions—a new level of governance, in contemporary parlance. This is, after all, only proper for countries where individualism has been long tamed by considerations of the public good and where government is not necessarily a dirty word; it may also have something to do with Europe being old and crowded.

Different methods of governance have developed for the wide variety of policy areas coming under the umbrella of European integration. They cover the whole spectrum from simple intergovernmental cooperation to outright federalism: federalism that in several countries still dares not speak its name. On the other hand, weak common rules and non-constraining forms of intergovernmental cooperation usually go hand in hand with low levels of integration on the ground and persistently wide diversity. There is nothing necessarily wrong with that, as long as it is compatible with economic and political fundamentals, and as long as the latter naturally include a conscious choice by a sufficient number of participants. It is up to the Europeans collectively to decide what they do together and what separately, and consequently what price they are willing to pay for further integration or continued fragmentation.

Interdependence is, of course, not a uniquely European phenomenon. It has increasingly characterised international relations during recent decades, and the accelerated pace of transnational forces has often led to exaggerated notions of a shrinking world and a global village: the sophisticated analyst from New York preaching globalisation to the tribesman in the Kalahari desert. Yet globalisation is not just a fad; it depicts real forces operating in the world today, striking down many of the barriers carefully and painstakingly built over the years by governments in the name of national autonomy, or simply for the sake of protecting special interests.

In most cases, regional interdependence in Europe today is substantially different from what we find at the global level in at least two important respects—intensity and governance—which are usually mutually reinforcing. The regional concentration of economic exchange is very high indeed in Europe, and this is intimately linked with a system of rules and regulations governing this exchange. This applies to almost all aspects of trade, although less so to financial markets where the regional tends to merge with the global. The extent to which such differences may be due to market fundamentals rather than to man-made rules is not always easy to establish.

Regional integration has served as an instrument of economic development, a catalyst for modernisation, and in many ways a kind of convergence machine for the benefit of the less developed countries of the European continent. This has reduced the geographical (as well as the political and cultural) distance between the core and the periphery. And economic development, coupled with modernisation, is still helping to strengthen the new democratic institutions in countries emerging from long periods of authoritarian and totalitarian rule. They all constitute integral parts of what is generally referred to as the process of Europeanization. These considerations also help explain why the periphery has a more rosy picture of the European Union, at least the one it has known so far, even though the challenge of adjustment has been much greater for it than for the core.

It has surely helped that a sense of solidarity has gradually developed among participants, which has been translated into, among other things, financial instruments of redistribution through the EU budget. Although limited, given the small size of the common budget, redistribution constitutes today a key element of the overall package deal behind European integration; and this is a highly important distinguishing feature of the EU. Solidarity has been manifested in mutual aid in a wide variety of instances, and also in explicit burden sharing, be it with respect to asylum policy or the costs of environmental protection. Burden sharing and redistribution of costs are, for example, a major component of the internal EU agreement linked to the Kyoto Protocol. A sense of community has been developing, albeit slowly, inside the EU; of course, it is still far short of the sense of community (*Gemeinschaft*, as the Germans would call it) to be found within old nation-states with a long common history strengthened by close bonds, shared symbols, and myths.

Common European policies and common institutions have also served as a means of projecting collective power and influence in international affairs. This has certainly been true of trade. Europeans have learned from experience that acting together was the only way of having a real impact in multilateral negotiations. However, not all have yet drawn the conclusion that the lessons learnt from external trade can be easily applied to other areas of policy, even less so as they move along the spectrum from so-called low to high politics. Thus, the shift from economic to political power has proved extremely difficult. Relations with the superpower across the Atlantic have usually acted as a dividing factor. The pursuit of a common foreign policy assumes that members perceive they have more interests in common than with outside countries, and are therefore prepared to sacrifice their independence of action (or simply the illusion of independence) in order to strengthen their collective negotiating power. This has not always been obvious, especially in those areas where regional self-sufficiency has been relatively low—security being a case in point.

European integration started basically as an economic affair, though with strong political undertones. Economics remains today the backbone of it all. For many years, integration helped to sustain a succession of virtuous circles, which helped strongly growing national economies while also bolstering the essentially permissive consensus of European citizens about further integration. It was very good as long as it lasted. For more than ten years now, the performance of most West European economies has been disappointing, certainly in comparison with the performance of the US economy even after the bursting of the stock exchange bubble.

The regional economy is influenced by the global economic environment which is, of course, not entirely something that European policy-makers can shape according to their wishes. Having just conceded the obvious, we may safely add that the eurozone (not to mention the sum of all EU economies) is big enough not to have to take the rest of the world as given. This assumes that member states act in a coordinated fashion, thus turning the EU into something more than the sum of its national parts (Sapir 2004). Macroeconomic management and the external dimension of EMU will therefore be crucial. They have not so far received their due amount of attention.

Many tools of economic policy are, of course, still in the hands of national governments. The big challenge for the near future will be whether they succeed, individually and collectively, in reconciling international competitiveness and internal structural reforms with the kind of politically stable and compassionate society that Western Europeans created in the aftermath of the Second World War. They need to handle with great care the problem of losers in times of rapid change and growing uncertainty. The new package should indeed include effective social safety nets and some of the means to enable people to adjust to the new economic environment. In trying to reform social and welfare policies, European countries will, however, continue facing an extremely difficult task as those with more secure jobs and/or accumulated generous pension rights ferociously resist change. In this respect, some countries will be more successful than others. There is both competition and solidarity in the European system, and this is manifested in both internal and external policies.

Notes

1 This chapter draws heavily on Tsoukalis (2005).

2 See also various chapters in Craft and Toniolo (1996).

3 For one of the best analyses, see De Grauwe (2005).

Further reading

This chapter relies heavily on the general arguments put forward in Tsoukalis (2005). For a historical treatment of the significance of the European integration project, see Craft and Toniolo (1996), and for a general treatment of the economic integration process see Pelkmans (2001). The significance of the internal market programme is also dealt with in Pelkmans (2001) and Tsoukalis (1997), whilst Majone (1996) deals with the specific issues arising from regulatory policy. The technical implications Of EMU are addressed by De Grauwe (2005), whilst the political economy of the process is especially the focus in Dyson (2000). Mair and Zielonka (2002) provide a treatment of the implications of enlargement, whilst Kierzkowski (2002) focuses on the relationship between European integration and globalisation. Finally, Sapir (2004) examines the overall economic package of regional integration and proposes a set of reforms.

Craft, N., and Toniolo, G. (eds) (1996), *Economic Growth in Europe Since 1945* (Cambridge: Cambridge University Press).

De Grauwe, P. (2005), *Economics of Monetary Union*, 6th edition (Oxford: Oxford University Press).

Dyson, K. (2000), *Elusive Union: The Process of Economic and Monetary Union in Europe* (Oxford: Oxford University Press).

Kierzkowski, H. (ed.) (2002), *Europe and Globalization* (Basingstoke: Palgrave).

Mair, P., and Zielonka, J. (eds.) (2002), *The Enlarged European Union: Diversity and Adaptation* (London: Frank Cass).

Majone, G. (1996) *Regulating Europe* (London: Routledge).

Pelkmans, J. (2001), *European Integration: Methods and Economic Analysis*, 2nd edition (Harlow: Pearson Education).

Sapir, A. *et al.* (2004), *An Agenda for a Growing Europe* (The Sapir Report) (Oxford: Oxford University Press).

Tsoukalis, L. (1997) *The New European Economy Revisited* (Oxford: Oxford University Press).

Tsoukalis, L. (2005), *What Kind of Europe? Revised and Updated Edition* (Oxford: Oxford University Press).

Web links

The best source for information on the EU's international economic and financial activities is the Europa web site, htpp://www.europa.eu.int/, where all of the main agencies and institutions provide access to policy statements, documents and other materials. Look especially for the pages dealing with Economic and Financial Affairs, with the Single Market and with Competition Policy. On monetary policy, see the web site of the European Central Bank, http://www.ecb.int/. The major economic and financial newspapers have web sites that offer a wide range of useful materials, for example http://www.ft.com/ (the *Financial Times*) and http://www.theeconomist.com/ (*The Economist*). For economic analysis, see for example the site of the Centre for Economic Policy Research in London (http://www.cepr.org/).

Chapter 12

The European Union as a Trade Power

Sophie Meunier and Kalypso Nicolaïdis

Contents

Summary

The EU is a formidable trade power. While trade liberalisation internally and externally have always been the essence of European integration, successive enlargements and the creation of the European Single Market have turned the EU into the world's largest trade power. The EU is responsible for making trade policy through a complex decision-making process that has often been contested politically but allows it to speak on behalf of its members in international trade negotiations. This chapter argues that not only does the EU derive some inherent power from trade, but that it is also increasingly prone to use trade as the backbone of its normative power. As a result the EU is now becoming a world power through trade, as one of the major actors shaping the multilateral trade agenda, and using access to its market strategically in order to obtain political concessions from its commercial partners. This chapter explores the determinants of the EU's trade power (both inherent and normative) and examines the contribution of trade policy to the power of Europe in the international system, both in the context of the World Trade Organization and in the broader framework of international relations.

Introduction

If there is any area in which the European Union (EU) has become an uncontested power in the international system, it is clearly in the field of trade policy. No wonder: trade is the EU's *raison d'être*. The objective of the 1957 Treaty of Rome was to create a customs union between the original six members of the European Community in which there would be no barriers to trade and a common external tariff would be applied to imports from third countries. From its very beginning, then, the Community became a single actor in international trade policy and almost immediately started talking on an equal footing with the United States in commercial negotiations. With its successive enlargements from six to 25 countries and the prosperous economies of its member states, the EU has become a formidable trade power and interlocutor in international trade negotiations.

Partly by design, partly by necessity, the EU entertains a very different relationship to power than the United States. It sees itself above all as a civilian and a normative power, apt at using non-military tools to achieve its goals in the rest of the world (Duchêne 1973; Hill 1990; Nicolaïdis and Howse 2002; Manners 2002). Trade is at the very core of the EU's civilian power. The sheer size of the European single market, which attracts the outside world both for the possibilities it offers and for the fear of being excluded, is an essential element of EU power. The collective character of European trade policy has enabled the EU to become a true rival to the United States. Yet the power of the EU in trade goes further than its impressive capacity to defend its own interests in international commercial negotiations. It also lies in its capacity to expand its own regulatory practices to the rest of the world and to use trade to promote internationally its own values and policies. In that the EU constitutes neither a rival to the US nor necessarily an ally, but it can be viewed as an 'alternative' for countries seeking a power anchor when disagreeing with the US. The principled positions taken by the EU in the beef hormones and the ongoing Genetically Modified Organisms disputes are evidence of this new European propensity to seek to shape the global rules of the game according to its own internal compromises.

In keeping with the driving themes of this volume, the present chapter explores the determinants of the EU's trade power and examines the contribution of trade policy to the power of Europe in the international system, both in the context of the World Trade Organization and in the broader framework of international relations. In doing so we argue that it is crucial to distinguish between the inherent power derived from trade and the use of trade as the backbone of normative power. We start by recounting how the EU acquired and retained competence to represent the member states in trade policy, from the Treaty of Rome to the latest debate around a new

European Constitutional Treaty. The second section provides an overview of the EU trade policy-making process, while the third section explores how its recent enlargement may transform the trade power of the EU. The fourth section moves on to asking whether and how, on this institutional basis, the EU can credibly be presented as a champion of multilateralism, including in the context of dispute resolution in the WTO. We conclude by assessing the EU as a world power in trade and through trade.

The road to European competence in trade

The common commercial policy is the most prominent EU policy to have been under supranational competence from the very beginning. Whether in bilateral, regional, or multilateral trade negotiations, Europe formally 'speaks with one voice' and negotiates through one agent, the European Commission. The very idea that nation states could give up such a key area of their external affairs was, and continues to be, revolutionary. But the granting of competence over trade to the supranational authority has not always been without political controversy (Meunier and Nicolaïdis 1999). While the expansion of the global trade agenda during the 1990s, notably to services, seemed to call for a parallel expansion of the scope of EU competence, several member states resisted further transfers of sovereignty, leading to a protracted battle over the issue of trade competence. This section explores the conflicts within the EU over the appropriate institutional design for trade policy-making, as reflected in the balance between competences exclusive to the EU and those shared with the member states.

The common commercial policy in the Treaty of Rome

As the nascent European Community's *raison d'être*, trade policy immediately came under supranational competence. In the field of trade, the Treaty of Rome was a revolutionary document. Not only did it contain unusually broad injunctions for achieving free trade internally, it also granted the new supranational entity an external personality with the authority to elaborate, negotiate, and enforce all aspects of trade relations with the rest of the world.[1] In practice, this was done through the establishment of a common commercial policy based on three principles: a common external tariff, common trade agreements with third countries, and the uniform application of trade instruments across member states.

Until the 1997 Amsterdam Summit, the Treaty of Rome's original wording of Article 113,[2] which grants the Community exclusive competence in 'trade' policy (without defining the term), remained almost unchanged (Devuyst 1992; Maresceau 1993). The provisions determining the trade policy-making process delegated authority from the individual states and their parliaments to the assembly of European states, acting collectively through the Council of Ministers. This approach can be understood in classical principal-agent terms: the member states (principals) have delegated their authority to conclude trade agreements to the European Community (agent), acting on their behalf. This contrasts with areas of 'mixed' competence (such as the negotiation of association agreements), where formal authority remains with the individual member states, in particular through parliamentary ratification. In both cases, the member states represent the ultimate authority, but in the former it is as voting parties in the EU structures, while in the latter it is through their sovereign parliament. The conduct of trade policy in practice reveals a second level of delegation, this time from the Council of Ministers (principals) to the European Commission (agent), which initiates the participation of the EU in international trade negotiations and negotiates on behalf of the member states.

The challenge to exclusive competence during the 1990s

During the two decades following the Treaty of Rome, the Commission successfully negotiated on behalf of its members two major trade rounds under GATT, as well as a host of bilateral trade agreements. Throughout the 1980s and 1990s, however, several developments challenged the clear foundations of the Community's trade competence.

The first of these challenges was the emergence of so-called 'new issues' (above all services) onto the international trade agenda in the mid-1980s. Issues such as aviation and product standards had been discussed already at the close of the Tokyo Round in 1979, but most member states considered these too domestically sensitive to leave entirely to the Commission.[3] The subsequent expansion of the world trade agenda onto policies traditionally not 'at the border' (e.g. tariffs and quotas) but 'inside the state' (e.g. national laws and regulations) forced an explicit internal EU debate on the issue of competence. Several member states, reluctant to give up forever entire new sectors of their trade policy, insisted on being granted their own competences with respect to the 'new issues', arguing that these were not covered under the original Treaty of Rome.

Another challenge was the creation of the new World Trade Organization (WTO), with a broader trade agenda than GATT, which forced the issue of trade authority to the fore (Devuyst 1995). The question of membership constituted an unavoidable legal challenge for the European Community, even though the rest of the world left it up to the Europeans to decide how this would be settled. The EC had never formally substituted the member states in GATT, whose creation preceded that of the Community. Since the GATT was only an 'agreement' with signatories but no members, the question of Community membership never formally arose. For all practical purposes, therefore, the EC—represented by the Commission—had been accepted by the other GATT partners as one of them. Moreover, formally replacing the member states by the EC could have a cost, since the individual voting rights of member states in GATT would give way to a single vote.[4]

In order to solve the competence dispute, the Commission asked the European Court of Justice for an 'advisory opinion' on the issue of competence. If member states were not going to compromise politically, perhaps their objection could be overruled legally. In November 1994, the European judges confirmed that the Community had sole competence to conclude international agreements on trade in goods.[5] In a controversial move, however, they also held that the member states and the Community shared competence in dealing with trade in the 'new issues'.[6] As we have argued elsewhere, the Court in effect had put the ball back in the politicians', court (Meunier and Nicolaïdis 1999; Nicolaïdis and Meunier 2002). To avoid future competence disputes, they would have to amend the treaty either by following the Court's opinion and enshrine this new sharing of sovereignty in the texts or by explicitly 'expanding' Community trade competence to include new issues.

From Amsterdam to Nice: a political solution to the competence dispute

The resolution of the competence dispute and the revision of Article 113 were tacked onto the broad agenda of the 1996 Inter-Governmental Conference (IGC), which was expected to design an institutional reform that would enable the Union to function with 25 members in the next millennium. Yet the member states could not agree to put the competence issue in trade to rest. The IGC culminated with the signing of the Amsterdam Treaty, in which the member states eventually agreed to a simple and short amendment to Article 113 (renumbered 133) allowing for future expansion of exclusive competence to the excluded sectors through a unanimous vote of the Council.[7] In trade policy, the Amsterdam outcome was a statement that extension of Community competence should be the result of case-by-case political decisions rather than some uncontrollable spillover. In effect, this decision amounted to a European equivalent of the US's fast track procedures, whereby Congress grants trade negotiating authority to the White House and United States Trade Representative (USTR) each time a new round of international negotiations is in sight.

Not surprisingly, it quickly became clear that the Amsterdam compromise on trade was not sustainable. Member states felt compelled to review the trade competence issue once more at Nice in December 2000, so soon after the hardly-fought battle in Amsterdam, for three main reasons. First was the significant increase in trade in services which had taken place since 1997. In order to capitalise on such growth, Commission trade officials, with Frenchman Pascal Lamy at the helm since September 1999, insisted that trade in services be transferred under the exclusive competence of the Community for reasons of efficiency, especially in view of the upcoming 'Millennium round' of multilateral trade negotiations expected to be launched in Seattle in November 2003.

Second, trade had suddenly become a hot political issue, as globalisation gave rise to a new brand of well-organised activists worldwide. The defeat of the OECD-based Multilateral Agreement on Investment in 1998—which aimed to facilitate international investment by ensuring that host governments treat foreign and domestic firms—was similarly interpreted by anti-globalisation activists as a victory against a text that would have limited the ability of national governments to regulate the protection of their culture, environment, natural resources and health, as well as ending the protection of their citizens from foreign investors. Trade was again highly politicised in the summer of 1999 when French sheep farmer José Bové and his companions very publicly destroyed a McDonald's in the French countryside in response to the retaliatory trade sanctions that the WTO had authorised the United States to take against the EU in the beef hormones and bananas cases (Meunier 2000a). This politicisation of trade reached its peak in December 1999 when the international trade talks in Seattle supposed to launch a new round of multilateral trade talks collapsed, amidst massive public demonstrations by anti-globalisation protesters.

All of these episodes were reflections of and further contributing factors to the increasingly contentious character of trade.[8] Specifically, anti-globalisation activists focused their attention on issues such as trade in cultural, education, and social services—issues that had been left open to further transfers of competence by the Amsterdam compromise.

Third, the prospect of the imminent enlargement of the EU also contributed to calls for revisiting the trade competence issue. Widening membership of the EU to many more countries, all with disparate and even contradictory interests, lent a double sense of urgency to the issue. On the one hand, and most obviously, external representation—like other policy areas—risked increased inefficiency at best, stalemate at worst. An arrangement originally designed for six members would likely no longer be adequate when the 'single voice' has to represent 25 different countries. On the other hand, the current members may have had an interest in 'locking in' their preferred institutional design before the widening to new members. The prospect of new entrants eager to use their veto power to block trade liberalisation in some sectors or, on the contrary, eager to favour liberalisation in other areas where existing members would prefer protection may have proven enough of an incentive for the existing members of the EU to settle the institutional question in Nice.

The final agreement reflected the bargaining dynamics of the negotiation. There was a general momentum at Nice to expand qualified majority voting, and Article 133 was to be no exception. Exclusive competence became the general rule for trade in services (Article 133.5). Exceptions to exclusive competence in order to satisfy residual national sensitivities were kept to a minimum and carved out under a 'positive list' approach. First and foremost, the Treaty enshrined the concept of 'mixed competence' developed by the Court in its 1994 jurisprudence as a new legal category. Particularly noteworthy is the explicit inclusion of the 'cultural exception' clause in Community law, with cultural and audiovisual services falling under mixed competence alongside education, social, and human health services. In addition, transport remained under a separate legal basis (Title V and Article 300). Finally, intellectual property was divided into two components: 'commercial aspects of intellectual property', which fall under exclusive competence, and all other aspects of intellectual property, which are shared. But the Council could decide by unanimity that the provisions relevant to exclusive competence can be extended to the latter—a last echo of the defunct Amsterdam compromise.[9] In EU parlance, the 'passerelle clause' had now been circumscribed to one last, sensitive, area of trade negotiations.

This outcome proved quite satisfactory for most member states: for France (adamant about cultural exception); for Great Britain (which cared more about the linkage with taxation); for Germany (which is happy about the result for air transport, and whose *Länder* are content with shared competence on culture); and for the pro-integration countries which can claim that the original spirit of the Treaty of Rome has been, at least to some extent, restored.

Trade policy in the EU Constitutional Treaty

The debate over competence and representation in trade policy was not closed with the Nice Treaty. When a Convention on the Future of Europe was convened in the Spring of 2002 to draft a constitution for Europe, many voices demanded a greater role for the European Parliament in trade. Indeed, these demands have increased as the reach of trade policy increased to politically sensitive issues that used to be the exclusive domain of domestic regulation, such as food safety and culture. A group of EU parliamentarians filed a constitutional amendment that would give the Parliament unprecedented powers in shaping EU trade policy, including the establishment of a right to a vote of assent in the Parliament for any significant bilateral and multilateral trade deals entered into by the EU. The Commission also pushed for a greater role for the parliament in trade policy, on the implicit grounds that a right to veto by the Parliament could provide Commission officials with greater leverage in international trade negotiations.

In response to these demands, the Convention introduced many important institutional changes with respect to trade policy—changes which were endorsed by the Intergovernmental Conference which followed and finally agreed on a Constitutional Treaty in June 2004 (to be ratified by 2006). First, the Constitutional Treaty opened up greater avenues for parliamentary control. Trade-related legislation, such as anti-dumping rules, will now be adopted according to the co-decision procedure—that is, jointly by the Council and the Parliament. The Commission is in charge of the implementation of these rules. The Parliament will be kept informed of the progress of trade negotiations and it will get to approve the conclusion of trade agreements. Formally, this will mean equal power of the Council and the Parliament over trade policy. In practice of course, the involvement of the Council through the on-going oversight of Commission activities (see below) still leaves the former in a stronger position.

The second institutional problem faced by the EU has been the challenge of keeping an efficient decision-making system in an enlarged Europe of 25 or even 30 member states. As we have seen, the rule of Qualified Majority Voting did not apply to all cases of trade policy which meant that the existence of a veto could lead to a paralysis of the system. The Constitutional Treaty which goes further than the 2000 Nice Treaty simplifies the trade policy-making apparatus by establishing that trade policy is an exclusive Community competence, whether in goods, services, intellectual property or foreign direct investment. The use of qualified majority voting is broadened correspondingly. There remains, however, one exception to this radical simplification: *l'exception culturelle*. Unsurprisingly, all French representatives at the Convention were adamant that matters of trade in cultural and audiovisual services constituted the critical French 'red line' and were even supported by a majority of member states, including Germany and Poland. The text actually states that the Council uses unanimity for the negotiation and conclusion of agreements in trade in cultural and audiovisual services when such agreements could jeopardise the cultural and linguistic diversity of the EU. In other cases, majority voting will apply.

If adopted, these institutional changes would make the EU function more effectively across the board. Its trade policy regime would become more similar to that of the US, where the Congress has the authority to grant negotiating authority to the president and to veto multilateral and bilateral trade deals. Perhaps most importantly, the deal embedded in the Constitutional Treaty would appear to represent a relatively stable equilibrium after a decade of haggling over the precise delineation of powers between the EU and the member states. Although there is still a mix of provisions for unanimity and QMV, and in some areas Community competence still coexists with residual member state competence or quasi-competence, key issues have thus either been settled or made subject to a predictable *modus vivendi*.

The EU trade policy-making process

How does the EU make decisions in an area which, for all relevant purposes, falls under its prerogative of exclusive competence? The key to this question is to understand the relationship between the Commission and the member states, which can be stylised as a principal-agent relation (Nicolaïdis 2000). We outline below the precise steps and specify the actors involved during each of these steps.

We first need to distinguish between four stages in the negotiation of international agreements: (1) the design of a negotiation mandate; (2) the representation of the parties during the negotiations; (3) the ratification of the agreement once negotiated; and (4) the implementation and enforcement of the agreement once it is brought into force. 'Here, we are concerned directly with the first three of these stages (the mandate, the negotiations and ratification), since the question of implementation and enforcement is covered by the discussion later in the chapter of the substance of EU trade policies.' It is important to compare procedures and the actors in charge at each of these stages in cases of 'exclusive' and 'mixed' competence.[10] Whether the Community is perceived to speak with 'one voice' is most relevant during the negotiations but is also affected by shared expectations about the ratification stage.

In theory, the core difference between exclusive and mixed competence comes at the ratification stage. Mixed competence in trade simply means that delegation of authority on the part of the member states is granted on an adhoc basis for negotiation purposes rather than systematically. Individual member states retain a veto both through unanimity voting in the Council and through ratification by their own national parliament. In practice, the difference is more blurred. On the one hand, exclusive competence does not guarantee a single voice: Member states might fail to find a majority behind a given policy and if so, their external front may crumble. More to the point, powerful member states still exercise an informal veto both at the mandate and the ratification stages, to the extent that the Luxembourg compromise extends to the trade area. Conversely, member states have managed to speak with one voice in areas of mixed competence or common foreign policy (as exemplified by 95% of the decisions taken in common in the United Nations). The principle of unity of representation through the Commission is valid under both configurations, even if in both cases, individual member states usually seek to reduce Commission autonomy to the extent tolerated by their partners. Nevertheless, the expression of dissent is dampened, the incentives for seeking compromise increased and the role of the Commission enhanced in areas of exclusive competence.

The negotiating mandate

The European Commission has the power to propose legislation, act as the guardian of EU treaties, and ensure that EU legislation is implemented by all members. The

Commission's role in the EU institutional edifice is to act in support of the collective goals and needs, independently of instructions from national governments. Therefore it is up to the Commission to elaborate proposals for the initiation and content of international trade negotiations (Johnson 1998; Meunier and Nicolaïdis 1999; Woolcock 2000; Meunier 2005). The initial proposals are made by staffers in the Trade Directorate ('DG Trade'), based like the rest of the Commission in Brussels. DG Trade assists, and answers to, the EU Trade Commissioner, nominated by the member states along with the 19 other commissioners for a five-year term (between 1999 and 2004, the EU Trade Commissioner was Frenchman Pascal Lamy; it is now Peter Mandelson, from Britain. DG Trade also oversees the use of trade policy instruments (see Box 12.1).

Once DG Trade has elaborated proposals for trade negotiations, the key policy discussions take place in a special advisory committee, the '133 Committee', named after Article 133 on trade policy.[11] It plays a key role in helping member states influence EU trade policy, even though its role is formally consultative only. The agenda of the 133 Committee is set by the Commission, in collaboration with the rotating presidency of the EU. The 133 Committee meets weekly at either the senior level or at the level of deputies. The senior members ('titulaires'), senior civil servants from the member states' national ministries as well as the director general of DG Trade, meet once a month in Brussels. In addition they meet in Geneva whenever there are WTO plenary sessions. These senior members serve on the committee for extended periods of time and have a good sense of what actions are politically acceptable within their state of origin. They only deal with the politically sensitive problems. The 133 Committee also meets three Fridays a month at the level of deputies, who are drawn from the member states' permanent representations in Brussels, sometimes from the national ministries, in addition to the director of the WTO unit within DG Trade and special experts. The deputies deal with the more technical issues. Additionally, there are also sub-committees of a sectoral nature (such as '133 textiles', '133 services', '133 steel'), which prepare the work for the 133 Committee. Matters are typically discussed until a consensus emerges and no formal votes are recorded.[12]

The Commission almost always follows the advice of the 133 Committee, since its members reflect the wishes of the ministers who ultimately can refuse to conclude the agreement negotiated by the Commission.[13] Once the Committee has amended Commission proposals, they are transmitted to the Committee of Permanent Representatives (Coreper)—a key group based in Brussels and composed of the member state officials who are national ambassadors to the EU, their deputies and staff. Coreper then transmits the negotiating proposal to the Council of Ministers, which has the power to establish objectives for trade negotiations (known as the 'negotiating mandate'). Composed of ministers from each government, the Council represents the national interests of the member states. The composition of the Council varies, depending on the subject matter under discussion. With respect to trade policy, the issues are often tackled by the General Affairs and External Relations Council (GAERC), where the member states are in principle represented by Foreign Ministers, although sometimes it is composed exclusively of trade ministers.

The Council then agrees on a negotiating mandate to hand out the Commission. The form of the actual mandate varies depending on the negotiation: in some cases the mandate takes the form of one or several directives, while in other cases the mandate is only a very vague document.[14] 'Negotiating directives' are not legally constraining: the negotiator can depart from those directives, but then takes the risk of having to sell the negotiating package to the Council at the end of the negotiation. Court jurisprudence and treaty articles spell out the cases in which policy decisions are made according to majority or unanimity. According to the 1957 Treaty of Rome, unanimity should have been used for external trade only until January 1966, the end of the transitional period. Majority voting would have been automatically instituted after this date, had France's De Gaulle not paralysed the functioning of Community institutions with the 'empty chair' crisis during the Kennedy Round. The crisis resulted in the 'Luxembourg Compromise', a gentleman's agreement according to which an individual member state could veto a decision otherwise taken according to qualified majority if it deemed that vital national interests were at stake. The subsequent addition of new member states increased the divergence of interests within the EC and rendered even more difficult the task of reaching a common bargaining position for international trade negotiations. The 1985 Single European Act attempted to establish the primacy of majority voting. With the exception of sensitive areas such as taxes, employee rights, and the free movement of persons, the member states agreed to use majority voting to legislate on all economic matters.[15] Since then, at least on paper, the Council agrees on a common external bargaining position for international trade negotiations on 'traditional' trade issues (exclusive of services and intellectual property) according to a 'qualified majority' system. This is a procedure under which member states are assigned different voting weights, based approximately on the size of their population, and by which roughly two-thirds of the votes are needed in order for a proposal to be accepted.[16] Nevertheless, in reaching a common bargaining position for international trade negotiations as in reaching most other policy decisions in the Community, member states have most often attempted to find a general consensus around a given issue without resorting to a formal vote. Almost none of the cases in which Council decisions have been contested to the level at which a formal vote was needed have involved trade issues, reflecting both the more general difference in EU policy-making between QMV as a legally ordained procedure and the reality, and the perceived importance of achieving unity on external policy matters.[17]

   The competence over external trade negotiations is therefore fairly centralised at the Commission and Council levels. Unlike in other fields of external agreements, such as the association agreements, the European Parliament has no formal say in the process. Subsequent Treaty modifications, such as the 1986 Single European Act, the 1991 Maastricht Treaty, the 1997 Amsterdam Treaty, and the 2000 Nice Treaty have not increased the role of the Parliament in the trade policy-making process. In practice, informal procedures exist for informing and consulting the Parliament: the Commission and the Council inform the Parliament of the conduct of international trade negotiations on an informal basis and may request the Parliament's approval before the formal ratification of an international agreement. Nevertheless, while it cannot veto trade legislation (unlike legislation in social policy, agriculture, and the internal market), the Parliament can hold hearings and issue reports on trade issues, thereby influencing indirectly the course of trade negotiations. Lately it has tried to exert greater clout over trade, especially those issues with a heavy regulatory component that have divided the EU and the US. The European Parliament was indeed the driving force behind the EU ban on aircraft engine hush-kits to meet noise standards, data protection issues that affect US firms, and broadcast and motion picture quotas. Perhaps this will change if the EU Constitutional Treaty is adopted.

The negotiations

Following the adoption of the negotiating mandate by the Council, the actual conduct of international trade negotiations for the EU is carried out by members of the Commission, acting under the authority of the Trade Commissioner. The situation during the negotiations may seem somewhat surrealistic: member states are allowed to observe but not speak in WTO plenary sessions. In principle, as long as they remain within the limits set by the mandate, Commission negotiators are free to conduct bargaining with third countries as they wish. In practice the negotiators' latitude and flexibility vary case by case, depending on the member states' willingness to give up control over the issue being negotiated. While they remain silent in plenary, member states' ambassadors usually do not shy away from informal corridor negotiations with EU counterparts. Moreover, the 133 Committee often meets in Geneva during the negotiations to ascertain whether the Commission remains with its mandate and to agree on changes in negotiating position. Thus if the EU Commissioner is envisaging a significant move, he needs to either call the capitals or call a meeting on the premise of the negotiations. This oversight often makes moves and concessions harder for the EU than for other trade partners, but it also gives it significant bargaining power (Meunier 2000b; Meunier 2005). From the member states' viewpoint, it is this oversight that makes it acceptable to issue vague mandates containing little indication of the actual positions to be taken in negotiation.

The ratification

At the conclusion of the negotiations, the trade agreement must be ratified. In cases of agreements falling entirely under EU competence (such as on textiles and steel), the Council approves or rejects the final text according to qualified majority voting—with the exception of some services and intellectual property negotiations where unanimity is the rule (Meunier 2005). In most cases, however, the ratification process is complicated by the 'mixed' nature of many of the big 'packaged' trade agreements, which must be approved both by the EU as a whole and by the individual member states. EU ratification occurs through adoption in the Council. As for member states, they ratify the trade agreement according to their own internal procedures, such as a vote in parliament. In practice, the Council always decides on the temporary implementation of the EU-only part of the agreement. The rest, subject to national ratification, is implemented later, often years. Hence, there is no room for big surprises at the ratification stage of the negotiation, since member states have had ample time to manifest their reservations during the course of the international negotiations.

The enlarged EU as a trade power

The EU enlarged to ten new countries in May 2004, the biggest enlargement ever since its creation. This did not trigger any immediate disruption of trade, since the transition had been prepared for a decade. Indeed, on the eve of enlargement, over 95% of the trade of the EU-15 with the new entrants was already free.

Structurally, enlargement will make the EU stronger in relation to its trade negotiating partners, because a larger single market is both a more attractive prize to outside economic players and a more costly opportunity loss in cases when a threat of being cut out is carried through. Enlargement increases the size of the single market (accounting for 18% of world trade and contributing to 25% of the world's GDP), augments the geographical size of the EU by 34%, and boosts the total population by 105 million to a total of $450 million.[18]

By joining the EU, however, the new entrants are bringing in a wealth of different histories and cultures, which also means different interests, priorities and sensibilities. These will have to be included and amalgamated in the definition of a common European position on trade, thus posing a challenge to the current institutional mechanisms. Pessimists argue that diversity could incapacitate the EU and bog down multilateral trade liberalisation. Substantively, they say it could also lead to common positions which are invariably the lowest common denominator and, therefore, to a protectionist bias of the EU in international trade negotiations. On the other hand, there is no doubt that through sheer arithmetics, enlargement will make internal EU negotiations more difficult to control for trade ministers; it can be argued that this in turn could further concentrate trade policy-making power in the hands of the Commission, which has a historical and functionalist interest in promoting trade liberalisation (Van den Hoven 2002). In short, the impact of the new members on the balance between protectionist and liberal forces in the EU overall is underdetermined.

Undoubtedly, however, EU enlargement raises several legal and political issues. The first is that the US and the new entrants have bilateral agreements on investment protection that do include provisions contrary to Community law (for instance with respect to investments in the audiovisual sector). Another issue is the negotiation which necessarily follows from the extension of the customs union to ten currently autonomous territories (known as Article 24 negotiation). In most cases, third countries will benefit from a drop in custom duties. Official EU calculations predict that enlargement will lead, overall, to a reduction in average tariffs from 9% to 4%.[19] In some highly visible cases, however, the pre-enlargement custom duties of the new entrants are lower (when not null) than those of the EU—leading to a rise after May 2004 and thus presumably trade frictions, in particular with the United States (similar to the 'chicken war' of 1963). Independent calculations show that enlargement will indeed lower industrial tariffs in the new entrants, but it may nearly double tariffs on agriculture, especially for products such as wheat, beef, and dairy products, which are all important in the EU trade policy at the WTO (Van den Hoven 2002).

From a political perspective, one could expect the new entrants to pursue a general policy line more favourable to the United States, as was suggested by Secretary Rumsfeld's quip on 'old Europe, new Europe' at the time of the Iraq war: it would seem that 'new Europe' is more open to the US economically as well as politically. But while the US administration can certainly be expected to pursue its strategy of 'divide and rule', the extension of qualified majority voting should limit the incidences when such tactics can work since it is getting harder to muster a blocking minority. On some issues, however, the new entrants will likely have trade interests contrary to those of the US. Analysts expect Poland and several other new entrants to become strong supporters of anti-dumping measures for basic industrial goods such as steel, chemicals, and textiles (Messerlin 2001; Van den Hoven 2002; Evenett and Verlmust 2004). Moreover, the countries that stand to benefit most from the generous EU agricultural provisions will not be inclined to make concessions on that issue. Once they gain access to CAP subsidies, they may strengthen the protectionist camp in the agricultural sector. Finally, since the services sector is still relatively weak in these countries, this may weaken internal EU support for greater services liberalisation in the WTO (Van den Hoven 2002).

The EU as champion of multilateralism?

We have now illustrated how almost all of trade policy falls under the exclusive net of the EU; how, under this configuration, the Commission negotiates on behalf and under the control of member states; and the potential impact of enlargement on those dynamics. How, then, does the EU exercise its formidable power in trade policy? We argue that it has been by asserting its central role in the multilateral system, less to uphold the value of multilateralism as a public good and more to promote the EU's own interest in this system. The EU has always claimed that its single market is a building block for multilateralism and often posits itself as champion of international law, including in the field of global economic governance (by contrast to the United States, for instance). Yet, it does continue to attract criticism. Can it genuinely pretend to defend developing countries in view of the amount of subsidies poured into its protectionist agricultural policy? Is it now the case that its highly differentiated approach to trade agreements around the world constitutes undue discrimination? Is the EU not trying to impose its own regulatory model as a condition for free trade instead of negotiating with world partners on an equal footing?

The European single market and world trade liberalisation

From its inception, the EU has played a central role in multilateral trade negotiations (Woolcock 1993; Young 2000, 2002; Smith, M. 2001; Meunier 2005). In the 1960s it introduced a new radical tariff-cutting formula which greatly reduced the transaction costs of negotiations. In spite of the rising trend of 'new protectionism' in the 1970s, the Europeans led the way in attacking so called non-tariff barriers. As the EU accelerated the pace of completion of its single market in the run-up to 1992, issues became more complicated. Quite logically, it required that firms wishing to export goods and services into the EU conform to its standards and regulations as well as to its conformity assessment procedures (Mattli and Buthe 2003). Since such requirements had not been consistently enforced before, the move initially spurred cries of 'fortress Europe'—indeed the external dimension of the single market had been dealt with a bit as an afterthought. But the EU Commission quickly sought to ensure that foreign firms be given a fair chance of access through opportunities to demonstrate their conformity to standards (Nicolaïdis and Egan 2001).

As the programme to complete the single market agreed to under the Single Act (1987–92) coincided with the Uruguay Round (1986–93), the EU progressively developed a strategy to export its approach to trade liberalisation to the global level, especially in dealing with trade in services, the core new area in both settings (Drake and Nicolaïdis 1992). Along with the US, it promoted the inclusion of 'new issues' (services, intellectual property rights, and trade-related investment measures) under the WTO which was created at the end of the Uruguay Round. Agriculture, however, has remained the glaring counter-example of liberalisation. By the end of the Uruguay Round in 1993, the EU did not look so good as a trade liberaliser, as the trade distortions engendered by the CAP led the US to build a coalition of GATT members against the European agricultural policy (Patterson 1997; Davis 2003). The Cairns group on its part mobilised against both US and EU farming support.[20]

But the issue is not only how much liberalisation, but also what kind of liberalisation and for whose benefit. During the 1990s, the developing world progressively came to question the 'grand bargain' agreed to during the Uruguay Round—namely, accepting to open up their markets to services and to enforce patents in exchange for greater access for their industrial products. The cost of the former turned out to be higher than many had foreseen, while increased access for third world exports often failed to materialise. Initially both the US and the EU resisted their attempt to revisit this bargain, while at the same time pushing for a continued expansion of the multilateral agenda to include issues such as linkage between trade access and labour and environment standards. The tension between OECD countries—including the EU—and the developing world culminated at Seattle in 1999. But in the years since, the EU has managed to establish, at least partly, a new reputation as a champion of multilateralism. Today it is the EU who is mobilising WTO members against the perceived US unilateralism on issues such as steel, taxation, and anti-dumping. Most importantly, the EU played a key role in launching the 'Doha development agenda', in November 2001, the first trade round avowedly aimed specifically at the welfare of the developing countries. There it promoted the adoption of a path-breaking declaration on trade and public health, which opened the way for legalising broad exemptions from intellectual property constraints by importing generic drugs to treat diseases like AIDS (a final agreement was finally accepted by the US in August 2003). Moreover, the EU sought to take the lead in making good on market access by launching in the run-up to the Doha Round the 'Everything but Arms' initiative (EBA), designed to offer preferential market access to the exports of the 48 least developed countries in the world. This initiative enabled the EU to change its image in the WTO by holding the high moral ground, even though it was not able then to have its approach adopted by the entire WTO membership.

Many voices, however, question the EU's genuine commitment to putting multi-lateralism at the service of development. Agriculture has at last become central stage in the Doha round, with developed countries being asked to reduce (if not eliminate) their trade-distorting farm subsidies and drastically decrease their tariffs, quotas, and non-tariff barriers. While the EU and the US had reached a common proposal on reform of the protection of their agriculture, this was not enough. The collapse of the WTO Cancun meeting in September 2003 was due to a great extent to differences over agricultural reform, especially over the issue of cotton, between the US, the EU and a group of developing countries led by Brazil and India (called the G-22). Perhaps more fundamentally, the meeting exposed a clash between an EU philosophy of trade liberalisation based on the design and enforcement of new multilateral rules reproducing the EU's own approach (the so-called 'Singapore issues'—investment, competition policy, government procurement, and trade facilitation) and the approach of most of the rest of the world, which continues to view trade rounds as fora for the exchange of reciprocal conditions. The abrupt end of the Cancun meeting testifies to this tension and left a great deal of uncertainty on how to proceed next with talks on agriculture, industrial goods, and the Singapore issues when agreements need to be reached in a consensual way in an organisation with 148 members.

In what direction is EU trade policy evolving? In the Spring of 2004, the EU made bold proposals in order to relaunch the multilateral trade talks. Most importantly, it offered to put on the table all agricultural export subsidies, provided that others do the same and that the final agreement offer an overall balanced package on agriculture. For decades the issue of agricultural export subsidies had been a sticking point in multilateral trade negotiations, so this is close to a revolutionary proposal (even if it is easy to argue that, in the long run, the EU has little choice over giving them up). The second EU proposal was to be more flexible on the so-called Singapore issues, which may mean abandoning them in the end, since most countries are not ready to launch multilateral negotiations on investment, competition, and public procurement. Finally, the EU proposed to give a special deal to the 90 poorest countries in the world, which could benefit from freer access to world markets while not opening up further their own markets. In August 2004, the Doha Round participants adopted a package of temporary agreements including commitments, such as the abolition of agricultural export subsidies.

Settling disputes in the WTO

The WTO differs from its predecessor, the GATT, not only because it is a bona fide organisation rather than a mere 'agreement' with a broader scope, but also and perhaps most importantly due to its significantly strengthened dispute settlement mechanism, in which the EU has been an active participant. In 2004, the EU was involved in 29 WTO disputes as both a plaintiff (16 cases) and a defendant (13 cases) with eight of its trading partners (Argentina, Australia, Brazil, Canada, India, Korea, Thailand, and the US).[21] In the majority of these cases (14 out of 29), the EU was paired against the US—11 times with the EU as the plaintiff (e.g. US Anti-Dumping Act and Foreign Sales Corporation) and only three times with the EU as the defendant (GMOs, hormones, and trademark/geographical indications).

Box 12.1 EU trade policy instruments

Trade Policy Instruments

The EU Commission, through DG Trade, also oversees the use of trade policy instruments, which are of the defensive and the proactive types.

Defensive instruments: '**Trade Defence Instruments**' (TDI) may be used to counter unfair trade practices by other countries, in accordance with WTO agreements. They consist of:

- **Anti-dumping measures:** used to counter dumping, which occurs when manufacturers from a non-EU country sell goods in the EU below the sales price in their domestic market or below the cost of production — this is the most frequent trade-distorting practice.

- **Anti-subsidy measures:** used to combat subsidies, which help to reduce production costs from abroad or cut the price of EU exports, with the consequence of distorting trade.

- **Safeguards:** the WTO allows a country to restrict temporarily imports of a product if its domestic industry is seriously injured by a surge in imports.

Proactive instruments: the '**Trade Barriers Regulation**' (TBR) enables companies to lodge a complaint with the EU Commission when they feel they encounter trade barriers that restrict their access to third country markets.

Source: http://europa.eu.int/comm/trade/issues/respectrules/tpi_en/htm

---

Such a high level of involvement has strengthened overall the power of the EU in trade. On one hand, some of the EU's trade partners have exercised their rights to demand change in EU trade practices (such as on hormone-treated beef and bananas), which has resulted either in compliance or in the willingness by the EU to incur retaliatory sanctions. On the other hand, participation in the WTO has enabled the EU to confront other trade partners, in particular the US, on a variety of unilateral actions (see Box 12.1). The following examples of recent and ongoing transatlantic trade disputes are evidence of the power of the EU in the multilateral trade arena.

Steel

In the Spring of 2002, the Bush administration unilaterally raised steel tariffs for a three-year period by 30% in order to protect its domestic steel industry from the problem of global overcapacity during a time of restructuring. The EU (and seven other countries)[22] launched a lawsuit at the WTO, which ruled that the tariffs were in violation of international trade rules. The WTO confirmed in November 2003 in its final ruling that the American tariffs are indeed illegal under international trade rules. Faced with the threat that Europe would impose 100% duties on $2.2 billion worth of US imports, ranging from Harley Davidson to underwear to citrus juices from Florida — products chosen mainly because of coming from swing-states crucial for the 2004 US presidential election — Washington dropped the tariffs in December 2003.

Tax breaks

In 2000 the EU asked the WTO to adjudicate on the so-called Foreign Sales Corporation (FSC) dispute, because this American law was believed to confer illegal export subsidies on many US companies by taxing exports more favourably than production abroad. In subsequent rulings, the WTO confirmed that the FSC constituted an illegal export subsidy and gave the US administration until November 2000 to withdraw its scheme. The US replaced the FSC law, but because the new law did not substantially modify the export subsidy scheme, the EU challenged it again in the WTO. In 2002 the WTO ruled again that these breaks were indeed an illegal subsidy and authorised the EU to impose $4 billion in retaliatory sanctions if the US law was not brought into compliance with WTO obligations. The Europeans, fearful of what the sanctions would do to their own economies given the size of the potential disruption to transatlantic trade (more than ten times larger than the beef and bananas sanctions combined), opted for patience and instead gave the Americans ample time to change their tax laws. In March 2004 the EU began to gradually implement some retaliatory sanctions on American exports. The law repealing the FSC was finally passed in October 2004 and is supposed to be implemented as of 2005 (with a transition period). The EU will lift the sanctions when the implementation of the new US law proves satisfactory.

Anti-dumping

In 2000 the WTO condemned the US 1916 Anti-Dumping Act for allowing sanctions against dumping not permitted under WTO agreements and gave the US one year to repeal the Act. In February 2004, given the non-compliance of the US, the WTO allowed the EU to retaliate by implementing a mirror regulation that would be applicable only to American products.

Genetically modified organisms

Since 1998, the EU has observed a moratorium on the approval of GMO products, and some member states banned the import and cultivation of some crops that had been approved prior to that date. The EU made this decision in response to popular concern about the long-term impact of GMOs on human health and the environment, although there was little scientific evidence to support these concerns, but no evidence either that GMOs are harmless (Pollack and Shaffer 2000; Vogel 2002; Rhinard 2004). This measure led to the suspension of exports of genetically modified corn from the US. The successive American administrations were hesitant at first to challenge at the WTO the issue of whether such public health concerns could legitimise protectionism. In May 2003, however, the Bush administration decided to finally file the suit against the EU at the WTO when it was learned that the EU had warned Zambia to refuse US donations of genetically modified corn and that many poor African nations had refused to experiment with GMO crops for fear that they could not sell them in Europe. Such a lawsuit, however, is politically risky. It may spark a backlash from European consumers, already quite nervous over food safety in the wake of the mad cow and foot and mouth diseases, and perhaps some consumer resistance in the US as well.

'Open bilateralism'? The limits of transatlantic trade cooperation

In spite of these disputes, the transatlantic trade partnership is characterised by a much greater degree of cooperation than conflict, owing to the unprecedented level of interdependence between the two sides of the Atlantic: in 2003 EU imports from the US represented a fifth of its imports while EU exports to the US represented a quarter of US exports.[23] While transatlantic economic cooperation is not new, the post Cold War era has been characterised by a much greater emphasis over economic and regulatory cooperation than ever before and the growing recognition by the US of the importance of the EU as an interlocutor over and above the member states (BP Chair Report, 2001). In the wake of the disputes surrounding the completion of the single market mentioned above the EU and the US signed a series of agreements to underpin their new transatlantic partnership—the Transatlantic Declaration (1990), the New Transatlantic Agenda (NTA 1995), and the Transatlantic Economic Partnership (TEP 1998). The idea of a Transatlantic free trade area was quietly abandoned given its potential implications for agriculture, as well as grander schemes for the total elimination of all industrial tariffs. Instead, these agreements served both to increase the scope of cooperation (creating a 'transatlantic marketplace') and to introduce more formal institutions to manage such cooperation. Especially with the NTA, and at the urging of the Transatlantic Business Dialogue, a special focus was introduced on regulatory cooperation to allow the trading partners to overcome their non-tariff barriers to trade.

One of the most innovative aspects of the new transatlantic cooperation was the signing in 1997 of a series of 'Mutual Recognition Agreements', from pharmaceuticals to telecoms. These agreements were certainly less ambitious than their inspirations—the mutual recognition directives enforced to complete the internal market of the EU—in that they only covered the recognition of conformity assessments rather than recognition of the standards themselves (Nicolaïdis and Egan 2001). But the difficulty of signing on to such agreements should not be under-estimated. US agencies like the Food and Drug Administration had to undergo a great deal of pressure before agreeing to transfer part of their regulatory authority to their EU counterparts. And accommodating the complex array of conformity assessment bodies operating in the US for electrical standards and the likes to the more coordinated system prevailing in the EU was no small feat. In fact it has proven impossible to extend the MRA approach beyond the original six to other products or to services where the US is notoriously plagued by regulatory fragmentation due to its federal structure.

In fact the EU has successfully negotiated a whole array of MRAs around the world, spearheading a movement towards trade-friendly regulatory reform without deregulation. Whether its approach can serve as a laboratory for regulatory cooperation under WTO remains to be seen (Nicolaïdis and Howse, 2002).

The EU's conditional support for regionalism

Last but not least, the EU has built over the last decade a complex web of preferential agreements which has come to encompass most of the planet. For several decades, the EU negotiated trade agreements only with its immediate neighbours (mainly to the East) and the former colonies with which it shared historical ties, mainly through the successive Lomé (later Cotonou) Conventions. Since the end of the Uruguay Round, which coincided with the signing of the North American Free Trade Agreements, the EU has become actively interested in negotiating regional agreements with a variety of other countries, mostly in Latin America, where the

---

Box 12.2 The Barcelona Process

The partnership between the EU and the Mediterranean countries is referred to as the 'Barcelona Process'. In the 1995 Barcelona Declaration, the then 27 Euro-Mediterranean Partners agreed on the establishment of a Euro-Mediterranean Free Trade Area by 2010, to be achieved through Association Agreements, negotiated and concluded with the European Union, together with free trade agreements between themselves. These association agreements also include respect for human rights and democratic principles as essential elements. More recently it has been decided to add clauses on fighting Terrorism, and on Non-proliferation of Weapons of Mass Destruction.

In addition to the EU member states, the parties to the Barcelona Process are: Algeria, Cyprus, Egypt, Israel, Jordan, Lebanon, Malta, Morocco, Palestinian Authority, Syria, Turkey, and Tunisia.

Source: http://europa.eu.int/comm/trade/issues/bilateral/regions/euromed/index_en.htm

---

EU has signed 'Global Agreements' (including free-trade) with Mexico in 2000 and Chile in 2002 (Sbragia 2004). An all-encompassing agreement with the customs union Mercosur (Argentina, Brazil, Paraguay, and Uruguay), aiming at the creation of a free-trade area with the European single market, is currently being negotiated. If concluded, this would be the first agreement between two customs unions. The EU has also signed regional association agreements through the 1995 Euro-Mediterranean partnership (also referred to as the 'Barcelona Process', see Box 12.2), with the goal of establishing a Euro-Mediterranean Free Trade Area by 2010. The EU negotiated a free trade agreement with South Africa in 2000.

This active pursuit of regionalism through bilateral agreements further reinforces the EU as a global power. In part a forced reaction to the US move towards regionalism in the 1990s, the new policy has increased EU power by restoring a level playing field for European companies competing in the lucrative Latin American markets. Regionalism has also enhanced the EU's normative power. In a way, the EU has acted as a 'globaliser' with Latin America, exporting its cultural and political dimensions along with its economic agreements (Sbragia 2004).

Conclusion: the EU as a power in and through trade

The EU is a formidable power *in* trade. If it is considered as one single economic unit, there is little doubt that it has become, since the last enlargement, the biggest trading block in the world. As a result its potential hegemonic power, based on the capacity to grant or withhold access to its internal market, has become as strong as the US. Moreover, its more than 40 years of experience negotiating international trade agreements on behalf of its members that have made the EU an essential player and a powerful bargainer in the multilateral trading system.

The EU is also becoming a power *through* trade. Increasingly, it uses market access as a bargaining chip to obtain changes in the domestic arena of its trading partners, from labour standards to development policies. Indeed, one of the central objectives of EU trade policy under trade commissioner Pascal Lamy has been to 'harness globalisation' and spread, through the negotiation of trade agreements, the European model of society to the rest of the world. One of the most interesting questions about European trade policy today is how far the EU will be willing or able to transform its structural power into effective influence and what will be its goals in establishing itself as a global power through trade. In particular, can the EU become an important foreign policy actor through the back door, by using trade instead of more traditional diplomatic or military means? As the 2004 bilateral agreement with Syria seems to indicate, the EU is now entering a new phase where it is increasingly ready and able to use its trade muscle to serve political goals, in this case controlling the proliferation of weapons of mass destruction. It remains to be seen, however, how effective such a policy will be in the long run, and whether the EU can escape the adjacent risk of (even benign) imperialism which comes from seeking to impose one's model onto the rest of the world.

Notes

1 The 1952 European Coal and Steel Community did not have external powers.

2 Article 113 was renamed Article 133 at Amsterdam.

3 At that point, they found a compromise solution whereby the Community concluded all the agreements of the Round, while the ECSC Tariff Protocol, the Standards Code and the Civil Aircraft Code were concluded jointly by the Community and the member states.

4 Since GATT operated by consensus, this had more symbolic than practical significance.

5 Including agricultural products and products covered by the European Coal and Steel Community and Euratom treaties.

6 Court of Justice of the European Communities, Opinion 1/94, 15 November 1994, I-123.
   (1) The Community has sole competence, pursuant to Article 113 of the

EC Treaty, to conclude the multilateral agreements on trade in goods.
   (2) The Community and its member states are jointly competent to conclude GATS.
   (3) The Community and its member states are jointly competent to conclude TRIPs.

7 The new Article 113(5) as finally adopted reads as follows: 'The Council, acting unanimously on a proposal from the Commission and after consulting the European Parliament, may extend the application of paragraph 1 to 4 to international negotiations and agreements on services and intellectual property insofar as they are not covered by these paragraphs.'

8 Meunier 2000b.

9 Article 133, para. 6: 'An agreement may not be concluded by the Council if it includes provisions which would go beyond the Community's internal powers, in particular by leading to harmonisation of the laws or

regulations of the member states in an area for which this Treaty rules out such harmonisation.

In this regard, by way of derogation from the first subparagraph of paragraph 5, agreements relating to trade in cultural and audiovisual services, educational services, and social and human health services, shall fall within the shared competence of the Community and its member states. Consequently, in addition to a Community decision taken in accordance with the relevant provisions of Article 300, the negotiation of such agreements shall require the common accord of the member states.

The negotiation and conclusion of international agreements in the field of transport shall continue to be governed by the provisions of Title V and Article 300.'

10 We leave out the enforcement stage, which is of lesser importance to our discussion.

11 The '133 Committee' is named after Article 133 §3.

12 The deliberations of the 133 Committee are not published, which is a complaint often raised by anti-globalisation groups like ATTAC. But with 26 delegations around the table, secrecy can only go so far.

13 See Hayes-Renshaw and Helen Wallace, H. 1997, 88.

14 On the formal vs. informal shapes of the negotiating mandate in trade policy, see Kerremans 2003.

15 See Moravcsik 1991 on the issue of voting in the Single European Act.

16 From 1995 to 2003, Germany, France, Italy and the United Kingdom each had 10 votes; Spain 8; Belgium, Greece, the Netherlands and Portugal 5; Austria and Sweden 4; Ireland, Denmark and Finland 3; and Luxembourg 2. 62 votes out of a total of 87 votes needed to be cast in its favour for a Commission proposal to be adopted. In other cases,

the qualified majority remained the same but the 62 votes had to be cast by at least 10 member states. The qualified majority requirements were changed by the 2001 Treaty of Nice and the 2004 Accession Treaty. A qualified majority will be obtained if the decision receives at least a specified number of votes and the decision is approved by a majority of member states. The weighing of the votes was also changed. See for instance http://www.europa.eu.int/comm/ igc2000/dialogue/info/offdoc/ guidecitoyen_en.pdf for a table of the new voting weights, including those of the candidate countries.

17 In 1994 only 14% of the legislation adopted by the Council was formally put to a vote and the subject of negative votes and abstentions (source: *Guide to EU Institutions*, The Council, Europa web server). Moreover, while in theory the consultation procedure (under which Commission proposals can be amended by the Council only unanimously) applies, in practice the Commission alters its proposal several times following the deliberations of the 133 Committee in order to ensure adoption by the Council (Garrett and Tsebelis 1996 argue that the consultation procedure gives the agenda-setting Commission the possibility to act strategically in presenting its proposals to the Council). Even during the height of the crisis created by French demands for a renegotiation of the Uruguay Round agricultural agreement between the EU and the US in 1993, member states insisted that the tradition of consensus be not broken. See also Devuyst 1995; Paemen and Bensch 1995; and Woolcock and Hodges 1996 on the EC negotiating process during the Uruguay Round.

18 Source: Commission of the European Communities, 'Trade implications of EU enlargement: Facts and Figures.' Brussels, 4 February 2004. http://europa.eu.int/comm/trade/

issues/bilateral/regions/candidates/
ff040204_en.htm.

19 Source: Commission of the European
    Communities, 'Trade implications of
    EU enlargement: Facts and Figures',
    Brussels, 4 February 2004.

20 The Cairns Group, founded in 1986,
    is a coalition of 17 agricultural
    exporting countries accounting for
    one-third of the world's agricultural
    exports. Its members are Argentina,
    Australia, Bolivia, Brazil, Canada, Chile,
    Colombia, Costa Rica, Guatemala,

Indonesia, Malaysia, New Zealand,
Paraguay, the Philippines, South
Africa, Thailand, and Uruguay.

21 EU Commission, 'General overview of
    active WTO dispute settlement cases
    involving the EC as complainant or
    defendant', Brussels, 7 April 2004.

22 Japan, South Korea, Norway, Switzer-
    land, China, New Zealand, and Brazil.

23 Source: EU Commission DG Trade,
    http://europa.eu.int/comm/trade/
    issues/bilateral/countries/usa/
    index_en.htm.

Further reading

The following is a selection of the very substantial literature about the EU's trade policies, which reflects both the legal and the policy analysis aspects of the topic. Some historical background is provided by Devuyst (1995), Johnson (1998), Woolcock (1993) and Young (2000, 2002). The specific issues of competence and of the trade policy process (including WTO negotiations) are dealt with by Meunier (2000, 2005), Meunier and Nicolaïdis (1999), Nicolaïdis and Meunier (2002), Smith (2001), and Woolcock (2000). Smith (2001) and Young (2002) provide analysis of the ways in which the changing nature of world trade has been reflected in EU trade policies.

Devuyst, Y. (1995), 'The European Community and the Conclusion of the Uruguay Round' in Rhodes, C. and Mazey, S. (eds) *The State of the European Union, volume 3* (Boulder, CO: Lynne Rienner).

Johnson, M. (1998), *European Community Trade Policy and the Article 113 Committee* (London: Royal Institute of International Affairs).

Meunier, S. (2000), 'What Single Voice? European Institutions and EU-US trade negotiations', *International Organization* 54/1, 103–35.

Meunier, S. (2005), *Trading Voices: The European Union in International Commercial Negotiations* (Princeton, NJ: Princeton University Press).

Meunier, S., and Nicolaïdis, K. (1999), 'Who Speaks for Europe? The Delegation of Trade Authority in the EU', *Journal of Common Market Studies* 37/3, 477–501.

Nicolaïdis, K., and Meunier, S. (2002), 'Revisiting Trade Competence in the European Union: Amsterdam, Nice, and Beyond' in Hosli, M., van Deemen, A., and Widgren, M. (eds) *Institutional Challenges in the European Union* (London: Routledge).

Smith, M. (2001), 'The European Union's Commercial Policy: Between Coherence and Fragmentation', *Journal of European Public Policy* 8/5, 787–802.

Woolcock, S. (1993), 'The European *Acquis* and Multilateral Trade Rules: Are They Compatible?' *Journal of Common Market Studies* 31/4, 539–58.

Woolcock, S. (2000), 'European Trade Policy' in Wallace, H., and Wallace, W. (eds) *Policy-Making in the European Union* 4th edition (Oxford: Oxford University Press), pp. 373–400.

Young, A. (2000), 'The Adaptation of European Foreign Economic Policy:

From Rome to Seattle', *Journal of Common Market Studies* 38/1, 93–116.

Young, A. (2002), *Extending European Cooperation: The European Union and the 'New'* *International Trade Agenda* (Manchester: Manchester University Press).

Web links

The first port of call for all matters of EU trade policy is the web site of the EU Commission, DG Trade: http://www.europa.eu.int/comm/trade/. Much useful information about the context for and the impact of EU trade policies can be obtained from the World Trade Organization and Organisation for Economic Co-operation and development web sites: World Trade Organization: http://www.wto.org/; OECD: http://www.oecd.org/home/. A good web site providing information and analysis about trade policies and the global political economy is that of the Washington-based Institute for International Economics: http://www.iie.com/.

Chapter 13

Enlargement and European Order

Karen E. Smith

Contents

Summary

In May 2004, the EU enlarged by ten countries, most of which are in Central and Eastern Europe. Enlargement has been the EU's principal response to the end of the Cold War: by enlarging, the EU hopes to consolidate the democratic and economic reforms in post-communist countries, and spread security and prosperity eastwards. Its enlargement policy has also involved the extensive use of carrots and sticks to encourage reforms, mainly through the application of membership conditionality. The 2004 enlargement, however, is only the beginning, as there are numerous other European countries in the membership queue. This chapter analyses the EU's key decisions on enlargement, and considers why the EU member states have agreed to such a radical reshaping of the European order.

Introduction

Enlargement of the European Union—or, more accurately, the prospect of enlargement—is the principal means by which the EU has tried to spread prosperity, democracy and security to the former communist countries of Central, Eastern, and South-eastern Europe. Though largely devoid of a long-term strategic vision of Europe, the EU has thus contributed significantly to shaping the post-Cold War European order.[1] It has been actively setting the 'rules of the game', the norms of domestic and international behaviour that should guide European states, as well as shaping the institutional structure in which those states are increasingly embedded. Incorporation within the EU is seen as a way to stabilise the new democracies and foster economic growth, but the EU has also used the promise of enlargement, if certain conditions are fulfilled, to influence the domestic and foreign policies of membership aspirants and encourage political and economic reforms, which are seen as necessary to ensure security in Europe. To an impressive extent, the EU's enlargement policy has been its most successful foreign policy.[2]

The EU has been able to exercise such influence because it has exploited its enormous 'power of attraction': the post-communist governments have repeatedly declared that they want to 'return to Europe', which they consider to entail membership of the EU (and NATO). The EU has made extensive use of both carrots and sticks in its relations with other European states, turning its soft power of attraction into quite coercive—though still civilian—power. As a result, the EU has become an ever more significant power with considerable impact on Europe.

The factors driving such heavy EU engagement in its neighbourhood are fairly obvious ones, including the need for stability and prosperity across Europe and a shared sense of responsibility for repairing the Cold War split of Europe. What is more surprising is that the policy response to these imperatives has been enlargement of the EU itself, rather than, say, an attempt to foster another strong regional grouping with which the EU could engage in inter-regional cooperation. The former communist states are much poorer and more agricultural than the EU member states, which has important implications for EU spending, and the extension of membership could have deleterious effects on both the functioning of the EU and the integration process. Although the member states have persistently sought to reduce the negative effects of enlargement—notably through a less-than-generous extension of benefits to new members—they were eventually prepared to assume the risks of enlargement: they shared a strong sense of responsibility for ensuring security in Europe and were convinced that enlargement was the way to do so, and they were persuaded that post-communist countries were enough like themselves that they could not reasonably be excluded from the EU.

Enlargement, in turn, has had and will have a very large impact on the EU. As has been the case with past enlargements, it will increase the EU's global 'weight' and expand its international interests. The increase in the number of EU member states from six to 15 did not bring the integration process to a halt, and certainly the looming eastern enlargement has in large part motivated three intergovernmental conferences on institutional reform (two led to the Amsterdam and Nice Treaties, while the latest led—finally—to the draft constitutional treaty). In practice, though, institutional reform has not been a precondition for enlargement and there are concerns that the May 2004 enlargement, which brought the number of member states to 25, will hinder decision-making, and that the EU cannot absorb many more new members. Former External Relations Commissioner Chris Patten has stated, 'There must be a line somewhere where the EU ends. We have almost got to the line' (Mahony 2003). But the 'line' after May 2004 still leaves numerous states on the outside, many of whom have repeatedly expressed their desire to join the EU, and the EU will have to decide how to manage their expectations. The 'ghost' of enlargement will hover over the EU's relations with its European neighbours for some time to come.

This chapter analyses the EU's enlargement policy by looking in more depth at the key decisions that it has made on enlargement. It tries to answer questions raised by the three perspectives outlined by the editors: (1) How and why have the member states reached agreement on enlargement?; (2) Why has the EU used enlargement as the principal policy instrument to respond to the new post-Cold War environment?; and (3) What has the EU's influence been on its European neighbours and on the shape of European order?

Concentric circles

The first important decision that the EU—then the European Community—took regarding enlargement was to put off the prospect by adopting a 'concentric circles' approach. Concentric circles would allow the Community to proceed with economic and political integration, while strengthening its relations with its European neighbours short of enlarging them.

The Community had responded relatively quickly to the collapse of communism in Europe by concluding trade and cooperation agreements with and extending technical assistance to the new post-communist governments. The collapse of communism in the fall of 1989 coincided with a very dynamic period in the Community's history: it was in the midst of completing the single European market and considering plans for an economic and monetary union. As a result, there was a general expectation—both within the Community and outside it—that the Community should take the lead in responding to the astounding events.

In June 1988, the Community and the Council for Mutual Economic Assistance (CMEA), the organisation for economic cooperation among communist countries, established official relations. As the 'price' for officially recognising the CMEA, the Community insisted on developing trade relations with the CMEA member countries on a bilateral basis, rather than with the CMEA as a whole (which would grant the Soviet Union, as the most powerful CMEA member, far too much influence). 'Bilateralism' allowed the Community to differentiate between the Central and East European countries (CEECs) and apply conditionality: those countries that were further ahead in the reform process concluded trade and cooperation agreements first (see Table 13.1). In this way, the Community encouraged reforms. Bilateralism effectively precluded the development of a regional framework for cooperation among the

CEECs (the CEECs also objected to any such suggestions as attempts to 'resurrect' the CMEA and obstruct their 'return to Europe'). Differentiation—distinguishing between countries on the basis of how well they meet given political and economic conditions—would come to have far-reaching consequences for the EU's relations with all of its European neighbours.

In late 1989, the Community extended aid through the Phare programme to help the new democracies implement economic reforms.[3] Again, aid was extended on a conditional basis, first to Poland and Hungary, then to other countries. Importantly, the Soviet Union never received Phare aid, a clear sign that relations with the Soviet Union were much more problematic than relations with those countries that had suffered under the Soviet Union's yoke.

The agreements and aid were not enough to meet the CEECs' expectations, which centred on acceding to the Community. These membership expectations sparked off a 'widening vs. deepening' debate within the Community. Some policy-makers (notably in France) argued that the Community should enlarge only after it integrated further, as a way of ensuring that a united Germany would be well secured to a more integrated European Union. Others (notably in the UK) argued that enlargement should occur first, because further integration would make it more difficult for the CEECs to join. There was little explicit discussion of *never* enlarging. This would have been difficult to justify: not only had its membership already doubled by the time of the collapse of communism (and, setting an important precedent, East Germany had been quickly incorporated into the EC in 1990 via its unification with West Germany), but the Rome Treaty also stated that any European state could apply to join the Community. Support within the EC for enlargement—though not universal—also closed off the option of never enlarging. The debate thus centred not on whether to enlarge, but when and how. Internal and external factors had to favour enlargement; in 1990–91, they did not, yet.

Instead in 1990 the Community compromised with the concentric circles approach, championed by European Commission President Jacques Delors and German Foreign Minister Hans-Dietrich Genscher (Allen 1992, 122). An integrated European Union would be at the centre (therefore the Maastricht Treaty was negotiated); in the closest ring to the EU would be the prosperous, small members of the European Free Trade Association linked to the EU via the European Economic Area, which extended the single European market to the EFTAns on 1 January 1994. The CEECs occupied the outer ring, to be connected to the EU by special association ('Europe') agreements, while the Soviet Union, off on the outer fringes of Europe, did not figure highly at all. By trying to keep everyone happy, the concentric circles approach resolved the widening vs. deepening dilemma, at least in the short run.

Europe agreements were to be strictly conditional; only countries clearly committed to democratic and market economic principles were eligible. The first to meet the grade were Czechoslovakia, Hungary, and Poland, in 1991 (see Table 13.1). Yugoslavia, in early 1990, was initially considered a prospective associate, but not even a year later it was clearly in deep trouble and was therefore kept outside all concentric circles (see Box 13.1).[4] Europe agreements provided for the gradual establishment of a free trade area, and for political dialogue on foreign policy matters. They also, despite resistance by several member states, made reference in the preamble to the associate's aspirations to join the EU.[5]

Table 13.1 The EU's agreements with its neighbours

Association agreements with Mediterranean countries (Year in force)	Trade and cooperation agreements (Year signed/ year in force)	Europe (association) agreements (Year signed/ year in force)	Partnership and cooperation agreements (Year in force)	Stabilisation and association agreements (Year signed)
Turkey (1963) (customs union in force, 1996)	Hungary (1988/1988)	Hungary (1991/1994)	Russia (1997) Ukraine (1998)	Former Yugoslav Republic of Macedonia (2001)
Malta (1971)	Poland (1989/1989)	Poland (1991/1994)	Moldova (1998)	Croatia (2001)
Republic of Cyprus (1972)	Soviet Union (1989/1990)	Czechoslovakia (1991)[a]	Armenia (1999)	In 2003, negotiations began with Albania.
	Czechoslovakia (1990/1990)	Czech Republic (1993/1995)	Azerbaijan (1999)	
	Bulgaria (1990/1990)	Slovakia (1993/1995)	Georgia (1999)	
	Romania (1990/1991)	Bulgaria (1993/1995)	In 1997, negotiations with Belarus were suspended due to violations of democracy and human rights there.	
	Albania (1992/1992)	Romania (1993/1995)		
	Estonia (1992/1993)	Estonia (1995/1998)		
	Latvia (1992/1993)	Latvia (1995/1998)		
	Lithuania (1992/1993)	Lithuania (1995/1998)		
	Slovenia (1993/1993)	Slovenia (1996/1999)		

[a] The Community signed a Europe agreement with Czechoslovakia in December 1991, but the breakup of Czechoslovakia on 1 January 1993 complicated matters. The Community then negotiated separate agreements with the Czech Republic and Slovakia.

At the end of 1991, the Soviet Union broke up. The Community's reaction to this was muted: it promised to conclude partnership and cooperation agreements with the new countries emerging from the Soviet federation (see Table 13.1), but these were considerably less generous than the Europe agreements and did not include any reference to EU membership. The Community also set up a separate aid programme for the former Soviet Union, TACIS, further indicating that the former Soviet republics were in the most distant concentric circle. The exception to this was the three Baltic republics, which, for historical, political, and geographical reasons, were soon incorporated into the circle with the other CEECs.

Box 13.1 The EU and the wars in the former Yugoslavia

The descent of Yugoslavia into bloodshed is the most stunning tragedy of post-Cold War Europe. The country had been the most 'western' of what were then known as East European countries, with a mixed economy and a non-aligned foreign policy, and was a popular destination for West European tourists. But instead of blossoming after the Cold War, it collapsed.

When Yugoslavia disintegrated into war in mid 1991, the European Community publicly assumed responsibility for trying to halt the violence. But its record in the wars in Croatia and Bosnia (1991–95) is dismal. Although active in the first year of the conflicts — sponsoring a peace conference, sending monitors to negotiate local ceasefires, imposing sanctions on Serbia/Montenegro — the Community did not greatly improve the prospects for peace. And in early 1992, it controversially recognised Slovenia and Croatia, after Germany broke ranks with a common position and declared that it would recognise the two republics. Even more controversially, it then recognised Bosnia-Herzegovina, while Greece blocked Macedonia's recognition until after it was renamed the Former Yugoslav Republic of Macedonia (FYROM). Moreover, several member states opposed sending a Western European Union force to back up their diplomacy; instead they contributed troops to a UN peacekeeping force.

These diplomatic failures contributed to a widespread loss of confidence in the EU as an international actor. From summer 1992, it was sidelined; it first worked *alongside* the UN to gain approval of a peace plan, without success, and then stood by as the Contact Group, composed of the US, Russia, the UK, France, and Germany, took over the diplomacy, and NATO enforced UN resolutions. In summer 1995, NATO's military activity increased in Bosnia, helping to establish the conditions for a peace agreement. In the end, the US alone mediated the Dayton peace plan, signed in Paris in December 1995, and NATO troops policed its implementation.

Following Dayton, in 1996 the EU devised a strategy to strengthen regional stability, promising trade relations, aid, and cooperation agreements if the South-east European countries (the republics of former Yugoslavia plus Albania) met conditions such as respect for democracy and human rights, and cooperation with their neighbours (Council of the European Union 1996). But the EU's approach was long-term; in the short run, it was harder to balance stability with a concern for democracy and human rights, and to deal with violence as it continued to erupt in the region. Hence, for example, Slobodan Milosevic's regime in Serbia was tolerated from 1995 to 1998 in the interests of maintaining peace in Bosnia-Herzegovina, while western governments supported Sali Berisha's barely-democratic government in Albania until it collapsed in 1997. The EU did not respond to the corresponding spread of disorder in Albania, even though Italy and Greece called on it to act. The large member states (above all Germany and the UK) did not want to add new commitments to their role in Bosnia, so instead Italy assembled a 'coalition of the willing', acting under a UN mandate, to help restore calm in Albania (see Silvestri 1997). Nor did the EU play a large role in the Kosovo conflict. In 1997–98, Serbia/Montenegro's leader, Slobodan Milosevic, pursued a brutal campaign to impose Belgrade's rule over Kosovo, a province of Serbia inhabited mostly by Albanian Muslims. The EU pressed Belgrade to cease offensive military actions, but was in no position to force Serbia to comply. After a peace conference failed in January 1999, NATO took the military initiative, bombing Serbia until its troops withdrew from Kosovo.

The Copenhagen European Council, June 1993

The very rational concentric circles approach did not last long; few countries were content to stay out of the inner core. While the rich EFTAns were fairly easy to embrace—and Austria, Finland, and Sweden acceded to the EU in January 1995—enlargement to the CEECs anytime soon posed problems, particularly because of the need for adjustments to the EU budget and policies such as the Common Agricultural Policy and structural funds (if the CEECs received the same benefits that the member states did, there would not be enough money in the EU's budget, so the Fifteen would either have to pay more into the budget or agree to cut the benefits they receive from it—which particularly affected net recipients such as Greece, Ireland, Portugal, and Spain). Who would pay for eastern enlargement? Even those member states (such as Germany and the UK) most supportive of eastern expansion seemed unwilling to do so.

But the CEECs' demands for a *promise* of eventual accession, made persistently throughout 1992, eventually became impossible to deny, especially as violence spread in the east (the former Yugoslavia, Albania, the Caucasus). A promise to enlarge would foster the reform process, by boosting reformers, and thus help ensure peace and security in Europe (see European Commission 1993, European Council 1993, 12).[6] But the promise was made only in June 1993 because until then, the Community was embroiled in internal difficulties, notably regarding the ratification of the Maastricht Treaty; once the treaty was ratified, enlargement could be agreed.

Box 13.2 The EU's membership conditions

The Treaty of Rome stated that 'Any European state may apply to become a member of the Community' (Article 237). The 1999 Amsterdam Treaty added that any European state that respects the principles of liberty, democracy, respect for human rights and fundamental freedoms, and the rule of law, may apply to become a member of the Union (Articles 5 and 49).

The Copenhagen European Council in June 1993 declared that membership candidate countries must have achieved:

- a functioning market economy with the capacity to cope with competitive pressures and market forces within the EU;
- stability of institutions guaranteeing democracy, the rule of law, human rights, and respect for and protection of minorities; and
- the ability to take on the obligations of EU membership including adherence to the aims of economic and political union (the *acquis communautaire*).

By 1999, the EU had formally added 'good-neighbourliness' to the list of conditions. The December 1999 Helsinki European Council stated that candidate countries must resolve outstanding border disputes peacefully, if necessary by referring them to the International Court of Justice (European Council 1999c, para. 4).

In June 1993, the Copenhagen European Council agreed that the CEECs could join the EU, if they satisfied certain conditions (see Box 13.2). The membership conditions—though not new, they had not been stated so explicitly before—helped to reassure reluctant member states that enlargement would not wreck the (apparently fragile) Union. The European Council declared: 'The Union's capacity to absorb new members, while maintaining the momentum of European integration, is also an important consideration in the general interest of both the Union and the candidate countries' (European Council 1993, 13). This was clearly designed to protect the 'club'; to ensure, as the Commission argued, that 'widening must not be at the expense of deepening' (European Commission 1992, 10).

Table 13.2 Applications for EU membership since 1987

Country	Date of application	Date of accession
Turkey	14 April 1987	—
Austria	17 July 1989	1 January 1995
Cyprus	3 July 1990	1 May 2004
Malta[a]	16 July 1990	1 May 2004
Sweden	1 July 1991	1 January 1995
Finland	18 March 1992	1 January 1995
Switzerland[b]	26 May 1992	—
Norway[c]	25 November 1992	—
Hungary	31 March 1994	1 May 2004
Poland	5 April 1994	1 May 2004
Romania	22 June 1995	—
Slovakia	27 June 1995	1 May 2004
Latvia	13 October 1995	1 May 2004
Estonia	24 November 1995	1 May 2004
Lithuania	8 December 1995	1 May 2004
Bulgaria	14 December 1995	—
Czech Republic	17 January 1996	1 May 2004
Slovenia	10 June 1996	1 May 2004
Croatia	21 February 2003	—
Former Yugoslav Republic of Macedonia	22 March 2004	—

[a] In 1996, Malta froze its membership application after an anti-membership party won elections. It was thus excluded from Agenda 2000 and Luxembourg European Council decisions. It later reactivated its application, and negotiations opened in 2000.
[b] Switzerland froze its membership application, after Swiss voters rejected participation in the European Economic Area in December 1992.
[c] Norway completed accession negotiations in 1994, but Norwegian voters rejected EU membership in a referendum (again, having done so in 1972).

The Copenhagen conditions were aimed at the six countries that had concluded or were negotiating Europe agreements: Bulgaria, Czech Republic, Hungary, Poland, Romania, and Slovakia. But events once again complicated the EU's policy. Four newly independent countries—Estonia, Latvia, Lithuania, and Slovenia—could not reasonably be kept in an outer circle, especially given that they had backers within the EU, and in December 1994, the Essen European Council affirmed that they met the conditions for Europe agreements and would thus be formally included in the membership queue (European Council 1994, point I.14). All ten CEECs then applied for membership between 1994 and 1996 (see Table 13.2). In June 1994, the Corfu European Council also extended membership invitations to Malta and, controversially, to the Republic of Cyprus (see Box 13.3). This was a response to the concerns of southern member states that the 'southern dimension' was being neglected in favour of eastern enlargement. While the six new prospective members did seem more likely candidates than other European countries, the expansion of the enlargement queue seems to reflect the exigencies of intra-EU balancing.

Thus, within a year and a half of the Copenhagen summit, an initially difficult decision on enlargement was extended—with little discussion of the implications for other European countries or European order. Admittedly, at this stage it looked unlikely that 'outsiders' were credible membership candidates, with South-eastern Europe still embroiled in war, and the former Soviet republics plagued by war, instability, and a general lack of progress in economic and political reform. Yet, the question surely arose: would the EU eventually expand to include all of Europe? Expanding the queue of applicants does mean that the EU can exercise influence over a greater number of countries, but, as will be seen below, this requires carefully managing both that queue and the implications of enlargement for the internal functioning of the EU.

Box 13.3 The EU and the Republic of Cyprus

In June 1994, the European Council decided that the EU would open negotiations with the Republic of Cyprus at the same time that it opened talks with the first wave of CEECs. This was controversial because the island is divided between the internationally-recognised Republic of Cyprus, where most Greek Cypriots live, and the unrecognised Turkish Republic of Northern Cyprus (TRNC), where most Turkish Cypriots live. In 1974, at a time of great ethnic violence amid attempts to unite Cyprus with Greece, Turkey invaded the island; the 'green line' (patrolled by UN peacekeepers) eventually divided the two communities. Turkish troops are still present in the TRNC, as are a large number of Turkish mainland settlers. In 1998, the EU opened negotiations only with the Republic of Cyprus, which negotiated on behalf of the entire island. The EU hoped that the promise of enlargement would push both sides towards a solution and did not threaten to exclude Cyprus if none was reached. But throughout 2002 and 2003 it also insisted that Turkey put pressure on the TRNC to accept an agreement on unification. In this sense, the EU was successful: in April 2004, a referendum in the TRNC accepted a UN plan on reunification. The Republic of Cyprus rejected it, yet on 1 May it still acceded to the EU. Since then, the EU has found it difficult to 'reward' the TRNC, given the latter's unusual legal situation and while the Republic of Cyprus blocks any EU move it perceives as contrary to international law. With this unsatisfactory state of affairs, EU-Turkish relations assume even more importance, with the potential to stabilise or destabilise the eastern Mediterranean.

Following Copenhagen, the EU launched a pre-accession strategy, primarily to help the CEECs adopt and implement the *acquis*. Another IGC was held to reform the EU treaties and thus prepare the EU for enlargement, principally by expanding the use of qualified majority voting and streamlining the EU's institutions. Although the resulting Amsterdam Treaty was disappointing in that regard (in fact, the Amsterdam 'leftovers' had to be resolved at a later IGC, which led to the Nice Treaty) the European Council nonetheless declared that the enlargement process could proceed.[7] In July 1997, one month after the Amsterdam IGC concluded, the European Commission published its opinions on the membership applications in a wide-ranging report entitled 'Agenda 2000' (European Commission 1997).

In the run-up to Agenda 2000, the EU actively used membership conditionality to influence the applicant countries. This went beyond merely encouraging them to implement the *acquis*: the EU criticised domestic political processes and outcomes, and foreign policy choices, and expressed strong preferences for particular changes. Conditionality was used to lay the basis for European security *before* enlargement. For example, during the Pact for Stability, a multilateral negotiating framework led by the EU between May 1994 and March 1995, the CEECs were encouraged to conclude 'good-neighbourly' agreements with each other on borders and the treatment of minorities. The EU also criticised domestic politics. During the period of Vladimir Meciar's government in Slovakia (1992–98), for example, the EU issued numerous warnings that Slovakia must meet democratic norms before it could join the EU. The EU's demands were not always met with full compliance, but the extent to which they were is still striking—and contributed to the view that membership conditionality is the EU's most powerful foreign policy instrument.

Obviously then, the pressure on the CEECs before the Commission issued its opinions in Agenda 2000 was quite high. But it was also increasingly apparent that other considerations besides conditionality would play a role in enlargement decisions, in particular the effects of those decisions on European order. There was debate within the EU over how many countries should join initially: should the EU go for a more easily manageable first enlargement, and only let in a few (two or three) CEECs? Or should it go for the big-bang approach, and let in as many as feasible, thus prioritising enlargement (and the vision of a peaceful and united Europe) over the deepening of integration among only some of Europe's states?

The Luxembourg and Helsinki European Councils

There was much concern about the impact of leaving countries outside. Each membership application would be judged on its merits; in principle, differentiation should spur progress with reforms. But the application of membership conditionality—part of, after all, a strategy to spread peace and security—could actually end up destabilising countries, as it isolates and excludes (for a time) some states from the benefits of EU membership (see Senior Nello and Smith 1998). Alienation from the EU could consequently reduce its leverage, and where relations between countries inside and those left out have been tense, enlargement could be particularly destabilising. The inclusion/exclusion dilemma has since dominated enlargement policy-making.

The EU tried to lessen the negative implications of differentiation in three success-ive ways: by taking a multilateral approach to relations with the CEECs and their neighbours; by establishing an inclusive 'accession process'; and by opening nego-tiations with all of them. Firstly, the EU tried to encourage multilateralism, mainly by granting aid to regional cooperation initiatives such as the Central European Ini-tiative and Pact for Stability projects. But this has not reduced the centrality of the bilateral relationship between the EU and each CEEC, which was dominated by the accession process.

The other two ways of lessening the impact of differentiation are in practice just ways of postponing it, because they deal with the impact of exclusion from member-ship negotiations, not from membership itself. The EU initially developed an inclus-ive 'accession process', launched at the same time as the decisions were made in 1997 to differentiate between two groups of applicant countries, and begin membership negotiations with only one of them.

In Agenda 2000, the European Commission recommended that membership ne-gotiations be opened with five countries: the Czech Republic, Estonia, Hungary, Po-land, and Slovenia (in addition to Cyprus). Although no candidate country met all of the membership conditions, these five states came closest to doing so. The other five CEECs did not, and of these, Slovakia was singled out as the only country which did not meet the political condition. The decision to include Estonia and Slovenia, in addition to the three countries traditionally considered the frontrunners (the Czech Republic, Hungary, and Poland), was influenced by NATO's June 1997 decision to ex-pand to only three countries in the first instance, the Czech Republic, Hungary, and Poland.[8] In December 1997, the Luxembourg European Council agreed with the Com-mission's recommendation, and in March 1998, membership negotiations formally began with Cyprus, the Czech Republic, Estonia, Hungary, Poland, and Slovenia. The EU's next round of enlargement would in the event be larger, partly in the interests of stabilising the Baltic and Balkan regions. But this still left the problem of stabil-ising the unlucky applicants.

Although accession negotiations were opened only with the 'Luxembourg Six', an-nual Accession Partnerships were drawn up for all the applicant countries, listing the objectives that the EU wanted each applicant to meet. The accession process kept up the pressure on all the applicants, since only those countries that met the membership conditions would join, while the remaining applicant countries were promised that if they made good progress in that respect, then they too could start accession talks.

However, the EU's strategy started to unravel within a year, paradoxically because it worked quite quickly. Latvia and Lithuania made rapid progress in meeting the conditions, while elections in Slovakia in September 1998 resulted in defeat for the Meciar government. As Geoffrey Pridham argues (2002, 963), while EU pressure had little effect on the Meciar government, it clearly had an impact on Slovak society. The new government under Prime Minister Mikulas Dzurinda sought to reverse Slov-akia's isolated position. Thus by late 1998, three more CEECs (plus Malta) were close to joining those already negotiating accession, leaving Bulgaria and Romania in the 'slow lane'.

Excluding Bulgaria and Romania became untenable, however, when war erupted between Serbia and NATO over the treatment of Kosovar Albanians in March 1999. The risks of further isolating Bulgaria and Romania—given the instability in their neighbourhood and the support they had given to NATO action—made it infeasible to leave them out of the next round of negotiations. In October 1999, the Commission recommended that the EU open negotiations with all of the applicant countries except Turkey: this would make a 'decisive contribution to stability and prosperity' in Europe, a political imperative for the EU (European Commission 1999, 30). Enlargement Commissioner Günter Verheugen made explicit the political reasons behind the proposals:

> The strategic recommendations are based on the assumption that we need a strong political signal in Helsinki. This is what the Member States want too. Like us, they have learned a fundamental lesson from the Kosovo crisis. … Let me be quite clear here: the Commission is proposing a change of strategy on political grounds. If we further subdivide the second group or put them on a back burner, we risk losing some countries along the way by depriving their reforms of a tangible, credible objective. Because the political consequences of this cannot be measured, no risk should be taken. (Verheugen 1999)

The Commission justified its recommendation by arguing that the six applicant countries met the *political* condition for membership (the most important), if not the other conditions. This also provided a convenient way to handle Turkey's membership application: negotiations would not open with Turkey because it did not (yet) meet the political condition, but Turkey would conclude an Accession Partnership with the EU (see Box 13.4).

The Helsinki European Council in December 1999 approved the Commission's recommendations, and opened negotiations with the six countries, because it was 'determined to lend a positive contribution to security and stability on the European continent' (European Council 1999b, para. 10). In February 2000, formal membership negotiations started with the 'Helsinki Six'. The EU would still complete talks with each country only as it was ready. While differentiation kept up the pressure on the candidates to meet the conditions, it further deferred the basic dilemma: at some point, countries would inevitably be excluded from the first round of eastern enlargement, whatever the political implications.

How can we explain these decisions of 1997–99? A rationalist perspective, as several observers have noted, does not help much. This explains such outcomes as intergovernmental compromises among member states that are bargaining on the basis of their material interests. But for Frank Schimmelfennig, the member states had far too divergent interests regarding enlargement. Instead, with a sociological approach, the Luxembourg European Council's decision to open negotiations with only five CEECs 'can be explained as the inclusion of those countries that have come to share its liberal values and norms' (Schimmelfennig 2001, 48). Schimmelfennig maintains that since the EU professed itself to be based on such norms, the CEECs argued successfully that the credibility of the entire integration project depended on a commitment to enlarge to other liberal democracies. Since the Luxembourg Six met liberal norms, reluctant member states were shamed into fulfilling the promise of enlargement. They were trapped by their own rhetoric. Helene Sjursen emphasises identity, and argues that the EU is motivated by a strong sense of duty to enlarge to

> **Box 13.4** The EU and Turkey
>
> The EU's relations with Turkey have historically been problematic and the member states have frequently been divided over how to handle the country. Turkey is a long-standing member of NATO and the Council of Europe, located in a very sensitive region (its neighbours include Syria, Iran, and Iraq). The Bosphorous, which cuts through Istanbul, is considered the geographical boundary between Europe and Asia; the big question is whether this geographical boundary disqualifies Turkey from EU membership. Turkey is a democracy, but there have been coup d'etats in the past and the military has long played a decisive role in politics. There have been human rights problems: torture has been practised; the freedom of speech has not been protected; and the use of force against Kurdish guerrillas has often caused civilian casualties. Turkey is also a very large and mostly agricultural country—which alone poses plenty of problems for the EU. Although the state is secular, its population is predominantly Muslim. It is this last characteristic that has been the focus, implicitly or explicitly, of debates regarding Turkey's membership bid.
>
> In 1987, Turkey applied for membership; in 1989, the Commission's opinion concluded that it would not be appropriate to open accession negotiations. Since then, the Commission, Council, and European Parliament have persistently raised problems regarding Turkey's human rights and democracy situation, and have declared that until those problems are resolved, Turkey cannot join the EU. But Turkey then watched the EFTAns and CEECs jump the membership queue, while various European politicians cited cultural and religious factors for its exclusion. It suspected that it would never become a member of the club even if it had a fully functioning democracy and exemplary human rights record. When the December 1997 Luxembourg European Council placed Turkey in its own separate category of applicant states, Turkey suspended its relations with the EU.
>
> The EU's leverage over Turkey diminished, and consequently the EU altered its policy. The Helsinki European Council in December 1999 classified Turkey as an official candidate, although it made it clear that membership negotiations would only be opened once the political conditions had been met. At the Copenhagen European Council in December 2002, the EU came under intense pressure from the US to open membership negotiations with Turkey (a crucial ally in the run-up to the war on Iraq). Instead, the EU agreed to consider opening negotiations in December 2004 if Turkey met the political conditions by then (including a resolution of the Cyprus dispute). The EU's influence increased, as the parliament passed several laws strengthening the protection of human rights and democratic principles, and Turkey did indeed play a positive role in fostering TRNC acceptance of the UN plan for Cyprus. Throughout 2004, debate continued as to whether Turkey had done enough, and while the European Commission was prepared to argue that it had, not all of the member states were enthusiastic about launching negotiations. Inside or outside, Turkey will clearly continue to pose significant challenges for the EU—for its institutions, common policies, and external relations.

fellow Europeans and overcome the division of Europe. This shared identity explains why the EU prioritised enlargement to the CEECs over Turkey, whose candidacy is accepted only on utility calculations (geostrategic benefits) rather than shared identity (Sjursen 2002, especially 502–9).

Undeniably, a deep sense of responsibility to enlarge to the democratising Central and East European states is an important motivation for enlargement, and the EU really had little choice but to enlarge, given its rhetorical and treaty-based commitments. But this still does not fully explain the decisions of the Luxembourg and Helsinki European Councils. We need to add more of a 'foreign policy' perspective to explain why particular decisions were taken: political and security considerations played a major role in these decisions (which also prompted the member states to overcome disagreements based on material interests). The Luxembourg decision encompassed five CEECs and designed an accession process for all of them in a deliberate attempt to be as inclusive as possible, more so than NATO at the time, and to lessen the negative effects of differentiation.[9] The Helsinki decision included two states that patently did not meet the membership conditions, but which could not be left out for political and security reasons. In other words, the implications for European security were a determining factor in decisions on the enlargement *process*; security was not just the anticipated result of enlargement itself, steps had to be taken to avoid instability along the way. In addition, the extensive pressure placed on the candidate countries to conform to the membership conditions does not fit comfortably with sociological explanations of enlargement. The EU used membership conditionality both to limit the potential negative consequences of enlargement for itself (hence prospective members must be functioning and competitive market economies, implement most of the *acquis communautaire*, and resolve their disputes with neighbours before they join), and to create the basis for a secure Europe by demanding political reform. Although it had to respond to the CEECs' demands to make good on its promises to overcome the division of Europe, the EU retained much leverage to influence the CEECs.

Big bang enlargement

The membership negotiations were marked by considerable haggling over the terms of entry (and particularly the financial benefits to be extended to the new member states), as well as delays caused both by slow implementation of the *acquis* by the CEECs and events such as looming elections in EU member states or the Commission's resignation in March 1999. *The* question in 2000–2001, however, was how many countries would conclude negotiations by the 2002 deadline agreed by the member states for any front-runners. In 2000, support for a 'big bang' enlargement—up to ten candidate countries joining at once—grew among observers, though not yet among all the member states. Taking in ten countries together would leave fewer on the outside (and thus minimise the problem of exclusion, particularly of Poland, whose membership preparations were not as advanced as several other CEECs), and necessitate only one large-scale (though daunting) adjustment by the EU. But acceptance of a big bang enlargement also risked disappointing the front-runners (would they then have to wait for everyone else to catch up?), and could reduce the pressure on all of them (if they are all going to get in, why make much of an effort to meet the onerous conditions?).

The Commission eventually joined the big bang bandwagon, thus tilting the debate in favour of this option. In early September 2001, Verheugen (2001) maintained that ten countries could join in the next round of enlargement: all of the candidates except for Bulgaria and Romania. The terrorist attacks on the US then reinforced the security rationale for the big bang option. In November 2001, the Commission declared that '[a] strong and united Europe is more important than ever before, against the background of the terrorist attacks of 11 September and subsequent developments', and stated that ten candidate countries could conclude negotiations by the end of 2002 (European Commission 2001b, 4). By late 2001, the big bang option was widely perceived to be a certainty. This made it all the more difficult for the EU to take any other decision, although French Foreign Minister Hubert Vedrine warned of the dangers of leaving Bulgaria and Romania out. Despite the doubts, the Laeken European Council stated that all but Bulgaria and Romania could be ready to conclude negotiations within a year, thus making its self-imposed deadline (European Council 2001c, para. 8).

In October 2002, the Commission maintained that the ten countries would be able to assume the obligations of membership from 2004 (European Commission 2002, 20–1). The last two months of 2002 were a dash towards the finishing line, with brinkmanship on both sides of the negotiating table, particularly over agriculture and financial matters (and the candidate countries were unhappy with the EU's stinginess on both). But at the December 2002 Copenhagen European Council, the deal was done; the ten countries acceded to the EU on 1 May 2004.

As for Bulgaria and Romania, the Copenhagen European Council stated that 'depending on further progress in complying with the membership criteria, the objective is to welcome Bulgaria and Romania as members of the European Union in 2007' (European Council 2002, 4). This is striking, because previous European Councils had been so hesitant to set a definite date for the accession of specific candidates. The risks of alienating Bulgaria and Romania were considered too great *not* to give a firmer indication of when those two countries might finally accede, although the pressure on them to comply with the conditions could be more difficult to maintain. Turkey, in contrast, was told that a decision on opening membership negotiations with it would be taken by the end of 2004.

So in spite of the tough bargaining, and the calculable and incalculable costs of enlargement, the EU still agreed to a very large first round of eastern enlargement. The sense of responsibility towards the candidate countries, the sense of shared European identity, the strategic imperatives favouring a big bang enlargement, and the fact that the EU could not have backed down from its promises without a serious loss of credibility and legitimacy all helped to sustain the momentum. But the successful management of the exclusion dilemma for the candidate countries has very profound implications for the EU's relations with other European states.

Relations with south-eastern Europe

Ever since the 1995 Dayton peace agreement, the EU has assumed more and more responsibility for the reconstruction, stabilisation, and integration of South-eastern Europe. Although it played little role in the Albanian and Kosovo crises (see Box 13.1), with the end of the Kosovo war the EU took the lead in constructing a post-war order in South-eastern Europe. It added a Stability Pact (modelled on the earlier Pact for Stability in Central and Eastern Europe) and Stabilisation and Association agreements (see Table 13.1) to its previous strategy. Most importantly, it explicitly extended the promise of eventual accession to the South-east European countries.

The German presidency proposed the Stability Pact in the midst of the Kosovo crisis, in April 1999, and specifically added that the EU should make a clear commitment that the countries in the region could eventually accede to the EU. This would encourage them to undertake political and economic reforms and to work on cooperating with each other (German presidency 1999, para. IV.1). The CFSP Common Position on the Stability Pact, of 17 May 1999, stated that the 'EU will draw the region closer to the perspective of full integration of these countries into its structures ... with a perspective of EU membership on the basis of the Amsterdam Treaty and once the Copenhagen criteria have been met' (Council of the European Union 1999, recitals, para. 7). The June 2003 Thessaloniki European Council then reiterated the membership promise. The perceived success of membership conditionality elsewhere meant that it was tempting to try to repeat that success in South-eastern Europe: this would be the key to EU influence in the region.[10]

The EU's strategy had a better chance of success as authoritarian regimes fell: Franjo Tudjman's regime in Croatia was replaced by a pro-Western government in early 2000, and Milosevic was toppled in October 2000. The EU also regained a considerable amount of self-confidence, and the member states have been much more willing to let it take the lead. For example, when inter-ethnic violence erupted in the Former Yugoslav Republic of Macedonia (FYROM) in early 2001, the EU led efforts to resolve the crisis, in close cooperation with NATO. From August 2001, a NATO force collected weapons from ethnic Albanian rebels, while the EU pressured the FYROM government to enact reforms enhancing Albanian minority rights. The EU took over the NATO mission in early 2003.

There are still numerous potential pitfalls ahead. There are justifiable concerns that 25 member states will find it more difficult to agree to enlarge further. Such concerns prompted the inclusion of a declaration on 'One Europe' in the accession treaty, in which the current and acceding member states fully support the 'continuous, inclusive and irreversible enlargement process' (European Union, Official Journal, 2003, 971). The 25 states supported the aim of enlarging to Bulgaria and Romania in 2007, and the decisions on Turkey's candidacy. But beyond averring that the 'Union will remain determined to avoid new dividing lines in Europe', there is no mention of further enlargement. It may thus prove difficult to convince all of the South-east European states that enlargement really will take place—though two states, Croatia and FYROM, responded with alacrity to the EU's promise and submitted membership applications (see Table 13.2), indicating some belief in EU rhetoric.

Furthermore, enlargement entails differentiation—difficult to reconcile with the demand that South-east European countries cooperate with each other. The EU has already faced this exclusion-inclusion dilemma, and has yet again taken what may seem like a small step, but which actually has quite profound implications for European order. In June 2004, the European Council agreed with a largely positive Commission opinion on Croatia's application, and stated that membership negotiations will begin with that country in 2005 if it meets the condition. It is thus more likely that once FYROM is considered ready, it too will begin negotiations, without having to wait for other South-east European countries to catch up. These decisions are particularly important because politics in the region are still tinged with extreme nationalism and minority rights issues remain volatile. The promise of enlargement, made in a clear attempt to encourage South-eastern Europe to embark on a post-national 'European' path, could have consequences that the EU has difficulty managing.

Relations with the 'wider Europe'

The enlargement commitments discussed above leave out the former Soviet republics, many of which have also expressed a desire to join the EU. Here the EU faces quite a dilemma: if it does not promise further enlargement, its influence could suffer; but if it does, the promise may lack credibility, as the countries are quite far from meeting the conditions, and it is not clear at all that an enlarged EU would be capable of taking decisions on further enlargement, much less enjoy public backing for doing so. Since 2002, it has struggled to formulate a coherent strategy for the 'wider Europe'—those countries that are much closer neighbours since 2004 (see Dannreuther 2003).

The extension of the EU's border in 2004 (and 2007) is, as Christopher Hill (2002, 97) has argued, 'the most important of all the foreign policy implications of enlargement'. Most notably, enlargement means the extension of Schengen rules, which create a 'hard' border. In particular, the new member states must impose visa requirements on nationals from neighbouring countries.[11] As Heather Grabbe (2000, 528) notes, 'erecting Schengen borders with difficult neighbours like Ukraine, Kaliningrad (part of Russia) and Croatia could upset delicately balanced relationships and stall cross-border economic integration'.

The EU's bilateral relations with the westernmost former Soviet republics have been plagued with difficulties. The member states have struggled to come up with a strategy for how to deal with Russia—witness the anodyne CFSP Common Strategy on Russia (European Council 1999a)—partly because Russia itself has had different approaches towards the west and partly because several member states (particularly the large states, France, Germany, and the UK) consider Russia to be too important a global player to let the EU lead in relations with it. Those relations have been at times very difficult, over issues such as NATO enlargement, the wars in Bosnia and Kosovo (where western diplomacy and military action was frequently criticised by Russia), and the wars in the break-away Russian republic of Chechnya (which has prompted considerable criticism of Russia in European circles, but little consistent action to back it up).

Ukraine poses yet a different set of problems: the EU seeks to boost its independence from Russia, but does not want to spark Russian concerns. Ukraine has repeatedly indicated that it wishes to join the EU, but its lack of progress on political and economic reforms has not helped its case for stronger relations with the EU. Belarus, meanwhile, has been languishing under authoritarian misrule, and has been isolated by the EU, while a simmering ethnic conflict has at times paralysed Moldova and therefore its relations with the EU. The EU has not been active in the Caucasus: rather the OSCE and UN have been at the forefront of conflict resolution efforts in Armenia, Azerbaijan, and Georgia.

The EU has tried to formulate a multilateral approach to relations with some of the former Soviet republics, initially through the European Conference. The European Conference was launched in March 1998, as a means of linking the EU and the 13 applicant countries (including Turkey above all). It entailed periodic meetings of the heads of state or government to discuss foreign policy problems and issues such as immigration or transnational crime, but not much resulted from the meetings, and Turkey in fact refused to participate in it for several years. In June 2001, the Göteborg European Council suggested inviting Moldova and Ukraine to the next meeting. Yet in October 2001, the European Conference was expanded to 40 participants, including EFTA members, the South-east European countries, Moldova, Russia, and Ukraine. Unless the European Conference becomes more than a 'talking shop', it cannot possibly effectively link the EU and wider Europe.

In early 2002, the UK in particular pushed for a more substantive 'wider Europe' initiative, which would be aimed at Belarus, Moldova, Russia, and Ukraine, but not the South-east European countries, already involved in the stabilisation and association process, or other western Soviet republics such as Armenia, Azerbaijan, and Georgia. In December 2002, the Copenhagen European Council agreed, but included the southern Mediterranean countries in the initiative, on the insistence of southern member states. In June 2004, after considerable lobbying by the Caucasian republics (and a peaceful 'revolution' in Georgia), the Council extended the initiative still further to Armenia, Azerbaijan, and Georgia.

In December 2002, Romano Prodi declared, 'We have to be prepared to offer more than partnership and less than membership, without precluding the latter' (Prodi 2002, 3). In March 2003, the Commission specified that the neighbours 'should be offered the prospect of a stake in the EU's Internal Market' (European Commission 2003a, 4). Increased economic integration and closer political cooperation would be conditional, and clear benchmarks for each country would be set out. In 2004, the Commission began preparing individual action plans—detailing objectives and benchmarks—for the most advanced neighbours. These are not new legal agreements; the agreements currently in force remain the key framework for relations.

Whether this will suffice to encourage reform can be doubted: several EFTAns, after all, decided that it was better to be inside the EU making decisions than just in the European Economic Area implementing them. Furthermore, the EU is hardly offering 'all but institutions'. The Commission was silent about agricultural trade liberalisation, which could boost growth in the neighbours but is too controversial for the member states to contemplate. Nor is any new aid yet on offer, and only limited visa-free access would be granted to some non-EU citizens.

There are two basic problems for the EU here. Firstly, unless it promises membership, it cannot overcome the dilemma of exclusion: 'No matter how frequently NATO and EU officials reiterate that they have no intention of redividing Europe, irrespective of how many "partnership" agreements they offer to non-members, the inevitable consequence of admitting some countries to full membership of the organisations and excluding others is to produce "insiders" and "outsiders"' (Light *et al.* 2000, 77). Secondly, the policy instruments available to the EU are inadequate. Far too little is on offer, both to encourage democracy, economic reform and so on from the 'bottom up' (via aid and the free movement of people), and to try to force governments to comply with political and economic conditions. Unless the EU can provide more resources to try to make up for the lack of a medium-term membership prospect, it is unlikely to exercise much influence in the former Soviet Union.

Conclusion

Although the EU may struggle to exercise influence in the former Soviet Union, its role in Europe is extensive and growing. Since the end of the Cold War, the EU has increasingly but emphatically 'flexed its muscles' in Europe, assuming responsibility for an ever expanding geographical area—primarily through enlargement and the expansion of its 'security community'. It is certainly a power in European international relations, and has reshaped the European order largely in its own image.

Enlargement policy was perforce a common one. Although they may have disagreed over aspects of the policy (such as the potential costs), the member states still had to reach agreement at the EU level. The member states could not escape from the fact that the EU was the focus of European countries' demands; this necessarily overshadowed their bilateral relations with them. Furthermore, those demands—notably for accession—could *only* have arisen within the Union context, and thus had to be handled in that forum. And once the member states had explicitly agreed on the prospect of eastern enlargement, there appeared to be no turning back.

Explaining why the member states have agreed to enlargement—when the costs are not only large (though uncertain) but unevenly distributed—requires the use of several theoretical approaches. Approaches that emphasise shared identity certainly help, as does recognition that the member states effectively had little room for manoeuvre—they could not realistically reject enlargement as a policy option. But we need to add geopolitical and security factors to the explanation: enlargement was considered a way to ensure European stability and security. Furthermore, the member states then had to deal incrementally with the geopolitical and security consequences that each successive enlargement decision created, and these factors dominated decision-making.

The challenges facing the EU are very significant indeed. It must first of all absorb the ten new member states, while still maintaining the capacity to engage with outsiders, and to enlarge further (to Bulgaria and Romania in the first instance). There is a danger that the enlarged EU will become so obsessed with internal reform (ratifying a new 'constitution' and then implementing it) that the outside world is neglected. The EU must also make credible its promises of enlargement—and of intensive engagement more generally—in South-eastern Europe, if it is to retain leverage, but must handle the consequences of differentiation very carefully. And finally, it must consider how to exercise influence in the former Soviet Union without holding out the promise of enlargement, even as the implications of EU expansion for those eastern neighbours are bound to create pressures for inclusion rather than exclusion.

Notes

1 The definition of 'order' here follows that of William Wallace (2001, 2): 'a relatively stable pattern of shared assumptions, rules and institutions which together constitute what Hedley Bull defined as not only a "state system", but more broadly also a "society of states"'.

2 The EU's enlargement policy is rightly considered 'foreign policy' — even though its aim is the eventual incorporation of the 'targets' into the EU — primarily because of the way the EU has used the prospect of membership to influence the domestic and foreign policies of those targets. The EU's policy towards its European neighbours is cross-pillar (and often led by the first, not second, pillar) — which may blind some observers to its foreign policy characteristics.

3 Aid to help implement democratic reforms was much slower in coming; the first Phare programme for democracy was set up only in late 1992. The Community clearly thought that the top-down pressure of conditionality would be enough to foster democratisation. After Yugoslavia proved that a democratic transition can go badly wrong, democracy aid was extended to the CEECs and to TACIS aid recipients. By 2002, Phare aid was over ε 1.5 billion a year (and total pre-accession aid topped ε 3 billion).

4 In December 1989, the European Council had stated that it would strengthen its relations with Yugoslavia, the Soviet Union and the Central and East European countries (European Council 1989, 14–15). A year later, Yugoslavia and the Soviet Union were undoubtedly in separate categories.

5 Turkey's association agreement with the EC mentioned the possibility of membership, which made many within the Community wary about even promising eventual membership. See Michalski and Wallace 1992, 120–4.

6 The link between democracy, protection of human rights, economic openness, and international security was already well-entrenched as a European norm, particularly in the principles of the Conference on Security and Cooperation in Europe (CSCE). Compliance with CSCE principles was an explicit condition for EU assistance and agreements.

7 Several member states — Belgium, France, and Italy — made it clear in a declaration attached to the Amsterdam Treaty that further reform would have to precede enlargement.

8 Estonia in particular seemed only a marginally (if at all) more suitable candidate than Latvia and Lithuania (which the latter two countries bitterly pointed out afterwards). The inclusion of only one Baltic country would expand the first round of enlargement but not scarily so, and would help reassure the Baltic republics that they were firmly within the EU's 'sphere of influence'.

9 On the inclusive nature of the accession process, see Friis (1998). Friis and Murphy (1999) point out that widening the first round of negotiations also ensured the support of southern and northern member states.

10 As the European Commission noted, 'the incentive for reform created by the prospect of membership has proved to be strong — enlargement has unarguably been the Union's most successful foreign policy instrument' (European Commission 2003, 5).

11 The effects of this can be seen most vividly with respect to Kaliningrad. When the Soviet Union broke up, the Russian region of Kaliningrad became

an outpost, so that to travel between Kaliningrad and the rest of Russia, Russian citizens must cross Lithuania and Latvia, or Poland and Belarus. The EU's insistence that new member states implement the Schengen *acquis* means that Russian citizens must possess a visa and valid passport to cross EU territory even though they are travelling between parts of Russia (European Commission 2001a, 4–5). Temporary arrangements specific to Kaliningrad were eventually agreed in 2002: Russians will be issued special travel documents to travel between Kaliningrad and the rest of Russia.

Further reading

All of the books below provide a good historical account of the EU's enlargement policy. Cremona (2003) includes chapters on the EU's policy towards South-eastern Europe and the effects of enlargement on the EU's external relations and its internal development. Barbé and Johansson-Nogués (2003) concentrate on the effects of enlargement on the EU's external relations. Schimmelfennig (2003) develops the theory of rhetorical entrapment.

Avery, G., and Cameron, F. (1998), *The Enlargement of the European Union* (Sheffield: Sheffield Academic Press).

Barbé, E., and Johansson-Nogués, E. (eds) (2003), *Beyond Enlargement: The New Members and New Frontiers of the Enlarged European Union* (Barcelona: Universitat Autonoma de Barcelona).

Cremona, M. (ed.) (2003), *The Enlargement of the European Union* (Oxford: Oxford University Press).

Grabbe, H., and Hughes, K. (1998), *Enlarging the EU Eastwards* (London: Pinter).

Mayhew, A. (1998), *Recreating Europe: The European Union's Policy Towards Central and Eastern Europe* (Cambridge: Cambridge University Press).

Schimmelfennig, F. (2003), *The EU, NATO and the Integration of Europe* (Cambridge: Cambridge University Press).

Smith, K.E. (2004), *The Making of EU Foreign Policy: The Case of Eastern Europe*, 2nd edition (Basingstoke: Palgrave).

Web links

The European Commission has several web sites on the EU's relations with Central, Eastern and South-eastern Europe. The Directorate-General for Enlargement handles relations with countries that have applied for membership (http://www.europa.eu.int/comm/enlargement/index.htm). Relations with South-eastern Europe and the former Soviet republics are the responsibility of the Directorate-General for External Relations: on the former Soviet republics see http://www.europa.eu.int/comm/external_relations/ceeca/index.htm, and on South-eastern Europe, see http://www.europa.eu.int/comm/external_relations/see/index.htm.

The European Parliament's web site on enlargement contains much useful information. See http://www.europarl.eu.int/enlargement/default_en.htm.

Finally, the Centre for European Reform in London has published numerous studies on enlargement. See their enlargement web page, http://www.cer.org.uk/enlargement/index.html.

Chapter 14

The Shadow of Empire: The EU and the Former Colonial World

James Mayall

Contents

Summary

The long shadow cast by colonialism over Europe's relations with the poorer states of the world gradually receded over the last decades of the 20th century. Not only are Europeans no longer on the defensive, but they no longer give the priority to development issues which was evident in the European Community's Lomé Conventions from 1975 on. The focus has shifted elsewhere, notably to eastern Europe, largely as the result of enlargement and the end of the Cold War. Nonetheless the EU, and in particular member states like Britain and France, continue to be a significant power in the Third World, and deeply implicated in the latter's processes of international relations. The EU is, however, more a force for modernisation than for integration, peace, and international order, however much it is concerned to promote these values.

Introduction

The contemporary international order is conventionally seen as resting on three major 20th-century developments. The first was the retreat of Western Europe from its commanding position in international politics. This retreat was brought about by the combined consequences of the Second World War, the rise of the two superpowers after 1945, and the loss of empire. The second was the 40-year-long Cold War that framed the strategic environment between 1946/7 and 1989/91. The third was the enormous expansion in the membership of international society. This last was, in turn, the product of European decolonisation and its ambiguous consequences for international relations, as a result of the interests the new states sought to protect and the international objectives they pursued.

While Western Europe was driven from its pole position in world politics after 1945, the collapse of the European empires was quite unlike the fall of previous empires in Europe or elsewhere. Traditionally, when empires collapsed they were either swallowed up or partitioned in a new territorial dispensation, or (if the territory was insufficiently attractive to neighbouring predators) lapsed into statelessness, a condition that 19th-century international lawyers conveniently labelled as *terra nullius*. Nothing of the sort happened after 1945. The emperors withdrew to their own homelands, where they remained infinitely more powerful, economically, politically, and strategically, than the successor states to which they transferred power. Britain and France also held permanent seats on the Security Council and, therefore, the ability to veto Afro Asian resolutions that they perceived to be against their own interests, a power that they did not hesitate to use.

Perhaps because they were relatively so powerful, but also because (with the exception of Spain and Portugal) the former imperial powers were also democracies, they continued to figure disproportionately in the world-views—and possibly also in the psychic make-up—of post-colonial political elites. The political class might recognise that power had shifted away from western Europe and that they were the beneficiaries of this shift, they might be attracted to American capitalism or Soviet communism, or like Pandit Nehru, they might dream of combining a western style polity with a socialist economy. All, however, had cut their political teeth not on these abstractions but in confronting, negotiating and sometimes even collaborating with Belgian, British, Dutch, French, Italian, Portuguese, and Spanish rule.

This meant that the new elites had direct experience of Europe, and not the United States, or the Soviet Union. Indeed, in the aftermath of empire, Europe continued to hold its former colonies—or at least their rulers—in thrall.[1] With the transfer of power, the new leaders moved into the positions and the properties vacated by the departing Europeans. For ordinary folk, the vast majority of whom were peasant farmers, no doubt life went on much as before, once the independence celebrations were over (Thakur 1995, 39).[2] But for the elite, the European legacy was so all enveloping, that there was no ordinary life to which they could revert. The imperial experience was so recent and so vivid, that Europe was almost invariably the model, on which the post-colonial state was based. But it was also available as a scapegoat, when governments failed to deliver a material dividend from independence. Ironically, a generation after the transfer of power, by when some post-colonial states had failed catastrophically, the Cold War came to an end and it was no longer so easy for the leaders of new states to blame the disaster on imperialism (Mayall 2005).

For opposition politicians, who lost out in the ferocious 'winner-takes-all' battles that were the hallmark of post-colonial politics in many states, the former metropole also often provided sanctuary. And, as colonial rule receded in time, increasing numbers of their countrymen, despairing of the opportunities at home, found their way to European countries, whose languages they spoke, and with whose culture they had at least an arms length familiarity. They came, legally when possible but often illegally as well. By the turn of the century about 3% of the British population were either immigrants from South Asia and the Caribbean or their descendants. Between 2000 and 2002 around 379,000 arrived from Commonwealth countries in Asia, Africa, and the Caribbean. In France there was a similar pattern, with the majority coming from north and sub-Saharan Africa (National Statistics 2004; Beaumel, Doisneau and Vatan 2003). As we shall see, their arrival created problems as well as opportunities, not merely for the host countries but for the EU as a whole.

The EEC, the predecessor of the EU, was in part conceived as a solution to the problem of internecine European nationalist rivalries, particularly between France and Germany. In the final period of imperialist rivalry before 1914, it had proved possible to reach agreement about dividing the spoils in Africa in order to preserve the European balance of power. When the imperial safety valve finally blew after two European-provoked world wars, the value of empire was called into question. Despite the number of look-alike, regional organisations modelled on the EU (most recently the African Union which has replaced the Organization for African Unity (OAU)). Europeans would be wrong to conclude that it is the European solution to the problem of national rivalries that has attracted political elites in the former colonies. The anti-colonial struggle was for the capture of the state, not the region, and post-colonial states have been amongst the strongest opponents of any evolution of international society that involves a dilution of the concepts of sovereignty, territorial integrity, and self-determination defined as European decolonisation, no less, but certainly no more. It was nationalism, learned from Europe, and then successfully turned against the imperial powers that was the strongest intellectual influence in shaping post-colonial relations with Western Europe. The EU model has been accepted—at least rhetorically—in many but not all parts of the former colonial world, albeit as a means of attacking the problem of under-development, not of confronting the problem of sovereignty.

Against this background, this chapter will seek to answer three questions, which arise under the three aspects of the EU's international relations which are the subject of this book:

- What has been the legacy of empire for the international system in general and the European system in particular; and how have these legacies shaped European relations with the former colonial world?

- How have the processes of EU decision making (and style) influenced bilateral and EU-wide relations with former colonies, and African, Asian, Caribbean, and Oceanic perceptions of the EU?

- To what extent is the EU viewed as a major power in its own right by the former dependencies of its member states and how influential is the European view of how the international order should be organised?

The EU as a system of IR and within the wider international order

The Cold War

The relationship between the European system and the former colonial world had its origins in the broader international system that was reconstructed after 1945. There were three features of this system that were crucial to the forging of Europe's post-imperial relations. The first two were features of what Raymond Aron once called the egalitarian order of law, the third of the hierarchical order of power, on which together the new system was based. The first feature—the fundamental rejection of the principle of empire as a legitimate political form—was initially resisted by the imperial powers. Britain and France, in particular, hoped that their colonial responsibilities would help them to re-establish their status as great powers after the war. But once Soviet anti-imperialism was added to the support for the self-determination of peoples that the Americans had made one of their war aims from the Atlantic Charter onwards, the writing was on the wall. The United Nations provided the setting for this pincer movement against the European empires. By 1960, only three years after the signing of the Treaty of Rome, the General Assembly passed Resolution 1514, on 'The Declaration on the Granting of Independence to Colonial Countries and Peoples'. Amongst its other provisions, it ruled that lack of preparation could no longer be used as a reason for delaying independence.

The second feature concerned the economic architecture of the new order. For the first time ever an attempt was made to establish an institutional infrastructure to embody the values on which an open multilateral world economy would need to be based. The International Monetary Fund (IMF), the International Bank for Reconstruction and Development or World Bank (IBRD), and the General Agreement on Tariffs and Trade (GATT) established the rules for the system as a whole. Some of these, including the immediate restoration of currency convertibility within a fixed exchange rate system, and the elimination of imperial trade preferences in favour of the most favoured nation (MFN) principle, proved unworkable in the short run. But they nonetheless established the standard for other multilateral and regional initiatives. In the case of Europe and its former colonies, this meant that the EEC had to be compatible with the GATT, which allowed a few exceptions to the MFN principle, the most notable being for customs unions and free trade areas.

Although Jacob Viner provided a celebrated theoretical justification for this exception (Viner 1950)—broadly where their creation would be trade-creating rather than trade-diverting—the exception reflected the recognition of a political reality, namely that where states were prepared to offer 100% preference, there was a presumption that they intended to change the political significance of their mutual borders. In other words, more was involved than merely discriminating in favour of one set of sovereign states and against another. The creation of the EEC as a Customs Union, however, immediately challenged the existing relationships between France, Belgium, and Italy—three original signatories of the Treaty—and their colonies, none of which in 1957 had achieved independence. These were based on various forms of colonial protection in metropolitan markets and the virtual closure of the colonial markets themselves to third country competition. The solution, insisted on by France, as the price of its signature, was the addition to the Treaty of Part IV, under which subsidised colonial exports were allowed to continue.

Britain was not a signatory of the Rome Treaty, although it too maintained an extensive system of imperial preferences. Indeed, the fact that these had been negotiated with the old Dominions (Australia, Canada, New Zealand, and South Africa), all sovereign states in their own right, was a major reason why the British had insisted that they could not unilaterally abolish preferences as the Americans had originally hoped. The compromise negotiated within the GATT was that there would be no new preferences, and that those that existed would be left to 'wither on the vine', as the result of the general reduction of tariffs in the successive rounds of multilateral negotiations through which world trade was to be liberalised. The British viewed Part IV as undermining this compromise and re-introducing the preferential principle on a permanent basis by the back door.

By this time, Britain's own plans for transferring power to their remaining colonies—or at least to those of them that they judged to be economically viable—were evolving fast. Sudan became independent in 1956, Ghana (then the Gold Coast) and Malaya in 1957, and the date was set for Nigerian independence in 1960. These countries, as well as the South Asian states that had preceded them to independence in the late 1940s, viewed the concept of association in Part IV with alarm. It reinforced their fears of a Fortress Europe, for which the EEC policy of food self-sufficiency was largely responsible. With the negotiation of the first Yaoundé Agreement in 1963, following the independence of the majority of francophone African states in 1960, the EEC attempted to make the new agreement conform with GATT by establishing a separate Free Trade Area with each of them, thus providing for the continuation of privileged access in both directions. The Commonwealth states were unimpressed and denounced the association as a form of neo-colonialism. In 1963, they persuaded Britain to support their challenge to the legality of the Agreement within the GATT (Mayall 1986, 326–30).

This challenge failed, largely because it brought the legal order, based on sovereignty, non-discrimination and MFN, into direct conflict with the hierarchical principles of power politics. These provided the third feature of the post-war system that shaped Europe's post-imperial relations. Even though the GATT had been designed in response to United States interests and values, the Americans were prepared to make an exception to the rules in order to underpin the strategy of containment, which they had developed after the onset of the Cold War.[3] The British were slow to acknowledge that, in American eyes, the primary value of the EEC was to provide a strong European pillar to support the arch of the Atlantic Alliance. Internal trade liberalisation had been part of the price that the west Europeans had had to pay for Marshall aid on which their reconstruction was based. The EEC's customs union was consistent with this aim, and if association technically was not, viewed from

---

Box 14.1 The evolution of the EU/ACP relationship

1957 Part IV Rome Treaty

Maintains privileged access to metropolitan markets for former colonies and extends preferential access for these associated territories to other EEC member state markets.

1963 First Yaoundé Agreement (renewed 1969)

Reciprocal preferential trade access between EEC member states and associated states.

European Development Fund (EDF) established as an *additional* source of concessionary finance.

Joint Council of Ministers, Joint Parliamentary Assembly, and Committee of Ambassadors established.

Under Arusha Convention of 1968 the East African Community Countries were linked to Yaoundé II, but do not participate in the political institutions.

1974 First Lomé Agreement (renewed 1979, 1984, 1990, 1995)

Former British colonies are included for the first time. Nigeria leads negotiations and agrees not to claim against the EDF.

African, Caribbean, Pacific (ACP) Group established with its own Secretariat in Brussels.

Reciprocity abolished.

STABEX (1979) and MINEX (1984) schemes set up to support ACP agricultural prices and to insure against a slump in mineral export prices. In 1998 South Africa becomes a signatory of the Lomé Convention but is excluded from the trade chapters. Signs a Trade, Development and cooperation agreement providing for an asymmetrical free trade area to be phased in over 12 years.

2000 Cotonou Agreement

Although based on the same principles of sovereignty and equality as previous agreements, the Cotonou Agreement seeks to encourage 'the smooth and gradual integration of the ACP countries into the world economy'. The signatories are committed to conclude WTO compatible Free-Trade Economic Partnership Agreements (EPAs) by December 2007.

Article 9 of the Agreement makes aid disbursement conditional on democratic governance and respect for human rights.

The Agreement entered into force in April 2003 and will run for 20 years.

Washington this was a small price to pay to secure democracy and stability in Europe. The peripheral nature of most of the countries involved, both economically and politically, no doubt helped the Americans to digest this pragmatic departure from their ideological principles. For their part, once it became clear that the charge of illegality and neo-colonialism would not stick, Commonwealth countries, starting with Nigeria in 1966 and the East African Community in 1968, came to terms and negotiated their own bilateral trade agreements with the EEC.

There was one major difference between these agreements and both Part IV and the first Yaoundé Convention. The latter was based on a reciprocal exchange of concessions, which the Commonwealth countries continued to reject on the grounds that there could be no equality between unequals. The dispute over reciprocity was not resolved until after Britain's accession to the Community in 1973. This confronted the Commonwealth states that were deemed to be associable with a stark choice. Either they would have to associate with the EEC on the same terms as the existing associated states, or they would lose preferential access to the British market and have to face competition from Latin American and other third world countries on equal terms. Faced with it the Commonwealth associables swallowed their pride and agreed to negotiate.

The decision was made easier because the benefits of the Yaoundé regime had not been sufficient to prevent the associated states from losing market share to stronger non-associated developing countries. In these circumstances they were prepared to abandon their commitment to reciprocity and to adopt the position of the UNCTAD (United Nations Conference on Trade and Development) Group of 77, which had successfully negotiated the General Special Preference (GSP) scheme on the basis of non-reciprocity. Their fears of being swamped by the stronger Commonwealth states were allayed by the Nigerian offer to lead the negotiations for the new Lomé Convention, on their behalf, and more importantly, to forego any claim on the European Development Fund (EDF).[4] Superficially, the argument had been about trade reciprocity—and about participation in the joint institutions established under the Yaoundé Conventions, which many Commonwealth states regarded as institutionalised neo-colonialism. In reality, it was the protection of their privileged access to aid funds, and the possibility of an additional source of such funds, that was of most concern to the majority of associated and associable states alike.

With the establishment of the first Lomé Convention in 1974, the European system was brought a step closer to the general north-south regime, favoured amongst others by the United States and Britain. Under it, developing countries were treated as a single constituency in multilateral negotiations. The substance of the Yaoundé and Lomé Conventions, and the way in which the European Community conducted its relations with former colonies within them, will be examined in the next section. For the moment it is sufficient to note that with British accession and the negotiation of the first Lomé Convention, the basic structure of the European post-colonial regime, and its relationship with the wider international system, was put in place. It did not fundamentally change until after the Cold War.

It has been said that, despite growing convergence, the European system established a pyramid of privilege within the broader system of north-south relations (Mishilani, Robert and Stevens 1981, 60–82). At its apex were the African, Caribbean, and Pacific states (ACP) whose 'partnership' under the Lomé Convention entitled them to special trade privileges and access to the EDF. A second tier was formed by the non-member Mediterranean countries, whose strategic proximity and traditional economic ties led to the negotiation of a series of bilateral trade agreements to protect market access in both directions, and to cushion the effects and slow the pace of adjustments made necessary as the result of European integration. At the base of the pyramid was the rest of the developing world, all those countries that were eligible for GSP and some of which—the South Asian states for example—were recipients of significant bilateral aid from particular EEC member states.

During the Cold War, the pyramid of privilege provided modest additional resources to some of the most disadvantaged states in the world. From this point

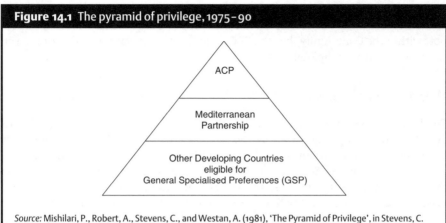

Figure 14.1 The pyramid of privilege, 1975–90

ACP

Mediterranean Partnership

Other Developing Countries
eligible for
General Specialised Preferences (GSP)

Source: Mishilari, P., Robert, A., Stevens, C., and Westan, A. (1981), 'The Pyramid of Privilege', in Stevens, C. (ed.), *EEC and the Third World: A Survey* (London: Hodder and Stoughton).

of view, the European post-colonial regime also played a useful, if subordinate role, in maintaining Western influence in the third world. In the early 1960s, President Kennedy had re-defined development assistance as a US strategic interest in combating Soviet and Chinese influence amongst the non-aligned. Nonetheless, foreign aid was always unpopular in the US Congress, and in 1963, the Clay Report recommended that, in the interests of burden sharing amongst the western allies, Africa should be the prime responsibility of the Europeans since the United States had no vital interests to protect there.[5] The policy seems to have been reasonably successful in driving a wedge between the Soviet Union and its African client states. When Angola, Mozambique, and Guinea-Bissau became independent following the Portuguese revolution, they joined the ACP states under the second Lomé Convention, despite the fact that all three countries had communist governments and the latter two had signed long term cooperation agreements with the Soviet Union.

Throughout the Cold War, EEC relations with the post-colonial world were confined to economic issues. The United States also paid only spasmodic attention to African politics between the end of the Congo crisis in 1964 and the Portuguese coup a decade later. Thereafter, whenever ACP countries were involved either directly or indirectly in conflicts with a bearing on the central east-west confrontation, the United States forgot about burden sharing and intervened either unilaterally or in bilateral cooperation with a particular ally. This was partly no doubt because NATO, the main vehicle for western security cooperation, could not at that time act out of area. But it was also because the EEC itself had not been designed with high politics in mind. Thus, following the Soviet invasion of Afghanistan, the US developed a Rapid Deployment Force with facilities in Kenya, Sudan, and later Somalia, totally overshadowing assistance efforts from other countries including the EEC. And once Henry Kissinger, as Secretary of State, had identified a threat to the west in the continued stalemate in the overlapping racial conflicts in southern Africa, he brought decisive pressure to bear on South Africa, in order to bring Rhodesia to the negotiating table. The US then cooperated with Britain in brokering the Zimbabwe settlement of 1980. From then on, and until the independence of Namibia in 1993 and majority rule in South Africa in 1994, the Americans remained actively engaged in southern Africa in close collaboration with Britain. Both countries lobbied for support within the Community, but the EEC as an institution was not a major player in the southern African diplomacy.

The post-Cold War order

The European system was established in the Cold War environment. Originally, its evolution was also partly driven by the need to protect west European democracy from the threat of communism. But structurally the system was quite independent of these considerations. Moreover, regardless of its underlying political rationale and in the case of the ACP countries, an explicitly political framework, the pyramid of privilege had been designed with economic and developmental, rather than security issues in mind. There was, therefore, no ostensible reason why Europe's post-colonial relationships should have been affected by the end of the Cold War. In practice, so massive a shift in the international landscape inevitably channelled the EU's relations with all countries in new directions.

So far as the Community's post-colonial system was concerned, the main consequences of the end of the Cold War were to weaken the defences of the ACP countries' special relationship with the EU, while simultaneously politicising it in new ways; and to increase the political salience of geopolitical considerations in the EU's emerging foreign and security policy. Let us consider these developments in turn.

At the height of the Cold War, when defection to the communist bloc was a serious option, the EEC had followed general international practice in being careful not to offend post-colonial sensitivities on the issue of sovereignty. In 1960, the Congo crisis provided a salutary warning of the dangers of identifying too closely with groups opposed to the government. When the Congolese army mutinied in the immediate aftermath of independence, Belgium sent in paratroopers to protect its nationals, only to find itself accused of designs to re-colonise the country. It is true that France had treaty relations with most of its former African colonies, which in some cases provided for the permanent garrisoning of French troops; and therefore allowed France to intervene as necessary to protect its allies when they were threatened by internal insurrection. But since such intervention was taken at the request of the incumbent government, it was the target of external criticism rather than official censure by the post-colonial government itself. Similarly, over most of the life of the Lomé system, France sided with its African allies in resisting pressure for access to the EDF to be made conditional on the human rights record of the recipient country.

On the issue of economic conditions, however, the Community generally tracked the policies favoured by the IMF and World Bank. These were ratcheted up in the early 1980s with the introduction of Structural Adjustment Programmes (SAPs) as a way of dealing with third world debt. Now, after the Cold War, the EU again kept pace with the more general western move to political conditionality, whose criteria of good governance, respect for human rights, and eventually multi-party democracy had to be met before aid could be disbursed—an epistemic consensus on these matters had emerged among western specialists. In 1994, eight African states—the Gambia, Equatorial Guinea, Liberia, Nigeria, Somalia, Sudan, Togo, and Zaire—had aid suspended or restricted for political reasons (Smith 2002, 186).

Article 9 of the Cotonou Agreement, which replaced the Lomé system in 2000, finally added to the existing principles of cooperation—equality between partners, self determination and the security of the EU/ACP relationship—the requirement that they be interpreted to include respect for human rights, democratic principles, and the rule of law.[6]

Cotonou marked a further stage in the folding of the EU system back into the global order established under the World Trade Organization (WTO). To meet WTO rules, preferences are to be phased out in favour of a return to reciprocal uncon-ditional MFN treatment, although in theory the *quid pro quo* for this forced conces-sion from the developing world is that their interests will be given special priority in the Dohar round of multilateral trade negotiations. Judging by the collapse of the Cancun summit in September 2003, and the many outstanding issues that remain to be settled after agreement in principle was finally reached in mid-summer 2004, formidable obstacles remain. The breakdown of the 2003 summit was engineered by the concerted action of dissatisfied developing countries, and there is currently little evidence that the EU is prepared to make significant concessions to cushion its ACP and former preferential trade partners from the costs of globalisation. Con-sequently the EU notion of a special relationship with developing countries looked rather threadbare. The interests of rich European societies pushed them not infre-quently into the same camp as the United States.

One reason, perhaps, is the paradoxical fact that under globalisation geo-politics appears to have become more rather than less important. With the collapse of the So-viet Union, the successor states and former Warsaw Pact countries in eastern Europe looked west, many of them aspiring to join NATO, the EU, or both. Not all could meet either the economic or political criteria for membership, but a combination of their aspirations, and the EU's core interest in a stable, peaceful and democratic Europe, was sufficient to revise the pyramid of privilege significantly. To some extent, indeed, the EU turned inwards, becoming in the process less interested in the global reach that its imperial past had provided.

As the EU's priorities changed, eastern Europe and the Commonwealth of Inde-pendent States (the CIS, viz the successor states to the former Soviet Socialist Re-publics) replaced the ACP countries at the top of the pyramid of privilege as the primary focus for EU aid and trade diplomacy. The Mediterranean retained its pos-ition. Indeed, the relationship was strengthened with the introduction of the Euro-Mediterranean Partnership Programme—the so-called Barcelona process—in 1995, providing for the creation of a Free Trade Area by 2010 and regular political as well as economic consultations. Meanwhile, the difference between the ACP and the rest of the developing world, which continued to occupy the base of the pyramid, became largely notional, although European consciences were partially salved by the recog-nition that the least developed countries (LDCs) stand in need of special protection within a globalised world economy. What this recognition will amount to in practice remains to be seen.

Two other systemic consequences of the end of the Cold War had ripple effects on the European system. The resurgence of ethnic, religious and national conflicts that accompanied the world-wide democratisation and economic deregulation of the 1990s led to accelerated migration, as those caught in the cross fire sought refuge and economic opportunities in the west. Much of the pressure on the EU came from the

Figure 14.2 The pyramid of privilege, 1990–2004

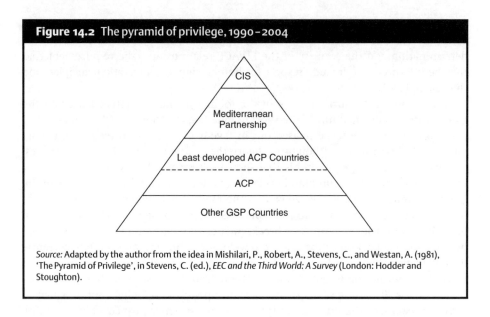

Source: Adapted by the author from the idea in Mishilari, P., Robert, A., Stevens, C., and Westan, A. (1981), 'The Pyramid of Privilege', in Stevens, C. (ed.), *EEC and the Third World: A Survey* (London: Hodder and Stoughton).

former Soviet Union and Eastern Europe, and European efforts to stem the flow in part explained the diversion of resources from the ACP countries referred to above. But there was also an upsurge in migration from South Asia and North and Sub-Saharan Africa. Although these flows fall outside the immediate scope of the EU's foreign and security policy, they raise important questions for it.

The enlargement of the Community to include Spain and Portugal in 1986 had already alerted Europeans to the potential dangers of illegal immigration once the proposed free movement of labour within the single market was implemen-ted. In this context Morocco—the traditional conduit for African immigration into Spain—was seen as the weakest link in the EU's defences, As Peo Hansen has noted, the Spanish enclaves of Melilla and Ceuta in particular 'have come to serve as hubs in the Union's escalating fight against the so-called mounting problem of illegal im-migration from Africa and elsewhere'. With the support of—and no doubt pressure from—the EU, the Spanish government has invested $120 m in constructing a sur-veillance radar system in the Straits of Gibraltar (Hansen 2002, 488). Given the spe-cial ties that different countries have with European Member States—Algeria with France, Morocco with Spain, Somalia with Italy, India, Pakistan, Bangladesh, and the Caribbean countries with Britain—as well as the different colonial experiences that shaped these ties, it is not surprising that the harmonisation of immigration policy within the EU remains a contentious subject.

Secondly, the failure by all European countries to integrate fully post-colonial im-migrants, particularly those from Moslem countries, into their own societies, com-pounded European fears for their own security. Their nervousness was increased with the accelerated rise of political Islam after the attacks on the World Trade Center and Pentagon in the United States in September 2001. As we shall see in the final section of this chapter, after an initial show of solidarity with the US, the war on terror—or rather the way the United States *chose* to prosecute it in Iraq—had a confusing and divisive impact on the EU.

The EU and the processes of international relations

The EU interacts with the former dependencies of its member states on all the major issues of the 21st century. As we have noted in discussion of the evolution of the European system, how it does so is partly a function of external developments and pressures, for example from the UNCTAD during the campaign for a New International Economic Order during the 1970s or as a result of the end of the Cold War between 1989 and 1991, but it also reflects the nature of the Union itself, its history, and the changing interests and priorities that new members have brought to it with each successive enlargement. The EU increasingly values a mix of hard and soft power in its external relations, and is well-placed to exercise both in relation to the poor states within its special, historical, zone of influence.

Until the intervention of 2004 in the Democratic Republic of the Congo, however, the EU (as opposed to individual member states) relied on structured diplomacy, through Lomé and EPC/CFSP. In terms of pure diplomatic style, the EU's relationship with the developing world uniquely combined qualities of ad hoc politicisation, legalism, and bureaucratic proceduralism, in part because of the historical baggage of colonialism. In the view of at least two of the original Rome Treaty signatories—Germany and the Netherlands—the Community should have pursued a global development policy from the outset rather than one that rested on the preservation of colonial relationships on a regional basis. They were forced to concede the principle of association, partly because France insisted on it, but also because France and Belgium could not reasonably be asked to abandon their colonies as customs union theory required. In other words, while the possession of colonies may not have been part of the vision of the new Europe, it created a genuine political problem that would have to be addressed. The same was true in relation to the Commonwealth, when Britain joined in 1973, and to a lesser extent when Spain and Portugal joined in 1986.

The British problem was reduced because, following the first French veto on British accession in 1963, the larger Commonwealth countries had seen the writing on the wall and had taken steps to diversify their economies. Spain and Portugal had close economic ties with Latin American countries, but no post-colonial responsibilities there. The main consequence of Spanish accession—the country was after all separated from Morocco by a mere 15 miles of water—was to strengthen the Community's links with the southern Mediterranean, and of Portugal's to add the Lusophone African countries to the ACP group. The steady widening of the EU/ACP partnership—from 18 African countries who signed the first Yaoundé Convention in 1963 to 77 signatories of the Cotonou Agreement in 2000—was thus not the result of a deliberate plan, but of the Union coming to terms, in a fairly haphazard way, with the political history of its member states.

The fact that not all these states were caught up in post-colonial networks meant that in the argument between the supporters of global and regional approaches to north south relations, the regionalists always had to face intra-European as well as external opponents. To this extent, the Cotonou Agreement, with its emphasis on making EU/ACP relations conform to WTO rules, represents not so much a

Table 14.1 The EEC/EC/EU and the former colonial world

Former Colonial Power	BELGIUM	FRANCE	ITALY	PORTUGAL	SPAIN	UK	OTHER [ ] Former Colonial Power
Year of Accession to EU	1957	1957	1957	1986	1986	1973	
AFRICA							
ACP State and Year of Accession	Zaire/DR Congo 1963 Burundi 1963 Rwanda 1963	Benin 1963 Burkina Faso 1963 Cameroon 1963 Central African Republic 1963 Chad 1963 Congo 1963 Cote d'Ivoire 1963 Djibouti 1979 Gabon 1963 Guinea 1975 Madagascar 1963 Mali 1963 Mauritania 1963 Mauritius 1975 Niger 1963 Senegal 1963 Seychelles 1979 Togo 1963	Eritrea 1995 Somalia 1963	Angola 1985 Guinea Bissau 1975 Mozambique 1984	Equatorial Guinea 1990 Cape Verde 1979 São Tomé and Principe 1979	Botswana 1975 The Gambia 1975 Ghana 1975 Kenya 1969 Lesotho 1975 Malawi 1975 Nigeria 1975 Sierra Leone 1975 South Africa 1997/2000 Sudan 1975 Swaziland 1974 Tanzania 1969 Uganda 1979 Zambia 1975 Zimbabwe 1984	Ethiopia [Independent State] 1975 Liberia [Independent State] 1975 Namibia [Germany, South Africa/UN] 1995

continues

Table 14.1 continued

Former Colonial Power	BELGIUM	FRANCE	ITALY	PORTUGAL	SPAIN	UK	OTHER [ ] Former Colonial Power
CARIBBEAN							
						Antigua and Barbuda 1984 The Bahamas 1975 Barbados 1975 Belize 1984 Dominica 1979 Grenada 1975 Guyana 1975 Jamaica 1975 St. Kitts and Nevis 1984 St. Lucia 1979 St Vincent and the Grenadines 1984 Trinidad and Tobago 1975	Dominican Republic [Independent State] 1984 Haiti [Independent State] 1990 Suriname [Netherlands] 1979
PACIFIC							
		Vanuatu [Condominium with UK] 1984		East Timor 2003		Fiji 1975 Kiribati 1979 Nauru 2000 Solomon Islands 1979 Tonga 1975 Tuvalu 1979 Vanuatu [Condominium with France] 1984	Cook Islands [N.Zealand] 2000 Marshall Islands [Japan/UN/US] 2000 Papua New Guinea [Germany/Australia] 1979 Palau [Japan/US] 1975 Federated States of Micronesia [Japan/US] 2000 Niue [Japan/US] 2000 Samoa [Germany/ N.Zealand] 1975

Source: Compiled by the author from information on the EU website (www.http://europa.eu.int/comm/development/index_en.htm)

complete break with the past as a change in the balance of power—or at least argument—within the Union itself.

The Community's Development Policy was slow to develop prior to the Maastricht Treaty of 1992. Nevertheless, compared with the bilateral relations that developed between many post-colonial and their former metropolitan governments, the EU system seems excessively formal. This may have been partly because the system originated in French colonial policy, which had envisaged the eventual assimilation of colonial populations and their participation in a French Community on theoretically equal terms—most of the first generation of francophone African leaders had served in the governments of the Fourth Republic. But it is also because the EU is not a state and could not act in external affairs as though it possessed a single will. Everything had first to be negotiated amongst the member states and then with either the ACP states collectively or, in the case of the Mediterranean countries, on a bilateral basis. These negotiations resulted in a series of five-year Conventions named after the African cities in which they took place. The first two (1963, 1969) were in Yaoundé, capital of the Cameroons, the next five (1974, 1979, 1984, 1990, and 1995) in Lomé, capital of Togo. In 2000, a new 20-year agreement was negotiated in Cotonou in the Republic of Mali (see Box 14.1).

Prior to the Cotonou Agreement, which includes some new features, all the Conventions retained the same essential structure. The belief that they constituted a model approach to north south relations was largely based on their institutional framework. EU/ACP cooperation—and in this respect Cotonou continues the tradition—is based on the principles of sovereignty and equality and overseen by a Joint Council of Ministers, a Committee of Ambassadors, and a Joint Parliamentary Assembly. The ACP also maintains a secretariat in Brussels to service the relationship on a day-to-day basis. All the Conventions have provided for preferential trade access (from 1974 on a non reciprocal basis) for the majority of ACP exports on terms better than those available within the GATT under the GSP. Under the first two Lomé Conventions two new schemes were introduced, first to stabilise the price of key agricultural commodities when they crashed (STABEX) and then, when it was realised that insufficient funds were available to include mineral exports in this scheme, another to provide insurance for mineral exporting states (MINEX). Together with the special protocols that were negotiated in 1990 to protect the European market shares of ACP banana, tobacco, rum, beef, and in the case of sugar also its price, these trade measures provided a higher level of protection to countries whose colonial history had been dominated by the development of a single commodity, than anything on offer at the global level.

The Conventions also initially provided automatic access to the EDF, which was separate from the EU budget and, in theory at least, additional to the bilateral aid programmes of the EU member states. In the ACP view, the amounts available under the EDF—it currently stands at ϵ 13.5 billion for the 2002–2007 period—have never been sufficient. It is true that the growth in the fund has not kept pace with the expansion of the ACP group itself, or with inflation, although the fact that there was almost ϵ 9 billion unspent from the previous Lomé Convention suggests that the administration of EU aid leaves much to be desired.

In theory, the administration of the Lomé system was intended to be the responsibility of both sides. ACP ownership of their own development strategy was symbolised by the National Indicative Programmes (NIPs), which they were required to draw up in consultation with the European Commission. In practice, the NIPs did not work well and, over the years, lost their major function of identifying national development priorities. The explanation seems to lie partly in the diversity and complexity of different aid and trade programmes, each with its own decision making procedures, partly in heavy-handed bureaucratic control, which is in turn a result of pressure on the Commission to account for the money spent to the European tax-payer, and partly because many ACP countries lack the capacity to manage the system effectively (Koulaimah-Gabriel 1997, 8).

Had the Lomé system led to significant additional trade and economic diversification, it might have generated the resources to overcome some of these problems, at least on the ACP side of the relationship. But it did not. Between 1970 and 1993, the ACP share of imports to the Community fell from 8.9% to 3%, and in relation to the share of imports from all developing countries from 23.8% in 1960 to 10.31% in 1993 (The Courier 1996).[7] Despite these failures, when the British and German governments suggested that the whole system might have outlived its shelf life and should be replaced by the general provisions of the liberalised international trade regime, the idea met with strong opposition from the ACP countries, but also from France, which not only regarded itself as the architect of the system but had also continued to benefit disproportionately from the award of contracts under the EDF. The EU eventually agreed to negotiate a new agreement, which would preserve the positive aspects of the relationship while smoothing the inevitable adjustment that ACP countries would have to make to survive in an increasingly deregulated global market.

Before turning to the changes introduced under the Cotonou Agreement, it is worth asking whether the Lomé system was indeed a form of institutionalised neo-colonialism, as third world Commonwealth governments had initially insisted and radical critics have always maintained? Certainly, European/ACP relations were (and remain) highly asymmetrical. The apparatus of partnership—the Joint Council, Committee of Ambassadors, and Joint Assembly—was well designed to enhance the *amour propre* of ACP leaders, and to propagate European styles and values amongst them. To this extent, the system can be viewed as a reasonably successful experiment in the exercise of 'soft power'. But in the end the ACP had to take what was on offer, regardless of how far it fell short of their demands. Moreover, the large South and South East Asian countries were excluded from membership from the start on the grounds that their problems—but also one suspects their potential—far exceeded the capacity of the European Community to satisfy their needs. In any case, their own governments made it clear that they were not interested in an association that, notwithstanding its rhetoric, would inevitably be organised along hierarchical lines.

If, therefore, neo-colonialism is interpreted as a system in which real power lies in the former metropolitan centres, while the subordinate partners, despite the trappings of independence, have little or no scope for independent action, the Community would be hard put to escape the charge. If, on the other hand, a neo-colonial relationship is essentially exploitative, designed to transfer wealth from the periphery to the centre, then its accuracy as a description of EEC/ACP relations is unconvincing. With few exceptions—the most obvious being the oil-producing countries—the ACP economies are amongst the most marginal in the world. When South

Africa, a stronger and potentially more competitive country, sought to join the Lomé Convention after the victory of the ANC in 1994, it took protracted negotiations before partial accession could be achieved in 1997 (Hill 2001). A further three years were needed for the EU/South African Trade Agreement to come into effect and even then without trade preferences. This certainly provides evidence of protectionist pressures within the community but hardly of neo-colonial motivation in respect of the rest of the ACP countries. Moreover, as we have seen, over the life of the Conventions, the importance of the ACP countries to the Community progressively declined, not merely in relation to other industrial markets but even in comparison to other countries in the developing world.

In any case, the collapse of communism rendered the debate over neo-colonialism largely irrelevant. In the 1970s, the dependency theorists had argued that the only way for third world countries to develop was to de-link from the capitalist world economy. Even before the end of the Cold War, this argument had lost much of its force, and with the failure of central planning as an alternative development model, its remaining purchase dissipated. The weakest countries were left to accept whatever order the powerful were prepared to organise on their behalf, or to put it more bluntly, to make do with whatever crumbs fell from rich country tables. Bilateral aid programmes were always more important than the EDF, but of the current EU member states, only two—the Netherlands and Denmark—have met the United Nations target for development assistance of 0.7% of GDP. The average in 2001 was 0.33%, scheduled to rise to 0.36% in 2006. It is perhaps not surprising, therefore, that ACP leaders should have been unwilling to give up one of the few associations in which their formal equality of status at least allows them to press their views, even if these seem increasingly Micawberesque.

The hope that 'something will turn up' rather than intellectual conviction has always characterised ACP willingness to follow EU fashions. Under the first Lomé Convention, 10% of the EDF was set aside for projects designed to promote regional integration. The intention was to counter the criticism that the Association had been designed to prevent diversification and to keep ACP primary producers dependent on their European patrons. Since the pattern of trade was slow to respond to this initiative, it led to the quip that African regional integration was limited to 10%. Similarly, the New Economic Partnership for Africa's Development (NEPAD), which was designed to put flesh on South African President Mbeki's 'African Renaissance' project, borrows self-consciously from European experience without paying close attention to African realities. To meet EU and OECD requirements that they should demonstrate ownership of their development strategies in order to qualify for debt relief and financial aid, African countries have introduced a 'peer review' system, borrowed from the original Organisation of European Economic Co-operation (OEEC) countries who were also required to demonstrate collective self help in order to qualify for Marshall aid. A NEPAD secretariat has been set up to work out modalities, but it remains to be seen how it will work.

It is too early to judge whether the Cotonou Agreement will revitalise the EU/ACP relationship or preside over its gradual disintegration. In its statement on the Community's development policy, issued in January 2001, the Council and the Commission did not altogether avoid self-congratulation. They suggested that the policy reflected:

Table 14.2 Overseas development assistance, 2000–2002: EU, EU member states, US, and Japan					
US $m					
	Actual		**As % GNI**		
	2001	**2002**	**2000**	**2001**	**2002**
EC	5961	6561			
EU MSs*	26,288	29,949	0.32	0.33	0.35
combined					
Of which					
Austria	533	520	0.23	0.29	0.26
Belgium	867	1072	0.36	0.37	0.43
Denmark	1634	1643	1.06	1.03	0.96
Finland	389	462	0.31	0.32	0.35
France	4198	5486	0.32	0.32	0.38
Germany	4990	5324	0.27	0.27	0.27
Greece	202	276	0.20	0.17	0.21
Ireland	287	398	0.29	0.33	0.40
Italy	1627	2332	0.13	0.15	0.20
Luxembourg	139	147	0.71	0.76	0.77
Netherlands	3172	3338'	0.84	0.82	0.81
Portugal	268	323	0.26	0.25	0.27
Spain	1737	1712	0.22	0.30	0.26
Sweden	1666	1991	0.80	0.77	0.83
UK	4579	4924	0.32	0.32	0.31
USA	11,429	13,290	0.10	0.11	0.13
Japan	9847	9283	0.28	0.23	0.23

*MS = member states.
Source: author's calculations from OECD data, 2003
(http://www.oecd.org/dataoecd/3/2/22460411.pdf).

The essential solidarity, which is an underlying feature of its international activity. The exercise of such solidarity must be seen as a major political challenge. In accordance with the principles upon which it is based the Union needs to put this message across in every forum and ensure that it is disseminated particularly in the other industrialised countries.

(European Council 2001a, para. 2)

What marks the Agreement off from its predecessors is not so much that it will run for 20 years as that, by the end of this period, EU specific trade protection will have been eradicated, except for the least developed countries. In this respect, solidarity no longer refers to the maintenance of a privileged trading relationship but to the aspiration for a fair international system from which poverty will have been eradicated—indeed, in recent years the concentration in all developed countries has been on helping the poorest of the poor, both poor states and the poorest within states. In other words, there is no longer a doctrinal split between the EU, the Bretton Woods Institutions or even the United States, although many Europeans would no doubt argue that the institutional framework of the EU/ACP relationship gives them a comparative advantage in responding sensitively to the transitional problems of particular countries. Admittedly, the statement did identify six areas—the link between trade and development, support for regional development and cooperation, support for macro-economic policies, transport, food security, and sustainable rural development—on which it plans to refocus its development effort under the new Agreement. But a sceptic might reasonably argue that these areas seem so broad (and so familiar) that it is unlikely that the Union will be able to use them to create a strategy that will avoid the duplication, bureaucratic mismanagement, and other pitfalls of the earlier Conventions.

The EU statement also emphasised 'the prime importance of the quality of the political dialogue with partner countries to ensure coherence between the policy pursued by the country and Community support operations' (European Council 2001a, para. 11). But since it is made clear that this dialogue is intended to concentrate on the role of good governance, transparency, human rights, the rule of law, democracy, and the participation of civil society, precisely those non-economic criteria that have marked all western development policies since the end of the Cold War, it is not immediately clear what the distinctive EU contribution to this process will be. Indeed, the EU statement implicitly recognises this dilemma when, having stated that its review of Community aid has been conducted 'in the framework of the debate on increasing the effectiveness of external Union action', it goes on to say that the success of its development policy 'will determine the European Union's credibility on the international stage' (European Council 2001a, paras 3–4). Much will depend therefore not on the legal and institutional peculiarities of the EU system but on how it acts as a power in its own right, and how it is perceived in this regard throughout the former colonial world. If it does not exploit the one-way street of its political dialogue with the ACP states it will seem weak; if it does, it will seem neo-colonialist.

The EU as a power in international relations

Some answers to the third question raised at the beginning of this chapter have been hinted at in the previous two sections. Despite the opposition of most former colonies to Cold War alliances, it was that strategic confrontation that created the conditions for their independence. At its outset, the support of both super powers for decolonisation had trumped the inclination of the British and French to delay the process. (The Belgians succumbed precipitately, but the weakest of all the imperial states, Portugal, hung on longest, partly because it lacked a democratic anti-colonial opposition, but partly also because it could exploit the US need for a military base in the Azores.) Once they had conceded independence, the former colonial powers had no choice but to develop policies to cover their imperial retreat. Indeed, to a large extent, British and French aid policies represented the price they had to pay to disengage from Empire and to preserve some influence over their former dependencies. They did not need any further ideological justification, although Part IV of the Rome treaty presented the French with an opportunity to spread some of the costs amongst the other signatories, not least Germany, which by this means amongst others literally paid a price for regaining some international respectability.

By contrast, the United States, the Soviet Union, and even the European Community needed a political justification for their third world policies. For reasons stemming directly from its origins after the Second World War, the European Community strongly endorsed a version of the democratic peace argument. From the start, therefore, it predicated its external policies on the exercise of soft rather than hard power. During the Cold War, for obvious reasons, little attention was paid to the democratic part of the theory, although it was a crucial assumption of intra-EEC relations. The fact that when the Treaty of Rome was signed, France was still engaged in a brutal colonial war in Algeria, was also conveniently ignored. Nonetheless, the European model of regional integration was widely exported around the developing world.

The model did not travel well. This was mainly because the circumstances faced by post-war European and post-colonial governments were so different. In Europe, integration was an economic solution to a political problem, whereas in most of Asia, Africa, the Caribbean, and Latin America, it was regarded as a political solution to an economic problem. The development problems of many of these countries, particularly those that associated with the Community under the Yaoundé and Lomé Conventions, were constrained by impoverished small populations. Not only did they not trade much amongst themselves—producing in the colonial fashion what they did not consume and consuming what they did not produce—but their domestic markets were in most cases too small to attract foreign investment. Enlarging the potential resource base and market by regional cooperation seemed to chart a way forward.

Most of these schemes failed for a combination of three reasons (Mayall 1995). First, since intra-regional trade was so small, and there was little to integrate, little did get integrated. Secondly, since all the members of post-colonial regions were poor, the relatively better off were reluctant to open their markets to their poorer neighbours or to share with them what little investment was available. Above all, new states—or rather their leaders—were reluctant to surrender the sovereignty they had so recently gained. Nevertheless, despite a dismal record during the 1960s and 1970s, the prestige of the European model was never totally eclipsed. Paradoxically, regionalisation enjoyed something of a renaissance in both Africa and Latin America during the 1990s as a response to the pressures of globalisation. Since economic liberalisation and democratisation were increasingly if perversely presented as two sides of the same coin, and since many of the East European states, whose velvet revolution had world-wide demonstration effects, aspired to EU membership, it seems likely that the EU's reputation was also enhanced.

Will reputational or soft power of this kind alone be sufficient to protect Europe's global interests in the 21st century? It seems doubtful. Here and there Europe may be the beneficiary of official anti-Americanism, or viewed as a more accessible and less problematic source of western technology and a cheaper source of western higher education, but in the end, as in the past, harder power is likely to exercise a magnetic attraction in the post-colonial world.

After 1960, superpower competition for clients allowed non-aligned states to obtain assistance from both sides and to promote their global agenda, e.g., through the establishment of UNCTAD and the subsequent formation of the Group of 77. Throughout the period, the EEC was viewed by the non-aligned as an important but subordinate part of the Western alliance system. In individual cases—e.g. Indian support for Bangladesh's secession from Pakistan, or Indonesian annexation of East Timor—the Cold War stand-off allowed non-aligned states a freedom of manoeuvre they might not otherwise have enjoyed. On issues of broader concern—e.g. the campaign to establish a New International Economic Order (NIEO), opposition to apartheid and confrontation with white minority regimes in Southern Africa—Europe was primarily viewed (as was the Commonwealth) as a conduit through which to bring pressure to bear on Washington.

It is not clear how much changed, even after the end of the Cold War, despite the increasing attention the EU now pays to conducting regular consultations—in the case of India even at Prime Ministerial level—with non associated South and South East Asian countries to which it is linked by non preferential trade agreements. But there is limited scope for a truly independent EU policy since, as we have seen, there was little to separate the European attitude to the putative new world order—supplementing economic with political conditionality for foreign aid and debt relief, support for democratisation and human rights—from that of the United States and the Bretton Woods institutions. The two partial exceptions concern the issue of intervention and support for the International Criminal Court (ICC). On the latter issue, there is a clear division between the EU and the US, but it also extends to the former colonial world (except for the ACP countries), with most of Asia and the Arab world, like the US, refusing either to sign or ratify.

The debate over intervention is more complex. To the extent that the EU shares the general enthusiasm for basing the post Cold War international system on democratisation, the protection of human rights, and the rule of law, and is prepared to impose political conditions on its economic assistance to promote these goals, it has already committed itself to a more interventionist style in international relations than was customary. It also responded to the epidemic of man-made and natural disasters that followed the end of the Cold War by establishing the European Community Humanitarian Aid Office (ECHO) in 1992. Since then it has funnelled humanitarian assistance to 85 countries, including 30 war zones. Its emergency aid—in 2003 it disbursed Ɛ 485m—is now comparable to the United States, and a new fast track procedure has been set up to enable it to respond more rapidly than in the past.

The more difficult question for Europeans was whether to sanction the use of military force to deal with these humanitarian catastrophes. Since the EU lacked a military capability, the initial European response to this question was channelled through the United Nations Security Council. Some of the bigger member states were part of the grand coalition which on UN authority forced Iraq to withdraw from Kuwait in 1991. British and French public opinion also played a major part in forcing western governments to intervene subsequently to protect the Kurds and the southern Iraqi Shia from Saddam Hussein's savage repression of their post war uprising. On this occasion, there was no return to the Security Council since it was known that a number of members opposed the concept of humanitarian intervention, viewing it as a cover for a new form of western imperialism. But throughout the dramas of 1990-1, collective European diplomacy was put in the shade (Nuttall 2000, 136-48).

Given their justifiable pride in having created a zone of peace in western Europe—probably the most effective security community anywhere in the world—it was the savage wars of the Yugoslav succession that presented the EU with its most serious challenge. The difficulty that the Union had in coordinating its policies, and after playing the leading part in the UN operations in Croatia and Bosnia, the humiliation it suffered when it was forced to hand over the initiative to the Americans, focused European attention on the weaknesses of its foreign and security policy and its lack of a capability to respond quickly to crises when they occurred even in Europe, let alone further afield. By the same token the crisis on the Community's own borders reinforced the EU's preoccupation with geopolitical issues and at first sight further weakened the position of its traditional ACP partners. The NATO Operation in Kosovo, which was again supported by EU member states, although with varying degrees of enthusiasm, was generally not popular outside Europe. Important third world countries such as India saw it as further evidence of the western willingness to flout international law (Schnabel and Thakur 2000).

Closer scrutiny suggests a more ambiguous outcome. The international fallout of the war on terror, which temporarily united the western world in 2001, and of the military occupation of Iraq in 2003, which divided it, make it more than usually difficult to predict the future direction of EU foreign policy, or its probable reception. But, despite their difference over Iraq—with the British supporting the American-led invasion of Iraq and the French leading the international opposition to it—the joint Franco-British initiative to create an EU military capability has gone ahead. The decision to establish a European Rapid Reaction Force was taken against the background of the UN and European failures in former Yugoslavia, but its first mission was carried out, by most accounts more or less successfully, in 2003 in the eastern Congo. While the implications of a European defence capability for NATO remain a contentious issue in trans-atlantic relations—and even within Europe itself—it thus seems possible that, as in the 1960s, the EU may replace the United States as the major external influence, at least in the strategically less sensitive parts of the former colonial world, and in particular in Africa. There are, however, clear geopolitical limits to Europe's influence. Notwithstanding the important European colonial presence in Asia, for example, the EU no longer has much leverage in this large and complex region, despite efforts to build on historic roles in Indo-China and South East Asia, and to build privileged partnerships with India and China. Where the United States is active, and large regional powers are emerging, tradition is insufficient to guarantee Europe a significant role—even if it secures a seat at meetings like ASEM (Asia-Europe Meetings).

Conclusion

What can be said, by way of conclusion, about the driving forces behind the evolution of the Community's post-colonial relations? Clearly, the long shadow cast by Empire has receded. The ACP association, which stood at the apex of the pyramid of privilege in the 1960s, above the Mediterranean and the other developing countries in Asia and Latin America, no longer occupies this position. But the shadow has not been eclipsed altogether, as testified not only by the Congo episode, but also by the controversial 1994 UN Operation Turquoise in Rwanda led by the French, and the

British role in Sierra Leone since 2000. There is no single explanation for the shifts in European priorities that have occurred over the period reviewed in this chapter. Certainly, the neo-colonial analysis favoured by the political left in the 1970s now seems not merely unconvincingly reductionist, but to have mistaken symptoms for causes. Three influences, which together must form part of any explanation, can nonetheless be identified. The first is the contrast between French and British decolonisation, and the way their respective policies carried over into the European Community; the second the process of enlargement; and the third the impact of external events, most particularly the end of the Cold War.

The French clung on much longer than the British to the quasi-federal idea of a French Community as a way of organising post-colonial relations within the United Nations. Their attachment to this idea ultimately stemmed from their imperial ideology of assimilation, contrasting with the British doctrine of indirect rule. Although the French conceded military defeat in Indo-China and political defeat in Algeria, their remaining colonies were far more closely integrated in the political and economic life of France itself than was the case anywhere in the British Empire. Moreover, the *dirigiste* policies favoured in France itself were extended to the colonies. The British view won the general argument by default since the attractions of full membership of the UN proved irresistible even to the most Francophile African leaders. But since Britain remained outside the EEC, it was the French style of diplomacy and their preference for the creation of political institutions through which they could continue to exercise influence that prevailed within the Community. When the British eventually joined in 1973, with help from the Germans and Dutch, the British were able to modify the way the Association worked but not its basic structure. Their own special relations with the large South Asian countries had to be conducted bilaterally, and to some extent through the Commonwealth. Only those countries whose economies were structurally comparable with the existing associates were allowed to join the privileged group.

Once this pattern was established, each successive enlargement led to an expansion of the ACP group but also to pressure on the hierarchy of the Community's relations. The Mediterranean countries had to be treated differently from the ACP because although their special interests, and interdependence with the Community, were recognised, conflicts over French policy towards Algeria and subsequently within the Maghreb itself ruled out a multilateral approach. But with Spanish accession in 1986 the geopolitical arguments for relations with North Africa demanded more attention. Moreover, the accession of Spain and Portugal—and the relentless pressure of market forces—also lent weight to the voices in the Community that had always favoured developing closer relations with Latin America and the ASEAN countries.

In the post-Cold War context, Portugal's support for the independence of East Timor also fuelled the shift away from a predominantly developmental approach to post-colonial relations. Finally, the collapse of communism and the end of the Cold War not merely changed the wider international environment in fundamental ways, but presented the EU with opportunities for eastward expansion, which also inevitably brought with them new political and financial problems. The always-latent ACP fear of a Fortress Europe may have been misplaced, but that the EU would in future be more preoccupied with the development problems of its own neighbourhood, partly at their expense, was undeniable.

Notes

1 Leopold Senghor, the first President of Senegal, cut short the first OAU Council of Ministers meeting in Dakar in 1963 when it threatened to interfere with his annual holiday in Normandy. In Yaoundé, in the mid 1970s, the major attraction for the elite was the arrival of the weekly supply plane, bringing fresh French vegetables from Paris, despite the abundance of locally grown alternatives. In Calcutta in the late 1980s, the ruling Politburo of the West Bengal Communist Party dined to the accompaniment of their favourite TV programme, 'Yes Minister'. It would not be difficult to find such anecdotal evidence from all over the post-colonial world.

2 In India, a post-independence survey to establish what the villagers thought of the changes in government since the end of British rule in 1947, had to be abandoned when it was discovered that the majority of peasants were unaware that the British had ever been there.

3 The GATT was salvaged by the US government as the one part of the Havana Charter for which they could secure Congressional support. The judged that the Charter as a whole, which aimed to establish an International Trade Organisation, contained too many departures from liberal principles to have any chance of success.

4 The Asian ex-colonies of the UK were excluded from Lomé, but did not in any case wish to enter, preferring bilateral agreements and a freedom from the kind of collective institutions that the Commonwealth African states were eventually persuaded to accept. On the Nigerian position, see Aluko (1981, 73–81).

5 President Kennedy had appointed General Lucius Clay to head the Foreign Aid Committee in the hope that his reputation as a conservative would ease the aid budget through the Congress (Schlesinger 1967, 473–7).

6 Article 9 also stipulates that good governance underpins the ACP-EU Partnership, although in a charming concession to realism it also notes that 'The Parties agree that only serious cases of corruption including of bribery... constitute a violation of this element.'

7 Quoted in Sophia Price, 'The Political Economy of the EU's external relations', paper presented to the ECPR Rotating Summer school, European Institute of the University of Geneva, p23. http://www.ulb.ac.be/iee/ecpr/index.htm.

Further reading

On decolonisation, good starting points are Holland (1985) and Smith (1978). The economic background is discussed in Maddison (1995) and Tomlinson (1999).

For the impact of the Cold War and of US foreign policy on European relations with the former colonial world, see Mayall (1971), Darwin (1988) and Bull and Louis

(1986). The early history of Africa's relations with the European Community, up to and including the abortive agreement between Nigeria and the EEC, is the subject of Okigbo (1967). Fawcett and Hurrell (1995) is a useful point of departure for studying the wider demonstration effect of the European model. EU development policy is discussed in Lister (1999) and Holland (2002), and the incorporation of ACP relations in the CFSP in Smith (2002). A WEU working paper (2004) examines the evolving security relationship.

Bull, H., and Louis, W.R. (eds) (1986), *The Special Relationship: Anglo-American Relations since 1945* (Oxford: Oxford University Press).

Darwin, J. (1988), *Britain and Decolonisation: The Retreat from Empire in the Postwar World* (London: Macmillan).

Fawcett, L., and Hurrell, A. (eds) (1995), *Regionalism in World Politics: Regional Organisation and International Order* (Oxford: Oxford University Press).

Holland, M. (2002), *The European Union and the Third World* (Basingstoke: Palgrave).

Holland, R. (1985), *European Decolonisation, 1918–1981: An Introductory Survey* (Basingstoke: Macmillan).

Lister, M. (ed.) (1999), *New Perspectives on European Union Development Cooperation* (Boulder, CO: Westview Press).

Maddison, A. (1995), *Monitoring the World Economy, 1820–1992* (Paris: OECD).

Mayall, J. (1971), *Africa: The Cold War and After* (London: Elek Books).

Okigbo, P. (1967), *Africa and the Common Market* (London: Longmans).

Smith, H. (2002), *European Foreign Policy: What it is and What it Does* (London: Pluto Press).

Smith, T. (1978), 'A Comparative Study of French and British Decolonisation,' *Comparative Studies in Society and History vol. 20/1, pp 70–102*.

Tomlinson, B. (1999) 'Imperialism and After: The Economy of the Empire on the Periphery', in Brown, J.M., and Roger Louis, W.M. (eds), *The Oxford History of the British Empire, Vol. IV, The Twentieth Century* (Oxford: Oxford University Press).

WEU (2004), *The European Union and Peacekeeping in Africa* (Doc. C/1880, Assembly of the WEU, 9 November).

Web links

The most useful web site for EU development policy activities and issues is the Europa site: http://www.europa.eu.int/pol/dev/. See also the web site of the ACP Secretariat: http://www.apcsec.org/, which presents a variety of documents and topics for discussion from the perspective of the EU's partners under the Cotonou Agreement. Many of the web sites cited in Chapter 15, on inter-regional relations, are also useful here.

Chapter 15
The EU and Inter-regional Cooperation

Nicole Alecu de Flers and Elfriede Regelsberger

Contents

Summary

Europe's emergence as a key player, if not 'power', in world politics, capable not only of responding to but also shaping the global challenges of the 21st century, has to be understood against the background of developments over the 1990s—both internal to the EU and international. Inter-regional cooperation has turned out to be one of the most attractive frameworks for both the EU and third countries to meet their respective foreign policy interests. It corresponds to the EU's own wish to pool national resources and to resolve conflicts through dialogue and negotiation, with all parties having an equal standing. It offers support to processes of regionalisation elsewhere in the world and enables the participating groupings to respond more effectively to globalisation, thus improving their profiles as collective actors. The notion of inter-regional dialogues covers a sometimes confusing variety of formats, which differ with regard to the objectives, the legal basis, the actors involved and the agenda. In terms of its geographic focus the EU's immediate neighbourhood (the Mediterranean Basin, the Western Balkans) has become the top priority while other traditional partners in Africa and Latin America, and to some extent also in Asia, rank second best.

Introduction

Gone are the days when the then EC was judged a political 'dwarf', with hardly any say in international politics. The completion of the EU Internal Market and the introduction of the Euro worked as driving forces towards a strengthening of Europe's profile in foreign and security policy. What became known as the Common Foreign and Security Policy (CFSP) set the priority on the stabilisation of Europe's immediate neighbourhood in the hope that, after the fall of the Berlin wall, its young and fragile democracies would turn towards the EU. Yet new threats and even wars also emerged from the region after the dissolution of Yugoslavia. The subsequent events, of 11 September 2001 and 11 March 2004, as well as the war against Iraq in 2003, have made obvious Europe's vulnerability towards new challenges like international terrorism, Islamist fundamentalism, and the spread of new weapons of mass destruction. They have reinforced the wish of the EU and its member states to have an active foreign policy and to pursue global strategies in close cooperation with other parts of the world.

This chapter focuses on one distinct feature of how the EU tries to respond to those international challenges: the system of the EU's relations with other groups of states. It describes both the conceptual framework and the real performance of inter-regional cooperation. Particular emphasis is placed on the dialogue formats which exist at the time of writing (2004) and which are geared towards some form of permanent structures. In order to better understand the complexity of these structures, the regions of the world are differentiated. Not surprisingly a number of dialogue formats are not treated extensively here, since they have either faded away (as did that with the Central and Eastern European countries once they became EU members), have been subsumed into other models (as with the Euro-Arab dialogue) and/or are to be understood as ad hoc working relations between the European Commission and third partners (like the numerous ties with regional groupings in Africa, e.g. the West African Economic and Monetary Union (WAEMU) or the Common Market for Eastern and Southern Africa (COMESA), but also in Europe, such as the Barents Euro-Arctic Council (BEAC) or the Black Sea Economic Cooperation (BSEC)).

Inter-regional cooperation as part of the EU's foreign and security policy

The relations of the EU and its member states with other groups of states are not an accidental development. They are a direct result of the EU construction proper and Europe's own posture as a regional organisation. Therefore the logic of inter-regional cooperation derives from the successful European model, which has transformed the relations between formerly warring parties into some sort of a cooperative structure where divergent interests are tackled and resolved by negotiation (Fawcett 1995, 23ff). Although not explicitly mentioned in the Treaty on European Union as one objective of the EU's role in the world, the EU and its member states hope that their model will be adopted by other regions/groups of states, thus fostering intra-regional processes and actors elsewhere (Regelsberger in Edwards and Regelsberger 1990, 3ff). Inter-regional cooperation is therefore neither bound to a specific geographical area nor oriented primarily towards safeguarding the EU's economic interests. Basic principles governing the EU's own integration, like the rule of law, democratic institutions, and a respect for human rights, are perceived as key values both to be 'exported' to other regions and to play an important role in the dialogue processes today. In times of global interdependence regional cooperation may also serve to establish alliances with other groups of states sharing similar economic and trade interests, thus increasing one's own negotiation power in international organisations like the World Trade Organization (WTO), or the various arms of the United Nations (UN). Furthermore, and of increasing importance, are new challenges like terrorism and organised crime, which have forced the EU—as reaffirmed in the EU's 'Security Strategy' of 2003—to put the emphasis on modes of 'effective multilateralism', with the UN at its core, but also through the establishment of 'strategic partnerships' with countries and regional groupings in the Middle East, Africa, Asia, and Latin America (*A secure Europe in a better world* 2003a; Council of the European Union 2004, 11f).

Inter-regional cooperation, however, is but one tool of the EU's international presence (Regelsberger 1998, 2). Others, like the permanent dialogues with the United States and Russia or the association and stabilisation/enlargement policies towards the newly emerging states in South Eastern Europe are similarly relevant and require the EU's serious attention. The relevance of inter-regional cooperation has changed—if not reached its limits—over time, not least due to new international challenges. The EU has recently been forced to set geographical priorities and to adjust its instruments, so as to have a concrete presence in the field, through such Joint Actions as election observation, or through special representatives in the Middle East and the Great Lakes region of central Africa (Forster and Wallace 2000, 482ff; Allen and Smith, M. 2002, 99). Furthermore, the demands have grown to equip the 'civilian' power EU with the military means which were urgently needed in the crisis management operations in Macedonia, Bosnia, and the Democratic Republic of Congo (Dembinski 2002).

Inter-regional cooperation as a foreign policy objective of the EU depends on the EU's capacity to perform as a viable interlocutor and to have appropriate instruments at hand. Since competences in the field of external relations are split between the EU organs and the member states, the number of participants and the requirements for intra-European coordination are high. The accession of another ten countries to the EU as from 1 May 2004 onwards has made the system even more complex. The political guidelines are usually defined in the CFSP framework and articulated at the highest political level, i.e. the European Council and the Council, while 'beefing' them up with substance, in the form of trade preferences, economic assistance or other sorts of financial aid, is traditionally the responsibility of the European Commission. Certain dialogue formats like the Asia-Europe Meetings (ASEM) or the 'Barcelona Process' involve a great number of other actors ranging from the business world to cultural organisations and the national parliamentary level, which in turn requires additional streamlining and coordination.

Traditionally the EU Presidency is the key actor. It not only carries the heavy burden of preparing the positions inside the EU. It is also responsible for coordinating the European *acquis* with that of the dialogue partners, and has to act as the chair at the respective meetings. At the same time the presidential term enables a government to set its specific mark on a preferred dialogue project, thus presenting itself as an active and successful 'player' in the name of Europe. Illustrative in this respect were the efforts of the German government in 1978 to start cooperation with the Association of South East Asian Nations (ASEAN), the Spanish initiative for the second European Latin American summit in Madrid in 2002, and the Portuguese endeavours to organise the second meeting of heads of state and government between Europe and Africa in 2003.

The constant growth of the dialogue commitments, together with the other increased responsibilities of the Presidency in the area of the CFSP and the European Security and Defence Policy (ESDP), have clearly revealed the shortcomings of the system of six-monthly rotating Presidencies. The ignorance from outside towards the EU spokesman when it is in the hands of a small EU member state—as demonstrated by the United States' attitude towards the Belgian government in the aftermath of 11 September 2001—together with the prospect of EU enlargement, have given rise to a fundamental reconsidering of the existing procedures since then. The European Convention and the subsequent Intergovernmental Conference during 2003–2004 agreed to replace the rotating Presidency for the Foreign Affairs Council (and other subordinate CFSP bodies like the Political and Security Committee [PSC]) by a permanent figure. Instead of confronting the dialogue partners with ever changing European 'faces', a greater permanence and profile is expected, in particular from the creation of a Union Minister for Foreign Affairs assisted by a new European External Action Service, to be composed of national diplomats from the member states, officials from the Council Secretariat and the European Commission. Until this proposal of the recent EU reform debate materialises (*Treaty Establishing a Constitution for Europe* 2004, Articles I-28; III-296), the constraints of the old system will continue and may require additional steps to pare down the existing dialogue obligations. However, here the EU finds itself in a tricky situation since cutting down the frequency and level of meetings, or reducing the number of EU participants in the Troika formula or the Presidency alone, may be interpreted by the other side as a general downgrading of its status. Equally, the EU's declared desire to extend its global international presence further, through bi-regional summits attended by a

Box 15.1 Historical overview on inter-regional cooperation

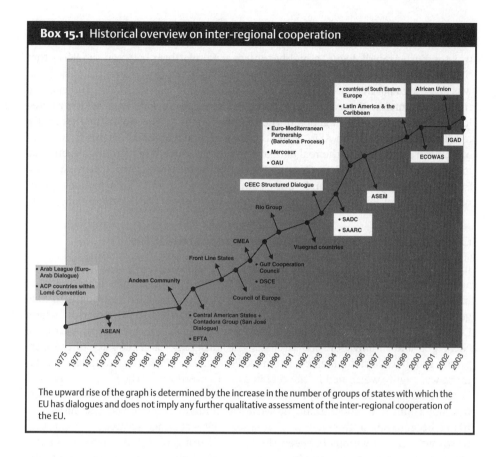

The upward rise of the graph is determined by the increase in the number of groups of states with which the EU has dialogues and does not imply any further qualitative assessment of the inter-regional cooperation of the EU.

huge number of high-level participants, calls for an even greater involvement of both EU and national representatives—and a heavier workload for the Presidency.

Old and new forms of cooperation—an historical overview

The origins—relations with Africa, the Mediterranean Basin, and ASEAN in the 1970s

The origins of the group-to-group approach can be traced back to the association agreements of Yaoundé I, II (1963 and 1969) and of Arusha (1968–9) linking a number of former colonies in Africa with the then EC, and extending after the first round of enlargement to cooperation with the signatories of the Lomé Convention of 1975. However, inter-regional cooperation at that time was more a response to specific historical ties than the expression of a genuine European foreign policy design. Group-to-group relations began to take further shape in the mid-1970s (see Box 15.1) when the crises in the Mediterranean Basin and the Arab-Israeli conflict forced the EC member states towards some sort of a collective role to respond to new external challenges and to safeguard the economic well-being of their countries. The result was the Euro-Arab dialogue, a highly controversial platform between the EC at that time and the Arab League, which faded away in the 1980s (Regelsberger 1998, 2) and was integrated partly into the framework of cooperation with the Mediterranean and the Gulf countries. Thereafter contacts were extended towards Asia, which ranked low on the foreign policy agenda of the member states at that time. The first ministerial conference between ASEAN and the then EC and its member states in 1978 has often been referred to as the real date of birth of the concept of a group-to-group dialogue which its protagonists (German Foreign Minister Hans-Dietrich Genscher and European Commissioner Claude Cheysson) wished to promote as a new model for both a consistent European foreign policy and the future of the international system.

Extension towards Central America and Europe in the 1980s

Inter-regional cooperation entered a remarkable period of growth in the 1980s, partly as an immediate answer to the explicit wish of the Europeans not only to react to international events but to shape them, partly as an immediate response to dangerous developments outside. It first expanded towards Central America, where Europe was eager and able to help pacify relations between the warring parties in Nicaragua and El Salvador, and to foster the intra-regional diplomacy of the Contadora group (Colombia, Mexico, Panama, Venezuela). While the European engagement was highly welcomed in the region as a counterpoise to the United States, the latter found it difficult to accept this new European presence in its immediate neighbourhood (Smith, H. 1995). Dialogue with the Contadora Group was also highly dynamic because Spain, then a new EC member state, attached particular importance to strengthening relations between the EC and Latin America. A further diversification took place with the establishment of regular contacts with the emerging Rio Group (which in its composition partly overlaps with the Contadora Group), mainly for economic reasons.

The political change in the Soviet Union in 1985 marked the start of a renewal of relations with the Central and Eastern European countries, which only a few years later were to become the most privileged group to be associated with the EU, finally entering as new members on 1 May 2004. With German diplomacy again in the vanguard, inter-regional cooperation was extended to the non-EC members of the Council of Europe and to the countries of the European Free Trade Association (EFTA) in order not to exclude them from joint European foreign policy positions. Most of them would then receive privileged access to the EU and the CFSP when they later became EU applicants.

The mid-1980s also saw the establishment of contacts between the EC and the Front Line States to the north of South Africa, an immediate political response to the increasing criticism of European tolerance of the Apartheid regime in Pretoria. Finally, regular diplomatic links were established with the Gulf Cooperation Council (GCC), to secure oil supplies and to promote trade, but also to demonstrate solidarity with those moderate Arab states threatened by the Iran/Iraq war and Islamist fundamentalism. Thus the already complex picture of inter-regional partnerships was further developed.

New regionalism after the end of the East-West divide

From the mid-1990s onwards, inter-regional cooperation has grown and diversified considerably. On the one hand this new regionalism has much to do with the EU's decision to enlarge to an EU of 25/27, thus associating the new democracies in Eastern Europe, plus Cyprus and Malta, with the objectives, instruments, and policies of the emerging CFSP as soon as possible; on the other hand the immediate, but not necessarily tranquil, European neighbourhood was to become the preferred area for EU action. The effects thereof were manifold: the focus on the candidate countries implied intensified links between them and the EU at all levels. Although those among the applicants which were most advanced in terms of political stability and economic development favoured an individual approach in their relations with the EU, 'Brussels' set the tone and insisted on a group-to-group basis, starting with the Visegrad Four—even if bilateral links, as through individual association agreements, were not completely excluded (Monar 1997b, 270).

Behind this strategy lay both organisational and political motives. The first related to the fact that the management of the CFSP, and in particular the dialogue commitments (both the group-to-group structures and the other numerous regular meetings with individual third countries), had reached its limits. An intolerable pressure of business was being imposed upon the Presidency. The other line of reasoning had to do with the EU's explicit desire to see intra-regional cooperation emerge as a key feature of the 'new Europe'. The Stability Pact, with its various round tables under the authority of an EU Special Representative, constitutes one mode. Another is the 'structured dialogue' which became the preferred forum to prepare the EU newcomers for accession, and which included regular information on the EU's international relations. For all those countries in the Western Balkans not yet able to fulfil the Copenhagen criteria for EU membership but eager to be associated as closely as possible with the EU, because of its attractiveness as a provider of political stability, security, and economic growth, another framework took shape. Initiated mainly by the Greek Presidency in 2003, an 'EU–Western Balkans Forum' was inaugurated. Designed as a regular group-to-group dialogue at a high political level, it complements the existing links between the EU and the countries of the region, known as the Stabilisation and Association Process (SAP), which precisely promote intra-regional cooperation as a precondition for closer ties with Brussels.

This somewhat Eurocentric approach had to be compensated by intensified relations with the countries of the 'south' as some, both inside and outside the EU, argued (Telò 2001, 182). The 'Barcelona Process', i.e. the Euro-Mediterranean Partnership between the EU and the countries bordering the southern and eastern shores, was designed along the model of the former Conference on Security and Cooperation in Europe (CSCE), today's Organisation for Security and Cooperation in Europe (OSCE). More than once the fate of the Barcelona Process has been endangered by the course of events in the Arab-Israeli conflict, and the dialogue structures are hardly sufficient to moderate the positions of the two conflicting parties (Gomez 1998). Most recently and as an immediate reaction to the escalation of violence in the Middle East and beyond, i.e. Iraq and the threat of terrorism, the EU is in the process of re-defining this cooperation towards an 'EU Strategic Partnership' (*Interim Report on an EU Strategic Partnership with the Mediterranean and the Middle East* 2004).

The EU's shift in regional priorities has not gone unnoticed in the other parts of the world. Whenever new regionalisation tendencies emerged after the end of the Cold War, the EU showed interest in supporting them as a means of stabilising international relations and of establishing regular ties with other collective actors. This was the case with the Southern African Development Community (SADC) and the Organization of African Unity (OAU—since 2002 the African Union (AU)), institutions to which the EU attaches considerable weight, hoping that they might play a key role in stabilising the African continent. In an attempt to offer some compensation for its policies towards Eastern Europe, the EU also offered the states of Africa a new (if mainly symbolic) 'strategic partnership', which is to manifest itself in regular high-level summit meetings. So far only one has taken place (in 2000), while EU internal divergences over the participation of Zimbabwe (centred on the Franco-British dispute over the application of sanctions to Zimbabwe) led to the cancellation of the second summit in 2003.

Yet another new 'strategic partnership' was designed for Latin America in 1999. Here again symbolism plays a major role. In order both to compensate for the focus on the 'near abroad' and to underline its role as a global player, the EU introduced this new bi-regional approach. The aim is to have meetings at the highest political level which will constitute the overarching 'roof' for all the other traditional sub-regional cooperation models the EU uses with Mercosur, the Andean Community, and the San José Group.

In the case of the renewed and intensified relations with Asia from the late 1990s, the factor of economic globalisation was decisive. Initially launched by non-governmental actors (i.e. business interests), governments on both sides felt the need to set up an institutional framework at both high political (summits) and expert levels, which would foster mutual trade and inter-regional economic cooperation, and which would lead to joint positions in the negotiations of international organisations like the WTO and the International Monetary Fund (IMF). Accordingly the Asia-Europe Meetings (ASEM) were set up in 1996, bringing together representatives of 35 countries in all.

The EU and inter-regional cooperation in action—main features

The EU and Africa

Inter-regional cooperation here is marked on the one hand by the historic links of several EU member states with the African continent, due to their colonial past. This is most obvious in the contractual relationship between the EU and the African, Caribbean, and Pacific countries (the ACPs), which over the years has also been diversified along the lines of specific political and/or economic sub-groupings in Africa (see Box 15.2). On the other hand, to the extent that Africa as a whole has managed to organise itself as a viable interlocutor, a new strategic partnership has been constructed since 2000.

Box 15.2 The dialogue in action — key structures

The dialogue partners listed below are grouped in alphabetical order by geographical area (Africa, Asia, Europe, Latin America, Mediterranean/Gulf region) and listed within each area in chronological order according to the start of inter-regional cooperation with the EC/EU.

Dialogue partners	Start/main events	Frequency and levels of meetings
ACP Group **(African, Caribbean and Pacific Group)** (at present 79 countries of Africa, the Caribbean and the Pacific)	• 1975 Lomé I Convention • 1979 Lomé II Convention • 1984 Lomé III Convention • 1989 Lomé IV Convention • 2000 Cotonou Agreement	• annual meetings of Council of Ministers • meetings of Committee of Ambassadors once per month • meetings of Joint Assembly twice a year
SADC **(Southern African Development Community)** (Angola, Botswana, Democratic Republic of the Congo, Lesotho, Malawi, Mauritius, Mozambique, Namibia, Seychelles, South Africa, Swaziland, Tanzania, Zambia, Zimbabwe)	• 1994 Berlin Initiative	• regular meetings at the level of foreign ministers and officials
OAU/since 2002: AU **(Organization for African Unity/African Union)** (53 out of the 54 countries in Africa)	• 2000 first EU-Africa Summit in Cairo • Cairo Declaration and Action Plan	• meetings at summit, ministerial and senior officials level
ECOWAS **(Economic Community of West African States)** (Benin, Burkina Faso, Cape Verde, Côte d'Ivoire, Gambia, Ghana, Guinea, Guinea-Bissau, Liberia, Mali, Niger, Nigeria, Senegal, Sierra Leone, Togo)	• 2000 initiation of high-level political dialogue	• regular meetings at ministerial and senior officials level
IGAD **(Intergovernmental Authority on Development)** (Djibouti, Eritrea, Ethiopia, Kenya, Somalia, Sudan, Uganda)	• 2003 first political dialogue meeting in the margins of the IGAD Summit in Kampala/Uganda	• meetings at ministerial level (EU Troika)

continues

Box 15.2 continued

ASEAN **(Association of South East Asian Nations)** (Brunei, Burma/Myanmar, Cambodia, Indonesia, Laos People's Democratic Republic, Malaysia, Philippines, Singapore, Thailand, Vietnam)	• 1978 first ministerial conference • 1980 Cooperation Agreement	• ministerial conferences every second year • meetings of senior officials between ministerial meetings • meetings of the Joint Cooperation Committee usually every 18 months • ASEAN Regional Forum
ASEM **(Asia-Europe Meeting)** (EU member states and European Commission with thirteen Asian countries (Brunei, Burma/Myanmar, Cambodia, China, Indonesia, Japan, Laos, Malaysia, the Philippines, Singapore, South Korea, Thailand, Vietnam))	• 1996 first ASEM Summit in Bangkok • 1998 second ASEM in London • 2000 third ASEM in Seoul • 2002 fourth ASEM in Copenhagen • 2004 fifth ASEM in Hanoi	• summit-level meetings every second year • ministerial-level meetings in the intervening years (although now normally once a year), foreign ministers and others • range of meetings at senior official and working levels • Asia Europe Business Forum, Asia Europe Foundation and other non-governmental organisations
SAARC **(South Asian Association for Regional Cooperation)** (Bangladesh, Bhutan, India, the Maldives, Nepal, Pakistan, Sri Lanka)	• 1994 initiation of political dialogue • 1996 Memorandum of Understanding between EC and SAARC Secretariat	• ministerial meetings
OSCE **(Organization for Security and Cooperation in Europe)** (55 member states from Europe, Central Asia and North America)	• involvement of the European Community in the Helsinki Process from its beginning • since 1989 official representation of the EC/EU at CSCE/OSCE meetings by a representative of the country holding the EU Presidency and a representative of the European Commission	• regular meetings at the beginning of each EU Presidency between the respective Troikas and the OSCE Secretary General at the ministerial level • regular gatherings at senior official and working party levels

continues

Box 15.2 continued

EFTA **(European Free Trade Association)** (at present: Iceland, Liechtenstein, Norway, Switzerland)	• 1984 Luxembourg Declaration • 1992 Agreement creating the European Economic Area (EEA)	• ministerial meetings • High-Level Contact Group • expert groups
Council of Europe (i.e. its non-EC/EU members)	• 1987 arrangement between European Commission and Council of Europe • 2001 Joint Declaration on Cooperation and Partnership	• twice yearly political-level meetings between the EU Presidency and the Commission, and as well as the Council of Europe Chairmanship and Secretary General
countries of South Eastern Europe (Albania, Bosnia and Herzegovina, Croatia, FYROM, Serbia and Montenegro)	• 1999 Stabilisation and Association Process (SAP) proposed • 2000 Zagreb Summit • 2003 EU-Western Balkans Summit of Thessaloniki	• EU-Western Balkans Forum (high political level, i.e. foreign ministers since end of 2003, ministers of justice and home affairs)
Andean Community (Bolivia, Colombia, Ecuador, Peru, Venezuela)	• 1983 first Framework Agreement on Cooperation • 1993 second Framework Agreement on Cooperation • 1996 Declaration of Rome • 2003 Political Dialogue and Cooperation Agreement	• ad hoc presidential and ministerial meetings • bi-annual meetings of Joint Committee; annual meetings of Joint Sub-Committees for Cooperation • special high-level dialogue on drugs
Central American States **('San José Dialogue')** (Costa Rica, El Salvador, Guatemala, Honduras, Nicaragua, Panama)	• 1984 ministerial meeting in San José[a] • 1985 Cooperation Agreement • 1993 Framework Cooperation Agreement • 2003 Political Dialogue and Cooperation Agreement • 2004 first summit meeting in Guadalajara, Mexico	• annual ministerial conferences • regular meetings of Joint Committee and Sub-Committee for Cooperation

continues

Box 15.2 continued

Rio Group (Andean Community + Central American states + Mercosur + Mexico, Chile, the Dominican Republic, as well as a representative from the Caribbean Community)	• 1990 Rome agreement	• annual ministerial meetings
Mercosur **(Common Market South America)** (Argentina, Brazil, Paraguay, Uruguay)	• 1995 Inter-regional Framework Cooperation Agreement • 13 rounds of association negotiations from 1999 to May 2004	• political dialogue at the heads of state/ government level, ministerial and senior officials levels • meetings of the EU-Mercosur Cooperation Council in 1999 and 2001
Latin America and the Caribbean (33 countries)	• 1999 first summit in Rio de Janeiro • 2002 second summit in Madrid • 2004 third summit in Guadalajara/Mexico	• summits between the heads of state/ government of Latin America, the Caribbean and the EU
Gulf Cooperation Council (Bahrain, Kuwait, Oman, Qatar, Saudi Arabia, United Arab Emirates)	• 1989 Cooperation Agreement	• annual meetings of foreign ministers at Joint Council/Ministerial Meetings • since 1995 talks of senior officials twice a year and at expert level
Euro-Mediterranean Partnership (**'Barcelona Process'**) (Algeria, Egypt, Israel, Jordan, Lebanon, Morocco, the Palestinian Authority, Syria, Tunisia, Turkey, Cyprus, Malta; Libya has observer status at certain meetings)	• 1995 Conference of EU foreign ministers in Barcelona • 2000 EU Common Strategy • 2003/2004 Wider Europe—New Neighbourhood Initiative/EU Strategic Partnership for the Mediterranean and the Middle East	• conferences of foreign ministers every 18 months and mid-term ministerial meetings • sectoral ministerial conferences • on average three meetings of the Euro-Mediterranean Committee per Council Presidency • numerous meetings at senior official and expert levels • Euromed Parliamentary Assembly and Cultural Foundation

[a] This meeting was attended by the EC ministers of foreign affairs and their equivalents from the Central American states and the Contadora Group (Colombia, Mexico, Panama, Venezuela).

The ACP Group, which at present comprises 79 countries, is the biggest group with which the EC/EU has group-to-group relations. They started in 1975 with the Lomé Convention which was a 'comprehensive trade and aid agreement' (Gibb 2000, 457) gradually made more sophisticated (Lomé II-IV, 1978–89), culminating in June 2000 in the Cotonou Agreement, which entered into force in 2003 and lasts for ten years. Furthermore, while under the Lomé Convention the ACP states were permitted to erect tariff barriers against European goods, whereas ACP (non-agricultural) exports had access to the European market (Gibb 2000, 457), the ACP countries and the EU are currently negotiating Economic Partnership Agreements by which all trade barriers between the EU and ACP sub-regions will be progressively removed (European Commission 2003b, 10). One aim is to support sub-regional integration processes in Africa. EU cooperation combined with specific funding instruments is already under way with a number of regional groupings, e.g. with the Economic Community of West African States (ECOWAS) and the Central African Economic and Monetary Community (CEMAC).[1]

Solidarity within African sub-regional groupings has been shaped by the fight against apartheid (Schmuck in Edwards and Regelsberger 1990, 49). This was the case with the Front Line States (Angola, Botswana, Mozambique, Tanzania, Zambia, Zimbabwe) with which the EC established contacts as early as in 1986. After the end of the apartheid regime in South Africa these contacts were transformed into a regular dialogue between the EU and the members (currently 14) of the Southern African Development Community (SADC) (Regelsberger 1998, 3). Initiated in 1994 under the German Presidency, cooperation includes regular ministerial sessions and a number of issues ranging from trade and development cooperation to matters of security, environment and cultural cooperation (European Commission 2003b, 32ff; Dembinski 2002, 32).

As with the dialogue at the sub-regional level, discussions within the ACP-EU Council, the Committee of Ambassadors and the Joint Parliamentary Assembly went beyond trade issues to include social and cultural problems, as well as such political issues as the promotion of democracy, good governance, the rule of law and human rights (Schmuck in Edwards and Regelsberger 1990, 46ff). This includes the definition and introduction of precise consultation and sanction mechanisms in the treaty, in case a signatory state should violate the basic principles of the agreement.

The continental-wide approach the EU has established with the Organization of African Unity (OAU)—today the African Union (AU)—has its roots in the mid-1990s when the European Council declared itself in favour of a more active role regarding the prevention of conflicts in Africa, particularly in the Great Lakes region, where the EU also has a presence through a Special CFSP Representative (Aldo Ajello) and where the EU military crisis management operation 'Artemis' was successfully conducted in 2003. Furthermore, the EU is ready to support other fora, such as the Intergovernmental Authority on Development (IGAD), which is attempting to resolve conflicts in the Horn of Africa.

EU pan-African relations gained a temporary new momentum in 2000 when African and European heads of state met for the first (and so far only) time in Cairo to create a framework for discussion of a wide range of topics of mutual interest. Besides the European concerns mentioned above, the priority issues of this dialogue are: external debt, the return of stolen cultural goods, conflict prevention, HIV/AIDS, food security, and the environment (European Commission 2003b, 7). The ambitious format and agenda (the Cairo Action Plan contains no fewer than 130 separate items) turned out to be less effective than initially assumed. Attempts have been made to streamline both the institutional set-up and the agenda of the dialogue at regular high-level meetings. There are also hopes that the recent (2001) New Partnership for Africa's Development (NEPAD) might be placed under the auspices of the AU.

The EU and the Mediterranean and the Gulf region

Geographic proximity and the direct vulnerability of Europe's political and economic well-being to developments on the southern shores of the Mediterranean and the Middle East region have been the driving forces for what is known today as the Euro-Mediterranean (Euromed) Partnership and the EU's cooperation with the Gulf Co-operation Council. The former was officially launched in 1995 at a foreign ministers' conference in Barcelona, with strong backing from the southern EU member states, eager to counterbalance the preoccupation of certain of their partners with Eastern Europe (Smith, K. 2003, 76). The relevance of the region has been further underlined by a Common Strategy—the newly established CFSP instrument to set priorities for the foreign policy agenda of the EU. The document passed by the European Council in 2000 recalls the existing principles and adds new important items for cooperation, such as combating terrorism and migration issues. The Euro-Mediterranean Partnership is the umbrella mechanism for the bilateral and multilateral relations of the EU with 12 (now ten) Mediterranean countries,[2] and covers three main areas of partnership: political and security; economic and financial (including the creation of a free trade area); social, cultural, and human relations. In the area of the political dialogue the Barcelona declaration set as its objective the establishment of 'a common Euro-Mediterranean area of peace and stability based on fundamental principles including respect for human rights and democracy' (European Commission 2003b, 22). Unlike the relations of the EU with other regional groupings such as with Mercosur or within ASEM, which are focused on trade and economic issues, the Euro-Mediterranean Partnership takes into account the fact that the economic, social, and political stability problems of the region are interdependent and therefore require a comprehensive strategy (Gomez 1998, 134), including the considerable EU subventions known as MEDA programmes—the second largest aid programmes for a group of countries in the EU budget.[3]

The 'Barcelona Process'—to the wider public most obvious in the form of the foreign ministers' conferences which take place approximately every 18 months[4]—has served as an important forum where the conflicting parties of the Middle East, particularly in times of tensions, may simply meet, without high expectations. Conversely, the deadlock in the peace process has reduced the chances for progress in the Euromed Partnership (Smith, K. 2003, 76), and has limited the participation of the Mediterranean side. For example, on several occasions Lebanon and Syria did not attend the ministerial sessions, so as to demonstrate their opposition to Israeli policy. Not surprisingly political issues like the establishment of a charter for peace and security in the region turned out to be too controversial to be agreed by all (Allen and Smith, M. 2002, 107). EU attempts to link aid more directly to the acceptance of the principles of good governance and to the question of human rights also met with reservations on the part of the dialogue partners.

The second, although much more limited, model of dialogue in the (wider) region is based on a Cooperation Agreement with the six member states of the Gulf Coopera- tion Council (Bahrain, Kuwait, Oman, Qatar, Saudi Arabia, and United Arab Emirates) since 1989 (Saleh 1999, 50).[5] On each side it is driven by both political and economic interests. The Gulf countries were together perceived as an attractive interlocutor to assist Europe's policy in the Arab-Israeli conflict and to help bridge tensions between the EU and such other key actors in the region as Libya, Iraq, and Iran. The safeguard- ing of energy supplies is crucial to the EU and is balanced by the considerable interest on the part of the oil-supplying countries in getting access to European markets. So far, however, cooperation has not advanced to mutual satisfaction. In particular, ne- gotiations on a free trade agreement have not yet been successfully concluded des- pite numerous foreign ministers' meetings in the Joint Council (normally on an an- nual basis), which is the highest political level responsible for defining the general guidelines for the cooperation (Saleh 1999, 51).[6]

The EU and Asia[7]

Inter-regional cooperation in relation to Asia has seen considerable change since the establishment of regular contacts between the then EC and ASEAN in the 1970s. Mo- tivated by both economic and political interests—i.e. European concerns to secure access to the prospering Asian economies, to improve the EU's foreign policy profile and to support intra-regional tendencies in Asia (not least as a means to reduce Soviet and US influence in the region)—the first conference of foreign ministers of the members of both the EC and ASEAN was convened as early as in 1978, setting a pattern for the future (Rüland 2001, 9ff). In 1980 the EC and the member countries of the ASEAN signed a Cooperation Agreement, which encompasses aspects of trade, economic and development policy.[8] The EU-ASEAN foreign ministers' conferences take place every second year, while since 1995 there have been senior officials' meet- ings which prepare the ministerial conferences (also at other levels). Additionally, a Joint Cooperation Committee (together with several sub-committees) was created, in which senior officials discuss the various cooperation activities (usually every 18 months), together with a so-called Eminent Persons Group of high-ranking public figures from both regions (Piening 1997, 147). Furthermore, the ASEAN Regional Forum, in which the Asian group meets regularly with its most important partners of the region and beyond, offers another opportunity for the EU (represented by the Troika) to discuss issues of a mainly political/regional security nature (Piening 1997, 147). The terrorist attacks of 11 September 2001 and others that followed in the region itself (e.g. Bali/Indonesia) added another dimension to the existing framework and highlighted the interest of both sides in collaborating bilaterally and multilaterally on these new threats.

Cooperation has not always been without tensions. The tabling of human rights and good governance issues met with reservations from ASEAN members, who perceived them as an unacceptable interference by the EU into their domestic af- fairs—provoking in part the debate on 'Asian values' (Rüland 2001, 18)—while Brussels insisted on discussing these principles, which have become central to the EU's international profile. The most contested issue here is the policy of the Burmese/Myanmar government, since 1997 a member of ASEAN, towards its political opposition. In order to protest against the constant violation of human rights in Burma the EU has decided on a package of sanctions which on several occasions have prevented Burmese representatives from taking part in EU-ASEAN meetings, at least in Europe, and which have led already to the postponement of such dialogue meetings in Asia.[9]

Since 1996 EU-ASEAN relations seem to have lost something of their status as a model, and increasingly compete with a new, much broader and more dynamic inter-regional dialogue: the Asia-Europe Meeting (ASEM). Born out of concerns from the business side and supported by several European governments (France, Germany, the United Kingdom) as a way of responding collectively to globalisation—and in particular to safeguard attractive markets in Asia (Rüland 2001, 22ff)—ASEM brings together the 25 EU member states and the European Commission, as well as Brunei, Burma/Myanmar, Cambodia, Indonesia, Laos, Malaysia, the Philippines, Singapore, Thailand, Vietnam, China, Japan, and South Korea. The desire to enlarge the Asian group towards Laos, Cambodia, and Burma has recently created serious tensions both between the groups and the Europeans themselves as to whether and how to allow Burmese participation at the ASEM summit in Hanoi, Vietnam, in October 2004. The opposing interests among the 25 of those on the one hand interested in safeguarding the established framework of inter-regional cooperation, and those on the other in enforcing sanctions against the Burmese authorities, had to be reconciled—in the end by accepting Burmese participation, albeit at a level below that of a head of state or government.

The ASEM process is to be understood as an informal and multi-dimensional dialogue and cooperation process which encompasses three broad areas: political, economic, and cultural, extended recently to include the fight against international terrorism. The first ASEM summit took place in Bangkok in 1996 and since then there have been summit-level meetings every second year: the second ASEM was held in London in 1998, the third in Seoul in 2000, the fourth in Copenhagen in 2002, and the fifth in Hanoi in 2004. In addition there are ministerial-level meetings (of the foreign ministers, the finance ministers, the economic ministers, and now also of the ministers of science and the ministers of the environment), which were intended to take place in the intervening years but are now normally once a year. Finally, the ASEM process includes a series of senior officials' meetings and gatherings at the working level, not to forget the numerous emerging contacts between business and the civil societies on both sides.

In contrast, the relations between the EU and the South Asian Association for Regional Cooperation (SAARC) have so far been rather limited, and subordinated to bilateral links (Smith, K. 2003, 78), including regular political dialogues with such individual countries as India and Pakistan. These have been reinforced in the course of the EU's involvement in the fight against international terrorism. Although SAARC has strong ambitions to reinforce links between its members it lacks political cohesion and has difficulties in discussing politically contentious matters (Piening 1997, 162). Nevertheless, since 1994 there have been dialogue meetings of the ministerial Troika, while, in order to intensify cooperation at the technical level, a Memorandum of Understanding between the EC and the SAARC Secretariat was signed in

1996 (Bhargava 1998, 6). Due to difficulties inside SAARC, however, this has yet to be implemented effectively.

The EU and Latin America[10]

Inter-regional cooperation between the EU and Latin America takes place regularly both at the bi-regional level and in specialised dialogues with various groups of countries (see Box 15.3). The bewildering multitude of different fora has to do with the initial political motivation of the Europeans to mediate among the conflicting parties (e.g. in Central America in the 1980s), widened later to economic and other global issues when intra-regional integration took shape, particularly within the Mercosur. Further impulses for a strengthening of the relations and in particular the inter-regional dimension stemmed from the EU's Eurocentric approach in the 1990s but also from a joint EU-Latin American interest in counterbalancing, to some degree, the strong US influence in the region, including the pressure to establish a pan-American free trade area.

Historically the Andean Community (which was originally named the Andean Pact) was the first group to establish contractual relations in the form of a Framework Agreement on Cooperation in 1983 (Piening 1997, 7). While the relations between the EC and the Andean Community (Bolivia, Colombia, Ecuador, Peru, and Venezuela) focused on commercial issues and development cooperation and were fairly desultory at first, they were reactivated in the 1990s (Smith, H. 1998, 163). A second and more extensive Framework Agreement on Cooperation was signed in 1993 (entering into force in 1998) while the 1996 Rome Declaration also led to a strengthening of relations. Since 1996 there have been ad hoc presidential and ministerial meetings between the EU and the Andean Community, usually in the margins of the meetings of the Rio Group or of the United Nations General Assembly. The 1993 Framework Cooperation Agreement also established a Joint Committee that meets every two years and joint Sub-Committees for Cooperation which have annual meetings. An institutionalisation of the political dialogue between the EU and the Andean Community is envisaged in the Political Dialogue and Cooperation Agreement of December 2003 (which still needs to be ratified).[11] At the meetings between the EU and the Andean Community topics such as progress in regional integration, democracy, the rule of law, and respect for human rights are discussed and the scope of the political dialogue will be further extended by the new Political Dialogue and Cooperation Agreement to include conflict prevention, good governance, migration, and counter-terrorism. Furthermore, since 1995 there has been a special high-level dialogue on drugs. In general terms, however, economic issues take priority in relations between the EU and the Andean Community.

As a response to the Central American conflict in the 1980s the EC entered into a foreign policy engagement with the Central American states (Costa Rica, El Salvador, Guatemala, Honduras, Nicaragua, and Panama) (Smith, H. 1995). The so-called San José Dialogue began with a meeting where all ten EC ministers of foreign affairs travelled to meet their equivalents from the Central American states and the Contadora Group (Colombia, Mexico, Panama, Venezuela) in September 1984 in San José (Piening 1997, 125). It was established in order to contribute to the democratisation and peace processes of the region. A Cooperation Agreement between the EC and

Central America was signed in 1985. Since then ministerial conferences of the San José Group have taken place on an annual basis. In addition, the EU-Central America Framework Cooperation Agreement of 1993 established a Joint Committee of high-level officials and a Sub-Committee for Co-operation to supervise the agreement and to prepare and implement the ministerial sessions. As the original aim of the San José Dialogue was largely achieved by the early 1990s, in that peace was restored to the region, the 1993 Framework Cooperation Agreement also provided for an extension of political cooperation. The focus of cooperation with Central America is now on issues such as regional integration, democracy, and human rights, but also includes rural development, disaster prevention, and reconstruction. Today the EU sees the dialogue mainly as a contribution to the strengthening of the still weak democratic governmental systems on the Central American isthmus (Piening 1997, 128). Recently (2003), the EU and the Central American countries negotiated a new Political and Co-operation Agreement which awaits ratification but which will further strengthen the relations. It could establish the conditions under which an Association Agreement, including a Free Trade Area, could be signed.[12]

EU relations with the Rio Group were also initiated in the second half of the 1980s to further the peace process in Central America. Initially the group was limited to countries of the region which were perceived as important political players (Argentina, Brazil, Colombia, Mexico, Panama, Peru, Uruguay, and Venezuela) to help stabilise the San José process.[13] Cooperation was institutionalised by the Rome agreement of December 1990, which provides for regular annual meetings of the foreign ministers where high importance is generally accorded to political issues (Piening 1997, 130). Meanwhile not only has participation been widened to include the whole Andean Community, the Mercosur and others, but the dialogue serves for wider political and economic cooperation including the fight against traffic in drugs and crime, thus somewhat overlapping with other existing formats (Smith, H. 1998, 160ff).

Seen from the EU side the most interesting format of inter-regional cooperation in economic terms relates to the creation of the Mercosur in 1991. As early as 1992 the EU stated its intention to consider some form of associated status with this partner (Smith, H. 1998, 161). An Inter-regional Framework Cooperation Agreement between the EU and its member states and the Mercosur and its party states was formalised in 1995 and fully entered into force in 1999. The Framework Agreement lists three main elements of the cooperation, namely political dialogue, cooperation, and trade issues, operating through a sophisticated institutional network. Since 1995 there have been political dialogue meetings at the levels of heads of government, foreign ministers, and senior officials.[14] In addition, meetings of the EU-Mercosur Cooperation Council took place in 1999 and 2001. The subsequent negotiations for a Political and Economic Association Agreement, conducted through 13 rounds of negotiations between the EU and Mercosur from 1999 through to May 2004, have not yet resolved all the difficult issues between the sides, mostly in the areas of agriculture and investments (Müller-Brandeck-Bocquet 2000).

In order to strengthen the long-standing political, economic, and cultural ties between Europe and Latin America, and to underline the EU's claim for a global presence in the world in the new millennium, a summit between the heads of state and government of the EU on the one side, and of Latin America and the Caribbean on

Box 15.3 Regional groupings in Latin America

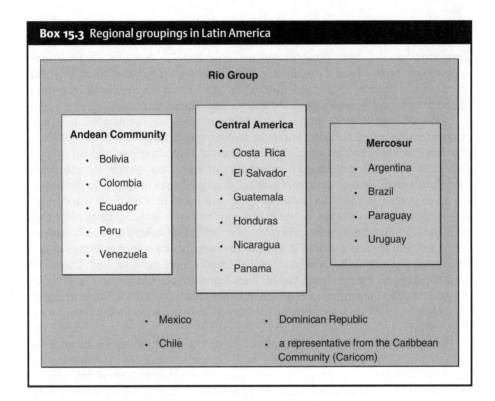

Rio Group

Andean Community

- Bolivia
- Colombia
- Ecuador
- Peru
- Venezuela

Central America

- Costa Rica
- El Salvador
- Guatemala
- Honduras
- Nicaragua
- Panama

Mercosur

- Argentina
- Brazil
- Paraguay
- Uruguay

- Mexico
- Chile
- Dominican Republic
- a representative from the Caribbean Community (Caricom)

the other, was held in Rio de Janeiro in June 1999 (Smith, K. 2003, 79). There an ambitious 'strategic' partnership between the EU and Latin America and the Caribbean was established which includes political, economic and cultural aspects (Müller-Brandeck-Bocquet 2000, 571ff). Similar to other inter-regional summits (ASEM, EU-Africa, Barcelona Process), meetings at the highest political level serve publicly to emphasise the overall importance of the dialogue. They offer a general exchange of views on a wide range of topics while the daily business has to be managed elsewhere. So far two EU/LAC summits have followed that in Rio (Madrid, May 2002, Guadalajara/Mexico, May 2004), offering further opportunities for the governments to articulate and strengthen their joint interests and to make commitments, particularly regarding social cohesion, multilateralism, and regional integration.

The EU and other regional groupings in Europe

Inter-regional cooperation inside Europe is marked by four different models (see Box 15.2 and Box 15.4). The first, politically now of less relevance given the shrinking composition of the non-EU group, is the EU's dialogue with the members of EFTA. The EC and EFTA[15] committed themselves to cooperation on a number of mostly economic and trade issues in the Luxembourg Declaration of 1984, and the creation of a group-to-group structure followed (Pedersen in Edwards and Regelsberger 1990, 98). Apart from ministerial meetings (of the foreign ministers, the economic ministers, the ministers of the environment, and the ministers of education) a High-Level

Contact Group and a number of expert groups were established (Regelsberger in Edwards and Regelsberger 1990, 21). In 1992 an Agreement creating the European Economic Area (EEA) was signed,[16] which allows the EFTA signatories to participate in the Single Market even if they did not wish to assume the full responsibilities of EU membership (Piening 1997, 53). Furthermore, EFTA countries are closely associated with the CFSP and regularly align themselves with the *acquis politique*.

The second model is of a particular kind since it unites the EU member states with a considerable number of other European states, not (yet) inside the EU but all also inside the Council of Europe, a legally-oriented institution often confused with the EU but actually pre-dating it. After a first exchange of letters in 1959 between the two institutions a more structured form of political dialogue began in 1987.[17] On the basis of an Arrangement between the European Commission and the Council of Europe high-level meetings are convened at which topics of mutual interest, such as respect for human rights and fundamental freedoms, the rule of law, education, and culture are discussed, and there is a shared interest in the concept of a common European judicial space. Since 1989 the twice yearly Quadripartite meetings—i.e. high-level meetings between, on the one hand, the EU Presidency and the Commission and, on the other hand, the Chairmanship and Secretary General of the Council—have deepened the cooperative process, resulting in 2001 in a Joint Declaration on Cooperation and Partnership.

The third category is again of a specific kind: The Organisation for Security and Cooperation in Europe (OSCE), the former CSCE, was initially designed to overcome the East-West divide in Europe. It could count on a strong and active voice on the part of the EC member states. After the fundamental changes of the pan-European scenery between 1989 and 1991, the agenda of the OSCE was increasingly dominated by new regional and intra-state conflicts. Again, expectations were high as to the EU's potential to contribute to greater stability and security among and inside OSCE member states. In contrast to other models of inter-regional cooperation in Europe, the role of the EU in the OSCE framework expresses itself through different modes of cooperation: regular meetings between representatives of the two sides at ministerial or senior official level seem to be of less relevance for concrete problem solving than the approaches which the EU pursues at the various OSCE levels in Vienna via the Presidency, the High Representative, and the European Commission. Support for the OSCE's endeavours for conflict prevention and crisis management in the field, for example in the Balkans through practical contributions from the CFSP, have considerably heightened the EU's profile.

Finally, the fourth category of inter-regional cooperation in Europe is particularly distinctive, since its final objective is the actual integration of the dialogue partners into the EU, and in the not too distant future. This is the relationship with the states of the old Warsaw Pact. Its forerunners were the contacts between the EC and the Council for Mutual Economic Assistance (CMEA),[18] which were established in 1985 and formalised by a Joint Declaration in 1988, although there was at that time no question on either side of discussions about membership (Lippert, in Edwards and Regelsberger 1990, 123). After the fall of the Berlin Wall the EC's relations with the Central and Eastern European countries were renewed via bilateral 'Europe Agreements' and a multilateral 'Structured Dialogue'. There the acceding countries enjoyed a privileged status and had the most direct access to information, and in

Box 15.4 Regional and sub-regional groupings in Europe[a] (besides the EU)

Pan-European Organisations

Council of Europe
(46 member states, incl. 21 countries from Central and Eastern Europe)

OSCE (Organisation for Security and Cooperation in Europe)
(55 member states from Europe, Central Asia and North America)

Western Europe

EFTA (European Free Trade Association)
(Iceland, Liechtenstein, Norway, Switzerland; before their accession to the EC/EU, Austria, Denmark, Portugal, Sweden and the United Kingdom were also members of EFTA)

Central and Eastern Europe

CEI (Central European Initiative)[b]
(Albania, Austria, Belarus, Bosnia and Herzegovina, Bulgaria, Croatia, Czech Republic, FYROM, Hungary, Italy, Moldova, Poland, Romania, Serbia and Montenegro, Slovakia, Slovenia, Ukraine)

Visegrad countries
(Czech Republic, Hungary, Poland, Slovakia)

CEFTA (Central European Free Trade Agreement)
(Bulgaria, Croatia, Romania)

South Eastern Europe

countries of South Eastern Europe
(Albania, Bosnia and Herzegovina, Croatia, FYROM, Serbia and Montenegro)

a Other sub-regional groupings (which are supported by the EU) include the Council of Baltic Sea States (CBSS), the Barents Euro-Arctic Council (BEAC), and the Black Sea Economic Cooperation (BSEC).

b In November 1989 an agreement was signed in Budapest by which the so-called Quadrilateral Cooperation between Italy, Austria, Hungary, and Yugoslavia was established. With the admission of Czechoslovakia in 1990, it became the Pentagonal Initiative and after the admission of Poland in 1991 it was renamed the Hexagonal Initiative. After the dissolution of the former Yugoslavia, the Republics of Bosnia and Herzegovina, Croatia and Slovenia became members in 1992, and the grouping was thenceforth known as the Central European Initiative.

part to EU policy formulation, in particular in relation to the CFSP (Regelsberger 2003).

With their full entry into the EU as of 1 May 2004 the focus in Brussels has shifted towards the remaining group in the immediate neighbourhood of the EU, viz those countries in the Western Balkans eligible for EU membership. Against the background of the previous wars in the former Yugoslavia and the EU's failure to achieve conflict prevention in the region, after the Kosovo war in 1999 the EU proposed a new design, in the form of the Stabilisation and Association Process (SAP) for the five countries in the region (Albania, Bosnia and Herzegovina, Croatia, the former Yugoslav Republic of Macedonia (FYROM), Serbia and Montenegro).[19] The SAP offers them the clear prospect of full integration into the EU provided that specific political and economic conditions are met. The conclusion of individual Stabilisation and Association Agreements (SAA) is currently under way. The purpose of these agreements is to help the individual countries to move closer to the standards which apply inside the EU based on a constant monitoring by Brussels. Another key element of the SAP is the promotion of intra-regional cooperation (Triantaphyllou 2003, 70ff), which also seems to work well in the framework of the Stability Pact for South Eastern Europe—another long-term approach the EU came up with in 1999 to promote political and economic stability in the region.[20] The importance of stabilising the Western Balkans was underlined by the summits in Zagreb in 2000 and in Thessaloniki during the Greek Presidency of 2003 (Triantaphyllou 2003). The latter launched the 'EU–Western Balkans Forum' as a group-to-group dialogue at a high political level with the particular aim of strengthening ties on foreign policy.

Conclusions

Inter-regional cooperation has helped the EU and its member states to pursue their stated objective of becoming a global power in international relations. It has enabled them to contribute to conflict prevention outside the EU borders and the better to respond to external challenges of different kinds. However, the group-to-group approach is but one instrument through which the EU and its member states pursue their interests in the world. While it may help in the definition of collective principles and negotiation positions in international fora, it is less suited to conduct crisis management operations in concrete situations.

Inter-regional cooperation encompasses a plethora of institutionalised and mainly treaty-based relations of the EU with other regional groupings all over the world, which have grown and been diversified over the years, although not necessarily along precise or consistent schedules and concepts. Faced with the numerous threats stemming from Islamist fundamentalism, ethnic conflicts, and fragile political systems around the EU, to mention but a few, today the regional focus is clearly on the EU's immediate neighbourhood. The objective, establishing a 'European Neighbourhood Policy' (ENP), including the southern Mediterranean countries, the GCC, Yemen, Iran, Iraq, and Libya, as well as the conflicting parties in the Middle East, together with the EU's new neighbours after the enlargement of 1 May 2004, ranks high on the foreign policy agenda. Inter-regional cooperation will be but one component to implement the stated objectives. Existing instruments and institutions may be used, but the focus will also be on the needs of individual countries, with particular emphasis on improving political dialogue. At the same time the EU wishes to continue, if not to deepen, its bi-regional partnerships with the countries in Africa, Latin America, and Asia (said to be strategic but in practice more symbolic), with the last-named having priority given the importance of ASEM. Some observers go so far as to describe the EU-ASEM link as a new dimension of inter-regionalism, characterised by a multitude of actors (governmental and non-governmental) working together in a system of checks and balances, with a collective interest in the joint management of global interdependence through common rules and mechanisms (Maull 2000, 143).

In principle inter-regional cooperation has worked towards greater consistency between the various pillars of the EU's external relations and has improved the EU's profile as a collective actor. However, the increasing number of commitments to collective dialogues, together with the concomitant problems of intra-EU coordination, imposes considerable strains on the well-known institutional weaknesses of the EU system. The debate on reform of 2003–2004 has led to some steps being taken which seem likely to improve the EU's profile as an international actor. The arrival of a Union Minister for Foreign Affairs should enable greater continuity and visibility compared to the formulae of a rotating Presidency plus the Troika, Commission spokesmen, and the High Representative. With the assistance of a well-established External Action Service s/he could become the key figure on the EU side, not only for the concept and the conduct of inter-regional cooperation but for the EU's overall capacity to perform as an actor and a viable interlocutor on the international stage.

Notes

1 Furthermore, as far as ECOWAS is concerned a high-level political dialogue with the EU was established in 2000.

2 Now that Cyprus and Malta have joined the EU, these states are Algeria, Egypt, Israel, Jordan, Lebanon, Morocco, the Palestinian Authority, Syria, Tunisia, Turkey and Libya currently has observer status at certain meetings. For the following see http://europa.eu.int/comm/external_relations/med_mideast/intro/index.htm.

3 MEDA stands for 'Mesures d'Accompagnement' and it is the principal financial instrument of the European Union for the implementation of the Euro-Mediterranean Partnership. In the framework of the MEDA Programme, technical and financial support is granted to accompany the reform of economic and social structures as well as the promotion of democratic processes in the Mediterranean partner countries. For the period 1995–99 the programme accounted for Є 3,435 million, and MEDA II for the period of 2000–2006 amounts to Є 5,350 million. Also see http://europa.eu.int/comm/external_relations/euromed/meda.htm.

4 There are also informal ad hoc meetings, supplemented by the Euro-Mediterranean Committee and a number of functional working

groups (European Commission 2003, 22; Dembinski 2002, 33).

5   For the following see especially http://europa.eu.int/comm/ external_relations/gulf_cooperation/ intro/index.htm.

6   There are also meetings of senior officials (twice a year) and at the level of working groups. Prior to 1995, a Joint Cooperation Committee which was subsidiary to the Joint Council and composed of senior officials met at least once a year (Saleh 1999, 65).

7   For the relations of the EU with the regional groupings and organisations in Asia (ASEAN, ASEM, SAARC), especially see http://europa.eu.int/comm/ external_relations/asean/intro/ index.htm; http://europa.eu.int/comm/ external_relations/asem/intro/ index.htm; http://europa.eu.int/comm/ external_relations/saarc/intro/ index.htm.

8   As Laos, Cambodia, and Burma/ Myanmar were not then member countries of ASEAN, protocols for the accession of Laos and Cambodia to the Agreement were signed in July 2000; however, because of the still unacceptable situation as to human rights and democracy in Burma/Myanmar the EU has so far not been willing to negotiate an extension of the Agreement to Burma/Myanmar.

9   After the accession of Burma/Myanmar to ASEAN in 1997 the EU did not accept its participation in the bi-regional dialogue, thus putting it on hold until April 2000.

10   For the relations of the EU with regional groupings and organisations in Latin America (Andean Community, Central American states, Rio Group, Mercosur), especially see http://europa.eu.int/comm/ external_relations/la/index.htm; http://europa.eu.int/comm/ external_relations/andean/intro/ index.htm; http://europa.eu.int/comm/ external_relations/ca/index.htm; http://europa.eu.int/comm/ external_relations/mercosur/intro/ index.htm.

11   The heads of state and government of the European Union and the Andean Community also stressed that, together with the strengthening of their cooperation on trade investment and economic relations, this agreement could lead to the negotiation of an Association Agreement including a Free Trade Area.

12   Furthermore, in May 2004 a first summit meeting of the heads of state and government of Central America and the EU Troika took place in Guadalajara, Mexico, in order to commemorate the 20th anniversary of the San José Dialogue.

13   In 1990 Chile, Ecuador, Bolivia, and Paraguay also became members of the Rio Group. In 2000 Costa Rica, El Salvador, Guatemala, Honduras, Nicaragua, and the Dominican Republic joined the Rio Group. In 1990 it was also decided that every year one country from the Caribbean Community would participate as a representative in the activities conducted by the Rio Group.

14   Since 1998 Chile has taken part and Bolivia has been present in these meetings.

15   Seven states were then members of EFTA: Austria, Denmark, Norway, Portugal, Sweden, Switzerland, and the United Kingdom. Finland joined EFTA in 1961, Iceland entered in 1970, and Liechtenstein in 1991. After the UK and Denmark had left EFTA to join the EC in 1973, Portugal in 1986 and Austria, Finland, and Sweden in 1995, the remaining EFTA partners of the EU are Iceland, Liechtenstein, Norway, and Switzerland.

16   See http://europa.eu.int/comm/ external_relations/eea/index.htm. However, in a referendum Switzerland voted to stay out of the EEA; Austria, Finland, and Sweden switched sides within the EEA when joining the EU in 1995, while Liechtenstein joined the EEA in 1995.

17 For the following see especially
    http://europa.eu.int/comm/
    external_relations/coe/index.htm.

18 The original members of the CMEA,
    which was founded in January 1949,
    were the Soviet Union, Bulgaria,
    Czechoslovakia, Hungary, Poland, and
    Romania; in February 1949 Albania
    joined the CMEA (it stopped parti-
    cipating in the activities of CMEA
    in 1961, however); East Germany
    became a member in 1950, Mongolia
    in 1962, Cuba in 1972, and Vietnam
    in 1978 (Yugoslavia was considered
    as an associate member, based on its
    1964 agreement with the CMEA).

19 For the following see especially
    http://europa.eu.int/comm/

external_relations/see/actions/sap.htm
and http://europa.eu.int/comm/
external_relations/see/sum_11_00/
index.htm.

20 The Stability Pact for South Eastern
    Europe is to be understood as a quasi
    permanent intergovernmental
    conference chaired by the EU Special
    Coordinator Busek, in which all the
    international donors, such as the
    EU, IMF etc. unite with representat-
    ives from the five Western Balkans
    countries, Bulgaria, Romania, and
    Moldova, to coordinate the projects.
    Here again intra-regional approaches
    are assessed as particularly important.

Further reading

There is hardly any academic literature
giving an overview of the present models
of inter-regional cooperation, except
for Edwards and Regelsberger (1990) which
does not cover events since the end of the
Cold War. The contributions in Telò (2001)
offer a detailed survey of theoretical
perspectives on regionalism and a comparative analysis of the EU and other regional
arrangements, as well as an inquiry into
the EU's evolving continental and global
role. While Piening (1997) gives an overview of the EU's relations with third states
on a region by region basis, K. Smith (2003)
provides an assessment of the EU's foreign
policy in relation to five core objectives,
including the encouragement of regional
cooperation (Chapter 4). On a more general
level, an account of the historical development of regionalism and its links with other
issues in contemporary international relations, as well as an examination of regional
cooperation in various parts of the world,
is provided by Fawcett and Hurrell (1995).
Furthermore, the annual reports of the
European Commission (1995 onwards; see

above) refer to the most recent main events
in the various dialogue formats. So, in part,
do the Council documents on the CFSP
(Council of the European Union 1999–2003;
see above).

Edwards, G., and Regelsberger, E. (eds)
    (1990), *Europe's Global Links: The European
    Community and Inter-Regional Cooperation*
    (London: Pinter Publishers).

Fawcett, L., and Hurrell, A. (eds) (1995),
    *Regionalism in World Politics: Regional Organ-
    ization and International Order* (Oxford:
    Oxford University Press).

Piening, C. (1997), *Global Europe: The
    European Union in World Affairs* (Boulder,
    Colorado/London: Lynne Rienner
    Publishers).

Smith, K.E. (2003), *European Union Foreign
    Policy in a Changing World* (Cambridge:
    Polity Press).

Telò, M. (ed.) (2001), *European Union and
    New Regionalism: Regional Actors and Global
    Governance in a Post-Hegemonic Era* (Alder-
    shot: Ashgate).

Web links

For coverage of EU policies and activities on inter-regional relations, the best web resources are to be found in the web site of the Council of the European Union on the
Common Foreign and Security Policy (CFSP): http://ue.eu.int/showPage.asp?
id=248&lang=en&mode=g and the European Commission's web site on External Relations: http://europa.eu.int/comm/external_relations/. The following sites are a sample
of those dealing with specific regions and regional organisations: http://www.acp.int/
Index.aspx?sessLang=1 (ACP States); http://www.sadc.int/ (Southern African Development Community, SADC); http://www.africa-union.org/(African Union); http://www.
ecowas.int/org (Economic Community of West African States, ECOWAS); http://www.
igad.org/ (Intergovernmental Authority on Development, IGAD); http://www.
aseansec.org/home.htm (Association of Southeast Asian Nations, ASEAN); http://www.
asemifoboard.org/ (ASEM InfoBoard); http://www.saarc-sec.org/main.php (South Asian
Association for Regional Cooperation, SAARC); http://www.osce.org/index.php
(Organisation for Security and Cooperation in Europe, OSCE); http://www.efta.int/
(European Free Trade Association, EFTA); http://www.coe.int/DefaultEN.asp
(Council of Europe); http://www.comunidadandina.org/endex.htm (Andean Commu-
nity); http://www.mercosur.org.uy/ (Mercosur); http://www.gcc-sg.org/home_e.html
(Gulf Cooperation Council, GCC).

Chapter 16

The EU and the United States

Michael Smith and Rebecca Steffenson

Contents

Summary

The United States has always been the most 'significant other' of the European integration project in the world arena. This chapter explores the implications of this factor for the international relations of the EU, first by introducing the key features of the EU-US relationship and by considering the ways in which these raise issues of analysis and policy. Second, the chapter explores the ways in which the EU-US relationship reflects and affects the workings of the EU as a system of international relations. Third, the chapter focuses on the ways in which the EU-US relationship affects the broader process of international relations. Finally, the chapter evaluates the ways in which the roles of the EU as a 'power' in international relations are shaped by its relationship with the US, and the ways in which this moulds the EU's role in exercising international power and pursuing international order.

Introduction

The European Union (and previously the European Community) has been intimately entangled with the United States since the very beginnings of European integration in the 1950s. In the areas of trade, monetary relations and economic management this gives the US a key role not only in the international policies of the EU, but also in the management of both the European economy and the broader global political economy. In the area of security, the European project has always been linked to and embedded in the European and world security order, whilst politically the EU and its predecessors have been a key part of the US-led group of liberal democracies. American influence stimulated the European project in two senses. On the one hand, the American federal system was an inspiration to European leaders, such as Jean Monnet, and to Americans who saw the European project as a means of creating a United States of Europe. On the other hand, European integration was inspired to a substantial extent, by the desire to match US and Soviet superpower, or at least to create a 'third force' in international relations (DePorte 1987; Winand 1993; Ellwood 1992; Heller and Gillingham 1996). This ambivalence—the US as a key partner and leader but also as a potential rival in world politics—has been central to EU-US relations and to the international relations of the EU ever since (Smith 1984; Smith and Woolcock 1993; Smith 1998a).

These two dynamics, producing what can be called 'competitive cooperation' (Smith 1998a), are visible in all three of the core components of transatlantic life. Separate but interconnected economic, political and security relationships define transatlantic relations and go a long way towards shaping both EU politics and the changing global order. In this context, dealing with the US has been one of the key tests of the extent to which the EU has developed into an effective international actor with a distinct set of policy positions and instruments. Partly as a consequence, the EU-US relationship has, some would say increasingly, been a subject of political and policy debate, attracting the attention and disagreement of those involved in shaping the key questions of world order (Smith 2004a; Todd 2003; Kagan 2003).

This chapter aims to explore the ways in which EU-US relations enter into the international relations of the EU, and to assess the implications for key areas of the EU's growing international activity. In the first section, the focus is on the changing shape and focus of the transatlantic relationship as it enters into economic, political and security questions. The following three sections address the key themes raised by this volume as a whole, by successively dealing with the impact of EU-US relations on the EU's system of international relations, on the EU's role in the processes of international relations, and on the EU's position as a 'power' in international relations.

The changing shape of EU-US relations

Economic interdependence has always been at the core of the EU-US relationship. European integration itself was closely connected with the economic reconstruction of Europe through the Marshall Plan in the 1940s and 1950s, and the European project has been closely linked to both the evolution of the 'western world economy' during the Cold War and to 'globalisation' in the 21st century. The EU and the US have been historically linked through trade and investment since the early 20th century at least, and this relationship increased in both depth and breadth as the

Box 16.1 The EU-US economic relationship in the early 2000s

By the early 2000s, according to European Commission figures (European Commission 2003c), this deeply embedded economic relationship accounted for 37% of world merchandise trade and for 45% of world trade in services (2002 figures). In 2002, two-way cross-border trade in goods and services (imports and exports) between the EU and the US amounted to more than € 650 billions (€ 412 billions in goods and € 238 billions in services), making the EU and the US each other's single largest trading partner; these figures represented about 21% of each partner's trade in goods alone; when it came to the rapidly-growing service trade between the two partners, transatlantic trade in 2002 represented 39% of EU and 35% of US total cross-border trade in services, and this amounted to 36% of total bilateral trade in goods and services. The EU and the US in 2000 also accounted for 54% of total world inflows of Foreign Direct Investment (FDI) and for 67% of total world outflows. By 2001, the US absorbed 49% of the EU's outward investment flows, and the EU 46% of US outward flows; EU investment was 54% of total investment in the US, and US investment in the EU was 69% of the total. Over a more extended period, nearly three-quarters of all foreign investment in the US in the 1990s came from the EU. As a result, the total accumulated investment by the EU in the US and the US in the EU amounted by 2001 to € 1500 billion — by far the largest investment relationship in the world.

'Western Alliance' grew during the 1950s and beyond. Box 16.1 summarises a number of features of this relationship as it existed in the early 2000s.

The very intimacy of this relationship, and the depth of its historical and institutional roots, give rise to a number of important trends in EU-US economic relations. The first of these trends concerns the consistent growth of the economic links between the EC/EU and the US: in other words, there has been a continuous deepening of economic links over a more than 50-year period, and these links have notably continued to deepen and widen even when transatlantic political or security relations have been troubled (for example, during the later years of the Cold War, or during the period leading up to the war in Iraq during 2002/2003). A second trend concerns the ways in which the EC/EU, through processes of economic growth and enlargement, has increasingly come to be seen as an economic superpower. Both the EU and the US are of continental size, are advanced industrial and service-based economies, and both are deeply entangled both with each other and with the development of the global economy. In other words, the EU-US relationship has become a partnership of equals, at least in economic terms (Peterson 1996; Guay 1999).

But this evidence also raises a number of questions about the nature of EU-US economic relations. Given the continuous widening and deepening of the relationships, is it fair to see the EU and the US as effectively 'integrated' within an Atlantic political economy? How far is it possible to see the EU and the US as global economic rivals, given the simultaneous rise of disputes and more extensive conflicts over trade, investment, competition and other areas of regulatory policy, and what are the implications of this? Is the EU, despite its apparent equality with the US in quantitative terms, actually able to mobilise its economic resources to achieve equal influence with the US, within both economic and other contexts? These and other economic issues will be addressed later in the chapter. Meanwhile, Box 16.1 provides information on some of the current indicators by which the significance of EU-US economic relations might be evaluated.

The EU-US relationship also reflects a number of fundamental political forces. The foundations of the European project and the transatlantic relationship were as much political as they were economic. The defeat of almost all of the European states during World War II, the de-legitimisation of governments and underlying regimes in all parts of Europe, coupled by the looming threat of Soviet political domination in Eastern Europe, played a key role in shaping the political complexion of the 'new Europe' after 1945. The US commitment to a western market system was thus paralleled by the desire to promote the strengthening of liberal democracies in Europe. The development and consolidation of anti-Communism in the 1950s, the development of European socialisms and 'Euro-Communism' in the 1970s and 1980s, and the spread of free market and liberal ideas in the 1980s reflect key phases in the development of the political relationship (Ellwood 1992; Heller and Gillingham 1996). It is difficult to establish the extent to which these events affected American engagement in Europe, but it is clear that consistent and deep relationships between European and American political and diplomatic elites underpinned Cold War Europe.

The political changes initiated by the end of the Cold War threatened to transform the composition of EU-US relations. Whilst the removal of the Soviet hold over Central and Eastern Europe created new scope for the extension of liberal democracy and market ideas, it also revealed some of the fault lines and key policy questions that had been at least partly masked by the Cold War. To what extent did the EU and the US really share common values? Was it possible for the EU to develop and export a different brand of democracy, underpinned by economic success and by the mechanisms in the Common Foreign and Security Policy? How would this find its expression in both the economic and the security challenges likely to face the 'winners' in the contest between western democracy and communism? These were not simply analytical or academic questions: they reflected the uncertainties of political and policy-making elites on both sides of the Atlantic (Peterson 1996; Smith and Woolcock 1993; Haftendorn and Tuschhoff 1993). As Box 16.2 shows, the sheer range of areas covered by political initiatives in the immediate post-Cold War period raised

---

Box 16.2 Examples of transatlantic political initiatives (post-Cold War)

- Declaration on Combating Terrorism
- Energy Research Co-operation Agreement
- Statement on Communicable Diseases in Africa
- EU-US Biotechnology Consultative Forum
- Declaration on the Responsibilities of States on Transparency Regarding Arms Exports
- Declaration on Common Orientation of Non-Proliferation Policy
- Precursors Chemical Agreement
- Joint Initiative on Trafficking in Women
- Caribbean Drugs Initiative

important questions of transatlantic coordination, not only among foreign ministries and the EU's external relations apparatus but also in areas previously seen as 'internal' or 'domestic' in their political impact. Here, as elsewhere, the EU-US relationship demonstrated a concentrated form of the questions that had to be addressed by all political leaders and foreign policy officials.

Inescapably, the economic and political factors outlined above have been linked to the security question (indeed, many of the initiatives listed in Box 16.2 are security issues in many respects, as well as indicators of political cooperation). The EU and its predecessors can plausibly be analysed as 'security communities', as they gather societies together in a pluralistic yet common framework. More directly, of course, there are two standard explanations for the origins of the European project: on the one hand, Franco-German rapprochement and the creation of a new framework for the prevention of armed conflict in western Europe, on the other hand the creation of economic and political conditions that would buttress the West in the conduct of the Cold War. Here, of course, the EC/EU was not and is not the only game in town. American influence over its European allies was well and truly cemented with the creation of NATO in the 1950s, embodying what has been seen as a transatlantic 'security community' (Sloan 2002).

For this purpose, it is possible to see the European integration project as part of the institutional underpinning of the Cold War in general, and the EC as part of the jigsaw that constituted the western alliance. But the EC was and remained throughout the Cold War a 'civilian power', contained as well as supported by the western alliance and subject to US security dominance, especially at the 'hard security' end of the spectrum. The security dominance of the US extended also to the economics of military production and the development of defence industries.

The EU-US relationship in security was thus both intimate and uneven during the Cold War, and it can plausibly be argued that the trend-lines of European and US strength within the relationship were far apart—in contrast to the relative and growing equality of the two parties in the economic sphere and the diversity at many levels of political organisation and ideas. But here too the end of the Cold War, combined with the development of new EU capacities, raised fundamental questions. How far might and should the EU aim to duplicate, complement, or even supplement the US in European security issues and in the broader security debate within the global arena? How far was the notion of 'civilian power' in the European project simply a reflection and rationalisation of subordination and containment by the US, and how far might that rationalisation be challenged as the Cold War structures themselves were challenged? Did the EU—or could it ever—represent an alternative model of security politics as well as a possible alternative economic or political model for the organisation of the post-Cold War world?

It is not surprising that the development of EU-US relations has been accompanied by debate, controversy, and the proposal of different, often strongly conflicting, models of the future of the relationship. As the European integration process gained momentum and spread into areas of foreign policy cooperation during the 1970s and 1980s, speculation about the future of the relationship became a focus of policy debate among political and economic elites on both sides of the Atlantic (Smith 1984). The end of the Cold War posed new challenges and opportunities for the economic, political and security domains, and in many cases linked them together in new and potent ways. It affected both the composition and the conduct of the relationship, which for the purposes of this chapter raises important questions about how we interpret the transatlantic alliance and the EU's position within it:

- If we conceive of the EU as a system of international relations, how exactly does this system relate to the presence of the US, to its dominance of key areas of policy development and to the inevitable collision between the EU and the US systems of policy-making and policy coordination?

- If we analyse the EU as part of the process of international relations, how do we factor in the ways in which the EU and the US interact, the changes that have occurred in these interactions, and the balance-sheet of advantage and disadvantage of the economic, political, and security domains?

- Finally, if we conceive of the EU as a power in international relations, how exactly does this power relate to the US and to US power in the 21st century, and how can this relationship help us to understand key questions and disputes over the establishment of international order, both in the global political economy and in the global security arena?

EU-US relations and the EU's system of international relations

In earlier chapters, this book has presented the EU's international relations in part as expressing a system of international relations within the EU itself, and a subsystem of the broader international system. In other words, the EU's member states and institutions comprise a complex and multi-layered system within which national policies are adjusted, 'European' policy positions are developed and revised, and actions are produced in a number of coexisting and overlapping contexts. This has important consequences for the ways in which the EU enters into and conducts international relationships, and many of the chapters in this book bear witness to the ways in which this can be demonstrated. For the purposes of this chapter, the most important focus is upon the ways in which the EU-US relationship shows the operation of the intra-EU system of international relations, and by implication also the ways in which the United States can enter into that system both as a contextual factor but also as, in some instances, a participant in the system itself.

The multi-level governance literature provides a logical analytical starting point for a discussion about the complex relationships between EU member states, European institutions, and the US. According to this literature the EU is characterised by shared authority and policy-making competencies across multiple levels of government—subnational, national and supranational (see also Marks *et al.* 1996). This has important effects on EU external policies, and it is not surprising that the 'US factor' inevitably enters into the many different levels at which EU policies are made (Pollack and Shaffer 2001). In the first instance, there are formal diplomatic relations between the EU and the US, especially via the Commission in the field of external economic policies. The member states also retain important economic re-lations with the US, and in a number of areas these national interests and policies are at least as significant as those determined collectively. This is especially true in monetary and investment policy, which differs greatly depending on membership or non-membership of the Eurozone. The coexisting and overlapping policy arenas al-low the US Administration, US state governments and private companies to intervene in many different areas. Many large US companies are so long-established in the EU that they are effectively 'European' in terms of their interests and their ability to ex-ert pressure. This means that in terms of international economic relations, the US can be seen almost as a direct participant in the EU's multi-level system.

Interestingly, the US too can be seen less and less as a unitary state, and more as a multi-level system of economic policy-making. It is thus important to highlight the shared competencies between separate national as well as state institutions in US for-eign policy making (Smith 1998a; Peterson and O'Toole 2001), which will not neces-sarily always agree among themselves about the positions to be adopted in relation to the EU. 'Cooperative federalism', in which powers and competencies are shared and treated as shared between levels, is another way of characterising the US decision-making structure (Nicolaïdis and Howse 2001). Shared authority affects the capacity of the US to exercise international relations, because as Peterson and O'Toole (2001, 300) argue, 'federalism usually gives rise to less formal intricate structures within which a large number of actors, each wielding a small slice of power, interact'. It is not clear how and to what extent this enables the EU collectively or through its many possible agents to intervene in US domestic economic and political processes, but it is clear that there are important respects in which the changing nature of the global political economy has led to a convergence of state forms on the two sides of the Atlantic.

Many scholars have begun to focus on multiple actors and multiple levels of in-fluence within international relations theory more generally (see Milner 1997; Risse-Kappen 1995; Putnam 1988). The idea that domestic and international politics are not separable, and that domestic agents—be they political institutions, domestic groups, state or non-state actors—influence international negotiations, is uniting a number of emerging IR theories. In this respect, the overlapping and interpenetrat-ing external relations systems of the EU and the US can be seen as a key example of growing trends in the international arena as a whole. But it is clear that the most concrete examples of this phenomenon can be found in the area of political eco-nomy—dealing with the choices made and the positions adopted by the EU and the US in respect of welfare and a widening range of social issues.

What happens when we look at the EU's system of international relations in the more political and security-related domains? Here, we have to consider the notions that statehood and strategic action by major players still shape a large number of international patterns, including those in which the EU and the US are increasingly engaged as part of the global security system. The relationships between the EU and its member states are very different in political and security concerns, as is the ca-pacity of the US to intervene and to exert influence in the system. Most specifically, the US ability to incite defection from common EU positions, to develop 'special re-lationships' with member states and to undermine the solidarity of the EU is greatly increased. This need not be a matter of conscious or explicit US policies; it can simply be a reflection of the different incentives and natural political leanings of the member states, as well as an indication of the more intergovernmental nature of the EU's institutional setup in the areas of Common Foreign & Security Policy (CFSP) and European Security and Defence Policy (ESDP).

There are thus effectively two parallel narratives of the EU-US relationship when we examine the EU's system of international relations (McGuire and Smith 2005). On the one hand there is the political economy narrative, which stresses the ways in which the EU has developed a powerful set of institutions and resources that can be used to undertake collective action in a range of contexts. These contexts are often 'domestic' as well as 'international': thus EU-US interaction occurs via many agents at a range of levels, from the global (for example, in the World Trade Organization (WTO)) through the European and then the national to the sub-national and the local. In the political-security domain, however, the narrative is very different. Although in many respects the EU's CFSP and ESDP have been developed because of the US—as a means of filling the gaps in US policies, or responding to the challenges of successive US administrations, especially during the 1990s and 2000s—they are also severely constrained by the dominance if not hegemony of the 'only superpower' when the questions are those of crisis and conflict, and of the commitment of real resources to the conduct of war or near-war operations. The incentives for EU member states to act collectively are very different in the two areas, with the balance between solidarity and defection or abstention only shifting slowly in the political and security area towards the 'European' level.

Examples of this contrast have been legion since the end of the Cold War, with the most important of them emerging from the 'war on terror' and the invasion of Iraq (see also Chapters 9 and 10 in this volume). Whereas in both of these cases the EU could maintain solidarity in the economic sphere, with the imposition of sanctions or the implementation of reconstruction programmes, the EU's system of international relations became subject to strains if not to disintegration as soon as the issues became those of 'hard security'. The collapse of European solidarity in the height of the Iraq crisis, leading to the stand-off between 'old' and 'new' Europe and to intense frictions between Britain and France in particular, seemed to indicate that wherever the US placed intense demands on the EU's foreign policy system there would be the likelihood of disintegration rather than a great leap forward in cooperation (Peterson and Pollack 2003).

But this is not the whole story: one of the other strands of development during the 1990s and beyond has been the growing scope of areas of 'soft security' and security activity engaging the 'internal' mechanisms of both the EU and the US (see also Chapter 10 in this volume). This picture highlights very different results from the story of EU-US security cooperation and competition. The EU's system in such areas as justice and home affairs, or environmental protection, or civil administration in the aftermath of conflict, possesses far greater resources for interaction with the US. Indeed, some have argued that in these areas the EU has a comparative advantage over the US bestowed by the enduring traces of 'civilian power'.

What implications does this system of shared competency, of penetrated decision-making, and of competing 'languages' of international relations carry for EU collective action? First, it is clear that the overlapping decision-making competency between the internal and external spheres of politics complicates the process of collective action. It is still difficult to gauge 'who speaks for Europe' (Allen 1998; Meunier and Nicolaïdis 1999; Meunier 2000b). Although the Commission is able to exercise strategic authority in some areas of policy-making, it is clear that institutional deficits and the lack of a single EU negotiating authority mean that the EU often suffers from a 'capabilities-expectations gap' (see Hill 1993, 1998a) (and even a simple 'capabilities' gap because there are just no instruments available), particularly in the foreign and security policy area. This gap has been visible even during many EU-US economic policy crises including those surrounding the Blair House Agreement in the course of the Uruguay Round (1992), the failed New Transatlantic Marketplace Agreement negotiations (1997–98) and most EU-US trade disputes (Peterson 1996; Pollack and Shaffer 2001; Petersmann and Pollack 2003). As noted above, it is starkly apparent in areas where the issues are those of 'high politics' and 'hard security', where the stakes are different if not higher and where the US's decisional capacity and institutional strength act as a competitive advantage. These 'gaps' in EU capacities for collective action are likely to be severely tested by EU-US relations, given the range and intensity of the encounters and their significance for 'internal' parties as well as the broader world arena (Smith 2004b).

EU-US relations and the processes of international relations

It will be evident from the argument so far that the transatlantic relationship is central to the broader processes of international relations. Despite the growing challenges from China, India, and others such as Brazil, the EU and the US are the two dominant actors in the capitalist world economy. They are central to the institutions of the global system, and they contain many of the most powerful military powers, including the dominant military power in the post-Cold War world. Thus, the development of transatlantic relations themselves is of great importance to the process of world politics, and their engagement with the wider world is highly significant to the operation of a host of broader economic, political and security processes. A number of key analytical dimensions connect EU-US relations and the processes of international relations.

First, it is important to look at the nature of the transatlantic relationship itself. Not all European-American relations are centred on the EU, and the persistence and evolution of NATO in particular means that the EU-US relationship is part of a 'multi-institutional' transatlantic system (Sloan 2002). Nonetheless, the EU-US relationship has been consistently at the core of this system, and has arguably become more central and more dominant as the EU has developed its foreign and security policies. During the 1990s, there was a consistent effort on both sides of the Atlantic to institutionalise EU-US relations and to provide a framework of rules and procedures, which would make them easier to manage (Pollack and Shaffer 2001). Thus came the Transatlantic Declaration in 1990, which established some broad principles of organisation. This was followed in 1995 by the New Transatlantic Agenda

(NTA) which greatly expanded not only the scope of the arrangement but also included more detailed areas of joint action between the EU and the US, and in 1998 by the Transatlantic Economic Partnership (TEP) which focused more specifically on the achievement of mutual recognition agreements and other technical agreements dealing with the management of trade and competition. As Figure 16.1 shows, these 'intergovernmental' arrangements were accompanied by efforts to construct non-governmental transatlantic dialogues and networks between business, environment, consumer, and labour groups (Pollack and Shaffer 2001; Steffenson 2005).

One implication of shared competency at different levels of decision-making is that it gives rise to 'intense transgovernmentalism' (see Wallace and Wallace 2000). The intra-EU process of decision-making is reflected in the way the EU forms relations with external partners, and there is no more convincing demonstration of this than in transatlantic relations. The EU-US process of institutionalisation has created a dense structure of decision-making processes that mirror in many respects the competency of the EU. For example, the TAD, the NTA, and the TEP have established three branches of governmental dialogue to accommodate the different competencies of EU external negotiators (Steffenson 2005; Pollack and Shaffer 2001). The economic ministerial dialogue, the foreign policy ministerial dialogue and the Senior Level Group form the head of three separate branches of transgovernmental dialogue. There is also a dense network of economic and political working

Figure 16.1 Transatlantic institutions (selected)

Intergovernmental	Transgovernmental	Transnational
	(Political)	
	NTA Senior Level Group NTA Task Force	Transatlantic Business Dialogue
EU-US Summits (soft security, economic issues)		
	(Economic)	
	TEP Steering Group TEP Working Groups	Transatlantic Consumer Dialogue
NATO Summits (hard security)		
	(Security)	
	CFSP Working Groups	Transatlantic Environmental Dialogue

groups, such as the NTA Task Force and the TEP working groups (see Figure 16.1). Transgovernmental networks are also prominent in the security relationship. However, the trajectory of development and the broader institutional context are very different in some respects, which again raises the questions about the extent to which the security domain, with its distinctive set of EU-US relations, power distribution and external challenges, can be governed, especially through joint processes in which the EU and the US act as relative equals.

Beyond the transatlantic arena, the post-Cold War period has clearly introduced new dimensions into the processes of international relations. In a number of areas the EU and the US often find themselves working in competition, rather than in some kind of strategic partnership. Take, for example, policies towards developing countries, where the EU has developed a wide-ranging and highly institutionalised set of relationships with the African, Caribbean, and Pacific countries (ACP), as detailed in Chapter 14 of this volume, and where as a result there is a tendency—not least within the EU itself—to see the Union as a 'development superpower' with an advantage over the Americans (see Table 16.1). With regard to global environmental management, the EU has at times acted as the leader of a broad coalition in the face of US intransigence and refusal to ratify major instruments such as the Kyoto Protocol (Bodansky 2003). In this and other areas of 'soft security', there is no doubt that EU-US competition is conducted on changing terms, with the EU's strategic assets becoming increasingly visible and important.

Still, the terms of engagement change, often dramatically, when the focus turns to the politics and other dimensions of 'hard security'. Here, in relation to the process of international relations, the EU has much less leverage. Some would argue, indeed, that US dominance in this field allows the EU to evade responsibility for international security processes, leaving it free to focus on those areas where its assets count (Kagan 2002, 2003). When it comes to the management of international conflicts, the past decade has made it abundantly clear that the EU is unlikely to act collectively or to exercise influence when the stakes are high. Whilst the EU might

Table 16.1 Comparative EU-US development aid

1. Volume of Official Development Assistance as percent of Gross National Product

	1950–1955	1960–1961	1970–1971	1980–1981	1990–1991	2002
EEC Members	.51	.64	.38	.41	.43	.35
US	.32	.56	.30	.23	.20	.13

2. Volume of net ODA (dollars, millions, 1990 exchange rate)

EEC Members	3.453	12.05	12.089	19.251	25.862	29.949
US	2.523	11.071	8.977	9.508	11.127	13.290

Source: Fuhrer (1996, 44); Quinlan (2003). The figures for 2002 indicate GNI rather than GNP.

be seen as the kinder, softer partner, it is not seen as a real player in many areas of 'hard security' and conflict management.

This conclusion seems to be borne out by the historical record. In successive conflicts during the 1990s, the Europeans passed up various opportunities to contribute collectively to conflict management. For example, many Americans felt, particularly in the early stages, that the conflict in former Yugoslavia was an opportunity for Europe to exercise its common foreign policy. In the end successive failures of EU collective action created conditions within which the US, with support from NATO allies and varying degrees of legitimation from the United Nations, was led to take decisive action (Peterson 2003; Zucconi 1996). Likewise the successive American engagements in the Gulf, leading eventually to the Iraq conflict of 2003, saw the EU left on the sidelines and hardly involved in either the military action or the post-war reconstruction and stabilisation. Former NATO Secretary-General Lord Robertson has made repeated comments blaming the EU member states for reinforcing a culture in which 'Americans fight wars and Europeans do the dishes' (Black 2002; see also Peterson 2003).

Despite its shortcomings, it can be argued that the EU's attempts to participate in international security processes are not completely ineffective. For example, Brussels is well equipped to deal with post-conflict management. The EU has played an important part in the post-conflict reconstruction of Afghanistan, and indeed there is a sense that the EU is the only actor that could do so. There has also been significant—and increasingly EU-centred—European engagement with regional conflicts, especially in sub-Saharan Africa where the member states have been able to take advantage of historical links with local parties. The EU does have an important role to play in international security, but as with all external policy areas, the size of its role is pre-determined by the commitment of its member states to act collectively (see Howorth, Chapter 9 in this volume).

There are other ways in which the EU attempts to counterbalance the dominance of the US in the process of international relations. These modes of activity and influence relate in many ways to less tangible forces and resources than those deployed either in the management of the global political economy or the management of international conflict (Manners 2002). In this area, therefore, it might be argued that the EU operates primarily as a 'normative power', reinforcing the idea that the discursive development of ideas and understandings matters in the social construction of international relations. Here, the EU's position in relation to the US, and its ability to exert leverage in a variety of contexts, is best understood when one evaluates how its interests, and thus its policy positions, are shaped by common ideas and values.

Many of the EU's most important disputes with the US are the result of underlying value differences—for example, the conception of risk as it relates to the precautionary principle, environmental burden sharing and consumer protection with regard to data privacy and food safety (for further examples in the trade field see Meunier and Nicolaïdis, Chapter 12 in this volume). There are also varying views amongst the member states on issues of neutrality and security (over the EU's internal security policy developments but also over external policies such as those towards the Middle East and the US plans for a Missile Defence system). In a number of areas this translates into quite profound differences about the power of 'critical dialogue' or the comparative merits of sanctions, force and diplomacy (Lindstrom 2003b: chapters 1–2). For instance, in approaching the problem of relations with 'rogue states' or the so-called 'axis of evil', the EU has shown a consistent tendency to emphasise the merits of critical dialogue in contrast to the US focus on more coercive measures including ultimately the threat of force. More generally, it can be argued that the EU places more emphasis on ideas and processes of conflict prevention in international relations rather than coercion or even pre-emption as preached and sometimes practised by the US.

Furthermore, the EU's efforts to pursue international, regional and bilateral co-operation are strongly shaped by ideas about 'best practice' within the EU. There is a conscious effort to export the model (or at least some of the key principles and structures) of European integration in developing regions such as central and eastern Europe and Latin America. The externalisation of practices used within the common market also applies to the EU's relations with major trading partners. For example, in the case of the expanding network of mutual recognition agreements for a range of products and processes, it is often the EU not the US that takes a lead in the negotiations. The contrast between the discourses of EU and US policies can be found in very powerful ways when it comes to handling inter-regional issues of human rights or environmental matters (see also Chapter 15 by de Flers and Regelsberger). As in the case of the areas mentioned earlier, it can be argued quite strongly here that the EU possesses and can exploit a form of comparative advantage in processes of international relations, many of which have become markedly more prominent in the post-Cold War world.

A further set of questions about the connections between EU-US relations and the broader international arena relates to the problem of global governance and the strengthening of multilateral institutions. To what extent does the EU shape the agenda of such international institutions, and how does that bring it into collision with the United States? To what extent has the EU developed a distinctive role and identity in areas where it interacts with the US (that is to say, in almost all areas of its activity)?

What is clear is that the capacity of the EU to act is wide-ranging but often conditional. Thus, there are some international organisations within which the Commission can speak and negotiate on behalf of the EU's members, such as the WTO and a number of global environmental organisations, but there are others where the EU's representation is mixed and its voice is less unified or consistent as a result. This means that on the one hand there are organisations where the EU as a whole can take a key role in agenda-setting, in negotiation, in coalition-building, and other aspects of international institutional life, and there are others where in order to achieve EU solidarity there has to be a continuous process of internal coalition-building and management. In addition, there is often some discursive confusion about not only who speaks for Europe but about whether there is any EU message, in terms of values or of expectations, to communicate. For example, in international monetary and financial institutions, there are effectively 'three EUs' for different purposes: the EU of 'Euroland', comprising the 12 Eurozone member states, the EU of 25 member states agreed on certain economic and financial positions, and the EU's member states as independent financial and monetary authorities with voices and votes of their own.

It is important in the context of international institutions to evaluate in more depth how the EU as opposed to the member states operates in international relations and to identify the ways in which this tension feeds into transatlantic relations. The EU is primarily a soft power and an economic power. This 'power inventory', including the power of ideas and values, can be mobilised, often in juxtaposition or in opposition to the US, in a variety of arenas, but it remains less substantial and less wide-ranging than that even of an internally-divided US. During the late 1990s and 2000s, the range over which the EU could deploy this kind of resource to affect the process of international political economy was significantly broadened with the introduction of the Euro, but as noted above, at least in the initial stages, this was subject to a number of limitations arising not only from the incomplete membership of the Eurozone but also from the imperfections of macro-economic management within the zone. Thus the impact of the Euro on the expectations of the US and other players and on the interactions between the EU and the US in international forums has to date been uncertain and patchy.

When it comes to the potential capacity of the EU to play a bigger role in the 'hard' part of the spectrum, as its own security policy develops, the story is even less clear. Still, there is already some evidence that the EU collectively has more of a capacity to make its voice heard on international security issues within international institutions. At times this has caused significant friction with the United States. Although Americans were initially annoyed by European security organisation, which seems to parallel if not duplicate NATO's functions, they soon come to realise that the EU is unlikely to rival NATO at least in the short term. In the longer term, the increasing development and institutionalisation of the ESDP and of the CFSP is likely to cut increasingly across US interests and make itself felt in organisations where the US has traditionally had a commanding role (Sloan 2002; Lindstrom 2003b).

There is a more general question about the ways in which we can characterise the EU's participation in international organisations. Do the member states have a higher capacity for collective action given their experience with European integration? Sbragia and Damro (1999) argue that the EU is able to adjust policies over time to international cooperation because the member states already have experience of working cooperatively. Nicolaïdis and Egan (2001) argue that in terms of regulatory cooperation—a policy area where the member states have a considerable level of integration—the EU has initiated the exporting of its policies in order to benefit from 'first mover advantage'. This means that in studying the EU as a contributor to international relations it is important to examine it as a model of governance. As the most advanced international organisation it has become both a target for anti-globalisation groups and an archetype of governance, given its emphasis on the participation of civil society.

The issue here is the extent to which these kinds of assets and trends bring the EU into collision with the US, and the ways in which these encounters are managed. What impact does EU-US discord have on the process of international relations as a whole? One set of implications relates to the EU's developing international role and the fact that in many areas of activity its international initiatives inevitably and immediately run into the positions and actions of the US. The EU has proceeded in part by trying to rival the US, in part by trying to contain it, and in part by trying to create new foundations for EU-US cooperation. The development of the EU's international role, and thus its contribution to the processes of international relations in a wide range of arenas, has been driven to a significant degree by this ambivalent relationship with the US and by the EU-US encounters to which it gives rise.

Box 16.3 Areas of EU-US cooperation on combating terrorism

- Support for United Nations Conventions on terrorism
- Financial Action Task Force on terrorist financing
- Work towards laws and regulations enabling asset freezing
- Strengthening regulation of financial institutions
- Increased law enforcement cooperation and intelligence
- EU-US agreements on extradition and mutual legal assistance
- Increased security of international transport: container security, passenger records
- Promote development, democracy and good governance

In the context of this role-initiation and role-development, it is important to re-member that in many respects the US role in the post-Cold War era has also been conditioned by the existence and the widening impact of the EU. There is a sense in which the EU takes up important elements of burden sharing which the US is either unwilling or unable to sustain, both within the global political economy and the diplomatic or security arenas. As can be seen from Box 16.3, in the area of counter-terrorism activity, the EU has been able to enter into a wide range of activities along-side the United States and in the context of a variety of international organisations. It is arguable that in key areas the EU has a greater 'capacity to cooperate' and to play constructive roles in newly developing international processes or institutions than does the US. The EU has gained legitimacy in a variety of international contexts, not only from its internal integration process but also from its representation of an in-creasingly distinctive 'European' position. One could draw the conclusion that the evolution of individual EU and US discourses and practices has had significant re-structuring effects on the broader world arena—in other words, that the EU has be-gun to establish itself as an independent and influential force in the definition and development of global governance systems. But one must never forget the problems that arise for the EU in the 'hard' end of the spectrum. Inexorably this point leads to the consideration of EU-US relations in the context of understandings about the EU as a 'power'.

EU-US relations and the EU as a power in international relations

The evolution of the EU as a 'power' in international relations has inevitably become a point of tension with the US (Gordon and Shapiro 2004; Kagan 2002, 2003; Kupchan 2003). As pointed out many times in other chapters of this book, and in the preceding section of this chapter, the development of EU power resources and the processes by which they are mobilised and deployed has followed a distinctive path, conditioned by the fact that the EU is an organisation which is ultimately founded on states. This accounts for the conditional grants of foreign policy power to the EU and for the ways in which the member states have retained their own distinct national preferences, positions and resources. In other words, it explains the fact that in many respects, the EU continues to be a 'civilian power' in the international arena and that its influence is largely confined to those areas that fall outside the realm of hard security and high politics.

As noted above, this has important implications for the ways in which the EU and the US interact, both in areas affecting the EU's system of international relations and in areas that relate more to the broader process of international relations. In this part of the chapter, the emphasis is rather different. Here the focus is on the ways in which the EU and the US express apparently different types or 'mixes' of power, on the ways in which this enters into the EU and US discourses and on the ways in which this affects EU-US relations. The EU-US relationship encompasses a number of profound ambiguities emerging from the internal evolution of both parties and their shifting roles in the broader world arena.

Examining the EU as a power in international relations raises fresh analytical and empirical puzzles. A first problem, and one that has led to intense debate on both sides of the Atlantic in the early 2000s, is the nature of power itself. Of course power is a major preoccupation of IR theory, and brings with it a huge accumulated baggage of ideas about resources and capabilities, about the combination and mobilisation of power and about the management of power both at the national level and at the level of world order. It is thus not surprising that the end of the Cold War launched an obsessive examination by scholars and policy-makers of the new power situation, in which the United States seemed to have an almost unqualified dominance especially in military affairs. An intense debate followed in the early 2000s around what came to be seen as two qualitatively different types of power, one American, one European.

Key to this debate was the idea that the EU was constructed around a predominantly 'soft' notion of power, focusing and rationalising the Union's interests as a 'trading state' with key interests in the economic and social realms. By focusing on soft power, the EU could logically focus on ways to achieve both economic gains and key welfare objectives. More negatively, it was argued by some that the EU version of power was a rationalisation of the Union's essential weakness, and that it had been since the beginnings of the European integration project. Some argued that EU leaders settled for a second best version of power, built on its comparative advantages, because they could not hope to match the major military powers in matters of 'hard security'. In any case these judgments were not just empirical: they were also essentially moral, identifying the Europeans as more likely to compromise with bad regimes and bad leaders than those who saw the real nature of the international power game. A phrase often quoted in the early 2000s was that, 'Americans were from Mars and Europeans from Venus', and there was no doubt for many American commentators where virtue lay when confronted with the 'axis of evil' and other threats to the new world order (see Kagan 2002, 2003; Smith 2004a).

By contrast, the logic of American power was seen as essentially rooted in the 'hard' end of the spectrum. It had resources and could address problems in a way that the Europeans simply could not envisage. During the 1990s, this disparity was most apparent in the capacity to intervene on a global scale. It was also made very apparent much closer to home for the EU, when the Union had to rely on the US to inject a large number of troops and other material into the former Yugoslavia at short notice (Zucconi 1996). The key here, however, is not just what happened in practical policy terms, but also what effect this had on the expectations and understandings of policy-makers on both sides of the Atlantic. Quite simply, the mind-set of policy-makers in the US, especially but not only during the first George W. Bush Administration of 2000–2004, was one that accommodated the possibility and even the probability of the use of military power (including its unilateral use), whereas such options were effectively foreclosed at the collective EU level (Smith 2004a). As explained earlier, this has had a significant effect on the ways in which major EU member states have perceived the incentives to operate at the EU level, and has also conditioned their readiness to defect at crucial moments of crisis and conflict management.

How far does this power disparity extend, and how far are its effects felt in the area of non-military power? It is clear that the EU is still predominantly an economic power, and that it most legitimately rivals the US in international economic arenas. The EU's economic position makes it a viable foreign policy actor, especially where the use of economic sanctions, aid or other inducements is in question; it has also invested considerable effort in its capacity to act as a soft power in terms of aid and development assistance, and to operate in arenas where institutions and regimes are still being formed, such as in the environmental domain. As a result, it is possible to argue that the EU can exert a growing amount of 'institutional power' through inter-national regimes and organisations, and that its capacity to construct wide-ranging international coalitions on certain issues gives it influence comparable to if not more impressive than that of the US. The EU is less able to establish collective preferences and understandings in the security field, but there is a sense in which the EU has inserted itself into an increasing range of situations as a diplomatic actor, and in which it might develop considerably greater capacity to supplant the US either with American agreement or with American 'absence' (cf. the situation in the Balkans).

To what extent does the US—in the shape of its political leaders and comment-ators or analysts—perceive the EU as a major power? There is a sense in which the answer to this question has remained constant since Henry Kissinger pronounced it as 'civilian' and 'regional' in the early 1970s. The EU is also increasingly seen (both by its member states and by outsiders) as a 'soft security actor', with a significant role in the European order and an increasing but often frustrating role in the broader diplomacy of world order. For example, the EU has functioned as a full contributing member of the so-called 'Quartet' group on the Middle East (with the US, the UN, and Russia), helping to produce the 'road map' for an Israeli-Palestine peace settlement which was published in 2003. The creation of the High Representative for Common Foreign and Security Policy—the post first held by Javier Solana—meant that the EU was equipped to play a more significant role in international diplomacy. A key ques-tion, though, is whether other key actors perceive the EU as a persuasive voice in international affairs. The EU has established a role in Afghanistan which might be seen as parallel to that assumed in the later stages of the Balkans conflicts, but do diplomatic and reconstructive functions give the EU the same status enjoyed by the US? Equally, the EU has a well-established role in the G7 and G8 groups of leading industrial countries, but it is not clear whether this has reinforced or weakened the perception of the Union as a key player in Washington, or indeed in the capitals of some member states who are also G7/G8 members.

This raises major questions about the EU's role in the broader international arena. Is it possible, firstly, that the EU can be seen as an alternative player to the US for diplomatic or even security purposes in situations of regional or local conflict? This possibility has at least been raised by the EU's actions in a number of conflicts, for example in sub-Saharan Africa, during the early years of the new century. Or should the EU, secondly, be seen as a balancing force for the US in a variety of institutional and other contexts, providing the 'soft cop' to balance the United States' 'hard cop'? Take for example the case of Iran's nuclear policies (see Box 16.4 below and Everts, 2004). This case seems to indicate that there was at least a tacit division of labour between the EU (especially three of its leading members) and the US in trying to handle and to defuse the possibility of Iran obtaining nuclear capacity. Whilst this one episode cannot be seen as typical, it is important at least to raise the possibility that the EU and the US could be more complementary than competitive in their uses of international power (Moravcsik 2003).

More typical is the third possibility apparent under George W. Bush's Administration: that the EU would be ignored, and even 'disaggregated' either as the result of deliberate US policies or as the result of the inevitable tensions between different positions within the EU, for example on Iraq (Howorth 2003; Lindstrom 2003b; Smith 2004b). In this case, the distinction notoriously made by Secretary of Defence Donald Rumsfeld between 'old Europe' (France, Germany, and their supporters) and 'new Europe' (the UK, Spain, and many of the newly-acceding states from central and eastern Europe) was intended to convey US opposition to apparent European feebleness,

---

Box 16.4 The EU, the US and Iran's nuclear programmes

During 2003–2004 differences surfaced between the EU member states and the US over how to handle nuclear weapons programmes in Iran. These tensions reflected a long-standing divergence of approaches, with the Europeans having emphasised the value of 'critical dialogue' with Tehran and the Americans having adopted a strategy based on containment or even 'rollback', Iran being one of the members of the so-called 'axis of evil'. The problem was also underlined by the transatlantic disagreements that had emerged during the build-up to and the conduct of the American-led attack on Iraq in 2003. In the case of Iran, however, there was a united EU position in favour of diplomacy and a multilateral solution; the UK, which had been the most loyal and substantial of the US's allies in the Iraq action, pursued a strongly 'Europeanized' line on Iran, and played a leading role through what became known as the 'EU3' group along with France and Germany. Having secured Iranian agreement to adhere to the Nuclear Non-Proliferation Treaty during 2003, the 'EU3' (supported by Russia) then decided to offer Iran incentives to suspend its work with enriched uranium, and to multilateralise the process through the involvement of the International Atomic Energy Agency in monitoring and surveillance. However, the Bush Administration did not endorse the package and explicitly canvassed the possibility of coercive sanctions or even a pre-emptive attack on Iran's nuclear facilities. The victory of George W. Bush in the US Presidential election of November 2004 seemed likely to create further tensions between the EU focus on 'soft power' and multilateral solutions, and the US emphasis on 'hard power' and the possibility of force. Although this could be seen as proof of an implicit division of labour, it could also be seen as a sign of further conflict to come.

but also to detach some of the more significant prospective new member states such as Poland.

It is apparent that the EU has faced, is facing and will always face a problem with the management of American power, and this will profoundly affect its developing international relations. The US is clearly a major factor in the uneven development of the EU's own international power position, both structurally and as the result of successive policies emanating from Washington. The United States is also, as noted earlier, present in the EU itself, both as the result of the American stake in Europe and as the reflection of the place Washington and its power occupy in the minds of European political leaders and officials.

In consequence, when discussion turns to the 'capability-expectations gap' in EU policies, Washington is both a major incentive for the gap to be closed and a major reason why in certain areas it may never be closed. This does not mean that the EU is not a 'power' in the international arena, but rather that its status has been, and will continue to be, embedded in a US-dominated western or global order. The President of the European Commission, José Manuel Barroso, during his confirmation hearings in July 2004, felt the need to make two apparently conflicting points during his testimony. On the one hand, he attacked the arrogance of the US and called for a more equal relationship between Brussels and Washington; on the other hand, he was at pains to emphasise his 'Atlanticist' credentials, his support for the US attack on Iraq and his commitment to support American policies in the 'war on terror'. To a greater or lesser degree, all EU leaders have to reconcile these components in the attempt to pursue the EU's international role after 11 September 2001.

Conclusion

This chapter has explored four key topics: the evolution of EU-US relations, the ways in which EU-US relations enter into the EU's system of international relations, the impact of EU-US relations on the EU's role in the process of international relations, and the ways in which the EU-US relationship feeds into the part played by the EU as an international 'power'. The key findings are as follows:

• The developing EU-US relationship has been a key force in shaping the development of the EU's international relations, but it is a force full of contradictions.

• In many respects, the US (both as a governmental and a private actor) is 'present' in the EU's system of international relations, and the EU-US relationship has played a key (and contradictory) role in development of the EU's foreign policy mechanisms.

• The EU-US relationship has been crucial in conditioning the development of the EU's participation in international processes, and it will continue to be a key factor shaping the EU's role in many international contexts, including key global institutions.

• As a result of the factors mentioned above, the EU's role as a 'power' in international relations must be seen at least partly in the light of its relationship with the US. This is so not only because of the dominant American position in a number of areas of international life, but also because of the way in which the US enters into the expectations and understandings of those making policies within the EU as well as their key international partners.

The overall conclusion from this discussion is necessarily nuanced and reflects a number of contradictory lines of development. In terms of international relations theory, it is clear that any analysis of EU-US relations raises major questions about 'power and interdependence' and the extent to which different worlds of international relations can coexist. EU-US relations also generate and crystallise key questions about the role of institutions in world politics and the ways in which they can be seen as sources of legitimacy as well as sources of information, support, and influence. More specifically, they also raise in a highly concentrated form questions about the possibilities and limits of collective action in international relations, both at the EU and at the global level. The EU and the US exist in conditions of intense yet uneven integration, within an international context full of uncertainty, and dealing with its most 'significant other' will remain a dominating item on the EU's international agenda.

Further reading

There is a vast literature on the general area of transatlantic relations, which has been a key focus of scholarship and debate since the 1940s. The list below gives a sample of the more recent commentaries and of the literature relating EU-US relations to broader problems of international relations. Peterson (1996), Guay (1999), and McGuire and Smith (2005) provide historical reviews as well as dealing with contemporary policy issues; each of them also links EU-US relations to issues of international relations analysis. The more specific debates about the end of the Cold War, the conflicts of the 1990s and the tensions over Iraq are dealt with by Gordon and Shapiro (2003), Kagan (2002), Peterson and Pollack (2003), Sloan (2002), and Smith and Woolcock (1993). Issues of political economy are covered by the general texts cited above and by Pollack and Shaffer (2001). The possible futures of EU-US relations are covered by many of the texts and specifically by Moravcsik (2003).

Gordon, P., and Shapiro, J. (2004), *Allies at War: America, Europe, and the Crisis over Iraq* (Washington DC: Brookings Institution).

Guay, T. (1999), *The United States and the European Union: the political economy of a relationship* (Sheffield: Sheffield Academic Press).

Kagan, R. (2003), *Paradise and Power: America and Europe in the New World Order* (London: Atlantic Books).

McGuire, S., and Smith, M. (2005), *The European Union and the United States: Competition and Convergence in the Global Arena* (Basingstoke: Palgrave/Macmillan).

Moravcsik, A. (2003), 'Striking a New Transatlantic Bargain'. *Foreign Affairs* 82/4, 74–89.

Peterson, J. (1996), *Europe and America: The Prospects for Partnership*, 2nd edition (London: Routledge).

Peterson, J., and Pollack, M. (eds) (2003), *Europe, America, Bush: Transatlantic Relations in the Twenty-First Century* (London: Routledge).

Pollack, M., and Shaffer, G. (eds) (2001), *Transatlantic Governance in the Global Economy* (Lanham, MD: Rowman and Littlefield).

Sloan, S. (2002), *NATO, the European Union and the Atlantic Community: the Transatlantic Bargain Reconsidered* (Lanham, MD: Rowman and Littlefield).

Smith, M., and Woolcock, S. (1993), *The United States and the European Community in a Transformed World* (London: Pinter/Royal Institute of International Affairs).

Web links

The most useful sites for information about EU-US relations in general are the Commission's Europa site (http://www.europa.eu.int), especially the trade and CFSP pages, and the web site of the Commission delegation in Washington DC (http://www.eurunion.org). See also the various US government web sites including that of the US Mission to the EU (http://www.useu.be/) and that of the State Department (http://www.state.gov). There is of course a huge variety of both governmental and commercial sites dealing with the wide range of EU-US issues: see for example the site of the Brookings Institution Centre on the US and Europe: http://www.brookings.edu/fp/cuse; or the site of the Institute for International Economics: http://www.iie.org.

Part IV

Evaluation and Conclusion

Chapter 17

A European Civilising Process?[1]

Andrew Linklater

Contents

Summary

One of the most famous portrayals of the EU casts it as a security community in which national governments have renounced the use of force between themselves and where mass publics are acquiring a palpable sense of 'we feeling'. Another celebrated approach depicts the EU as a civilian power committed to ending power politics between the member states and in the world at large. These reflections on the EU can be linked with what some sociologists call 'the civilising process' — the process in which individual European societies became pacified and the members of national populations came to identify more closely with one another between the 16th century and the present day. One of the three questions discussed in this chapter is whether it is useful to regard the EU as an experiment in taking the civilising process beyond the nation-state — and not just within Europe. What specifically is the relationship between the EU's role in transforming political community on the continent and its conduct towards the rest of the world?

How the EU should behave towards other societies is the second key question which is raised in this chapter. What moral criteria should be used to decide whether the EU is realising its potential as a civilian power in world affairs? What should the EU as a civilian power aim to achieve in future? Although the study of 'the civilising process' is a sociological one, it offers some clues as to how to approach normative questions of this kind. One of its central empirical claims is that all societies must ask how their members can satisfy their basic needs without injuring, demeaning, frustrating and in other ways *harming* each other time and time again. It is a small step from here to the question of what any society *should* do to prevent harm to its inhabitants and indeed to the members of other societies. The EU has tried to persuade neighbouring states to abolish the death penalty but should it take this moral stance? More specifically, what should the EU do to ensure that its attempt to build closer cooperation in Europe does not cause unnecessary harm to people who live elsewhere? A third question is whether a moral audit of the EU would reveal significant achievements in promoting common interests without harming the members of other societies or major deficiencies which the EU should aim to reduce in future.

Introduction

In May 2000 the German Foreign Minister, Joschka Fischer, described the EU as a regional political system based 'on the rejection of the European balance-of-power principle and the hegemonic ambitions of individual states that had emerged following the peace of Westphalia in 1648' (quoted in Kagan 2003, 56). Many observers share Fischer's view that the EU's greatest achievement has been to end the addiction to realpolitik which dominated the continent for almost four centuries. Analysts have argued that the EU demonstrates that classical realists and neo-realists are wrong to insist that anarchy condemns states to compete for military power and to become embroiled in major wars. They maintain that Western Europe has been the site for an important experiment in transforming political community (Linklater 1998). The region has self-consciously broken with the 'totalising project' in which states placed loyalty to the nation above other possible objects of identification. Efforts to promote respect for linguistic and cultural differences *within* Europe's nation states have been accompanied by measures to reduce the moral and political significance of national differences *between* sovereign political communities. Steps to devolve power to the domestic regions have developed in tandem with the endeavour to establish transnational political institutions and solidarities. The EU is rightly credited with promoting new forms of international cooperation which have brought an end to the appalling suffering caused by modern war. One of its greatest achievements has been to help end the historical antagonism between France and Germany. However, the EU has also been concerned with promoting greater respect for the linguistic and cultural differences which can be found within each of its member states.

With the end of the bipolar era, the EU moved to the larger canvass of enlarging the organisation to assist post-socialist societies which were struggling to achieve economic prosperity and political stability. To its earlier project of eliminating war between the European powers, the EU added the new challenge of encouraging democratic politics and respect for human rights across the continent. In large part because of their ties with the former colonies, members of the EU have been active in providing development assistance to poorer societies and in defending human rights on a global scale. It is striking that the project of transforming political community in Western Europe has come to be linked with this broader set of international con-cerns—that the values which EU members have used to develop a regional political identity have led them to reflect on the role the organisation should have in world affairs. In this respect the EU is no different from all political associations in having to ask what its internal value-commitments mean for its behaviour towards the rest of the world.

Two images of the EU

It is useful to comment on two influential characterisations of the EU before consid-ering links with the sociological analysis of the civilising process in the next section of this chapter. The aim here is to show how various portraits of the organisation focus on dimensions of social and political change which lie at the heart of empir-ical studies of the civilising process. It should be stressed from the outset that dis-cussions of the civilising process have mainly concentrated on long-term patterns of social and political life *within* modern European states: there has been less emphasis on any changes in the ways in which sovereign states behave towards one another. The argument that follows is that the idea of a civilising process can be usefully ex-tended to include developments at the international level (Linklater 2004). The aim is to show that the EU can be regarded as a major experiment in developing a complex civilising process in international politics.

Two views of the EU are especially relevant to the analysis of the EU as a civilising process. The first is Karl Deutsch's idea of the 'security community'—a community whose members no longer regard force as a legitimate means of resolving political differences and who display significant capacities to communicate with each other, at both elite and mass levels. This he first observed in the North Atlantic area, but then also in the European Economic Community (Deutsch 1957). Taylor (1996, 156–7) contributes to the discussion of 'we feeling' by noting how the EU has had an import-ant role in promoting trust between the peoples of France and Germany. He argues that the EU has made significant inroads into the 'in-group—out-group mentality' which underpinned suspicion, geopolitical competition, and violence between the two societies. He adds that the EU has had some success in encouraging 'a degree of popular identification with the Community which (is) ahead of the perceived level of utilitarian reward'. In other words, support for the EU cannot be reduced to in-dividual or social calculations of immediate self-interest (although these considera-tions underlie loyalty to all political associations). Support rests in part on the belief that the project of economic and political integration will benefit most of Europe's peoples over time.

A second example is Duchêne's frequently cited notion of the EU as a civilian power which introduces 'a new stage in political civilisation', one that replaces the balance of power with the attempt 'to *domesticate* relations between states, includ-ing those of its members and those with states outside its frontiers'. The civilian power aims 'to bring to international problems the sense of common responsibility and structures of contractual politics which have in the past been associated almost

---

Box 17.1 Norbert Elias

Norbert Elias was born in Breslau, Germany in 1897 and died in 1990. Initially a student of philosophy and medicine, Elias was drawn towards the new field of Sociology. In 1933, shortly after Hitler's rise to power, Elias left Germany for Paris and then London where he completed his major work, *The Civilizing Process*, first published in Switzerland in 1939. Over the next quarter of a century Elias published little, although he continued to refine his thesis about the civilising process. In 1954, at the age of 57, Elias was appointed to his first permanent academic position in the Department of Sociology at the University of Leicester. In the last 30 years of his life, Elias published prolifically, and his work gradually came to be recognised as one of the most significant contributions to sociological thought in the 20th century.

---

exclusively with "home" and not foreign, that is *alien*, affairs' (Duchêne 1973—italics above in original). Manners (2002) develops Duchêne's theme in an interesting discussion of Normative Power Europe. He uses this expression to describe the EU's commitment to global moral causes such as the abolition of the death penalty (which has had, however, no effect on the US Government). His argument is that the dominant self-images of the EU have encouraged a foreign policy stance which aims to end what its members regard as unnecessary suffering caused by a cruel form of punishment.

There are several parallels between those interpretations of the EU and the analysis of the civilising process which was undertaken by the leading European sociologist, Norbert Elias (1897–1990). Those characterisations of the organisation suggest that it is meaningful to regard the EU as evidence of a civilising process 'beyond the nation-state'—not that Elias saw the EU in these terms. Indeed Elias, who was rare amongst sociologists in reflecting on relations between states, did not believe there was much evidence of a civilising process in international relations. In common with exponents of the Hobbesian or realist approach, he was sceptical that the civilising process could develop outside the state, where centralised institutions monopolised control of the instruments of violence and maintained social and political order. In fact, the EU demonstrates that Elias was unduly pessimistic about what European states could achieve in their relations with each other and with the rest of the world. Here it is worth pausing to note that pessimism about what is possible in international politics has often led analysts to believe that moral and political philosophy are relevant to domestic politics where there is evidence of social progress, but hardly relevant to international politics which display the same depressing regularities across the millennia. The success the EU has had in blurring the contrast between domestic and international politics invites philosophical reflections about what the EU should aim to achieve as a normative power committed to promoting community in international relations. Prior to considering these issues it is necessary to provide a brief overview of Elias's sociology of the civilising process.

Norbert Elias on 'the civilizing process'

Elias claimed to have discovered important long-term patterns of change within modern European states between the 15th and 20th centuries. He argued that these societies were pacified in this period; their inhabitants came to enjoy levels of personal security which simply did not exist in the Middle Ages (Elias has been accused of exaggerating the differences between the Middle Ages and modern Europe, but we cannot consider that here). He maintained that over five centuries the citizens of modern states came to identify more closely with each other (but not with the members of other states to any discernible extent). One of the consequences was that Western European societies came to find public acts of cruelty such as public execution and violent punishment morally repugnant. Support for Elias's analysis of the modern West can be found not only in the development of such taboos against violence, but in increasing concern about cruelty to animals and children. This form of analysis immediately raises questions about whether developments in international criminal law since the Nuremberg and Tokyo trials and the growth of the universal human rights culture since the Universal Declaration of Human Rights in 1948 point to the existence of a global civilising process.

It is essential to stress that Elias did not argue that modern European societies are more civilised than other places. Admittedly, his language can easily lead to this interpretation; however, his primary task as a sociologist was to understand how Europeans came to see themselves as a civilisation which was entitled, so they once believed, to colonise other societies and to enslave other peoples. Far from endorsing this world-view, Elias set out to comprehend its development. He was also keen to stress — we shall come back to this later — that all civilising processes, and not only the one he analysed in the modern West, are accompanied by 'decivilising processes' and tendencies. In other words civilising processes simultaneously check aggressive inclinations *and* create new possibilities of violence and domination.

Elias's conception of the civilising process can be reduced to six basic points. The first is that from the 1500s onwards the modern state succeeded in monopolising control of the instruments of violence; it was able to pacify society by bringing its physical power to bear on violent tendencies in society. A second point is that the greater personal security made higher levels of social and economic interdependence possible. A third point is that over time 'self-control' and 'internal' checks on aggressive inclinations grew in importance relative to the state's need to use its physical power to maintain personal security; the necessity for greater self-control came to be 'taken for granted' as the populations of each modern society became increasingly interdependent (Elias 1996, 34). Here, it is worth noting a parallel with Michel Foucault's later account of the importance of self-monitoring as against external compulsion for the organisation of modern societies (see also Smith 2001). Foucault believed that this change marked the development of new forms of power rather than the progress of society. Some of Elias's observations about long-term changes in Europe seem to suggest that modern societies have progressed beyond the Middle Ages, but he was keen to stress that the civilising process was accompanied by more sinister forces.

A fourth point is that the trend towards greater control of aggressive tendencies was accompanied by a tendency 'to identify more readily with other people…regardless of social origins'. In particular, attitudes to cruelty and suffering changed fundamentally over five centuries. Some examples of this long-term trend have already been given. An essential part of the civilising process is that anything distasteful or disgusting—including the slaughter of animals—has been hidden 'behind the scenes' if not eliminated (Fletcher 1997, 21; 2000, 161ff). Elias believed this practice reflected changing sensibilities towards violence.

A fifth point is that the Europeans' belief that these developments demonstrated their 'inborn superiority' over other peoples had disastrous consequences for the continent in the 1930s and 1940s. During the 19th and 20th centuries, Europeans

---

Box 17.2 Elias on the civilising process

'If members of present-day Western civilized society were to find themselves suddenly transported into a past epoch of their own society, such as the medieval-feudal period, they would find there much that they esteem "uncivilized" in other societies today…They would, depending on their situation and inclinations, be either attracted by the wilder, more unrestrained and adventurous life of the upper classes in this society, or repulsed by the "barbaric" customs, the squalor and coarseness…encountered there.' (N. Elias, 1992, p 147)

'That physical security from violence by other people is not so great in all societies as in our own is usually not clearly realized.' (N. Elias, 2001a, p 48)

'We no longer regard it as a Sunday entertainment to see people hanged, quartered, broken on the wheel…As compared with antiquity, our identification with other people, our sharing in their suffering and death, has increased.' (N. Elias, 2001a, pp 2–3)

'One can see (the) growing internalization of the social prohibition against violence and the advance in the threshold of revulsion against violence, especially against killing and even against seeing it done, if one considers that, in its heyday, the ritual of English fox-hunting, which prohibited any direct human participation in the killing, represented a civilizing spurt. It was an advance in people's revulsion against doing violence, while today, in accordance with the continued advance of the threshold of sensitivity, not a few people find even this representative of an earlier civilizing spurt distasteful and would like to see it abolished.' (N. Elias, 1986, p 163)

'In ancient Greece and Rome we hear time and time again of infants thrown onto dungheaps or in rivers…Until the late nineteenth century there was no law against infanticide. Public opinion in antiquity also regarded the killing of infants or the sale of children—if they were pretty, to brothels, otherwise as slaves—as self-evident. The threshold of sensibility among people in antiquity—like those of Europeans in the Middle Ages and the early modern period—was quite different from that of the present day, particularly in relation to the use of physical violence. People assumed that they were violent to each other, they were attuned to it. No-one noticed that children required special treatment.' (N. Elias, 1998c, pp 142–3)

'So far, the civilizing of human beings and the standards of civilization have developed completely unplanned and in a haphazard manner. It is necessary to form a theory so that, in the future, we may be able to judge more closely what kind of restraints are required for complicated societies to function and what type of restraints have been merely built into us to bolster up the authority of certain ruling groups.' (N. Elias, 1998b, p 145)

came to think that terrible cruelty belonged to the past or was typical of uncivilised peoples who had yet to emulate their process of social and political development. This myth of superiority left them unprepared for Fascism and for the attempt to destroy European Jews. A sixth and final point was that it was too simple to regard the Nazi death camps as evidence of regression to a more barbaric past. The Nazis' genocidal project revealed that new totalitarian possibilities were made possible by the civilising process. The attempt to exterminate the Jews employed a vast bureaucracy which administered genocide yet without directly involving the mass of the population in the use of violence. Complex questions exist about whether Nazi genocide was evidence of the dangerous side of the civilising process or an example of its underdevelopment in the German society, but they cannot be discussed here. Nonetheless, enough has been said to explain why Elias (1996, 173) observed that the 'civilization of which I speak is never completed and always endangered'.

A global civilising process?

It is important to comment briefly about Elias's views about international relations before using his approach to reflect on the EU. The crucial point to make is that he did not think the civilising process had made much impression on relations between states between the 15th and 20th centuries. His analysis was essentially realist. States had competed relentlessly for power and security in the absence of a global monopoly of force. They had encouraged their populations to believe that relations between states and relations between citizens were governed by different moral codes: they had tolerated—and at times encouraged—the use of force in the conduct of their external relations while loudly proclaiming their achievement in eradicating violence in the relations between members of the same society (Elias 1996, 461). Elias did not think this 'curious split' within Western civilisation was about to be—or would ever be—healed.

The problem with this argument, it might be suggested, is that it inclines too sharply towards vulgar realism. Elias did refer in passing to the important development of new regional international organisations such as the EU—and others have provided ways of building on this possibly more optimistic dimension of his remarks on world politics by arguing that member states have come to be bound together by 'new standards of decency' (Smith, K. 2000). Elias argued that emotional responses to suffering in war and genocide had changed perceptibly as part of the larger historical trend towards popular aversion against cruelty. There was some evidence of the development of a 'global conscience' in human affairs—and the development of a European public opinion in response to the war in Iraq can be regarded as a recent example of this trend. But Elias was convinced that the civilising process was a precarious achievement and that emotional repugnance to excessive violence was prone to crumble rapidly when individuals or societies confronted new threats to safety and security.

Sociologists and political scientists have not devoted much time to the question of whether the European Union has revealed how the civilising process can develop

---

Box 17.3 Elias on international relations

'The ancient Greeks. . .who are so often held up to us as models of civilized behaviour, considered it quite a matter of course to commit acts of mass destruction, not quite identical
to those of the National Socialists but, nevertheless, similar to them in several respects. The
Athenian popular assembly decided to wipe out the entire population of Melos, because the
city did not want to join the Athenian colonial empire. There were dozens of other examples
in antiquity of what we now call genocide.' (N. Elias, 1996, p 445)

'The wars of the seventeenth century were cruel in a somewhat different sense to those
of today. The army had, as far as possible, to feed itself when on foreign soil. Plunder and
rapine were not merely permitted, but were demanded by military technique. To torment
the subjugated inhabitants of occupied territories. . .was, as well as a means of satisfying
lust, a deliberate means of collecting war contributions and bringing to light concealed
treasure. Soldiers were supposed to behave like robbers. It was a banditry exacted and organized by the army commanders.' (N. Elias, 1998a, pp 22–3)

'We (may be) entering an era in which it will no longer be individual states but unions of
states which will serve mankind as the dominant social unit.' (N. Elias, 2001b, pp 164–5)

'We may surmise that with continuing integration even larger units will gradually be assembled under a stable government and internally pacified, and that they in their turn will
turn their weapons outwards against human aggregates of the same size until, with a further integration, a still greater reduction of distances, they too gradually grow together and
world society is pacified.' (N. Elias, 2000, p 255)

'We are nowadays more strongly aware than ever before that an enormously large part
of humanity live their entire lives on the verge of starvation. . .Many members of richer
countries feel it to be almost a duty to do something about the misery of other human
groups. . .in actual fact relatively little is done. The feeling of responsibility which people
have for each other is certainly minimal, looked at in absolute terms, but compared with before it has increased.' (N. Elias, 1996, p 26)

'The fact that we have not yet learned how to curb wars. . .lends support to the assumption that. . .what we call modern times represents a very early rather than a late stage of development. I like best the suggestion that our descendants, if humanity can survive the violence of our age, might consider us as late barbarians.' (N. Elias, 1991, pp 146–7)

---

beyond the nation state (a partial exception is Kapteyn, 1996). But if we think about
what Deutsch, Duchêne and others have written about security communities, civilian
power status and normative power Europe, then similarities with Elias's type of analysis quickly become apparent.

There are parallels, for example, between Deutsch's conception of a security community which no longer regards force as a legitimate means of resolving differences between societies that share a sense of 'we feeling', and Elias's analysis of
pacification and the development of mutual identification between human beings
who belong to the same nation state. Parallels exist between Taylor's focus on how
the EU has eroded the 'in-group—out-group mentality' especially in the relations
between France and Germany and Elias's interest in widening emotional identification between the members of modern states. Duchêne's notion of civilian power,
which attempts 'to domesticate relations between states', bears comparison with
Elias's account of what preceded this 'new stage in political civilisation', namely the
civilising process within the European state. Manners' account of normative power

Europe which is committed to the abolition of the death penalty in other societies immediately brings to mind Elias's analysis of changing orientations to cruelty and suffering in Europe over the last few centuries.

All of these analyses deal with similar political and psychological phenomena: the pacification of human affairs and the internalisation of constraints on violent behaviour. But of course, the analysis of such developments within the EU assumes precisely what Elias tended to reject, namely the existence of a civilising process between states that have not submitted to institutions which have monopoly control of the instruments of force. The approaches to the EU which have been discussed can

---

Box 17.4 Conceptions of the EU

'Given sufficiently widespread compliance habits and other favorable circumstances, a political community may become effectively integrated and thus come to function as a security community, so that war among its constituent populations is neither expected nor in fact probable. Integration into a security community may be, but need not be, accompanied by a formal amalgamation or merger of political institutions.' (Karl Deutsch, 1957a, p 42)

'Europe as a whole could well become the first example in history of a major centre of the balance of power becoming in the era of its decline not a colonised victim but the exemplar of a new stage in political civilisation. . .The European Community's interest as a civilian group of countries long on economic power and relatively short on armed force is as far as possible to *domesticate* relations between states, including those of its members and those with states outside its frontiers. This means trying to bring to international problems the sense of common responsibility and structures of contractual politics which have in the past been associated almost exclusively with "home" and not foreign, that is *alien*, affairs.' (Francois Duchêne, 1973, pp 19–20)

'Europe's attainment is normative rather than empirical. . .It is perhaps a paradox. . .that the continent which once ruled the world through the physical impositions of imperialism is now coming to set world standards in normative terms.' (Richard Rosecrance, 1988, p 22)

'The concept of normative power is an attempt to suggest that not only is the EU constructed on a normative basis, but importantly that this predisposes it to act in a normative way in world politics.' (Ian Manners, 2002, p 252)

'The Union is founded on the principles of liberty, democracy, respect for human rights and fundamental freedoms, and the rule of law, principles which are common to the Member States.' (Article 6(1) of the 1997 Amsterdam Treaty)

'In its relations with the rest of the world, the Union shall uphold its values and interests. It shall contribute to peace, security, the sustainable development of the earth, solidarity and mutual respect among peoples, free and fair trade, eradication of poverty and protection of human rights, and in particular children's rights, as well as to strict adherence and development of international law, including respect for the principles of the United Nations Charter.' (Article 3, section 4 of the 'Draft Treaty Establishing a Constitution for Europe')

'The [accession negotiations about enlarging the EU] are not about future relations between "us" and "them", but rather about relations between the "future us". It is this process of the external becoming internal which gives accession negotiations such extraordinary interest.' (G. Avery, 1995, p 4)

'The transmission of the European miracle to the rest of the world has become Europe's new *mission civilisatrice*. . .Europeans have a new mission born of their own discovery of perpetual peace.' (Robert Kagan, 2003, p 61)

be regarded as correcting Elias's overly pessimistic interpretation of what is possible in relations between states; each might be said to describe how some of the forces which Elias described (the widening of the scope of emotional identification, the growing aversion to cruelty and suffering, and the rise of internal checks on aggressive inclinations) have come to be embedded in a widening European system of international relations. Studies of the EU can be usefully connected with the approach that Elias took in his investigation of the civilising process. Although Elias did not describe the EU as a new stage in the development of the civilising process, this is a useful way to think about the organisation. It can be regarded as an example of the trend in which domestic value-commitments have gradually come to influence relations between the European powers and their conduct towards the rest of the world. The conclusion of this section, then, is that *the EU needs to be understood against the background of institutional developments and psychological and emotional changes which can be traced back over several centuries. It can be regarded as an important new phase in the civilising process—or as a 'new stage in political civilisation' in Duchêne's phraseology.*

The changing nature of political community in Europe

The EU is a political experiment in taking the civilising process beyond the nation state. It is thus important to evaluate it in the context of wider changes in the normative structure of international society. This section considers some of these changes and their influence on the development of the political communities of Europe. We shall then turn to how the changing nature of political life within Western Europe has come to be associated with a distinctive role for the EU in world affairs. On this basis it will then be possible to show how a moral audit of the EU can be conducted.

Three recent accounts of changing global norms are directly relevant to this part of the analysis. They are Neta Crawford's examination of growing revulsion against notions of racial supremacy and the cruelties of colonial domination over the last two centuries (Crawford 2002); Heather Rae's detailed historical account of how 'ethnic cleansing' has come to be regarded as an offence against the universal human rights culture especially following the end of the Second World War (Rae 2002); and Ward Thomas's analysis of what he calls the 'bombing norm' (that is, the aspect of the *ius in bello* concerned with limiting unnecessary suffering to civilian populations in times of war) in the second half of the 20th century (Thomas 2001). These new norms have changed the normative structure of contemporary international society; they have been among the main reasons for the radical project of transforming political communities across Europe.

The EU was established to eradicate unnecessary suffering from Western Europe whether caused by interstate war or by economic collapse, as during the Depression. The Second World War was a total war which resulted in unprecedented civilian deaths and casualties. This epoch witnessed the revival of doctrines of racial supremacy and associated forms of slave labour in Europe itself—the continent which had prided itself in supposedly having banished these evils from its politics. It saw the forced expulsion of peoples and systematic genocide without parallel in Europe's recent history. The founders of the EU envisaged the development of new forms of political community which would eradicate cruelty by establishing new transnational structures of economic and political cooperation which have come to be coupled with measures to devolve power to minority nations and protect human rights in Europe. Many visions of the EU have looked beyond the nation state to new forms of political community which are more internationalist (in the sense of reducing the moral and political significance of difference between citizens and foreigners in the member states) and more sensitive to linguistic and cultural differences (in the sense of encouraging devolution in an envisaged 'Europe of the regions'). These visions have been accompanied by the idea that the EU should redistribute some wealth from the more to the less affluent regions if it is to build a new form of international political community underpinned by feelings of solidarity.

The EU's first, if indirect, task was to pacify relations between France and Germany, and it has long been centrally involved in trying to abolish violence from the continent. Some observers regard the EU's commitment to the 'rejection of force' as evidence of a growing 'moral consciousness' in global affairs, one in which 'self-enforced rules of behaviour' replace the age-old reliance on the external constraints imposed by the balance of military power (Cooper, quoted in Kagan 2003, 57). This stress on self-constraints raises the question of how far the EU has taken the six features of the civilising process 'beyond the nation state'.

The first point to make is that the EU has revealed that separate states can make progress in developing a regional civilising process without transferring all their powers to a new sovereign authority. Admittedly, this experiment in regional political cooperation presupposes the existence of stable monopolies of power which belong to a common civilisation, have shared interests in preventing the return of a violent past, and value close cooperation to deal with the challenge of economic globalisation. The second point is that the establishment of this zone of peace has permitted the development of high levels of social interdependence. The third is that 'self-control' and 'internal' checks on aggressive inclinations have grown in importance across the territories that belong to the European security community. The fourth is that peoples in the EU have come 'to identify more readily with other people. . .regardless of social origins' and to develop some shared responses to human suffering (as in the case of violations of human rights and excessive violence to civilians in war). The fifth point is that the violence of the first half of the 20th century damaged Europe's belief in its 'inborn superiority' and encouraged efforts to move beyond all forms of ethnocentrism.

The sixth point arising from this application of Elias's thought to Europe's place in the world is that despite the evident progress being made there are still persistent dangers that the EU will generate its own decivilising processes. We come back to this later. Certainly, many interpretations of the EU advise against investing too much hope in the association. Some realists have argued that the first stages of regional cooperation were largely the result of Europe's desire to harness its collective resources in the era of superpower dominance, and in any case were underwritten by NATO. In short, the association has been held together by common interests and external support, and will only survive as long as these common interests—which are a result of Europe's declining geopolitical significance—last (see also Bull 1982). A recent assessment of Europe's troubled relationship with the United States since the terrorist attacks of 11 September 2001 restates the point that the EU's commitment to peaceful change in world politics reflects its military and political weakness (Kagan 2003). Adopting the moral high ground, it is argued, is an attempt to compensate for the lack of influence in a world dominated by the United States.

On this view the European civilising process may be little more than skin deep, amplified for effect under conditions of relative military weakness, and largely dependent on the nature of contemporary global economic and political challenges. The point can be elaborated by noting that references to civilian power or normative power Europe do not alter the fact that the EU was famously indecisive over how to respond to human rights violations in the former Yugoslavia and divided over whether or not to support the US decision in 2003 to secure regime change in Iraq. Many argue that loyalty to the nation state is much greater than emotional identification between the member states of the EU and that compassion for the poor in one's own political community greatly exceeds sympathy for peoples in other parts of Europe. For such reasons it may be necessary to be sceptical about the EU's capacity to have a civilising role in world affairs.

Questions about the depth of a civilising process in Europe—and about the extent to which the EU has or will acquire a distinctive voice and influence in world affairs—raise old issues about the relative importance of interests and ideas or identities in political life which have been central to recent debates between 'rationalist' and 'constructivist' theories of international relations. It is significant that the sceptics do not deny that moral ideas have influenced the development of the EU; it is also worth noting that moral concerns about ethnic cleansing and human rights violations, about the use of force in world politics and about unnecessary civilian suffering in war, are now important elements in public orientations to international politics—as government and public responses to the Yugoslav wars and to the 2003 war against Iraq demonstrated. To acknowledge that the EU is influenced by such moral considerations leads to the philosophical question of what moral principles should govern its conduct towards the rest of the world. What are the moral values that the EU should seek to promote in its own region and in the wider world? What does the EU's project of transforming political community within Europe mean for its conduct towards other parts of the world, and how, therefore, should the EU promote its role as a civilian power?

Preventing harm in world politics

The idea of the civilising process is useful in suggesting how to answer these questions. Here it is worth recalling that the civilising process deals with the question of how human beings can satisfy their fundamental needs without 'destroying, frustrating, demeaning or in other ways *harming* each other' over and over again (Elias 1996, 31, my italics). All societies have to protect their members from what they (or in effect the most powerful) regard as serious forms of harm. Exactly the same question arises over relations between the members of an international society of states or regional security community. They must also address the problem of how to promote their respective interests without causing unnecessary harm to each other. Modern international law makes explicit reference to this issue. The international law of human rights, the law of war and environmental law oblige states not to cause 'unnecessary suffering' in war, to avoid 'serious bodily and mental harm' and to avoid harming the natural environments of other states and the global commons. An important question is whether it is possible to identify various forms of harm which the EU should strive to avoid if it is to fulfil its aspirations to be a civilising force in world politics.

The argument of this section is that at least seven forms of harm exist in international politics. A global civilising process can be said to exist if national governments are committed to avoiding some or all of these forms of harm. The extent to which the EU is important in promoting a global civilising process depends on how seriously it attempts to avoid these examples of harm.

The seven forms of harm can be usefully sub-divided into two main groups. The first set includes three forms of harm where human beings deliberately set out to injure others. They are:

- Deliberate harm that governments and/or societies do to the members of other communities. Examples include: acts of aggression; attempts to maximise the suffering of combatants and non-combatants during military conflict whether through deliberate acts of violence against civilians or cruelty to prisoners of war; deliberate attempts to cause hardship and suffering by imposing economic costs on other peoples; and racist and xenophobic portrayals of other peoples which are designed to degrade or humiliate them. It need hardly be added that these forms of harm have been dominant features of international relations for millennia.

- Deliberate harm that governments do to their own citizens, as when torturing them or otherwise abusing their human rights. This second form of harm has become especially central to world politics since the end of the Second World War. In Europe and elsewhere, it has meant challenging the classical Westphalian principle that governments are not answerable to the international community for how they treat their subjects or citizens.

- Deliberate harm that non-state actors do to the members of different societies. Key examples are discussed in Wyn Rees's chapter in this volume (see Chapter 10). They include violence caused by international terrorist organisations, and by transnational criminal organisations which trade in illicit drugs or engage in the traffic of women and children for the purpose of 'sexual slavery'.

As noted earlier, Elias maintained that the civilising process was largely concerned with controlling violent intentions and aggressive impulses; it was especially concerned with reducing cruelty to other human beings and to non-human animals. But reducing cruelty is not all there is to the civilising process, as the following quotation reveals: 'the extent and depth of people's mutual identification with each other and, accordingly, the depth and extent of their ability to empathize and capacity to feel for and sympathize with other people in their relationships with them' are no less important indicators of the existence of a civilising process (Elias 1996, 109). This observation raises the question of whether the civilising process requires not only efforts to protect individuals and groups from deliberate physical or emotional injury, *but also* positive steps to protect them from harm which can occur in other ways. The next four forms of harm look beyond deliberate attempts to cause mental and/or physical injury. They are:

• Unintended harm where, for example, a government or business enterprise unknowingly damages the physical environment of another society. (Since the Stockholm Conference on the Environment in June 1972, various international conventions have insisted that states have obligations to ensure they do not cause accidental damage to their neighbour's physical environment or to the global commons.)

• Negligence where, for example, a state or business enterprise knowingly submits others to the risk of harm. The failure to ensure that those involved in hazardous industries have adequate health and safety provision is a case in point. (Since the Bhopal incident of 1984 this question has loomed large in discussions of the extent to which transnational business enterprises work with a double standard of morality in world affairs—specifically with how far lower standards of health and safety, and a higher exposure to risk, should apply in poor societies hungry for foreign investment.)

• Harm through unjust enrichment where, for example, members of affluent societies benefit unfairly from protectionist strategies, from export subsidies, from the vulnerability of foreign producers who may have to sell their products cheaply on the world market and from the rules of global commerce which favour the strong and disadvantage the weak.

• Harm through acts of omission where, for example, a person or community fails to take measures to alleviate the suffering of others in circumstances where there is no, or little, cost to itself. This is the most complex and controversial of the forms of harm described above. Legal systems take different positions on the extent to which individuals should be punished for failing to rescue others (see Feinberg 1985 and 1986 on this topic and on the question of what counts as an excessive risk for potential rescuers to bear). In world politics, there is no consensus about whether the failure to intervene to prevent genocide is an example of harm; and there are no laws which make the failure to rescue a punishable offence. But some philosophers argue that the failure to rescue can cause harm by inviting the vulnerable to conclude that the question of whether they survive or perish is of no concern to those who are able to help them. This question is hardly abstract. It confronts Italian and Spanish governments every week in summer, as boatloads of illegal immigrants attempt the trip across the Mediterranean, often in unseaworthy vessels provided by unscrupulous criminal gangs. To their credit the EU states always decide to rescue those in peril, but then have to decide whether they have further obligations of hospitality, or whether to repatriate the new arrivals.

It is possible to use this typology of forms of harm for two purposes: first, we can ask the empirical question of whether a regional association such as the EU is taking steps to avoid or prevent these forms of harm. It would be possible to undertake this inquiry in the spirit of value-freedom, that is without supposing that political efforts to avoid harm are necessarily desirable. Second, this typology may also be used to conduct a moral audit of the EU and to seek to ascertain how far it is a force for good in world politics and how far it falls short of aspirations to be a civilian power. The case for combining these two modes of analysis is that it is not fruitful to assess the EU's performance in combating forms of harm in isolation from developments in other regions of the world's political system or from sectors which include the NGO community. We need to ask whether the EU is lagging behind other regions and sectors in identifying and tackling forms of serious harm, and whether there is any evidence it is at the forefront of progressive developments.

What are the most progressive developments and highest moral ideals which must be kept in mind when assessing the EU's conduct towards other societies? Arguably, they include:

- efforts to tame the use of interstate violence, not least by defending the need for the multilateral authorisation of military power as opposed to the unilateral resort to force;
- attempts to minimise suffering in war and to use moral and at times physical sanctions against human rights violators;
- measures to combat transnational crime and international terrorism without dangerous encroachments on civil liberties and invasions of privacy;
- a regard for ways in which industrial processes may spoil the environment of neighbouring states, create health hazards for other peoples, and place added burdens on the global commons;
- a commitment to ensuring that vulnerable peoples are not exposed to hazards which affluent populations are unprepared to tolerate in their own societies;
- a concern about forms of unjust enrichment in which powerful groups benefit from the disadvantaged position of others in the world economy;
- a sense of shame or guilt when those who are capable of releasing the most desperate from hunger, disease, and extreme poverty, without significant costs to themselves, fail to do so.

Some of the most progressive concrete developments in world politics in recent times include the development of international criminal law and the establishment of the International Criminal Court, advances in global environmental law and calls for radical measures to deal with global warming and climate change; sensitivity to the plight of the vulnerable as expressed in concerns about child labour and sweatshop industries, and in support for fair trade and for ethical investment; and the apparent development of a 'global conscience' which makes the powerful unwilling to look on passively while others suffer. These developments are evidence of the existence of a global civilising process—however modest and precarious—which is concerned with reducing cruelty in world affairs and with widening emotional identification to include the members of other societies, especially the most vulnerable. They are important reference points as we turn to our final task, of reflecting on what a preliminary moral audit of the EU reveals about the conduct of its external relations.

Auditing the EU

In their introduction the editors argue that one 'of the important tasks for academic observers now is to conduct an audit' of what the EU has achieved (p. 15). They ask 'who and what is the EU for, in its international relations?', and call for further reflection on what it should 'be trying to achieve' (*Ibid*). The claim that the EU has attempted to take the civilising process beyond the nation state raises precisely this last question, of what the EU *should* seek to achieve. These are some of the most interesting questions about the EU, and yet largely neglected because historical and empirical approaches to regional cooperation have dominated the field and because theoretical approaches have mostly been concerned with explaining institutional developments rather than with subjecting them to an ethical assessment. Many analysts will assume that disputes about ethical principles are a reminder of the subjective nature of moral preferences. On what grounds, they might ask, is any moral audit of the EU to be established? How are the values which underpin such an assessment to be selected?

International legal conventions which outlaw 'serious bodily and mental harm' suggest one answer to these questions. They prompt the observation that one way of conducting a moral audit is to ask whether the EU has been at the centre of global initiatives to establish commitments to reduce harm to individuals. This is an immensely complex undertaking which must be left to experienced students of the EU. The main task of this section is to encourage discussion and debate about its successes and failures, and to do so principally by drawing on observations contained in preceding chapters of this volume.

A preliminary moral audit might conclude that the EU has made progress with respect to each of the seven forms of harm mentioned, but also risks damaging its own values in other respects which include hardening the boundaries between Europe and the rest of the world:

- The EU's successful early commitment to promoting peace in Western Europe has encouraged its members to extend the '*Pax Europea*' by enlarging the EU to include former socialist societies (Tsoukalis, Chapter 11). As part of this project, it has insisted that states which are joining the EU should display 'good neighbourliness', for example in the attempt to promote the peaceful settlement of territorial disputes (see Karen Smith, Chapter 13). Its experience of collaboration and consultation has led to efforts to export regionalism to other areas (with limited success) and to promote multilateralism including reliance on the UN system. The EU's support for multilateralism in principle can be contrasted with the Bush Administration's willingness (as in the end with that of the British Government) to by-pass the UN Security Council in the build-up to the 2003 Iraq War.

- The EU's general commitment to the global human rights culture and to the development of international criminal law (see Smith 2001 and Karen Smith, Chapter 13) is evident in the attempt within its own region to promote respect for individual human rights, minority rights, the rule of law, and democracy on the part of those acceding to the EU (Spain, Portugal, and Greece in the 1970s and the former members of the socialist bloc at the present time). Externally, it is present in the use of conditionality clauses in an increasing number of trade and cooperation agreements.

• The EU's efforts to deal with international terrorism and transnational crime by creating transnational forms of policing and surveillance, and its steps to enhance the internal security provisions of the aspirant states prior to admitting them to the Union represent the internationalisation of the state, in that national borders are less important than the common external frontier. This can be regarded as a major extension of the civilising process described by Elias.

• Regarding environmental harm, the EU has an important role in 'standard setting' which includes broad support for the precautionary principle; that is, to take such care as not to cause unintended harm to future generations and other societies. It has promoted the shift away from traditional notions of statecraft which insist on 'the absolute sovereignty of every nation...within its own territory' to the internationalist commitment illustrated by Principle 21 of the Stockholm Agreement of 1972, which claims that states have a duty not to cause harm to the environment of neighbouring states or to the global commons.

• Regarding harm caused by negligence, the EU is committed to international environmental obligations such as those contained in the 1989 Basel Convention on the Control of Transboundary Movements of Hazardous Wastes and their Disposal. They establish the duty of prior notification of and consultation with states that may be affected by a potentially harmful activity, and the duty to cooperate to prevent the transfer to other states of any activities and substances which may cause severe environmental degradation or be harmful to human health.

• The EU is credited with recognising that globalisation 'raises fundamental questions of governance' since together 'with its undeniable wealth-creating effects, globalization often brings along greater inequalities, social disruption, and environmental damage, the kinds of negative externalities that those benefiting from globalization prefer to ignore' (Tsoukalis: Chapter 10 above). It has played a leading role in promoting debt relief; it is also a major aid donor, the largest in the world if national aid programmes are included. This role, in addition to its concerns about 'the rights of workers and distributional justice' (ibid.), reveal a commitment to promoting 'social democratic normative goals' in world politics. By linking aid with the wider issues of democracy and human rights, the EU offers an alternative to US policies (see Smith, M. and Rebecca Steffenson, Chapter 16).

• The EU was accused of weakness in responding to human rights violations in the former Yugoslavia. Precisely how it should respond to external humanitarian challenges is one of the most complex questions facing the organisation. Against the view that such an organisation should acquire military power precisely so as to become a 'good international citizen' with the capacity to intervene in civil conflicts, Karen Smith (2001, 192) argues that 'the EU should remain true to its civilian power roots, and renounce the potential to use force, just as this potential has effectively been eliminated among its member states'. The point is that between indifference to suffering in other countries and military intervention lie many alternative strategies which include measures to promote democracy and human rights, and efforts to ensure economic stability. Where such policies fail, the EU can demonstrate its good international citizenship by supporting efforts to bring about political reconstruction.

Its contribution to civilian policing in Kosovo and to peacekeeping in Macedonia (see Michael E. Smith, Chapter 8) are important examples of its attempt since the end of the Kosovo war to take 'the lead in constructing a post-war order in South-eastern Europe' (see Karen Smith, Chapter 13).

One must also ask whether the EU's efforts to enlarge the boundaries of moral and political community may create new forms of social exclusion and new hierarchies between peoples. In Elias's terms, the question is whether the European civilising process can proceed without generating decivilising tendencies. On the deficit side of the EU's performance, it is necessary to include at least the following:

• The recurrent fear that Europe will close in on itself, as the idea of 'Fortress Europe' suggests (see Rees above, Chapter 10). This is no longer a matter of economics alone, as it was during the debate over the Single Market. In particular, there are fears that efforts to create a European political identity could lead to sharpening differences between, for example, Europe and the Islamic world.

• Economic assistance to 'outsiders'—as an intended consequence of the EU's expansion to the East—may come to mean that 'an increasing number of (the) young and worse-off will be turned into privileged citizens of the Union, although after long transitional periods intended to placate the fears of those already in. Immigration will remain a hot political issue, and much will depend on how the economic situation develops' (Tsoukalis, Chapter 11).

• An additional danger is that the EU will become less humane because of legitimate public fears about international terrorism and transnational crime. In particular, the extent to which the EU can sustain humane conduct towards refugees and asylum seekers given public concerns about resource capabilities and anxieties about criminal elements and terrorism is a crucial matter. Many fear that that new political structures are being created which pose a threat to civil liberties and which escape democratic accountability; they are concerned that the way in which it polices its borders 'inevitably involves coercion, discrimination, and sharp distinctions between citizens and non-citizens' (Peterson and Smith 2003, 213). Again, the danger is that the EU will create distinctions between responsible citizens and dangerous outsiders which are just as pernicious as the old national distinctions between insiders and outsiders which it has been committed to leaving behind.

• The 'credibility' of the EU 'as the generous partner of poor countries will continue to be severely tested' as long as 'the European agricultural fortress keeps many of the exports of the less developed countries out of European markets' (Tsoukalis, Chapter 11; see also Meunier and Nicolaïdis, Chapter 12). Related forms of vulnerability arise from the fact of agricultural subsidies which harm competitors in other countries, and from 'dumping' surplus production in overseas markets.[2]

• There is the fear that humanitarian assistance will lead the EU to acquire some of the features of an imperial power—a notion endorsed, albeit in terms of a new, imperialism-by-consensus, by Robert Cooper, a senior adviser to High Representative Javier Solana (Cooper 2002).

The main reason for an ethical audit is to decide how far the EU has succeeded in calling public attention to the forms of harm which befall individuals and groups in world politics, and in directing its political resources to the alleviation of that harm.

The EU can point to many achievements in promoting, within its own region and beyond, a civilising process which prefers the peaceful resolution of disputes to the use of force, privileges multilateralism over unilateralism, and entails the enlargement of sympathies to include the members of societies who are the victims of human rights violations. Of course, states and regional political organisations are no different from the individuals which comprise them, in falling short every so often of the moral standards they claim to live by. As we have seen, the EU is especially vulnerable to the accusation that it erects barriers against weaker producers that wish to sell in its market, that there is a hardening of attitudes towards refugees and immigrants which may create sharp distinctions between the European heartland of secure democracies and the outer world of instability and danger, and that efforts to create a European identity run the risk of replicating—albeit weakly—'the in-group—out-group mentality' of the nation state. For many the challenge the EU faces is one of moving beyond monopolistic states, without creating centralised institutions and strong accompanying transnational loyalties which rest on the fear of and hostility towards outsiders. If it succeeds in this pluralist project it may be able to avoid the decivilising processes and tendencies which are present in all social and political arrangements.

Conclusions

Joschka Fischer's claim that European international relations have long been dominated by power politics was quoted in the introduction to this chapter. Realists have argued that a stark contrast between domestic and international politics has been a feature of European and world politics since the 1648 Peace of Westphalia. As they see it, domestic political progress which includes the establishment of health, welfare, and educational systems has proceeded without any parallel developments in relations between states. The struggle for power and recurrent war meant that emotional identification with the state or nation towered over transnational loyalties. Current policy-makers, as we saw earlier with Joschka Fischer, tend to agree with this interpretation, and consciously react against the realist narrative.

The EU now poses a clear and deliberate challenge to traditional power politics. Europe is the region where sharp divisions between domestic and international politics have declined in importance. The existence of the EU has raised intriguing questions about how far a regional civilising process can develop without the physical constraints associated with the existence of a monopoly of force. Few could have predicted this development in 1945 when France and Germany ended their third major conflict in 70 years. We may view the development of the EU as an example of the planned extension of the civilising process beyond the nation state—as an effort to create new forms of political community in Europe which are more internationalist in outlook, more sensitive to the existence of linguistic and cultural differences within nation states and more willing to redistribute wealth towards the less affluent societies of the region. These values also inform the EU's relations with other parts of the world. Whether they will become more central or decline in importance in this respect is a central question for students of the EU, and of its international relations.

Notes

1 I am especially grateful to Christopher Hill and other participants in the workshop on the International Relations of the EU held at Loughborough University in September 2003 for their comments on an earlier version of this paper. I am grateful to Stephen Mennell for advice and comments.

2 There is, after the Geneva agreement in the context of the World Trade Organization of July 2004, at last a chance that these subsidies will eventually disappear. After the unity the developing countries showed at Cancun in September 2003, the EU has made concessions under pressure.

Further reading

For a good short summary of Elias's study of the civilising process, see Kilminster and Mennell (2003). Fletcher (1997) is an accessible longer study. Elias (2000 and 1996) are two books which are especially relevant to the themes discussed in this chapter. Studies of European integration which deal with themes related to Elias's study of the civilising process include Deutsch (1957) (see also Adler and Barnett (1998)), Duchêne (1973), Manners (2002), and Taylor (1996). Kagan (2003) is a provocative discussion of recent differences between American and European approaches to international relations.

Adler, E., and Barnett, M. (eds) (1998), *Security Communities* (Cambridge: Cambridge University Press).

Deutsch, K. *et al.* (1957), *Political Community and the North Atlantic Area: International Organization in the Light of Historical Experience* (Princeton: Princeton University Press).

Duchêne, F. (1973), 'The European Community and the Uncertainties of Interdependence', in Kohnstamm, M., and Hager, W. (eds) *A Nation Writ Large? Foreign Policy Problems Before the European Community* (London: Macmillan).

Elias, N. (1996), *The Germans* (Cambridge: Polity Press).

Elias, N. (2000), *The Civilizing Process: Sociogenetic and Psychogenetic Investigations* (Oxford: Blackwell).

Fletcher, J. (1997), *Violence and Civilisation: An Introduction to the Work of Norbert Elias* (Cambridge: Polity Press).

Kagan, R. (2003), *Paradise and Power: America and Europe in the New World Order* (London: Atlantic Books).

Kilminster, R., and Mennell, S. (2003), 'Norbert Elias' in Ritzer, G. (ed.) *The Blackwell Companion to Major Contemporary Social Theorists* (Oxford: Blackwell).

Manners, I. (2002), 'Normative Power Europe: A Contradiction in Terms?' *Journal of Common Market Studies* 40/2, 235–58.

Taylor, P. (1996), *The European Union in the 1990s* (Oxford: Oxford University Press).

Web links

Copies of *Figurations: The newsletter of The Norbert Elias Foundation* can be found at www.usyd.edu.au/su/social/elias/figsframe.html. The site contains short papers on different aspects of the civilising process and some reflections on the significance of Elias's thought for the study of international relations. Newsletters 17, 19, and 20 are useful in this regard. The Fornet network, whose outputs are to be found at http://www.fornet.info, generates discussion of ethical as well as analytical aspects of EU external relations.

Chapter 18

Acting for Europe: Reassessing the European Union's Place in International Relations

Christopher Hill and Michael Smith

Contents

Summary

This chapter presents the major common findings of the volume, while also stressing the different approaches and specialist areas covered by the contributors. It re-examines the usefulness of the major schools of International Relations theory as applied to the EU's external relations, seeing all as applicable in varying ways even if liberalism and its variants tend to generate most insights. It then moves on to the EU's substantive impact (or lack of it) on world politics, which has grown steadily in broad terms albeit with obvious gaps and setbacks. The three lenses introduced in Chapter I, whereby the EU is analysed as a system of international relations, as a participant in wider international processes and as a power, are then revisited to make possible the overall conclusions: (1) that the EU can no longer be treated as a peculiar side-issue in international relations, and must now be fully integrated into the academic study of the subject; (2) that the EU has significant powers as well as a wide-ranging presence in the international system, even if it may not yet be termed 'a power'.

Introduction

This is a lengthy book, because the role of the European Union in international relations at the start of the 21st century amounts to a great deal, across a wide variety of issue-areas. Such an extensive treatment would not have been easy to justify even two decades ago, but now there are three main reasons for it: (a) the fact that the EU itself generates a significant quantity of international relations, with an increasing impact on third parties; (b) the converse, namely that the international system is increasingly implicated in the development of the EU itself, in shaping its external strategies but also the everyday lives of its citizens; (c) the increasing mutual relevance of the academic literature of International Relations, and the specialist study of EU external relations, previously connected only by a slim isthmus.

Our focus in this concluding chapter is on two overarching questions, which subsume the dimensions referred to above and the various themes and approaches outlined in the three introductory chapters. The first asks about the extent to which our analysis of the EU's international relations has added both to our general understanding of real-world international relations (lower case), and the theoretically-driven academic subject of International Relations (upper case) which seeks to establish a framework for understanding how the world works. The second asks about how we should think about the place of the EU in contemporary international society, drawing on theory as well as the burgeoning amount of empirical material now being generated. What kind of actor is it, what kind of functions does it fulfil, and what is the trajectory of its development?

The EU and the perspectives of international relations

In Chapter 2 Filippo Andreatta (after looking at the classical federalist and neo-functionalist accounts) surveyed the main theoretical approaches in International Relations of relevance to the EU's external behaviour. He summarised these under the headings of realist, liberal, and some 'alternative' schools of thought.

Realism

Of these three approaches realism seemed the least promising, centring as it does on unitary states and the international condition of anarchy. The EU is not a unitary state (nor about to become one) and it also transcends anarchy in its internal condition, just as it seeks to modify it in the wider international system. The studies which constitute the empirical core of this book do, however, suggest that realism can provide some insights for our purposes. It can, for instance, help to explain why the CFSP has so far been a relative failure—how can sovereign states be expected to renounce their national freedoms of manoeuvre in the interests of a long-term solidarity? It might also throw light on why, nonetheless, the EU has begun to develop a defence dimension. *Pace* John Mearsheimer's gloomy predictions, the Europeans have reacted to the end of the Cold War not by falling on each other's throats but by starting to huddle together for protection as the United States not only finds other interests beyond European security but even becomes a source of problems which Europe think they need to reinsure against (Mearsheimer 1990). Andreatta makes the point that European Political Cooperation/Common Foreign and Security Policy (EPC/CFSP) might be seen as an extraordinarily enduring and special kind of alliance, designed to deal with friends as well as putative enemies. It is an alliance which has gradually expanded its scope and responsibilities, as Europe's external environment has become less stable. To splice a little constructivism onto realism, Venus may be starting to become more like Mars, or even vice versa. The gender stereotypes may be breaking down.

This reference to the views of Robert Kagan indicates that an adapted form of realism, at least, might cast light on the successes of EU foreign policy as well as its failures (Kagan 2003). Kagan himself has begun to recognise this (Kagan 2004). Neo-realism, given its highly systemic perspective and stress on the balance of power, seems to have relatively little to tell us about the EU's place in the world. The latter is more a 'pole' than a 'power', at least unless one qualifies the frame of reference by referring to the international political *economy* rather than the overall international system, which is generally understood in macro-political terms. Even with a concept like 'multipolarity', which Waltzians have little time for, the EU's role is difficult to define clearly. Classical realism, by contrast, has a stronger historical component and therefore stresses the particular circumstances in western Europe which have given birth to the distinctive construction known as the CFSP/CSDP (Common Security and Defence Policy), partial, stuttering but still indispensable. It is also more likely to make sense of the paradox that the major member states continue to play an important role alongside the evolving collective diplomacy. Britain and France, have, if anything, reasserted their ambitions to be major players during the last ten years, while Germany, Italy, Spain, and now Poland have discovered the confidence to identify and assert national interests, through the very process of foreign policy cooperation.

Liberalism

It may be that a realist form of liberalism is best suited to explain these paradoxes, as with Andrew Moravcsik's theory of 'liberal intergovernmentalism' which has become so prominent in the analysis of the EU's internal politics (Moravcsik 1998). This adapts realism to take account of the 'two-level game' decision-makers play between the two chess-boards of the domestic environment and the EU institutions, and to allow for the possibility of lasting cooperation, through 'grand bargains'. Liberal intergovernmentalism has only just begun to be applied to the EU's external policies, even if it has some potential in this area (Moravcsik 2003). The CFSP and the external aspects of pillar III are evidently intergovernmental, and even the evolution of the common commercial policy may be seen as subject to intermittent bargains between the bigger states (see chapters by Tsoukalis and Meunier/Nicolaidis, above). Yet here too we need to add something, taken from the broad church of liberalism.

Catherine Gegout (2003) has pointed out that the CFSP cannot be fully explained without reference to history and to the functioning of institutions—combined in the form of 'historical institutionalism'. The wider role of the EU, including its economic, development, and societal impact on the world, also requires more contextualisation than simple bargaining models can provide. Yet the liberal IR perspectives which have most commonly provided such contextualisation are themselves widely divergent, both in the particular focus of their interests and in their assumptions about the capacity of actors to generate lasting structures of cooperation (Carlsnaes 2004). Most contributors to this volume take a broadly liberal view of international relations (or are liberal realists), but they span the range from those who see institutions as having a transformational and socialising effect on the prospects for common action (for instance, Vanhoonacker, Smith, M.E.), to those who see the EU's liberal values as significantly constrained by the logic of the international system, and subject to the glacier-like progress of historical change (Howorth, Mayall). Some issues tend only to be highlighted in the first place by a liberal set of assumptions, as with accountability, or interdependence (Lord, Tsoukalis). In terms of Andreatta's three schools of liberalism—republican, commercial, and institutional—the first is only implicitly supported in this volume, in the sense that it is largely taken for granted that relations between member states represent a form of the 'democratic peace', and that by extension relations with new members, and prospective new members, are subject to the same kind of domestication (Smith, K.E.). Indeed, it is clear that the EU regards its 'power of attraction' to be sufficiently strong to pull even those neighbours with only a remote chance of accession into its irenic orbit. Linklater's view that the EU represents a 'civilising' impulse in international relations is closely related to this republican version of liberalism.

Commercial liberalism is more obviously central to the EU's external relations, and has been from the beginning, even with the evident tension between the model of free trade represented by the common market and that of protectionism embodied in the customs union. It can be argued, in the Cobdenite tradition, that the commitment to a civilian power foreign policy is rooted in a system which has privileged trade liberalisation—and indeed transnational relations more generally—as an instrument of integration between states, and which assumes that the EEC model can be exported elsewhere. The fact that economics is the main instrument employed by EU foreign policy thus far complicates the matter, in that while the use of cooperation agreements and foreign aid helps to bind countries together, economic sanctions are inherently coercive, and represent realist more than liberal values.

The other element of commercial liberalism which is clearly born out by a detailed look at the international relations of the EU is the latter's capacity to provide a site of agency in the complex and glutinous processes of interdependence. The chapters by Tsoukalis, and Meunier and Nicolaïdis, demonstrate the extent of the Union's trade power, both in terms of defending pure economic interests and as a way of promoting wider values, epitomised in the phrase 'normative power' (Manners 2002). Integration as an overall process, not just the common commercial policy, is then to be seen as 'a highly developed system for the joint management of interdependence', notably dense within the region itself, but almost as important in terms of Europe's relations with north America, the Middle East, parts of Asia and the ex-colonial states. From the macro viewpoint the EU can be seen as a vehicle of globalisation, but to its citizens—current and potential—it seems to have the scale of resources and the decision-making apparatus required to tackle the dilemmas arising from globalisation, for instance in the WTO, the international financial institutions and the G8. In this context the fact that even these illustrious sites of global governance have a limited capacity to moderate the winds of economic change is less important than the EU's prestige within them.

A liberal economic zone like that of the European Union actively encourages free enterprise, as it has done with the Single Market project and the Lisbon agenda. This in turn creates much space for transnational enterprises, cultural and political as well as economic, to operate outside direct governmental control, and thus to cause difficulties for the member states. Such is the price for the stimulus to growth represented by the huge marketplace of the EU and EEA combined—now c. 460 million—and it is exerting pressure on the continental model of a social market economy. It is no accident that the most 'flexible' economy in the EU, with one of the lowest rates of unemployment, is that of Britain, which has also absented itself from the common monetary project. Yet it will therefore be excluded from decision-making over the management of the eurozone, including the increasingly important external dimension of the common currency. By the same token it keeps out of the Schengen arrangements in part so as to manage its influx of economic migrants, and thus compromises the notion of a single, 'hard' external border for the EU (Rees, Chapter 12).

The dictates of commercial liberalism therefore cut two ways for the EU and its member states. A further demonstration of the fact is the inevitable and regular clashes between the United States and Europe. The latter's *organised* economic power represents competition for the US as well as a potential partnership in the management of the world economy. Accordingly Washington has always been ambivalent about encouraging European integration, even if it has usually concluded that the long-term advantages outweigh the short-term pains. But if Americans do not always take seriously the foreign policy pronouncements of the presidency or (latterly) the High Representative, they always pay the closest attention to the activities of the Trade Commissioner or Ecofin. They have learned through prolonged disputes since the early 1960s (over everything from soya beans to pipelines, from bananas to Boeing) that the EU knows how to win. As Smith and Steffenson show in Chapter 16, despite its heterogeneity, in the area of trade the EU can stick to a policy, negotiate hard, and play the same games with transnational lobbying that the US itself is adept at. Moreover—and this testifies to the broader common interests which underpin the transatlantic relationship—however sharp the disagreements in the economic field, they have remained compartmentalised, so as to leave the strategic alliance largely unscathed. This was particularly true during the Cold War, when 'linkage' was seen as a dangerous game, whether by the US hinting at a possible troop withdrawals if the Europeans did not fall into line on the anti-OPEC cartel in 1973–74, or the European outrage at US extra-territorial legislation leading to questions about the value of the western alliance. Such spats refocused attention on common interests, and brought both sides back into line. Since 1991, however, it is arguable that a more fluid and competitive international environment has led implicit linkages to rise closer to the surface, and the Europeans have begun to define themselves and their common interests more in terms of competition with a globalisation defined more readily as Americanisation. Economics and politics thus inexorably converge, not least with the drive during the administration of George W. Bush to export values as well as goods with which the Europeans are in competition (Tsoukalis 2003, 192–200).

Alternative approaches

The 'alternative' approaches which Andreatta analysed in Chapter 2 range from the orthodox but partial, to the radical and structural. It would be possible to group the latter under the heading of 'critical' theories, but this would do justice neither to the particular strand of critical theory deriving from the work of Jürgen Habermas, nor to the ability of all theories to interrogate some conventional assumptions.

Among the partial theories which throw light on the EU's international relations, Foreign Policy Analysis (FPA) is the most prominent. Indeed, it can hardly be avoided if one wishes to probe the complex processes of decision-making involved in the generation of Europe's 'foreign policy' (White 2001). Bureaucratic politics within the Commission and the Council Secretariat, distinctive 'domestic' constituencies for leaders to defer to, and serious problems of coherence and legitimacy all demand the attention of the middle-range theories generated within FPA. There is fertile ground here for future scholarship.

Other approaches go yet further in contesting the notion of more or less objective interests determining Europe's external behaviour. Institutionalisation, or in this context 'Europeanisation', suggests that states are influenced by common rules and procedures to draw ever closer together. The contributors to this volume would disagree on the extent to which this is happening, or is inexorable, but few would disagree with Wong that the EU has come to constitute an ever more powerful point of reference in international relations, both for its member states and for its neighbours. This is a minimal but useful definition of Europeanization.

Constructivists would wish to go further, by saying that shared understandings of what constitutes Europe's role and interest in the world are gradually giving *meaning* to the material position of the EU, a position which cannot speak for itself, as it were. The perceptions of the actors—including third parties—help to give Europe its international identity and thus some of its capabilities (Bretherton and Vogler 1999, 28–32). This approach informs not just Wong's discussion of Europeanization, but also Linklater's argument that the EU is presenting itself as a civilising force in international relations, and is increasingly being seen as such by outsiders.

Robert Cooper's extension of this focus on identity, to the effect that the EU represents a high point of post-modernism in its breakdown of the distinction between domestic and foreign affairs, is not taken up explicitly in this book, although plenty of attention is given to the multi-level nature of its system for producing external policy (Cooper 2003). The side of his argument which deals with policy substance, however, attracts strong support. Cooper argued that the EU needed a commitment both to the multilateralism which is its own defining feature, and to the possession of more of the traditional kind of hard, or military power (ibid., 164–72). This view is developed in the chapters by Howorth and Rees, while de Flers and Regelsberger show how extensive is the Union's pursuit and promotion of multilateral diplomatic partners like itself. As Smith and Steffenson indicate, while the EU cannot hope to match the hard power of the United States, it has concluded that in order to deal with Washington on more equal terms it needs to go beyond cooperation towards some more state-like capabilities. In effect, it has to move from a loose to a tight form of multilateralism.

At the other end of the spectrum, neo-Marxist structuralism finds little favour these days as either an explanation or a prescription for European policy, but Mayall reminds us of its importance in shaping critical attitudes towards the treatment of the Third World in the 1960s and 1970s, in parts of which it still lives on, leading to complaints about the Lomé and Cotonou agreements as neo-colonialism (Smith, H., 2002). Europeans themselves should bear in mind this tradition of thought, despite the collapse of communism. We do not like to think of ourselves as a conservative, wealthy force in international society, but that is how it appears to the poor majority. Three decades ago in an under-rated book Johan Galtung warned that the European Community was doomed to exercise structural power in the sense of being able to determine the life-chances of the exploited Third World (Galtung 1973, 38–47, 55–86, but see Keukeleire (2003), for a more neutral use of the term 'structural power'). The differences between Europeans and Americans from this perspective are much less than we tend to think, especially given the reappearance in Europe of confidence in a civilising mission, or 'liberal imperialism' (Cooper 2002). If Europe has great economic power, then that implies an international hierarchy working to its advantage. This may be difficult to reconcile with its hopes to represent a new kind of order, or civility, for others to follow.

The place of the EU in the international system

Against this theoretical background, of inevitably competing interpretations, what can we say about the *substance* of the EU's place in the international system? If realism tends to scepticism over Europe's collective capabilities, liberalism has the opposite tendency. Ideological preferences infect each, as with the variety of alternative possibilities. The latter highlight strengths and weaknesses in specific issue-areas and/or parts of the world, while allowing for a discussion of what might be immanent—or merely just possible. Amidst this cacophony, there are some points to make about what the EU cannot do, but also about the positive functions it performs in the international system.

What the EU is not

There are three things which it is clear the EU is *not*, in terms of its international role:

- It is *not* a straightforward 'pole' in a multipolar system. Such a system does not yet exist, given the huge inequalities of wealth and military power that still obtain between the US and even states like China and India. What is more the EU does not possess cumulative power across all major dimensions—although it aspires to do so. Its strength in trade production is not yet matched even in the areas of finance and environmental policy, while its strengths in diplomacy and development aid are intermittent and patchy at best. The EU is indeed a major point of reference for other states, and possesses a distinct 'power of attraction' (Munuera 1994), but despite French ambitions it is as yet well short of being able even to constitute an equal pillar in the western alliance.

- Yet the EU is *not* merely a subordinate sub-system of western capitalism, and/or a province of an American world empire, as in their different ways both the 'no global' movement and Al-Qaeda believe. The United States certainly has a privileged position in terms of access to European decision-making, with some particularly 'special' relationships with member states and individuals (it should not be forgotten that Javier Solana is an ex-Secretary-General of NATO) as well as a formal Transatlantic Partnership with the EU. It often succeeds in dividing and ruling the Europeans, as well as over-shadowing them in high politics. What it does not do, however, is to control them, or persistently manipulate the CFSP as an instrument of its global strategy. The EU very often stands up to Washington, at least in terms of taking a different line, and where it has the power—as in trade policy—it is not above forcing a show-down. The US has twice backed away in tussles over the key politico-legal-economic issue of extra-territoriality, over the Siberian gas pipeline in 1982 and the Helms-Burton legislation over Cuba in 1996. This is because the US needs European support often enough not to be able to take it for granted. It thus has to make concessions. Insofar as a division of labour approach is sometimes visible (as possibly in 2003–2004 over Iran) this is as much on European as on American terms.

- The EU, and still less its international policies, is *not* a channel by which political agency is surrendering to the forces of functionalism and globalisation. Although European integration has favoured international free trade rather than mercantilism, this does not mean that the EU has signed its own death warrant. Rather, it has given Brussels a more significant place in the regulation of the international economy, as growth has been achieved and the major states of Europe have embarked on more path-breaking projects, from the Single Market to EMU and the 'open method of co-ordination' (Wallace and Wallace 2000; Peterson and Shackleton 2002, 91). Thus the EU itself has acquired more powers in international relations—even if it is still far from having all the necessary attributes of statehood—without robbing its member states of their own national identities. Alan Milward may be right that the European Economic Community 'saved' the nation-state in the 1950s and 1960s (Milward 1991, 2000). It may still be helping to do so with the ex-Soviet satellites in the post-Cold War era. But if this trend has slowed, and gradually the states are relinquishing some of their capacity to exercise sovereignty, the study of the EU's international relations could lead no-one to suppose that the gates are being opened to a tidal wave of globalisation. The EU is neither so economically liberal nor so powerless that it is at the mercy of wider forces. Indeed, this is precisely why so many Europeans are attempting to strengthen the EU: as a means of *managing* globalisation. Thus the interplay of the international environment with the EU institutions has led to a renegotiation of the place of government, not its undermining, and to the creation of a para-statal entity alongside the traditional nation states, to handle those tasks with which they might otherwise struggle.

The EU's positive contributions

Turning to the more positive side of the equation, on the basis of the analyses presented in this book we can see that the European Union fulfils certain distinctive functions in the international system, and is likely to continue to do so for the foreseeable future. Firstly, whatever the general truth of the 'democratic peace' hypothesis, the EU does represent a settled bloc of constitutional relations, and a zone of peace, in the international system. Indeed, it has created a regional form of international *society*. This might or might not represent a building block for the overall nature of international relations, but it is acknowledged and respected across the world as a major political (as well as economic) achievement.

Secondly, and as a consequence of this achievement, the EU represents a model for other regional organisations. It is true that this has been the case for nearly 50 years, and yet nothing has come near to emulating the EU's success—perhaps the result of a certain idealism on both sides as to what the model entails (Nicolaïdis and Howse 2002). At the end of 2004, a new attempt to emulate the EU was even announced by the unlikely trio of Kenya, Uganda, and Tanzania. Nonetheless, many less mature groupings have sought bloc-to-bloc relations, as Alecu de Flers and Regelsberger demonstrated in Chapter 15. In doing so they have had to deepen their own internal structures, while following the EU in keeping foreign policy a purely intergovernmental process. The idea of regional integration, however, remains strong precisely because of the existence and growth of the EU.

To turn Schmitter's idea of the 'external federator' on its head, one could say that the need to deal with a rich and powerful EU draws other states into cooperative ventures, *especially* in their international relations (Schmitter 1969). This is as true of the Southern African Development Committee (SADC), most of whose members feared the consequences of a bilateral deal between South Africa and the EU, as it is of the Asia-Europe Meeting (ASEM), which was set up precisely to create an inter-regional diplomacy which did not previously exist.

The third practical function fulfilled by the EU in world politics is that of a reference point inside other international organisations. With the steady increase in the number of sovereign states created since 1945 the universal institutions are now large and unwieldy, with evident spaces for leadership and caucuses to grow up—not least as an alternative to a US diplomatic hegemony. That the EU does not act as one in the UN Security Council is a huge gap in its portfolio, which damages its image as much as it undermines capabilities, but elsewhere there are signs of ever greater coordination. One scholar has recently observed both that 'representatives from other UN member states charge that nothing gets accomplished in many UN bodies unless the Europeans are on board', and that there is 'compelling evidence that European voting cohesion has grown rather dramatically in the UN General Assembly over the course of the 1990s' (Laatikainen 2004, 4). The influence of the EU is equally felt in the functional organizations such as the World Health Organization and the International Atomic Energy Agency (witness Iran's willingness to work with the IAEA and the EU, but not the US, in late 2004). In the major international economic organisations the EU presence is of great significance in the WTO, and the OECD, but more subordinate to the US and individual member states in the IMF and World Bank. This might change once the Union has got used to possessing the legal personality which is provided for in the draft Constitutional Treaty.

Still at the level of outsiders' perceptions, the EU clearly represents the hopes of many, from Russia and China through Canada and Japan to the Third World, for some kind of political counter-balance to the United States. Few hold illusions about the possibility—or desirability—of Europe rivalling the US in military terms, and thus balancing its power in the classical manner. What is seen as possible is an alternative articulation of western interests, with more understanding shown of the underlying reasons for conflict than is currently on view in Washington. In the poorer countries, save those irredeemably in the US orbit, there is a hope that the EU and its members might be able to restrain Washington, and also to encourage it (as to some extent has indeed happened) down the road of debt relief and overseas development aid. In a unipolar world, where the phrase 'hyperpower' is not mere hyperbole, only a grouping of the rich states stands much chance of 'balancing' the US, and that only in a purely diplomatic sense. The EU is the prime candidate to lead such activity, and even it is significantly constrained—by internal divisions, by prudence and by genuine identification with many US positions.

The last of the five substantive functions that the EU fulfils in international relations is that to which Linklater's chapter draws particular attention, namely the actualisation of certain principles of conduct in foreign policy. This is related to our first point about Europe being a building-block of constitutionalism in international order, but it refers more to the power of example. It is a Hegelian point, about the realisation of what might otherwise remain ideas and principles. Just as Mayall shows how the collective action embodied in the EU has enabled European states to free themselves from the mind-set and unpleasant associations of colonial overlordship, so Linklater demonstrates that the activities of the EU have raised a series of important questions about how to promote common interests in international relations without harming or unnecessarily antagonising others.

The idea of 'civilian power' has been central to this process, in stressing the utility of benign means, and widely shared, 'milieu', goals over such matters as the environment or new forms of governance for a turbulent world. But in recent years the EU has gone beyond this somewhat sloganistic notion to more practical methods of standard-setting, such as the promotion of a human rights culture, and of transnational processes of justice and criminal investigation. The latter cuts both ways, in that the scale of the EU and the cooperation it fosters can increase the power of surveillance and policing over ordinary citizens, thus tipping the balance of world politics even further in favour of the big battalions. But this is a tension which has been evident in the EU right from its birth.

System, process, and power

We began this book by arguing that no one theory, or approach, was suitable for the complex tasks of explaining, understanding, and prescribing for the international relations of the European Union. In this case, one size definitely does not fit all, given the multiplicity of policies, actors, and levels of decision-making involved in the relations between 25 member states, at least three major collective institutions, and well over 200 third states and international organisations—to say nothing of the plethora of non-governmental organisations and other outputs of civil society. We therefore suggested a three-part model as a way of coming to terms with not just multi-level governance but also manifold diplomacy: the EU as a *sub-system* of international relations; as enmeshed in the *processes of general international relations*; and as an actual and potential *power* in the world. We now take these three sets of issues in turn, as a means of auditing the Union's performance, in the light of the specialist accounts which make up the bulk of this book.

The EU as a sub-system of international relations

The politics which takes place inside the EU is that of the demi-monde, neither fully domestic nor authentically international. The trajectory may be that of 'Europeanization', but we are still some distance from reaching the end-point of such a process, especially in relation to foreign policy-making. Nonetheless, the level of trust which has been achieved between member states is unprecedented in the history of international relations between sovereign units, and the range of instruments which the units have available to them in dealings with each other is spectacularly narrower than it would have been half a century earlier. If international relations still exist between the member states, they do so in a manner which is much transformed from the usual understanding of the term.

This quality of domestication is both what attracts outsiders to seek membership and what is called into question by them. Although it is tempting to project into the future the line of progress from the past we cannot be wholly sure that the arrival of ten, perhaps ultimately 15–20, new members within a few decades will not have more effect on the Union than it has on them. Enlargement may turn out to have re-imported some international relations to the Union's internal affairs, or at least to have complicated its internal functioning. What is more, the current expectation of yet further rounds of enlargement makes the very distinction between the EU and its environment, between internal and external, ambiguous and contentious.

Another aspect of the EU as sub-system which has been carefully dissected here, particularly in the chapters of Part II, is that of the EU's existence as a means of co-ordinating the interests and preferences of member states for the purposes of collective action in world politics. Seen from outside the EU represents a dense set of interactions, and a sophisticated decision-making process, albeit one that is too complex to be easily understood, or manipulated. Although third parties do not easily penetrate into the EU sub-system, it does happen. The United States is the main 'Trojan horse', but Iceland, Norway, and Turkey also have inside tracks. Canada and

Japan have had regular high-level summits for more than ten years and other 'strategic partnerships' are being formulated towards India and China. Conversely, EU policy-making is not insulated from other networks and international organisations, whether the UN Security Council or the international financial institutions. On several occasions, for example, European development policy has taken its cue from the World Bank.

The institutions of the Union clearly play an important part in making the European sub-system of international relations work. Vanhoonacker shows how 'historical institutionalism' has gradually shaped and consolidated key practices. These may or may not strengthen Europeans' hands in the world, according to political viewpoint, but they are certainly now difficult to unstitch. For example, while the Commission's part in EU external relations has been weakened in recent years, with the decline in its general position, it remains a key player in the Common Commercial Policy, in conjunction with the Council and the Article 133 Committee. Institutions and policies interact to produce various forms of path-dependency.

Yet there is also a considerable degree of heterogeneity. Lord shows how such accountability and legitimacy as exist in relation to external policy within the EU the product of interplay between the European Parliament and national legislatures, while Nuttall makes explicit the three kinds of 'consistency' problems which bedevil the Union in dealing with outsiders: horizontal (between policies); institutional (between pillars); and vertical (between the EU and national policies). Much of this, as Nuttall argues, may not matter too much. Indeed it may be a perfectly sensible way of providing actions 'fit for purpose', and of avoiding the conflicts inherent in trying for too much symmetry. On occasion it may also usefully confuse third parties. But there can be no dispute that it is perceived internally as causing sufficient problems to have preoccupied generations of officials, in attempts to dream up solutions for the inconsistencies evident to, and sometimes exploited by, outsiders.

Wong shows how Europeanization may render some of these problems redundant in the long run, but his focus on the Common Foreign and Security Policy makes it clear that there is still quite a distance to travel before that point is reached. It is here that problems of vertical consistency are most pronounced—surfacing to disastrous effect during the build-up to the Iraq war in 2002–2003, to the point where there was a complete schism between two intra-European camps. Such dramas belie the long-term processes of convergence also observable in underlying foreign policy attitudes, and in the more effective work being done out of the spotlight, on subjects as diverse as Macedonia and North Korea. The Union may make mistakes in its foreign policy, but it has a systemic capacity to acknowledge them, and often to learn, as has been clear in the Balkans since Dayton. It is indeed a 'foreign policy system' in the broad sense, including the Commission, the High Representative and his Secretariat, and the member states, which all engage in a continuous if not always harmonious process of mutually constituting discussion, and some action (Hill 1991).

The EU and the general processes of international relations

All actors are solipsistic, but the EU is at the benign end of the spectrum, and surprisingly open in most of its activities. 'Fortress Europe' was never more than a squawk of fear or hostility from nervous outsiders. Given the commitments to free trade, enlargement, civilian power, and democratisation it would be difficult not to become interpenetrated with the wider processes of international relations. Even the worries about Schengen and the 'hard' external border of the Union are exaggerated. The arrangements to monitor the common frontiers are a consequence of free movements within the EU, and in any case are no worse and no better than those implemented by any given nation state.

The EU is enmeshed with its neighbours, with other international organisations, and with the functional processes of rule and law-making. To some, indeed, this process seems to have gone so far as to call into question its very actorness. The boundaries between value-systems and processes of governance (if not physical frontiers) may become so fuzzy that 'Europe' and the EU blur into each other, or that the latter stands more for a set of principles than a distinctive and defendable set of interests (Smith, M. 1996a; Christiansen et al. 2000). Furthermore enlargement, especially if it involves too much expansion too quickly, might lead the EU to become more like the OSCE than its former self, more a framework than an 'action organisation' (Hill 2002, 107). Variable geometry might then mean not just inner groups pursuing 'structured' or 'enhanced' cooperation, but also limited groups which extend to outsiders—as already happens with the Schengen group, but was resisted when Turkey attempted to leap from the dying Western European Union straight into the ESDP process.

A more reasonable interpretation, and one born out in large part by the contents of this volume, is that the EU is both a key part of the multilateral structures of world politics, and a player of growing resource and influence in its own right. As Michael E. Smith says above (p 174) it 'will continue its erratic though progressive development as a unique global actor'. Smith demonstrates how many resources the Union disposes of, and the range of instruments this translates into. Not all are easily useable for political (that is, foreign policy) purposes, but they all help 'to shape not only the regional future of Europe, but also the international environment on which that future depends'. Diplomatic, economic, and now some limited military tools are all available to the EU, based on a population nearly 60% bigger than that of the US and a far deeper involvement in international processes than that of the world's only superpower. This is not to say that the EU rivals the US in power; on most indicators, including the perceptions of third states, it does not come close. But its wealth, history, range of contacts, and potential all mean that the fate of the Union is bound up with that of the international system as a whole—and possibly vice versa. This is why so many regional organisations continue to seek privileged relationships with the EU. Furthermore, as Smith and Steffenson argued in Chapter 16, between them the US and the EU dominate the agenda of international politics, in a relationship of 'competitive cooperation'. When they cooperate, they can determine many outcomes; when they disagree, the political space that then opens up defines the opportunities for other states.

To some extent it is the issue-area which determines the nature of the EU's role in the wider system, with the EU being much more central to international processes in economics than in the high politics of, say, arms control or Security Council reform. Nonetheless, as the agenda of foreign policy widens, this distinction is itself being eroded (Hill 2003, 4). The result is more to heighten Europe's profile and status than to damage it, as the greater role for domestic and transnational actors favours an organisation like the EU which stresses openness in politics, and multi-level forms of governance. It is revealing, for example, that in policy terms (at least) the three-pillared structure of the Maastricht Treaty has broken down: 'Justice and Home Affairs' increasingly involves international issues, and often cooperation with third states; the CFSP now extends to defence, and can only work at all through liaison with the external economic policies of Pillar I, and with the 'homeland security' aspects of Pillar III. On this basis it is clear that the Union has been flexible enough to allow issues to inter-relate, and accumulate, where the flow of events demanded it.

There are, however, two important issues still unresolved in terms of the EU's involvement in international processes. The first is the fact that while issues have de facto begun to flow into each other, the differentiation of decision-making procedures remains. The draft Constitutional Treaty attempts to make the operation of EU external relations easier (indeed, arguably this is its main thrust, despite having been conceived as a way of enabling the EU institutions to cope better with enlargement), but even assuming that the Treaty will be ratified, it will not unify procedures or make it much easier for outsiders to understand the basis on which a particular decision is taken. As Nuttall says in this volume, 'even if the pillars formally disappear, de facto problems of consistency will remain'. The new figures of the elected President and the Foreign Minister will still be subject to the constraints and complexities arising from intergovernmentalism in the CFSP and JHA co-existing with the Community method in pillar I. Furthermore, in their mutual relations these two personalities may also add yet another discordant note to the policy-making process.

The geographical dimension is the second major issue outstanding. The EU needs to take a position on whether it wishes its engagement with the international system to be largely regional, in its own neighbourhood, global, as an aspirant superpower with pretensions to be heard on all major issues and crises, or neither, in the sense that geography is not the main criterion for action, rather being supplanted by functional, political, or other concerns 'on their merits'. This is less a matter of hard and fast choice than of balance between competing considerations. The regional and the global cannot be mutually exclusive categories when the territory of one powerful neighbour stretches as far as Vladivostok, or when some member states still have territorial possessions in the Pacific or south Atlantic. Still, decisions have to be taken on priorities, and where European resources can be best made to count. Has the Security Strategy of December 2003 made a tacit judgement, for example, that the US is no longer so committed to Europe and that the Union must now concentrate on its own immediate security, making common cause with like-minded neighbours? Or do the two statements in the Strategy, on the one hand, that 'in an era of globalisation, distant threats may be as much a concern as those that are near at hand', and on the other that there is a 'need to develop a strategic culture that fosters early, rapid, and where necessary, robust intervention' reveal a new globalist ambition? (European Council 2003a). The tenor of the document is certainly globalist: 'an active and capable European Union would make an impact on a global scale'; but the failure so far to envisage anything like the resources needed to give meaning to the rhetoric leaves the position ambiguous if not contradictory. While the theory is global, current practice is necessarily regional.

The EU as a power in the world

However much emphasis the EU places on multilateralism and interdependence, it will still be judged by many, and particularly the bigger states in the world, on the criterion of power. How capable are the Europeans, collectively, of defending—and asserting—their own interests, even against the opposition of others? Is Robert Kagan right in seeing the EU's distinctive international posture, including the idea of civilian power, as a mere rationalisation of painful weakness (Kagan 2003)?

The first response to this kind of scepticism is that international power is divisible. In some policy arenas, generally insulated from others, the Union does indeed have considerable capacity to achieve its ends and to ensure that its positions are factored into the calculations of others. Indeed, it could without exaggeration be said that the EU is an economic superpower because of its weight in world trade, the increasing strength and importance of its common currency, and its sheer size and wealth. In the UN Human Development Index for 2004, the established EU members (not including those which joined on 1 May 2004) occupied 15 of the top 26 places in a table of 177 countries which aggregates life expectancy, literacy, and education together with the familiar measure of GDP per capita. This makes the EU a relatively conservative power, in the sense of having interests in the status quo. Yet, as Giuseppe di Lampedusa demonstrated in *The Leopard*, to retain your advantages you need to move with the times, and the Europeans have been willing and able to force the United States into compromises at the WTO, to seek changes in Third World regimes through the political conditionality attaching to their development policy, and to use their leverage on those states in their orbit which wish for accession or special relationships.

It is on the dimension of 'hard power' that the EU justifies Kagan's jibe. Although strictly speaking the term should cover any attempt at coercion, including economic sanctions (where the Europeans generally have more leverage than the US), it is mostly associated with military force. Howorth shows how, given the zero baseline the EU started from in 1998, progress in recent years has been surprisingly rapid. But there is still a long way to go in terms of coordination, spending, and technological advance before the Union can attain a level of coordinated and autonomous military strength which is consonant with its size and wealth. The small operations in 2003–2004 in the DRC, in Macedonia and Bosnia are admirable in their way, but they would not be sufficient even to prevent the outbreak of large-scale fighting in these countries, let alone to defeat a determined national force in the way the US did over Kosovo and in Iraq.

Since St. Malo in 1998, the Europeans have decided that soft power is not enough, while realising that serious military capability will take at least a generation to achieve. They thus seek to square the circle by fostering a stable external environment in which multilateralism figures prominently, whether through stressing the importance of the UN or working with other compatible organisations such as NATO and the OSCE. Moral conviction and example are important, but they will do little in the short-term in intractable conflicts or against intransigent adversaries. Moreover they will carry little force if the EU itself appears to be behaving in a disreputable fashion.

This is the ultimate dilemma for the contemporary EU: should it attempt to de-velop its capabilities according to conventional definitions of power, including the military element, when this might put at risk the very (irenic) values which Europe has come to stand for in international relations? The emphasis on conflict prevention as an instrument of external action from the late 1990s is not surprising in this con-text, as it seems to offer an escape-route from the dilemma. Yet since wishing does not make it so in international politics, conflict prevention remains a necessary but insufficient platform for external strategy. Even here, conventional power is often necessary in order to bring warring parties to the table, as the tragic stalemate over Palestine in the absence of serious American peace-making illustrates.

What about Europe's *impact*? How may we judge what kind of a power it is or might be in world politics? Naturally we may all draw our own political and moral conclu-sions about the desirability of various actions, and of possibilities like militarisation and/or superpowerdom. But in terms of making as objective an assessment as pos-sible of the extent to which the EU makes a difference to outcomes, we need to con-sider both perceptions and the actual pattern of events.

On the perceptions side, the EU's impact needs to be measured against the expect-ations of both insiders and outsiders (Hill 1993, 1998a). Since the St. Malo initiative these two sets of views have not diverged markedly. The forging of the ESDP has been seen as a serious development by many, including a Turkey fearful over exclusion, and a US determined on the primacy of NATO. The failure to meet the Headline Goals in 2003 produced a corresponding disappointment, while the public splits over Iraq have lowered expectations over both political and military capability as never before. European public opinion expected more of the Union in this crisis than at any previ-ous time, and its failure strengthened the arguments of the CFSP-sceptics. That said, hope springs eternal for the integrationists and for those in need, so that there have been continued calls for effective EU action in such diverse places as Darfur (the Su-dan), the Congolese–Rwanda border, and the Ukraine, encouraged by the increa-singly effective EU presence in the Balkans. Looked at in historical perspective, the EU probably has more impact across more issues in world politics than it did 20 years ago, but since expectations have risen in parallel, it gets less credit.

The other side of this coin is over-stretch. But this is only likely if the EU places too much emphasis on the exercise of power, and an ability to make a difference in the great conflicts of international politics. If it accepts, for the time being, that at least it has a significant presence throughout international relations, plus a distinct-ive and relatively unthreatening identity, there are benefits to be had which might outweigh the obvious frustrations of a self-denying ordinance. For at the operational (that is, not just the psychological) level the EU does have a significant impact. Israel might have contemptuously destroyed buildings funded by the EU for the Palestinian Authority, but that was itself a recognition of the fact that European resources were being brought to bear to the Palestinian advantage; the persistent exercise of a car-rot and stick policy toward Libya was probably as important as the invasion of Iraq in enabling Colonel Ghaddafi to come in from the cold; the support given by High Representative Solana and then the European Parliament to the Ukrainian opposi-tion in early December 2004 helped achieve a re-run of the contested elections in that country.

These are only three examples from recent years. They could be multiplied. What is clear is that the EU both *has* power, and *is* a power of a certain kind in international relations, even if these claims must be qualified by reference to geography and issue-area. More generally, it has most external impact either in the purely trade and regulatory areas, or at the interface of economics and politics, where it has a distinct advantage. But even in matters of classical diplomacy the critical mass represented by 15 (now 25) states acting in unison (when they do) can be impressive, while the small but useable military capabilities now available have given the EU a physical presence in certain key flash-points. It need no longer be a question of hand-wringing from a distance.

In some respects the EU fits Stephan Keukeleire's model of 'structural power', followed by Simon Nuttall in this volume (Keukeleire, 2003, but see the discussion above of Galtung's different use of the term). This stresses how an actor often seeks to shape the overall environment in which it and its peers operate (see also Wolfers 1962). The European Union does have the capacity to shape some important aspects of the structures, or milieux, affecting other states' choices. Measured by absolute standards this power will be found to be limited and inconsistent, but assessed in relative terms against the capacities of other actors, the EU looks like one of the most significant members of the international system. China and India have bigger populations, and the potential to be superpowers which the EU may not choose, or be able, to follow. But they are still far from reaching that status, and their influence now is primarily regional. Russia still has more sway than it is given credit for, in the wake of the collapse of the USSR, but it is hobbled by internal problems and on the defensive geopolitically. Only the US has more capacity to influence the shape and evolution of international politics than the EU.

Conclusions

In this chapter we have sought to do justice to the complexity of our subject, and to the detailed analysis provided by our contributors. But it is also important to take the broad view and to summarise the common findings of the book. They are fivefold:

1. *An understanding of the EU's evolution cannot be achieved without reference to the international dimension.* This apparent truism is necessary because of the neglect of international relations and foreign policy evident in most mainstream political science approaches to European integration over the last 40 years. Whether it is Haas (neo-functionalism) or Moravcsik (liberal intergovernmentalism), or even Hoffmann (liberal realism), the issue of the meaning of European foreign policy cooperation for the international system, and conversely the impact of international relations on the EU, has been of marginal concern (Haas 1964; Moravcsik 1998; Hoffmann 1995). There have been exceptions, as with aspects of the worth of the lawyer Joseph Weiler, but for the most part these issues have been pursued only by European foreign policy specialists, such as Ginsberg (Weiler 1999; Ginsberg 1989, 2001). Their work has gradually broadened out to include political economy and transnational issues but it

has generally not been picked up on by those not already on the same expert circuit. Mearsheimer, for example, has taken some dramatic positions on Europe's international relations, but has based them on axiomatic realism rather than bother with the specialist literature on the EU (Mearsheimer 1990, 1994–95). The result is that much high-profile political science, especially in the United States, simplifies the EU's international activities by looking at them through the lens of comparative politics or neo-realism, neither of which is fit for the purpose.

2. *The EU is a significant presence in the international system, along most dimensions.* Economically it is a major player; politically it represents an alternative voice within the West—yet also, paradoxically, the USA's most valued set of allies; militarily, it has finally entered the lists, and in only six years has made notable, practical progress; culturally Europe represents one of the greatest concentrations of artistic and scientific endeavour, and possesses a raft of internationally admired educational resources. In short, Europe counts. The EU represents a new 'quality' of international relations, and to some degree a distinct sub-system. It is also deeply implicated in the wider, regulatory, processes of the international system—political, institutional, legal, social and normative.

3. *The academic subject of International Relations needs to place the EU's external activities nearer to the centre of its concerns.* This is true of both theory and empiricism, and to some extent also of the EU more generally. Too often in the past the EU has been dependent on some major event or policy—such as the 1973 oil crisis, or the Single Market initiative, to attract wider intellectual attention, when the truth is that it is an inherently important and now an enduring experiment in international cooperation, with an accumulated capacity to shape the external environments of most other actors. On the empirical side no student of the post-Cold War order, whether unipolar or potentially multipolar, can neglect the EU. Even those who take the view that national foreign policies still hold sway in Europe need to relate their studies, of Germany or France, Spain or Poland, to the CFSP framework in which they are played out. Specialists of other regions, equally, are increasingly likely to take Europe's activities into account as they attempt to explain the regional dynamics of international relations. This is most obviously true of the ex-CIS or the Middle East, but the EU is a notable factor also in Africa, and in parts of Asia and Latin America.

Theoretically, IR will benefit from incorporating the EU more fully into its *Weltanschauung*. Whether we are interested in the behaviour of states, international organisation, political economy, the impact of domestic politics, ethical foreign policy, human rights, conflict resolution, identity, or other central issues in the subject, the study of the EU in the world has much to teach us. Given the range of the EU's international activity and its evident capacity to transform a range of international relationships, the days have passed of being able to bracket it out as a theoretical anomaly.

4. *The EU fits distinctively, but without excessive strain, into the general categories of International Relations scholarship.* Realism, liberalism, and structuralism, or post-positivisms of various kinds may all be applied—and increasingly are being—to the problems of explaining and understanding the EU's international roles. So long as the original purpose is not forgotten, there will be significant gains from this encounter. Even if

the EU is deemed *sui generis*, the definition still depends on comparisons with other kinds of actors. Comparative analysis, as generated in IR principally by Foreign Policy Analysis, is indispensable in identifying those aspects of the political and decision-making processes which are to be found in the EU as well as in states, and those which can only be understood from the inside, out.

5. *The EU is better thought of as having powers, than as being a 'power'.* Its forms of presence vary, its impacts are not necessarily cumulative and its power is not therefore always fungible. But the EU is now much nearer being a coherent power than when Johan Galtung discussed its coming superpower status in 1973, and even realists no longer find it so inconceivable that it might actually reach that point during the present century. Enlargement, complexity and 'the logic of diversity' are the major obstacles, as well as sharp normative disagreements among the citizens of Europe as to its desirability. Third states will also not stand idly by if they see their interests as threatened by growing European power. At the least they will play on internal divisions, which in an increasingly large and diverse Union is not so difficult. In any case whether super power is, or should be, the *telos* of the EU will remain a hotly contested subject. What is not in dispute is the fact that the international relations of the Union are now a subject of immense political and intellectual significance.

References

Adler, E., and Barnett, M. (eds) (1998), *Security Communities* (Cambridge: Cambridge University Press).

Aggestam, L. (2000), 'Germany' in Manners, I., and Whitman, R. (eds) *The Foreign Policies of European Union Member States* (Manchester: Manchester University Press).

Ágh, A. (1999), 'Europeanisation of Policy-Making in East Central Europe: The Hungarian Approach to EU Accession', *Journal of European Public Policy* 6/5, 839–54.

Allen, D. (1978), 'The Euro-Arab Dialogue', *Journal of Common Market Studies* 16/4, 323–42.

Allen, D. (1992), 'West European Responses to Change in the Soviet Union and Eastern Europe', in Rummel, R. (ed)., *Toward Political Union: Planning a Common Foreign and Security Policy in the European Community* (Boulder, CO: Westview Press).

Allen, D. (1998), 'Who Speaks for Europe? The Search for an Effective and Coherent External Policy', in Peterson, J., and Sjursen, H. (eds), *A Common Foreign Policy for Europe? Competing Visions of the CFSP* (London: Routledge).

Allen, D., and Smith, M. (1990), 'Western Europe's Presence in the Contemporary International Arena', *Review of International Studies* 16/3, 19–38.

Allen, D., and Smith, M. (2002), 'External Policy Developments', in Edwards, G., and Wiessala, G. (eds) *The European Union: Annual Review of the EU 2001/2002* (Oxford: Blackwell).

Allen, D., Rummel, R., and Wessels, W. (eds) (1982), *European Political Cooperation: Towards a Foreign Policy for Western Europe* (London: Butterworth Scientific).

Aluko, O. (1981), *Essays in Nigerian Foreign Policy* (London: Allen and Unwin).

Andréani, G., Bertram, C., and Grant, C. (2001), *Europe's Military Revolution* (London: Centre for European Reform).

Aron, R. (1966), *Peace and War: A Theory of International Relations* (Garden City, NJ: Doubleday).

Arquilla, J., and Ronfeldt, D. (2001), *Networks and Netwars: The Future of Terror, Crime, and Militancy* (Santa Monica, CA: Rand).

Art, R. (1996), 'Why Western Europe Needs the United States and NATO', *Political Science Quarterly*, 111/1, 1–37

Avery, G. (1995), 'The Commission's perspective on the EFTA accession negotiations', Sussex European Institute Working Paper No. 12 (Falmer: University of Sussex).

Axelrod, R., and Keohane, R. (1993), 'Achieving Cooperation Under Anarchy: Strategies and Institutions', in Baldwin, D.A. (ed.), *Neorealism and Neoliberalism* (New York: Columbia University Press).

Barbé, E. (1996), 'Spain: The Uses of Foreign Policy Cooperation' in Hill, C. (ed.) *The Actors in Europe's Foreign Policy* (London: Routledge), 108–29.

Barbé, E., and Izquierdo, F. (1997), 'Present and Future of the Joint Actions for the Mediterranean Region' in Holland, M. (ed.) *Common Foreign and Security Policy: The Record and Reform* (London: Pinter).

Beaumel, C., Doisneau, L., and Vatan, M. (2003), *La situation demographique en 2001: Mouvement de la population* (Paris: INSEE).

Beetham, D. (1991), *The Legitimation of Power* (Basingstoke: Macmillan).

Beetham, D. (1994), *Defining and Measuring Democracy* (London: Sage/ECPR).

Beetham, D., and Lord, C. (1998), *Legitimacy in the European Union* (London: Addison-Wesley Longman).

Bellamy, R., and Castiglione, D. (2002), 'Legitimizing the Euro-"Polity" and its Regime' *European Journal of Political Theory* 2/1, 7–34.

Bellier, I., and Wilson, T.M. (eds) (2000), *An Anthropology of the European Union: Building, Imagining and Experiencing the New Europe* (Oxford: Berg).

Bhargava, K.K. (1998), 'EU-SAARC: Comparisons and Prospects of Cooperation'. Discussion Paper C15 (Bonn: Center for European Integration Studies).

Bigo, D. (1999), 'The Landscape of Police Cooperation', in Bort, E., and Keat, R. (eds), *The Boundaries of Understanding. Essays in Honour of Malcolm Anderson* (Institute of Social Sciences, University of Edinburgh).

Bigo, D. (2000), 'When Two Become One: Internal and External Securitisations in Europe' in Kelstrup, M. and Williams, M. (eds) *International Theory and the Politics of European Integration* (London: Routledge).

Biscop, S., and Coolsaet, R. (2003), *The World is the Stage: A Global Security Strategy for the European Union*. Policy Paper 8, *Notre Europe* (Paris) accessed in May 2004 at: http://www.notre-europe.asso.fr

Black, I. (2002), 'Europe's dreams of muscle dashed', *The Guardian*, December 6.

Bobbitt, P. (2002), *The Shield of Achilles: War, Peace, and the Course of History* (London: Penguin).

Bodansky, D. (2003), 'Transatlantic Environmental Relations' in Peterson, J., and Pollack, M. (eds) *Europe, America, Bush: Transatlantic Relations in the Twenty-first Century*. (London: Routledge).

Bort, E. (2000), 'Illegal Migration and Cross-Border Crime: Challenges at the Eastern Frontier of the European Union', in den Boer, M. (ed.), *Schengen Still Going Strong* (Maastricht: European Institute for Public Administration).

Bretherton, C., and Vogler, J. (1999), *The European Union as a Global Actor* (London: Routledge).

Buchan, D. (1993), *Europe: The Strange Superpower* (Aldershot: Dartmouth).

Bull, H. (1977), *The Anarchical Society: A Study of Order in World Politics* (London: Macmillan).

Bull, H. (1982), 'Civilian Power Europe: A Contradiction in Terms?' *Journal of Common Market Studies* 21/2, 149–64.

Bulmer, S. and Burch, M. (1999), 'The Europeanisation of Central Government: The UK and Germany in Historical Institutionalist Perspective', *ARENA Working Paper* 99/30 (Oslo: ARENA).

Buzan, B., Jones, C., and Little, R. (1993), *The Logic of Anarchy: from Neo-Realism to Structural Realism* (New York: Columbia University Press).

Buzan, B., Waever, O., and de Wilde, J. (1998), *Security: A New Framework for Analysis* (Boulder, CO: Lynne Rienner).

Cameron, F. (1997), 'Where the European Commission Comes in: From Single European Act to Maastricht', in Regelsberger, E., de Schoutheete, P., and Wessels, W. (eds) *Foreign Policy of the European Union: From EPC to CFSP and Beyond* (Boulder, Co and London: Lynne Rienner).

Cannizzarro, E. (ed.) (2002), *The European Union as an Actor in International Relations* (The Hague: Kluwer).

Caporaso, J. (1996), 'The European Union and Forms of State: Westphalian, Regulatory, or Post-Modern?' *Journal of Common Market Studies*, 34/1, 29–52.

Carlsnaes, W. (2004), 'Where is the analysis of European Union foreign policy going?', *European Union Politics*, 5/4, 495–508.

Carlsnaes, W., and Smith, S. (eds) (1994), *European Foreign Policy: The EC and Changing Perspectives in Europe* (London: Sage).

Carlsnaes, W., Sjursen, H., and White, B. (eds) (2004), *Contemporary European Foreign Policy* (London: Sage).

CEPS (Centre for European Policy Studies) (2001), *Reshaping Europe's Borders: Challenges for EU Internal and External Policy* (Brussels: CEPS).

Chalk, P. (2000), 'The Third Pillar on Judicial and Home Affairs Cooperation, Anti-Terrorist Collaboration and Liberal Democratic Accountability', in Reinares, F. (ed.), *European Democracies Against Terrorism: Governmental Policies and Intergovernmental Cooperation* (Aldershot: Ashgate).

Christiansen, T, Petito, F., and Tonra, B. (2000), 'Fuzzy Politics Around Fuzzy Borders: The European Union's 'Near Abroad', *Cooperation and Conflict*, 35/4, 389–415.

Clapham, A. (1999), 'Where is the EU's Human Rights Common Foreign Policy, and How is it Manifested in Multilateral Fora?' in Alston, P. (ed.), *The European Union and Human Rights* (Oxford: Oxford University Press).

Cole, A., and Drake, H. (2000), 'The Europeanisation of the French Polity: Continuity, Change and Adaptation', *Journal of European Public Policy*, 7/1, 26–43.

Coleman, K. (2004), 'Network Centric Warfare', *Directions Magazine*, 14 May.

Cooper, R. (2002), 'The new liberal imperialism', *The Observer*, 7 April.

Cooper, R. (2003), *The Breaking of Nations: Order and Chaos in the Twenty-First Century* (New York: Atlantic Monthly Press, London: Atlantic Books).

Corbett, R., Jacobs, F., and Shackleton, M. (1995), *The European Parliament* (London: Cartermill).

Corkill, D. (1999), *The Development of the Portuguese Economy: A Case of Europeanisation* (London: Routledge).

Cornish, P. (1997), *Partnership in Crisis: The US, Europe and the Fall and Rise of NATO* (London: Pinter for the Royal Institute of International Affairs).

Cornish, P. (2004), *Artemis and Coral: British Perspectives on European Union Crisis Management Operations in the Democratic Republic of Congo, 2003.* Unpublished Report, King's College London.

Cornish, P., and Edwards, G. (2001), 'Identifying the development of an EU "Strategic Culture" ', *International Affairs* 77/3, 587–604.

Council of the European Union (1996), 'Council conclusions on the principle of conditionality governing the development of the European Union's relations with certain countries of south-east Europe', *EU Bulletin* No. 4.

Council of the European Union (1999–2004), *Annual Report From the Council to the European Parliament on the main aspects and basic choices of CFSP, including the financial implications for the general budget of the European Communities, 1998–2003* (Brussels).

Council of the European Union (1999), 'Common Position of 17 May 1999 concerning the launching of the Stability Pact of the EU on south-eastern Europe (1999/345/CFSP)', OJ L133, 28 May.

Council of the European Union (2002), 'Council Framework Decision of 13 June 2002 on Combating Terrorism', Brussels.

Cowles, M.G., Caporaso, J., and Risse, T. (eds) (2001), *Transforming Europe: Europeanization and Domestic Change* (Ihtaca, NY: Cornell University Press).

Craft, N., and Toniolo, G. (eds) (1996), *Economic Growth in Europe Since 1945* (Cambridge: Cambridge University Press).

Crawford, N.C. (2002), *Argument and Change in World Politics: Ethics, Decolonization and Humanitarian Intervention* (Cambridge: Cambridge University Press).

Croft, S., Redmond, J., Rees, W., and Webber, M. (1999), *The Enlargement of Europe* (Manchester: Manchester University Press).

Daalder, I. (2003), 'The End of Atlanticism', *Survival* 45/2, 147–66.

Dannreuther, R. (ed.) (2003), *European Union Foreign and Security Policy: Towards a Neighbourhood Strategy* (London: Routledge).

Davis, C.L. (2003), *Food Fights over Free Trade: how international institutions promote agricultural trade liberalization* (Princeton, NJ: Princeton University Press).

De Grauwe, P. (2005), *Economics of Monetary Union*. 6th edition (Oxford: Oxford University Press).

de Schoutheete de Tervarent, P. (1980), *La coopération politique européenne* (Brussels: F. Nathan Editions Labor).

de Schoutheete de Tervarent, P. (1986), *La coopération politique européenne*, 2nd edition (Brussels: F. Nathan Editions Labor).

Deighton, A. (ed.) (1997), *Western European Union, 1954–97: Defence, Security, Integration* (Oxford: St Antony's College).

Deighton, A. (2002), 'The European Security and Defence Policy', *Journal of Common Market Studies* 40/4, 719–42.

Dembinski, M. (2002), 'Kein Abschied vom Leitbild "Zivilmacht". Die Europäische Sicherheits- und Verteidigungspolitik und die Zukunft Europäischer Außenpolitik', HSFK-Report 12/2002 (Frankfurt am Main: Hessische Stiftung Friedens- und Konfliktforschung).

Den Boer, M. (1997), 'Wearing it Inside Out: European Police Cooperation Between Internal and External Security', *European Foreign Affairs Review* 2/4, 491–508.

Den Boer, M. (1999), 'The European Union and Organized Crime: Fighting a New Enemy with Many Tentacles', in Viano, E. (ed.), *Global Organized Crime and International Security* (Aldershot: Ashgate).

Dent, C. (1999), *The European Union and East Asia: An Economic Relationship* (London: Routledge).

Denza, E. (2002), *The Intergovernmental Pillars of the European Union* (Oxford: Oxford University Press).

DePorte, A. (1987), *Europe Between the Superpowers: The Enduring Balance*, 2nd edition (New Haven, CT: Yale University Press).

Deudney, D. (1995), 'The Philadelphian System: Sovereignty, Arms Control and Balance of Power in the American States Union, ca. 1787–1861', *International Organization*, 49/2, 191–228.

Deutsch, K. (1968), *The Analysis of International Relations* (Englewood Cliffs, NJ: Prentice-Hall).

Deutsch, K., et al. (1957), *Political Community in the North Atlantic Area: International Organization in the Light of Historical Experience* (Princeton: Princeton University Press).

Deutsch, K. (1957a), *Political Community at the International Level: Problems of Definition and Measurement* (London: Archon Books).

Devuyst, Y. (1992), 'The EC's Common Commercial Policy and the Treaty on European Union: An Overview of the Negotiations', *World Competition*, 16/2, 67–80.

Devuyst, Y. (1995), 'The European Community and the Conclusion of the Uruguay Round' in Rhodes, C. and Mazey, S. (eds), *The State of the European Union, volume 3: Building a European Polity?* (Boulder, CO: Lynne Rienner).

Doyle, M. (1983), 'Kant, Liberal Legacies and Foreign Affairs', *Philosophy and Public Affairs* 12, 205–35 and 323–53.

Drake, W., and Nicolaïdis, K. (1992), 'Ideas, Interests and Institutionalization: Trade in Services and the Uruguay Round' *International Organization* 46/1, 37–100.

Duchêne, F. (1972), 'Europe's Role in World Peace', in Mayne, R. (ed.), *Europe Tomorrow: Sixteen Europeans Look Ahead* (London: Fontana).

Duchêne, F. (1973), 'The European Community and the Uncertainties of Interdependence', in Kohnstamm, M., and Hager, W. (eds), *A Nation Writ Large? Foreign Policy Problems Before the European Community* (London: Macmillan).

Duke, S. (2002), 'Preparing for European Diplomacy?' *Journal of Common Market Studies* 40/5, 849–70.

Duke, S. (2003), *The Convention, the Draft Constitution and External Relations: Effects and Implications for the EU and its International Role* Occasional Paper 2003/W2 (Maastricht: EIPA).

Dyson, K. (2000), *Elusive Union: The Process of Economic and Monetary Union in Europe* (Oxford: Oxford University Press).

Edwards, G. (1997), 'The Potential and Limits of the CFSP: The Yugoslav Example', in Regelsberger, E., de Schoutheete de Tervarent, P., and Wessels, W. (eds) *Foreign Policy of the European Union: from EPC to CFSP and Beyond* (Boulder, CO: Lynne Rienner).

Edwards, G. (1998), 'Common Foreign and Security Policy: Incrementalism in Action', in Koskenniemi, M. (ed.) *International Law Aspects of the European Union* (The Hague: Kluwer).

Edwards, G. (2000), 'Europe's Security and Defence Policy and Enlargement: The Ghost at the Feast?' European University Institute *Working Papers* RSC No. 2000/69 (Florence: European University Institute).

Edwards, G., and Regelsberger, E. (eds) (1990), *Europe's Global Links: The European Community and Inter-Regional Cooperation* (London: Pinter Publishers).

Elias, N. (1986), *The Quest for Excitement: Sport and Leisure in the Civilizing Process*, Elias, N., and Dunning, E. (eds) (Oxford: Blackwell).

Elias, N. (1991), *The Symbol Theory* (London: Sage).

Elias, N. (1992), *Time: An Essay* (Oxford: Blackwell).

Elias, N. (1996), *The Germans* (Cambridge: Polity Press).

Elias, N. (1998a), 'The Expulsion of the Huguenots from France', in Goudsblom, J., and Mennell, S. (eds) *The Norbert Elias Reader* (Oxford: Blackwell).

Elias, N. (1998b), 'An Interview in Amsterdam', in Goudsblom, J., and Mennell, S. (eds) *The Norbert Elias Reader* (Oxford: Blackwell).

Elias, N. (1998c), 'The Civilizing of Parents', in Goudsblom, J., and Mennell, S. (eds) *The Norbert Elias Reader* (Oxford: Blackwell).

Elias, N. (2000), *The Civilizing Process: Sociogenetic and Psychogenetic Investigations* (Oxford: Blackwell).

Elias, N. (2001a), *The Loneliness of Dying* (London: Continuum).

Elias, N. (2001b), *The Society of Individuals* (London: Continuum).

Ellwood, D. (1992), *Rebuilding Europe: Western Europe, America and Postwar Reconstruction* (London: Longman).

European Commission (1992), 'Europe and the Challenge of Enlargement', *EC Bulletin Supplement* 3/92 (Brussels: European Commission).

European Commission (1993), 'Towards a Closer Association with the Countries of Central and Eastern Europe', SEC (93) 648 final, 18 May.

European Commission (1995–2004), *General Report on the Activities of the European Union, 1994–2003* (Brussels/Luxembourg: Office for Official Publications of the European Communities).

European Commission (1997), 'Agenda 2000: For a Stronger and Wider Union', *EU Bulletin Supplement* 5/97.

European Commission (1999), 'Composite Paper: Reports on Progress Towards Accession by Each of the Candidate Countries', Brussels, 13 October.

European Commission (2000), 'Communication as the Reform of the Management of External Assistance', Rev. 8., Brussels, 16 May.

European Commission (2001a), 'The EU and Kaliningrad', COM (2001) 26 final, Brussels, 17 January.

European Commission (2001b), 'Making a Success of Enlargement: Strategy Paper 2001 and Report of the European Commission on the Progress Towards Accession by Each of the Candidate Countries', Brussels, 13 November.

European Commission (2001c), *Perceptions of the European Union: A Qualitative Study of the Public's Attitudes to and Expectations of the European Union in the 15 Member States and the 9 Candidate Countries* (The Optem Report), Brussels, September.

European Commission (2002), 'Towards the Enlarged Union: Strategy Paper and Report on the Progress towards Accession by Each of the Candidate Countries', COM (2002) 700 final, Brussels, 9 October.

European Commission (2003a), 'Wider Europe—Neighbourhood: A New Framework for Relations with our Eastern and Southern Neighbours', COM (2003) 104 final, Brussels, 11 March.

European Commission (2003b), *Africa and the European Union* (Brussels/Luxembourg: Office for Official Publications of the European Communities).

European Commission (2003c), *EU-US Bilateral Economic Relations*, European Union Factsheet published on the occasion of the EU-US Summit, Washington, 25th June 2003. Accessed at http://www.eurunion.org/.

European Council (1989), Strasbourg, Conclusions of the Presidency, 8–9 December, *EC Bulletin* No. 12.

European Council (1993), Copenhagen, Conclusions of the Presidency, 22–23 June, document no. SN 180/93.

European Council (1999a), 'Common Strategy of the European Union on Russia', document no. 8199/99, 12 May.

European Council (1999b), Helsinki, Presidency Conclusions, 10–11 December.

European Council (2001a), 'The European Community's Development Policy—Statement by the Council and the Commission', January. http://europa.eu.int/comm/development/lex/en/council20001110_en.htm,

European Council (2001b), 'Presidency Conclusions', 22 October, Ghent.

European Council (2001c), Laeken, Presidency Conclusions, 13–14 December.

European Council (2001d), Laeken, Presidency Conclusions 14–15 December 2001. Annex One. 'Laeken Declaration on the Future of the European Union', in Rutten (2002, 112–18).

European Council (2002), Copenhagen, Presidency Conclusions, 12–13 December, document no. SN 400/02.

European Council (2003), 'Presidency Conclusions', 12 December, Brussels.

European Council (2003a), *A Secure Europe in a Better World. European Security Strategy*, Brussels, 12 December.

European Monitoring Centre for Drugs and Drug Addiction (2000), *Annual Report on the State of the Drugs Problem in the European Union*, Lisbon.

European Parliament (2000a), *Report on the Progress Achieved in the Implementation of the Common Foreign and Security Policy During 1999* (Brok Report) (Brussels: European Parliament).

European Parliament (2000b), *Report on the General Budget for 2001* (European Parliament, Council..) (Ferber Report) (Brussels: European Parliament).

European Parliament (2001a), *Report on the Progress Achieved in the Implementation of the Common Foreign and Security Policy* (Response to the Council of Ministers Report on CFSP During 2000) (Brok Report) (Brussels: European Parliament).

European Parliament (2001b), *Report on Proposal for a Regulation on the Protection of Individuals with Regard to the Processing of Personal Data by the Institutions and Bodies of the Community* (Paciotti Report) (Brussels: European Parliament).

European Parliament (2001c), *On the Financial Regulation Applicable to the General Budget of the European Communities* (Dell'Alba Report) (Brussels: European Parliament).

European Union Official Journal, 2003, 'Joint Declaration: One Europe', OJ L 236, 23 September.

Europol (2000), *1998 Situation Report on Organised Crime*, The Hague, 1 January.

Europol (2001), *2000 EU Organised Crime Situation Report*, The Hague, http://www.europol.eu.int/content.htm

Evans, P., Jacobson, H., and Putnam, R. (eds) (1993), *Double-Edged Diplomacy: International Bargaining and Domestic Politics* (Berkeley: University of California Press).

Evenett, S., and Vermulst, E. (2004), *The Politicization of EC Anti-Dumping Policy: Member States, their Votes, and the European Commission*. Working Paper, University of Michigan (Ann Arbor, Michigan: University of Michigan).

Everts, S. (2004), *Engaging Iran: a test case for EU foreign policy*. (London: Centre for European Reform).

Everts, S., and Keohane, D. (2003), 'The European Convention and EU Foreign Policy: Learning from Failure', *Survival*, 45/3, 167–86.

Fawcett, L. (1995), 'Regionalism in Historical Perspective' in Fawcett, L., and Hurrell, A. (eds) *Regionalism in World Politics: Regional Organization and International Order* (Oxford: Oxford University Press).

Featherstone, K. (1998), '"Europeanisation" and the Centre-Periphery: The Case of Greece in the 1990s', *South European Politics and Society* 2/1, 23–39.

Feinberg, J. (1985), *The Moral Limits of the Criminal Law, Vol. 2: Offence to Others* (New York, Oxford: Oxford University Press).

Feinberg, J. (1986), *The Moral Limits of the Criminal Law, Vol. 3: Harm to Self* (New York, Oxford: Oxford University Press).

Forster, A. (1999), 'EU and Southeast Asia Relations: A Balancing Act', *International Affairs* 75/4, 743–58.

Forster, A., and Wallace, W. (2000), 'Common Foreign and Security Policy: From Shadow to Substance?' in Wallace, H., and Wallace, W. (eds) *Policy-Making in the European Union*, 4th edition (Oxford: Oxford University Press).

Fortescue, J. (1995), 'First Experiences in the implementation of the Third Pillar Provisions', in Rieber, R., and Monar, J. (eds) *Justice and Home Affairs in the European Union: The Development of the Third Pillar* (Bruges: College of Europe).

Friedrich, C. (1968), *Trends in Federalism* (New York: Praeger).

Friis, L. (1998), '"The End of the Beginning" of Eastern Enlargement—Luxembourg Summit and Agenda-Setting', *European Integration Online Papers (EioP)*, 2 (7) (http://eiop.or.at).

Friis, L., and Murphy, A. (1999), 'The European Union and Central and Eastern Europe: Governance and Boundaries', *Journal of Common Market Studies*, 37/2, 211–32.

Führer, H. (1996), *The Story of Official Development Assistance*. Available at http://www.oecd.org/dataoecd/3/39/1896816.pdf

Gaddis, J. (1985), 'The US and the Question of a Sphere of Influence in Europe', in Riste, O. (ed.), *Western Security: The Formative Years* (Oslo: Universitetsforlaget).

Galloway, D. (2001), *The Treaty of Nice and Beyond: Realities and Illusions of Power in the EU* (Sheffield: Sheffield Academic Press).

Galtung, J. (1971), 'A Structural Theory of Imperialism', *Journal of Peace Research* 13/2, 81–118.

Galtung, J. (1973), *The European Community: A Superpower in the Making?* (London: Allen and Unwin).

Garcia, G., and Le Torrec, V. (2003), *L'Union Européenne et les Médias, Regards Croisés sur L'Information Européenne* (Paris: L'Harmattan).

Garrett, G., and Tsebelis, G. (1996), 'An Institutional Critique of Intergovernmentalism' *International Organization* 50/2, 269–99.

Gärtner, H., Hyde-Price, A. and Reiter, E. (2001), *Europe's New Security Challenges* (Boulder: Lynne Reinner).

Geddes, A. (2000), *Immigration and European Integration: Towards Fortress Europe?* (Manchester: Manchester University Press).

Gegout, C. (2002), 'The Quint', *Journal of Common Market Studies* 40/2, 331–44.

Gelpi, C. (1999), 'Alliances as Instruments of Inter-Allied Control', in Haftendorn, H., Keohane, R., and Wallander, C. (eds), *Imperfect Unions: Security Institutions Over Time and Space* (Oxford: Oxford University Press).

German Presidency (1999), 'A Stability Pact for South-Eastern Europe', 12 April, http://www.bundesregierung.de/english/01/0103/3810/index.html.

Gibb, R. (2000), 'Post-Lomé: The European Union and the South' *Third World Quarterly* 21/3, 457–81.

Gilpin, R. (1981), *War and Change in World Politics* (Princeton, NJ: Princeton University Press).

Ginsberg, R. (1989), *Foreign Policy Actions of the European Community: The Politics of Scale* (London: Adamantine).

Ginsberg, R. (1999), 'Conceptualising the European Union as an International Actor: Narrowing the Capability-Expectations Gap', *Journal of Common Market Studies*, 37/3, 429–54.

Ginsberg, R. (2001), *The European Union in International Politics: Baptism by Fire* (Lanham, MD: Rowman & Littlefield).

Glarbo, K. (1999), 'Wide-Awake Diplomacy: Reconstructing the Common Foreign and Security Policy of the European Union', *Journal of European Public Policy* 6/4, pp. 634–51.

Goertz, G., and Diehl, P. (1992), *Territorial Changes and International Conflict* (London: Routledge).

Goetz, K., and Hix, S. (eds) (2001), *Europeanised Politics? European Integration and National Political Systems* (London: Frank Cass).

Gomez, R. (1998), 'The EU's Mediterranean Policy: Common Foreign Policy by the Back Door? in Peterson, J. and Sjursen, H. (eds), *A Common Foreign Policy for Europe? Competing Visions of the CFSP* (London: Routledge).

Gomez, R., and Peterson, J. (2001), 'The EU's Impossibly Busy Foreign Ministers: "No-one is in Control"', *European Foreign Affairs Review* 6/1, 53–74.

Gordon, P., and Shapiro, J. (2004), *Allies at War: America, Europe, and the Crisis over Iraq.* (Washington DC: Brookings Institution).

Gowa, J. (1989), 'Bipolarity, Multipolarity and Free Trade', *American Political Science Review*, 83/4L, 1245–56

Grabbe, H. (2000), 'The Sharp Edges of Europe: Extending Schengen Eastwards', *International Affairs*, 76/3, 519–36.

Grant, R. (2000), *The RMA: Europe Can Keep in Step*. Occasional Paper 15 (Paris: WEU Institute for Security Studies) available at http://www.iss-eu.org

Grieco, J. (1995), 'The Maastricht, Treaty, Economic and Monetary Union, and the Neo-Realist Research Programme', *Review of International Studies* 21/1, 21–40.

Grieco, J. (1996), 'State Interests and International Rule Trajectories: A Neo-Realist Interpretation of the Maastricht Treaty and European Economic and Monetary Union', *Security Studies* 5/3, 261–305.

Grieco, J. (1997a), 'Systemic Sources of Variation in Regional Institutionalization in Western Europe, East Asia and the Americas', in Mansfield, E., and Milner, H. (eds), *The Political Economy of Regionalism* (New York: Columbia University Press).

Grieco, J. (1997b), 'Realist International Theory and the Study of World Politics', in Doyle, M., and Ikenberry, J. (eds), *New Thinking in International Relations Theory* (Boulder, CO: Westview Press).

Grilli, E. (1993), *The European Community and the Developing Countries* (Cambridge: Cambridge University Press).

Guay, T. (1999), *The United States and the European Union: the political economy of a relationship*. (Sheffield: Sheffield Academic Press).

Guyomarch, A. (2001), 'The Europeanisation of Policy-Making' in Guyomarch, A. *et al.* (eds), *Developments in French Politics* (Basingstoke: Palgrave).

Guyomarch, A., Machin, H., and Ritchie, E. (eds) (1998), *France in the European Union* (Basingstoke: Macmillan).

Haas, E. (1958), *The Uniting of Europe: Political, Economic, and Social Forces, 1950–1957* (Stanford: Stanford University Press).

Haas, E. (1961), 'International Integration: The European and the Universal Process', *International Organization* 15/3, 366–92.

Haas, E. (1964), *Beyond the Nation-State: Functionalism and International Organization* (Stanford: Stanford University Press).

Haas, P. (1992), 'Introduction: Epistemic Communities and International Policy Coordination', *International Organization*, 46/1, 1–35.

Habermas, J. (2003), 'Why Europe Needs a Constitution' in Eriksen, E., Fossum, J. and Menendez, A. (eds), *The Chartering of Europe: The European Charter of Fundamental Rights and its Constitutional Implications* (Baden-Baden: Nomos).

Haftendorn, H., and Tuschhoff, C. (1993), *America and Europe in an Era of Change* (Boulder, CO: Westview Press).

Haine, J.-Y. (dir.) (2003), *From Laeken to Copenhagen: European Defence—Core Documents III*. Chaillot Paper 57 (Paris: EU Institute for Security Studies) available at http://www.iss-eu.org

Haine, J.-Y. (dir) (2003a), 'European Strategy: First Steps', *EU-ISS Newsletter* 7 (July) available at http://www.iss-eu.org

Hall, P., and Taylor, R. (1996), 'Political Science and the Three New Institutionalisms', *Political Studies* 44/5, 936–57.

Hanf, K., and Soetendorp, B. (1998), 'Small States and the Europeanisation of Public Policy' in Hanf, K., and Soetendorp, B. (eds), *Adapting to European Integration: Small States and the European Union* (London: Longman).

Hansen, P. (2002), 'European Integration, European Identity and the Colonial Connection', *European Journal of Social Theory* 5/4, 483–98.

Hansenclever. A., Mayer, P., and Rittberger, V. (1997), *Theories of International Regimes* (Cambridge: Cambridge University Press).

Harlow, C. (2002), *Accountability in the European Union* (Oxford: Oxford University Press).

Harmsen, R., and Wilson, T. (eds) (2000), *Europeanisation: Institutions, Identities and Citizenship* (Amsterdam: Rodopi).

Hassner, P. (1968), *Change and Security in Europe II: In Search of a System*, Adelphi Paper 49 (London: International Institute for Strategic Studies).

Hayes, J.P. (1993), *Making Trade Policy in the European Community* (London: Macmillan).

Hayes-Renshaw, F., and Wallace, H. (1997), *The Council of Ministers of the European Union* (London: Macmillan).

Hayward, J., and Menon, A. (eds) (2003), *Governing Europe* (Oxford: Oxford University Press).

Heisbourg, F. (2000), 'Europe's Strategic Ambitions: The Limits of Ambiguity', *Survival* 42/1, 5–15

Heller, F., and Gillingham, J. (eds) (1996), *The United States and the Integration of Europe: Legacies of the Postwar Era* (New York: St Martin's Press).

Henderson, K. (ed.) (1999), *Back to Europe: Central and Eastern Europe and the European Union* (London: UCL Press).

Héritier, A. (1997), 'Policy-making by Subterfuge: Interest Accommodation, Innovation and Substitute Democratic Legitimation in Europe—Perspectives from Different Policy Areas', *Journal of European Public Policy* 4/2, 171–89.

Heurlin, B. (1996), 'Denmark: A New Activism in Foreign and Security Policy', in Hill, C. (ed.) *The Actors In Europe's Foreign Policy* (London: Routledge).

Hill, C. (1990), 'European Foreign Policy: Power Bloc, Civilian Model—or Flop?' in Rummel, R. (ed.), *The Evolution of an International Actor: Western Europe's New Assertiveness* (Boulder, CO: Westview Press).

Hill, C. (1991), 'The Foreign Policy of the European Community' in Roy Macridis (ed.), *Foreign Policy and World Politics*, 8th edition, (New York, Prentice Hall).

Hill, C. (1993), 'The Capability-Expectations Gap, or Conceptualising Europe's International Role', *Journal of Common Market Studies* 31/3, 305–28.

Hill, C. (1993a), 'Shaping a Federal Foreign Policy for Europe', in Hocking, B. (ed.) *Foreign Relations and Federal States* (Leicester: Leicester University Press).

Hill, C. (ed.) (1996), *The Actors in Europe's Foreign Policy* (London: Routledge).

Hill, C. (1998a), 'Closing the Capability-Expectations Gap?' in Peterson, J. and Sjursen, H. (eds), *A Common Foreign Policy for Europe? Competing Visions of the CFSP* (London: Routledge).

Hill, C. (1998b), 'Convergence, Divergence and Dialectics: National Foreign Policies and the CFSP' in Zielonka, J. (ed.), *Paradoxes of European Foreign Policy* (The Hague: Kluwer).

Hill, C. (2001a), 'The European Union and South Africa', in Broderick, J., Burford, G., and Freer, G., (eds.), *South Africa's Foreign Policy: Dilemmas of a New Democracy* (Basingstoke: Palgrave).

Hill, C. (2001b), 'The EU's Capacity for Conflict Prevention', *European Foreign Affairs Review* 6/3, 315–34.

Hill, C. (2002), 'The Geopolitical Implications of Enlargement', in Zielonka, J. (ed.), *Europe Unbound: Enlarging and Reshaping the Boundaries of the European Union* (London: Routledge).

Hill, C. (2003), *The Changing Politics of Foreign Policy* (Houndsmill: Palgrave)

Hill, C., and Wallace, W. (1996), 'Introduction: Actors and Actions' in Hill, C. (ed.), *The Actors in Europe's Foreign Policy* (London: Routledge).

Hilpold, P. (2002), 'EU Development Cooperation at the Crossroads', *European Foreign Affairs Review* 7/1, 53–72.

Hine, R. (1985), *The Political Economy of European Trade* (Brighton: Harvester-Wheatsheaf).

Hinsley, F. (1963), *Power and the Pursuit of Peace: Theory and Practice in the History of Relations Between States* (Cambridge: Cambridge University Press).

Hocking, B., and Smith, M. (1987), *Beyond Foreign Economic Policy: The United States, the Single European Market and the Changing World Economy* (London: Cassell-Pinter).

Hocking, B., and Spence, D. (eds) (2002), *Foreign Ministries in the European Union: Integrating Diplomats* (Basingstoke: Palgrave).

Hoffmann, S. (1966), 'Obstinate or Obsolete? The Fate of the Nation-State and the Case of Western Europe', *Daedalus* 95, 862–915.

Hoffmann, S. (1995), 'Balance, Concert, Anarchy, or None of the Above', in Hoffmann, S. (ed.) *The European Sisyphus* (Boulder, CO: Westview Press).

Hoffmann, S. (2000a), 'La France dans le Monde, 1979–2000', *Politique Etrangère* 2/2000, 307–17.

Hoffmann, S. (2000b), 'Towards a Common Foreign and Security Policy?' *Journal of Common Market Studies* 38/2, 189–98.

Holland M. (ed.) (1991), *The Future of European Political Cooperation: Essays on Theory and Practice* (London: Macmillan).

Holland, M. (1995), *European Union Common Foreign Policy: From EPC to CFSP Joint Action and South Africa* (Basingstoke: Macmillan).

Holland, M. (2002), *The European Union and the Third World* (Basingstoke: Palgrave).

Holland, S. (1990), *UnCommon Market: Capital, Class and Power in the European Community* (London: Macmillan).

Hollis, M., and Smith, S. (1991), *Explaining and Understanding International Relations* (Oxford: Clarendon Press).

Holsti, K. (1992), *International Politics: A Framework for Analysis*, 6th edition (Englewood Cliffs, NJ: Prentice-Hall).

House of Lords (1996), *27th Report on the Scrutiny of European Business*. Select Committee on European Legislation (London: HMSO).

House of Lords (2003), *Select Committee on European Union*. 12th Report (London: HMSO). See http://www.publications.parliament.uk

Howorth, J. (2000), *European Integration and Defence: The Ultimate Challenge?* Chaillot Paper 43 (Paris: WEU Institute for Security Studies) available at http://www.iss-eu.org

Howorth, J. (2003), 'European Defence and the Changing Politics of the European Union: Hanging Together or Hanging Separately?' *Journal of Common Market Studies* 39/4, pp. 765–90.

Howorth, J. (2003), 'Reconcilable Differences: Europe, the US and the War in Iraq', http://www.thepolitic.org/news/2003/05/13/International/Reconcilable.Differences 433176.shtml, May 13

Howorth, J. (2004), 'Discourse, Ideas and Epistemic Communities in European Security and Defence Policy', *West European Politics* 27/2, 29–52.

Howorth, J., and Keeler, J. (eds) (2003), *Defending Europe: The EU, NATO and the Quest for European Autonomy* (New York: Palgrave/Macmillan).

[Human Security] (2004), *A Human Security Doctrine for Europe: The Barcelona Report of the Study Group on Europe's Security Capabilities*.

Hunter, R.E. (2002), *The European Security and Defense Policy: NATO's Companion or Competitor?* (Santa Monica, CA: Rand).

Hurd, D. (1981), 'Political Cooperation', *International Affairs* 57/3 383–93.

Huysmans, J. (2002), 'The European Union and the Securitisation of Migration', *Journal of Common Market Studies* 38/5, 751–78.

[IISS] (2003), 'EU Operational Planning', *Strategic Comments* 9/10.

Ikenberry, J. (ed.) (2002), *America Unrivaled: The Future of the Balance of Power* (Ithaca, NY: Cornell University Press).

Interim Report on an EU Strategic Partnership with the Mediterranean and the Middle East, prepared by the Presidency, the Council Secretariat and the Commission, Brussels, 22 March 2004.

Jenkins, C., and Smith, J. (2003), *Through the Paper Curtain* (Oxford: Blackwell/Royal Institute of International Affairs).

Jervis, R. (1976), *Perception and Misperception in International Politics* (Princeton, NJ: Princeton University Press).

Joergensen, K.E. (2002), 'Making the CFSP Work', in Peterson, J., and Shackleton, M. (eds) *The Institutions of the European Union* (Oxford: Oxford University Press).

Johnson, M. (1998), *European Community Trade Policy and the Article 113 Committee* (London: Royal Institute of International Affairs).

Jopp, M. (1997), 'The Defence Dimension of the European Union: The Role and Performance of the WEU', in Regelsberger, E. de Schoutheete de Tervarent. P., and Wessels, W. (eds) *Foreign Policy of the European Union: From EPC to CFSP and Beyond* (Boulder, CO and London: Lynne Rienner).

Kagan, R. (2002), 'Power and Weakness: Why the United States and Europe see the World Differently', *Policy Review,* 113. Available at http://www.policyreview.org/JUN02/kagan.html

Kagan, R. (2003), *Paradise and Power: America and Europe in the New World Order* (London: Atlantic Books).

Kagan, R. (2004), 'Embraceable EU', *The Washington Post,* 5 December.

Kaiser, K. (1971), 'Transnational Relations as a Threat to the Democratic Process', *International Organisation* 25/3, 706–720, Reprinted in Keohane, R., and Nye, J. (eds) (1973) *Transnational Relations and World Politics* (Cambridge, MA: Harvard University Press).

Kaplan, L. (1996), 'NATO After the Cold War', in Wiener, J. (ed.), *The Transatlantic Relationship* (New York: St Martin's Press).

Kapteyn, P.J.G. (1996), *The Stateless Market: The European Dilemma of Integration and Civilization* (London: Routledge).

Kassim, H. (2003), 'The European Administration: Between Europeanisation and Domestication' in Hayward, J., and Menon, A. (eds), *Governing Europe* (Oxford: Oxford University Press).

Kassim, H., Peters, B.G., and Wright, V. (eds) (2000), *The National Coordination of EU Policy* (Oxford: Oxford University Press).

Kassim, H., and Menon, A. (2003), 'The Principal-Agent Approach and the Study of the European Union', *Journal of European Public Policy* 10/1, 121–39.

Katzenstein, P. (ed.) (1996), *The Culture of National Security: Norms and Identity in World Politics* (New York: Columbia University Press).

Kelstrup, M., and Williams, M. (eds) (2000), *International Relations Theory and the Politics of European Integration: Power, Security and Community* (London: Routledge).

Keohane, R. (1983), 'The Demand for International Regimes', in Krasner, S. (ed.) *International Regimes* (Ithaca: Cornell University Press).

Keohane, R. (1984), *After Hegemony: Cooperation and Discord in the World Political Economy* (Princeton, NJ: Princeton University Press).

Keohane, R. (1989), *International Institutions and State Power: Essays on International Relations* (Boulder, CO: Westview Press).

Keohane, R. (1989), 'International Institutions: Two Approaches' in *International Institutions and State Power: Essays in International Relations Theory* (Boulder, CO: Westview Press).

Keohane, R. (2002), 'Ironies of Sovereignty: The European Union and the United States', *Journal of Common Market Studies* 40/4, 743–65.

Keohane, R., and Nye, J. (1977), *Power and Interdependence: World Politics in Transition* (Boston: Little, Brown).

Keohane, R. Nye, J., and Hoffmann, S. (eds) (1993), *After the Cold War: International Institutions and State Strategies in Europe* (Cambridge, MA: Harvard University Press).

Keohane, R., and Martin, L. (1995), 'The Promise of Institutionalist Theory', *International Security* 20/1, 39–51.

Keukeleire, S. (2003), 'The European Union as a Diplomatic Actor: Internal, Traditional and Structural Diplomacy', *Diplomacy and Statecraft* 14/3, 31–56.

Keukeleire, S. (2004), 'EU Structural Foreign Policy and Structural Conflict Prevention', in Kronenberger, V., and Wouters, J. (eds), *The European Union and Conflict Prevention: Legal and Policy Aspects* (The Hague: T.M.C. Asser Press).

Kierzkowski, H. (ed.) (2002), *Europe and Globalization* (Basingstoke: Palgrave).

Kiessler, K.K. (2003), 'The Political and Security Committee. Insights into EU Decision-Shaping: Role, Strengths and Weaknesses of the "Linchpin" of CFSP and ESDP'. Masters thesis (Bruges: College of Europe).

Koenig-Archibugi, M. (2000), *La costruzione di una politica estera e di difesa commune per l'Unione Europea. Interessi nazionali e scelta instituzionale*. PhD Dissertation, Università degli Studi di Firenze.

Koenig-Archibugi, M. (2002), 'The Democratic deficit of EU Foreign and Security Policy', *The International Spectator* 37/4, 61–73.

Koenig-Archibugi, M. (2004), 'Explaining Preferences for Institutional Change in EU Foreign and Security Policy', *International Organization* 54/1, 137–74.

Koulaimah-Gabriel, A. (1997), *The Geographic Scope of EC Aid: One or Several Development Policies?* ECDPM Working Paper Number 42, December, http://www.ecdpm.org/Web_ECDPM/Web/Content/FileStruc.nsf/0/1CF47E7621D155

Krasner, S. (1999), *Sovereignty: Organised Hypocrisy* (Princeton, NJ: Princeton University Press).

Krehbiel, K. (1991), *Information and Legislative Organization* (Ann Arbor, MI: University of Michigan Press).

Krenzler, H.-G., and Schneider, H. (1997), 'The Question of Consistency' in Regelsberger., E., de Schoutheete de Tervarent, P., and Wessels, W. (eds) *Foreign Policy of the European Union: from EPC to CFSP and Beyond* (Boulder, CO/London: Lynne Rienner).

Kupchan, C. (2000), 'In Defence of European Defence: An American Perspective', *Survival* 42/2, 16–32.

Kupchan, C. (2002), *The End of the American Era* (New York: Knopf).

Kupchan, C. (2003), 'The Rise of Europe, America's Changing Imperialism, and the End of US Primacy', *Political Science Quarterly*, 118/2, 205–31

Laatikainen, K. (2004), 'Assessing the EU as an actor at the UN: Authority, Cohesion, Recognition and Autonomy', *CFSP Forum*, 2/1, 4–9. http://www.fornet.info

Ladrech, R. (1994), 'Europeanisation of Domestic Politics and Institutions: The Case of France', *Journal of Common Market Studies* 32/1, 69–87

Laffan, B., and Stubb, A. (2003), 'Member States', in Bomberg, E. and Stubb, A. (eds), *The European Union: How Does it Work?* (Oxford: Oxford University Press).

Laffan, B., and Tannam, E. (1998), 'Ireland: the Rewards of Pragmatism', in Hanf, K., and Soedentorp, B. (eds), *Adapting to European Integration: Small States and the European Union* (London: Longman).

Lake, D. (1996), 'Anarchy, Hierarchy and the Variety of International Relations', *International Organization* 50/1, 1–33.

Larsen, H. (1997), *Foreign Policy and Discourse Analysis: France, Britain and Europe* (London: Routledge).

Lavenex, S. (1998), 'Asylum, Immigration and Central-Eastern Europe: Challenges to EU Enlargement', *European Foreign Affairs Review*, 3/2, 275–94.

Lehmann, J.-P. (1992), 'France, Japan, Europe and Industrial Competition: The Automotive Case', *International Affairs* 68/1, 37–53.

Leonard, M. (2000), *The Future of Europe* (London: Foreign Policy Centre).

Lepgold, J. (1998), 'NATO's Post-Cold War Collective Action Problem', *International Security* 23/1, 76–106.

Lequesne, C. (1993), *Paris-Bruxelles: Comment se fait la politique europeénne de la France* (Paris: Presses de la Fondation nationale des Sciences Politiques).

Light, M., White, S., and Löwenhardt, J. (2000), 'A Wider Europe: The View from Moscow and Kyiv', *International Affairs*, 76/1, 77–88.

Lindstrom, G. (2003a), *The Galileo Satellite System and its Security Implications.* Occasional Paper 44 (Paris: European Union Institute for Security Studies) available at http://www.iss-eu.org

Lindstrom, G. (ed.) (2003b), *Shift or Rift: assessing US-EU relations after Iraq.* (Paris: European Union Institute for Security Studies).

Linklater, A. (2004), 'Norbert Elias, the "Civilizing Process" and International Relations', *International Politics*, 14/1, 3–35.

Lippert, B., and Becker, P. (1998), 'Structured Dialogue Revisited: The EU's Politics of Inclusion and Exclusion', *European Foreign Affairs Review* 3/3, 341–66.

Lipson, C. (2003), *Reliable Partners: How Democracies Have Made a Separate Peace* (Princeton, NJ: Princeton University Press).

Lodge, J. (1984), 'European Union and the First Elected European Parliament: The Spinelli Initiative', *Journal of Common Market Studies* 22/4, 377–402

Lodge, M. (2000), 'Isomorphism of National Policies? The "Europeanisation" of German Competition and Public Procurement Law', *West European Politics* 23/1, 89–107.

Lord, C. (2004), *A Democratic Audit of the European Union* (Basingstoke: Palgrave Macmillan).

Lord, C., and Beetham, D. (2001), 'Legitimizing the EU: Is there a "Post-Parliamentary Basis" for its Legitimation?' *Journal of Common Market Studies* 39/3, 443–62.

Lord, C., and Magnette, P. (2004), 'E Pluribus Unum? Creative Disagreement About Legitimacy in the EU', *Journal of Common Market Studies* 42/1, 183–202.

Luif, P. (1998), 'Austria: Adaptation Through Anticipation', in Hanf, K., and Soetendorp, B. (eds), *Adapting to European Integration* (London: Longman).

Lynne-Jones, S., and Miller, S. (eds) (1996), *Debating the Democratic Peace* (Cambridge, MA: MIT Press).

MacLeod, I., Henry, I., and Hyett, S. (1996), *External Relations of the European Community* (Oxford: Oxford University Press).

Magnette, P. (2003), *Contrôler l'Europe: Pouvoirs et Responsabilité dans l'Union Européenne* (Brussels: editions de l'Université de Bruxelles).

Mahony, H. (2003), 'EU of 25 is almost full, says Patten', *EUObserver.com*, 29 December.

Mair, P., and Zielonka, J. (eds) (2002), *The Enlarged European Union: Diversity and Adaptation* (London: Frank Cass).

Majone, G. (1996), *Regulating Europe* (London: Routledge).

Mandelbaum, M. (1996), *The Dawn of Peace in Europe* (New York: Twentieth Century Fund Press).

Manners, I. (2002), 'Normative Power Europe: A Contradiction in Terms?' *Journal of Common Market Studies* 40/2, 234–58.

Manners, I., and Whitman, R. (eds) (2000), *The Foreign Policies of European Union Member States* (Manchester: Manchester University Press).

Manners, I., and Whitman, R. (2003), 'The "Difference Engine": Constructing and Representing the International Identity of the European Union', *Journal of European Public Policy* 10/3, 380–404.

March, J., and Olsen, J. (1984), 'The New Institutionalism: Organizational Factors in Political Life', *American Political Science Review* 78/3, 734–49.

March, J. (1989), *Rediscovering Institutions: The Organisational Basis of Politics* (New York: Free Press).

March, J. (1995), *Democratic Governance* (New York: Free Press).

March, J. (1998), 'The Institutional Dynamics of International Political Orders', *International Organization* 52/4, 943–70.

Marcussen, M., Risse, T., Engelmann-Martin, D., Knopf, H., and Roscher, K. (1999), 'Constructing Europe? The Evolution of French, British and German Nation State Identities', *Journal of European Public Policy* 6/4, 614–33.

Maresceau, M. (ed.) (1993), *The European Community's Trade Policy after 1992: The Legal Dimension* (Dordrecht: Nijhoff).

Marks, G., Hooghe, L., and Blank, K. (1996), 'European Integration from the 1980s: State-Centric v. Multi-Level Governance', *Journal of Common Market Studies*, 34/3, 341–78.

Martin, L. (1992), *Coercive Cooperation: Explaining Multilateral Economic Sanctions* (Princeton, NJ: Princeton University Press).

Mattli, W., and Buthe, T. (2003), 'Setting International Standards', *World Politics*, 56/1, 1–42.

Maull, H.W. (2000), 'Europa und Ostasien: Eine neue Dimension des Inter-Regionalismus?', in Schubert, K., and Müller-Brandeck-Bocquet. G. (eds), *Die Europäische Union als Akteur der Weltpolitik* (Opladen: Leske + Budrich).

Mayall, J. (1986), 'Africa in Anglo-American Relations', in Louis, W.R., and Bull, H. (eds), *The Special relationship: Anglo-American Relations since 1945* (Oxford and New York: Oxford University Press).

Mayall, J. (1995), 'National Identity and the Revival of Regionalism', in Fawcett, L., and Hurrell, A. (eds), *Regionalism in World Politics* (Oxford: Oxford University Press).

Mayall, J. (2005), 'The Colonial Legacy', in Chesterman, S., Ignatieff, M., and Thakur, R. (eds), *Making States Work: State Failure and the Crisis of Governance* (Tokyo: United Nations University Press).

Mayes, D. (ed.) (1993), *The External Implications of European Integration* (Brighton: Harvester-Wheatsheaf).

Mazey, S., and Richardson, J. (1996), 'EU Policy-Making: A Garbage Can or an Anticipatory and Consensual Policy Style?' in Mény, Y., Müller, W., and Quermonne, J.-L. (eds), *Adjusting to Europe: The Impact of the European Union on National Institutions and Policies* (London: Routledge).

McGuire, S., and Smith, M. (2005), *The European Union and the United States: Competition and Convergence in the Global Arena* (Basingstoke: Palgrave/Macmillan)

Mearsheimer, J. (1990), 'Back to the Future: Instability in Europe After the Cold War', *International Security* 15/1, 5–56.

Mearsheimer, J. (1994–5), 'The False Promise of International Institutions' *International Security* 19/3, 5–49.

Menon, A. (2004), 'From Crisis to Catharsis: ESDP After Iraq', *International Affairs* 80/4, 631–48.

Menon, A., Nicolaïdis, K., and Welsh, J. (2004), 'In Defence of Europe—A Response to Kagan', *Journal of European Affairs* 2/3, http://www.eupolicynetwork.org.uk/JEA2-3.pdf

Mény, Y., Müller, P., and Quermonne, J.-L. (eds) (1996), *Adjusting to Europe: The Impact of the European Union on National Institutions and Policies* (London: Routledge).

Messerlin, P. (2001), *Measuring the Costs of Protection in Europe* (Washington, DC: Institute for International Economics).

Meunier, S. (2000a), 'The French Exception', *Foreign Affairs* 79/4, 104–16.

Meunier, S. (2000b), 'What Single Voice? European Institutions and EU-US Trade Negotiations', *International Organization* 54/1, 103–35.

Meunier, S. (2005), *Trading Voices: The European Union in International Commercial Negotiations* (Princeton, NJ: Princeton University Press).

Meunier, S., and Nicolaïdis, K. (1999), 'Who Speaks for Europe? The Delegation of Trade Authority in the EU', *Journal of Common Market Studies* 37/3, 477–501.

Meunier, S., and Nicolaïdis, K. (2001), 'Trade Competence in the Nice Treaty', *ECSA Review* 14/2, http://www.eustudies.org/NiceTreatyForum.html

Michalski, A., and Wallace, H. (1992), *The European Community: The Challenge of Enlargement* (London: Royal Institute of International Affairs).

Miles, L. (2000), 'Sweden and Finland' in Manners, I., and Whitman, R. (eds), *The Foreign Policies of European Union Member States* (Manchester: Manchester University Press).

Milner, H. (1997), *Interests, Institutions and Information: Domestic Politics and International Relations* (Princeton, NJ: Princeton University Press).

Milward, A. (1984), *The Reconstruction of Western Europe* (London: Methuen).

Milward, A. (1991, 2000), *The European Rescue of the Nation-State* (London: Routledge).

Mishilani, P., Robert, A., Stevens, C., and Weston, A. (1981), 'The Pyramid of Privilege', in Stevens, C. (ed.), *EEC and the Third World: A Survey I* (London: Hodder & Stoughton).

Missiroli, A. (2002a), 'Coherence, Effectiveness and Flexibility for CFSP/ESDP', in Reifer, E., Rummel, R., and Schmidt, P. (eds), *Europas ferne Streitmacht* (Hamburg: Mittler).

Missiroli, A. (ed) (2002b), *Enlargement and European Defence After 11th September*, Chaillot Papers 53 (Paris: European Union Institute for Security Studies).

Missiroli, A. (2003), *From Copenhagen to Brussels: European Defence—Core Documents IV*. Chaillot Paper 67 (Paris: EU Institute for Security Studies) available at http://www.iss-eu.org

Mitrany, D. (1933), *The Progress of International Government* (London: George Allen and Unwin).

Mitrany, D. (1943), *A Working Peace System* (Chicago: Quadrangle Books).

Mitrany, D. (1975), 'The Prospect of Integration: Federal or Functional?' in Groom, A.J.R., and Taylor, P. (eds), *Functionalism: Theory and Practice in International Relations* (London: University of London Press).

Mitsilegas, V., Monar, J., and Rees, W. (2003), *The European Union and Internal Security: Guardian of the People?* (Basingstoke: Palgrave Macmillan).

Monar, J. (1997a), 'The Finances of the Union's Intergovernmental Pillars: Tortuous Experiments with the Community Budget', *Journal of Common Market Studies* 35/1, 57–78.

Monar, J. (1997b), 'Political Dialogue with Third Countries and Regional Political Groupings: The Fifteen as an Attractive Interlocutor', in E. Regelsberger, P. de Schoutheete de Tervarent, and W. Wessels (eds), *Foreign Policy of the European Union: From EPC to CFSP and Beyond* (Boulder, CO/London: Lynne Rienner).

Monar, J. (2000), 'An "Area of Freedom, Justice and Security"? Progress and Deficits in Justice and Home Affairs', in Lynch, P., Neuwahl, N., and Rees, W. (eds) *Reforming the European Union—From Maastricht to Amsterdam*, (Harlow: Pearson).

Morata, F. (1998), 'Spain: Modernization through integration' in Hanf, K., and Soetendorp, B. (eds), *Adapting to European Integration* (London: Longman).

Moravcsik, A. (1991), 'Negotiating the Single European Act: National Interest and Conventional Statecraft in the European Community' in Keohane, R., and Hoffmann, S. (eds), *The New European Community: Decisionmaking and Institutional Change* (Boulder, CO: Westview Press).

Moravcsik, A. (1993), 'Preferences and power in the European Community: a liberal intergovernmentalist approach', *Journal of Common Market Studies*, 31/4, 473–524.

Moravcsik, A. (1998), *The choice for Europe: Social purpose and state power from Messina to Maastricht* (Ithaca, NY: Cornell University Press and London: UCL Press).

Moravcsik, A. (2003) 'Striking a New Transatlantic Bargain'. *Foreign Affairs*, 82/4, 74–89.

Morgenthau, H. (1973), *Politics Among Nations: The Struggle for Power and Peace* 5th edn (New York: Knopf).

Müller-Brandeck-Bocquet, G. (2000), 'Perspectives for a New Regionalism: Relations between the EU and the MERCOSUR', *European Foreign Affairs Review* 5/4, 561–79.

Müller-Brandeck-Bocquet, G. (2002), 'The New CFSP and ESDP Decision Making System of the European Union', *European Foreign Affairs Review*, 7/3, 257–82.

Muller-Wille, B. (2004), *For our Eyes Only? Shaping an Intelligence Community within the EU.* Occasional Paper 50 (Paris: EU Institute for Security Studies) available at http://www.iss-eu.org

Munuera, G. (1994) *Preventing Armed Conflict in Europe: lessons from Recent Experience.* Chaillot Paper 15/16 (Paris: Western European Union Institute for Security Studies).

National Statistics (2004), *International Migration: Migrants entering or leaving the United Kingdom and England and Wales*, 2002 (London: Office for National Statistics).

Neuwahl, N. (1993), 'Foreign and Security Policy and the Implementation of the Requirement of "Consistency" under the Treaty on European Union', in Twomey, P. and O'Keeffe, D. (eds), *Legal Issues of the Maastricht Treaty* (Oxford: Hart).

Nicolaïdis, K. (2000), 'Minimizing Agency Costs in Two-Level Games: Lessons from the Trade Authority Controversies in the United States and the European Union', in Mnookin, R., and Susskind, L. (eds), *Negotiating on Behalf of Others* (Thousand Oaks, CA: Sage).

Nicolaïdis, K., and Egan, M. (2001), 'Regional Policy Externality and Market Governance: Why Recognize Foreign Standards?' *Journal of European Public Policy* 8/3, 454–74.

Nicolaïdis, K., and Howse, R. (2001), *The Federal Vision: Legitimacy and Levels of Government in the US and the EU* (Oxford: Oxford University Press).

Nicolaïdis, K., and Howse, R. (2002), '"This is my EUtopia…": Narrative as Power', *Journal of Common Market Studies*, 40/4, 767–92.

Nicolaïdis, K., and Meunier, S. (2002), 'Revisiting Trade Competence in the European Union: Amsterdam, Nice and Beyond' in Hosli, M., van Deemen, A., and Widgren, M. (eds) *Institutional Challenges in the European Union* (London: Routledge).

Nicoll, W., and Salmon, T.C. (2001), *Understanding the European Union* (Harlow: Longman).

Nuttall, S. (1992), *European Political Cooperation* (Oxford: Clarendon Press).

Nuttall, S. (1994), 'Keynote Article: The EC and Yugoslavia—*deus ex machina* or *machina sine deo?* In Nugent, N. (ed.) *The European Union 1993: Annual Review of Activities* (Oxford: Blackwell).

Nuttall, S. (1996), 'Japan and the EU', *Survival* 38/2, 104–20.

Nuttall, S. (1997), 'Two Decades of EPC Performance', in Regelsberger, E., de Schoutheete de Tervarent, P., and Wessels, W. (eds) *Foreign Policy of the European Union: From EPC to CFSP and Beyond* (Boulder, CO/London: Lynne Rienner).

Nuttall, S. (2000), *European Foreign Policy* (Oxford: Oxford University Press).

Nuttall, S. (2001), '"Consistency" and the CFSP: A Categorisation and its Consequences'. LSE European Foreign Policy Unit Working Paper No. 2001/3, available at http://www.lse.ac.uk/Depts/intrel/EuroFPUnit.html

Nuttall, S. (2004), 'On Fuzzy Pillars: Criteria for the Continued Existence of Pillars in the Draft Constitution', *CFSP Forum* 2/3, http://www.fornet.info

Nye, J. (1971), 'Comparing Common Markets: A Revised Neo-Functionalist Model', in Lindberg, L., and Scheingold, S. (eds), *Regional Integration: Theory and Research* (Cambridge, MA: Harvard University Press).

Nye, J. (1990), *Bound to Lead: The Changing Nature of American Power* (New York: Basic Books).

Øhrgaard, J. (1997), 'Less than Supranational, More than Intergovernmental: European Political Cooperation and the Dynamics of Intergovernmental Integration', *Millennium* 26/1, 1–29.

Olsen, J.P. (2002), 'The Many Faces of Europeanisation', *Journal of Common Market Studies* 40/5, 921–52.

Olsen, J.P. (2002), 'Europeanisation', in Cini, M. (ed.), *European Union Politics* (Oxford: Oxford University Press).

Olson, M. (1982), *The Rise and Decline of Nations* (New Haven, CT: Yale University Press).

Olson, M., and Zeckhauser, R. (1996), 'An Economic Theory of Alliances', *The Review of Economics and Statistics* 48/3, 266–79.

Oneal, J. (1990), 'The Theory of Collective Action and Burden-Sharing in NATO', *International Organization* 44/3, 379–402.

Paemen, H., and Bensch, A. (1995), *From the GATT to the WTO: The European Community in the Uruguay Round* (Leuven: Leuven University Press).

Pastore, F. (2001), 'Reconciling the Prince's Two "Arms". Internal-External Security Policy Coordination in the European Union', Occasional Papers 30 (Paris: WEU Institute for Security Studies).

Patterson, L.A. (1997), 'Agricultural Policy Reform in the European Community: A Three-Level Game Analysis', *International Organization* 51/1, 135–65.

Pelkmans, J. (2001), *European Integration: Methods and Economic Analysis*, 2nd edition (Harlow: Pearson Education).

Pentland, C. (2003), 'Brussels, Bosnia and Beyond: The European Union's Search for a Role in South Eastern Europe' in Pentland, C. (ed.), *Bridges to Peace: Ten Years of Conflict Management in Bosnia*, Special Edition of *Queens Quarterly*, 145–64.

'Petersberg Declaration', *Europe Documents*, No. 1787, 23 June 1992.

Petersmann, E.-U., and Pollack, M. (eds) (2003), *Transatlantic Economic Disputes: The EU, the US, and the WTO* (Oxford: Oxford University Press).

Peterson, J. (1996), *Europe and America: The Prospects for Partnership*. 2nd edition (London: Routledge).

Peterson, J. (2003a) 'The US and Europe in the Balkans' in Peterson, J., and Pollack, M. (eds) *Europe, America, Bush: transatlantic relations in the twenty-first century* (London: Routledge).

Peterson, J., and O'Toole, L. Jr (2001) 'Federal Governance in the United States and the European Union: A Policy Network Perspective' in Nicolaïdis, K., and Howse, R. (eds) *The Federal Vision: Legitimacy and Levels of Governance in the United States and the European Union* (Oxford: Oxford University Press).

Peterson, J., and Shackleton, M. (eds) (2002), *The Institutions of the European Union* (Oxford: Oxford University Press).

Peterson, J., and Pollack, M. (eds) (2003), *Europe, America, Bush: Transatlantic Relations in the Twenty-first Century* (London: Routledge).

Peterson, J., and Smith, M.E. (2003), 'The EU as a Global Actor', in Bomberg, E., and Stubb, A. (eds), *The European Union: How Does it Work?* (Oxford: Oxford University Press).

Pettit, P. (1997), *Republicanism: A Theory of Freedom and Government* (Oxford: Oxford University Press).

Philippart, E., and Winand, P. (eds) (2001), *Ever-Closer Partnership: Policy-Making in US-EU Relations* (Brussels: PIE-Peter Lang).

Phinnemore, D. (2000), 'Austria' in Manners, I., and Whitman, R. (eds) *The Foreign Policies of European Union Member States* (Manchester: Manchester University Press).

Piening, C. (1997), *Global Europe: The European Union in World Affairs* (Boulder, CO/London: Lynne Rienner).

Pierson, P. (1996), 'The Path to European Integration: a Historical Institutionalist Analysis', *Comparative Political Studies*, 29/2, 123–63.

Pinder, J. (1991), *European Community: The Building of a Union* (Oxford: Oxford University Press).

Pippan, C. (2004), 'The Rocky Road to Europe: The EU's Stabilisation and Association Process for the Western Balkans and the Principle of Conditionality', *European Foreign Affairs Review* 9/2, 219–46.

Pollack, M. (1997), 'Delegation, Agency, and Agenda Setting in the European Community', *International Organization* 51/1, 99–134.

Pollack, M. (2003), *The Engines of European Integration: Delegation, Agency and Agenda-Setting in the EU* (New York and Oxford: Oxford University Press).

Pollack, M. (2004), 'The New Institutionalisms and European Integration', in Wiener, A., and Diez, T. (eds), *European Integration Theory* (Oxford: Oxford University Press).

Pollack, M., and Shaffer, G. (2000), 'Transatlantic Conflict over Genetically Modified Organisms' *Washington Quarterly* 23/4, 41–54.

Pollack, M., and Shaffer, G. (eds) (2001), *Transatlantic Governance in the Global Economy* (Lanham, MD: Rowman and Littlefield).

Powell, W., and Dimaggio, P. (1991), *The New Institutionalism in Organizational Analysis* (Chicago: Chicago University Press).

Pridham, G. (2002), 'EU Enlargement and Consolidating Democracy in Post-Communist States—Formality and Reality', *Journal of Common Market Studies*, 40/3, 953–73.

Prodi, R. (2002), 'A Wider Europe—A Proximity Policy as the Key to Stability', Speech to the Sixth ECSA-World Conference, Brussels, 5–6 December, SPEECH/02/619.

Putnam, R. (1988), 'Diplomacy and Domestic Politics: The Logic of Two-Level Games' *International Organization* 42/3, 427–60.

Quinlan, J. (2003), *Drifting Apart or Growing Together: The Primacy of the Transatlantic Economy* (Washington, DC: Centre for Transatlantic Relations).

Quinlan, M. (2002), *European Defense Cooperation: Asset or Threat to NATO?* (Washington, DC: Woodrow Wilson Center Press).

Radaelli, C. (1997), 'How Does Europeanisation Produce Domestic Policy Change? Corporate Tax Policy in Italy and the United Kingdom', *Comparative Political Studies* 30/5, 553–75.

Rae, H. (2002), *State Identities and the Homogenisation of Peoples* (Cambridge: Cambridge University Press).

Ravenhill, J. (1985), *Collective Clientelism: The Lomé Conventions and North-South Relations* (New York: Columbia University Press).

Regelsberger E. (1997), 'The Institutional Set-Up and Functioning of EPC/CFSP', in Regelsberger, E., de Schoutheete de Tervarent, P., and Wessels, W. (eds) *Foreign Policy of the European Union: From EPC to CFSP and Beyond* (Boulder, CO/London: Lynne Rienner).

Regelsberger, E. (1998), 'Group-to-Group Dialogues—A Prominent Role in the EU's External Relations?' *CFSP Forum* 2/1998, 2–3.

Regelsberger, E. (2003), 'The Impact of EU Enlargement on CFSP Procedures and Policies—Some Mixed Results', in Neuhold, H., and Sucharipa, E. (eds), *The CFSP/ESDP After Enlargement—A bigger EU = a stronger EU?* (Vienna: Diplomatic Academy).

Regelsberger, E., de Schoutheete de Tervarent, P., and Wessels, W. (1997), 'From EPC to CFSP: Does Maastricht Push the EU Toward a Role as a Global Power?', in Regelsberger, E., de Schoutheete de Tervarent, P., and Wessels, W. (eds) *Foreign Policy of the European Union: From EPC to CFSP and Beyond* (Boulder, CO/London: Lynne Rienner).

Reif, K., and Schmitt, H. (1980), 'Nine Second-Order National Elections: A Conceptual Framework for the Analysis of European Election Results', *European Journal of Political Research* 8/1, 3–45.

Rhein, E. (1996), 'Europe and the Mediterranean: A Newly Emerging Geographical Area', *European Foreign Affairs Review* 1/1, 79–86.

Rhinard, M. (2004), 'Negotiations and Multi-Level Games: The Role of the European Union in the 2000 Cartagena Protocol Negotiations', paper presented to the American Political Science Association Annual Meeting, Chicago, IL, September.

Riker, W. (1964), *Federalism* (Boston: Little, Brown).

Riker, W. (1975), 'Federalism', in Greenstein, F., and Polsby, N. (eds), *Handbook of Political Science* (Reading: Addison-Wesley).

Riker, W. (1995), 'European Federalism: The Lessons of Past Experience', in Hesse, J., and Wright, V. (eds), *Federalising Europe? The Costs, Benefits and Preconditions of Federal Political Systems* (Oxford: Oxford University Press).

Risse-Kappen, T. (ed.) (1995) *Bringing Transnational Relations Back In: Non-State Actors, Domestic Structures and International Institutions* (Cambridge: Cambridge University Press).

Risse-Kappen, T. (1996), 'Exploring the Nature of the Beast: International Relations Theory and Comparative Policy Analysis meet the European Union', *Journal of Common Market Studies*, 34/1, 53–80.

Risse, T. (2004), 'Social Constructivism and European Integration', in Wiener, A., and Diez, T. (eds) *European Integration Theory* (Oxford: Oxford University Press).

Rosamond, B. (2000a), *Theories of European Integration* (Basingstoke: Palgrave Macmillan).

Rosamond, B. (2000b), 'Europeanization and Globalization' in Harmsen, R., and Wilson, T. (eds), *Europeanization: Institutions, Identities and Citizenship* (Amsterdam: Rodopi).

Rosencrance, R. (1986), *The Rise of the Trading State: Commerce and Conquest in the Modern World* (New York: Basic Books).

Rosencrance, R. (1998), 'The European Union: a new type of international actor?', in Zielonka, J. (ed.), *Parodoxes of European foreign policy* (The Hague: Kluwer Law International).

Ruggiero, V., and South, N. (1995), *Eurodrugs: Drug Use, Markets and Trafficking in Europe* (London: UCL Press).

Rüland, J. (2001), 'ASEAN and the European Union: A Bumpy Interregional Relationship'. Discussion Paper C95 (Bonn: Center for European Integration Studies).

Rummel, R. (ed.) (1990), *The Evolution of an International Actor: Western Europe's New Assertiveness* (Boulder, CO: Westview Press).

Rummel, R. (1996), 'Germany's Role in the CFSP: "Normalität" or "Sonderweg"?' in Hill, C. (ed.) *The actors in Europe's Foreign Policy* (London: Routledge).

Rummel, R. (1997), 'The CFSP's Conflict Prevention Policy' in Holland, M. (ed.) *Common Foreign and Security Policy: The Record and Reforms* (London: Pinter).

Rummel, R. (2002), 'From Weakness to Power with the ESDP?' *European Foreign Affairs Review* 7/4, 453–72.

Russett, B., and Oneal, J. (2001), *Triangulating Peace: Democracy, Interdependence and International Organization* (New York: Norton).

Russett, B. *et al.* (1993), *Grasping the Democratic Peace* (Princeton, NJ: Princeton University Press).

Rutten, M. (dir) (2001), *From Saint-Malo to Nice: European Defence — Core Documents.* Chaillot Paper 47 (Paris: WEU Institute for Security Studies) available at http://www.iss-eu.org

Rutten, M. (dir) (2002), *From Nice to Laeken. European Defence: Core Documents II.* (Paris: European Union Institute for Security Studies) available at http://www.iss-eu.org

Saleh, N. (1999), 'The European Union and the Gulf States: A Growing Partnership', *Middle East Policy* 7/1, 50–71.

Salmon, T., and Shepherd, A. (2003), *Toward a European Army: A Military Power in the Making?* (Boulder, CO: Lynne Rienner).

Sandholtz, W. (1996), 'Membership Matters: Limits of the Functional Approach to European Institutions', *Journal of Common Market Studies* 34/3, 403–29.

Sandholtz, W., and Stone Sweet, A. (eds) (1998), *European Integration and Supranational Governance* (Oxford: Oxford University Press).

Sangiovanni, M.E. (2003), 'Why a Common Security and Defence Policy is Bad for Europe', *Survival* 45/3, 193–206.

Sapir, A. *et al.* (2004), *An Agenda for a Growing Europe* (The Sapir Report) (Oxford: Oxford University Press).

Sbragia, A. (2004), 'Competitive Regionalism, Trade Liberalization, and Globalization: The EU and the Americas' paper presented to Conference of Europeanists, Chicago, IL, March.

Sbragia A., and Damro, C. (1999), 'The Changing Role of the EU in International Environmental Policy' *Government and Policy*, theme issue on European Union Environmental Policy at 25, Vol. 17, 53–68.

Scharpf, F. (1996), 'Democratic Policy in Europe', *European Law Journal* 2/2, 136–55.

Scharpf, F. (1999), *Governing in Europe: Effective and Democratic?* (Oxford: Oxford University Press).

Schimmelfennig, F. (2001), 'The Community Trap: Liberal Norms, Rhetorical Actions, and the Eastern Enlargement of the European Union', *International Organization*, 55/1, 47–80.

Schimmelfennig, F. (2003), *The EU, NATO and the Integration of Europe: Rules and Rhetoric* (Cambridge: Cambridge University Press).

Schlesinger, A.M. Jr (1967), *A Thousand Days* (London: Mayflower-Dell).

Schmalz, U. (1998), 'The Amsterdam Provisions on External Coherence: Bridging the Union's Foreign Policy Dualism?' *European Foreign Affairs Review* 3/3, 421–42.

Schmidt, V. (2002), *The Futures of European Capitalism* (Oxford: Oxford University Press).

Schmitt, B. (2000), *From Cooperation to Integration: Defence and Aerospace Industries in Europe.* Chaillot Paper 40 (Paris: WEU Institute for Security Studies) available at http://www.iss-eu.org

Schmitt, B. (2003), *The European Union and Armaments: Getting a Bigger Bang for the Euro.* Chaillot Paper 63 (Paris: EU Institute for Security Studies) available at http://www.iss-eu.org

Schmitt, H., and Thomassen, T. (2000), 'Dynamic Representation: The Case of European Integration', *European Union Politics* 1/3, 340–63.

Schmitter, P. (1969), 'Three Neo-Functional Hypotheses about European Integration', *International Organization* 23/1, 161–66.

Schmitter, P. (1974), 'A Revised Theory of European Integration', in Lindberg, L., and Scheingold, S. (eds), *Regional Integration: Theory and Research* (Cambridge, MA: Harvard University Press).

Schnabel, A., and Thakur, R. (eds) (2000), *Kosovo and the Challenge of Humanitarian Intervention: Selective Indignation, Collective Action and International Citizenship*, Part Four: Selected International Perspectives (Tokyo: United Nations University Press).

Schroeder, P. (1976), 'Alliances 1815–1945: Weapons of Power and Tools of Management', in Knorr, K. (ed.), *Historical Dimensions of National Security Problems* (Lawrence, K: University Press of Kansas).

Senior Nello, S., and Smith, K. (1998), *The European Union and Central and Eastern Europe: The Implications of Enlargement in Stages* (Aldershot: Ashgate).

Shearer, A. (2000), 'Britain, France and the Saint-Malo Declaration', *Cambridge Review of International Affairs* XIII/2, 283–98.

Silvestri, S. (1997), 'Conflict Prevention and Crisis Management in the Balkans: The Albanian Test Case', *The International Spectator*, 32/3–4, 87–99.

Sjursen, H. (2001), 'The Common Foreign and Security Policy: Limits of Intergovernmentalism and the Search for a Global Role' in Andersen, S., and Eliassen, K. (eds), *Making Policy in Europe*, 2nd edition (London: Sage).

Sjursen, H. (2002), 'Why Expand? The Question of Legitimacy and Justification in the EU's Enlargement Policy', *Journal of Common Market Studies*, 40/3, 491–513.

Sloan, S. (2002), *NATO, the European Union and the Atlantic Community: the Transatlantic Bargain Reconsidered* (Lanham, MD: Rowman and Littlefield).

Smith, D. (2001), *Norbert Elias and Modern Social Theory* (London: Sage).

Smith, H. (1995), *European Union Foreign Policy and Central America* (New York: St. Martin's Press).

Smith, H. (1998), 'Actually Existing Foreign Policy—Or Not? The EU in Latin and Central America', in Peterson, J., and Sjursen, H. (eds), *A Common Foreign Policy for Europe? Competing Visions of the CFSP* (London: Routledge).

Smith, H. (2002), *European Union Foreign Policy: What it is and What it Does* (London: Pluto Press).

Smith, K. (1999), *The Making of EU Foreign Policy: The Case of Eastern Europe* (London: Macmillan).

Smith, K. (2001), 'The EU, Human Rights and Relations with Third Countries: "Foreign Policy" with an Ethical Dimension?' in Smith, K., and Light, M. (eds), *Ethics and Foreign Policy* (Cambridge: Cambridge University Press).

Smith, K. (2003), *European Union Foreign Policy in a Changing World* (Cambridge: Polity Press).

Smith, M. (1984), *Western Europe and the United States: The Uncertain Alliance* (London: George Allen and Unwin).

Smith, M. (1990), 'The Devil You Know: The United States and a Changing European Community', *International Affairs*, 68/1, 103–20.

Smith, M. (1996a), 'The European Union and a Changing Europe: Establishing the Boundaries of Order', *Journal of Common Market Studies*, 34/1, 5–28.

Smith, M. (1996b), 'The EU as an International Actor', in Richardson, J. (ed.) *European Union: Power and Policy-Making* (London: Routledge).

Smith, M. (1998a), 'Competitive Co-operation and EU/US Relations: Can the EU be a Strategic Partner for the US in the World Political Economy?' *Journal of European Public Policy* 5/4, 561–77.

Smith, M. (1998b), 'Does the Flag Follow Trade? "Politicisation" and the Emergence of a European Foreign Policy' in Peterson, J., and Sjursen, H. (eds) *A Common Foreign Policy for Europe? Competing Visions of the CFSP* (London: Routledge).

Smith, M. (2001), 'The European Union's Commercial Policy: Between Coherence and Fragmentation', *Journal of European Public Policy* 8/5, 787–802.

Smith, M. (2004a), 'Between Two Worlds? The European Union, the United States and World Order' *International Politics* 41/1, 95–117.

Smith, M. (2004b), 'A Europe That Can Say No? Collective Action Problems in EU Responses to the George W. Bush Administration'. Paper presented at the American Political Science Association Annual Meeting, Chicago, September.

Smith, M. (2004c), 'The European Union, the United States and Asia: A New Trilateralism?' in Cowles, M.G., and Dinan, D. (eds) *Developments in the European Union 2* (Basingstoke: Palgrave/Macmillan).

Smith, M., and Woolcock, S. (1993), *The United States and the European Community in a Transformed World* (London: Pinter/Royal Institute of International Affairs).

Smith, M., and Woolcock, S. (1999), 'European Commercial Policy: a leadership role in the new millennium?' *European Foreign Affairs Review*, 4/4, 439–62.

Smith, M.E. (2000), 'Conforming to Europe: The Domestic Impact of EU Foreign Policy Cooperation', *Journal of European Public Policy* 7/4, 613–31.

Smith, M.E. (2003), *Europe's Foreign and Security Policy: The Institutionalization of Cooperation* (Cambridge: Cambridge University Press).

Smith, M.E. (2004), 'Toward a Theory of EU Foreign Policy-making: Multi-level Governance, Domestic Politics, and National Adaptation to Europe's Common Foreign and Security Policy', *Journal of European Public Policy* 11/4, 740–58.

Snyder, G. (1997), *Alliance Politics* (Ithaca, NY: Cornell University Press).

Spinelli, A. (1972), 'The Growth of the European Movement Since the Second World War', in Hodges, M. (ed.), *European Integration* (Harmondsworth: Penguin).

Stares, P. (1996), *Global Habit: The Drug Problem in a Borderless World* (Washington DC: Brookings Institution Press).

Steffenson, R. (2005), *Managing EU-US Relations: Actors, Institutions and the New Transatlantic Agenda* (Manchester: Manchester University Press).

Stevens, C. (ed.) (1981), *EEC and the Third World: A Survey I* (London: Hodder & Stoughton).

Stone Sweet, A., and Sandholtz, W. (eds) (1998), *Supranational Governance: The Institutionalization of the European Union* (Oxford: Oxford University Press).

Stone Sweet, A., Sandholtz, W., and Fligstein, N. (eds) (2001), *The Institutionalization of Europe* (Oxford: Oxford University Press).

Storbeck, J. (2003), 'The European Union and Enlargement: Challenge and Opportunity for Europol in the Fight Against International Crime', *European Foreign Affairs Review*, 8/3, 283–8.

Strange, S. (1993), *States and Markets: An Introduction to Political Economy* (London: Pinter).

Suganami, H. (1989), *The Domestic Analogy and World Order Proposals* (Cambridge: Cambridge University Press).

Szukala, A., and Wessels, W. (1997), 'The Franco-German Tandem' in Edwards, G., and Pijpers, A. (eds) *The Politics of European Treaty Reform* (London: Cassell).

Szymanski, M., and Smith, M.E. (2005), 'Coherence and Conditionality in EU Foreign Policy: Negotiating the EU-Mexico Global Agreement', *Journal of Common Market Studies* (forthcoming).

Tams, K. (1999), 'Functions of a European Security and Defence Identity and its institutional Form', in Haftendorn, H., Keohane, R., and Wallander, C. (eds), *Imperfect Unions: Security Institutions Over Time and Space* (Oxford: Oxford University Press).

Telò, M. (ed.) (2001), *European Union and New Regionalism: Regional Actors and Global Governance in a Post-Hegemonic Era* (Aldershot: Ashgate).

Telò, M. (2001), 'The European Union and the Challenge of the Near Abroad', in Telò, M. (ed.), *European Union and New Regionalism: Regional Actors and Global Governance in a Post-Hegemonic Era* (Aldershot: Ashgate).

Terriff, T. (2003), 'The CJTF Concept and the Limits of European Autonomy', in Howorth, J., and Keeler, J. (eds), *Defending Europe: The EU, NATO and the Quest for European Autonomy* (New York: Palgrave Macmillan).

Tewes, H. (2002), *Germany, Civilian Power and the New Europe* (Basingstoke: Palgrave).

Thakur, R. (1995), *The Government and Politics of India* (Basingstoke: Macmillan).

The Courier (1996), special issue: *EU-ACP Cooperation in 1994* (Brussels, Steffen Smidt).

Thomas, W. (2001), *The Ethics of Destruction: Norms and Violence in International Relations* (Ithaca, NY: Cornell University Press).

Todd, E. (2003), *After the American Empire: The Breakdown of the American Order* (New York: Columbia University Press).

Tofte, S. (2003), 'Non-EU NATO Members and the Issue of Discrimination' in Howorth, J., and Keeler, J. (eds) *Defending Europe: The EU, NATO and the Quest for Autonomy* (New York: Palgrave Macmillan).

Tonra, B. (2000), 'Denmark and Ireland' in Manners, I., and Whitman, R. (eds), *The Foreign Policies of European Union Member States* (Manchester: Manchester University Press).

Tonra, B. (2001), *The Europeanisation of National Foreign Policy: Dutch, Danish and Irish Foreign Policy in the European Union* (Aldershot: Ashgate).

Tonra, B. (2003), 'Constructing the Common Foreign and Security Policy: The Utility of a Cognitive Approach', *Journal of Common Market Studies* 41/4, 731–56.

Tranholm-Mikkelsen, J. (1991), 'Neofunctionalism: Obstinate or Obsolete? A Reappraisal in the Light of the New Dynamism of the EC' *Millennium* 20/1, 1–22.

Triantaphyllou, D. (2003), 'The Balkans between stabilisation and membership', in Batt, J., Lynch, D., Missiroli, A., Ortega, M., and Triantaphyllou, D., *Partners and neighbours: A CFSP for a wider Europe*, Chaillot Papers No. 64 (Paris: EU Institute for Security Studies).

Tsoukalis, L. (1997), *The New European Economy Revisited* (Oxford: Oxford University Press).

Tsoukalis, L. (2003), *What Kind of Europe?* [Revised and updated edition, 2005] (Oxford: Oxford University Press).

Twitchett, C.C. (1981), *A Framework for Development: The EEC and the ACP* (London: Allen and Unwin).

United Nations High Commissioner for Refugees (1999), *Statistics: Asylum Applications in Europe, 1999* (New York: UNHCR).

United States National Security Council (2002), *The National Security Strategy of the United States*, available at http://www.whitehouse.gov/nsc/nss.html

Van den Hoven, A. (2002), 'Enlargement and the EU's Common Commercial Policy'. ECSA-Canada Conference, Toronto, May.

Van Eekelen, W. (1998), *Debating European Security, 1948–1998* (Brussels: CEPS).

Van Oudenaren, J. (2001), 'E Pluribus Confusio: Living with the EU's Structural Incoherence', *The National Interest*, Fall, 23–36.

Vasconcelos, A.de (1996), 'Portugal: Pressing for an Open Europe', in Hill, C. (ed.) *The Actors in Europe's Foreign Policy* (London: Routledge).

Vasconcelos, A.de, and Joffé, G. (eds) (2000), *The Barcelona Process* (London: Frank Cass).

Venusberg Group (2004), *A European Defence Strategy* (Gutersloh: Bertelsmann).

Verheugen, G. (1999), 'Enlargement: Speed and Quality', Speech in The Hague, 4 November 1999, Rapid document SPEECH/99/151.

Verheugen, G. (2001), 'Debate on EU Enlargement in the European Parliament', Strasbourg, 4 September 2001, Rapid Document SPEECH/01/363.

Viner, J., (1950), *The Customs Union Issue* (London: Stevens & Sons).

Viola, D. (2000), *European Foreign Policy and the European Parliament in the 1990s* (Aldershot: Ashgate).

Vitorino, A. (2001), 'Strategies of the EU and the US in Combating Transnational Organised Crime', Conference Speech, Gent, 24 January.

Vogel, D. (2002), 'The Hare and the Tortoise Revisited: The New Politics of Consumer and Environmental Regulation in Europe' *British Journal of Political Science*, 33/4, 557–80.

Wallace, H., and Wallace, W. (2000), *Policy Making in the European Union.* 4th edition (Oxford: Oxford University Press).

Wallace, W. (1983) 'Less than a Federation, More than a Regime: The Community as a Political System', in Wallace, H., and Wallace, W. (eds) *Policy-Making in the European Community*, 2nd edition (Chichester and New York: John Wiley).

Wallace, W. (1994), *Regional integration: The West European Experience* (Washington, DC: Brookings Institution).

Wallace, W. (1999), 'Europe After the Cold War', *Review of International Studies* 25/5, 201–23.

Wallace, W. (2001), 'Rethinking European Order: West European Responses, 1989–97—Introduction', in Niblett, R., and Wallace, W. (eds), *Rethinking European Order: West European Responses, 1989–97* (Basingstoke: Palgrave).

Wallerstein, I. (1979), *The Capitalist World Economy* (Cambridge: Cambridge University Press).

Waltz, K. (1979), *Theory of International Politics* (London: Addison-Wesley).

Waltz, K. (1993), 'The Emerging Structure of International Politics', *International Security* 18/2, 44–79.

Waltz, K. (2000), 'Structural Realism After the Cold War', *International Security* 25/1, 5–41.

Ward, A. (1998), 'Frameworks for Cooperation Between the European Union and Third States', *European Foreign Affairs Review* 3/3, 503–56.

Wayman, F., and Diehl, P. (eds) (1994), *Reconstructing Realpolitik* (Ann Arbor: University of Michigan Press).

Weale, A. (1999), *Democracy* (London: Macmillan).

Weber, K. (1997), 'Hierarchy Amidst Anarchy: A Transactions Cost Approach to International Security Cooperation', *International Studies Quarterly* 41/2, 321–40.

Weiler, J. (1999), *The Constitution of Europe: 'Do the New Clothes have an Emperor?' and Other Essays on European Integration* (Cambridge: Cambridge University Press).

Weiler, J. (ed.) (2000), *The EU, the WTO and the NAFTA* (Oxford: Oxford University Press).

Wendt, A. (1987), 'The Agent-Structure Problem in International Theory', *International Organization* 43/3, 335–70.

Wendt, A. (1992), 'Anarchy is What States Make of it: The Social Construction of Power Politics', *International Organization* 46/2, 391–425.

Wendt, A. (1999) *Social Theory of International Relations* (Cambridge: Cambridge University Press).

Western European Union (1988), *The Reactivation of WEU: Statements and Communiqués, 1984-1987* (London: WEU).

Westlake, M. (1999), *The Council of the European Union* (London: Cartermill).

White, B. (2001), *Understanding European Foreign Policy* (Basingstoke: Palgrave Macmillan).

White Paper (2004), *European Defence: A Proposal for a White Paper* (Paris: EU Institute for Security Studies).

Whitman, R. (1998), *From Civilian Power to Superpower? The International Identity of the European Union* (London: Macmillan).

Wiessala, G. (2002), *The European Union and Asian Countries* (London: Sheffield Academic Press/Continuum for UACES).

Winand, P. (1993), *Eisenhower, Kennedy and the United States of Europe* (New York: St Martin's Press).

Wolfers, A. (1962), *Discord and Collaboration: Essays on International Politics* (Baltimore, MD: Johns Hopkins University Press).

Wong, R. (2002), 'French Foreign Policy, Asia and Europe', paper presented at LSE-Birmingham University Workshop on 'Foreign Policy and Europeanisation', London, 5th June, available at http://www.lse.ac.uk/Depts/intrel/pdfs/EFPUfrenchforpolasiaeurope.pdf

Wong, R. (2005 forthcoming), *The Europeanisation of French Foreign Policy* (Basingstoke: Palgrave/Macmillan).

Woolcock, S. (1993), 'The European *Acquis* and Multilateral Trade Rules: Are they Compatible?' *Journal of Common Market Studies* 31/4, 539-58.

Woolcock, S. (2000), 'European Trade Policy: Global Pressures and Domestic Constraints', in Wallace, H., and Wallace, W. (eds) *Policy-Making in the European Union*, 4th edition (Oxford: Oxford University Press).

Woolcock, S., and Hodges, M. (1996), 'EU Policy in the Uruguay Round: The Story behind the Headlines' in Wallance, H., and Wallance, W. (eds) (1996: 301-24).

Wright, V. (1996), 'The national Coordination of European Policy-making: Negotiating the Quagmire', in Richardson, J. (ed.) *European Union: Power and Policy-making* (London: Routledge).

Young, A. (2000), 'The Adaptation of European Foreign Economic Policy: From Rome to Seattle', *Journal of Common Market Studies*, 38/1, 93-116.

Young, A.R. (2002), *Extending European Cooperation: The European Union and the 'New' International Trade Agenda* (Manchester: Manchester University Press).

Youngs, R. (2001), *The European Union and the Promotion of Democracy: Europe's Mediterranean and Asian Policies* (Oxford: Oxford University Press).

Zielonka, J. (1998a), *Explaining Euro-Paralysis* (Houndsmills: Macmillan).

Zielonka, J. (ed.) (1998b), *Paradoxes of European Foreign Policy* (The Hague: Kluwer).

Zielonka, J. (1998c), 'Policies Without Strategy: The EU's Record in Eastern Europe' in Zielonka, J. (ed.) *Paradoxes of European Foreign Policy* (The Hague: Kluwer).

Zielonka, J. (ed.) (2002), *Europe Unbound* (London: Routledge).

Zucconi, M. (1996), 'The European Union in the Former Yugoslavia', in Chayes A., and Chayes A. (eds) *Preventing Conflict in the Post-Communist World: Mobilizing International and Regional Organizations* (Washington, DC: Brookings Institution).

Index

decision to expand 280
enlargement 286
EU unlikely to rival 356
European Security and Defence Identity
within 54
exclusive role of 180
expansion 144
gratitude towards 60
guarantees of non-aggression between ESDP
and 186
implications of a European defence capability
for 313
less well suited to coping with non-military
risks 208
members not belonging to EU 81
members then outside EU 160
military capability independent of 143
most of Europe's defence capability
coordinated
in 169
need to specify division of labour between
ESDP,
UN and 172
operation in Kosovo 313
partnership with 196
procedures copied 194
questioning of the value of 61
regarded as having a global mission 60
reluctance of many states to forego 60
resolution of EU working relationship
with 186
Secretary-General 163, 354, 395
successful attack on Kosovo 169, 172
survival of 26
under threat 55
US determined on the primacy of 403
US security guarantee delivered via 195
war between Serbia and 281
see also IFOR; SHAPE; WEU
Nazis 373
'near abroad' 324
'near neighbourhood' model 13
Nehru, Jawaharlal (Pandit) 293
Neighbourhood Policy (2004) 48
neoclassical economics 227
neo-colonialism 296, 297, 394
debate over 308
institutionalised 298, 307
neofunctionalism 24, 34, 136
federalism and 20-2, 23
neoliberal institutionalists 30
neoliberals 231
neo-Marxism 33
neo-realism 25, 368, 390
NEPAD (New Economic Partnership for Africa's
Development, 2001) 308, 330

Netherlands 60, 147, 165, 303, 308
military capacity 191
removal of internal borders 207
success in attracting Japanese FDI 148
networking 138
neutrality 56, 61, 80, 169, 186, 197, 241
revised 139
new entrants 258, 259
influence of 13
new Europe 60, 360
stand-off between old and 350
'New Neighbourhood Policy' 62
New Transatlantic Agenda (1995) 48, 168
New Transatlantic Marketplace Agreement
negotiations (1997-8) 351
New York 96, 212
New Zealand 296
newly independent countries 278
NGOs (non-governmental organisations) 58, 73,
74, 130, 131
NHAIs (National High Authorities of
Intelligence) 200
Niblett, R. 5
Nicaragua 322, 333
Nice Council/Treaty (2000-01) 42, 46, 51, 54, 73,
82, 83, 84, 107, 160, 251, 256
general momentum to expand QMV 252
IGCs leading to 271, 279
Nicolaides group 83
Nicolaïdis, Kalypso 14, 60, 86, 248, 249, 251, 254,
255, 260, 264, 349, 351, 354, 356, 384, 391, 396
Nicoll, W. 71, 73
NICs (Newly Industrialising Countries) 41
competitive challenge of 49
NIEO (New International Economic Order) 43,
195, 312
campaign (1970s) 303
Nigeria 296, 297, 298, 300
NIPs (National Indicative Programmes) 307
non-compliance 44
non-reciprocity 298
Nordic countries, *see* Scandinavia
Normative Power Europe 370, 374
norms 28, 32, 139, 159
agreed, powerful internalisation of 126
'bombing' 376
CEECs and 46
democratic 279
global 376
internalisation of 144, 146
liberal 281
political 47
shared 146
North Africa 44, 76, 147
cannabis imported from 210
migration from and through 45, 213, 218, 302

Index compiled by Frank Pert